PC Security and Virus Protection

The Ongoing War Against
Information Sabotage

Pamela Kane

M&T Books
A Division of MIS:Press, Inc.
A Subsidiary of Henry Holt and Company, Inc.
115 West 18th Street
New York, New York 10011

Limits of Liability and Disclaimer of Warranty
The Author and Publisher of this book have used their best efforts in preparing the book and the programs contained in it. These efforts include the development, research, and testing of the theories and programs to determine their effectiveness.

The Author and Publisher make no warranty of any kind, expressed or implied, with regard to these programs or the documentation contained in this book. The Author and Publisher shall not be liable in any event for incidental or consequential damages in connection with, or arising out of, the furnishing, performance, or use of these programs.

All products, names and services are trademarks or registered trademarks of their respective companies.

Library of Congress Cataloging-in-Publication Data

Kane, Pamela
    PC security and virus protection: the ongoing war against information sabotage / Pamela Kane.
       p. cm.
    Includes index.
    ISBN 1-55851-390-6 : $39.95
      1. Microcomputers--Access control 2. Computer viruses. I. Title.
QA76.9.A25K34   1994
005.8--dc20   94-14134
                                                        CIP

97 96 95 94   4 3 2 1

Publisher: Steve Berkowitz
Associate Publisher: Brenda McLaughlin
Project Editor: Debra Williams Cauley
Development Editor: Jono Hardjowirogo
Copy Editors: Kristin Juba and Jack Donner
Technical Editor: Padgett Peterson
Production Editor: Eileen Mullin
Associate Production Editor: Amy Carley

Dedication

From the Lady of the Virus Security Institute to the Gentlemen of the Virus Security Institute:

Harold Highland, Ross Greenberg, Jon David, Padgett Peterson, Frisk Skulason, Alan Solomon, Chris Fischer, Klaus Brunnstein, Vess Bontchev, Yisrael Radai, and Bill Caelli.

With respect, affection, and sincere thanks.

And to HWs, one and all.

Table of Contents

Acknowledgments

It's frequently argued that the entire body of knowledge about computer viruses and computer security is reposed in a relative (or virtual) handful of people. Taken in the grander scheme of things, this is probably true. However, to thank everyone who has contributed to this book through an E-mail note, a paper bound in the proceedings of one conference or another, a posting on VIRUS-L, a magazine article, or a book is simply impossible.

That said, there are people who MUST be thanked. First, the eleven other Founding Members of the Virus Security Institute: Dr. Harold Joseph Highland, Ross Greenberg, Dr. Jon David, Padgett Peterson, Frisk Skulason, Chris Fischer, Dr. Alan Solomon, Dr. Klaus Brunnstein, Vesselin Bontchev, Yisrael Radai, and Dr. William Caelli.

From this gathering of security eagles, a few must be singled out: Yisrael Radai for his work on Microsoft Anti-Virus included both in the body of the book and in the Appendix; Vesselin Bontchev for patiently answering endless questions and providing the data from the Virus Test Centre at the University of Hamburg that is found throughout the book. Alan Solomon's own virus history was the jumping off point for Chapter Two. Thanks to Padgett Peterson for, once again, a fine technical edit and his contribution on LAN security. For Harold Highland, who wrote the Foreword and provided much needed support and understanding, there are never enough thanks.

PC Security and Virus Protection

Thanks, next, to Ken van Wyk who moderates VIRUS-L and always had the answer…sometimes before the question was asked.

High praise to Sara Gordon for her interview with Dark Avenger and sharing in the experience of being women in this almost completely male-dominated field.

Sincere thanks and a smile across the miles to Belden Menkus who has taught me more than I will probably ever realize.

Special kudos to Rob Rosenberger who helped not only in the research for this book (a stellar repeat performance!) but, with Ross Greenberg, contributed the treatise on Virus Myths and Realities.

Jack Holleran at the National Computer Security Center and Les Gotsch at NCSC's Dockmaster provided invaluable insights into highly secure situations and communications.

At M&T Press, thanks to Jono Hardjowirogo, a co-survivor of other wars, and to Steve Berkowitz who pulled us both out of the fire. Debra Williams Cauley has been a steady hand throughout the process.

When I needed to venture outside our tight little world of computer viruses and security for reality research, Lt. David L. Citro of the Delaware State Police, Debra Korr of ABC Insurance, and Benjamin Reich, Philadelphia lawyer extraordinaire, were there. Thanks to Ed Williams for his marvelous tale of poorly behaved humans and software and for our long friendship that's been enhanced by the addition of Catherine Laughton Williams to the inner circle.

Special thanks to my cousin, C.R. Jones III, Conservator of the New York State Historical Association and the Farmers' Museum in Cooperstown, NY, for researching his vast collection of 1950s comic books to ensure a proper citation for walkie-talkies and wrist radios.

Thanks, as ever, to my mother who—at 81—is STILL waiting for me to write a book that she can understand but, nonetheless, adds each new title to her ever-growing collection. And dusts them regularly.

A salute to my father whose mantra, "Every day's work every day," comes clearly to me each morning as I sit down to write. As the old Irish blessing goes, "May God be good to him." God may have met his match with Dad and they're probably teeing off at the 7th hole of the Celestial Golf Course at this very moment. And I think God wouldn't dare NOT to be good to Dad. They have both been very good to me.

The kids' indulgence in the process is, possibly, the result of long experience. "Oh, Mom, are you writing ANOTHER book and are you on deadline AGAIN?" Yeah, guys. I am. Thanks to Rob, Max, Liz, JT and Libby.

The last and best thanks, as always, to my partner in the adventures of my life and work—Andy Hopkins. Without Andy there would be no disk in the back of this book. Without Andy there would be no reason to get up in the morning to hear Dad telling me "Every day's work every day."

Sincere thanks to all.

Foreword

For many professionals in computer security: PC security is an oxymoron and virus protection is self-inflicted punishment.

Real PC security is not attainable. Virus protection is needed because users have not yet rebelled against existing hardware architectures and inadequate operating systems to force suppliers to redesign existing computer systems to be easy to use, easy to secure, and invulnerable to viruses.

Professional computer security means:

[a] protecting computers and their services from all natural and man-made hazards,

[b] providing assurance that the computer performs its critical functions correctly, and

[c] assuring the user that there are no harmful side-effects.

In the world of mainframes, and even with minicomputers, a system's security is a shared responsibility among a core of computer professionals. Some of the security functions are built into the hardware. Some are part of the operating system. Many are totally automated, untouched by human hands. That world is free from computer viruses.

No user stops to make backups. This chore is supervised by an individual, or even a staff, responsible for maintaining backup tapes, indexing the library, and providing lookup and restore services. There are special programmers who update executable programs and utilities when new versions are received. Operations staff periodically test the health of the system. Users are not even aware of these changes. A user with a problem calls the computer center's technical support staff.

In the world of the personal computer, you, the user, must take time to make backups. *You* update software when newer versions arrive. *You* are responsible for the health of your system. If there's a problem it's you who must wade through the lengthy, poorly-written manuals, and wait endlessly on hold for the vendor's technical support. And you must sit idly by while antivirus programs scan the hard disk and make integrity checks.

With large systems there is a professional staff to perform various security functions. With a PC, the user is chief cook, bottle washer, and floor sweeper. And in their spare time the user must also go hunt for computer viruses.

Probably the biggest PC security threat is the user. Most are unaware of what it takes to maintain a healthy system. Even those in the know, too often do not take the time to do the whole job.

In this book, Pamela Kane provides you with the basic checklists to keep your system virus-free and humming. This book is written in a friendly tone. It avoids typical computerese and technical jargon. It is sparing in its use of obscure technical terms and helps you understand a specific problem or master a security feature without a dictionary or a degree in computer science.

Pamela Kane unlocks the secrets of PC operation so that you are prepared for possible disasters and understand how to avoid them before they occur. If they occur, in spite of your best efforts, you're prepared to handle them. This book provides an excellent explanation of computer viruses and offers excellent help in protecting your system from attack.

This book takes you beyond virus protection and into the larger world of PC security to help you protect your equipment and data. Enjoy learning how you can help keep your PC secure so that it's always available for your use.

Dr. Harold Joseph Highland, F.I.C.S.
Editor-in-Chief, *Computers & Security*
April 1994

Introduction

It's been quite a while since a major book about computer viruses was written—perhaps because things in the virus world have moved so quickly in the past few years that anyone who had the solid background to write about the problem was too busy working on it.

Things have, at long last, settled down—at least for the moment. The Prophets of Doom who grabbed world-wide headlines have slunk away. A more scientific approach—through the efforts of EICAR, CARO and VSI—is in place. Computer viruses have become part of a larger picture called SECURITY.

Rather than imagining shadowy spectres lurking behind half-closed doors, we are beginning to know the names and faces of those who would sabotage our data.

As we move into a new day of awareness, it is time for a new look at computer viruses and a new look at our personal computers and creating secure environments.

If you think you "know" about computer viruses, it is a safe bet that you don't. If you think your PC—either at home or in a work environment is secure—you're probably wrong. If you believe that the antivirus program you have on your computer is keeping you safe from tomorrow's disaster, think again.

That's why it was time for a new book that draws on the collective experience of virus fighters (and virus *writers*) around the world.

This book goes from the absolute basics—understandable to even the greenest novice user—to concepts that perhaps only a few thousand people, world-wide, will understand or care about.

Take What You Need and Leave the Rest...

This is a book you will come back to, time and again. But if it's in your hands, you already care about protecting your PC from viruses (that's why there's the disk in the back) and about the larger issues. If you can't wait to test the PANDA Utilities in the back, rip out the disk, install it and, please, RTFB (read the book) for how they work and what they do.

After that, settle down in a comfortable chair and begin to read, secure in the knowledge that your PC is as well-protected as any in the world.

How Long Till My Soul Gets It Right? — Part I

There are some things that our own hearts and souls just can't countenance. Why would ANYONE write a computer virus, much less spread it around to innocent users? That age of innocence is past. Computer viruses are a fact of life in the mid-'90s; all of us are at risk. In the first chapters of this book you'll learn the basics, including the words that the media seems to purposely misunderstand or miscommunicate. There's a chronology of the explosion of the virus problem, and a debunking of the myths that have surrounded computer viruses since Day One. Sara Gordon's conversations with the world's most famous (infamous) virus writer, Dark Avenger, provide a fascinating insight into the "who" behind the phenomenon. These first three chapters will help you "get your arms around" the computer virus question.

Risky Business — Part II

This part of the book examines, both in everyday and technical terms, what the security risks facing today's PCs, their owners, and their owners' data are. Everyone can understand a burglary—it's more difficult to understand how a mismatched operating system and a utility program can spell data disaster. Here, the functions of hardware, software, and common sense are pulled apart and put back together again. At the end of this group of chapters, you will be able to put together your own disaster recovery plan, know how to keep your data safe and secure, and how to combat your own worst enemy—yourself.

The Seven Percent Solution — Part III

These chapters examine, in close technical detail, just how hardware and software work together (or, sometimes, at swords' points) toward reaching security and antivirus solutions. There's a discerning look at Microsoft's late entry into the antivirus field, MSAV, released with DOS 6.0. The differences between the various antivirus approaches are discussed in detail and there's a clear-eyed look at the "experts" in the field. In the last chapter, be prepared to have your socks roll up and down a few times when we talk about what's coming tomorrow. (And you thought today was bad enough!)

Appendices — Part IV

Here's where you'll find the accumulated knowledge of experts around the world. Appendix A is the FAQ (Frequently Asked Questions) document from Internet's VIRUS_L forum. If you have a specific question, chances are you'll find the answer here. Appendix B is an in-depth look at Microsoft's new antivirus program, its strengths and weaknesses. Appendix C represents years of work and cooperation among members of international antivirus groups and lists every virus known at the time of publication. In addition, you'll see which viruses are running around "in the wild" and how often they appear.

The Disk in Back — Part V

Here is the documentation for the legendary DR. PANDA UTILITIES, now in a new incarnation as PANDA PRO. Not too long ago, one of the European antivirus vendors announced that it was "impossible" for any product to reliably find a virus called "Number of the Beast." PANDA PRO does. We will not fall prey to the temptation to say we find 100% of all viruses, known or unknown, but we're still waiting for one to show up we can't find.

Combination Lock

With the information found in this book and the software bound into the back, you have all the essential information you need to not only use locks but to build them from scratch to protect your PC and its data.

Why This Book is for You

Most of us fear computer viruses—and well we should. Almost 4,000 of them are ready, willing, and eager to chomp their way through our systems. This book teaches you how to identify and understand viruses, and then supplies you with the antiviral software to combat and protect your valuable PC data.

If you want to know how viruses work, how our PC's operating systems almost *encourage* them to work, or learn about the strange symbiosis between virus writers and those who would block their efforts, this book is for you. A contemporary history of viruses is provided, along with an exhaustive A-to-Z catalog of viruses in current circulation, describing each one in detail and how to defend against it.

Virus vulnerability is not the only danger to your PC. You have a significant investment in your computer, your programs, and your data. Securing your PC means learning to plan for disasters, identify hardware and software risks, and securing your data. In this book, you'll confront your enemies—real or imagined.

You'll learn just what dangers—random acts of God, pets or terrorists, for example—can compromise your system and the data it holds. For instance, your local power monopoly can bring your PC to its knees in time of heavy power use without a by-your-leave or warning. The drunk driver who hits an electrical switching station couldn't care less how many files you have open under Windows when the collision knocks out the power for miles around. Even for an instant.

The burglar who sees your laptop next to your briefcase isn't interested in the corporate secrets that may be stored on the hard drive; he's interested in the resale value of something that returns big bucks per portable ounce. There's another kind of thief, though. The one who knows that your corporate secrets *are* on the laptop. He couldn't care less about the value of the computer itself.

This complete overview of viruses and security on the PC platform helps you pinpoint your system's vulnerabilities and shows you how to address them. With this step-by-step approach to protecting your equipment and data, you'll be well-prepared in the war against information sabotage.

Viruses and Security: The Basics

Almost ten years have passed since the distribution of the first destructive programming targeted at personal computers; seven years have passed since the first computer viruses in wide circulation made their appearances. Still, people—people who should know—don't seem to know what the term *virus* means. In November, 1993, the *New York Times* termed a time bomb set by an annoyed programmer as a virus. In this chapter, *virus* (which Sanford Sheridan acronymized in the late 1980s as Vital Information Resources Under Siege) will be explained, torn apart, and put back together again.

The general perception—and common misconception—seems to be that any destructive program, run on any computer, is a virus. Not so.

Perhaps such ignorance was excusable in the late 1980s when a mere handful of people had even the first clue as to what the term might mean. The folks at G.C. Merriam, publisher of the Merriam-Webster family of dictionaries, called *computer virus* the 1988 term of the year.

It wasn't until 1993, however, that the term was actually defined in print in *Merriam-Webster's Collegiate Dictionary*: "a computer program usually hidden within another seemingly innocuous program that produces copies of itself and inserts them into other programs and that usually performs a malicious action (as destroying data)."

In November 1988, the prestigious Information Systems Security Association convened a symposium of the fifty "best and brightest" in the security/virus field to examine the emerging problem. Notable among the events was the inability of the assembled company to agree on a working definition of the term *virus*.

It's a pity that the *Dallas Morning News* hadn't talked to either group before printing this definition: "a virus [is] a program that can order a computer to replicate itself." Even though the price of PCs has fallen dramatically since the early days, the idea of getting several computers for the price of one, merely by adding a virus, is tempting.

What a Virus Is

First off, the *Dallas Morning News* folks had two words right: *program* and *replicate*. To be nit-pickingly correct, a virus is program code, that is, a set of instructions to be executed by the computer when a program infected by the virus is run. The second essential component of a virus is that it must replicate. Some replications are relatively simple. The infamous Michelangelo virus simply copies itself to any diskette that's used in an infected machine. The highly sophisticated polymorphic viruses infect each program file with slightly altered versions of the infecting code.

So, remember that a virus is a program that replicates. A virus does not necessarily have to do anything destructive, it just has to spread.

What a Virus Isn't

A virus isn't a time bomb or logic bomb like the one described in the *New York Times*. It also isn't a *worm* like the program young Robert Morris, Jr., sent flying across the ARPAnet in November 1988. A virus also isn't a *Trojan horse*, which does its dirty work (usually) upon the first execution of the program. These types of programs are usually loosely classed as *malware* and will be thoroughly dissected later in this chapter.

How Viruses Spread

There are two basic types of viruses (we consider the term *virii* to be precious and pretentious): *program infectors* and *boot sector infectors*. For the purposes of clarity, programs are executable code, usually with the file extensions of .EXE or .COM. They are infected when a program infected with a virus writes the virus code into another .EXE or .COM file. The next time the newly infected program is run, it will infect other .EXE or .COM files. The previous program will, usually, infect as well.

A *boot sector infector* (BSI) is passed at the time of disk access—which can be as simple as the DIR command—even if no operations are performed on the disk. It enters a PC when the computer is booted from an infected disk.

It's not this simple, of course. Later in this chapter, I'll look at infection methods in detail.

Where Viruses Are

Funny thing. Even though the percentage of known viruses weighs heavily toward program infectors (a ratio of ten program infectors to one boot sector infector according to the Virus Research Center at the University of Hamburg), at least 50 percent of infections occurring "in the wild" are boot sector infectors. Cynical veterans of the virus wars have an explanation for this. It doesn't take a great deal of programming skill to write a program infector; you can even download a virus-writing kit from renegade bulletin boards complete with pull-down menus and a mouse interface. Writing a boot sector infector is much more difficult, and it's easy to see why a well-written boot sector infector enjoys more success.

Not only are the talented virus writers to blame for this. Writing an antivirus product that reliably finds and destroys boot sector infectors is an even more difficult task—one that only a precious few developers have bothered to learn. Some of the most popular antivirus programs, in terms of units sold, notably Central Point Anti-Virus and its offspring, Microsoft Anti-Virus which is included with DOS 6, can't find a previously unknown or slightly modified boot infector. Thus, it's very possible that there are infected PCs all over the world spreading boot sector infectors to every disk with which they come in contact. It's also a possibility that the owners of those PCs don't even know they may be infected because they're running an antivirus program and believe that they're safe. After all, if you run an antivirus program and a big banner appears on the screen stating, "This PC is CERTIFIED Virus-Free!" you'd believe it, wouldn't you? But you shouldn't!

A Beginning Viral Lexicon

Following are the basic "dirty words" in the world of viruses. These simple definitions lay the foundation for the in-depth technical discussion that follows in the next section.

- **Malware:** An emerging word that covers any computer program with a destructive component. All viruses are malware, but not all malware contains a virus. Trojan horses, worms, and logic bombs are also malware.

- **Virus:** The key words in the definition of virus are *program* and *replicate*; destructive action is not a requirement in the strictest definition, but the street definition includes it.

- **Program infector (a/k/a file infector):** The virus inserts itself into an executable program and attempts to spread. Some infect any executable (.COM, .EXE, .PRG, .SYS, .OVL, or .MNU), while others infect only .COM files or .EXE files.

- **Direct program infector:** When a file containing the virus is executed, the virus attempts to infect one or more files as part of its run-time activity.

- **Resident program infector:** These viruses hide in RAM as soon as the infected program is run and infect each and every subsequent program as soon as it is executed (some resident program infectors add certain parameters before infection takes place). Resident viruses are more efficient than direct infectors.

- **Fast infector:** These viruses infect files on any access (such as a scanner examining the disk) instead of an execution.

- **Boot sector infector (a/k/a system infector, boot record infector):** These can affect either the DOS boot sector or the PC's master boot record on its hard drive. Theoretically, they are hard to catch because the PC must be booted with an infected diskette in the A drive, but after they are in place, they infect every diskette that's used.

- **Multi-partite virus (a/k/a boot-and-file virus):** The best (or worst) of both worlds. These viruses can infect both program files and boot sectors.

- **File system virus (a/k/a cluster virus):** This type of virus changes directory table entries so that it sneaks in before the program the user intends to run.

- **Stealth virus:** Stealth viruses specialize in forgery. They make a copy of good information, store it where the virus can find it, and redirect calls from antivirus products to the clean information while the dirty work goes on.

- **Companion virus:** Companions take advantage of the DOS hierarchy of executable files. A .COM file always executes before an .EXE file with the same name. Companion viruses build a .COM file with the same name as an existing file so that, when the user types the file name, the virus file runs first and then calls the good file.

- **Polymorphic virus:** The point of polymorphs is, arguably, to evade signature scanning techniques. As the virus spreads, it rewrites its own code strings so the child is not identical to the parent.

- **Mutation engine:** This particularly nasty set of code can turn any virus into a polymorphic virus.

- **Scanner:** An antivirus program that searches through the files on a disk for the presence of viruses. The standard technique for scanners is a signature check. These are developed by taking a "fingerprint" of each virus known to the developer and searching for it.

- **Integrity checker:** These antivirus programs compare files with a model created when the integrity checker was installed. Changes to files can often indicate virus activity.

- **Behavior blocker:** Behavior blockers don't actively seek viruses. Rather, they attempt to stop the sorts of destructive activity that viruses often attempt.

Plumbing the Depths

The following paragraphs were taken from the VIRUS-L FAQ (Frequently Asked Questions) file. VIRUS-L is a moderated forum on the Internet in which antivirus researchers participate. It is moderated by Dr. Kenneth van Wyk of Carnegie Mellon University, Pittsburgh, Pennsylvania, and is sponsored by Lehigh University, Bethlehem, Pennsylvania, where one of the first virus attacks on PCs took place.

The entire VIRUS-L FAQ documentation is included as Appendix B.

NOTE

What are computer viruses (and why should I worry about them)?

According to Fred Cohen's well-known definition, a COMPUTER VIRUS is a computer program that can infect other computer programs by modifying them in such a way as to include a (possibly evolved) copy of itself. Note that a program does not have to perform outright damage (such as deleting or corrupting files) in order to be called a virus. However, Cohen uses the terms within his definition (e.g. "program" and "modify") a bit differently from the way most anti-virus researchers use them, and classifies as viruses some things which most of us would not consider viruses.

Many people use the term loosely to cover any sort of program that tries to hide its (malicious) function and tries to spread onto as many computers as possible. (See the definition of "Trojan".) Be aware that what constitutes a program for a virus to infect may include a lot more than is at first obvious—don't assume too much about what a virus can or can't do!

These software pranks are very serious; they are spreading faster than they are being stopped, and even the least harmful of viruses could be fatal. For example, a virus that stops your computer and displays a message, in the context of a hospital life-support computer, could be fatal. Even those who created the viruses could not stop them if they wanted to; it requires a concerted effort from computer users to be "virus-aware," rather than the ignorance and ambivalence that have allowed them to grow to such a problem.

What is a Trojan Horse?

A Trojan Horse is a program that does something undocumented which the programmer intended, but that the user would not approve of if he knew about it. According to some people, a virus is a particular case of a Trojan Horse, namely one which is able to spread to other programs (i.e., it turns them into Trojans too). According to others, a virus that does not do any deliberate damage (other than merely replicating) is not a Trojan. Finally, despite the definitions, many people use the term "Trojan" to refer only to a *non-replicating* malicious program, so that the set of Trojans and the set of viruses are disjoint.

According to Dr. Fred Cohen's definition, a virus is a program that makes a copy of itself. To this we add "without the knowledge or approval of the user." Certainly the program COMMAND.COM can make a copy of itself if the user types **COPY COMMAND.COM A:**. This does not make COMMAND.COM a virus even though it contains the code necessary to make a duplicate of itself or any other program.

Not all destructive programs can be classed as Trojans either. Surely COMMAND.COM has the ability to delete files and FORMAT has the capability of destroying all the files on a disk. Yet the user is, or should be, fully aware of the risks associated with the use of these programs. Or maybe not! The latest versions of DOS include programs to UNFORMAT a disk and to UNDELETE files—presumably to protect users who were unaware of the consequences of DELETE and FORMAT.

Anatomy of a Virus

A computer virus is so named because it acts much like its organic counterpart. A virus contains enough protein to be classified as organic, but cannot live and reproduce without a host organism to supply other organic material. A computer virus is more like a hitchhiker than an organic virus. It is a set of computer instructions that hitches a ride on a legitimate program or replaces the instructions of a legitimate program. Computer viruses do not feed off the host like their organic counterparts, but the host program is used to hide the activities of the virus and cause the virus instructions to be activated without the user knowing it. To be classified as a virus, the code must contain instructions that copy the virus code to another host. This is one property that all computer viruses have in common. Other properties may include installation in memory of the virus code to aid in subsequent infections, stealth, mutation, trigger, and damage. Not all viruses have all of these properties. While some viruses merely infect, others can cause catastrophic damage to the computer's file system.

The PC Hardware and Viruses

The personal computer with the "Intel Inside" has become the target of the majority of computer viruses. Commonly called the PC, the IBM PC and compatibles all share a common microprocessor family. Starting in 1981 with the first IBM PC, which set the standard for desktop computing, all PCs have a hardware architecture based on the Intel 86 series of chips.

The Intel 8086 was the first of the popular microprocessors to address more than 64K of memory and calculate in 16-bit binary digits. The Intel 8088, which was used in the first IBM PCs, was essentially the same as the 8086, except that data was moved to and from memory in 8-bit binary digits called bytes instead of the 16-bit binary digits of the 8086. Both of these processors calculate memory addresses in 20-bit digits, giving the processor a capacity of 1M of memory (2^{20} or 1,048,576 bytes). Two internal 16-bit registers at a time are used in memory address calculation, a segment register and an offset register. The segment register divides the 1M address space into 65,536 paragraphs that begin every 16 bytes. Because the offset register is 16 bits wide, it can contain numbers up to 65,535 or 64K. The 1M of address space is thus divided into 65,536 overlapping segments, each of which can be 65,536 bytes long.

The next generation of IBM PC was the PC AT, which featured the Intel 80286. The 80286 has a memory address capability of 24 bits instead of 20 bits like the older 8086 and 8088 (16M as opposed to 1M). Additionally, the 80286 is a dual mode processor. It can act just like an 8086 in real mode or it can extend the capabilities in protected mode. When operating in protected mode, the processor can isolate memory addresses so that one process has no access to another process's address space. One of the problems encountered when programming for the 80286 was that it could not easily switch from real to protected mode and back. This problem was solved in the next generation.

The next processor in the Intel series, the 80386, added a 32-bit address capability and 32-bit calculation. In addition to solving the problem of real and protected mode switching, the 80386 also has a virtual 8086 mode that enables the processor to act like the older processor without switching from protected mode.

Subsequent additions to the series, the 80486 and Pentium (not 80586), add more instructions to the processor's calculating capabilities, on-chip memory caching to speed memory access, and some extra internal registers for calculations and memory addressing. One thing that Intel tried to do with each new processor was to make it backwardly compatible with its predecessors. All the newer processors can operate in real mode and carry out all the instructions meant for the 8086. (There is one notable exception. The instruction MOV CS,AX, which loads the code segment from a register is only supported in the 8088 and 8086. Several viruses use this instruction and do not work on newer processors.)

What this backward compatibility means for the user is that any software written for the older chips almost certainly works with the newer ones too. What this means to the person who writes viruses is that all Intel-based computers can operate in real mode where any program can have access to any conventional memory address. This and the fact that there are millions of PCs sitting on desktops throughout the world has made them the target of more viruses than any other computing platform. If other types of desktop computers—such as Apple, Atari, and Commodore—had the installed base of the Intel-based computers, they would also be a tempting target.

Another of the frequently asked questions is whether a virus written for a Mac can attack a PC or vice versa. The answer is simply no. Because a virus consists of a series of instructions to the microprocessor, and each brand of microprocessor uses different instructions, there is no way a virus can cross from one type of computer to another. Even computers that use compatible file structures, such as the PC and the Atari ST, use different processors. The PCs Intel 80x86 instructions are interpreted differently by the Atari's 680x0 family of processors. If you cannot trade programs from one machine to another, then you cannot trade viruses.

There is a least one virus that attempts to infect source code. Source code is the text that is compiled into the processor instructions that make up a program. Whoever wrote this virus may have been trying to infect across platforms, apparently hoping that the source code would be compiled for different computers and make the virus spread. However, source code is plain text and the added instructions are fairly easy to spot, so the virus has not been successful in the field.

Operating System and Viruses

Another controlling factor in virus spread is the *operating system*. The majority of PCs use the Microsoft or IBM operating system called DOS, a three letter acronym for disk operating system. There are many disk operating systems, but the one usually mentioned as just plain DOS is in reality IBM's PC-DOS or Microsoft's MS-DOS. These two brand names are twins, and their operating systems function essentially alike. Any program written for PC-DOS will also work with MS-DOS. Other operating systems used on PCs, such as OS/2 and UNIX (the operating system used by most mainframe computers), are not compatible with DOS. Programs written under UNIX or OS/2 do not operate with DOS even though the processor is compatible. The reverse may not be true. OS/2 provides DOS compatibility, so many programs written for DOS can operate under OS/2.

Some viruses, particularly boot infectors, can operate across operating systems, but the majority cannot. If a virus uses DOS functions, it is not viable in another operating system. Boot infectors operate before the operating system is loaded and may be written so that they make no use of the operating system at all. These viruses pose a threat to all PCs regardless of the operating system.

Infection Methods

Most PC viruses can be broken down into two major types: *boot infectors* and *program infectors*. This section examines each type and explains in more detail how they can infect your system.

Program Infectors

To understand how viruses infect files, you must first know how a file stored on a disk is loaded into memory and run as a program. A program file on disk contains the code necessary for the central processing unit (CPU) to perform some useful task. There may also be sections of a program file that contain data used by the program and not part of the instructions to the processor. There may also be sections of the file that contain neither instructions nor data but are merely place holders for areas that will be used for data while the program is running.

A program file is merely the magnetic image of the program stored on the disk. After the file is loaded into memory, and the operating system switches the CPU to begin processing the instructions contained in the program, the program file becomes what is called a process. Memory areas that do not get control of the CPU are not considered processes, even if there is valid instruction code in that area.

All MS/PC-DOS processes have an entry point and at least one exit point that returns control of the CPU to the process that loaded it, usually COMMAND.COM. At least one process is always running, even if the computer appears to be sitting idly waiting for input. When the DOS prompt appears on the screen, COMMAND.COM is in control, constantly monitoring the keyboard for input. While COMMAND.COM is the most commonly used command interpreter or top level process of the operating system, it is by no means the only one that can be used. Many systems replace COMMAND.COM with another top level process that can be defined in the configuration file CONFIG.SYS. One thing all top level processes share is that they exit to themselves. If they do not, the operating system halts.

MS/PC-DOS uses two types of program files. Both contain executable code; the difference is in how the program is loaded into memory by the operating system. In the original design of the IBM PC, there were only a few internal DOS commands. These are functions that remain in memory at all times, such as DIR, COPY, and ERASE. When COMMAND.COM interprets these commands, it jumps immediately to the processes that control the action. All external DOS commands are contained on the DOS disk and are loaded into memory, processed, and then discarded from memory. These short command files are designated with the file extension .COM, for command. These files must fit within one segment of memory (64K) and are binary images of the system memory. DOS loads a .COM file as is into memory and transfers control to the first byte of the file. Because the load address may vary, any memory reference must be as a relative offset, not an exact location, a restriction that is not hard to implement.

Although the original idea that .COM files were to be an extension of the operating system's internal commands has long since disappeared, the .COM extension is still supported for any program that can fit within a 64K memory segment.

Application programs are designated with the extension .EXE, for executable. These files are not direct memory images, can be any length up to the amount of available memory, and need the help of the DOS program loader to run. These files contain a header with information for the loader including, entry point, stack segment, and size of the program. There is also a relocation table that lists the parts of the program where memory references must be adjusted to reflect the actual load address. The header is not loaded into memory as a part of the program, but is used by DOS to load and convert the remainder of the file and begin to process the program at the entry point.

It is interesting to note that the extensions .COM and .EXE are arbitrary and are not used by the DOS load and execute function. In early versions of DOS, the load and execute function was contained in the COMMAND.COM program, but later versions of DOS only use COMMAND.COM to locate an executable file. The actual load and execute function is part of the operating system. Because the user types only the file name, with no extension, there is no distinction among internal DOS commands, external DOS commands (.COM), and program files (.EXE). COMMAND.COM first searches an internal table of commands and only then begins a file search.

COMMAND.COM first adds the extension .COM to the typed command and searches the default directory for a file by that name. If this search fails, the extension .EXE is added to the command, and the default directory is searched again. COMMAND.COM then searches for a file with the .BAT extension. Batch files are not program files that contain processor instructions but files that contain further instructions to COMMAND.COM in text form. If COMMAND.COM cannot find a matching file with either a .COM, .EXE, or .BAT extension, it then begins a search in each directory named in the PATH variable in the environment. The first time COMMAND.COM finds a match on either a .COM or .EXE extension, it loads the file into memory and transfers control to the entry point. Finding a BAT extension ends the search, and COMMAND.COM processes the instructions in the batch file.

Before loading a program into memory, DOS builds a 256-byte program segment prefix (PSP). What follows the PSP is dependent on the type of file. COMMAND.COM loads a .COM file into the bytes immediately following the PSP and then begins processing at the first byte of the program.

DOS also loads .EXE files into memory immediately following the PSP. Any segment references in the program are patched to reflect the address where the program begins. The stack registers are set according to the instructions contained in the .EXE header. Finally, the entry point is determined by values also set in the .EXE header, and the process begins at this point.

How does DOS determine if the program is an .EXE or a .COM? Not by the file extension, but by the first two bytes of the file. Executable (.EXE) programs contain the ASCII characters *MZ* (the initials of Mark Zbikowski, one of the developers of DOS) as the first two characters. Regardless of the program's file extension, if the first two characters are *MZ*, the file is loaded as an .EXE file; otherwise, the file is loaded as a binary memory image. Keep in mind though that COMMAND.COM will not find a program that does not have either an .EXE or .COM extension unless it is modified to search for a different extension.

Companion Viruses

There is a subclass of program infectors called *companion viruses*, which take advantage of the DOS program search hierarchy. While some researchers deny that companion viruses are truly viruses, their existence cannot be denied. A companion virus creates an entire program with the same base file name as an .EXE program, except with a .COM extension. This file is marked as hidden so it will not appear in normal directory searches. When the user types the file name of the program at the DOS command prompt, DOS runs the hidden .COM file instead of the .EXE file. A companion virus stays hidden by explicitly calling the .EXE file after it is finished doing what ever it is programmed to do. Thus, the user who types 123 on the command line actually runs the companion program 123.COM, which then runs 123.EXE.

What 123.COM actually does (other than running 123.EXE) is entirely dependent on the code within 123.COM. At the very least, the companion virus will attempt to find another .EXE program and make a copy of the virus as a .COM file under the same name.

While a companion program may be proficient at propagating copies of itself within the system, it is difficult to spread from PC to PC. The normal COPY *.* command will not copy a hidden file nor will the companion be copied if the .EXE program is explicitly copied. The only way a companion virus can propagate from machine to machine is if it intercepts the DOS function interrupt and waits for a COPY command and then performs the copy function for itself.

A companion virus makes no change to the program file and is therefore missed by many antivirus programs. Whether it should be classified as a true virus or as a separate Trojan horse program is an exercise left to academics. The result is the same to the user: The program he or she intends to run is corrupted. Virus or not, a companion program is definitely malware.

Overwriting File Infectors

An overwriting file infector is a virus that replaces a portion of the program's code with the virus code. This act can often disable the host program, making the presence of the virus immediately apparent to even the most unsophisticated user. If a user types **123** at the command prompt (or selects **Spread Sheet** from a menu), and the computer hangs or garbage appears on the screen, it's a pretty good indication that the 123 program is not what it used to be.

Some overwriting viruses are so unsophisticated as to write the virus code over the first part of the file. In the case of an .EXE file, this act destroys the header information (including the .EXE signature *MZ*), and the file is loaded as a binary image just like a .COM file. The virus gets control and does its work, but the original program is destroyed in the process. If the virus does not exit to DOS and tries to continue with the destroyed program, there is a good possibility that the computer will simply hang, and the user will have to reboot to continue.

Other overwriting viruses are extremely sophisticated and use overwriting as a method of stealth (see the "Stealth" section later in this chapter). In this case, before the virus infects, it attempts to analyze the host file to identify a block of space that will not be executed. This space could be an uninitialized data area or stack area. The virus then overwrites this area of the file and sets the entry point to jump to the virus code. When the virus finishes its work, the original entry point is restored, and the program is run as normal. The fact that the host program overwrites the area used by the virus in memory is of no consequence because the virus code is disposable after it has run. As long as the virus code remains in the file, the virus can run again the next time the program is executed.

An overwriting virus has the advantage of not adding to the file length. This makes identification difficult for the casual user. A simple DIR will not indicate any change in the host file. Scanning and integrity checking antivirus software have little trouble in identifying the infected host unless the virus uses other means of stealth.

One of the first identified PC viruses, the so-called Lehigh virus, was an overwriting virus of the COMMAND.COM program used as a command processor in most PCs. This virus placed its code in an area of COMMAND.COM that was used as a stack and was represented by a large block of binary zeros in the file. The original Lehigh virus left its mark by allowing the date and time fields of the directory entry to change, a mistake not often repeated in later viruses.

Pre- and Post-Pending File Infectors

The other two subclasses of file infecting viruses are the pre- and post-penders. Both of these types of viruses add the virus code to a host program file. The pre-pending virus adds code to the beginning of the file; the post-pending adds code to the end of the file.

Post-pending is the easiest to accomplish from a programming stand-point because the entire file does not need to be read into memory. A DOS function will easily allow new bytes to be written to the end of a file. All the virus has to do is get the length of the file, read the first few bytes so the entry point can be changed, and then add the virus code to the end of the file. The virus code is already in memory; after all, this is the program that has control. Searching for a program file, altering the file, and then writing the changes to disk are all tasks easily performed with simple DOS function calls.

Pre-pending viruses are a little more difficult from a programming stand-point because the entire file must be read into memory, the virus code written to disk, and the host program file written to the end of the virus code. This takes more time because there is more disk access than needed for a post-pending virus. Time is the enemy of viruses. A noticeable slowdown in system performance can raise a warning flag that even a novice user can spot.

Infection Methods

There are two methods the viruses use to infect files. One type of virus runs only when an infected program is run and terminates immediately. The other is a resident infector which, once run, remains in memory. Regardless of which method a virus uses, there is one cardinal rule: The virus *must* get control of the processor.

Nonresident Infectors

Nonresident viruses get control when the host program is run. The majority of them reside at the entry point of the host program or alter the entry point to indicate the virus code. There are a few that patch themselves into the logic of the host program and gain control at a certain point in the operation of the process, but these are rare. After a nonresident virus is in control, there is one procedure that it must perform: make a copy of the virus on another program. If it is not capable of propagating it is, by definition not a virus.

The method of making a copy varies with the virus. Because a nonresident virus runs only when the host program is executed, it must make the most of its one-time opportunity. It may attempt to infect every file on the system, but this noticeably delays the start of the host program. It may attempt to infect every file in the default directory, but this could affect the spread of the virus. Some viruses only attempt to infect one other file. While this method produces little delay in the host program's operation, it greatly reduces the opportunities for the virus to spread throughout the system and to other PCs.

> In testing various viruses, I introduced a slow spreading nonresident infector to the DOS subdirectory of a test machine. The virus attached itself to the first program it found in the directory, APPEND.COM. However, APPEND is a program that I never use. After removing the infecting host, the virus never spread because the new host program was never run. Maybe this is a good reason to leave those unused programs on the disk!

Resident Infectors

Resident infectors are by far the more dangerous of the virus types. These viruses remain in memory after the host program has terminated and get control by hooking one or more of the interrupts. The most common interrupt hooked is the DOS function interrupt (33), although the disk BIOS interrupt (19), keyboard interrupt (9), and timer interrupt (26), are commonly used.

A resident infector leaves itself in memory either by using the DOS *terminate and stay resident function* (TSR) or by manipulating the memory allocation scheme to reserve a block of memory that will not be used by subsequent programs. The interrupt vector table is adjusted to enable the virus code to get control periodically.

When a resident infector hooks the DOS function interrupt 33 any time a subsequent program calls a DOS function, the virus examines the function request and takes action. It can infect a program any time a program file is opened, closed, or executed. In fact, the actions that could trigger a resident virus are almost unlimited, and some have not even been tried.

Another common action taken by resident infectors is an attempt at stealth (see the "Stealth" section later in this chapter), the only way a virus can hide from antivirus software. There is no way a stealth virus can hide if it is not resident, and it cannot be resident unless it is run. This is one of the reasons all reputable manufacturers of antivirus software advise users to reboot from a DOS disk in drive A when checking for viruses. However, only 1 percent of users bother to reboot before checking for viruses. Of the remaining 99 percent, 10 percent do not reboot before checking for viruses, and 89 percent do not even bother to check for viruses.

System or Boot Infectors

A boot infector is a class of viruses that does not use a program file as a host, but replaces the bootstrap loader found on the first sector of all disks and diskettes. Because boot infectors get control before the operating system is loaded, they are completely operating system independent. Whether the PC runs MS/IBM-DOS, OS/2, UNIX, or any other operating system, the machine is vulnerable to boot infectors.

When a computer is turned on or reset, the power on self-test (POST) routine built into the ROM attempts to load the very first sector of a diskette in the first drive (drive 0). If the diskette does not respond, the ROM routine then attempts to load the first sector of the hard disk (drive 0x80). After the sector is loaded into memory at address 0000:7c00, control is transferred to that point. The bootstrap load program contained in the first sector is one of the only PC programs loaded at a specific memory address.

The first sector of a diskette is different from the first sector of a hard disk, but both accomplish the same basic task of beginning to load DOS. The boot sector of a diskette contains a small program that loads the diskette directory and searches for the DOS file, IO.SYS or IBMBIO.COM, depending on the brand of DOS the PC is using. After that file is located, it is read into memory, and control is transferred there to continue the loading of the operating system. If the diskette does not contain the IBMBIO.COM or IO.SYS file, the loader prints the following message and waits for a keypress: "Non-system disk. Replace and press any key." After a key is pressed, the boot sector is reloaded, and the process is repeated. The boot sector of a diskette contains a data area that describes the layout of the diskette, known as the BIOS parameter block (BPB).

The first sector of a hard disk contains a small program that locates the DOS boot sector for the hard disk, a sector similar to the boot sector of a diskette. The first sector also contains a data area that describes the partitioning of the hard disk, whether it is one large disk or several smaller disks. Because the first sector contains the partitioning information, it is often erroneously referred to as the partition sector. The preferred term for this sector is the master boot record (MBR).

The program code in the MBR locates the DOS boot sector (DBS), reads it into memory, and terminates by passing control to the *DOS boot record* program. The DOS boot record contains the same instructions and data as the first sector of a diskette. In effect, the MBR is just an extra step in the start-up procedure that is unique to hard disk systems.

Because both the DOS boot record of a diskette and the master boot record of a hard disk contain program code that gets control from the CPU before any programs are run, they have become a target of viruses. Also, most users are unaware of the program code contained within the MBR and DBS because it does not appear in the disk directory.

Most boot infector viruses (but not all) move the legitimate boot sector somewhere else on the disk and overwrite the first sector with the virus code. Because DOS, which is loaded after the boot virus has had control, must read the BIOS parameter block of a diskette and the partition data of a hard disk, the virus must be able to return this information to DOS; otherwise, the system will crash before it has even booted. Either the virus must include the BPB or the partition data or it must return the legitimate boot sector when requested.

Therefore, most boot infector viruses remain in memory and intercept disk BIOS calls to the boot sector so that the legitimate sector, regardless of where it is on the disk, is read by DOS. The virus also uses its memory-resident status to check on the infection status of a diskette. Every time a noninfected diskette is accessed, the virus is written to the diskette. After a hard disk has been infected, there is little reason to check again because the hard disk does not change.

The only way a PC can get infected is by attempting to boot from an infected diskette. Like all statements involving viruses, that one is for the most part true, but a little bit false. There are program infectors that are called droppers that also infect the boot sector. Thus, it is possible to get a boot infector through a program, although it is rare. For the most part, boot infector viruses are passed from machine to machine by passing infected diskettes among different users. However, even the act of passing an infected diskette to a clean machine does not guarantee that the virus will spread. The user must reboot the clean machine with the infected diskette locked into drive A. Incidentally, the infected diskette does not have to contain the DOS files to pass the infection. The virus is contained in the boot sector, not the DOS files. Even if the user gets the error message "Non-system disk. Replace and press any key," the virus has already infected the computer. Don't be lulled into a false sense of security by a nonsystem diskette. It can be just as dangerous as a diskette containing the DOS system files.

The boot sector can contain only 512 bytes of code, which is rather short for a truly elaborate program. Either the virus must be relatively simple or it must appropriate extra segments somewhere on the disk. The first boot sector virus, the so called Pakistani Brain virus, marked several sectors on the disk as bad and used them for extra code. Other boot sector viruses use only one sector. As with file infectors there is no hard and fast rule.

There is also no rule that determines where the virus places the legitimate boot sector (if it saves it at all). Most hard disk partitioning schemes leave blank several sectors at the beginning of the disk following the MBR that could be used by the virus. However, diskettes do not have an MBR, and the sector following the boot sector is used for the beginning of the *file allocation table* (FAT). Additionally, there are many different sizes and configurations of diskettes, the primary transmission device of boot infectors. Unless the virus has accounted for all the differences between diskette types and hard disks, it cannot hope to spread, which is the primary raison d'être of a virus.

Some viruses, like the Pakistani Brain virus, mark bad sectors in the FAT, but that sends out a flag that something is wrong. Other viruses use the last sector of the root directory for additional storage in the belief that the user will not have enough files to fill the entire root directory. Other viruses manipulate the partition data to shorten the first partition by several sectors. A few viruses do not use any sector other than the MBR or boot sector.

Other Infectors

There should always be another category when discussing computer viruses. I would tell you how many viruses there are, however, that number would be outdated long before you read this. Let's just say that there are more viruses now than when you began reading this book. There will be even more before you are finished. Some will be (if you pardon the term) successful and infect many machines before defensive measures to combat them are taken. Others will die a quick (and justified) death because they are poorly written. Needless to say, with the proliferation of computer viruses, no discussion can adequately depict and categorize all of them.

Other means of infection that have been seen include manipulation of the file directory and FAT so that a legitimate program's directory entry points to the virus instead of the program. This invalidates the directory and the FAT and would be reported by CHKDSK if the virus could not fool DOS. Like the companion virus, the virus code does not actually reside as an attachment to the host's program file. Instead it uses DOS tricks to make the system do something it was not designed to do. I will again leave it as an exercise for academics as to whether this trick should be classified as a true virus.

Installation

Installation is a phenomenon peculiar to resident viruses. Some viruses work only when the designated host program is run and then terminate. A resident infector remains in memory after the host program exits and continues to infect files or boot sectors until the computer is rebooted.

One of the first known viruses, and still one of the most prevalent, Jerusalem is a resident infector. When the host program is run, the virus code is activated first. The virus searches memory to see if it has been previously installed, and if not, appropriates an area of memory and alters the DOS function interrupt to point to the virus. When the host program terminates, the virus code remains in memory and gets control every time a DOS function call is made.

The next time a program name is entered, COMMAND.COM makes a DOS function call to load and execute that program. The virus code activates and copies the virus code in memory to the program file. The first versions of the virus had no check as to whether an .EXE file was already infected so the program file grew each time it was run. Eventually, the file was too big to load into memory, and DOS issued an error message. In later versions of the virus, this problem has been fixed.

There are many methods a virus can use to install its code in memory. Regardless of which method the virus uses, it must make some provision to ensure that another program does not use that area; otherwise, the machine will probably crash. Some viruses install themselves in low memory in a portion of the interrupt table not often used. Others attempt to use the upper memory areas. Most use a DOS function to allocate a permanent block of memory or manipulate the DOS memory block information.

Boot infectors also remain in memory after the virus code runs when the PC is started. Because DOS is not active at the time the virus is first run, a boot infector usually copies the virus code to the top of user memory, points the disk BIOS interrupt to the code, and adjusts the memory byte that indicates how much memory is installed. Every time a disk is accessed, the virus code gets control from the interrupt and infects the disk being accessed, thus passing the virus along.

Any virus that remains in memory must take control of the processor from time to time. The usual method is to alter the interrupt vector table stored at the beginning of memory. An interrupt is one of the methods the processor uses to transfer process control from one part of memory to another. Some interrupts are caused by the processor itself; others are caused by hardware such as the keyboard, timer, and disk. A large number of interrupts, known as software interrupts, are reserved for programs to use. The binary instruction 11001101 followed by a number between 0 and 255 causes the processor to save the current state of the flags register, the code segment register, and the instruction pointer register. Process then continues at the 4-byte segment:offset indicated by the entry in the interrupt vector table corresponding to the interrupt number. Interrupt vectors point to processes called *interrupt service routines* (ISR), which process the interrupt and return control of the processor to the instruction following the interrupt call.

The interrupt vector table is not protected by the operating system in the PC. Any program can change the values stored in this table and cause the interrupt to process at a different location. Additionally, a process can save a previous vector and pass control onto that location upon exit. This chaining of interrupt processes is commonly performed by legitimate ISRs. While this adds a great deal of flexibility to programming, it also makes the system vulnerable to unwanted processes.

Several interrupt vectors are used by the operating system. The most commonly used interrupt is the DOS function interrupt 33 or 21 hex. (Few use the decimal notation when discussing interrupts, so INT 21 is commonly understood to be the hexadecimal notation for interrupt 33.) Almost all of the DOS functions dealing with the file system are available to programs using INT 21. Any process may intercept DOS function calls before DOS processes them and alter them accordingly. A virus can intercept the call to execute a file and infect it before DOS processes the request. If the virus subsequently chains the function request to DOS, the user is unaware that anything took place, despite the added time it took to process the virus activity.

Point-Counterpoint: Stealth

Ever since the first PC viruses began appearing in the late 1980s, attempts have been made at hiding the virus from the user. If the user can recognize the presence of a virus, it will be eradicated. The success of a virus is dependent on making a large number of copies that can be spread to other PCs. A virus that proudly announces "Hi, I'm a virus" would be unlikely to spread very far. Stealth became more of a factor in viruses with the advent of antivirus programs (see Chapter 12), and viruses now attempt to hide not only from average users but also from antivirus programs as well.

Many viruses contain messages of one sort or another that are often used to name the virus. Often these messages are hidden by coding the text to avoid being spotted by utilities that print the contents of a file. Even before the first viruses appeared, Trojan horse programs that erased a disk contained messages that mocked the user. One of the first to appear was a program called NUKE-LA, which purported to be a graphic of LA LA Land being blown away in a thermonuclear holocaust. Instead, the program erased the disk and printed the text "Arf Arf." The program CHK4BOMB merely reads a program file and prints any ASCII text found in the file. CHK4BOMB was written for a local bulletin board systems (BBS) operator in Wilmington, Delaware, who put it on his board for other BBS operators. Although it was not written as an antivirus program, ten years later it can still be found on BBS and FTP sites around the world. Although CHK4BOMB is of dubious value in stopping the threat of viruses, it began an industry and the cat and mouse game between those bent on destruction and those trying to prevent it. A simple coding of the text message within the program prevents programs like CHK4BOMB from spotting suspicious messages.

The Pakistani Brain virus, a boot infector, tries to hide and announce its presence at the same time. The diskette volume label proudly prints "(C) BRAIN" when the user looks at the directory. Yet if the user tries to read the boot sector with a debugging program, the Brain virus intercepts the request and returns the legitimate boot sector instead of the infected one.

The Lehigh virus, an early file infector, overwrites an area of COM-MAND.COM normally filled with zeros and used as a run-time stack. The length of the file does not increase, which makes the presence of this virus difficult to spot.

The first antivirus program was an integrity checker that compared a known good copy of COMMAND.COM with the file copy. It was written specifically to combat the Lehigh virus. This was soon followed by a scanning antivirus program that checked a file for several viruses by looking for a specific set of bytes known to be in the virus. The horses were out of the gate. The race between the antivirus producers and the virus writers was on. Could a virus be written that could fool the antivirus programs? This was the beginning of stealth viruses.

Most viruses have some sort of stealth in that they appear invisible to the average user. Modest attempts at stealth include resetting the read-only attribute to enable the virus to append to the program file. Many users falsely believe that setting this attribute will protect them from viruses. Most viruses keep the same date and time stamps as the uninfected file as a means of hiding from the average user.

These modest attempts at stealth are no match for antivirus programs, so viruses have become more and more proficient at hiding. In trying to fool antivirus programs, stealth viruses must be resident in the system. If they are, they can play tricks with DOS and hide the true file length and, in some cases, themselves.

Any time a DOS call is made to request the directory listing of the file, a stealth virus can adjust the length to reflect the length the file should be, not what it actually is. This can cause problems with the DOS CHKDSK program, which calculates the number of Fs the file should have in relation to its length and reports the discrepancy.

The Number of the Beast virus can hide itself entirely from antivirus programs as long as the virus code is resident in memory. When DOS allocates disk space for a file it does so in allocation units which may be 1, 2, 4, or 8 sectors long depending on the disk size. On average, half of the last allocation unit is unused by the file. Number of the Beast uses this slack space to save the first portion of the program file and overwrites the beginning of the file with virus code. The length in the directory listing does not change and matches the number of allocation units, so CHKDSK sees no error. Whenever the file is read, the virus code intercepts the DOS call and returns the program exactly as it should be.

Because stealth measures, such as that used by Number of the Beast are dependent on the virus being resident in memory, most antivirus scanners look through memory for resident infectors before beginning a scan of the files. Some very sophisticated viruses try to prevent this activity so they can remain hidden from memory searches, but this requires programming and system knowledge greater than 99.9 percent of the people who write viruses have and are thus very rare.

Stealth is no match for antivirus software, whether scanner or integrity checker, if it is not resident in memory. This is why all antivirus packages warn the user to turn the computer off and reboot from a write-protected, uninfected DOS diskette. However, busy users do not always take the trouble. Antivirus programs take long enough to run as it is. Adding the time to turn the computer off, rebooting from a disk, and then rebooting from the hard disk after the antivirus program is finished is probably too much to ask. If you paid for the antivirus software, you may pay for not using it correctly.

Point-Counterpoint: Mutation

When asked at an antivirus conference why scanners were so much more prevalent than integrity checkers, Dr. Alan Solomon replied, "Marketing." Dr. Solomon, being no fool, markets Dr. Solomon's Anti-Virus Toolkit, which contains one of the best virus scanners, FINDVIRUS. Whatever the reason, antivirus scanners have become such a force in the marketplace that viruses are beginning to use another stealth method, mutation, to hide from scanners. (For a full discussion of antivirus solutions, see Chapter 11.)

Antivirus scanners rely on finding a series of bytes in a file that can be identified as a particular virus. To counteract this, viruses are encoded so that the numbers stored in the file are not the same as the numbers used as processor instructions. When the virus activates, it decodes the file so that the processor can execute the virus instructions. If the virus uses the same coding scheme on each replication, a scanner can be programmed to look for the encoded instructions in the file. However, if the encoding scheme changes on each infection, a scanner is faced with an almost infinite number of possibilities. This is a so-called polymorphic virus. Each infection of the virus is different from the infection that preceded it.

Extracting a recognizable pattern from the virus becomes an impossible task with one exception. There must be at least a few unencoded instructions in the virus so the rest of the program can be decoded. It is in this section of the virus that the antivirus scanner must look. Virus writers know this, and the decoding portion is often padded with do-nothing instructions that change from copy to copy, making identification much more difficult.

Trigger

The early Trojan horse program NUKE-LA did its damage immediately. While some viruses do no damage other than replicating, many contain sections that attempt to alter the file system or completely destroy it at a certain time. If a virus destroys immediately upon infection, it would not only erase the disk, but would most likely destroy itself in the process. Therefore, many viruses have some sort of trigger mechanism that only takes effect under certain circumstances.

Some viruses keep a counter that triggers when a certain number is reached. The Lehigh virus waits until it has copied itself four times before triggering any damage. The Jerusalem virus has several triggers. After the virus has been resident for 30 minutes, it slows the system to a fifth of normal speed. There is also a trigger based on the system date, triggering damage on any Friday the 13th.

Many viruses check the system date as a trigger and go into the damage phase only on certain days. Unfortunately, there are so many viruses that there is probably one for any day of the year.

Damage

Exploding monitors, flaming printers, and melting modems are the stuff of science fiction. Missing or erroneous information is the stuff of real computer viruses. Unfortunately, it is a lot easier to replace a melted modem than a customer database gathered over years of business, but such is the damage that can be caused by viruses.

Some viruses cause no real permanent damage. Some appear to be just cute and print "Your PC is stoned" or cause the letters on the screen to fall to the bottom line in a heap. Some viruses do nothing but replicate. Other viruses, however, can make every bit of information on a disk disappear forever.

The damage phase of some viruses is perhaps the most dangerous aspect of this phenomenon. For whatever reason, there are viruses programmed to destroy data. There has been widespread media coverage of just a few of the potentially catastrophic viruses, but there are hundreds of viruses that can cause just as much, if not more, damage than the ones that have created a media feeding frenzy and a windfall profit for antivirus software producers. If there were not this potential for damage, viruses would still be a nuisance but by no means the danger they are today.

Virus damage is usually concentrated on the file system. Because of the openness of the DOS file system where every program can have access to every file, damaging the files is easy. Even without the help of a virus, the file system is subject to damage. Older files can easily be overwritten by newer files with the same file name. Rebooting in the middle of a DOS operation can corrupt the directory or vital file allocation table (FAT). Just entering **DEL *.***

can cause needed information to be lost. There are many "stupid user tricks" that can remove information from the files as effectively as any virus.

Some file damage from a virus can be subtle. A virus can change the values stored in a spreadsheet program or the fields in a database. Sometimes this type of damage may go unnoticed for a long time. After the damage is noted, reconstruction may be impossible.

Some viruses delete program files. The widespread Jerusalem virus erases every program that the user tries to run on any Friday the 13th. Other viruses may erase random sectors of the disk. Even seemingly benign viruses like Stoned overwrite the last sector of the root directory, which may lead to lost files if this sector is used by the directory.

The absolute worst is a virus that destroys the entire file system. Because DOS stores vital information on the first sectors of the disk, corruption of just a few sectors could make the entire disk useless. Even if these sectors were restored, the files that occupy the remainder of the disk may be inaccessible.

Many viruses can get the user to destroy the file system. Even a virus with no trigger and no damage section could cause the user to go into a panic and reformat the entire disk in an attempt to get rid of the virus. Many posts to the VIRUS-L bulletin say in effect, "I did a low-level format and still did not get rid of the virus." Not only is a low-level or logical format never necessary to remove a virus, it also may be ineffective. All it does in most cases is destroy all the data carefully stored on the disk. There are better and less damaging ways to remove a virus from a disk. Virus removal and data recovery are addressed in Chapter 11.

How Many Different Viruses Are There?

There are thousands of viruses, and hundreds more are appearing all the time. However, many viruses are lab viruses, and only one or two samples exist. Many more are unsuccessful in the wild because they are poorly written and do not replicate well. There are also hundreds of named viruses that have never been seen in the wild, that is outside of the collection of antivirus researchers. People who write viruses often send a sample to an antivirus researcher or post them on one of a number of BBSs devoted to viruses. These viruses are never released into the wild, but still acquire names. Perhaps less than ten percent of all viruses have actually infected users' systems.

Those viruses actually appearing in the wild and infecting unsuspecting users are still numbered in the hundreds. Although hundreds of new viruses are reported each week, only rarely will one infect a lot of computers. Most of the new infection outbreaks are reported where there is a concentration of shared computers, such as at a university. Even these viruses seldom spread beyond the immediate confines of the campus.

Because only about ten percent of the viruses are boot infectors, it would seem that file infector viruses would get spread further and faster. Program files can be easily transferred by modem from user to user. There are many computer BBSs that offer programs via modem. The Internet contains hundreds of sites that offer software from around the world. On the other hand, with the exception of a few dropper viruses, that is program viruses that infect the boot sector, the transmission of boot sector viruses requires a disk to be physically transported from one PC to another and then used to boot the system. The surprising fact is that most of the widespread computer viruses are boot sector infectors.

Contrary to popular belief, sharing of software over BBSs and through shareware is not the most common method of virus transmission. People who trade programs are much more virus aware than the average user and tend to be the ones who religiously test programs with the latest antivirus software. Therefore, boot sector viruses seem to be much more common in the wild than their numbers would indicate. Almost half of the known virus attacks have been by boot sector viruses. There are a couple of reasons for this.

Boot sector viruses are not easily spotted. A conscientious user may spot a file that has grown larger, but the boot sector is generally never seen. It sits there on every diskette whether it is bootable or not, activating every time a computer is booted from a diskette. Starting a computer with a diskette in drive A is not as uncommon an occurrence as you might think. Many users turn off the computer at the end of the work day with a data diskette still locked into the drive. The next day, they arrive at the office, turn on the computer, and fail to notice that drive A contains a diskette. Even though the computer will not boot from a diskette that does not contain DOS, if the diskette is infected, it will install the virus and infect the hard disk. Subsequently, the virus is activated every time the computer is started and infects every diskette used in the computer. As diskettes are passed from worker to worker, the virus spreads. Depending on the virus, this spreading may go on for months before someone notices. Someone may take a diskette home from time to time. Even a data diskette with no DOS system files can spread the virus outside of the confines of the original site. Even after the virus has been discovered at a work site, some diskettes may have been stored away or removed from the premises and never checked for the virus. These diskettes can start the cycle all over again.

There is another way that a boot sector virus can gain a fast foothold: through a mass distribution of an infected diskette. Commercial software diskettes and preformatted blank diskettes have been suspected (but never proved) to be the origin for several large boot sector virus outbreaks. A software company usually relies on a duplication service to make the thousands of diskettes needed to distribute a program. Because the software company knows the length of the program files, it is highly unlikely that they would allow distribution of a diskette with a different file size, which would indicate a file infector virus. However, there is no guarantee that a boot sector virus was not introduced somewhere before the master diskette was sent out for duplication. Even if the software company checks the master diskette with an antivirus scanner, there is a chance that the diskette may be infected with a virus or a version of a virus unknown to the scanner. Releasing an infected diskette could have disastrous consequences.

Nothing is more frustrating than working for hours on a project, attempting to save data on a diskette, and then finding that you have to format a new one. With some programs, you have to quit the program, format the diskette, and rerun the program, re-creating the data. Therefore, many companies now offer the convenience of preformatted diskettes. You just pull a new one out of the box, insert it in the drive, and save your data. No formatting is necessary. But does that preformatted diskette contain a hidden boot sector virus?

Companies that mass produce diskettes and program diskettes can always deny that their diskettes were the root cause of a virus outbreak. Sure, the diskette is infected, but did the infection spread to the diskette from the user or to the user from the diskette? There is no way to know. The companies that distribute infected diskettes know, but it is in their best interest to deny culpability and claim that the user's machine was the source of infection. Only a few companies have gone public and admitted that they distributed programs on infected diskettes. No diskette company has ever admitted that its blank disks were infected.

> After an electronic highway first—the distribution of the Clinton administration's monster health plan document on diskette rather than on paper—at least one recipient complained that the health care plan was infected for reasons other than fuzzy thinking. The culprit virus was variously said to be Michelangelo or other boot sector infectors. Because the claim was never substantiated it's probably safe to assume that the disks were run on an infected machine.

Now that you know what viruses are and aren't and have the nomenclature well in hand, the next chapter will take you on a tour of "Virusland," a theme park that is not particularly amusing.

A Contemporary Virus History

The beginning of the virus phenomenon, as most understand it, can be accurately date stamped "Fourth Quarter, 1987." In October, (c)Brain entered the wild in the United States at the University of Delaware. On November 18, the Lehigh virus was discovered at Pennsylvania's Lehigh University. In December, Jerusalem was discovered at Hebrew University in Israel.

Other than the time frame, this trinity of viruses did not have much in common. (c)Brain is a boot sector infector and, in the grander scheme of things, relatively benign because it wasn't programmed to actually perform any destructive deeds. Lehigh infected only COMMAND.COM files and contained destructive code designed to activate on a counter basis. Jerusalem infected both .COM and .EXE files and contained a trigger date to destroy data.

There's no question that (c)Brain was written by a computer shop owner in Lahore, Pakistan. It's commonly accepted that Jerusalem is an Israeli product. And it's highly probable that Lehigh is U.S. grown because it's never been seen in the wild outside the country.

Was it just a coincidence that three very different viruses, from three corners of the world, burst forth within a matter of months, all in university settings? Maybe not. To understand the virus situation of today, it's necessary to understand the building blocks that had been in place for quite a long time.

A Basic Virus Chronology

We will begin with a quick look at the 30 years or so that have gotten us to where we are today. Later in this chapter, the most recent happenings will be examined in greater detail.

1949 — John von Neumann

In 1949 John von Neumann wrote a most unusual paper titled "Theory and Organization of Complicated Automata." This was not the sort of thing to arouse much interest, even though it did put forth his theory that computer programs could multiply and included what, technically, was a model of a computer virus. Why no interest? It would be several more years before the first practical electronic computer came on the scene.

Bell Labs in the '50s

Von Neumann's theories were put into practice in the heady scientific atmosphere of Bell Labs where stretching the envelope, in almost any way at all, was the order of the day. There, three brilliant young programmers—H. Douglas McIlroy, Victor Vysottsky, and Robert Morris, Sr.—invented and played a game called Core Wars. Even so long ago biological terms were applied. One player's "organisms," really computer code, attacked the "organism" population of his opponent's code. The winning player was the one with the largest "organism" count at the end of the game.

It's unlikely that such activities would be tolerated at a computer research center these days, but the term "play" is still in wide use when it comes to experimentation with computers.

1983 — Core Wars Goes Public

Core Wars was too good a secret to be kept and soon spread to other ultra high-tech sites, notably MIT and the Xerox research site, PARC, in Palo Alto, California. The secret was, however, kept fairly close until 1983 when Ken Thompson, the developer of the original version of UNIX (in reaction to MULTICS) received one of the computer industry's most prestigious honors, the A. M. Turing Award. Legend holds that Thompson, with more than a bit of glee, told of Core Wars and suggested that the august scientists attending the awards presentation also start playing!

Also in 1983, Fred Cohen, a graduate student, was writing his doctoral thesis. In his work, he described replicating computer programs and coined the term *virus*. There are those who would argue that viruses simply did not exist until Cohen's definition. They would be wrong.

1984 — *Scientific American*

In the historic May issue, *Scientific American* offered its readership an unparalleled opportunity. In an article describing Core Wars, there was also an invitation to send $2 for a set of programming instructions.

1985 — First PC Malware

The first Trojan horse programs for the PC/MS-DOS platform appeared on user bulletin boards around the country. Masquerading as useful programs in some cases (EGABTR) or cool games (NUKE-LA) in others, they were highly destructive but relatively easy to defeat.

1986 — Chaos and VIRDEM

In December 1986, Ralf Burger, a German programmer, introduced his demonstration virus, VIRDEM, at the Chaos Computer Congress. In his writings, Burger appears to be a disciple of Cohen, determined to go the master one better. In 1987 Burger published a book in German, complete with recipes for writing viruses. It was translated into English and released in the United States in 1988.

1987 — October

In October 1987, (c)Brain, the first virus to be found in the wild in the United States, was discovered at the University of Delaware. The Lehigh virus was identified at Lehigh University the following month, and in December the Jerusalem virus was discovered at Hebrew University.

1988 — Stoned

Stoned, the first master boot record infector, appeared in 1988. Two of its aliases, New Zealand and Australian, indicate its likely geographical source. Later that year, the first formal virus conference was held.

1989 — January: Dark Avenger

The Dark Avenger virus, the first fast infector, seen in 1989, proclaimed in its code that it was written in Sofia (Bulgaria) and carried a copyright notice of 1988–1999. You'll meet the writer of this virus in Chapter 3.

The first huge virus scare came in October 1989. Two viruses, Jerusalem (Friday the 13th) and Datacrime (any day after Columbus Day, October 12) were scheduled to hit concurrently.

The 1990s

The V2Px series of viruses, the first heavily polymorphic code, showed up early in 1990. Usually dated in December 1991, the first known virus bulletin board is opened by Todor Todorov in Sofia, Bulgaria. Even more attention was focused on Bulgaria. Along with the advent of virus BBSs, virus creation toolkits begin to appear that same year.

The second widespread virus scare, centered on the Michelangelo virus, swept the world in 1992. Virus Awareness Day was observed in 1993, but nobody noticed.

A Closer Look

Telling what happened when in the history of viruses without the why component doesn't tell much. Follow along as the first four viruses became six, then seven, then thousands. Here we will see the growth of two industries—

the virus writers and their adversaries, the antivirus product vendors. Since those first days, a weird symbiosis has developed. Each group feeds upon the other. A small universe has been developed with the forces of good fighting the forces of evil. Strangely, each side believes in its own righteousness.

The Four Horsemen Of The Apocalypse

The Stoned, (c)Brain, Lehigh, and Jerusalem viruses provide a representative sample of the first virus wave. You may begin to ask why? Arguably, Burger's VIRDEM was a lame initial attempt to bring the (nonexistent, except in theory) problem to public attention. Clearly, Burger was aware of Cohen's work on large computers. Given the relatively simple operating system of the PC and the languages available for addressing the machine (the recipes include versions for Assembler, BASIC, and Pascal), writing a virus for a PC was a day at the beach compared with Cohen's experiments.

Cohen, in fact, has always stated that he had precious little time to perform his experiments. The administrators of the large systems he wished to use to prove his theories were, understandably, somewhat disinclined to allow him freedom to infect the systems for which they were responsible with something called a virus.

The PC presented no such problems to those who would experiment with replicating code. If one could turn a PC on, one was the system administrator.

Cohen's work, followed by Burger's presentation to the Chaos Club and subsequent distribution of VIRDEM, could not go unnoticed in the burgeoning field of computer science. Leading edge computer science professors around the world were soon challenging their students to write self-replicating code.

(c)Brain

(c)Brain can't be blamed on a college programming project, but the author was definitely university aware. Amjad Farooq Alvi and his brother, Basit Farooq Alvi, owned a business in Lahore, Pakistan—Brain Computer Services. Among other things, Brain developed proprietary software, and the brothers were becoming more than a little annoyed that people were pirating their programs. Their response was to write the (c)Brain virus to protect their products. The brothers also had a passing understanding of Pakistani copyright law which seemed to exempt computer programs. They soon developed a thriving sideline business in selling bootleg copies of top-of-the-line PC programs such as Lotus 1-2-3 for the Pakistani equivalent of a couple of dollars.

Word spreads almost as fast as viruses. American visitors to Lahore heard of the brothers Alvi and began to avail themselves of the incredible software bargains. Somehow, the Alvi brothers decided that Americans buying the copies were violating U.S. copyright law (but Pakistanis weren't?), so they began to add (c)Brain to copies purchased by U.S. nationals.

I'm still a bit unclear on why Lahore would be a tourist mecca for American college students, but the fact remains that enough copies were carried back to university computation centers to make (c)Brain a cause célèbre.

A Case Study

The following study was written in 1988 by Anne Webster of the University of Delaware, about the first (c)Brain infection identified in the US.

In October of 1987 an unusual number of users at the University of Delaware microcomputing sites were reporting problems with their data disks. At the same time, users of the general-access microcomputing facilities began reporting difficulty running certain software packages. Site personnel investigation of the problems found one similarity: all of the user and site discs with problems had volume labels that read "(c)Brain." As it turned out the labels were put there not by the site personnel or by the users, but by a computer virus. Internally, the virus was christened the "Brain" virus, though it later became known by its international description, the "Pakistani" virus.

The University of Delaware, with more than 17,000 undergraduate, graduate, and continuing education students, and several thousand faculty and staff, has more than 4000 microcomputers operating in labs, classrooms, dorms, and homes. Up to 500 of these are in general-access microcomputing facilities, open to anyone with a University of Delaware ID. Traffic is high at the microcomputing centers, with larger sites typically averaging about 1500 sign-ins during a typical week of the school year.

Site attendants and users start up most of the site computers from floppy diskettes since relatively few are hard-disk systems. Users either borrow site-owned software from a site service desk, or they bring in their own software for use with site equipment. Although the majority of site users are students, many university employees use the general-access facilities or have student employees who use the facilities for university work.

Once the virus was discovered, computing support personnel immediately notified the campus community by sending a memo to all university faculty and staff describing how to tell that a disk was infected and how to "disinfect" it. First, we recommended that users check their disks by using the DOS CHKDSK command. If the diskette had a volume label of "(c)Brain" or if it had 3072 or more bytes in bad sectors, then it was suspect. Users could clean up a diskette by first booting with a clean (non-infected) diskette, then transferring files from the infected diskette to a freshly formatted one using the DOS COPY command, and finally reformatting the infected diskette. Users were told not to use the DISKCOPY command, since making an exact duplicate of the disk would copy the virus as well as the files. Computer support personnel volunteered to assist anyone needing help and to doublecheck any questionable diskettes.

At this point we didn't yet know the extent of infection on campus or any details/limitations of the virus. While site personnel checked several thousand site-owned diskettes for infection to determine the scope of the virus problem, other Computing Services staff looked at the virus in more detail. Fortunately, only two general access sites were found to have infected disks: at one site about half of the most frequently used IBM disks were infected (about 75) and at another only 12 were infected. We felt fortunate that so few disks were infected and believed that the site operating procedures already in place at the sites helped account for the generally low infection rate. These are the major features:

1. All DOS boot diskettes have write-protect tabs or are "notchless" disks.

2. Site applications software (e.g., WordPerfect, Lotus 1-2-3) generally is not bootable.

3. Systems are booted with their own DOS disk (e.g., site system #1 uses DOS disk #1, system #2 uses DOS disk #2, etc.).

Meanwhile, computing professionals were learning more about the virus, how and when an infected disk would infect other disks, and the safest way to clean up a disk after infections. Our explorations were empirical; first, we learned that a system must be booted with an infected diskette in order to go on to infect other diskettes. We were happy to discover that only the 5.25" diskettes were affected by the Brain virus. And after intentionally infecting data diskettes but finding no file damage per se, we concluded that while hundreds of users *might* be using infected diskettes, a very small percentage were actually experiencing problems with them. Nevertheless, we suspected that repeated use of a diskette would increase the likelihood that a user would have problems with that diskette.

The unrestricted nature of computing site use at a university is an integral part of the learning environment. This makes many of the security recommendations suggested for business use inappropriate in this environment. A handful of virus filter and virus protection programs were obtained for evaluation, but none were adopted for general use.

Computing support personnel posted signs in the sites instructing the users about safe cleanup procedures and offering assistance. During the height of the virus season, site assistance checked every diskette that was returned from loan before returning the user's ID. Users were asked if we could check their [personal] disks as well. In that way, we were quickly able to arrest the infection and at the same time educate many of the users about the virus threat. To recover files that had been corrupted by infection, staff consultants used Norton Utilities. Although no comprehensive list of users with corrupted files exists, staff estimates the number to be only a couple of dozen.

Since the virus outbreak in the fall of 1987, the University of Delaware has been essentially free of the virus, but we still check the 200 or so most frequently used site diskettes periodically to ensure that they are free of the Brain virus, and we either use notchless diskettes for system startup or we check each morning as the systems are booted to make sure we are starting with non-infected system disks. We continue this check procedure because we suspect the

Brain virus may still be lurking on student diskettes (disks set aside for the semester, perhaps?). We will stay on the alert and will clean up the spurious user-diskettes that become infected as they come to our attention. We also continue to emphasize the importance of backing up important files because, ultimately, the user is responsible for his or her own data or diskettes.

Today, the University of Delaware has thousands of PCs in use in public access sites that are networked across campus and linked to Internet. According to campus computing officials, they can't remember the last time (c)Brain was seen at the University of Delaware.

How things have changed.

NOTE Another reason for the almost complete disappearance of the (c)Brain virus is the mass migration to 3.5" floppy diskettes that has taken place during the past several years. Surprisingly this wasn't the first time that a migration to a newer hardware or processor served as a solution to a long-standing virus problem. Consider the following.

Late Out of the Gate

Horsemen 5 and 6, viruses known as Cascade (falling letters) and Italian (ping pong or bouncing ball) also appeared in 1987. The Italian virus enjoyed brief popularity but, unfortunately, didn't work on anything but 8088 or 8086 (pre-AT) computers. As the installed base upgraded, Ping Pong died. Cascade, on the other hand, has remained a stalwart, still reliably showing up on all lists of viruses found in the wild. Cascade did something revolutionary: most of the code was encrypted with only a small amount of code in the clear. This may be the virus most responsible for the explosion of the scanner technique of virus protection. The chronological virus count clearly shows the danger that viruses pose to computing.

Dr. Alan Solomon of S&S International, creator of Dr. Solomon's Anti-Virus ToolKit, calls 1988 a virus-friendly year. Nobody except antivirus product developers seemed to take the problem too seriously, allowing the already existing viruses to spread—unnoticed and undetected. As Solomon points out, three of those very early viruses, Stoned, Cascade, and Jerusalem spread so far and wide that they will probably never be completely eradicated.

Virus writers got a boost in 1988 when a small antivirus company, trying to drum up business, released a demonstration virus known as Virus-B, it was intended to show potential customers just what might happen if a virus were running wild on their sites. With Burger's book in several foreign translations (complete with recipes) and Virus-B available to almost anyone who asked for it, the stage was set for 1989, The Year of the Computer Virus.

By the end of 1988, virus conferences had been held both in the United States and the United Kingdom. In the United States, ISSA joined with one of the then Big 8 accounting firms, Deloitte Haskins & Sills, to invite the 50 best and brightest in the field to confer. In Britain, Dr. Solomon's company held a seminar that "actually explained what a virus was and how they worked."

Basically, all hell broke loose—or was supposed to—on October 13. In the US, radio, television, newspapers, weekly news magazines, every public medium in existence predicted double trouble and a mega-disaster when the Jerusalem (Friday the 13th) and Datacrime viruses were due to strike on the same day.

Not much was happening on the virus-writing front except a few improved versions of Jerusalem being shipped around and the discovery of Datacrime. Datacrime was found by a gentleman in Holland. It was sent to a research team in the United Kingdom who disassembled it and discovered that while it had a serious payload (wiping out a hard disk's file allocation table on any date after October 12) it was not memory resident so it would be unlikely to spread far or fast.

By 1989, IBM was beginning to take the virus issue seriously (IBM itself had been hit with Cascade the year before) and went public with its first scanning program in September 1989.

In the two weeks before Doomsday, anyone who knew anything about viruses was a hot media property—to the point that the author of this book found herself on "Good Morning America" explaining Datacrime "in terms Joan Lunden can understand."

On that fateful Friday, virus researchers around the country and the world were very busy. Their activity? Calling up other virus researchers to see if they had heard of any major attacks. Nobody had.

While the United States was working itself up over Friday the 13th, programmers in Bulgaria and Russia were warming up to make 1990 a shocking one.

As the decade ended, the rules changed. By 1990 most antivirus products available relied on scanning techniques. With the advent of polymorphic viruses, a simple scan no longer worked. In the United States, Mark Washburn had improved Burger's Vienna virus and made it polymorphic. In Bulgaria, the shadowy figure still known only as Dark Avenger produced a polymorphic virus bearing his sobriquet.

The first virus exchange bulletin board appeared in 1990. The theory was simple. To become a member all you had to do was upload a virus you had written. That done, you had access to all the other viruses written by fellow members—including source code! No longer did a disk carrying a virus have to travel by student backpack from Pakistan to tiny Delaware; they could be sent around the world as fast as a phone line could carry them.

An important step was taken at the end of 1990. *EICAR*, the European Institute for Computer Antivirus Research was formed in Hamburg.

Alan Solomon refers to 1991 as the year of glut. New viruses were being produced at a furious rate—by year's end over 1,000 viruses would be identified. It also was the year of product marketing glut as Symantec (Norton Anti-Virus), Central Point Software (CPAV), X-Tree, and Fifth Generation flooded the trade press with advertisements for their "new" antivirus products. Never mind that these companies were far better known for other kinds of products; they saw a golden marketing opportunity and jumped on the bandwagon.

As more and more virus exchange BBSs came to life, more and more would-be virus authors went to work and the chase was on. With each new virus, a new search string had to be identified and added to a product.

Polymorphic viruses became more than a laboratory curiosity in 1991. In April, Tequila got loose and spread like wildfire. Some vendors were hot on its trail and had a fix within short order—others didn't. In late summer, Europe was invaded by the Maltese Amoeba virus, another polymorph.

The year 1992 was the year of "The Little Boy Who Cried Wolf"—the massive Michelangelo scare of March 6. This vapor-drama changed, possibly forever, the way the computer virus problem would be viewed. Or, at least, how much attention the media would pay to the problem.

This was also the year when virus writers set up open warfare against antivirus products. Improvements to polymorphic code, stealth techniques, companion techniques, and the Mutation Engine (MtE) were the order of the day. The goal was no longer to write a virus and spread it. It was to write a virus that would evade—or even cripple—existing products.

In the virus world, 1993 was the year of the calendar. For unknown reasons, calendaring the hit date of every virus known to humankind became the marketing *ploy du anne*. If nothing else, it did demonstrate how many viruses there are, if not how many are in wide circulation, or how likely you are to be a victim.

As beta versions of Microsoft's DOS 6.0 were distributed, unauthorized copies found their way to virus exchange bulletin boards and a whole new crop of viruses, targeted to specifically defeat Microsoft Anti-Virus, appeared.

It was also a year of consolidation and cashing in. Smaller developers gladly sold their businesses to higher stakes players. Companies who hadn't been able to stand up to the stiff competition and excessive advertising budgets of the major companies quietly went under. But the machine kept running. By year's end there would be over 2,500 known viruses.

In 1993 the two existing research groups, EICAR and CARO, were joined by the Virus Security Institute, whose stated goal is to provide practical and accurate information about viruses and security. The virus list maintained at the Virus Test Center at the University of Hamburg continued to grow. CARO member Joe Wells disseminated a monthly analysis of viruses in the wild and the frequency of their occurrence. At long last, the virus problem was being dealt with in a more scientific manner.

Five Little Viruses and How They Grew

It seems like viruses have been everywhere, forever. The following chart (Figure 2.1), assembled by Virus Security Institute member Padgett Peterson, shows the growth of known viruses.

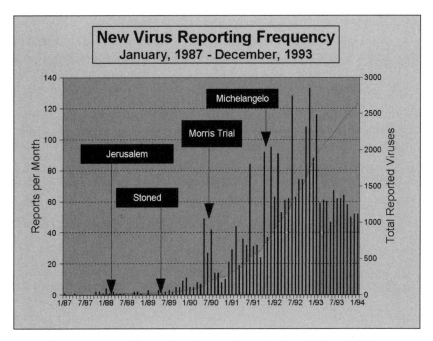

Figure 2.1   The number of reported viruses from 1987 to 1993.

The Mighty Virus Hunters

The antivirus jungle has become a more peaceful place with cooperation among most researchers and vendors being the order of the day. Through their exchanges more and better information about viruses is available.

At the end of Appendix C you will find two remarkable charts. In the industry, they are referred to as the Wild List and the Freq list. Look at them carefully. Often, when one virus appears in multiple places (Wild List) it won't be long before it appears over and over again in the same place (Frequency List). On the other hand, it might also mean that it had been frequent before but, as more and more vendors added that particular virus to their hit lists it's not as common any longer. These lists are updated monthly and, for the truly curious, are interesting to follow.

What Does It Mean for the Future?

The history of computer viruses will continue to be written. A few countries have already begun to take aggressive steps to prosecute individuals who knowingly distribute viruses. Some organizations, notably the Electronic Freedom Foundation, can be predicted to lobby aggressively for individual rights with a PC. In the United States, First Amendment rights will probably take center stage.

If nothing else, the rapprochement reached among the leading vendors and researchers will ensure that as much information as possible is shared within the community and that can only benefit the computing public at large.

Chapter

3

Virus Myths And Mysteries

In this chapter, the most common myths about computer viruses are described and debunked. Also, you'll meet the world's most famous virus writer, the Dark Avenger.

Myths And Realities

The following treatise, now in its tenth edition, was written by Rob Rosenberger with the able assistance of Ross Greenberg, creator of the legendary FluShot antivirus program. Rosenberger's particular interest in the subject comes as a professional shareware writer. When rumors began to circulate that users should avoid shareware to stay clear of viruses, Rosenberger went to work.

The alert reader may note that some of Rosenberger's and Greenberg's definitions aren't exactly the same as those already put forth in this book. That's okay. They know what they're talking about, too. This information is also a fine companion piece to the VIRUS_L.FAQ in Appendix B.

A number of myths have surfaced about the threat of computer viruses. There are myths about how widespread they are, how dangerous they are, and even myths about what a computer virus really is. We want you to know the facts.

The first thing you need to learn is that a computer virus falls in the realm of malicious programming techniques known as Trojan horses. All viruses are Trojan horses, but relatively few Trojan horses can be called a virus.

That having been said, it's time to go over the terminology we use:

- **BBS** or **Bulletin Board System**. If you have a modem, you can call a BBS and leave messages, transfer computer files back and forth, and learn a lot about computers. (What you're reading right now, for example, most likely came to you from a BBS.)

- **Bug.** An accidental flaw in the logic of a program which makes it do things it shouldn't be doing. Programmers don't mean to put bugs in their programs, but they always creep in. Programmers often spend more time "debugging" programs than they do writing them in the first place. Inadvertent bugs have caused more data loss than all viruses combined.

- **Hacker.** Someone who really loves computers and who wants to push them to the limit. Hackers have a healthy sense of curiosity: they try doorknobs just to see if they're locked, for example. They also love to tinker with a piece of equipment until it's just right. The entire computer revolution itself is largely a result of hackers.

- **Shareware.** A distribution method for quality software available on a try before you buy basis. You must pay for it if you continue using it after the trial period. Shareware authors let you download their programs from BBSs and encourage you to give evaluation copies to friends. Many shareware applications rival their retail-shelf counterparts at a fraction of the price. (You must pay for the shareware you continue to use—otherwise you're stealing software.)

- **Trojan horse.** A generic term describing a set of computer instructions purposely hidden inside a program. Trojan horses tell programs to do things you don't expect them to do. The term comes from the legendary battle in which the ancient city of Troy received a large wooden horse to commemorate a fierce battle. The "gift" secretly held enemy soldiers in its belly and, when the Trojans rolled it into their fortified city...

- **Virus.** A term for a very specialized Trojan horse which spreads to other computers by secretly infecting programs with a copy of itself. A virus is the only type of Trojan horse which is contagious, much like the common cold. If a Trojan horse doesn't meet this definition, then it isn't a virus.

- **Worm.** A term similar to a Trojan horse, but there is no "gift" involved. If the Trojans had left that wooden horse outside the city, they wouldn't have been attacked from inside the city. Worms, on the other hand, can bypass your defenses without having to deceive you into dropping your guard. An example would be a program designed to spread itself by exploiting bugs in a network software package. Worms usually come from someone who has legitimate access to the computer or network.

- **Wormers.** What we call people who unleash Trojan horses onto an unsuspecting public. Let's face it, these people aren't angels. What they do hurts us. They deserve our disrespect.

Viruses, like all Trojan horses, purposely make a program do things you don't expect it to do. Some viruses will just annoy you, perhaps only displaying a "Peace on earth" greeting. The viruses we worry about will try to erase your data (the most valuable asset of your computer!) and waste your valuable time in recovering from an attack.

Now you know the differences between a bug and a Trojan horse and a virus. Let's get into some of the myths:

All purposely destructive code spreads like a virus.

Wrong. Remember, "Trojan horse" describes purposely destructive code in general. Very few Trojan horses actually qualify as viruses. Newspaper and magazine reporters tend to call almost anything a virus because they often have no real understanding of computer crime.

Viruses and Trojan horses are a recent phenomenon.

Trojan horses have existed since the first days of the computer; hackers toyed with viruses in the early 1960s as a form of amusement. Many different Trojan horse techniques have emerged over the decades to embezzle money, destroy data, fool investors, etc. The general public really didn't know of this problem until the IBM PC revolution brought it into the spotlight. Banks still hush up computerized embezzlements to this day because they believe customers will lose faith in them if word gets out.

Viruses are written by teenage hackers.

Yes, hackers have unleashed viruses—but so has a computer magazine publisher. And according to one trusted military publication, the U.S. Defense Department creates computer viruses for use as weapons. Trojan horses for many decades sprang from the minds of middle-aged men; computer prices have only recently dropped to a level where teenagers could get into the act. We call people "wormers" when they abuse their knowledge of computers. You shouldn't fear hackers just because some of them know how to write viruses. This whole thing boils down to an ethics issue, not a technology issue. Hackers know a lot about computers; wormers abuse their knowledge. Hackers as a whole got a bum rap when the mass media corrupted the term.

Viruses infect 25% of all IBM PCs every month.

If 25% suffer an infection every month, then 100% would have a virus every four months—in other words, every IBM PC would suffer an infection three times per year. This mythical estimate surfaced in the media after researcher Peter Tippett wrote a complex thesis on how viruses might spread in the future. Computer viruses exist all over the planet, yes—but they won't take over the world. Only about 500 different viruses exist at this time; many of them have never existed in the wild and some have since been completely eliminated from the wild. You can easily reduce your exposure to viruses with a few simple precautions. Yes, it's still safe to turn on your computer!

Only 500 different viruses? But most experts talk about them in the thousands.

The virus experts who claim much larger numbers usually work for antivirus companies. They count even the most insignificant variations for advertising purposes. When the Marijuana virus first appeared, for example, it contained the word "legalise," but a miscreant later modified it to read "legalize." Any program which can detect the original virus can detect the version with one letter changed—but antivirus companies count them as two viruses. These obscure differentiations quickly add up. And take note: the majority of new computer viruses discovered these days are only minor variations on well-known viruses.

A virus could destroy all the files on my disks.

Yes, and a spilled cup of coffee could do the same thing. You can recover from any virus or coffee problem if you have adequate backups of your data. Backups mean the difference between a nuisance and a disaster. You can safely presume that there has been more accidental loss of data than loss by all viruses and Trojan horses.

Viruses have been documented on over 300,000 computers [1988].

Viruses have been documented on over 400,000 computers [1989].

The Michelangelo virus alone was estimated to be on over 5,000,000 computers [1992].

These numbers originated from John McAfee, a self-styled virus fighter who craves attention and media recognition. If we assume it took him a mere five minutes to adequately document each viral infection, it would have taken four man-years of effort to document a problem only two years old by 1989. We further assume McAfee's statements included every floppy disk ever infected up to that time by a virus, as well as every computer involved in the Christmas and Internet worm attacks. (Worms cannot be included in virus infection statistics.) McAfee prefers to "estimate" his totals these days and was widely quoted during the Michelangelo virus hysteria in early 1992. Let's do some estimating ourselves by assuming that there are about 80 million IBM PC-compatible computers around the world. McAfee's estimate meant one out of every 16 of those computers not only had a virus of some type, it specifically had the Michelangelo virus. Many other virus experts considered it an astronomical estimate based on the empirical evidence.

Viruses can hide inside a data file.

Data files can't wreak havoc on your computer—only an executable program file can do that (including the one that runs every time you turn on or reboot a computer). If a virus infected a data file, it would be a wasted effort. But let's be realistic: what you think is data may actually be an executable program file. For example, a batch file on an IBM PC contains only text, yet DOS treats it just like an executable program.

Some viruses can completely hide themselves from all antivirus software, making them truly undetectable.

This myth ironically surfaced when certain antivirus companies publicized how they could detect so-called Mutation Engine viruses. The myth gained national exposure in early 1993 when the Associated Press printed excerpts from a new book about viruses. Most viruses have a character-based "signature" which identifies it both to the virus (so it doesn't infect a program too many times) and to antivirus software (which uses the signature to detect the virus). A Mutation Engine virus employs an algorithm signature rather than a character-based signature—but it still has a unique, readily identifiable signature. The technique of using algorithm signatures really doesn't make it any harder to detect a virus. You just have to do some calculations to know the correct signature—no big deal for an antivirus program.

BBSs and shareware programs spread viruses.

Here's another scary myth, this one spouted as gospel by many "experts" who claim to know how viruses spread. "The truth," says *PC Magazine* publisher Bill Machrone, "is that all major viruses to date were transmitted by [retail] packages and private mail systems, often in universities." [*PC Magazine*, October 11, 1988.] What Machrone said back then still applies today. Over 50 retail companies have admitted spreading infected master disks to tens of thousands of customers since 1988—compared to only nine shareware authors who have spread viruses on master disks to less than 300 customers since 1990. Machrone goes on to say,"bulletin boards and shareware authors work extraordinarily hard at policing themselves to keep viruses out." Reputable sysops check every file for Trojan horses; nationwide sysop networks help spread the word about dangerous files. Yes, you should beware of the software you get from BBSs and shareware authors, but you should also beware of retail software found on store shelves. By the way, many stores now routinely re-shrinkwrap returned software and put it on the shelf again. Do you know for sure only you ever touched those master disks?

My computer could be infected if I call an infected BBS.

BBSs can't write information on your disks—the communications software you use performs this task. You can only transfer a dangerous file to your computer if you let your software do it. And there is no "300bps subcarrier" by which a virus can slip through a modem. A joker who called himself Mike RoChenle ("micro channel," get it?) started this myth after leaving a techy-joke message on a public network. Unfortunately, some highly respected journalists got taken in by the joke.

So-called boot sector viruses travel primarily in software downloaded from BBSs.

This common myth—touted as gospel even by "experts"—expounds on the supposed role bulletin boards play in spreading infections. Boot sector viruses spread only if you directly copy an infected floppy disk, or if you try to boot a computer from an infected disk, or if you use a floppy in an infected computer. BBSs deal exclusively with program files and don't pass along copies of boot sectors. Bulletin board users thus have a natural immunity to boot-sector viruses in downloaded software. (And since the clear majority of infections stem from boot sector viruses, this fact alone exonerates the BBS community as the so called primary source for the spread of viruses.) We should make a special note about "dropper" programs developed by virus researchers as an easy way to transfer boot sector viruses among themselves. Since they don't replicate, "dropper" programs don't qualify as viruses. These programs have never appeared on BBSs to date and have no real use other than to transfer infected boot sectors.

My files are damaged, so it must have been a virus attack.

It also could have happened because of a power flux, or static electricity, or a fingerprint on a floppy disk, or a bug in your software, or perhaps a simple error on your part. Power failures, spilled cups of coffee, and user errors have destroyed more data than all viruses combined.

Donald Burleson was convicted of releasing a virus.

Newspapers all over the country hailed a 1989 Texas computer crime trial as a virus trial. The defendant, Donald Burleson, had released a destructive Trojan horse on his employer's mainframe computer. The software in question couldn't spread to other computers, and prosecuting attorney Davis McCown claimed he "never brought up the word virus" during Burleson's trial. So why did the media call it one?

1. David Kinney, an expert witness testifying for the defense, claimed Burleson had unleashed a virus. The prosecuting attorney didn't argue the point and we don't blame him— Kinney's claim may have actually swayed the jury to convict Burleson.

2. McCown gave reporters the facts behind the case and let them come up with their own definitions. The Associated Press and *USA Today*, among others, used such vague definitions that any program would have qualified as a virus. If we applied their definitions to the medical world, we could safely label penicillin as a biological virus (which is, of course, absurd).

Robert Morris Jr. released a benign virus on a defense network.

It supposedly may have been benign, but it wasn't a virus. Morris, the son of a chief computer scientist at the U.S. National Security Agency, decided one day to take advantage of bugs in the software which controls Internet, a network the Defense Department often uses. These tiny bugs let Morris send a worm throughout the network. Among other things, the "Internet worm" sent copies of itself to other computers—and clogged the entire network in a matter of hours due to bugs in the worm module itself. The press called it a virus, like it called the 1987 Christmas worm a virus, because it spread to other computers. Yet Morris's work didn't infect any computers. A few notes:

1. Reporters finally started calling it a worm a year after the fact, but only because lawyers on both sides of the case constantly referred to it as a worm.

2. The worm operated only on Sun-3 and VAX computers which employ the UNIX operating system and which were specifically linked into Internet at the time of the attack.

3. The 6,200 affected computers cannot be counted in virus infection statistics (they weren't infected).

4. It cost way less than $98 million to clean up the attack. An official Cornell University report claims John McAfee, the man behind this wild estimate, "was probably serving [him]self" in an effort to drum up business. People familiar with the case estimated the final figure at slightly under $1 million.

5. Yes, Morris could easily have added some infection code to make it both a worm and a virus if he'd had the urge.

6. Internet gurus have since fixed the bugs Morris exploited in the attack.

7. Morris went on trial for launching the worm and received a federal conviction. The Supreme Court refused to hear his case, so the conviction stands.

The U.S. government planted a virus in Iraqi military computers during the Gulf War.

U.S. News & World Report in early 1992 claimed the National Security Agency had replaced a computer chip in a printer bound for Iraq just before the Gulf War with a secret computer chip containing a virus. The magazine cited "two unidentified senior U.S. officials" as their source, saying "once the virus was in the [Iraqi computer] system…each time an Iraqi technician opened a 'window' on his computer screen to access information, the contents of the screen simply vanished." Yet the *USN&WR* story shows amazing similarities to a 1991 April Fool's joke published by *InfoWorld* magazine. Most computer experts dismiss the *USN&WR* story as a hoax—an "urban legend" innocently created by the *InfoWorld* joke. Some notes:

1. *USN&WR* continues to stand by its story, but did publish a "clarification" stating "it could not be confirmed that the [virus] was ultimately successful." The editors broke with tradition by declining to print any letters readers had submitted about it.

2. Ted Koppel, a well-known American news anchor, opened one of his "Nightline" broadcasts with a report on the alleged virus. Koppel's staff politely refers people to talk with *USN&WR* about the story's validity.

3. *InfoWorld* didn't label their story as fiction, but the last paragraph identified it as an April Fool's joke.

Viruses can spread to all sorts of computers.

The design of all Trojan horses limits them to a family of computers, something especially true for viruses. A virus written for IBM PCs cannot infect an IBM 4300 series mainframe, nor can it infect a Commodore C64, nor can it infect an Apple Macintosh. But take note: some computers can now run software written for other types of computers. An Apple Macintosh, with the right products, can run IBM PC software for example. If one type of computer can run software written for another type of computer, then it can also catch viruses written for the other type of computer.

My backups will be worthless if I back up a virus.

No, they won't. Let's suppose a virus does get backed up with your files. You can restore important documents and databases and spreadsheets—your valuable data—without restoring an infected program. You just reinstall the programs from master disks. It's tedious work, but not as hard as some people claim.

Antivirus software will protect me from viruses.

There is no such thing as a foolproof antivirus program. Viruses and other Trojan horses can be (and have been) designed to bypass them. Antivirus products also can be tricky to use at times and they occasionally have bugs. Always use a good set of backups as your first line of defense; rely on antivirus software only as a second line of defense.

Read-only files are safe from virus infections.

This common myth among IBM PC users has appeared even in some computer magazines. Supposedly, you can protect yourself by using the ATTRIB command to set the read-only attribute on program files. Yet ATTRIB is software—what it can do, a virus can undo. The ATTRIB command cannot halt the spread of most viruses.

Viruses can infect files on write-protected floppy disks.

Another common IBM PC myth. If viruses can modify read-only files, people assume that they can also modify files on write-protected disks. However, the disk drive itself knows when a floppy has a write-protect tab and refuses to write to the disk. You can't override an IBM PC drive's write-protect sensor with a software command.

We hope this dispels the many computer virus myths. Viruses DO exist, they ARE out there, they WANT to spread to other computers, and they CAN cause you problems. But you can defend yourself with a cool head and a good set of backups.

The following guidelines can shield you from viruses and other Trojan horses. They will lower your chances of getting infected and raise your chances of recovering from an attack.

1. Implement a procedure to regularly back up your files and follow it religiously. We can't emphasize this enough! Consider purchasing a user-friendly program or a tape backup device to take the drudgery out of this task. You'll find plenty of inexpensive programs and tape backup hardware to choose from.

2. Rotate between at least two sets of backups for better security (use set #1, then set #2, then set #1...). The more sets you use, the better protection you have. Many people take a "master" backup of their entire hard disk, then take a number of "incremental" backups of files which have changed since the last time they backed up. Incremental backups might only require five minutes of your time each day.

3. Many IBM PC computers now have a "BIOS option" to ignore floppy drives during the bootup process. Consult your computer's documentation to see if you can set this option. It will greatly reduce your exposure to boot sector viruses (the most common type of computer virus).

4. Download files only from reputable BBSs where the sysop checks every program for Trojan horses. If you're still afraid, consider getting programs from a BBS or "disk vendor" company which obtains files direct from the authors.

5. Let a newly uploaded file "mature" on a BBS for one or two weeks before you download it (others will put it through its paces).

6. Consider using a program that searches (scans) for known viruses. Almost all infections involve viruses known to antivirus companies. A recent version (no more than four months old) of any scanning program will in all probability identify a virus before it can infect your computer. But remember: there is no perfect antivirus defense.

7. Consider using a program that creates a unique "signature" of all the programs on your computer. Run this software once in awhile to see if any of your program files have been modified—either by a virus or perhaps just by a stray gamma ray.

8. DON'T PANIC if your computer starts acting weird. You might have a virus, but then again you might not. Immediately turn

off all power to your computer and disconnect it from any local area networks. Reboot from a write-protected copy of your master DOS disk. Don't run any programs on a "regular" disk—you might activate a Trojan horse. If you don't have adequate backups, try to bring them up-to-date. (Yes, you might back up a virus as well, but it can't hurt you if you don't use your normal programs.) Set your backups off to the side. Only then can you safely hunt for problems.

9. If you can't figure out the problem and you don't know what to do next, just turn off your computer and call for help. Consider calling a local computer group before you call for an expert. If you need a professional, consider a regular computer consultant first. (Some "virus removal experts" charge prices far beyond their actual value.)

Meet The Mutation Engine Mystery Man

"We dedicate this little virus to Sara Gordon, who wanted to have a virus named after her." Thus began one of the more bizarre communications in the history of the virus/antivirus industry. It took place between Gordon and the man who is known as Dark Avenger, or DAv. The dedication to Gordon was contained in the code of the mutation engine which set the virus world back on its heels.

Over a period of five months in 1992, the U.S.-based Gordon corresponded by electronic mail with DAv in Bulgaria. Following are excerpts from those conversations which were originally printed in *Virus News International*.

Sara Gordon (SG): Some time ago in the Fidonet virus echo, you were told that one of your viruses was possibly responsible for the deaths of thousands, you responded with "**** you" (obscenity). Let's assume for a moment that the allegation is true. If one of your viruses was used by someone else to cause such a tragic situation, how do you really feel?

Dark Avenger (DA): I am sorry for it. I never meant to cause tragic incidents. I never imagined that these viruses would ever affect anything outside the computers. I used the nasty words because the people who wrote to me said some very nasty things to me first.

SG: Do you mean you were not aware that there could be any serious consequences with the viruses? Don't computers in your country affect the lives and livelihoods of people?

DA: They don't. Or at least at that time, they didn't. PCs were just very expensive toys which nobody could afford and nobody knew how to use. They were only used by some hotshots (or their children) who had nothing else to play with. I was not aware that there could be any consequences. The virus was so badly written that I never imagined it would leave the town. I only imagined it could leave the neighborhood. It all depends on human stupidity, you know. It's not the computer's fault that viruses spread.

SG: It is said that many people working for the government and companies in Bulgaria had computers at that time. Is this not the case?

DA: I don't know who said that but it's not true. Actually, at that time, most of the people in Bulgaria did not even know what IS a computer. If it was so, where did all those computers go? I don't think everyone in Bulgaria has them now.

SG: Did you have access to modems at that time? Did you ever make use of virus exchange systems to send your viruses? I've seen your name on some of the mail coming from those systems.

DA: At that time I did not have access to a modem and there were no virus exchange systems. I think I've been on some of them but that was much later. I never made any "use" of them, I was just fooling with them. Actually, I've been on almost no vx systems, using that name.

If you saw my name somewhere, it was probably just some imposter, not me. You know, when I have called any of them, they (the sysops) insist I have written many more viruses than I have.

It's very difficult, when you're DAv and you upload a virus, to make the impression that you didn't write it.

...

SG: People have wondered why you wrote your first virus. Why did you do it and do you have any regrets?

DA: I wrote it because I had heard about viruses and wanted to know more about them but nobody around me could tell me anything. So I decided to write my own one. I put some code inside it that intentionally destroys data and I am sorry for doing it.

SG: Couldn't you have asked someone who had a virus to show you one?

DA: I knew nobody who had a virus. In fact, I think that at that time, nobody in Bulgaria had one. Did you?

...

SG: Where did you hear about viruses? What in particular caught your interest?

DA: There was a magazine called *Computer For You*, the only computer magazine in Bulgaria at that time. In its copy of May 1988 there was a stupid article about viruses and a funny picture on its cover. This particular article was what made me write that virus.

Of course, that was not the first time I heard about viruses. I was interested in them and thinking of writing one a long time before that. I think that the only idea of making a program that would travel on its own and go to places its creator could never go was the most interesting thing for me.

The American government can stop me from going to the U.S. but they can't stop my virus. Ha ha ha ha ha ha ha ha.

...

SG: How do you feel about the destruction of data?

DA: I think it's not right to destroy someone else's data.

SG: Then why did you put destructive code in viruses?

DA: As for the first virus, the truth is that I didn't know what else to put in it. Also, to make people try to get rid of the virus, not just let it live. At that time, I didn't think any data in PCs could have great value.

SG: Do you mean the data in PCs in Bulgaria is of no value?

DA: As I said (or did I?), at that time there were not many PCs in Bulgaria and they were only used by a bunch of hotshots (or their kids) who didn't have what to play with.

Nobody wanted or needed computers to get their work done but they still had to stick to their workplaces and they had to do something at that time. Usually they were just drinking coffee and talking to each other, but some of them who had PCs were playing with them.

PCs basically were just a part of the furniture and a very expensive one. So I just hated it when some asshole had a new, powerful 16MHz 286 and didn't use it for nothing, while I had to program on a 4.77MHz XT with no hard drive (and I was lucky if I could ever get access to it at all).

Actually, I don't know why am I saying all this. The real answer is: I don't know. AND, I didn't care. I also don't care very much now, I'm afraid. I just want the other people to leave me alone.

...

SG: Do you feel responsible if someone else uses one of your viruses to cause harm to a person's machine?

DA: No. If they wanted to cause harm, they wouldn't need my viruses, they could simply type format C: or something else that is much more effective.

...

SG: What about the fact that you are giving people the idea, by creating such clever viruses?

DA: Ideas are not responsible for people who believe in them. Or use them. Or abuse them. Also, I didn't write them to "provide" anybody with anything ... I just wrote them for fun. I couldn't care less for all the suckers that would see/use them. They were not supposed to make such a mess.

SG: What do you think about the new crop of virus writers, like Phalcon/Skism, nUkE, etc.?

DA: I think they are a bunch of kids most of whom seek "fame" (and achieve it very easily with the help of antivirus people. Most of them are not good programmers at all.

...

SG: How long do you plan to continue writing viruses?

DA: I don't. I never planned it.

SG: You misunderstand the question. Are you going to continue writing viruses?

DA: I don't know that. It depends on what happens to me.

SG: What do you mean?

DA: I mean, I will not normally write and spread any destructive virus code, unless something extraordinary happens. Well, not if they put me in jail.

If they do and I ever go out, I would not be in the mood for programming. It is not and was not a crime to write the viruses, so I don't think that should happen. I just am not interested in writing them now.

...

SG: Have you ever considered making an antivirus product, other than the fake doctor.exe which actually is a virus?

DA: I have considered it many times, of course. But antivirus products are as useless as viruses. I don't think I will ever make a real one. As for doctor.exe, it's not fake. It really does the job it says it does.

SG: Why do you say they are useless? Don't you think they help protect the users from common viruses?

DA: The users spend much more money on buying such products and their updates than they would lose on data damage because of viruses.

The a-v products only help the users to empty their wallets. Besides, viruses would spread much less if the "innocent" user did not steal software and if they worked a bit more at their workplace, instead of playing games. For example, it is known that the Dark Avenger virus was transported from Europe to U.S.A. through some (of course stolen) games.

...

[Speaking of "innocent users"]

I cannot be held responsible because of where my virus went and what it did. You cannot be responsible for your children's actions. But, as I said, I am sorry that I put the destructive code in.

About those people, I don't know! Usually this (or any) virus does not do any damage but in most cases people panic and do more damage than the virus ever would.

Those people, I don't know, I never met them and I don't know if it was true what was said. Sometimes they use the wrong antivirus programs and they do the damage for them.

[He makes a prediction]

Sooner or later they will have REAL trouble, not toys like MtE or Commander Bomber, and not from me.

SG: What would make you want to write another virus?

DA: I cannot tell. Maybe if I got an extraordinary idea—a very good one or a very bad one. I already have one and I'm tempted to implement it but it's not really extraordinary.

Maybe if somebody pays me big bucks for it, I would want to do it.... But there is a big difference between "want" and "can."

[In response to Gordon's question asking whether she would know DAv if she met him in person]

I don't know. Did Lois Lane recognize Superman in his day-job suit?

I'm not suggesting he is a hero; by all means he is not, despite his reputation in the underground.

Yet it remains to be seen; is he really a mild-mannered, ordinary chap, or a superhero/anti-hero—and, if the latter, on which side is he fighting—does he even know himself?

The Biggest Mystery of All

Who writes viruses? You know Dark Avenger's story. What about the hundreds or thousands of other who have written one virus, or twenty, or a hundred?

The popular perception of a virus writer is a maladjusted acne-ridden, late-teens or early 20s social misfit, fueled by JOLT! cola and Cheetos. In the United States, this may be true. But United States viruses are lame by comparison to those produced in other parts of the world. Looking back at the successful viruses—those which have spread far and wide and created media circuses surrounding them—it's clear that they've all come from somewhere outside the country.

For a virus to be "good"—in the sense that it does spread, undetected, and takes a firm foothold before being discovered and combatted—requires a level of programming skill that the usual nerd does not possess. Arguably, the people best suited to write viruses are those who are capable of disassembling them and understanding what's inside—the antivirus product developers themselves.

To write a minor virus variant, all it takes is a load of source code (probably downloaded from a virus exchange BBS or sent by a "friend") and the ability to change a few words within the code itself. In fact, one Jerusalem variant, known as Jerusalem IRA, contains the name of the author of this book.

The Jerusalem virus, in its initial incarnation, was scheduled to perform Trojan Horse functions on any Friday the 13th. The "hack" to create Jerusalem IRA scheduled random screen messages memorializing the dates of death or imprisonment of IRA members. It's an ironic coincidence that a woman currently in prison is also named Pamela Kane. (Pamela is a very common first name for women in the United Kingdom and Kane is almost the Irish equivalent of Smith.)

What does this tell us? A new virus can be created by anyone with minimum programming skill. Variants of existing viruses will continue to appear and be presented to the antivirus community—through virus exchange BBSs or other methods—as a challenge. It's a sad waste of valuable resources since antivirus products that depend upon scanning techniques MUST keep adding each new strain as it appears.

It really doesn't matter WHO writes viruses or why. It's unlikely that a virus-writer profile such as the one developed for airplane hijackers back in the 70s can ever be developed. And, even if it were, what to do about it? Could there be a policing system—similar to airport security—that keeps someone matching the profile from ever telecommunicating with another person or passing a diskette to another person? Even if the person were, ultimately, to be identified and prosecuted, the damage would already have been done.

Antivirus product developers are among the most talented programmers in the world. They have access to far more information about how viruses work than even the best-connected would-be virus writer.

Most current virus traffic reminds one of the tigers chasing each other around the tree in the now politically incorrect story "Little Black Sambo." So long as it's a badge of honor to have one's new virus listed at the Virus Test Center, that may be enough for most of the miscreants.

The truly cagey, truly dedicated virus writer is working in secret and won't show off his or her work to anyone. Far better to have it discovered in the wild after it has spread to the four corners of the earth. Are people like that working today? Possibly. But such a person would have to have access to all the antivirus products available today (not too difficult), have disassembled them to analyze their weaknesses (somewhat more difficult), and have the world-class programming skills to bypass them all (extremely difficult!). Not only that, the writer of the next virus to burst on the scene and take over the world must have a method of distribution that ensures the virus spreads far and fast before its first infection is detected.

Possible? We can only wait and see.

Risk Assessment And Disaster Recovery

Several years ago at a security and virus conference, I was asked to address the problem of physical security of computers. A visual aid was indicated. I marched into the room with three props: a large cardboard box, about the size that would contain a case lot of paper towels; a pair of small boxes, courtesy of General Mills; and a huge trash bag. The boxes were covered with Mylar and the bag was Mylar. Pretty flashy. The message was even flashier.

The large box, I explained, represented a business's main computer. It could be a monster IBM, or it could be a CRAY II. Did the conference goers know where their main computers were located? Oh, yes. Nodding heads and satisfied smiles all around. The Cheerios-sized boxes are the mini-computers. A VAX or two, maybe? Nods. And you know where all your mini-computers are, don't you? More smiles, more nods. Of course.

Then the fun began. Inside the Mylar bag were thousands of styrofoam "peanuts." They made a lovely mess on the floor and began to scatter about. These are your PCs. The follow-up questions: Do you know for sure how many PCs your company has? Do you know where they are? Is there any central management for them as there is for the mainframe? These questions turned smug satisfaction into the bald realization that managing PCs is almost an exercise in managing the unmanageable.

There's no doubt that any organization knows just where its company cars are at a given time, including how many and who is using them. This is not the case with PCs. Home users are more likely to know where their one or two PCs are, but they can be more vulnerable to other problems, such as theft.

Exit, Stage Left: Taking PC

As a case in point, an international business behemoth gave a technical management employee his golden handshake and walking papers. He was instructed to report to a security office at a designated time to turn in his company credit cards, his passes to the various buildings, his keys—all the accoutrements of employment. The security officer went down a standard checklist. Forms were presented for signing and were signed and countersigned. Go in peace. "Um, but, what about…" began the former employee. "That's all, you're done. Good luck." Fortunately for Behemoth, Inc., a sense of ethics and honor prevailed. "What about this 486 laptop?"

The company was exquisitely concerned about its intellectual property and had reams of signed agreements about that. It was extremely careful to make sure that all keys were returned, but did it know about the $4,000 notebook PC loaded with proprietary programs?

It Works Both Ways

One of Behemoth's competitors promoted a talented system designer to (at last!) an office with a window. Company policy did not allow taking the PC belonging to the cubicle to the new windowed location. The designer carefully backed up her entire PC to tape so she could reinstall her work on the PC that belonged to her new space. She loaded the backup tapes, a few family photographs, and her personal files into boxes and carried them to the new office. (The official company files had to be moved by the Official Records Retention Squad.) Also in the box was a brand-new, high-speed modem that the woman had purchased herself rather than hassle the purchasing hierarchy.

Before leaving the hated cubicle for the last time she followed company policy and wiped the PC's hard drive and reformatted it.

She had waited, discreetly, until after office hours to move her personal effects. She used her new key to her new office and placed the box on the floor behind the door. She carefully locked the office and went home. Come Monday, no box. The weekend cleaning crew had thrown it away. Worse, they had not just thrown the box into the dumpster, they had emptied the box into the dumpster. A few hours later, the trash was collected, and years of work on backup tapes were gone.

If the policymakers had been thinking a little more clearly, they would have written a policy that ensured a replacement PC was properly installed and running before the first was reformatted. They also would have made sure that tapes with proprietary data were stored under lock and key.

Non-Traditional Shopping

A "48 Hours" television program focusing on political correctness referred to looters as "non-traditional shoppers." Stealing computers is certainly a non-traditional approach to acquiring them. And it's next to impossible to get technical support from the source. There are two reasons to steal hardware: the intrinsic value of the PC or peripheral and the value of the data contained on the machine. There's little one can do to deter the truly determined professional alternative shopper, but one can make the mission a bit more difficult.

First, don't issue invitations. Smart crooks like sure things. If you purchase new equipment, don't put the empty boxes out for the trash collector. If you decide not to save them in case of a return to the manufacturer, break the boxes down so they don't scream "Expensive Computer Stuff!" to the alert passerby with a larcenous bent.

Next, make it tough. Desktop PCs can be cabled to an immovable object. There are special engraving tools that enable you to emblazon your social security number or other identifier to the case of the system unit. A Magic Marker works just fine for the plastic parts of your PC.

Acts of God and Other Powers

Electricity is a computer's best friend, and worst enemy. Whether it's the ultimate power sending a lightning bolt from the sky or your local power monopoly sending a surge through its lines, your PC can be in big trouble. When power surges or fails, the minimum damage will probably be loss of whatever was in RAM at that moment.

N O T E

Be especially aware of the mini-surges or drops—the ones that just cause a flicker or an instant reboot of the machine. This is referred to in the electricity business as a *power brown*, but it can turn the rest of your day black, indeed. What can happen is that RAM is not completely cleared, and whatever data is in RAM can be corrupted. It might not be immediately obvious. So, in the case of a brown, the best thing to do is turn the PC completely off at the switch, wait, and then turn it back on again.

Surge protectors and ground fault interrupters should be on every outlet in which a PC is plugged. They're some insurance but can't protect against a lightning strike or full power outage.

Wise users unplug PCs at the wall socket (not just turn off the system unit or the surge protector) during thunderstorms. However, there's no way to predict when a delivery truck is going to hit the local transformer, knocking it out of service.

Of course, prepared users have a good and current backup so that a power outage would probably only affect a small amount of their work. It's even better (and you're even safer) if your software routinely backs up to a file, which probably wouldn't be affected by an outage.

Electricity run amok inside electronic devices presents a serious risk. It isn't always external electricity, either. One day, after steadfastly promising to replace the power supply that was sounding a bit funky, I discovered that it was too late. The video ROMs, soldered into the motherboard, were fried. And, the computer business being what it is, I found it was cheaper to replace the entire system unit than buy a new motherboard.

As an exercise in observing alternative shoppers, I placed the case, stripped of everything useful I could take out of it (except the offending power supply), and placed it atop a trash can on a busy street. A betting pool quickly formed. Four cars slowed down and looked. The fifth stopped, and the passenger, with furtive looks in all directions, snagged the useless case.

What Is a Disaster?

A software disaster is fairly simple: not having a good and current backup to put you back in business right away. Physical disasters are more complicated, not as easy to prevent, and can have far-reaching consequences. All the backups in the world are useless without a computer to put them on.

The 1993 bombing of New York's World Trade Center provides a good starting point for a hypothetical disaster. (The disaster recovery plans of those actually involved will be fodder for security conferences for years to come.) What if your company were located in a building that became a target for a mad bomber? It's a reasonable assumption that evacuation of personnel is uppermost in everyone's mind. The system of mailing backups to an outside location that protects your main computer resources works like a charm, but there's nobody there to gather the data and trundle it away. Yesterday's backups are safe in a vault five miles away, but what about the data that had accumulated today? And what about the data stored on individual PCs that has not been backed up in weeks, months, or years—or, if it has, is on tapes stored in desk drawers?

However, because this is a hypothetical situation, assume a miracle or two. The main computers were connected by high-speed modem to redundant systems far away from the explosion, and an exact duplicate of the system exists. Every employee had backed up every bit of essential data just seconds before the blast and, fervently loyal to the company, had left personal effects behind to carry the tapes. Are we still in business?

No. Where is the office space, where are the computers, where is the telephone system? These form the infrastructure of the business. What about the employee security passes that might have been left behind?

Obviously, even with miracles, companies are still not disasterproof. The sad fact of the matter is that, even if companies employ disaster-relief providers, the relief suppliers hope to collect serious money for services that will probably never be used. For them it is simply not feasible to maintain space and support systems for every client in the case of a single major disaster.

Arguably, these services should not accept more clients in a single structure than they can properly take care of if the whole building goes. A careful manager would make sure that, when negotiating a contract, that it's the case. In the grander scheme of things, such an event is not likely, and there are many consulting companies that would be happy to assist in disaster recovery planning.

What's the Worst That Could Happen?

That's a subjective question, and one that can only be answered by a company's information systems manager. Even a home PC has a manager, its owner or user.

The following checklist, developed by Jack Bologna of *Computer Security Digest* is a good starting place to figure out just what your risks are and how you should prepare for emergencies:

> ☐ Do you fully realize the value of your PCs, the software, the applications, and the data being used on your PC? Some simple math often shows that users have no idea what their complete system—not just the hardware—is really worth.
>
> ☐ Has the amount of possible financial loss from disaster, criminal act, accident, and so on, been determined? This ties directly to the value of the system but with the added cost of being out of business.
>
> ☐ Is the selection and purchase of PCs controlled? This can be important on several levels, not the least of which is the proliferation of gray market sales where standard warranties may not be in place.
>
> ☐ Has the effect of short- and long-term downtime of PCs been determined? Could downtime result in loss of business, customer or employee dissatisfaction, or loss of revenue?

☐ If one PC is shut down, can another be utilized for necessary processing?

☐ Do outsiders have access to your PCs? The ramifications of outside access range from stealing data or programs to trashing a system by purposefully or accidentally inserting a computer virus.

☐ Has a test disaster been conducted? Remember fire drills?

☐ Have emergency procedures been established in case of disaster or criminal act?

☐ Has a specific individual been assigned to the selection, purchase, and control of PCs?

☐ Is there PC equipment accountability?

☐ Has a physical inventory been conducted of all PC equipment? Do your PC users attend classes that instruct them on proper system handling and magnetic media handling?

☐ Are the PC users informed of their security and control responsibilities?

☐ Have written policies and procedures been prepared and implemented that govern the security and control of microcomputer equipment and applications?

☐ Are stringent controls placed on any PC use that could affect the accounting records of your company?

☐ Are there adequate controls to protect against the invasion of privacy?

☐ Are your internal/external auditors aware of your computer systems?

☐ Does the disaster recovery plan take into account multi-location PC operations?

☐ Have arrangements been made to replace the microcomputer hardware and software in case of disaster?

☐ Has someone been assigned responsibility for disaster planning?

If you're only one person with only one PC, you will look at this checklist somewhat differently than an information services specialist or manager with responsibility for hundreds or thousands of machines. Looking is the important part. Most users, regardless of how or where machines are used, will find something here that rings a bell.

Vulnerability Assessment

Most of the following items are beyond your control. Consider them in terms of what needs to be done if one of them happens.

Hardware	Electro-mechanical device failure
	CPU failure
	Disk unit head crash
	Tape drive failure
	Environmental problems, such as dirt, dust, and smoke
	Circuit failure
	Power problems, including spikes and drops
Software	Operating system problems
	Logic errors
	Programming errors
	Faulty design
	Insufficient testing
	Algorithmic errors, such as rounding and truncation
	Poor or lost documentation
	Computer viruses
Magnetic media	Physical damage of medium
	Equipment malfunction
	Software problems
	Operator error
	Operator mishandling
	Erasure
	Overwrites
	Computer viruses

Physical security and site security	Is the perimeter security adequate?
	Is the building's security adequate, including access control, proper lighting, alarm systems, and environmental controls?
	Is internal site security adequate, including access control, hardware security devices, alarm systems, and environmental controls?
	Are doors and docks secure; are keys or combinations controlled, combinations changed frequently, and control logs kept?
	If card access systems are used, are cards controlled?
	Is the work area secured during nonworking hours? Have policies and procedures been developed for access control?
	Is access to electrical power controlled and secure? Are floors and ceilings watertight?
	Is there sufficient ventilation around PCs?
	Is the PC placed near a window where people can view the materials being processed or where sight of the PC might tempt a thief?
	Are furnishings fire resistant?

Hardware

Hardware failures tend to be dramatic and obvious. Whether you have replacement parts on hand and install them yourself or whether you must go to a computer repair shop, you've lost time and money. Don't lose data, too.

In case of such a failure, you should have a good and current backup, either on tape, floptical, or disk. If you have a warning of an impending hardware problem (funny noises coming from a disk drive, for example) immediately take whatever steps you can to back up anything not included in your backups.

It's likely that your system will break down or display an error message like "301." (301 tells you that the CPU can't find the keyboard, even though you know it's right in front of you.) Be thankful that you have a good and current backup.

Software

Software problems are the common cold or 24-hour flu of computing. Some people suffer more, some people suffer less, and some people develop life-threatening complications.

Consider just what a software problem can mean to you and your data. With the exception of your operating system (DOS), most software is application specific. Product A develops data to be used with product A. Product B develops data to be used with product B. A second exception is utility software—the sort used for disk and data management which is used system wide.

In the next two chapters, I examine the risks to (and from) both hardware and software.

Hardware Risks

Your hardware can be at risk, or it can put your data at risk—or both. Here is a recent example from my memory book of disasters: I decided to write the columns I was going to FedEx to a magazine on a floppy disk. I saw no reason why not—all I had to do was back up to tape, and I could avoid cluttering up my ancient, too-small hard drive. Very efficient, indeed. After printing and closing the document, I remembered that I had forgotten to take out the double spacing. When I tried to re-open the document, the floppy drive made a grinding sound, and the word processor displayed the message "Data Error Reading Drive A: Retry? Cancel?"

Some headstrong word processing programs just don't understand the Cancel command. I removed the diskette and took it to another machine. Unfortunately, the other machine didn't have the word processing program on it, but it could read the disk's directory. I turned my attention to the original machine's floppy drive and tried a directory of another disk. Again, the drive made a grinding noise, and I received a message: "Data Error Reading Drive A: Abort? Retry? Fail?" I had one dead floppy drive.

Luckily I had a replacement drive waiting for just such an occasion. After finding a screwdriver, removing the case, and gagging at the amount of dust and fluff clogging the floppy drive, I replaced the drive. All this activity took twenty minutes at most because I had a replacement drive and a screwdriver close at hand. When I fired up the word processing program again, I found the file had been damaged beyond all recognition. It takes about twice as long to rekey an 800-word column as it does to replace a floppy drive.

There's a lot to be learned from this experience, not the least of which is the codependency between your hardware and your data. For a professional writer, a single hour without working hardware is an hour lost forever. For a professional writer working on a close deadline, it's a disaster.

I made two major mistakes: not keeping the PC as clean as it should be and not backing up the material immediately after I closed it the first time. On the plus side, I had the needed replacement part close at hand and I had hard copy to work from. Since some hardware problems are inevitable, it behooves users to think of when, not if, a problem will occur and to be always prepared for the worst.

The Codependency Problem

Without hardware you're nowhere. People tend to think of hardware as their largest dollar investment; they know exactly how much they paid for that new LaserGem printer or the 40G hard drive to run all those essential Windows applications. (They also know how much they paid for all that software.) Hardware failures tend to be immediate and dramatic. More often than not, they're expensive.

On the other hand, it is not that difficult to get replacement parts, find a repair person, or even borrow or rent another PC. You are back in business if you have your data.

In another memorable personal incident, my power supply had been making ominous noises, and the simple phone call to order a replacement wasn't at the top of my priority list. It should have been. Turning the PC off and on once too often resulted in electrical rebellion on the part of the power supply. It went south, taking all the video ROMS (soldered to the motherboard) with it. Of course, a deadline loomed. A frantic call to a friend resulted in a loaner system unit. I popped the hard drive containing most of my new book into the replacement and continued to work. A few days later, my new power supply arrived and was installed. The monitor's display looked like Bill the Cat had been experimenting with PC Draw on a bad day. A high-level technical conference ensued, the gist of which being that the SIMMs must be bad. I ordered new SIMMs, waited, installed them, and found that Bill the Cat was still around and active. After three or four other wrong guesses, I identified the video RAMS as the culprits. The entire process took almost two weeks.

The time involved could have been a disaster if an identical PC wasn't almost instantly available so that the hard drive could simply be dropped in. A rental unit would have required installing word processing programs, communications programs, and the software needed to restore from the tape drive. The problem could have been averted entirely by simply listening to the power supply on its last gasps and replacing it.

Risky Business

It's time to bite the bullet and, instead of skipping over the checklist as you probably did in the previous chapter, assess your own risk situation.

Money, Honey

Just what have you paid, over time, for your home and office PC equipment? If you're a corporate supervisor, what has your company paid? What is it worth to you to protect that investment?

Next, consider what your hardware is worth today. What is its worth to you as long as it continues to function reliably and what is its worth as a trade-in?

As you begin to assess the financial risk of hardware, be aware that the cost of repairing an older PC or peripheral may not be cost effective. In fact, it might be more than purchasing a replacement with more power and more speed. When you add in the down time for troubleshooting, ordering repair parts, carrying the equipment to a repair shop, and so on, you may well be better off making a quick phone call for next-day delivery of whatever you need.

As PCs have become more and more reliable, it has become more and more difficult to get the ones that go bad repaired. Gone are the days of computer stores in every strip mall with repairmen in the back room wielding screwdrivers. Calling a service company can be an experiment in terror. They can get to your site within 48 hours, but like plumbers, there's a walk-in-the-door charge. If you choose a carry-it-in approach, you must first find a place to carry it to. They are scarce in the mid-1990s. The "free" repairs that come with a new purchase's warranty can become costly if they take days and days to accomplish.

When thinking about your dollar investment, it's a lot easier if you have a home business or activity that has enabled you to depreciate your equipment. (Current IRS Rapid Write-Off rules allow you to take up to $17,500 in deductions for new equipment in the purchase year.) Years back, the "decimal theory" was developed for appliance failures. If the refrigerator, dishwasher, or whatever, was over ten years old and would cost more than $100 to repair, it was time for a new one. It's not that easy to develop a theory for PCs, but a good rule might be if you're more than two chips behind, replace it. In other words, if your 286 PC decides to take a dive and the current standard is 486, go for it. Later on, your might consider repairing the 286 (worth about $250 on the street) and keeping it around as a backup.

Don't get caught with your electronic pants down. Watch the ads in the newspaper or trade publications for current prices, find a repair person before you need one, and find a good book about troubleshooting hardware problems before you're in the position of having to make a decision.

Down Time

Down time can have a very real cost and very real consequences. If the hardware takes data down with it, the cost can increase exponentially. The more you depend on your computer, the more it can cost.

Only you can decide what your down time tolerance and costs are. Writers, programmers, researchers, architects, and anyone whose business is computer intensive will have a different tolerance than folks who use their PCs to do optional office-type work at home, play games, keep track of the stock market, or to cruise the electronic highway. If a day or two without a working PC won't change your life, your options are open.

The idea of keeping an extra PC around isn't as strange as it sounds. AT class machines can be purchased at used PC stores for the proverbial "song" and can get you back in business rapidly. Here in Wilmington, Delaware, a store called Second Source reconditions and sells them for $400. If your cost of one day's down time exceeds that figure, run, don't walk, to such a supplier, if your essential applications' needs are met by the technology. It's also possible to pick up a used PC by reading the classified ads (unfortunately, most people have an inflated idea of what their aged equipment is worth), from a nearby company doing a massive technology upgrade (if the employees don't snap them all up first), or just by putting the word out that you're looking.

Just make sure that you have a method to load your work onto the backup machine. A stack of 3.5" disks don't do much good when your backup machine has two 5.25" drives. If you back up to tape, make sure that the software to run the tape system is already installed on the second PC and that you know how to restore data selectively if your alternate PC has a much smaller drive than your main machine.

There are solid reasons for purchasing an extra PC in advance. You can have the drive loaded with your essential software so all you need to do is restore your backups and go. It's also possible that your local dealer may not always have stock on hand. The farther away you are from a good hardware source, the more essential the redundant PC will be.

If you're clever (or lucky) enough to purchase a spare with the same configuration as your top-drawer PC, it makes sense to set up the hard drive, remove it from the PC, and stick it in a drawer somewhere. If the hard drive fails, you just install the spare, restore from your backups, and keep going.

There's also a good argument for just purchasing a spare hard drive that's identical to your PCs, loading your applications, and putting it safely away. A hard drive is the most likely thing to go bad on a PC.

If, and when you upgrade to a bigger, faster, and better system, you might want to avoid the temptation to snag a few extra bucks by selling your old system. It's the cheapest insurance you'll ever buy.

Hang on to What You've Got

Consider the "alternate shoppers" mentioned in Chapter 3. There is always a risk of theft to anything expensive and relatively portable. If a burglar breaks into a place of business, it's likely that the goal is business equipment or the petty cash box. Home burglaries are a bit different. Smart thieves go for the items they know how to fence. Most crooks prefer to take the VCR, TV, stereo, camera, or silver. Computers aren't at the top of the garden-variety thief's wish list, but there's one exception: laptops.

Hardware and software solutions for data protection are covered later in this book. For now, concentrate on hanging on to your hardware.

There's a chunk of common wisdom that says "This site protected by Wombat Electronic security systems" stickers provide the most effective deterrent going. It may be true. Burglars are, arguably, not the smartest people in the world, but they are smart enough to pick on the easiest hits, not the most difficult.

It's hard to put a computer under your mattress, in a fake beer can, or in a closet semi-protected by a dead bolt. (As a practical matter, locked closets are incredibly attractive to our felonious friends; the more locks, the more attractive.) Thus, of all your prized possessions, your PC is probably going to be the most obvious—if not the most attractive—to an alternative shopper.

Make It (Appear to Be) Tough

Something as simple as draping a length of bicycle chain around your monitor and system unit is a remarkable deterrent to a burglar intent on getting as much as possible, as quickly as possible. You can go to greater (and more secure) lengths by purchasing cable tie-downs that attach to solid and immovable objects. Engraving your social security number or other identifier on your equipment is not nearly as effective as scrawling your name all over it with a Magic Marker. However, the engraving technique is somewhat more aesthetically attractive. Whether or not the equipment can be fenced doesn't matter much if it's already gone.

You can't absolutely prevent a burglary but you can be careful about whether your home or office appears attractive to thieves. Your local police are good sources for information about what equipment is popular with thieves and ways to be careful and prudent. Most people wouldn't put the antique silver service inherited from Great-Aunt Elsie on a table in a lighted front window, so don't put your computer there either. What I mentioned in Chapter 3 bears repeating: Don't put boxes that clearly say "There is a computer in this place" out with the trash. When going on vacation, give as much care to your computer hardware as you would to your flat silver, jewelry, or anything else portable and of great value.

Give more care to your precious backups and original installation software. That's the subject of the next chapter.

Insurance

Look at your policies. Business owners will have different coverages and types of policies than home PC owners. Make sure that you understand what your policy says, rather than what an aggressive agent says. The key words in most comprehensive policies that cover computer hardware are *of like kind*. If your PC Jr (remember those?) is stolen, there's almost no way your insurance carrier can replace it with an item of like kind. What they'll do is figure out how much you paid in the first place, depreciate it, and give you a check for the calculated actual cash value (about $2.95). Another possibility if you have a highly comprehensive policy is that they'll figure out that your PC Jr was the lowest-end PC around when you purchased it and give you a check for what they consider to be the lowest-end PC available at the time of the loss. On the other hand, you might make out like a bandit if you have an old PS-1 ripped off. An unwary claims adjustor might just provide you with a hot new model. Keep in mind, however, that all claims will result in a closer look at your policy, and insurance fraud is, almost always, a felony.

Good PC Housekeeping

Any beginner's book about PCs will give you the basics. Don't put your PC next to a heat source; make sure that it has plenty of room to breathe; don't pour JOLT! cola on the keyboard. Although it's not likely that readers of this book are beginners, it's still prudent to go back to PC kindergarten for a few reminders.

It's silly to assume that even the most anal-compulsive PC user will never smoke, drink, eat, or keep pets around a PC (pets are less likely in office settings, of course), but it's important to consider how to do these things with the least possible impact on expensive hardware.

If you must smoke around a PC, use a smokeless ashtray, keep the ashtray at least an arm's length from your system unit, and never empty an ashtray into the wastebasket in the same room as the PC is located. Furthermore, smoke in the ambient air will make dust, cat fluff, and Kleenex fallout stick harder to the PC.

Liquid on the keyboard is, for the most part, a transient problem. Develop a habit of always keeping your coffee cup or soda can at an arm's length from the computer. If you do spill on the keyboard, turn the PC off immediately. Disconnect the keyboard at the back of the system unit and turn it upside down on an old towel. If you spill a lot of liquid on the keyboard, pull the keys off as soon as you've drained the worst of it out. Your DOS manual will have a nice drawing of a keyboard so you'll know where to put the keys back. (Removing the space bar is not recommended.)

Pets are a bit trickier. A former office cat, Willard the Disinterested, has been immortalized in countless articles about computing with pets, but he's worth another look. Willard was a "mon-cat"; he liked to sleep on top of the monitor. Practically, it wasn't that much of a problem. Every now and then his tail would descend in front of the screen. However, not only were little bits of Willard dander getting into every part of the PC, Willard only had two tricks: eating and sleeping. The more Willard ate, the more his bulk increased until one day gravity took over. He slid down the back of the monitor into the tangle of cables connecting everything to everything else. (Real PC professionals never screw their cables in so the results were startling.) Willard never slept on top of the monitor again.

Another office cat, Pansy, used to sleep in the well of a LaserJet printer. Cleaning corona wires has an added dimension with long cat hairs clinging.

You probably don't want to think about what happened when a small (but very aggressive) kitten by the name of MicroBeast flung himself onto shoulders connected to hands that were installing hundreds of dollars worth of SIMM chips.

Overt actions aside, pet "stuff" gets into the air around your computer. Dander is measured in microns as are skin flakes from the human body and lots of other things that are contaminants in our everyday lives.

Even June Cleaver couldn't keep a house clean enough to really be healthy for a PC. Try this simple challenge: Find something black, preferably shiny, and put it next to your PC. Observe it at regular intervals. See how soon a thin coating of dust collects. Put an unlabeled black disk in your least-used floppy drive. Observe it at intervals. What you see on the disk is about 1/1,000,000 of what's pulled through your PC by the internal fan.

What can you do? One possible solution is to install hundreds (if not thousands) of dollars worth of air filters on your home HVAC system. This approach is excellent for keeping the gunk in the air moving efficiently past PCs rather than just staying put. Depending upon the results of your test, you may want to consider an ultra-high efficiency portable air cleaner. They're not cheap; one that cleans the air ten times an hour in a 10x20 room is almost $200. However, tests with the cleaner in place reliably show that it takes five times as long for the slight coating of dust to appear.

It's a good idea to check the air intake slots on the front of your PC (these include the floppy drives) on a regular basis. If you see fluff or gunk, use a small vacuum cleaner to remove it. Every now and then, remove the

Chapter 5: Hardware Risks

case from the PC and inspect the innards. If it's icky, use a very soft brush and your little vacuum cleaner to tidy things up. Externals can be easily cleaned with a lintless cloth dampened with a bit of household cleaner.

NOTE

Never spray a cleaning product directly onto any part of a computer.

Leaping Laptops

With the advent of these small, go-anywhere computers, an entire new security problem has developed. People steal them for a variety of reasons. The knowledge that they're theft prone has created a subset of problems. Their owners tend to put them in "safe," but potentially damaging, locations: the trunks of cars. In most climates, spring and fall are safe enough for trunk storage. However, don't try it in the dead of winter in International Falls, Minnesota, or the middle of summer in Atlanta, Georgia. If you must put your portable in the trunk, give it plenty of time to return to normal temperature before trying to start it up. Even then, an extreme temperature may damage the storage media, if not the PC itself.

The risks to the data on a stolen laptop are covered in Chapter 7, but it's your job to keep your data from being stolen in the first place. If you're the kind of person who would leave a $5,000 Rolex watch on the dresser when you leave your hotel room, leave your laptop there, too.

Stealing a laptop, however, is a lot easier for a crook than checking out who checks into a hotel. A laptop on the front seat of a car (locked or not) is easy prey. A laptop on the seat next to you on a train, in an airport, or anywhere is even easier if the thief has a quick getaway plan. If your home or office is burglarized, the laptop is an easy prize.

Not long ago, a consultant was standing outside an office building chatting with a group of clients. When the conversation was over, she reached down for the notebook computer she had placed on the sidewalk next to her feet. No notebook, and neither she nor her associates had seen anything or anyone. Not only was her notebook gone, but all the work she'd done at the client's site that day. Of course, she had made backups before leaving the office but they were in the case with the computer. When asked if she had put her purse on the sidewalk, too, her shocked response was "I would never do that." Slowly, she came to the realization that a lipstick, a few credit cards, and $20 in cash were not as valuable as her notebook computer.

Hard Facts About Hardware

Hardware is the most vulnerable part of any system. It can't be backed up and restored. It's expensive. You, as manager of your system(s), must determine the level of protection and redundancy you need—or the cost of not having it.

Software Risks

The most important word in this chapter—indeed the most important word associated with the art and science of computing—is *backup*. If a disaster occurs and you have a good and current backup of your system, you can be back to work just as soon as you find replacement hardware. Sadly, backing up is often at the bottom of users' priority lists.

In this chapter I will examine the various methods of backing up after looking at the ways software can play tricks on users.

Old Software, New Tricks

Utility software is often closely tied to a particular version of DOS because of the operations performed on the structure of DOS itself. It should be (and almost always is) downward compatible, meaning that it will run with all previous DOS versions, but nobody can guarantee upward compatibility when a new DOS version comes out. A well-behaved utility will issue a warning or refuse to run. This gives you the opportunity to send a few dollars for an upgraded version. There is always the possibility that the vendor of your cherished program has left the field, and you're left with the choice of staying with your old DOS version and using the program you've become so dependent upon or finding a replacement.

A poorly behaved utility might simply run amok under a new DOS version causing untold damage. When you change DOS versions, check your utilities. Microsoft made a major change to the underlaying structure of DOS in version 4. While this change was not apparent to the casual user, many utilities that accessed DOS structures directly would no longer work. Another change that Microsoft made in version 4 allowed hard disks of greater than 32 megs. Even the published routines for accessing the disk sectors directly were changed so that many utilities such as the popular Norton Utilities would not work under DOS 4.0 if the disk were larger than 32 megabytes.

Most of the utility programs that are included with DOS are version specific and will simply not run under a different version. You will see the message "Wrong DOS version" if you try to run a DOS utility from version 3 when you have started the computer with DOS version 4. For this reason it is a good idea to always copy all the new DOS utility programs onto the hard disk when changing DOS versions. The Microsoft trend is to now include a SETUP program which saves the old version of DOS in a separate directory, and copies all the new files from the distribution diskette to the hard disk. Unless you plan to go back to an earlier version of DOS, you can delete the old DOS program files.

Upgrading applications software is not without its own hazards. Word processing programs are notorious for including a routine that will turn documents created under a previous release into the current format. Unfortunately, these conversion programs don't always work as advertised. Even chancier are the ones that purport to take a document created with TypeWrite and turn them into VerbPerfect. Most word processing programs use extra characters in addition to the text to indicate type style, margin settings, and formatting information. A feature of one word processing program may not even be supported in another, and therefore a conversion program will not be able to add the appropriate code to the document during the conversion.

A major NY lawfirm had been using the IBM Displaywriters for composing documents from the late 1970s into the early 1980s when they switched to IBM PCs for word processing. The natural choice for the firm was IBM's DisplayWrite II word processing program which retained the documents using EBCDIC coding instead of the normal ASCII code used by most PC programs. This was followed by an upgrade to DisplayWrite III in the mid 1980s to add the enhanced functions of that program to the word processing department. The older documents were mostly compatible since the program came from the same vendor, IBM.

In the late 1980s, management decided to switch to WordPerfect for various reasons. After the switch, they discovered that none of the DisplayWrite documents would work with their new word processing program. This became a major headache in that lawfirm documents are often based on boiler plate paragraphs taken from previous documents. Additionally, legal documents have very specific formatting which no commercial conversion program at the time was equipped to handle. As a consequence the firm had to commission a custom program to convert all existing documents from DisplayWrite format (either II or III) to the WordPerfect format. The expense of a custom program plus the person hours involved in converting thousands of documents exceeded all the savings in switching from one package to another.

The best test of the efficacy of a conversion program is to create a special test document loaded with formatting codes and other fancy stuff and run it through the system. But even the best conversion utility may not be able to translate all the formatting codes from one system to another. Each document may need to be hand converted once the general conversion allows the other word processing package to read the files.

Database programs and spreadsheet programs can be as difficult to convert as word processors; running a test file through a new release is always a smart move. *Never* make a test with an original file. *Always* make a copy and work with that. If the new version of the program does not save the old version's file, and it does not convert correctly, you could possibly lose hours of work.

Backups or archived files are another area where the files are version specific. Disk backups using the DOS BACKUP program created under one DOS version often can't use RESTORE under another DOS version. This shouldn't be a big problem when you upgrade to a new release since, of course, you'll do a complete system backup as soon as the new DOS version is loaded. Not! But it could make a difference if you have to move your data to another PC because of hardware failure. Take the time to note the DOS version on all backup disks and keep the original DOS installation disks in a safe place. If you must restore files that were created using DOS version 3.3 to a machine that runs DOS 6.2, just boot the PC from the 3.3 diskette and use the

BACKUP on the diskette to transfer the files. Make sure you don't restore the DOS files too, since that will cover over the DOS 6.2 files of the same name on the second PC.

If you use a special backup program other than DOS, keep copies of previous releases of your archiving program close at hand or on your PC until you're sure that nobody is using that version any longer. No matter what kind of backup program you use, make sure you have the RESTORE portion of that program copied to a diskette. Most archive and backup software compresses the data to make more efficient use of diskette space when backing up files. Even if you have a backup of the entire hard disk, the data on the backup is not usable until it is restored. You can't use the backup program from the backup. If the hard disk crashes and the program that you need to restore your data was on the hard disk, there is no way to restore the data to a new disk or another machine if you don't have a copy of the restore program. All you have are forty-two disks of backed up data with no way to restore it.

Always make a bootable diskette with the hidden DOS files and COMMAND.COM as well as a copy of the restore program. If you are a guru, you should probably add DEBUG.COM to your emergency boot disk too. Check the CONFIG.SYS and AUTOEXEC.BAT files. Copy any files named in those startup files to the diskette in the same directories named in CONFIG.SYS and AUTOEXEC.BAT. Then copy both of those files to the emergency diskette. This way your computer can be started with the same configuration that is used when booted from the hard disk.

Broken Windows

Some people have stunning success running non-Windows applications under Windows. Others are less fortunate and end up with garbled data or worse. These effects seem to be capricious at best. It's no help if you've been working happily in Microsoft Word (not the Windows version) under Windows for weeks if not months and, suddenly, the Microsoft family throws a rock through your Windows and a few thousand carefully chosen words are nowhere to be found. This happened. To me! Fortunately the autosave option was turned on and little work was actually lost, but it could have been worse. Without autosave, the words are only saved in memory, not on disk. A power failure or program glitch can send hours of work into the bit bucket and nothing can get them back.

Most programmers who write for the Windows environment are aware that a file should never remain in the Open state. Windows pretends to be a multitasking operating system on a single tasking machine. A user can get click-happy and open the same file many times in different applications. If the person who programmed the application skipped the part about using files properly with Windows, all sorts of strange things may happen to your data.

Windows can also play strange tricks with utility programs that access the hardware directly or bypass DOS. Most DOS program are "Windows aware" and some refuse to run in a Windows session. Other utilities are not aware that Windows is in control and assume the user is at the DOS prompt. Remember that even when you click on the DOS icon, and get a full screen DOS prompt, Windows is still in control. Some internal functions that the programs assumes are available may fail. You could end up holding a mouse, and not much else.

What's in a (File) Name

We all know that a file needs at least a first name, up to eight alpha-numeric characters. Like FILENAME. Files can also have a last name, the extension, separated from the first name by a period: FILENAME.EXT. Many programs automatically create the extensions such as .DOC, .DBF, .TXT, and so on. DOS is smart enough not to allow you to put anything but alphanumeric characters in a file name or extension but not smart enough to know when you already have a file with that name on your disk.

The DOS COPY command is particularly stupid. If you try to copy a file called MYDOC.DOC from the A drive to your hard drive (or, for that matter, from one subdirectory to another) and there's already a MYDOC.DOC on the target drive, does DOS care? No. Always do a directory of a target drive when you use the COPY command if you are worried about overwriting existing files.

Late Breaking News: With the release of DOS 6.2 on February 1, 1994, the COPY command *finally* includes a confirm to overwrite an existing file. (Only 6.2 versions to realize that oversight!) But even then you must be careful. If you use one of the DOS wildcard characters, ? or *, you get three choices when DOS encounters an existing file, "FILENAME.EXT exists Overwrite? (Yes/No/All)." Answering **A** for All will suppress the warning on any other duplicate filenames.

Even supposedly sophisticated programs aren't that smart. Microsoft Word is nice enough to tell you that the file (actually, a file by that name) already exists. Do you want to replace it? To anyone accustomed to working in Word, the Yes response is so automatic as to be hazardous to the original file with the same name. In this situation, take a clue from Big Blue's old motto: Think.

Ok, if you don't like to think, there is another solution. In the latest DOS versions a utility called UNDELETE can be added to the AUTOEXEC.BAT file to make a hidden SENTRY directory on any drive. When this option is added, a file is never truly deleted but just moved to the SENTRY directory. Even overwritten files are moved to the SENTRY directory before the new file is written. The UNDELETE program can search this directory and restore any file that has been deleted or overwritten. As the disk fills up, the oldest files are really deleted from the SENTRY directory to make space, but there is a good chance that recently deleted files can be recovered intact.

RTFB

This is an acronym for a somewhat impolite statement that's said, probably thousands of times a day, by tech support people around the world. In English, the operative words are *read the book*. An alternate is RTFM for manual instead of book. There is even an archive site on the Internet maintained at MIT called RTFM which contains files of frequently asked questions (FAQs) on almost any subject.

There are a number of reasons to read the book, not the least of which is figuring out how to install your software. Admittedly, the book is not always interesting reading (especially DOS manuals) and may explain why there are so many aftermarket titles on the shelves of the computer book section of your bookstore. The book may also be a simple README.DOC file on your disk if your new program is shareware or distributed similarly. Even many shrink-wrapped commercial software contains READ.ME or README.NOW files which explain updates which went into effect after the manual was published. After all, it's a lot easier and quicker to make a file than a four-color, glossy, hard-bound manual.

Before installing and working with a new program, there are a few essentials any careful user ought to know. First, how to stop the installation program if it becomes clear that something may be going wrong. Pressing Ctrl-Break may not work.

Next, make sure that you know what your emergency keys are in the new program. Even though F1 has become a more or less *de facto* standard for Help across the industry, F1 in WordPerfect is Cancel. F1 used as Exit and Don't Save could be a disaster. RTFB.

Good documentation will include a list of error messages, usually at the back of the book. Know the error messages associated with a program and those generated by DOS. When you see an error message do nothing unless you are absolutely certain you know what it means and what the consequences of your action may be. For undocumented programs (perhaps collected from your local BBS), you can check the imbedded text—where the error messages ought to be—with LABTEST.

The book can also tell you (but may not) whether there are any known conflicts with other programs. This is particularly important with programs that need TSR status to operate. If the program routinely changes executable files (to reflect changes in formatting of data or screen display, etc.), be aware that some antivirus programs may signal the changes. (PHYSICAL will; you may want to exclude such programs from checking.) I take a more technical look at TSR programs and the havoc they can wreak later.

Death by Installation

Installation programs are convenient. Just type **INSTALL** and press **Enter**, and your new software does all the work for you. Sometimes, however, it may do a couple of jobs you didn't have on the list.

When a program runs you usually think in terms of "I am running COOLBASE, and the file that's running is COOLBSE.EXE." Not so. COOLBASE, an imaginary relational database, is probably opening and closing a large number of files that are subsets of COOLBASE and storing extracted data in temporary locations called buffers. DOS, when installed, tells your PC just how many files and buffers can be open at a given instant. The default is 8 files and 15 buffers although the buffers default depends on the amount of memory in the system. These are puny amounts for any serious application. Thus, the number of files and buffers in the DOS default can be changed in the CONFIG.SYS file.

To see what's in your CONFIG.SYS file, type **CONFIG.SYS** and press **Enter** at the DOS prompt. The contents of the file will display on your screen. You should see one line that says "FILES=*XX*" and another that says "BUFFERS=*XX*." If you don't, you're still running with the original DOS settings. This is highly unlikely.

One of the kindnesses of software developers is making sure that your CONFIG.SYS file is proper for their software by appending the number of files and buffers needed by their program. Unfortunately, you may have other programs that are needier.

What happens is that the install program appends its requirements to CONFIG.SYS. The lines in CONFIG.SYS are read sequentially, so the ones read last are the ones that stick in bootup. Thus, a new program could define a much smaller requirement, causing your needier programs to not run. Read the book to see what's in INSTALL.BAT or, if the idea of the book is too odious, simply toss in the first installation diskette and type **TYPE INSTALL.BAT** and press **Enter**.

There's a fairly easy fix. Using DOS COPY, copy CONFIG.SYS to a floppy in case of emergency. Next, run your install program. Then, before you do anything else, go back and edit out the FILES= and BUFFERS= lines that were added to CONFIG.SYS. Remember, you will have to reboot your computer to have CONFIG.SYS read in properly.

While you're at it, print out and make a copy of AUTOEXEC.BAT before you start the installation. There's a possibility that your new program might require a TSR loaded with AUTOEXEC. And that other TSRs already there might not welcome the newcomer in the last slot. Some particularly naughty installations will overwrite AUTOEXEC.BAT in its entirety but most will save the old file under a filename such as AUTOEXEC.OLD.

It's always easier to go back to where you were than to start over entirely.

Custom Tailoring

Many larger programs offer a variety of custom options to the user. Word processing programs, for example, enable you to set up numerous style sheets, macros, document formats, printer descriptions, and so on. It can take a long time to tweak the software to just where you want it to be. Should your software go south, you've lost all that tweaking time and have to start over. It doesn't make much sense to backup software that's sitting on the shelf ready to go. It does, however, make a lot of sense to back up your customizations. Read the book to find out which files hold that information and back them up to a disk.

True custom software, written to your (or your company's) order—usually at great expense and over a seemingly endless period of time—has its own set of problems, particularly during the development and testing period. Custom programmers don't have the luxury of huge beta testing pools where anything that might go wrong will be discovered. Usually, the customer does the final testing—usually with their own proprietary data. The importance of backing up before installing a new iteration of custom code can't be overemphasized. Neither can the importance of making sure that all PCs running the custom software are running exactly the same version.

Pirates of the Caribbean

Software piracy is, put plainly, a bad deal for everyone. The developer doesn't get paid, and the user doesn't get the manual, the (sometimes questionable) services of the vendor's technical support group, or the opportunity to upgrade to a newer version.

In the earliest days, vendors fiddled around with various theft-protection schemes including key disks that had to be in place before the program would run or only allowing a single installation from one set of disks. Users in general howled about this but the die was finally cast against copy protection when the U.S.'s largest buyer of computer software, the government, refused to purchase copy-protected software. Today, many games are still protected to a greater or lesser degree, but the government doesn't buy too many games.

As soon as the user base figured out that COPY *.* would yield a perfectly functional copy of the software, bootleg copies were everywhere. In fairness, the earliest PC users may not have understood the concept of licensing software and may have believed that they owned it and could do anything they pleased with it, including putting it on ten or a hundred separate PCs.

One client, a medium-sized law firm, paid for a license in a very expensive accounting package. After the package was up and running and one section of the firm's billings were on time for the first time in several years, a senior partner demanded that the software be put on his secretary's PC so she could do his billings. No can do, the partner was advised and the concept of licensing was explained. The partner chose not to understand and insisted. The license agreement was placed under his nose. He still refused to accept that the firm did not own the software.

Far more common, though, with the proliferation of home PCs was the simple ripping off of basic software (spreadsheets, word processors, and utilities) from office machines. At the same time, businesses would install a few genuine packages and load other machines with bootlegs.

Today, corporate users are as worried about their employees violating their site licenses as they are about the employees bringing in viruses. It's cheaper and easier to clean up a few infected machines than to pay a huge fine to MonsterSoft, Inc. and be seen across the world of commerce as a common thief.

The Software Publishers' Association in Washington, D.C. was created not only to lobby for the industry but to police piracy. It's not likely the software police will show up in your second floor study, though. They're after bigger fish. Still, don't do it.

Awareness is key. One day in a bookstore, a nice middle-aged lady asked what book would be good to teach her college-aged daughter WordPerfect. Why, the beginner's manual that comes with the package is terrific—you don't need any other books to get started. A few mumbles later, it became clear that daughter's copy of WordPerfect was pirated. ("Everybody does it.") Why, then, just put this book, and this book, and that book in your shopping bag and walk out of the bookstore. ("But that would be stealing!")

Exactly. Pirating software is no different than stealing a book, a candy bar, or a new Ferrari from the showroom floor.

If you wouldn't steal it from the shelf, don't steal it from a PC.

Shareware

The whole concept behind shareware is try it. If you like it, send money and share with your friends so that they will send money, too. It's a wonderful concept but sometimes it doesn't work to the benefit of the person who wrote the program. People try it. People like it. People share it with their friends. People don't send money.

The two earliest PANDA programs, CHK4BOMB and BOMBSQAD, were released before the PANDA Systems utility software development company was founded. These programs were not shareware; in fact, they were just little programs written to help out a local BBS sysop. He passed them on to a friend, and that friend passed them on, and so on. Today, ten years later, any Archie on Internet shows locations where these two programs can be downloaded. (Don't bother, you've got MONITOR and LABTEST, the descendants of those programs, on the disk in this book.)

Even more interesting, there's an offering called TRAPDISK.COM now in circulation that is, according to the program's author Andy Hopkins, based on CHK4BOMB. The documentation is clear: "In the spirit of Mr. Hopkins' original program, feel free to copy and distribute this program." Given the reasonable estimate of half a million copies of this little program floating around, Mr. Hopkins tries hard not to think what might have been (a villa on the Spanish Riviera?) if everyone who had used (and liked) CHK4BOMB had sent him a few dollars.

There's good shareware, there's great shareware, and there are mediocre offerings. Then there's dangerous shareware. Dangerous shareware isn't limited just to programs containing computer viruses or Trojan horses; any poorly behaved, poorly tested, poorly documented program can be just as dangerous as the more famous malware. It's a good idea to check out shareware offerings with others who have used it and get their opinions before firing it up on your PC. It's also worth the cost of an E-mail or a phone call to the developer to check the file size, file date, and, if you're really technical, a checksum of the file to make sure you've got a clean copy.

A decent source for checking out shareware and public domain (free) software is ZiffNet. Each program is described and rated by the Ziff folks. ZiffNet connections can be expensive in terms of on-line download time. If you find a program you're interested in, you may want to check out a local, no-charge BBS to see if you can find it.

Keep in mind that shareware writers depend upon the income from their programs. The possibility of an intentionally added virus or Trojan is about the same as Bill Gates using OS/2.

Do, however, be wary of a new program that shows up on your favorite BBS. Let someone else be the guinea pig. Follow the notes on the BBS to see what sort of success others have before you make your leap. If a pal passes you a shareware program, practice "safe hex" by scanning the disk before putting it in your PC. Boot from a known clean DOS disk before running it and turn off the PC immediately afterward. And, if you do like it, send money.

Simply Stupid Stuff

Pogo was right: "We have met the enemy and he is us." Some cynics would add that the only way to contemplate infinity is the collective stupidity of computer users. Now, nobody likes to feel stupid, but the fact is users are the single greatest danger to software. What are the stupidest things users can do? No problem. This list is almost entirely from personal experience. (Feel free to laugh out loud at any point and enjoy a voyeuristic look at the follies and foibles of an "expert" complete with fallacious rationalizations.)

The first anecdote comes to us from Ed Williams, a real guru who can take a PC apart chip by chip and put it back together with no parts left over.

I was having a problem with a DOS 6.2 double-spaced disk drive so I used the Norton Diagnostics. Big problem because I didn't have a 6.2 toolkit.

Here's what happens. When DOS boots up, if it finds special DOUBLE SPACE file then it mounts the DOUBLE SPACE data file as drive C: and renames the disk it booted from, then sets up the environment and runs COMMAND.COM. This is really neat because it means that all of DOS (including your CONFIG.SYS and AUTOEXEC.BAT) can be compressed.

Well, the Norton Diagnostics doesn't want double space running, so it renames the special file (so DOS won't find it), writes a little autoexec on the boot drive (not what you think of as C:) and reboots. Once it is booted again it does its diagnostics. When it is done it is supposed to change the special file back, remove its own little AUTOEXEC.BAT from the boot drive, and reboots again to get back to the original configuration. Here's what really happens. It does *not* change the special file back; it does remove its own AUTOEXEC.BAT and reboots.

This gives you a C: drive with nothing on it. Oh, nothing really is missing because all your stuff is on the DOUBLE SPACE disk which isn't mounted. Now that really neat trick of having all of DOS on the compressed drive seems really stupid because you need the DOS tools to mount the double space drive so you can get at your DOS tools. There are only three things you can do now; well—four really. Out of disgust you could give your PC to me.

1) Boot from a floppy that is cleverly set up to boot your PC back to the proper configuration (i.e., has the special file and knows what to do to setup the environment on YOUR PC).

2) Get a 6.2 bootable floppy with COMMAND.COM and ATTRIB.EXE on it, reboot, use ATTRIB to make the DBL-SPACE.BIN file visible so you can copy it to C:.

3) Reformat the drive and start over.

Which would you choose?

PS: Norton has an upgrade to their 7.0 software so this won't happen. I think you should get it before you need it.

Maybe Ed should have gotten it before he needed it. Of all the additions to the DOS 6+ version, DBLSPACE has caused more problems than any others. Not only for users, but for Microsoft itself. Legal problems aside, any altering of the data on the hard disk is risky. Whether it's for compression or protection, if the data on the hard disk is not readable without a proprietary program to decode the data, it can become useless. PANDA's prime directive: "Make sure you have a copy of the program needed to restore the data on some media that cannot be destroyed."

Some other amazing "stupid computer tricks" come to us from PANDA System's Andy Hopkins, the main programmer behind PANDA UTILITIES.

Stupid Computer Tricks? Well, maybe a couple. I guess like most programmers, I'm immune to data loss. Backup? Why bother, it can't happen to me. I know everything there is to know about the computer.

I do my programming on a state-of-the-art (well it was yesterday) computer which sits next to a not so state-of-the-art IBM PC model 1 from 1981 with an external hard disk. The old PC is great for testing antivirus software against the real thing, because I can merely turn off the external hard disk and nothing can get destroyed. Drives the viruses crazy too. Whoever thought you could get a drive not ready error from a hard disk?

The only problem is that the 3.5" disks of the programming machine are not compatible with the 5.25" disks of the test machine. It seemed ridiculous to tie up two phone lines to transfer programs from one machine to the other when a simple null modem cable would do the trick. So I went to the local computer supply store, priced null modem cables and thought, why pay that much when I can make my own. Soldering iron in hand with a few connectors and wire, I proceeded to make a null modem cable. In retrospect I probably should have RTFB. It would make a better story if I said there was a shower of sparks equal to the closing ceremonies of the Lillehammer Olympics, but there was nothing. Literally nothing. It just didn't work. I disconnected the wires, started the computer again and noticed that the mouse didn't work. Nor did the COM ports. The old antique PC worked fine. The new state-of-the-art machine refused to admit that there were any asynchronous ports attached to the machine. I like fried chips, but only from Frito-Lay, not on the PC motherboard. It only cost a couple of hundred dollars to fix, plus the price of a null modem cable at Radio Shack.

Like many computer users who began before the age of the GUI, I actually like to work from the DOS command line. When I was growing up we set traps for mice behind the ice box, [showing his age, Ed.] we didn't drag them across a rubber mat and tap them twice. The cats did that.

I have also been bitten by the unforgiving nature of the DOS commands.

```
C>DEL *.*
Delete all files in current directory <Y/N>?
```

Of course I want to delete all the files, why else would I type that command! How stupid does this computer think I am? "Y"!

I thought I was in a different directory at the time, so the computer deleted all the files I really wanted to save and kept the ones I wanted deleted. Question answered.

In Andy's defense it should probably be noted that his natural curiosity led him to discover that the deleted files were not really gone, and he could get them back once he learned the structure of DOS. Fortunately for all of us he did learn and has written some marvelous programs.

Our next anecdotes come from yours truly, the author. I hereby publicly admit that I, too have produced a stupid human trick or two with the computer.

Of course a virus and security "expert" has far different computing standards than the rest of the world. Mine are far sloppier than any other computer user I know: I let cats sleep on top of the monitor; I keep the dog near my feet in winter where she can roll over onto the power strip; I don't label diskettes; I use my tape backup unit as a convenient place to put unpaid bills; and I frequently try to do three things at once. Each of these practices has led to a greater or lesser disaster at least once.

But my worst set of tricks has to do with my absolute belief in my steel-trap memory and procrastination. One day I looked at a large stack of unlabeled, sort of labeled, and mislabeled diskettes on my desk and decided, with a surprising flood of zeal, to do something about them. I had become less than enchanted with remembering (sometimes) that the long document about Bulgarian virus writers was on the tan disk whose label said "Microsoft DOS 6.0 Beta version 6.22." I carefully slid the disks, one by one, into the A: slot and typed DIR A:>LPT1 (the command that prints out a directory of A:). As each directory listing slithered out of the printer, I carefully put the diskette on top of the page. They made a tidy pile on the floor next to my desk—there was no room on top of the desk, of course. I would worry about how to label them later. I decided to toast my heroine-like efforts with an appropriate beverage and left the office area. During my brief absence, one of the office cats, MicroBeast, was not content to let sleeping dogs lie and rudely awakened MagaByte, the Corgi. Their initial travels took them straight through my tidy stack of still unlabeled disks and directories.

Most writers are highly imaginative. It goes with the territory. Working, as I do, in an environment where computer viruses are as commonplace as beer cans in a college fraternity house, I have set up stringent rules for my "writing machine." It is the one machine in the whole lash-up that can

NEVER be used for testing ANYTHING. It will NEVER be attached to any sort of network anyone is fooling around with. I NEVER download anything but text files from online services. No new software goes on this machine before it's tested elsewhere with a backup of the complete hard drive. NOBODY is allowed to touch it except children in great time of need ("Mom, this term paper is due in 25 minutes and I GOTTA use your grammar checkers and printer!") Only tested data disks from other IN-HOUSE machines go into the floppy drives. Arguably, it may be the safest PC in the country. So, what do I think any time there is the slightest anomaly in a process? V-I-R-U-S!

And I didn't learn my lesson back in the sixties when I was the proud possessor of one of the finest collection of 45 r.p.m. records in the small town where I grew up. One sunny summer day they became a mass of molten vinyl in the back window of somebody's car on a trip to the lake. In the late '80s I did the same thing to a stack of 5.25"-floppies, though in a slightly more elegant location—the World Trade Center in New York.

If there's one Stupid Human Trick I try not to get involved in, it's answering a question when I don't know the answer. Guesswork can be the stupidest trick of all.

Over the years, I have collected interesting questions that I either did or didn't know the answer to. The long-term favorite came via E-mail from a user in Peoria. "If DOS will tell you BAD command or file name why can't it say 'GREAT command or file name'?". Some questions remain great mysteries of life.

The Last Word

BACKUP! BACKUP! BACKUP! BACKUP!

Data Security

This chapter examines the subject of securing your data, not from the hazards of rogue programs such as viruses and Trojan horses, but from the prying eyes of others. If you operate your computer in the privacy of your home or in a secure location where no one has access except yourself, you probably don't need to take any further steps to secure your data. However, if your computer is in a location in which others can easily gain access, you may need to take further steps to assure that they cannot access your data. Privacy is a personal matter. How much or how little you need is strictly up to you.

The personal computer was originally envisioned as a personal computer, that is, one user running one program at a time. As such there is no easy method for implementing the type of security seen in the mainframe world. Mainframes have elaborate protection schemes against one user accessing information created by another unless authorized to do so.

DOS allows every user access to almost all the program and data files on the system. While DOS files have an attribute byte associated with them that determines how the DIR command accesses the files, there is a program included with DOS that can easily change the attribute associated with a given file. This attribute byte contains a rudimentary permission setting on the file. A file can be marked as read-only, meaning that it cannot be altered or deleted. Files cannot be marked as executable. This function is handled by the DOS program loader and the file extension of .COM or .EXE.

In the UNIX world, files are given attributes by user, group, and system. A file may be any combination of executable, readable, and writeable for the authorized owner, the members of a group, or the whole system. Thus, a user who wants to keep his or her data and programs from prying eyes can set the attributes accordingly. Only the creator of the file and the system manager have the ability to change the file permission attributes.

Networked PCs can implement permission settings on files available across the network, but a single PC still leaves the data available to anyone who happens to be using that computer. Anyone who sits before a PC can access and copy anything on the system. Such rudimentary security measures as hiding a file from a normal directory search can be easily subverted by someone using the ATTRIB command to remove the hidden attribute. Almost anyone with a knowledge of DOS knows how to unhide a file.

To provide security on a DOS machine, the user needs to install a security system that enables the user to access the data but prevents an unauthorized person from seeing, altering, or copying the files. There are many programs on the market that purport to protect your programs and data. Like any other program you buy, a security system should fit your needs. The test of the program is how it actually works, not how good the blurbs on the box say it is. Let a computer-savvy person try to break it before you buy it.

Copy Protection

Early in the PC game, program producers came to the realization that making a copy of a popular program was as easy as typing COPY *.* A:. Every time a program was copied, that was one less sale, or at least the vendor thought so. In reality, many people who use pirated copies of software would not have bought the program anyway, so the effect on sales is probably minimal. However, in a company setting, a business with multiple PCs could buy only one copy of a program and install it on many computers. If the producer has a one-copy-per-machine policy for sales, then it indeed loses money if the program is copied.

Before the hard disk became a necessity, copy protection was easy. Because the program was always run from diskette, the original program disk was altered so that normal DOS functions could not copy it. Instead of the 512 bytes per sector of a normal diskette, the program diskette had one or more tracks formatted with another capacity. The program can tell DOS how to read the odd sectors and refuse to operate if those sectors are not there. Unless the program tells DOS how to access the odd sectors, DOS cannot read and copy them.

After the hard disk became the standard for personal computing, users rebelled at having to use a diskette to run a program. They wanted to be able to copy the program to the hard disk and run it from there. The next step was to enable the user to copy the program, but require a key disk in drive A. The key diskette contained a section that was intentionally damaged by laser. A PC could not write to this sector because the oxide had been damaged. The copy-protection portion of the program prompted for the key disk, wrote to the sector, and tried to read back the data. If it could, the program determined that this was not the key disk and refused to run.

Both of these (an several other) copy-protection schemes relied on a test of the diskette and a decision whether to proceed or not. It was trivial for a determined pirate to rewrite the program code to merely skip the test and decision and proceed directly to the program. This, and the fact that the largest purchaser in the world, the U.S. government, refused to buy copy-protected software, led to the quick demise of copy protection in business software.

Today, copy protection is relegated to games and other personal software. Copy protection by documentation seems to be the current preferred method. Many games begin with a random question that can only be answered by those having a copy of the documentation. Other game packages produce a code wheel that cannot be photocopied as easily as the documentation. Again, single users who pirate software are probably unlikely to buy it anyway, so copy protection may be more of a frustration to legal users than a method to ensure corporate profits.

PC Security

Copy protection only prevents (or makes more difficult) the duplication of programs. It cannot prevent an unauthorized person from running the program on an authorized PC. The computer is completely open to anyone who sits before the keyboard. Because PC hardware and DOS have no security provisions, an add-on product is needed if you want to protect your data and programs.

Because of the design of the computer, security systems can make it difficult, but not impossible, to view data or run programs. Not even the mainframes can provide absolute security, as the hackers known as the CHAOS Club have proven time and time again. To see how even the most security-conscious system can be compromised, read Clifford Stoll's *The Cuckoo's Egg.*

PC security can be divided into three broad categories: system security, program security, and data security. A system security scheme will prevent unauthorized access to the computer. Program security involves limiting access to only certain programs. Data security systems prevent unauthorized access to program data files.

Most software security involves the use of a password known only to an authorized user. Regardless of how clever the security algorithm, the password becomes the weak link in the security chain. Like a safe with a combination lock, anyone who knows the combination can compromise security. Most computer break-ins involve someone knowing or guessing a password. If you write down the password so you don't forget it, you run the risk of someone discovering your password. Many people tend to choose the same password, with the word *password* being the most common. Also, don't overlook the possibility of someone holding a gun to your head and demanding to know the password.

The flip side of an unauthorized person guessing or discovering a password, is forgetting your own password. If you lose the key or combination to a safe, you can call a locksmith. The contents of the safe are not altered in any manner, so after you break the lock, you can recover the material inside. However, many computer security programs encode the contents of the disk. The password becomes the decoding key and without it the data recorded on the disk cannot be used. While some cryptologists insist that there is no such thing as an unbreakable code, it may only be breakable by the super computers at the National Security Agency (NSA). Presumably NSA is more concerned with the vital interests of the United States than in decoding the data on your hard disk when you forget the password.

System Security

The most effective way to secure the system is to make sure that no one else has access to the computer. Locking the PC in an office or a secure desk may be one of the most effective ways of assuring privacy. In this case, the PC is as secure as any object in that location.

Some PCs cannot be physically secured. A notebook or laptop computer is particularly vulnerable to theft. Business people by the thousands now carry portable computers on trips. When you look in the waiting area of any airport, you will see dozens of harried executives trying to juggle a carry-on bag, garment bag, brief case, laptop computer, and ticket. Perhaps the most vulnerable place for a traveling business person is the airport rest room. A quick thief could grab the laptop, exit the rest room, and mingle with the crowd while you are in a compromising situation.

The problem of theft can be mitigated somewhat if the laptop does not contain any confidential data. The computer is undoubtedly covered by insurance, and the data can be restored from backups. However, if the data is confidential, as so much business data is, you run the risk of the data falling into the wrong hands. Industrial espionage is not just the subject of fiction, but a real risk of doing business. Regardless of the thief's motive for lifting the laptop, there are steps you can take to ensure that no one else can use the computer.

A password boot program can prevent anyone who does not know the password from using the data and programs on the computer. It's possible to alter the small program that starts the computer so it cannot proceed without a proper password. Although the computer can be started with a diskette in drive A, the hard disk can be rendered invisible to the operating system. Like any software-protection method, a password boot program can be broken by someone who knows how to do it. How secure it is may depend on who is trying to break it and why.

A thief who steals a laptop (or desktop) computer may have no interest in the data and may be just interested in acquiring computer equipment. In this case, the equipment is more valuable to the thief than the data, and you probably don't need to fear unauthorized use of your data. After the thief realizes that the system is secured, he may either abandon the computer or reformat the hard disk, thus destroying all the data.

If the thief is truly after the data instead of the equipment, the security system should be designed so that the data is destroyed if the system is broken. Naturally, combining system security with data encoding enhances the privacy of the data.

Program Security

There are situations where a PC should only run certain programs. Unlike a UNIX system, where execute permission can be given to a group of programs, DOS will execute any program with a .COM or .EXE extension. If you don't want the user to run certain programs, your only choice is to delete those programs from the hard disk. You are still faced with the fact that a user can run any program from a diskette or copy any program onto the hard disk.

Consider the hypothetical case of Ms. Grumby, the PC manager of the medium-sized XYZ Corp. Her group consists of ten PCs networked for word processing and FAX transmission. Additionally, her data processors often transmit and receive data from sales reps in the field via modem. Only a couple of her group members are particularly computer savvy; the rest know only about the three applications they use: word processing, FAX, and communications software.

Occasionally, Ms. Grumby has observed members of her group hard at work zapping alien space invaders instead of composing the latest in a never ending stream of truly important memos from the Big Guy. An audit of the hard disk contents of her group showed an amazing array of unauthorized programs stored in a multitude of subdirectories. To top it off, she suspects that two computer-savvy employees are helping the others make copies of the company's licensed software for home use, despite the many memos she has written explaining why this is illegal.

Ms. Grumby needs program security. Short of ordering diskless workstations for her group, what she needs is a security program that prohibits the use of any unauthorized software. Additionally, she needs a program to prevent her users from copying programs to and from the hard disk. The network software provides that type of protection between the user and the server, but DOS provides no protection for the PC.

Depending on the situation, there are several security utilities that can provide program protection in a DOS environment. Like all DOS software solutions to security problems, it is possible to break the protection. When deciding on a package that provides security, test it first by having a local computer-savvy user try to bypass the protection. If the users are not very sophisticated, you may not need a very complicated protection program. On the other hand, make sure that the security cannot be bypassed my merely booting the PC from a diskette or pressing the Break key before the protection program is loaded in the AUTOEXEC.BAT file.

Many security programs are loaded by lines contained in CONFIG.SYS. Unlike AUTOEXEC.BAT, the Break key is not enabled while DOS carries out the CONFIG.SYS commands. However, since the arrival of DOS 6.0, the user can bypass CONFIG.SYS by pressing a function key during the boot process. This addition to the boot process has left several security programs vulnerable.

Data Security

All files are in effect data files. Some files contain data that consists of instructions to the processor and are considered program files. The remaining files are data files that can be used by your programs to provide you with meaningful information. These are the most valuable files you own. Letters and memos, addresses and phone numbers, and account and inventory information are all forms of data stored in files. This information may or may not be of a proprietary nature. If you want to keep it confidential, you must install some sort of security system because, again, DOS is no help.

The most common way to secure data is through encoding. All computer data is encoded. There is no *A* in computer language, so the computer encodes the keyboard symbols into digital numbers. Although there are several standard methods for encoding standard alphanumeric symbols into computer digits, the most commonly used method in PCs is the American Standard Code for Information Interchange (ASCII). This standard converts letters, numbers, and symbols into 128 different binary digits. The computer handles the task of conversion. When you type a letter on the keyboard, that letter is converted to a binary digit and is stored in memory. The video monitor converts the binary digit stored in memory to a readable letter, number, or punctuation mark and displays it on the screen.

Like all codes, the trick to ASCII is knowing the key. The key is what translates from plain text to code and back to plain text. The key to ASCII is a well-known chart that lists the binary equivalent of alphanumeric characters. ASCII is a straight substitution code. The numerals *0* through *9* are represented with the binary numbers 48 through 58. The letter *A* is always 65, *B* is 66, and so on. Lowercase letters begin with code 97. Each symbol (such as *, !, or ?) has its own ASCII digit equivalent. Even the space, which appears to be nothing, is represented by the binary digit 32.

For computer purists, I should probably point out that the keyboard does not generate the ASCII equivalent of the key being pressed. The keyboard sends a number representing which key is pressed to the computer. When a key is released, the same number plus 128 is sent to the computer. It is software within the computer, called the keyboard driver, that converts the key press information into the equivalent ASCII binary digits by examining which key is pressed and which key is released. Pressing the *A* key does not necessarily mean that the ASCII *A* is sent to the computer. All the keyboard tells the computer is that key number 31 has been pressed. When the key is released, the keyboard sends the number 159 (31 plus 128) to the computer to indicate that key number 31 has been released. All PCs have a built-in routine within the ROM-BIOS (read-only memory, basic input output system) that converts from keyboard scan code to ASCII. A device driver, such as KEYBOARD.SYS, included with DOS and loaded by CONFIG.SYS can override the built-in conversion.

The output to the video monitor is even more complicated than the input from the keyboard. The display hardware performs the task of generating readable characters on the screen from the ASCII digits stored in memory. With newer PCs, this conversion can also be overridden by a device driver loaded by CONFIG.SYS.

Because ASCII is a standard, all PCs and most mainframe computers know the key to decoding the binary digits. ASCII encoding is therefore useless as a security shield. Thus, it might seem easy to protect the privacy of your data by using a different encoding scheme than ASCII. Because the input and output are controlled by software drivers, you could conceivably develop a proprietary encoding system not based on ASCII, letting the drivers convert from keyboard input to screen output using a code derived from another key. If someone tried to view the data using an ASCII translation, the screen would be filled with gibberish.

However, the flaw in this system is that most programs expect to receive input and generate output based on the ASCII character set. Even if the input device driver converted a press of key number 31 into the binary digit 13 and displayed the symbol *A* on the screen, if a 13 was in video memory, an application program would interpret the 13 as the ASCII equivalent of pressing the Enter key. Therefore, even though the device drivers could recognize the new code, a program would interpret the input as a press of the Enter key.

The alternative is to encrypt the data on the disk. Encryption has been a part of military technology since Hannibal crossed the Alps with camels disguised as elephants. Until the advent of computer technology for the masses though, cryptography was the milieu of spies and espionage. Lives and countries literally depend upon the flow, yet confidentiality, of information. Elaborate, yet slow, encryption techniques have developed over the centuries, with machines taking over the encoding and decoding process during the twentieth century. During World War II, the Germans relied on their Enigma machine to send coded messages to embassies and troops. The Enigma was just a bit larger than a typewriter, and a series of dials could be set to any one of multiple keys that would both code and decode messages automatically. Unless you had a machine and the current key, the code was unbreakable. Their so-called unbreakable code was easily broken by the Allies after covertly acquiring an Enigma machine.

The dawn of the computer age has made encryption much easier and code breaking a much more difficult task. Unlike a straight replacement code such as ASCII, modern encryption techniques involve complex mathematical algorithms that make breaking the code an almost impossible task. Computers can do the math in the wink of an eye to encrypt and, given the proper key, decrypt messages, or data. Computers can also use this mathematical skill to break a cipher lacking a key. The question of whether or not there is an unbreakable cipher is one that is hotly debated among cryptologers and mathematicians. The government approved data encryption standard (DES) appears to be unbreakable. But skeptics ask, "Why would they approve it if they cannot break it?"

One notable authority who has worked in the field since the Enigma of World War II has flatly stated that there is no unbreakable code if a person is willing to spend the time, money, and manpower on breaking it. The time needed to break any code is dependent upon the number of messages, to whom and from whom the message is sent, and the subject of the message. If the general subject of the message is known, then the task of breaking the message becomes easier. Also, the more messages there are that use the same key, the easier breaking the code becomes. If one can obtain a clear text copy of an encoded message, then with today's computing power breaking the key is a snap.

In considering an encryption system for a PC, the one question to ask is how much is it worth to someone trying to break the code. Surely the IRS will not devote hours of supercomputer CPU time to deciphering your recipe for hot crab dip. But would a competitor devote the hours necessary to discover your company's plans for a left-handed spurling flange?

The weakness of any encryption is the key used to decrypt the data. Whoever possesses the key can unlock the message. When the Allies stole the Enigma machine during World War II, they also needed to steal the key to using the machine. This key consisted of the settings on the machine that would make enciphered text readable. There were literally thousands of combinations of settings on the Enigma machine, and the war would have been over before all the combinations could have been tried. The key was changed daily and knowing one key did not necessarily mean that the next intercepted message would use the same key. Fortunately for the Allies, the person who developed the keys used a regular pattern. The daily keys were sent out on a monthly basis and, after the first few days of the month, the pattern began to reveal itself and the keys could be inserted into the Allies' copy of the Enigma machine.

Regardless of how sophisticated the cipher, anyone who possesses the key can decipher the data. On the other hand, losing the key can mean losing the data. Computer programming can be thought of as an analogy. Computer program languages are text instructions that indicate the steps a program is to follow to carry out a task. After this source code is written, a special program called a compiler translates the written instructions into computer instructions. Looking at computer instructions themselves gives little indication as to exactly what steps the program follows or what the original source code looked like. The only way to change the program is to change the source code and recompile the program. If the source code is missing or destroyed, the program code cannot be easily modified. One of my favorite cartoons among the many taped to the refrigerator depicts a gloomy grave side scene in which one of the mourners turns to the widow and says "This may be a bad time, but did he happen to mention anything about source code?"

Consider the consequences of losing your key if you encode your data. Consider also the consequences to your company if you are the only one who knows the key to the encrypted data on your PC and you get hit by the number 17 bus on your way home from work. While less secure than committing the key to memory, you should always store a copy of the key in a safe place. A trusted third party or a bank safe deposit vault would be a relatively secure place to store your decryption key.

Secure Communications

Electronic mail communication is becoming the norm among computer users throughout the world. You can type a message on your computer and send it literally to the ends of the earth almost instantly. While not as fast as telephone conversations, E-mail has the advantage of the recipient getting a permanent record of your message.

How does a message get from here to there on the electronic highway, and who can read that message? These are questions that have lead to the development of the public key concept of encryption. You have two encryption keys: a public key and a private key. The public key can be used by anyone who wishes to communicate with you. They use your public key to encrypt the message, and upon receipt you use your private key to decrypt the message. The process of encryption and decryption can be done automatically using computer software.

One of the most widely used public key encryption programs, PGP, is written by Philip Zimmerman and distributed free of charge. Philip even distributes the source code so that one can use his program on any computer from PCs and Macs to Vaxes and IBM mainframes. In the documentation that accompanies the program, Philip outlines the rationale behind encrypting E-mail messages:

Why Do You Need PGP?

It's personal. It's private. And it's no one's business but yours. You may be planning a political campaign, discussing your taxes, or having an illicit affair. Or you may be doing something that you feel shouldn't be illegal, but is. Whatever it is, you don't want your private electronic mail (E-mail) or confidential documents read by anyone else. There's nothing wrong with asserting your privacy. Privacy is as apple-pie as the Constitution.

Perhaps you think your E-mail is legitimate enough that encryption is unwarranted. If you really are a law-abiding citizen with nothing to hide, then why don't you always send your paper mail on postcards? Why not submit to drug testing on demand? Why require a warrant for police searches of your house? Are you trying to hide something? You must be a subversive or a drug dealer if you hide your mail inside envelopes. Or maybe a paranoid nut. Do law-abiding citizens have any need to encrypt their E-mail? What if everyone believed that law-abiding citizens should use postcards for their mail? If some brave soul tried to assert his privacy by using an envelope for his mail, it would draw suspicion. Perhaps the authorities would open his mail to see what he's hiding.

Fortunately, we don't live in that kind of world, because everyone protects most of their mail with envelopes. So no one draws suspicion by asserting their privacy with an envelope. There's safety in numbers. Analogously, it would be nice if everyone routinely used encryption for all their E-mail, innocent or not, so that no one drew suspicion by asserting their E-mail privacy with encryption. Think of it as a form of solidarity. Today, if the Government wants to violate the privacy of ordinary citizens, it has to expend a certain amount of expense and labor to intercept and steam open and read paper mail, and listen to and possibly transcribe spoken telephone conversation. This kind of labor-intensive monitoring is not practical on a large scale. This is only done in important cases when it seems worthwhile.

More and more of our private communications are being routed through electronic channels. Electronic mail is gradually replacing conventional paper mail. E-mail messages are just too easy to intercept and scan for interesting keywords. This can be done easily, routinely, automatically, and be undetectable on a grand scale. International cablegrams are already scanned this way on a large scale by the NSA. We are moving toward a future when the nation will be crisscrossed with high-capacity, fiber-optic data networks linking together all our increasingly ubiquitous personal computers. E-mail will be the norm for everyone, not the novelty it is today.

The Government will protect our E-mail with Government-designed encryption protocols. Probably most people will trust that. But perhaps some people will prefer their own protective measures.

Senate Bill 266, a 1991 omnibus anti-crime bill, had an unsettling measure buried in it. If this non-binding resolution had become real law, it would have forced manufacturers of secure communications equipment to insert special "trap doors" in their products, so that the Government can read anyone's encrypted messages. It reads: "It is the sense of Congress that providers of electronic communications services and manufacturers of electronic communications service equipment shall insure that communications systems permit the Government to obtain the plain text contents of voice, data, and other communications when appropriately authorized by law." This measure was defeated after rigorous protest from civil libertarians and industry groups.

In 1992, the FBI Digital Telephony wiretap proposal was introduced to Congress. It would require all manufacturers of communications equipment to build in special remote wiretap ports that would enable the FBI to remotely wiretap all forms of electronic communication from FBI offices. Although it never attracted any sponsors in Congress because of citizen opposition, it will be reintroduced in 1993.

Most alarming of all is the White House's bold new encryption policy initiative, under development at NSA for four years, and unveiled April 16th, 1993. The centerpiece of this initiative is a Government-built encryption device, called the "Clipper" chip, containing a new, classified NSA encryption algorithm. The Government is encouraging private industry to design it into all their secure communication products, like secure phones, secure FAX, etc. AT&T is now putting the Clipper into all their secure voice products. The catch: At the time of manufacture, each Clipper chip will be loaded with its own unique key, and the Government gets to keep a copy, placed in escrow. Not to worry, though—the Government promises that they will use these keys to read your traffic only when duly authorized by law. Of course, to make Clipper completely effective, the next logical step would be to outlaw other forms of cryptography.

If privacy is outlawed, only outlaws will have privacy. Intelligence agencies have access to good cryptographic technology. So do the big arms and drug traffickers. So do defense contractors, oil companies, and other corporate giants. But ordinary people and grassroots political organizations mostly have not had access to affordable "military grade" public-key cryptographic technology. Until now. PGP empowers people to take their privacy into their own hands. There's a growing social need for it. That's why I wrote it.

How it Works

It would help if you were already familiar with the concept of cryptography in general and public key cryptography in particular. Nonetheless, here are a few introductory remarks about public key cryptography.

First, some elementary terminology. Suppose I want to send you a message, but I don't want anyone but you to be able to read it. I can "encrypt," or "encipher" the message, which means I scramble it up in a hopelessly complicated way, rendering it unreadable to anyone except you, the intended recipient of the message. I supply a cryptographic "key" to encrypt the message, and you have to use the same key to decipher or "decrypt" it. At least that's how it works in conventional "single-key" cryptosystems.

In conventional cryptosystems, such as the U.S. Federal Data Encryption Standard (DES), a single key is used for both encryption and decryption. This means that a key must be initially transmitted via secure channels so that both parties can know it before encrypted messages can be sent over insecure channels. This may be inconvenient. If you have a secure channel for exchanging keys, then why do you need cryptography in the first place?

In public key cryptosystems, everyone has two related complementary keys, a publicly revealed key and a secret key. Each key unlocks the code that the other key makes. Knowing the public key does not help you deduce the corresponding secret key. The public key can be published and widely disseminated across a communications network. This protocol provides privacy without the need for the same kind of secure channels that a conventional cryptosystem requires.

Anyone can use a recipient's public key to encrypt a message to that person, and that recipient uses her own corresponding secret key to decrypt that message. No one but the recipient can decrypt it, because no one else has access to that secret key. Not even the person who encrypted the message can decrypt it.

Message authentication is also provided. The sender's own secret key can be used to encrypt a message, thereby "signing" it. This creates a digital signature of a message, which the recipient (or anyone else) can check by using the sender's public key to decrypt it. This proves that the sender was the true originator of the message, and that the message has not been subsequently altered by anyone else, because the sender alone possesses the secret key that made that signature. Forgery of a signed message is infeasible, and the sender cannot later disavow his signature.

These two processes can be combined to provide both privacy and authentication by first signing a message with your own secret key, then encrypting the signed message with the recipient's public key. The recipient reverses these steps by first decrypting the message with her own secret key, then checking the enclosed signature with your public key. These steps are done automatically by the recipient's software.

Philip Zimmerman continues his observations on the use of personal encryption later in the documentation for PGP:

Vulnerabilities

No data security system is impenetrable. PGP can be circumvented in a variety of ways. Potential vulnerabilities you should be aware of include compromising your pass phrase or secret key, public key tampering, files that you deleted but are still somewhere on the disk, viruses and Trojan horses, breaches in your physical security, electro-magnetic emissions, exposure on multi-user systems, traffic analysis, and perhaps even direct cryptanalysis. For a detailed discussion of these issues, see the "Vulnerabilities" section in the PGP User's Guide, Special Topics volume.

Beware of Snake Oil

When examining a cryptographic software package, the question always remains, why should you trust this product? Even if you examined the source code yourself, not everyone has the crypto-graphic experience to judge the security. Even if you are an experi-enced cryptographer, subtle weaknesses in the algorithms could still elude you.

When I was in college in the early seventies, I devised what I believed was a brilliant encryption scheme. A simple pseudorandom number stream was added to the plaintext stream to create ciphertext. This would seemingly thwart any frequency analysis of the ciphertext, and would be uncrackable even to the most resourceful Government intelligence agencies. I felt so smug about my achievement. So cock-sure. Years later, I discovered this same scheme in several intro-ductory cryptography texts and tutorial papers. How nice. Other cryptographers had thought of the same scheme. Unfortunately, the scheme was presented as a simple homework assignment on how to use elementary cryptanalytic techniques to trivially crack it. So much for my brilliant scheme.

From this humbling experience I learned how easy it is to fall into a false sense of security when devising an encryption algorithm. Most people don't realize how fiendishly difficult it is to devise an encryption algorithm that can withstand a prolonged and determined attack by a resourceful opponent. Many mainstream software engineers have developed equally naive encryption schemes (often even the very same encryption scheme), and some of them have been incorporated into commercial encryption software packages and sold for good money to thousands of unsuspecting users. This is like selling automotive seat belts that look good and feel good, but snap open in even the slowest crash test. Depending on them may be worse than not wearing seat belts at all. No one suspects they are bad until a real crash.

Depending on weak cryptographic software may cause you to unknowingly place sensitive information at risk. You might not otherwise have done so if you had no cryptographic software at all. Perhaps you may never even discover your data has been compromised.

Sometimes commercial packages use the Federal Data Encryption Standard (DES), a good conventional algorithm recommended by the Government for commercial use (but not for classified information, oddly enough—hmmm). There are several "modes of operation" the DES can use, some of them better than others. The Government specifically recommends not using the weakest simplest mode for messages, the Electronic Codebook (ECB) mode. But they do recommend the stronger and more complex Cipher Feedback (CFB) or Cipher Block Chaining (CBC) modes.

Unfortunately, most of the commercial encryption packages I've looked at use ECB mode. When I've talked to the authors of a number of these implementations, they say they've never heard of CBC or CFB modes, and didn't know anything about the weaknesses of ECB mode. The very fact that they haven't even learned enough cryptography to know these elementary concepts is not reassuring.

These same software packages often include a second faster encryption algorithm that can be used instead of the slower DES. The author of the package often thinks his proprietary faster algorithm is as secure as the DES, but after questioning him I usually discover that it's just a variation of my own brilliant scheme from college days. Or maybe he won't even reveal how his proprietary encryption scheme works, but assures me it's a brilliant scheme and I should trust it. I'm sure he believes that his algorithm is brilliant, but how can I know that without seeing it? In all fairness I must point out that in most cases these products do not come from companies that specialize in cryptographic technology.

There is a company called AccessData (87 East 600 South, Orem, Utah 84058, phone 1-800-658-5199) that sells a package for $185 that cracks the built-in encryption schemes used by WordPerfect, Lotus 1-2-3, MS Excel, Symphony, Quattro Pro, Paradox, and MS Word 2.0. It doesn't simply guess passwords—it does real cryptanalysis. Some people buy it when they forget their password for their own files. Law enforcement agencies buy it too, so they can read files they seize.

I talked to Eric Thompson, the author, and he said his program only takes a split second to crack them, but he put in some delay loops to slow it down so it doesn't look so easy to the customer. He also told me that the password encryption feature of PKZIP files can often be easily broken, and that his law enforcement customers already have that service regularly provided to them from another vendor.

In some ways, cryptography is like pharmaceuticals. Its integrity may be absolutely crucial. Bad penicillin looks the same as good penicillin. You can tell if your spreadsheet software is wrong, but how do you tell if your cryptography package is weak? The ciphertext produced by a weak encryption algorithm looks as good as ciphertext produced by a strong encryption algorithm. There's a lot of snake oil out there. A lot of quack cures. Unlike the patent medicine hucksters of old, these software implementors usually don't even know their stuff is snake oil. They may be good software engineers, but they usually haven't even read any of the academic literature in cryptography. But they think they can write good cryptographic software. And why not? After all, it seems intuitively easy to do so. And their software seems to work okay.

Anyone who thinks they have devised an unbreakable encryption scheme either is an incredibly rare genius or is naive and inexperienced. I remember a conversation with Brian Snow, a highly placed senior cryptographer with the NSA. He said he would never trust an encryption algorithm designed by someone who had not "earned their bones" by first spending a lot of time cracking codes. That did make a lot of sense. I observed that practically no one in the commercial world of cryptography qualified under this criterion. "Yes," he said with a self assured smile, "and that makes our job at NSA so much easier." A chilling thought. I didn't qualify either.

The Government has peddled snake oil too. After World War II, the U.S. sold German Enigma ciphering machines to third world governments. But they didn't tell them that the Allies cracked the Enigma code during the war, a fact that remained classified for many years.

Even today many UNIX systems worldwide use the Enigma cipher for file encryption, in part because the Government has created legal obstacles against using better algorithms. They even tried to prevent the initial publication of the RSA algorithm in 1977. And they have squashed essentially all commercial efforts to develop effective secure telephones for the general public.

The principal job of the U.S. Government's National Security Agency is to gather intelligence, principally by covertly tapping into people's private communications (see James Bamford's book *The Puzzle Palace*). The NSA has amassed considerable skill and resources for cracking codes. When people can't get good cryptography to protect themselves, it makes NSA's job much easier.

NSA also has the responsibility of approving and recommending encryption algorithms. Some critics charge that this is a conflict of interest, like putting the fox in charge of guarding the hen house. NSA has been pushing a conventional encryption algorithm that they designed, and they won't tell anybody how it works because that's classified. They want others to trust it and use it. But any cryptographer can tell you that a well-designed encryption algorithm does not have to be classified to remain secure. Only the keys should need protection. How does anyone else really know if NSA's classified algorithm is secure? It's not that hard for NSA to design an encryption algorithm that only they can crack, if no one else can review the algorithm. Are they deliberately selling snake oil?

I'm not as certain about the security of PGP as I once was about my brilliant encryption software from college. If I were, that would be a bad sign. But I'm pretty sure that PGP does not contain any glaring weaknesses. The crypto algorithms were developed by people at high levels of civilian cryptographic academia, and have been individually subject to extensive peer review. Source code is available to facilitate peer review of PGP and to help dispel the fears of some users. It's reasonably well researched, and has been years in the making. And I don't work for the NSA. I hope it doesn't require too large a "leap of faith" to trust the security of PGP.

According to a security authority with whom I spoke, the encryption used in the PGP program is not unbreakable. Because the sender and recipient of the message are known, and the subject matter is often a part of the message header which is sent in clear text, much of the crypronalysists job is already done. Public keys by their very nature use the same key for every message, so there could be a number of messages available from which to extract the key.

Environmental Questions—LANs

No discussion of data security would be complete without looking at the world of Local Area Networks (LANs). For that, one of the world's leading experts on LANs, Padgett Peterson of Martin-Marietta takes over:

LANs have been around for a long time, longer than the acronym has existed. Somewhere far back in recorded history (but after the invention of the fixed disk) some lazy individual got tired of the sneaker-net and decided to just plug two computers together and exchange files that way.

By the time the PC was introduced, networks were common and the biggest problem was writing good ASCII-EBCDIC converters for tying IBM mainframes with the rest of the world. The DOD ARPAnet (predecessor of the Internet) was alive and well. As PCs began to compete for corporate office space, often they sat next to the 3270 terminal that corporate America used to read their E-mail via PROFS.

Inevitably, someone said "why have two" and one of the earliest add-in boards was the DCA 3270 board (Irma) that allowed the PC to be both a PC and a terminal.

The IBM world being a bit stodgy, this was about as far as it went. However, just in case, IBM brought out a special PC-3270 model easily recognizable with its double row of twenty-four function keys at the top of the keyboard.

Very quickly software sprang up to allow asynchronous communications. One of the first was a PD program called PC-Talk that ran in interpretive BASIC, and was fast enough to handle the 300 baud modems of the day. 1200 baud put a strain on it that could be alleviated by compiling the program with the optional (and expensive) BASIC Compiler offered by IBM.

For the professional, there was also the BASIC Professional Development Kit for the truly dedicated (and wealthy—prices in the early eighties were very mainframe-like).

To engineers, the VAX was the platform of choice, so third party software houses were quick to bring out VT-100 emulators. Since everyone had preferred terminals and all were a bit different, a wide variety of emulation choices existed. Today this is still reflected in the ability of the user to choose such exotic terminals to emulate as the Heath H-19, Televideo 901, or DEC VT-52.

The next logical step was for the PC to automate keystroke entry. Why enter the same thing over and over again when the PC could enter it for you? And so began the concept of script files.

Then someone had the idea that they were paying $135 an hour to connect to the computers and most of it was spent on slow keyboard entry. Why not create the files on these cheap PCs and just do the mainframe entry in a burst mode. Today CompuServe and other on-line systems providers do much the same thing for the same reason.

The next step came sideways. People like to exchange programs, but programs are not the same as Text files. There are three major differences:

1) While they use all eight bits of a byte, ASCII text is confined to a subset in the first seven bits.

2) If there is a corrupted/lost bit in a text file, the writer can fix it easily. In a program, the system is liable to crash.

3) In text, a line terminator is expected every so often.

Terminal use is different. To many systems ctrl-S (19h) is an XOFF command and generally tells a host to stop sending data. In fact, for many systems the only safe characters are ASCII numbers, letters, and punctuation. These occupy the range from 20h to 5Ah, or the 3Bh (59) characters found on a conventional typewriter.

Fixes were needed and not long in coming. One of the first was TekHex introduced by the Tektronix Corporation, better known for its oscilloscopes. TekHex incorporated three major attributes:

1) It converted 8-bit hex data into 7 bit printable ASCII characters.

2) It incorporated error detection in the form of checksums and size on every line.

3) It created properly terminated lines that were a maximum of 48 characters long. The only drawback was that a program grew in a ratio of about 5/4. A program which started out as 2K bytes in binary would become about 2.5K in TekHex.

To reduce the amount of data to be transmitted, compression techniques (SEA, ZIP, ARC, etc.) got their start—not for disk savings but to minimize file transmission times. Before the breakup of Ma Bell, long distance rates were many times what they are today.

So when an engineer would create a particularly nice PC program (and there were few applications to choose from then), she would TekHex it and upload it to a public directory on the mainframe where everyone could download it. Cumbersome, slow, but the start of the server concept.

Still, connect times were expensive. A small group of recent grads from Brigham Young University, calling themselves the Superset, began working on a six-week contract from Novell Data Systems (a supplier of printers and Z-80 based CPM minis). They developed a disk-serving operating system to support CPM based on a Motorola 68000 processor. The contract was extended several times and became the basis for Novell Netware.

NDS went bankrupt shortly thereafter and was reorganized as Novell Inc. The server remained 68000-based until a version (2.0) was introduced in 1986 that allowed a PC-AT to be used as a server. Later "Portable Netware" was introduced that would permit still more platforms to be used. Among these platforms was the VAX, having now come full circle from being an expensive mini to being a not-so-expensive server.

Meanwhile topologies abounded—Starnet, Token Ring, and Arclan just to name a few. The IEEE issued a set of standards, 802.1-802.5, to define packet-based communications. As late as 1989, the battle over which would be supreme still raged. IBM was championing Token Ring but the little guys—in an attempt to stay away from the IBM dominated SNA (System Network Architecture)—were championing X.25, IEEE 802.3 Ethernet (first developed in the late '70s at the Xerox Palo Alto Research Center, better known as PARC.)

At the time, considerable bandwidth was being spent on the obsolescence of the TCP/IP network protocol with many learned people saying that it was doomed.

In the end, finances ruled and today there is no question who are the winners: Novell, TCP/IP, and Ethernet. These are the foundations on which the Information Superhighway will be built. The government has decided on the last two, and corporate America in 1994 is solidly behind Novell. An abundance of cheap hardware has made the real difference with good Ethernet adapters breaking under $100 a year ago and today available for $50. In counterpoint Token Ring adapters still are at the $400 mark.

A major element is that Ethernet is so easy to install, with thin coaxial cable good for 1500 meters being literally "plug and play." For large installations, twisted pair (10Base-T) is more complex to install but cheaper in the long run since the wiring can be standard twisted pair telephone wire and connections can be via a jack in the wall rather than a serial transceiver in the cable.

So today, we have very large installations tying together thousands of clients instantaneously. It did not take long to find out that such an installation is an equally effective breeding ground for viruses.

In 1991 I was asked to help with a company that was experiencing a massive Jerusalem attack. The virus had gotten into the executable E-mail file and had infected nearly 2000 clients in the course of a morning.

At the time the answer was to take down the server, disinfect it, check the clients, disinfect them, and then bring the system back up. The company said they could not do that since they stood to lose millions of dollars a day.

The solution was to create a special login script that would check for the virus when a client logged in and, if the client was infected, print a message, send a duplicate to tech services, and terminate the login. Problem solved.

Today such login scripts have become commonplace but such scripts are not enough and will not work on any LAN that does not have a scripting process (most peer-to-peer LANs do not).

Instead the answer is layered responses and can be accomplished with a checklist.

1) Protect the server files. All LANs provide a mechanism to determine who has access to a file. They can be made Read- or Execute-only if necessary. Earlier we said that the attributes on a PC are easy to turn off. True, but LAN attributes are enforced by the server and a virus on a client cannot affect them.

   If an unruly application requires that it have write permission to its own directory, then put the master copy in a protected directory and each time a client requests it, copy from the master before execution. This way clients always get a fresh (and uninfected) copy.

2) Examine the client. Virtually every virus scanner today provides a means for a "memory only" scan that can be made part of the login script. Better is to have a corporate-wide antivirus program in use and a "verifier" file in the login script. This method is fast and can permit fast updates when

a new version comes out. If the script can verify which version is on a client, if updates are needed, appropriate files can be automatically copied and invoked over the LAN. Some weapons of viruses can be used against them.

3) Keep LAN-trained personnel handy to keep everything running smoothly.

Viruses can spread like wildfire on an unprotected LAN, but the client-server separation can also be used to restore a mainframe-like division that a virus cannot cross, and to provide the level of support that once only mainframers once had available. LANs can be our destruction or salvation.

Conclusions

There is probably no one way of totally securing a PC's data—whether free-standing or as part of a LAN—against a determined adversary. Given the opportunity, time, money, and manpower, almost any security plan can be overcome. If you think you need to secure your data, make sure that anyone who tries to compromise the security system would have to use more time, money, or manpower than the data is worth.

Risks You Haven't Even Thought of Yet

This chapter is primarily the result of years of sky-pilot conversations with one of the icons of the security industry, Belden Menkus. After a serendipitous chance meeting in the speakers' lounge at PC Expo in New York in 1989, we became fast friends, sharing an interest not only in what is but what might be in the world of security. Menkus has the uncanny ability to take the smallest event, cogitate for a while, and then, in his piquant way, say, "What if ..."

Over the time of our friendship and frequent telephone conversations, we've not only written articles together but also spun out hypothetical events that scare even us. In the nature of most hypothetical situations, they're based on current events—and well they should be. It's on today that tomorrow is built.

Should they scare you? Should they scare the people used in the examples? That's for you to decide.

The Sixteen-Minute Problem

Everyone remembers Rosemary Woods' erasure of 16 minutes of dictation tape and how its absence contributed to the fall of Richard Nixon. There was a similar problem with Oliver North. And there may yet be a problem with Vincent Foster. (We don't try to overwork the crystal ball any more than necessary.)

In recent decisions by the United States District Court for the District of Columbia it was held that the Federal Records Act of 1950 applies to electronic communications and media.

Public Law 101-510, Div. A, Title V, goes like this:

> "If anyone with the custody of any such record, proceeding, map, book, or other similar thing, willfully and unlawfully conceals, removes, mutilates, obliterates, falsifies, or destroys the same, shall be fined not more than $2,000 or imprisoned for not more than three years, or both; and shall forfeit his office and be disqualified from holding any office under the United States. As used in this sub-section, the term office does not include the office held by any person as a retired officer of the Armed Forces of the United States."

The current cases are instantly recognizable: *U.S. v. Poindexter* and *U.S. v. North*. It's interesting to note that this didn't seem to deter Oliver North from running for elective office even though his conviction, if it had been upheld, would have prohibited him from holding bureaucratic office.

What does all this mean? Simply put, due diligence is required to preserve those records in exactly the same way that every scrap of paper produced in the White House (or, in Poindexter's case, the National Security Council) is subject to retention. (This is not to say that every scrap of paper must be retained, but it is subject to a decision on whether or not it should be.)

North, of course, failed to realize one of the simplest truths of electronic media. That a Delete command doesn't mean it's gone forever.

The history of politics is filled with late-night document shreddings, ditching of documents over bridges, claims of Executive Privilege, and other equally shady stuff. It's much easier to get rid of electronically stored information than hard copy.

It's entirely possible that another political scandal could come along with no records whatsoever because the weasels involved were smart enough to be able to get rid of any electronic paper trail. And a short sentence and a small fine for failure to retain records would be far preferable to having the full depths of malfeasance plumbed by prosecutors and media (who would have a field day with the Freedom of Information Act).

A dandy solution would be to make sure that all electronic traffic subject to the Records Retention Act of 1950 is backed up to secure, off-site locations and kept for a long time.

The Clinton administration's initiative to speed the country along the "electronic highway" may be ill-advised without some careful consideration of the potholes along the way.

Broken Records Retention

Before PCs were on every desk, production (and retention) of documents was a fairly straightforward procedure. After a document was typed, it (or one of several carbon copies of it) was put in a file. In law firms, huge files held every draft of important documents. In chemical companies, every lab report, every submission to the EPA, everything was saved in hard copy. The people doing the typing may not have known why they were keeping copies of everything, but keep them they did.

Before PCs, the practice of the "CYA memo" was in full bloom. Managers and subordinates flung them back and forth and saved them just in case.

With the advent of the paperless office and the efficiency and speed of electronic communication, to say nothing of the individual control of what flies back and forth, things have changed for the scarier.

In a fairly innocuous example, let's use two individuals engaged in an illicit love affair rather than something more serious—like industrial espionage. They communicate though an on-line service like Delphi or Prodigy or through the Internet gateways on their work PCs. Using a text editor, Stephanie composes a note to Steve, writing the text to a floppy drive she keeps in her bottom desk drawer for just this purpose. She then goes on-line and sends it. The diskette goes back into the drawer. (If Stephanie's really smart she will have used a utility to completely obliterate what she wrote.) Steve signs on to his E-mail, reads Stephanie's turgid words, sighs lustily, and deletes the message. Where did it go? Is it gone forever? Just about. As soon as the next batch clear runs through Steve's host, it is. If Steve fails to delete (or read) the message, it will stay around until the time comes for his system to delete retained/unread mail.

Stepping it up just a bit, let's say that Mr. Menkus and Ms. Kane decide to become involved in something a little more sinister like consulting (for mega-bucks) to federal employees on how to hide their electronic tracks and destroy records in direct violation of Public Law 101-510. Of course, we'd want our electronic discussions to be as secure as possible so we'd use our accounts on a system funded and supported by the federal government. We're both on a system classed as B-2 by the Department of Defense "Orange Book." The definition is a "Trusted Computer System" using the evaluation criteria of August 15, 1983, updated in December 1985. (There are only two higher classifications than B-2: B-3 and A-1.) What records would the government keep of our electronic mail? A log file—that MENKUS sent a message to PSKane on a certain date at a certain time, or vice-versa. Nothing else. And that for only three months. The only time the contents of back and forth messages would be available to be read by anyone else is before mail is picked up by the recipient or if it's held in the mailbox and not deleted. In reality, the messages might hang around a bit longer if the tapes haven't been cleared but it's unlikely that anything would remain by the time we were found out.

It's no more difficult to tap data lines than voice lines but it's easier to listen to voices than translate bits and bytes. If nobody's tapping, and your data and host system are secure to the Orange Book standard of B-2? Cool.

A more expensive, but still more secure, option is opening up a phone line between the two PCs and typing away using a communications program. The line still could be tapped but there would be no record whatsoever except what the conspirators saved for themselves.

Back to Records Reality

Extreme examples out of the way, consider the simplest communications. A quick E-mail that contains a significant typographical error could cause untold problems. Before PCs, a letter or memo was usually dictated, then typed, read by the typist, read by the sender, and then sent. Today, people read, write, and send—sometimes without thinking or proofreading.

Even if a text record of the electronic communication is retained on both ends, it still contains the error. It puts a nasty turn on "CYA."

Virus writers have taught us how simple it is to alter a file leaving the date and time stamp intact and without altering the checksum. It follows that files could be tampered with in a similar fashion in government or business settings for a multitude of reasons. Conversely, even using a different word processing program but the same printing font, a document could be retyped with a few changes and put in place of the original. How would a decision be made on which version is the real document? This is a thorny question, made thornier by the fact that the guts of most high-powered printers are exactly the same as those of photocopiers. Is there a way to tell a good photocopy from an original?

Desktop publishing programs present the opportunity for great amusement. Carefully excise an article from the *New York Times*, *Wall Street Journal*, or any other newspaper. Set your font to match the newspaper's exactly and write anything you want, the more outrageous, the better. Slide your work into the open space and make tracks to the photocopier. This little ploy is guaranteed to create consternation on the part of the victim until a real copy of the paper is located.

Not everyone wants to alter or otherwise futz around with data. Some people just want to keep a proper record, possibly as required by their records retention rules. The cards are stacked against people in a number of ways.

Floppy disks are cheap but seem to have acquired the status of gold ingots in some office supply rooms. Personnel are encouraged to reuse old diskettes, thereby destroying whatever data might have been on them. In other settings, the office workers think they're doing their employer a favor by saving 14 cents and using the same disk several times.

Another remarkable time-saving trick can result in loss of data. There are secretaries who are very proud of discovering that a few keystrokes can be saved be reusing the same headers for memos or letters to frequent recipients of their boss's correspondence. Just open up the last one, change the date, delete the text, and start typing.

Unless awareness is raised and records retention standards are expanded to include data diskettes, the paperless office may become the powerless office if, say, a federal agency becomes interested in its activities and flings a subpoena *duces tecum* in their direction.

Radio-Free Security

One of the national news magazines reported that Hillary Rodham Clinton is quite enamored of portable walk-around phone technology. Indeed, the walk-around phone has become almost essential for the busy folks of the '90s. How many people (including the First Lady) realize that cord-free luxury seriously compromises the privacy of telephone calls? When you pick up the portable, you're sending your voice via radio frequencies back to the base unit. Ordinary people report hearing their neighbors' phone conversations when they're trying to listen to NPR, Rush Limbaugh, or Howard Stern. To the listener, depending on who's listening and why, it might be an annoyance or a source of very useful information.

It's not hard to imagine a rotating team of fellows in trench coats taking turns stopping to rest on a bench in Lafayette Square (across Pennsylvania Avenue from the White House) tuned into Mrs. Clinton's frequency and recording her phone calls. As a practical matter, we hope that the White House security office doesn't allow walk-around phones in the building or that you won't undertake confidential conversations on one either.

Cell Biology

Cellular phones are orders of magnitude scarier than the radio signals of a portable phone. After all, you can't send data from a portable phone, you can only send data from the line that it's attached to. Anyone who can hack into the cellular carrier can pick up anything that's being transmitted, record it, and pick it apart later. Call your boss to talk marketing strategy from an AirPhone? There may be listeners. The President of the United States calls the President of Mexico (discussing NAFTA, of course) from Air Force One? There are listeners. It's a fair guess that the President's phone calls are scrambled but it doesn't take a dedicated unscrambler too much time to figure out the methodology.

It requires a court order to tap regular telephone lines; all it requires is a bit (okay, a lot) of technical knowledge to snag anything that comes into a satellite dish. What if Tonya Harding had approved the attack on Nancy Kerrigan from her truck phone and someone happened to be listening in?

Transmitting proprietary data over cellular links can be even more risky. Magazines touting the uses of portable technology are more than happy to tell you just how to send the sales reports or the marketing plans back to the home office from your carphone, laptop, and portable modem. They never seem to discuss the idea that your data is out there for anyone else to grab. It's only a matter of time before you'll be able to hook your modem into a data jack in the back of the airplane seat, and corporate espionage specialists will be able to pinpoint with stunning accuracy just when you're likely to transmit.

Walkie Talkies

Plus ça change, plus c'est la même chose. That's French for "the more things change, the more they remain the same." (Just a touch of class for the reader.) Walkie talkies, little hand-held wireless transmitters and receivers, are back. Not only are they back, they're being heralded as a brand new technology. In fact, the first-ever trade show for wireless communications will take place in mid-1994.

Back in the mid-1950s it was possible to order a truly dandy walkie talkie set from Ace comic books. It may be that today's aficionados of walkie talkies either have fond memories or no memories of this. The basic technology has been enhanced a bit: for example, there are docking stations to recharge the wireless devices these days.

Are today's walkie talkies any different than the Dick Tracy wrist radios? Not much. And eavesdropping on a walkie talkie can be accomplished by clever 11-year-olds.

If you ever visit a commodities exchange and feel your dental work vibrating, it's all those brokers wirelessing back and forth. How easy might it be to tap in and either use the information for your own benefit or, even more fun, skew what's going back and forth?

'Tis The law, M'lord

British courts are still deciding cases of data theft based on 14th century law. Even if someone copies data from a computer and uses it for a benefit, so long as the original data remains on the machine, no theft has occurred. What will it take to get the United Kingdom into this century?

Of course it makes sense when a vassal steals the master's cow that the vassal has the cow and the master doesn't. But what if both have the same cow and the vassal can get more milk from her? Silly proposition, of course, but this opens the door for even sillier arguments as cases of espionage based on computer data will surely come to the forefront.

Software license agreements are quite clear and have been pretty much sorted out over the past ten years. One copy on one computer at any one time. Period. But how can you steal something that the original owner still has?

A left-field take on this might be that any recorded data is protected by U.S. copyright the minute it is reduced to readable form. In other words, the minute you type (or hand write) an epic poem celebrating Lorena Bobbitt's contributions to the practice of outpatient surgery you have a right to take action against anyone who takes your words and uses them. All you have to do is prove you reduced those words to writing first. But what about a customer list? Ad copy for a two-minute commercial during the Super Bowl is probably more protectable than parts numbers or customer lists for left-handed spurling flanges. And what about the design plans for those infamous spurling flanges? It really doesn't make much difference. After a competitor has *your* data, you're in trouble. One of the charms of the civil court system in the United States is that you have to prove that you were damaged by another and to what extent.

This book is not the place for a lengthy discussion on evolving law about industrial espionage through theft of electronic data. Suffice to say that that laws will come and, as is the way of the law, will come with exquisite slowness.

This book is the place to make you aware of the value of the data on your PCs, on your backups, or wherever it might be stored. If you protect it, it can't be stolen.

Does Mother Nature Have PMS?

The 1993–1994 spate of natural disasters in the United States made many people wonder just who or what had annoyed Mother Nature quite so thoroughly. The floods in the midwest, the earthquake in California, and the intensely bitter cold that lasted almost forever along the East Coast extracted a toll far beyond the human interest stories shown on the TV news.

When the earthquake hit Los Angeles, the city lost most of its electrical power. But so did places as far north as Washington State—for two days. There are lots of telemarketing businesses in Washington, many of them were flat out of business. If those companies were feeling litigious, whom would they sue? Will a standard insurance policy cover a "proximate cause" that's two states away and is, after all, an Act of God? Or is it the fault of the power companies in California?

Nearer the epicenter, there was not only outright and visible destruction but some more subtle effects. In one building, apparently undamaged, the fiberoptic cable snaking through the walls was damaged beyond repair.

OSHA would have been mighty unhappy—to say nothing of individual employees—if midwestern businesses had tried to continue their operations without water in the workplace. Their insurance companies would not have been happy, either, if sprinkler systems were not operable. Nomad-like, entire companies and their computing equipment had to move to the high ground at great expense.

During the worst of the East Coast deep freeze, electrical power companies all along the Boston to Washington D.C. corridor instituted rolling blackouts, taking down the power in selected areas for 15 minutes. There was no way to post a schedule of just when this would happen in a given area; people were in the dark in more ways than one. Massive mainframes were, undoubtedly, protected by UPS systems; individual PCs and the work on them was at the mercy of whoever was pulling the plug (a computer?). The ice storms that accompanied the cold brought down electrical and telephone lines from Kentucky to New Hampshire.

Is UPS a Downer?

UPS (Uninterrupted Power Supply) systems are the best power backup available at the moment. Their response time to a power drop or outage is incredibly quick, measured in the pica-seconds. Most computers protected by UPS have one job and one job only when the UPS goes on: shut down. Depending on the complexity of the system and just what was going on at the moment of power loss, the shut-down could take the entire time that the

UPS keeps the machine up. What happens in the case of rolling blackouts? Would any work ever get done?

For a real downer, read the product literature. There are more caveats and disclaimers than you'd be exposed to before open-heart surgery. The stability of the batteries is also at issue; in the future, gas-powered UPS systems will have to become the rule.

What if your UPS is just a tad bit late out of the gate? Any data in read-write memory can be compromised. This is what happens to the lowly PC in the brown electrical condition: the power doesn't drop far enough to reboot the system, just enough to scramble whatever's in RAM.

Doc in the Box

Experiments have already begun (to the screams and howls of the animal rights people) in the area of remote surgery. In theory (and in limited testing) a surgeon can be hundreds or thousands of miles from the patient. The operating site is visualized on a computer screen, and the surgeon directs robotics (under supervision of actual medical personnel) to perform the operation by using equipment similar to joysticks.

This is really just a logical extension of existing surgical techniques that employ fiberoptics. The only difference is that the surgeon is not physically present in the operating room. Obviously, the key is the proper transmission of the data (joystick movement) from the remote site to the operating room. The flow of data back and forth from operating room to the surgeon's site is critical even if the patient's condition isn't. The least interruption or scrambling of data from either end could result in a critical situation for the patient.

Remember, the joystick movement isn't a cause and effect situation. It's the rapid translation of the movement into data that can be sent, received, and translated back to the movement of the surgical instrument.

It's hard to imagine just why this particular research is important because it's harder to imagine it in application. It's even harder to imagine the amount of malpractice insurance a long-distance surgeon would have to carry. What's not hard to imagine is what could happen if the data link were compromised.

Too Public Utilities

As computers get smarter and smarter (actually, the computers stay just as dumb as they always were, the programming gets more and more sophisticated), more and more activities will be run in an unattended mode. Long-distance telephone companies brag on television about their immediate-response computer-switched routing. The massive East Coast outage in the summer of 1990 proved how effective that can be. Monitoring demand for electrical power or water or natural gas can be done much better by a computer than any team of humans ever could. So, it makes sense that more and more of these utilities will be managed by computers.

You may think this is good because computers are faster (and cheaper) than real people. However, and this a big however, public utilities are regulated and the regulatory bodies want and need the ability to monitor performance. Assuming that the computers managing the delivery of the utility product are in highly secure locations, the management of the utility company will need to get into them from time to time. There must be data links (phone lines or satellite) from the computers to the points of delivery and monitoring locations. What fun for a dedicated hacker to tap in (the gateway is already there, it just has to be found) and spend an enjoyable afternoon turning the power in the entire state of Colorado off and on. How much worse if the system could be compromised in such a way that disaster monitoring was turned off. What if an earthquake took out the data links or the monitoring stations so that the computer didn't know to turn off the gas?

Hold the Phone

Individuals have become totally dependent on Mr. Bell's invention. Computers have become equally dependent. When phone service is disrupted, people begin to freak out. Computers don't do that; they just sit quietly, unable to send or receive data. The people whose business depends upon those computers and that data, do however, freak out. The technology exists to keep a queue of data on hold in the sending computer until it receives a confirmation from the receiving computer that the data is there and written. In highly secure or highly regulated environments, this technology is (or should be) used. In other settings, however, it's often not used due to cost and (supposed) expediency.

Whither Viruses?

As the symbiosis and synergy between virus writers (and virus exchange bulletin boards) and scanner developers grows, one of two things will happen. Either a truce will be called or things will spin out of control to an exponential degree. A middle ground doesn't seem likely.

Clearly, scanning technology—identifying each new virus as it shows up and searching for (and destroying)—can't continue in any practical way. On the other hand, antivirus scanners are usually far enough ahead of widespread distribution that anyone who's willing to go through the hassle of endless updates will be ahead of the game.

We believe that the scanner (virus signature) approach will have to be abandoned in favor of generic detection programs that only have to be updated as soon as a new method of infection is developed.

PC-based viruses as they are today will become as bothersome as swatting mosquitoes on a summer night or burning citronella candles to keep them away. What is to be feared are the lessons learned from the virus writers and malevolent hackers to intrude on secure systems.

Simply Intolerable

As dependence on computer transactions increases—from money machines to remote surgery—the tolerance for downtime shrinks to an almost infinitesimal amount. The tolerance for any interruption of data transfer or processing almost ceases to exist. The cost of an electronic highway without on- and off-ramps or alternate routes is terrifying to those who take the time, as we have, to think about it.

The Role of Hardware and Software in Solutions

The PC was not, is not, and may never be a secure computer. This may seem to be a harsh statement in a book that is supposed to tell you how you should secure your data and protect your programs, but it is the unfortunate truth because of the basic design of the PC since it was introduced in 1981.

There have been lots of solutions proposed along the way, right down to putting public key encryption on either add-in boards or on CMOS. The cost of solutions like that should send system managers running straight back to mainframes. In this chapter, you'll begin to understand why PCs as they are known today are problematical, at the least.

To understand the problems of designing either hardware or software security solutions, you need to understand what's inside that little gray box on your desk. If you understand how the PC works, you will understand the difficulty of finding a security solution in either hardware or software. You may even save a few bucks by resisting the temptation to buy the latest dingle or dongle that claims to protect your PC from a security breach.

First you'll look at the history of the PC and then open the cover to see what bits of information you can glean from the inside. Finally, you'll take all those little black chips apart to find out what you are really paying for.

History 101

IBM began by creating the mainframe and the microcomputers. In 1981, the PC for business personal computing was introduced. There were computers before then, even little boxes that would sit neatly on a desk and do word processing and spread sheets. Nothing IBM did in 1981 was truly innovative or ground breaking as far as the microcomputer industry was concerned. What IBM was able to accomplish was to put their marketing skill and reputation into a small box and establish a standard for a fledgling industry. IBM's open architecture policy assured that third parties would develop both hardware and software that would work with the IBM PC. That policy also meant that other manufacturers could copy the IBM specifications and produce PCs that would work with the third-party hardware and software at a cost below that of the original IBM PC. As the market penetration of the PC grew over that of IBM's rivals, the standard became more and more entrenched so that today even IBM has a difficult time overcoming some of the shortcomings that evolved in 1981.

Before IBM's PC, the microcomputer was generally used by hobbyists. The ALTAIR microcomputer was merely a fancy calculator and not suitable for business use. Radio Shack's TRS-80 had the marketing advantage of Tandy's hundreds of retail outlets, but was still limited in what it could do. The basic unit was a keyboard that contained all the computer circuits, a black and white monitor, and an audio cassette that could be plugged into the keyboard as a data storage medium. You could take your TRS-80 into the local Radio Shack and get a memory upgrade that would take it from 4K to a whole 16K. By the late 1970s, you could even purchase a disk system and printer for the TRS-80. A modem that operated at 300 bits per second would enable you to communicate over the telephone if you could find anyone else who had one.

The real spur to IBM was probably the two Steves, Jobs and Wozniak, who built a computer literally in their garage and, being Beatles fans, named it the Apple after the Beatles' record label. The Apple was much more adaptable to business use than the TRS-80, but lacked Radio Shack's marketing outlets. The success of any microcomputer depended on getting business to use it. The price was often too steep for the individual who saw them as fancy Atari video games (Nintendo and Sega had not arrived yet). It was software that pushed the microcomputer into the business world. Wordstar, a word processing program, dBASE, a data base program, and VISICALC, a spread sheet program, probably sold more TSR-80s and Apples than any Radio Shack or Apple marketing representative. Those three programs formed the basis of almost all programs used in business today.

As the 1980s began, more and more of these little machines started popping up on desktops across corporate America. Every time an IBM representative went to see a client, he or she would see these little wonders sitting on a desk. Sure, IBM sold those big behemoths that sat behind glass doors with men in white coats taking requests for computing time. And, although IBM's original marketing plan was to place the PC in the homes of the new baby boomers who were achieving management status, they perhaps inadvertently made decisions that put the little computers on the desks of corporate America.

A group of computer engineers was sent to an oversize garage in Boca Raton, Florida, and were told to produce a microcomputer at a price that was competitive with Apple and Radio Shack. And produce it fast, before any of the other brands became entrenched in the marketplace.

Produce they did. The result of their labors was the first microcomputer to bear the IBM label on the box, the IBM PC. Inside the box, however, hardly anything bore the IBM label. The PC was patched together with already produced parts that were reliable, but not really state of the art. IBM even bypassed the thousands of programmers on the corporate payroll and leased an operating system from a young fellow named Bill Gates who as a college student had helped develop the BASIC programming language. Bill Gates, being both a programming and business genius, turned his IBM connection into Microsoft Corporation.

Even though there was nothing really new in the components used in the IBM design, put together the PC could run rings around the competition. The design is modular in both hardware and software. Only the microprocessor, the basic 64K of memory and the built-in read-only memory chips are on the master circuit board. All additional devices including disk drives, monitor, printer, and up to 512K of memory are attached to the system through plug-in modular circuit cards that can be easily changed. There are even a few spare slots where you can plug in additional cards. This means that the IBM PC can be set up and configured in thousands of different ways to suit almost any computing need.

In announcing the PC, IBM did something that was completely unheard of in the computing industry. They published the complete specifications of both the hardware and operating system and encouraged third parties to produce software and additional hardware for the system. Through years of experience in the business machine field, IBM apparently knew that hardware sells only if someone needs the software. Look at the television industry before World War II. Television was a laboratory curiosity. There were few stations capable of broadcasting TV, so few sets were sold. Following the war, more and more cities got TV stations, so more and more people bought the sets. Who would want a TV if there were nothing to receive?

Because the target market was the middle manager working at home, by the time the PC hit the street, IBM had already developed (or bought) the big three business packages and made them work on the PC. Because all work and no play is anathema to many, IBM also sold a text-based adventure game. However, it was the addition of thousands of software programs developed by others and hundreds of hardware add-ons that made the IBM standard the de facto standard it remains today. Instead of the managers using the PC for work at home, the PC became a new office status symbol.

Secure In Success

There is no doubt that the IBM PC was successful in bringing personal computing to homes and businesses throughout the world. Successful it is. Secure it is not. The concept of the PC was to bring the power of computing to the masses. In order to design a computer that is inexpensive enough to sit in everyone's home, some of the security of the mainframes and minis had to be sacrificed. By ignoring the issue of data security, the PC became vulnerable to viruses and other malware. To understand why, you must look under the hood to see what makes it tick. Now don't go removing the cover of your fancy 486DX2 66MHz super VGA with a local bus TurboClone yet. I'll use a somewhat simpler PC to explain how the thing works. This is the

IBM PC, serial number 0105221, purchased in December 1981 for a bit over $5,000. It still works, although thanks to the modularity of the design, almost none of the original components are still under the cover. In its original form, this PC was an 8088 running at 4.77MHz with 64K of memory, one single-sided diskette drive, a monochrome text-only monitor and a dot-matrix printer. It's primitive by today's standards, but was priced about the same as a fully loaded high-speed desktop PC is today. The amazing fact remains that the software written for this seemingly ancient PC will still work on today's computers.

Because the original design (a bit simpler than in today's computers) set the standard by which we compute today, let's take the cover off and see what makes it tick. When engineers and computer types speak of hardware, they use a lot of acronyms and techno-babble, making the discussion difficult to understand. I'll try to help you uncover the way a computer works without resorting to overly technical language. First, look at the parts you can actually see.

Undercover Cop

Under the hood is a green, fiberglass epoxy board with row upon row of matte black microchips pushed into sockets that are connected by a network of copper-colored wires embedded in the epoxy. Long before Saddam coined the phrase "mother of all battles," this was referred to as the "mother of all circuit boards," or simply the motherboard. One of these microchips is larger than the others and has 40 little silver feet sprouting from the bottom. This is the Intel 8088 microprocessor, the central processing unit (CPU) and the brains behind the computer. The other chips on the motherboard are read-only memory (ROM), random-access memory (RAM), and a bunch of other stuff of interest to electrical engineers that helps make the computer go.

Taking up the right-rear quadrant of the motherboard is a silver box that contains the 63.5-watt power supply with the big red switch protruding through to the outside of the box. From the power supply, four cables supply electricity to the various components. Two cables are connected to the motherboard, one to the diskette drive, and the fourth just hangs there awaiting the purchase of another diskette drive.

Toward the rear of the motherboard are five slots that can be used for expansion cards. Each slot has 62 connections (31 on a side) to the motherboard.

Through these connections, an adapter board can send and receive data, and address and control information directly from the microprocessor and other little chips on the motherboard. The path from the microprocessor to the adapter cards is referred to as the *bus*. Those who are really curious can wade through the IBM Technical Reference Manual for the PC (IBM part number 6025005) which is probably no longer available.

On our primitive PC, two of the slots already have cards in them. One card is the diskette controller; it has a flat cable between it and the diskette drive at the front of the motherboard. The end of the cable has another connector waiting for another diskette drive. The rear of the diskette adapter card has a connector to accommodate two more external drives for a total of four.

Another slot is occupied with the display adapter card. This card actually controls two different devices, the monochrome display and the printer. There are connectors on the back of the adapter card for each of these peripherals. The original PC could be ordered with one of two different display monitors, the monochrome or a three-color graphics display. Monochrome was text only, but the color monitor could display graphics in three colors plus black. The color display adapter card did not include the printer adapter, so a separate printer adapter card was available for PCs with the graphics adapter. With a diskette, color display, and a printer, three of the five slots were occupied.

IBM offered several adapter cards to fill the remaining two slots. You could get a card that added up to 192K of memory which, with the 64K on the motherboard, gave a total of 256K. An asynchronous communications adapter that could be connected to a modem for phone communications was available for the original PC as well as a joystick adapter for playing games.

One other device connection was standard on the IBM PC, the cassette connector. Radio Shack had used a standard audio cassette player for data storage for years, so IBM put a connector at the back of the PC for one. We have yet to meet anyone who actually used a cassette player for data recording, so it's safe to assume that this option was not what sold the PC.

Many small companies leaped at the chance to provide adapter cards for the PC. With only five slots and five standard adapters, the opportunity to make multi-use adapter cards launched many companies on the road to success. A multipurpose card containing a printer port, a modem port, and additional memory could take the place of three different cards, leaving two precious slots for additional cards.

The concept of an individually configurable PC may add a lot to the marketability of the computer, but it leaves it vulnerable. In order to use an almost limitless selection of add-in components, the PC has to have an open architecture. This means that the basic design is available to both hardware and software producers as well as anyone who might have evil intentions. The virus theories of Dr. Fred Cohen which were outlined in Chapter 1 can easily become a reality on a standardized machine with open architecture. To understand why, you have to understand what makes a computer work.

Inside the Insides

But what makes it go? How do all these pieces interact and produce meaningful data? Should I care? Why can't I protect my data? Let's look at all those little black chips and see if we can make some sense out of what they do. After all, it is the hardware that allows a programmer to write all those wonderful spread sheets, word processors and communications programs. It is also the hardware that lets the malcontents write viruses that can destroy the work you perform on the computer. In the case of the PC, it is the hardware that makes it extremely difficult to protect our data from others.

The heart of any computer from the speedy CRAY to the lowly PC is the CPU. In the PC, the CPU is contained on one small microcircuit whose size belies its complexity. In simple terms, the CPU is an expensive calculator that can add, subtract, multiply, and divide numbers. It can also send and receive numbers over the data bus (exact change only, driver does not carry cash). In reality, the CPU is not even that smart. It can only calculate in the most basic of numbers, binary digits, which may explain why it is called a binary computer.

A Bit of Binary

A binary digit is the simplest of numbers, 1 or 0, on or off. Since birth, people tend to think of numbers in the decimal system, which is based on their number of fingers. Ten digits, from 0 to 9, make up the decimal system. Need a larger number? Add another place to the left and start from 0 again (10). Each place to the left represents a power of 10: 10 is 10 to the first power, 100 is 10 to the second power (10x10), 1,000 is 10 to the third power (10x10x10), and so on. There is a direct relationship to the power of 10 and the number of zeros that follow the 1: 10 to the 23 power is just a 1 followed by 23 zeros.

The binary system works the same way except that there are only two numbers, 0 and 1. Need a larger number? Add a place just like in the decimal system and begin again at 0. The real problem in understanding the binary system is that we use the same symbols for both decimal and binary. The symbols *10* mean ten in decimal system yet they represent two in the binary system. Each place to the left in binary is a power of 2. 10 can be thought of as 2 to the first power, 100 as 2 to the second power (2x2=4), 1000 as 2 to the third power (2x2x2=8), and so on. Like the decimal system there is a direct relationship to the power of 2 and the number of zeros that follow the 1.

It's just a little strange to think of 1010 as the number of fingers on both hands. Because people are taught the decimal system from birth, it is often easier to add a little *b* to the end of a binary number to indicate that it is binary and not decimal. Therefore, 1010b is the binary equivalent of 10.

Computers would be easier to understand if they used the decimal system instead of binary numbers. So why binary? The answer is in electronics. It is easy to represent a number as the presence of electricity (voltage) or the absence of electricity in a circuit. It is a much more difficult task to design a circuit that discriminates among 10 different voltage levels. Unfortunately, if numbers are to be represented by the presence or absence of electricity in the circuit, one must use the binary system.

How Many Nibbles in a Byte?

Obviously, because each place in a number can only represent two different values, numbers must contain many places to be of any value. Again the electronic circuitry within a computer dictates the number of places a binary number can have. The most commonly used unit of binary digits is eight places and is called by definition a *byte*. In the decimal system, eight places can represent a number that is about one tenth of Bill Gates' net worth (99,999,999). In the binary system, however, eight places is closer to my net worth (255 in decimal). Nevertheless, 256 different combinations of digits (0 through 255) can represent all of the letters (upper- and lowercase), all of the numbers, and all of the punctuation marks commonly used in the English language, and there are more than 128 number left over.

For numerical computation, 255 is a rather small number. Somewhat larger units than a byte are needed. Two bytes is a 16-bit unit called by computer people a *word* and can represent numbers between 0 and 65,535. A *double word* is 32 bits and can represent numbers from 0 to 4,294,967,295.

Oh, by the way. There are 2 nibbles in a byte. A nibble is defined as a 4 bit binary number.

Negative Thinking

Notice that all these binary numbers are positive integers, but computers also need to deal with negative integers. Because there is nothing in the computer that resembles the + and - signs used in everyday math, computer designers need a method to designate whether a binary number is negative or positive. Although there can be several ways to do this, the IBM standard uses what is known as the *twos compliment method* of designating negative numbers. It seems at first a little strange, but here's how it works. To make the negative of a positive binary number, all the bits are reversed and then one is added to the result.

To make an easy to understand example, consider a two-bit binary number. An unsigned two-bit binary number can be 00 (0), 01 (1), 10 (2), or 11 (3). A signed two-bit binary number can be 00 (0), 01 (1), 10 (-0), or 11 (-1). Because there is only one positive integer (01), take the twos compliment by reversing the bits (10) and adding 1 (11). Now as any college sophomore engineering student can tell you, adding 1 and -1 will give a result of zero. Test the computer model with binary numbers using the twos compliment method: 01+11=100 (in binary). However, because you only have two digits, the 1 in the third place is lost giving 01+11=00, or the correct result.

When a byte is used as a signed number, the last bit (on the left) becomes the sign bit. Now there are 128 positive combinations (0 to 127) and 127 negative combinations (-127 to -1). In using units larger than a byte, the same principle holds true. The highest positive integer is half the unsigned capacity of the unit.

Get Real

This leaves the problem of representing real numbers, those with fractional parts. How does one represent 49.95 in binary? This is an exercise for the programmer. The 8088 can operate only on signed and unsigned binary integers. Real numbers are calculated by software using several different methods.

What's New?

Perhaps the only truly innovative step IBM took in designing the PC was to choose the Intel 8088 microprocessor as the CPU. The other personal computer to date had used 8-bit processors, but the 8088 was a 16-bit processor, although it sent and received data in 8-bit chunks so it could be compatible with the devices already on the market. The Intel 8086 microprocessor was the same internally as the 8088, except it sent and transmitted data in 16-bit chunks which, while faster than the 8088, was not compatible with the diskette drives and printers that were already on the market.

Even though the CPU chip was a radical departure from the chips used in other microprocessors, it was still not capable of addressing the problems of data vulnerability inherent in microprocessors. If nothing else, the pure success of the IBM-PC was to add to the problem of viruses. Since virus code is specific to the processor, as was detailed in Chapter 1, the fact that millions of computers shared the same microchip made it much easier for a virus to spread from place to place. To understand why a virus, or any program for that matter, can only run with a specific processor, you need to understand how a processor works.

Transistors

The electronic component that makes a desktop computer possible is the *transistor*. These devices were developed in the late 1940's as a replacement for the vacuum tubes that were used in electronic circuits. A transistor is made of two slightly different kinds of silicon, the n-type and the p-type. Electrons can flow from the n-type to the p-type, but not from the p-type to the n-type. Transistors are simply a sandwich of either p-type silicon as the bread and n-type as the meat (a pnp transistor) or n-type as the bread and p-type as the meat (a npn transistor). One piece of bread is called the collector and the other the emitter. The meat is called the base. If a small current flows between the base and the emitter, a larger current flows between the collector and the emitter. If there is no current in the base/emitter circuit, there is no current in the collector/emitter circuit. Thus, a transistor, as used in a computer, acts as a miniature electric switch to turn the current in a particular circuit on or off.

Through the years, engineers have made the transistor smaller and smaller, so small in fact that thousands of them can now be placed on a circuit board smaller than a thumbnail. These subminiature circuit boards are called integrated circuits (ICs for short) and are what you see socketed on the larger circuit boards of the computer. Actually, you can only see the case of the IC which is often much larger than the actual chip inside so the connecting wires (feet) will fit into the sockets.

Inside the ICs, many transistors are connected together to form what is called a *flip/flop circuit*. A flip/flop circuit is an electronic switch that can remember whether it is on or off. A small momentary current to one of the two inputs (SET) turns the output on until another small momentary current to the other input (RESET) turns the output off. This on or off state can represent a binary digit. On is 1 and off is 0. Or it could be that on is 0 and off is 1, it doesn't matter as long as the circuits are consistent. This is the basic electrical circuit in a computer, and one IC may contain several, hundreds, or thousands of flip/flops.

Other transistor combinations form what are called *logic gates*. These are made from two flip/flop circuits wired together. The concept of the gate is that two different digital inputs result in one digital output. There are several different combinations of logic gates used in computers. The OR gate produces an "on" for an output if either of the two inputs are on. The AND gate produces an "on" output only if both inputs are on. The complements of these two are the NOR, which produces an "off" output if either of the two inputs are on, and the NAND, which produces an "off" output only if both inputs are on. Another logic gate is the exclusive (XOR) gate, which produces an "on" output only if both inputs are different—one on, one off. In electronic terms, on is defined as having a voltage from 3 to 5 volts, and off means that the voltage is somewhere between 0 and 0.7 volts. Because the voltage is not precise, the two states of a digital signal are referred to as high and low.

Knowing each and every type of logic gate and how to construct a flip/flop circuit is not important unless you are considering a career in electrical engineering. However, knowing that there are such things inside the microprocessor chip is important in the general understanding of how computers perform their magic. Interaction of these logic gates which are designed into the processor are what allows the computer to compute. The program codes in your software are merely electrical pulses which interact with these gates. In the Intel family of chips, there is no built in method of preventing program instructions from processing, even if they are not authorized by the user. To see why, you need a short course in how program instructions are executed by the CPU, and what they do.

Register Here for Computer Class

Several groups of flip/flop circuits inside the microprocessor are arranged into what are known as registers. The 8088 contains 14 different registers each of which is capable of holding 16 bits of information. What this means is that each of these registers is capable of storing, in binary form, any number from 0 to 65,565. Just storing a number is what memory does, so the registers within the CPU are wired together through logic gates so they can be altered according to an specific instruction. An instruction is just another binary number that activates certain logic gates so that the bits within a register can be altered in some way.

The number of instructions a processor can carry out depends on how the processor is designed. The 8088 can act on 135 different instructions. The instructions are divided into several categories which in the 8088 are Data Transfer, Arithmetic, Logic, Control Transfer, and Processor Control. Before diving head first into the rich instruction set of the 8088, let us take a side trip down memory lane.

Memories Are Made of This

Memory, like a register, is a special circuit that contains binary digits. In the PC, memory is an 8-bit binary digit called a byte by definition. Each byte has a unique associated binary address that in the original PC is a 20-bit-wide digit. Prior to the IBM PC, microcomputers used a 16-bit address that made the maximum memory address 65,565, or 64K. With 20 bits, the maximum address is 2 to the 20th power minus 1, which is 1,048,575, or 1M. Remember the 62 lines that connect to the bus? Twenty of these lines are address lines, one for each bit of the address. And some of those extra chips that only concern electrical engineers? These chips contain logic gates that decode the address and make sure that the correct memory byte is accessed.

N O T E   The prefix *kilo* generally means one thousand and *mega* means one million. In computers you get more than you pay for when talking kilo and mega. Kilo is not 1,000, but 2 to the 10th power (1,024). Mega is 2 to the 20th power (1,024 kilos or 1,048,576). In the future, you may have to calculate a *giga*, which is a kilo of megas (1,073,741,824).

Unlike registers, which are wired together to perform many tasks, memory can only perform one function, storing a bit pattern. The CPU can retrieve the contents of a memory address by placing the address on the address bus and activating the control bus line called the read request line. The memory chips sense the read request, decode the address, and then copy the contents of that address onto the data bus. (There are enough busses in the typical PC to satisfy the transportation needs of many medium-size communities.) The CPU can also copy the contents of a register to memory by placing the address of the memory byte on the address bus, sending a write request on a special line designed for that purpose and placing the 8 bits of data on the data bus.

If memory is 8 bits and the CPU register is 16 bits, how can the CPU read from and write to the memory? This is why IBM's engineers chose the 8088 instead of the 8086. The 8088 is designed to read and write the data to and from memory 8 bits at a time. To write 16 bits, the processor merely divides the data into two 8-bit chunks and sends the first half to the designated memory address and the second half to the next higher address.

Memory comes in two flavors, RAM and ROM. *RAM* is a misnomer for random-access memory. In the technical reference for the original PC, the term RAM is never used, it is referred to as read/write memory or R/W. Whether you call it RAM or R/W (which is hard to pronounce), this is the memory that can be changed by the processor. The data byte in each address can be accessed and changed by the processor, hopefully with a purpose and never randomly. *ROM* stands for read-only memory, and as the name implies, this memory can be accessed by the processor, but not changed. When the computer is first turned on, the R/W contains no data, all bytes are 0. The ROM, being permanent, contains the instructions that get the processor started.

The 8088 can address up to 1M (or 1,024K) of memory. IBM set specifications on how this memory was to be used in the PC. The first 1,024 bytes are reserved for the interrupt vector table which will be explained shortly. The next 256 bytes comprises a data area that holds information about the system. The next 654,080 bytes of RAM (if installed) are available for user programs. This means the first 640K, less the data area and vector table, are available for programs, while the upper 384K of memory is reserved for other purposes. The area beginning at 640K through 768K is reserved for a video display to use, although the original monochrome used only 4K and the color display used only 16K of this 128K reserved area. The 208K from 768K to 976K is reserved but not used in the original PC. The remaining 48K from 976K to the top of memory is dedicated to ROM, although the PC uses only to the top 40K of this space. The ROM contains the instructions that get the processor up and running and the basic input/output (BIOS) routines that enable programs to interface with the keyboard, monitor, parallel port (printer), serial port (modem), disk drives, and data cassette. IBM manufactured PCs also contain a BASIC program in the ROM.

Another way the processor communicates with the devices connected to the computer is through the *I/O* (for input/output) channel. Like memory, the I/O channel consists of an address on the address bus and a byte of data on the data bus. The 8088 uses the same data and address busses for the I/O channel and memory, but different control lines. The I/O channel is used to read data from and send data to peripheral devices such as the disk drive, modem, and printer, any device that does not have a dedicated memory space within the PC. The monitor uses a combination of I/O channel and dedicated memory to display characters or graphics on the screen.

Addressing by Pushing the Envelope

Returning to the CPU, look at the problem of addressing memory. The address bus is 20 bits wide, which allows 1M of memory. Because the CPU registers are 16 bits wide, there is a 4-bit discrepancy that becomes immediately apparent. How can one place a 20-bit address on the bus with a 16-bit register? Apparently it was simple for the Intel engineers, but for others the process is rather complicated.

Four of the 14 registers in the 8088 are dedicated to addressing memory and are used for no other purpose. These registers are called the *segment registers* and are named with two letter acronyms. They are code segment (CS), data segment (DS), stack segment (SS), and extra segment (ES). But what is a segment? A segment is basically the upper 16 bits of the memory address. The lower 4 bits are derived from what is called the offset into the segment which is stored in one of the other registers. The processor calculates the memory address by shifting the contents of the segment register 4 bits to the left and adding the contents of the designated offset register. The result is a 20-bit address. Programming memory addresses with an Intel CPU is really a lot more complicated than it sounds.

Unless you are programming the 8088, it really does not matter whether you understand the mechanics of how the CPU forms an address. However, from a security point of view it is important to remember that the entire address space of the PC can be accessed by putting the appropriate values into the processor's registers. Memory can contain either data or processor instructions, but the distinction is entirely up to the program. It is the software that determines how to interpret each byte of data in the address space of the computer. The hardware itself can not make a distinction between the two. This is where the operating system comes into play—to make sure that the processor is fed a continuing stream of logical instructions from memory, and not some random data byte which has been stored in another area of memory. Because the hardware cannot determine the purpose of a byte of data stored in memory, the PC becomes vulnerable to viruses which treat program instructions like data and add the virus code to the program code. If the processor could determine the type of data stored in a certain memory location, it would be much more difficult for viruses to spread. Most larger computers do store data and code in separate areas of memory and can prevent the areas containing code from being changed, but the 8088 cannot protect certain memory addresses. A closer look at the register set of the 8088 will detail the interaction of memory and registers.

The 8088 Register Set

The combination of the code segment register and the instruction pointer register indicates to the processor where in memory to find the next instruction. When the processor fetches an instruction, the instruction pointer is incremented to point to the next instruction. However, the instructions do not necessarily have to be arranged in consecutive bytes in memory. Some instructions, called jumps, indicate to the processor that the next instruction should come from somewhere else in memory rather than the next byte in sequence. Because addressing involves two registers, there are several jump instructions available. A jump instruction can affect just the offset register (instruction pointer), called a near jump, or both the segment register (code segment) and offset register, called a far jump.

Some of the remaining ten registers in the CPU are dedicated for special purposes. The instruction pointer (IP) works in conjunction with the code segment (CS) to produce the 20-bit address of the next instruction upon which the CPU will act. The stack pointer (SP) is used in conjunction with the stack segment (SS) register to address a last in, first out stack for temporarily saving and retrieving register data in memory.

Of the remaining eight registers, four are designated as general-purpose registers, but each has special functions. The accumulator (AX) is the primary calculation register for math functions. The base register (BX) is used primarily as an address offset to the data segment register. The count (CX) register is used to count repeating instructions. The data register (DX) is used to store data. Although these are 16-bit registers, there are instructions that can treat each as two 8-bit registers. Thus the AX register can be divided into its high half and low half as the AH and AL registers. Likewise, BX can be divided into BH and BL, CX into CH and CL, and DX into DH and DL. Therefore, the 8088 can have either four 16-bit general-purpose registers or eight 8-bit general-purpose registers, depending on the instruction. As general-purpose registers, there are many instructions that involve these registers besides the special functions from which they derive their names.

Three of the remaining four registers are generally used for addressing, although the instructions are not limited to that purpose. The source index (SI) register is usually used in conjunction with the data segment for addressing memory. The destination index (DI) register performs the same function as the extra segment register, and the base pointer is generally used with the stack segment to address memory. While forming addresses is the primary function of these registers, they are by no means limited to this function. The instruction set is rich in tasks for these registers.

Surely the architecture of the 8088 registers could lend itself to protecting certain areas of memory. Since memory is segmented, there could be a protection of the code segment against writing to memory, and a protection against executing code in the data segment. Unfortunately there is no such protection built into the 8088 processor. Any segment register can point to any memory address whether there are instructions or data stored there.

Run This Up the Flag Register

The remaining 16-bit register is used for a very special purpose. It is called the flags register (FLAGS) and is used sort of like a scratch pad during calculations. Of particular importance are the zero flag bit and the carry flag bit. The zero flag is set if the result of a calculation is 0. For example, if the instruction says "subtract the contents of the AX register from the contents of the DX register" and both registers contain the same value, the result is 0, and the zero flag is set. The next instruction might then examine the zero flag and take action according to how it is set: "Examine the zero flag and if it is 1, skip the next 30 instructions."

In reality, the 8088 cannot do subtraction, only addition. However, as you learned in seventh grade arithmetic, subtraction can be the same as adding a negative number. To perform a subtraction, the processor negates a number by taking the twos compliment (reversing the bits and adding 1) and then adding the two numbers together.

If the result of adding two registers has a carry out of the leftmost bit, that bit goes into the carry flag bit in the flags register. This sets the carry flag if the result of a subtraction is negative or if the result of an addition is greater than the capacity of the register. For instance, in the instruction subtract AX from DX, if AX contains a 3 and DX a 2, the computer converts the 3 to the twos compliment and adds the contents of the DX register (2). The result is -1, which is stored as all 1s, and the carry flag is set to indicate an overflow of the result.

Just as there are instructions that examine the zero flag, there are instructions that examine the carry flag and direct the processor to take action depending on whether the flag is set or not. As a group, these instructions are called conditional instructions and make a computer follow a certain set of logical rules rather than act as an expensive calculator. The compare instruction tells the CPU to compare two registers (or a register and a memory location) by subtracting one from the other without storing the result. This instruction can be followed by one or more instructions that examine the flags. If the zero flag is set, then both are equal because subtracting one from the other produced a result of zero. If the carry flag is set, then one register contains a larger number than the other. If the carry flag is not set, then the first register contains a number smaller than the other.

Programmers can jump to a different set of instructions depending on how the zero and carry flags are set. These instructions are called conditional jumps, and the processor will jump to different instructions if the flag is set but continue with the next sequential instruction if the flag is not set. Some of the conditional jumps are jump if equal, jump if not equal, jump if greater, and jump if lesser and most combinations of these. There are 16 different conditional jumps available with the 8088, which enables the computer to follow a logical path through the instructions, performing different tasks depending on the data.

Call if You Find Work

Another method the 8088 uses to change the instruction sequence is the call instruction. Unlike the jump or conditional jump instructions, the call instruction makes the processor act on instructions stored out of sequence in memory, but returns to the point following the call when it gets a return instruction. In this way the processor can execute a subroutine and then return to the point just after the call instruction. To do this, the 8088 uses the stack, an area of memory addressed by the stack segment, stack pointer pair or registers. A call instruction pushes the return address (the next instruction's address) into the memory area indicated by SP and IP, and then jumps to the memory location indicated by the call instruction for the next set of instructions. When the return instruction is encountered, the 8088 pops the return address from memory into the instruction pointer and continues reading instructions from the point right after the call. Real techies will note that the 8088 has two different call instructions and two different return instructions. A near call and near return only use the instruction pointer register, and the far call and far return use both the code segment and instruction pointer registers.

We Interrupt This Discussion...

There is one other method the 8088 uses to execute instructions elsewhere in memory than in sequential order. This is the interrupt. Like the call instruction, the interrupt instruction executes a subroutine and then returns to the next instruction in sequence, with a subtle difference. As the name interrupt implies, this instruction tells the processor to stop what it is doing right now and do something else then return to what it was doing. The call instruction tells the processor where in memory to begin executing the next set of instructions, but the interrupt instruction contains an interrupt number between 0 and 255. This number is used as an index into a special memory area called the interrupt vector table, which is always located at the beginning of memory. The interrupt vector table stores the memory address of the instructions that are executed for each of the interrupt numbers, called the interrupt service routine. When the processor receives the instruction that says "interrupt number 33," it checks the interrupt vector table in low memory for entry number 33 and begins to execute the instructions at the address stored there. The last instruction of this interrupt service routine is an interrupt return, which tells the processor to resume processing at the instruction it was previously dealing with.

There are three kinds of interrupts. The first is an interrupt generated by the processor itself, and in the 8088, these interrupts number 0 through 8. A good example is interrupt 0, which is the divide by zero interrupt. If an instruction attempts to divide by 0, which is impossible in our number system, the processor itself generates interrupt 0 and calls the routine indicated by the address stored at memory location 0. This usually prints "divide by zero" on the screen.

The second kind of interrupt is a hardware interrupt. There is a special chip on the motherboard called the interrupt controller chip that is tied directly to the processor's interrupt lines. Any device such as the keyboard, disk drive, or modem can generate an interrupt request (IRQ) to the processor. For instance, every time you press a key on the keyboard, the keyboard generates an interrupt 9 through the interrupt controller, and the CPU processes that keystroke before continuing what it was doing. It looks in the ninth entry in the interrupt vector table for the address of the keyboard service routine and then jumps to those instructions. When the keyboard service routine has finished, there is an interrupt return instruction that tells the CPU to continue what it was doing before the key was pressed.

The third method of generating an interrupt is through a software interrupt. This is just another instruction in the sequence like the add, jump, or call instruction. However, the processor looks up the address of the interrupt service routine in the interrupt vector table just as if it were a processor or hardware interrupt.

The concept of interrupts adds a great deal of flexibility to the Intel 8088 computers. All of the peripheral devices such as the keyboard, disk drive, monitor, and printer are accessed through different interrupts. If a device is added or a device is changed, the routine that services that device can be easily changed by setting the interrupt vector to point to a different place in memory.

All of the instructions which cause the processor to fetch instructions from a different area of memory are what differentiates a computer from a calculator. The Interrupt instruction, however, is what makes the PC such a versatile machine. It is the only instruction in which the new memory address is not hard coded into a program. All of the other instructions require that the program know where the next instruction is stored. The Interrupt, on the other hand, uses an area of memory to store those addresses. This means that any program can affect how other programs operate merely by changing the interrupt address in memory. It also means that viruses and other malware can change those addresses for not so legitimate purposes. Since the 8088 cannot prevent the Interrupt Vector Table from being changed, the system becomes wide open to attack.

The Deep Freeze

One of the more common causes of a system crash or freezing of the computer is when a program overwrites the memory area reserved for the interrupt vector table. If the memory locations in the interrupt vector table do not point to a section of memory with valid processor instructions, the logic of the program is interrupted. The processor begins to receive instructions from an area of memory that does not contain proper instructions, but random data that may or may not contain one of the 135 instructions the CPU can process. The result is a runaway processor, and the only recourse is a complete restart of the system. Often the interrupt generated by the keyboard is overwritten, making the Ctrl-Alt-Del reset impossible, and the only solution is to turn the power off and start again.

Hickory Dickory...

There is one other component in the PC that is important to understand, and that is the clock. One of those other chips on the motherboard is a quartz crystal oscillator that generates a pulse of electricity at a set interval. In the 8088, the clock operates at 1.44 million times per second (1.44MHz). Every time the clock ticks, the processor does something, sort of a kick in the pants to get moving. In fact, all the circuits in the PC are tied to the clock tick so that the whole system can operate in some semblance of order. Even the mouse runs up this clock. The processor does not carry out one whole instruction for each tick of the clock, just a part of the instruction. For example, take a simple "copy memory location 555 into register BX" instruction.

First, the 8088 must fetch the instruction pointed to by the CS:IP register pair. Then the address is calculated by converting the DS register and 555 into a 20-bit address. Next, the address is placed on the address bus. The memory is told to send the contents of the byte onto the data bus. Then the processor waits until the memory circuits place the data on the bus and signal that it is there. After the processor knows the data is on the bus, it is copied from the bus into the BX register. Finally, the instruction pointer register is incremented to point to the next instruction. Each of these steps takes at least one tick of the clock. To fetch one byte from memory takes at least 18 ticks of the clock in the 8088. One of the improvements in modern processors is that common instructions take fewer clock ticks.

To get a byte of data from an I/O channel, say in reading data from a disk, the processor must wait for the byte to be ready, read the byte from the I/O port into the AL register (the only register available for this operation), and then send that byte to memory. This operation takes at least 29 ticks of the clock to perform in the 8088. Because receiving and sending data between memory and the I/O ports is such a common occurrence, IBM equipped the PC with direct memory access (DMA) circuits. The DMA chips are small processors that can wait for an I/O port to signal that a byte is ready and then direct the I/O port to place that byte on the data bus while simultaneously signaling memory to read the data bus. This action takes only 5 clock ticks and leaves the 8088 out of the operation entirely. The DMA circuits can also do memory-to-memory transfers, but this operation takes almost as much time as the 8088 and is seldom used.

While talking the "Jurassic Park" of processors in examining the 8088, the principle is the same with all of the Intel processors in the family. Modern processors are much faster. An 80486 processor can complete the memory-to-register instruction in just one tick of a clock, operating up to 16 times faster than the 8088.

The clock which controls the CPU should not be mistaken for the clock which reports the system time and date. This clock, although part of the same electronic circuit, operates at a different frequency from the CPU clock. The clock which controls the system time interrupts the CPU at a set rate, and calls an interrupt service routine which updates a memory byte. Any program can examine this byte and determine the time of day based on the value stored in memory. In fact there are several software interrupts which will perform the calculations and report the time and date upon request. Many viruses use this information as a trigger for their payload as outlined in Chapter 1.

An Instruction in Software

Having a box with all this marvelous electronic hardware inside is worthless without the instructions that make it work. Every time the clock ticks, the processor fetches another instruction from the memory location pointed to by the CS:IP register pair. The instructions are the software that controls the hardware.

When the computer is turned on, the CS register contains all 1s and the IP register contains all 0s. The very first instruction is fetched from this memory location, 16 bytes from the very top of memory. At this time, all RAM contains nothing, therefore the ROM is the only source of instructions for the processor. The instructions contained in the ROM begin to start the process that tests all the circuits in the computer and begin to fill the R/W with data. This first process is referred to by the four-letter acronym *POST* (power on self-test).

When the POST is past, the built-in instructions in the ROM begin the process of loading the operating system into R/W. Disk drive 0 (which is eventually called A) spins, and the instructions in ROM direct the computer to read the very first 512 bytes on the diskette into memory. If there is no disk in the drive, or the drive does not exist, the original PC instructions jumped to the cassette basic routines that were contained in ROM. There was no hard disk available with the original PC. Today's computers attempt to read the diskette in the first disk drive and then try the hard disk if there is no diskette in the drive.

After the first 512 bytes of instructions are read into memory from the disk, the ROM instructions tell the processor to jump to the address of the first byte of those instructions. The instructions stored on the first part of the disk, called the boot sector, continue the process of loading the operating system into memory from the disk. The disk operating system, called DOS, consists of the basic instructions that make the computer go and help other programs access the input and output devices. DOS is always in memory, interpreting keyboard commands, reading and writing data to and from devices, and managing memory usage.

Memory Police

All computers have an operating system. On mainframe computers, the operating system sets priorities as to which users and which programs can do what. Users are restricted as to which files they can access and what areas of memory are available. Often many users or many programs are running all at once without interfering with one another. DOS, however, is designed as a single-user system and offers no file or memory protection.

In the DOS system, if a program says "read the file containing secret data into memory and display it on the screen," DOS does it. If a program says "change the memory area that controls the DOS functions so I can get control first," DOS does it. DOS is an equal opportunity employer, giving every program it runs an equal opportunity to employ DOS to screw things up. However, any protection DOS might use is limited by the hardware design. While DOS assigns memory to a program, it contains no police function, and a program is free to alter memory anywhere in the system. Because all memory is accessible to any program, any controls that DOS might put in place could be easily bypassed.

What is needed for security is a "memory police" for the PC. To a certain extent, the newer processors in the Intel line are set up with circuits that act as memory police. The concept of privilege level is borrowed from mainframes and minicomputers. Only programs that run at the highest privilege level can access the total range of memory. Programs and processes at lower privilege levels can only access certain assigned areas of memory and I/O channels. Naturally, only processes with the highest privilege level can grant a higher privilege level to other processes.

The Intel processors 80x86, where *x* is a 2, 3, or 4, as well as the Pentium (which should be the 80586), can all operate in what is called *protected mode*. In these more sophisticated processors, addresses in the registers no longer contain the physical address of memory. Instead of addresses, programs use selectors that are converted into physical addresses by the processor. In conjunction with the proper operating system, any program that attempts to select an address outside of a specific range is denied access. By using selectors instead of actual memory addresses, the hardware can protect the memory locations that contain processor instructions. This code area can be isolated from data area so that a program cannot make changes to it. Such protection of specific memory areas can go a long way to preventing the type of activity used by certain viruses. Therefore, in protected mode, the processor provides hardware-specific privileges to a user or program. An operating system that uses this concept of privilege levels can also deny access to certain functions and to certain files. Naturally, any function that would change the operating system and the way it grants privileges would be prohibited to any process except those operating at the highest level. Unless a user can attain access to the computer using the highest privilege level, he or she can be locked out of certain areas including the areas that grant access.

For compatibility with the older 8088/8086 processors, the 80286 and above processors can also operate in real mode, which more or less mimics the 8086 and allows complete access to the first megabyte of memory. When the processor is initialized at power on, it operates in real mode. Only under software control does it switch into protected mode. All versions of DOS up to this writing have operated the processors in real mode and only switch to protected mode to take advantage of the extra memory above the 1M limit. The combination of DOS and the real mode of the processors does not lend itself to providing the user with a secure computer. Additionally, any operating system that provides compatibility with DOS files can leave the system open to security breaches by allowing the files to be accessed by a restart from a DOS-bootable disk in drive A.

The problem with security (and several other issues) goes way back to IBM's original vision of the PC. While IBM was certainly foresighted in the design of the PC in allowing for expansion of not only the hardware but the software as well, they certainly did not envision the uses for the PC that users want today. The original thought that the PC would be for home use by one user only, made incorporating the security that was implemented in most mainframes and minicomputers unnecessary. The fact that the PC now has the speed, memory, and processing power to act as a multitasking, multi-user workstation was not considered when the standards were produced. The PC still is basically a one-user, one-task machine.

Integrated Circuits

That's a lot of really technical stuff. But the virus and security problem of PCs leads right back to the chips on the motherboard. To try to design a solution without a thorough knowledge of the inner workings of your computer can lead you to accept on faith the word of the so called experts. There are snake oil salesmen all around you promising the "perfect" solution to the virus and security problems with your system.

Now you know what happens, why it happens, and what could happen when things don't work the way they are supposed to. There are no perfect solutions to all the ills that can befall us, whether from hardware or software. At least not yet. Knowledge is power. The more you understand the inner workings of your PC and its processes, the better prepared you are to integrate yourself in the solution process.

A Look at Microsoft Anti-Virus

With the introduction of DOS 6.0, Microsoft Corporation took a giant step that many industry observers would have believed impossible only a few short years ago: including an antivirus program, Microsoft Anti-Virus (MSAV), in the package with the operating system software.

Even though IBM had developed an antivirus product years before, Microsoft did not acknowledge the existence of viruses (or the weaknesses of the operating system that enabled them to flourish on the platform) until the release of DOS 6.0.

MSAV is a slightly pared down version of the Central Point product, Central Point Anti-Virus (CPAV). Though the details of the agreement between Central Point and Microsoft are foggy, it's clear that as poorly as the Central Point product performs in testing, the Microsoft product is worse.

Test Results?

A Dutch publication, *Personal Computer Magazine*, performed a test in November 1993. The magazine assembled a large test bank (11,383 infected files—not 11,383 different viruses) with the assistance of the Dutch Virus Strategy Group (VSG) a collaboration of researchers, government installations, and private companies.

Products were tested in three categories: normal viruses (.COM and .EXE infectors, which were all at least one year old); new viruses, less than a year old; and 40 different polymorphic-type viruses using about 5,000 different replicants of them.

Table 11.1 Test results

Antivirus program	Normal	New	Poly
Thunderbyte TBAV 6.05	99	99	99
Sophos Vaccine 4.38	97.9	83	88.4
F-Prot Pro 2.09	98	85.6	83
McAfee Viruscan - VShield 106	94.1	60.5	92.1
Dr. Solomon's Tool Kit 6.54	96.7	61.3	62.9
Vaccine Professional 1.21	94.5	40.9	74
IBM Antivirus 1.03	92.9	61.5	47.7
Norton Antivirus	71.5	20	40
Microsoft Anti-virus	70	19.8	27

The magazine reported that Central Point Anti-Virus crashed on a significant number of viruses and was not included in the final test results. Thus, at least once MSAV outscored its parent, CPAV.

N O T E

It doesn't take a rocket scientist to determine that MSAV is at the bottom of the list in all three categories. In fairness, it should be pointed out that no memory-resident capabilities were tested and that for practical reasons no boot sector infectors were tested. It seems that Microsoft took an already poor product (CPAV) and made it even worse.

A simple hit test (you might want to say efficacy test) is only a single indicator of the performance of a product. An in-depth analysis of an individual product is time-consuming, tedious, and requires a great deal of technical skill and knowledge.

A Real Technical Review of Microsoft Anti-Virus

Last spring, Yisrael Radai, a virus specialist at the Computation Center of the Hebrew University in Jerusalem, prepared a broad-based technical review of MSAV, part of which follows in digested form. (Radai is known throughout the antivirus community for his initial work with the Jerusalem virus and his continuing outstanding efforts in the field.) The complete review is included in Appendix B.

Testing Conclusions

- **Known virus scanning**: This part of the software scores lower than most other scanners in speed and at or near the bottom of nearly every comparison in terms of percentage of viruses detected. For example, according to the VSUM certification of October 31, 1993, MSAV detects 48.7% (last place in a field of eleven, in which the leader detected 95.5%). Moreover, it cannot detect viruses within compressed executables. Updates of scan patterns and disinfection procedures are available, but probably very few users of MS-DOS 6 will bother obtaining them because of the inconvenience and expense.

- **Generic monitoring**: VSafe has eight optional types of generic monitoring and supplies them in a manner that is more flexible than most other programs of this type. However, there is considerable room for improvement in some of the monitoring capabilities. Some viral tricks (e.g., companion viruses or viruses that rename, infect, and restore the names of the executables) are completely undetectable by VSafe. Further more, the monitoring can be completely disabled by loading certain values into certain registers and calling a certain interrupt, and there are already some viruses that do this.

- **Integrity checking:** There is no integrity checking on boot sectors or the master boot record, hence an unknown boot-record infector will not be caught. On files, the integrity checking can be bypassed by deleting the checksum database (as several existing viruses do) or by modifying only parts of the file beyond the first 63 bytes and preserving the file length. It does not detect companion viruses. The checksum algorithm is not key dependent, hence for any given file all users will have the same checksum; this could be exploited to forge checksums. The decision to maintain a separate database for each directory is a poor one, because it not only wastes disk space, but also greatly hinders the blocking of some of the security holes.

- **Default options:** Some are poorly chosen, namely Anti-Stealth is set off and Check All Files is set on.

- **Conflicts with other anti-viral software:** Scan patterns containing wildcards are not encrypted, causing "ghost positives" when other scanners scan memory after MSAV or VSafe has been activated. No other widely-used scanner (except CPAV) fails to take some measure to prevent such false alarms.

- **General conclusions:** One of the things that differentiates a good antivirus program from a mediocre one is whether the developers try to predict what types of tricks a virus writer might use to bypass the product's protection. Software should be modified accordingly to provide the most secure product possible. Some developers have done this, but it is evident that the developers of MSAV/VSafe have made very little effort in this direction.

Because of its many security holes and the fact that the Microsoft software will probably become the *de facto* standard, virus writers will probably turn more and more to writing new viruses that target specific weaknesses of the generic part of the software.

Will the software be modified to correct these problems? Probably yes, for minor bugs. However, blocking some of the security holes would require such a radical redesign of the whole system that it seems highly unlikely. If past experience is an indicator, even the problems with less drastic solutions will take years to be corrected, if at all.

As an example, people complained for years that the developers did not bother to encrypt the scan strings in CPAV and VSafe. Thus, when running another scanning program after CPAV was run or when VSafe was active, the scanner would find those strings (or parts of them) in memory buffers or in the CPAV.EXE and VSAFE.EXE files themselves, producing false alarms. The problem was apparently partially fixed a year or two ago, but it took far too long for even this partial correction to be made.

Despite suggestions to Microsoft that it include validation or protection as part of the operating system, it has chosen, instead, to utilize add-on software. True, many people who purchase DOS 6.0 may now install antivirus software for the first time, however, they will be under the false impression that they are protected.

Is It Better Than Nothing?

There's a compelling argument to be made that any product that reliably catches the 20 or 30 most common viruses is good enough. Unfortunately, neither CPAV nor MSAV reliably catches certain common viruses. There's an equally compelling argument that a product with Microsoft's name attached will be assumed by the general public to be the finest product available, thus leading to a false sense of security.

Although *PC Magazine* rated CPAV, along with Norton Anti-Virus (NAV), as Editor's Choice, professional testing groups have shown the effective performance of CPAV to be seriously flawed as compared with other products. (Its usual rating is below the top ten for efficacy.)

A Major Failing

Every careful computer user knows to scan incoming diskettes for possible viruses before using the disk or installing its contents on a PC. Every careful computer user ought to know that it makes no sense to install an antivirus product on a PC that's not believed to be clean.

Strangely, Microsoft has chosen not to include a scan of the target hard drive as part of the MSAV installation process. Thus, the unwary user could install the program on a PC with a virus already active. The first time MSAV is run, it could become infected itself, possibly with a virus like Satan Bug which is designed to disable MSAV. But it gets better. A truly clever virus would not only infect MSAV to make it ineffective, it would also drop a boot sector infector onto every diskette scanned by MSAV.

So, to be practical, one should scan both the Microsoft distribution diskette and the PC's hard drive with another product before installing MSAV. And, because it's almost impossible to get your hands on a product that's not quantifiably superior to MSAV, why not continue to use that product and leave MSAV on the shelf?

A Lawyer's Dream?

The following article, researched and written by the author of this book, appeared in the Spring '93 issue of *Information Security News*. It sheds some light on the possible pickle Microsoft could find itself in.

FORBES magazine has recently declared Bill Gates, President of Microsoft Corporation, to be the richest man in America. At just about the same time, beta versions of Microsoft's DOS 6.0—including an antivirus product—were released into the testing community.

Within hours, if not days, of the first copies of DOS 6.0 reaching the hands of Microsoft's beta testers, 6.0 was in the hands of lots of other people, too. DOS 6.0 is a heavy download favorite on pirate bulletin board systems around the world. A flotilla of new viruses have appeared that directly target Microsoft Anti-Virus, disable it, insert a new virus in the space that's been cleared, and leave the user none the wiser. Some particularly charitable virus writers are even posting recipes on how to "crack" MSAV on underground -boards.

Early testing of Microsoft Anti-Virus finds little difference from its parent program, Central Point Anti-Virus, which reliably scores near the bottom in scanning efficiency and is considered by many industry experts to be a seriously flawed product. The most current VSUM certification results, dated October 23, 1992, show Central Point at 67.2% against a library of 1,509 viruses. The product was third from the bottom in a field of 18.

If a thoughtful observer puts a few factors together: Bill Gates' obvious personal wealth, the stature of Microsoft as virtually the only provider of operating systems for most PCs, the proliferation of new computer viruses that can't be trapped by most existing antivirus technology, the direct targeting of Microsoft Anti-Virus, the known lacks in the parent program, and the litigious nature of Americans in general, there's a strong temptation to send Mr. Gates an ancient Credence Clearwater Revival album and suggest he listen, carefully, to "I See A Bad Moon A'Rising."

What kind of nasty weather could be on the horizon for Microsoft? A user who gets a computer virus after installing DOS 6.0 and Microsoft Anti-Virus just might figure, "Bill Gates. Microsoft. Deep Pocket. Litigation."

With the help of a real Philadelphia lawyer, Benjamin Reich of Lightman and Associates, a series of theories and questions were developed and presented to four of the country's leading attorneys who specialize in the emerging law surrounding computer crime and liability. Two main theories quickly sorted out.

First, through advertising or offering a product for sale, Microsoft makes certain warranties, express or implied, that the product is "fit" for the purpose of its intended use. What if it's not? That's covered by the law of contracts. Second, if a product is known to be unreasonably dangerous and likely to cause damage to its consumer, liability could result. This area is covered by the law of torts. The burning question, and the one upon which any eventual litigation might be based, is whether a vendor knows—or should have known—that either the product wasn't fit for its intended (and advertised) purpose or was unreasonably dangerous. The vendor's knowledge is key, regardless of whether a suit might be brought based in either of the legal theories, contracts or torts.

Jean Pechette, a partner at Gordon & Glickson in Chicago, sees both theories as possible. "If a product is defective and the vendor reasonably should have known it, and the customer can show that losses were reasonably foreseeable to the vendor, or if the vendor makes false or misleading warranties, the vendor might be faced with liability under a number of tort and statute-based theories as well as traditional breach of contract and Uniform Commercial Code theories. With Microsoft as the 'deep pocket,' this case is a plaintiff's lawyer's dream." Pechette specializes in high-tech litigation; her firm sponsored the Illinois Anti-Virus Act (January 1, 1990) which deals specifically with computer viruses.

Reich prefers the theory known as "strict liability in tort." He cites the example of the exploding Ford Pinto automobile as an example of an "unreasonably dangerous" product. "If Microsoft releases DOS with antivirus software which is already known to be vulnerable to certain forms of virus attack, and there are other forms of virus protection which are either less vulnerable or invulnerable, then it follows that Microsoft Anti-Virus is unreasonably dangerous.

It would be unreasonably dangerous for two reasons, Reich theorized. "Since it would not be 'state of the art' and since it would invite virus attacks on a user's computer which would take advantage of known vulnerabilities, just as UNIX's vulnerabilities invited the attack by Robert Morris."

Mark Rasch, who prosecuted Robert Tappan Morris in the Internet litigation, now an Associate with Arent, Fox, Kintner, Plotkin and Khan in Washington, admits the attractiveness of litigation against Microsoft. "There would certainly be a strong incentive—not only by users of Microsoft's anti-viral products, but also by persons affected by computers using them, to attempt to go after Microsoft—as the deep pocket.

"If the use of the anti-viral software in the new release of DOS has the effect of making computers *more* vulnerable to attack rather than more secure, a court could find them liable for breach of contract, breach of express or implied warranties of fitness and intended use and merchantability as well as for negligence and strict product liability."

Boston's Lee Gesmer, a partner in Lucash, Gesmer and Updegrove, specializes in representation of high technology companies. He argued the conservative side by putting forth four defenses that Microsoft might employ. First, a vendor can disclaim all warranties in their standard software license agreement. Second, under the Uniform Commercial Code, vendors can limit their liability to "repair and replacement" of defective software. Third, strict liability (for damages) usually only applies to personal injury, not damage to property. Fourth, the harm that might come to a user is not caused by the software, it's caused by the malicious intent of a third party (the virus writer).

Vincent Amberly, a partner at Mason, Fenwick and Lawrence in Washington, DC, and the former Program Advisor for the Deceptive Practices Program at the Federal Trade Commission takes still another view. "A company such as Microsoft which has developed a good reputation for knowledge of the computer industry could likely be held to a higher standard of computer knowledge than a typical new start-up company."

Amberly suggests that Microsoft be mighty careful in their advertising of Microsoft Anti-Virus. "If Microsoft's advertising contains blatant misrepresentations, it could be a classic case of deceptive advertising claims and actionable under the federal law. If, as Reich posits, "There's one thing certain, there will be litigation," there's less certainty about how things will come out.

Computer law is in its infancy; this could be a case—or series of cases—that not only the plaintiffs who stand to benefit from Microsoft's deep pocket but their attorneys who stand to blaze new legal paths could find very compelling. Mark Rasch draws a practical conclusion. "Ultimately, the question will lie with a court or jury."

If this article showed nothing else, it showed that four lawyers had four very different ideas about the same subject

A Self-Fulfilling Prophecy?

In October of 1993, just a few months after Microsoft Anti-Virus was released, the following message went out from Microsoft to the users of DOS 6 and, presumably, MSAV:

If you were one of the people who ordered the DOS Anti-Virus Update offered with the Microsoft MS-DOS 6.0 update, Sydex feels there is something you should know.

Version 1.1 of the DOS Anti-Virus Update (MSAV) erroneously identifies CopyQM versions 3.00 through 3.05 as containing the "Virus Cruncher" virus and specifies that the files COPYQM.COM, CQMENU and VIEWCONF.COM should be deleted. These files, as distributed by Sydex, DO NOT CONTAIN THE INDICATED VIRUS.

The "Cruncher" virus is, in fact, a legitimate virus, having surfaced in the Netherlands sometime around June, 1993.

As far as Sydex has been able to determine, the false virus indication arises from Sydex's use of Teddy Matsumoto's DIET executable file compressor, which is a public domain compressor similar in function to PKWare's PKLITE or François Bellaard's LZEXE
compressors.

Both DIET and the relevant versions of CopyQM were in wide
circulation long before the emergence of the "Cruncher" virus.

MSAV and its updates are produced by Central Point Software,
not Microsoft. Sydex contacted Central Point and reported the problem in August [1993] after the indication was reported to us
[Microsoft] by a user of both CopyQM and MSAV. Central Point, for
its part, ignored our letters and so we were forced to turn the matter
over to our attorney. At this time, Central Point has acknowledged to
Sydex that a false indication is produced by MSAV 1.1 and that the
subsequent update, MSAV 1.2, does not produce the indication.
However, Central Point has not notified MSAV 1.1 customers about
the false indication of the "Virus Cruncher" virus in CopyQM.
Microsoft investigated the situation and confirms that MSAV 1.1 produced false virus indications of CopyQM.

It is noteworthy that none of the other leading virus detectors
tested by Sydex committed the same error, even though several of
them do recognize the "Cruncher" virus.

Sydex obviously does not benefit from the accusation of virus
infection made by MSAV 1.1. The issue of damage to Sydex's reputation still needs to be resolved between Central Point Software,
Microsoft and Sydex.

It's interesting to see how quickly Microsoft moved to distance itself as far as
possible from responsibility for the false positive on CopyQM. Note, particularly, the disclaimer that MSAV is produced by Central Point Software, not
Microsoft. It's safe to assume that Sydex's legal counsel are dancing in the
streets at the prospect of both Microsoft and Central Point Software as defen-
dants in a damage suit.

A Developer's Nightmare

Truth is, sometimes, stranger than fiction. The following fictionalized scenario, based on persistent rumors within the industry (as well as a firm fact trail chased down by one of the most respected researchers in the world), should make any developer shiver in its corporate boots:

1. X was a university student and a member of a class directed to write replicating code.

2. X's father owned a PC store. X used one of father's store PCs to test code.

3. Father's clients began to experience problems that were caused by X's project virus, ZAPOID.

4. Source of original ZAPOID infection, which quickly spread around the world, was father's store and the university computers.

5. Son goes into his father's business, and business becomes an antivirus product developer.

6. A major software company purchases the technology from X and father. Soon, another major software company licenses the technology and distributes a version of the product with its own proprietary products.

Balancing Act

Perhaps the kindest thing to be said about MSAV is that it's worth exactly what a user pays for it...theoretically, nothing. If including MSAV with DOS 6 does nothing more than put Microsoft's validation of the virus problem on record and raise user awareness, then perhaps its mere existence can be seen as a service to the public. It's obvious from the Sydex incident that Microsoft doesn't want to have much to do with MSAV. Smart users shouldn't either.

Three types of Antivirus Program:-

① Virus scanner

Do Antivirus Programs Work?

A nyone trying to sell you an antivirus program will insist, often in very expensive four-color ads in national publications, that antivirus products do, indeed, work. Never mind that. As seen elsewhere in this book, the products with the largest advertising budgets are often the poorest performers.

It's not like the Abraham Lincoln maxim of finding all of the viruses some of the time, some of the viruses all of the time. What it comes down to is that antivirus products work in different ways and that some of them work better than others. However, none of them can find all of the viruses all of the time.

At this time there are three types of antivirus programs in widespread use. By far the most popular are the virus scanners, programs that look for a particular virus in a file or in the boot sector. Integrity checkers, like the PANDA Systems PHYSICAL included with this book, attempt to detect changes in a file that indicate the presence of a virus. Behavior blocker's, such as TSRMON and MONITOR, which are also included with this book, attempt to prevent destructive or potentially destructive virus activity.

All three antivirus methods have pluses and minuses. Taken alone, each approach is inadequate. Used together, all three approaches provide adequate but not complete security from viruses. No system has yet been devised that will provide absolute protection on a PC platform. Because of the nature of the PC, it is doubtful that one solution can be devised.

In this chapter, you will see references to the Galactic Avenger III virus. There is no such thing (yet). This virus will be used as a generic virus for discussion purposes only and has no relationship to any actual virus.

Scanners

A scanning antivirus program attempts to find a virus by identifying a series of bytes in a file unique to that particular virus. This series of bytes is often called the virus signature, but antivirus researchers refer to this series as the scan string. The signature is also a series of bytes unique to a particular virus, but not necessarily the series of bytes for which a particular antivirus scanner searches. In this discussion, the signature is considered to be the scan string.

There is no one right way to write an antivirus scanner, but there are an infinite number of wrong ways. The only certain criteria are the following:

1. The scanner must report *every* incidence of a virus that is present.
2. The scanner must *never* report a virus if the virus is not present.
3. The scanner must be able to identify *every* virus.

Failure in any one of these criteria leaves the system open to virus attack. How these criteria are met is up to the programmer or programming team responsible for the antivirus scanner.

Perhaps it should be added that the antivirus product must meet the criteria not only in the testing suite but also in the field. If, for instance, the Galactic Avenger III virus is known to be in the testing file GALAVG3.EXE, a simple directory search for that file name would reliably find that particular virus when the antivirus scanner was run against the test suite. However, the scanner would fail miserably in the field.

Search Strings

Scanner programmers must develop a specific scan string for each and every virus. Therefore, they need access to either an actual sample of the virus or to a scan string developed by an independent researcher. In both cases someone must analyze the virus' instruction code and data areas and find something that is absolutely unique to that particular strain of virus.

The scan string of a virus is a series of values that appears in no other file except an infected file. The string does not necessarily have to be of consecutive bytes nor does the signature have to be only one series of bytes. Furthermore, the signature string may be a series of bytes found at a certain point in the infected file, adding location as a parameter to value.

A scan string should also be an area of code that cannot be easily modified. Targeted alteration of a virus is a real problem in the field. If a scanner gains widespread popularity, it becomes the target of those seeking to counter the capability of a scanner to detect a particular virus. If the signature code can be altered to accomplish the same function as before, the scanner will not be able to identify the altered virus. Technically, the modification will be a new strain of the virus, and a new signature will be needed to identify it. Consider the following code section from Galactic Avenger III, which was chosen by GrottyWare as a scan string:

```
MOV       BX,CS
PUSH      DS
MOV       DS,BX
MOV       ES,BX
```

The values (in hex) of this section are 8c cb 1e 8e db 8e cb.

This string of instructions occurs 57 bytes from the GAIII entry point and might be considered a signature. However, there are several ways to write the instructions, for example:

```
PUSH      DS
MOV       BX,CS
MOV       DS,BX
MOV       ES,BX
```

Now the hex values are 1e 8c cb 8e db 8e cb.

The string is still seven bytes long and accomplishes the same function—loading all the segment registers with the CS value—but a direct comparison of the bytes will fail. If the scanner is sophisticated enough, it will look for these seven bytes in any order 57 bytes into the file. Therefore, even the following rearrangement would be flagged as a signature:

```
PUSH        DS
MOV         BX,CS
MOV         ES,BX
MOV         DS,BX
```

The signature would now contain the hex string 1e 8c cb 8e cb 8e db. These are still the same seven values, but in a slightly different order. What happens if different registers are used?

```
PUSH        DS
MOV         AX,CS
MOV         ES,AX
MOV         DS,AX
```

Now the signature values are 1e 8c c8 8e c0 8e d8. Only four of the seven bytes are the same, and these could be in any order.

The proposed signature seems to be inadequate due to the ease of modification, but a closer look at the instruction set could help the situation.

The purpose of the code is clear. The contents of the DS register must be pushed on the stack and the value of the CS register transferred to the DS and ES registers. The instruction 1e must appear somewhere in the seven bytes and must be before the DS register is loaded with the new value.

The instructions must contain three MOVs, one from a segment register and two to a segment register. The register-to-register MOV instruction is two bytes long. The first byte is binary 100011d0. The third bit of the first byte of the MOV instruction contains the direction flag. If the bit is set, it is from a segment register; if it is cleared, it is to a segment register. Therefore, the values of the first byte can be either 8c or 8e. In the example, there must be one 8c (from segment register) and two 8e (to segment register) values. The byte following the 8c must contain the three-bit code for the CS register. The first three bits of the second byte contain the destination register and can be any value. The next three bits (bits 3, 4, and 5) are set to 001 to indicate the CS register. Bits 6 and 7 are both set to indicate that the MOV instruction is from register to register. The register chosen as the destination (lower three bits) becomes the source register for the two move to segment register instructions (bits 3, 4, and 5). The lower three bits indicate the destination register (000 for ES and 011 for DS). Therefore, the byte following 8e will be binary 11xxx000 or binary 11xxx110, where *xxx* is the register value found in the MOV *rr*,CS instruction.

Using a class of instructions rather than actual instructions makes the signature less likely to be modified and missed by the scanner, but it is not 100 percent foolproof, as shown in the following code fragment:

```
PUSH        DS
PUSH        CS
POP         DS
PUSH        DS
POP         ES
NOP
NOP
```

This translates into 7 hex bytes as 1e 0e 1f 1e 07 90 90.

The function performed is exactly the same as the string found in GAIII, but even a careful scan as outlined above would fail to find the signature. The virus would be missed by the scanner if someone were to alter the code in this manner, although the basic functions of the virus would be unaltered.

If this alteration of the virus code were not in the signature section, the scanner would continue to identify the virus as GAIII because alteration outside the signature has no effect on identification. If all antivirus scanners used the exact same signature and signature identification method for a particular virus, any rearrangement of the signature code would lead researchers to label the resulting virus as a new strain, perhaps GAIV. In reality, all scanners use different methods of signature checking, and an alteration as described above would be targeted to only one scanner. Because the targeted scanner would be forced to issue a new release to catch the modification, the programmers must make a decision.

The altered virus is essentially the same as the original, but the targeted scanner will not identify it. The choice for the company is to either search for another area in the code to flag as the signature or keep the original signature which will identify all unaltered occurrences of the virus and add another signature to the scan to identify the modified virus. This is a choice that could be affected by marketing decisions. The competition can identify either version of the virus as GAIII because the signature they use lies outside the altered code. Therefore, the targeted company can issue a new release of the scanner that differentiates between the two versions of the same virus and claim to identify 1,239 viruses whereas the competition can identify only 1,238.

False Positives

Finding a string of values that cannot be easily altered without destroying the function of the virus is only part of the battle. If the scanner chose the signature of the GAIII virus as the instruction PUSH DS, hex 1e, it would probably find that instruction 100 percent of the time. There is also a high probability that it would find that common instruction in every executable file! It would be almost the same as printing a directory of the disk and identifying every file as being infected with GAIII. Every incidence of GAIII would be reported without fail. Does this make the scanner 100 percent reliable?

Naturally, the scanner must identify the signature only in infected files and issue no false positives. What are the chances that a particular set of instructions used as a virus signature appears in a legitimate program? If machine instructions were merely a random series of byte values between 0 and 255, it would be easy to calculate the odds of one value following another (1 in 256). A statistician could calculate the odds of any number of consecutive identical bytes appearing in two different files. The larger the number of bytes, the more the odds would approach zero. That same statistician would also caution that, although the odds approach zero, they can never be zero.

Of course, machine instructions are not random values. There is a certain logic behind programming. There is a greater probability that a MOV instruction will appear in a program than a JNO (jump no overflow) instruction. There is also a high probability that the PUSH BP instruction is followed by MOV BP,SP because those instructions are commonly used by compilers to set a stack frame for local variables. Therefore, the odds of one value following another varies and in some cases may be higher than purely random chance while in other cases lower. Identifying a virus signature requires that the values chosen have the lowest possible odds of following one another. The odds can be made even lower that the signature will appear in a noninfected file by choosing a string that appears at a specific location within the virus code. Statistically speaking, however, there can never be a signature string that is 100 percent unique. Because there are a finite, although large number of program files, 99.9 percent may be good enough for practical purposes.

The only way to be sure that a signature will not trigger a false positive in a legitimate program is to test the scanner against them all. Think of the hard disk that could contain a copy of every program ever written for the PC! Obviously, the scanner companies must rely on reports from the field for false reports. Unfortunately, if a company's product sounds a false alarm when scanned by antivirus software, the user often blames the company for sending him an infected disk. The company may go out of business and be under indictment before a false alarm is suspected.

Missed Positives

The third criterion for virus scanners is to identify every virus. Most scanner companies would add the word *known* after *every*, but this is of little consolation to the user who is infected by the unknown virus. The result is that the computer is infected.

Most computer infections are caused by a small number of well-known viruses. The famous 80/20 rule can apply in that more than 80 percent of the infections are caused by less than 20 percent of the viruses. Therefore, testing only for known viruses may be adequate in most cases. A scanner that does not know the second strain of Galactic Avenger III is just as good as one that does because GAIII exists only in the imagination of this author. The odds of an infection of GAIII are zero, and a scanner that did not check for this virus would still be 100 percent accurate. However, a scanner that does not know about the Jerusalem virus would certainly be of lesser value even if it could identify all versions of GAIII. If the odds of a given PC being infected by Jerusalem are 100,000 to 1, then the scanner would be accurate 99,999 times out of 100,000 or 99.999 percent of the time. Of course, the system that did not use the scanner would also be clean of Jerusalem 99.999 percent of the time.

Another common cause of missed positives for virus scanners is the mutating virus. In Chapter 1, you will find a full discussion of mutating viruses. Because a mutating virus looks different in every generation, it is almost impossible for a scanner to develop a specific signature. There are a few bytes of virus code that must not be mutated to decode the remainder of the virus. It is this section for which scanners must develop a search string if they are to have any hope of identifying the virus. Some mutating viruses even alter this part of the code with each generation by adding or subtracting nonfunctional instructions.

Integrity Checkers

Integrity checking antivirus programs are designed to detect changes in files brought about by virus activity. There are several advantages that integrity checkers have over scanners in identifying a virus attack, but there are some disadvantages as well.

Integrity checking involves making a calculation of the state of a program file before it is infected and warning the user when the state of the program file changes. The one obvious disadvantage is that a virus must be active before an integrity checker notices the change. Scanners, of course, indicate the presence of a virus before any infection can take place. On the other hand, integrity checkers do not have to know about a particular virus and are less prone to missing one.

Integrity checkers use several methods to test the validity of a program file. Most have one or more data files associated with them that store some sort of signature of the file. The contents of this signature vary depending on the antivirus program. Some store just the file length and time and date stamps. Other schemes involve a checksum of the file or a more complicated cyclical redundancy check of the contents of the program file. Whichever method is used, the signature of the program is stored so that the integrity checker can periodically compare the stored signature with the current signature. If there is a difference, the user is notified.

Integrity checking antivirus programs come in two flavors. A stand-alone program makes a check of the integrity of the files only upon request when the antivirus program is run. A resident checker can check the integrity of a file every time the file is accessed. If the stand-alone program is not used often, a virus could infect many files before such activity is noticed. A resident checker, however, can notify the user the first time a file is changed, so that a virus infection can be halted immediately.

False Alarms

There are several conditions that can raise false alarms when checking the integrity of a program. The most obvious is an upgrade to existing software. Obviously, a new version of the software will have a different signature than the existing one. If the integrity checker is not aware that the software has been deliberately changed, it will report the change.

Some programs have the capability to self-configure. While the latest programming practice is for a program to read a configuration file, some programs still modify the executable according to the user's configuration desires. If the executable file is changed, an integrity checker will probably flag it.

Resident integrity checkers can often be programmed to deal with legitimate activity such as self-modifying programs and new version installation. This reduces or eliminates this type of false alarm.

How the change is reported depends on the antivirus package. Some indicate that a virus is in the system, while others only indicate that the program has changed since the last time it was checked. An even kinder program may query the user about any deliberate changes before screaming about a virus attack.

Missed Positives

Integrity checkers are much less subject to missed positives than scanners with one very notable exception: a previously infected file. Because the integrity scanner looks for changes in the program file, a previously infected program will not be changed by an attached virus. Some may say that integrity scanning is akin to aiming a revolver at your foot and pulling the trigger to see if it's loaded. Actually, it's more like aiming at plastic ducks in a shooting gallery that uses mostly blanks. If the duck is hit, you replace it with a new duck and throw away the gun. This analogy assumes that the integrity checker is resident and checks the duck after every shot. If the integrity checker is not used on a regular basis, you must think of a whole line of shooters in a gallery. One has a loaded gun and mows down a raft of ducks. The ducks are easily replaced from the new duck shelf, but which shooter has the loaded gun? Depending on the integrity checker, you may not know and may have to do some investigating.

Consider the same analogy with a scanner or no antivirus software at all. If a scanner misses a virus or the files are never checked, you would never know that the ducks are being hit until one day the gallery does not open for business because they have run out of ducks.

Mutating viruses have no effect on integrity checkers. Unlike with scanners, it does not matter what the virus looks like. The only criterion is that the program file changes. A mutating virus may change each host file differently, but as long as the file is changed integrity checkers can spot it.

Targeted Attacks

Integrity checkers are potentially as subject to targeted attacks as scanners, but the attacks take a great deal more skill than just altering a few bytes of the scan string. A virus could be written so that the signature of the program with the virus code added would remain the same for a particular integrity check. Of course, whoever wrote the virus would have to know how the integrity checker calculates the signature and program the virus accordingly. By the beginning of 1994, there were no viruses that attempted to fool integrity checkers in this manner.

A more practical approach might be a virus that alters the data file associated with a certain brand of integrity checker. There are several viruses that attempt to do this. The Antimon and PandaFlu viruses are two viruses that attempt to disable PANDA System antivirus software. The following list was supplied by antivirus researcher Vesselin Bontchev of the University of Hamburg:

- The Tequila virus removes the checksum added to the files by McAfee Associates' Scan product.
- The Encroacher virus deletes the files with checksums created by Central Point Anti-Virus (CHKLIST.CPS).
- The Satan_Bug virus removes the checksums added by McAfee Associates' Scan and disables the immunization modules added by Central Point Anti-Virus.
- The Peach virus deletes the Central Point Anti-Virus CHKLIST.CPS file.
- The Groove virus deletes the databases of signatures created by several products, including Norton Anti-Virus, NOVI, Central Point Anti-Virus, FindVirus, Untouchable, and ViruSafe.

Besides these, there are certainly many others. The easiest way for an antivirus developer to counter a directed attack on the data file is to enable the user to specify the name of the file. This prevents a virus from searching for a specific name. PANDA Systems is one of the few antivirus developers who give the user such control.

Since the introduction of MS-DOS 6.0, Microsoft has included Microsoft Anti-Virus (MSAV) with DOS. This program is in reality a stripped-down version of Central Point Anti-Virus (CPAV). In the opinion of more than one antivirus researcher (those without a product to sell), CPAV rates near the bottom of tested antivirus programs. MSAV not only inherits the low rating of CPAV, but became a virus target even during the beta (test) versions of DOS 6.0. Before MS-DOS 6.0 even hit the market, there were viruses that could disable its features. Because it becomes the de facto standard by being included with DOS, more and more viruses are targeting this particular antivirus product.

A virus has no control over the environment of the host computer. Therefore, a targeted attack on one particular integrity checker would have no effect in environments where that particular checker was not used or where another type of antivirus program was installed.

A generic approach to fooling integrity checkers (as well as scanners) is through stealth. In Chapter 1, you will find a full discussion of stealth techniques. However, even the most clever stealth virus can be defeated if the user starts the computer from a known noninfected DOS diskette after turning the power off for several seconds.

Heuristics

If it walks like a duck, quacks like a duck, and swims like a duck, it's probably a duck. That may be the best way to describe the latest tact being taken by antivirus programs. Heuristics is an attempt to identify a virus by examining what a program might do. Integrity checkers point out what a virus has done. Scanners can identify viruses by a known signature or scan string.

Heuristics is an attempt by antivirus programmers to look at a program file and, without actually executing the program code, see if the program might contain a virus. This may sound like it's done with smoke and mirrors, but with so many viruses in existence it has become fairly easy to see what techniques viruses use to infect other files. Heuristics is an attempt to examine the code for these techniques and flag the file as suspicious before it is run. The drawback to this technique is the large number of false positives that can be generated by legitimate programs and the number of missed positives on truly innovative viruses. Therefore, heuristics is not the total answer, but just one more step in the battle against viruses.

Eradication

Disinfection of files and eradication of viruses are often a part of antivirus scanners, but are seldom included with integrity checkers. For a disinfecting program to work, the programmers must first have an absolute identification of the infecting virus. Presumably, the programmers know how a virus such as Galactic Avenger III works and how much code it has added to the host file and where it was added. It is a simple matter to reverse the process of infection, leaving the host program clean.

All DOS users already possess a powerful program than can quickly eradicate a virus from any program file. This program is called DOS. No identification of the specific virus is needed, only the commands DEL and COPY and the original disk of the infected program. (Some programs may need to be installed rather than copied.) DOS can even deal with a boot infector on a hard disk by using the FDISK program with the /mbr parameter. This rewrites the start-up code to the master boot record. Rewriting the DOS boot record is done with the SYS command.

Nevertheless, many users feel more comfortable with a product that is designed to remove virus infections than with the DOS commands readily available. How do these programs work? Take the imaginary Galactic Avenger III virus as an example.

GAIII is classed as a resident .EXE infector, meaning that after an infected program is run, the virus code remains in memory and gains access through INT 21, the DOS function interrupt. Any time a program (or DOS) calls INT 21, the resident GAIII code checks the AX register for function 4b00 (hex), the load and execute program function. Using the pointer to the file name in the DS:DX register pair, the virus code first examines and saves the file attributes, time, date, and length. Then the virus changes the attributes to enable writing and opens the file and checks the first two bytes for the .EXE signature ASCII MZ. If the file is an .EXE file, the virus reads the .EXE header to determine the initial CS:IP (entry point) of the program. Then the virus reads the file beginning at the entry point to determine if the program has been previously infected. Only if the program is an uninfected .EXE file does the infection take place. The CS:IP entry point in the header is adjusted to a point past the length of the file, and the file length entry in the header is adjusted to account for the length of the virus code. The original file entry point is saved within the virus code at its termination point, and the virus code is written to the end of the file. The date and time of the file are restored to the original values, the file is closed, and the attributes are returned to their original state, which may have been read-only.

To restore the program file to the original, a disinfecting program must know a great deal about the GAIII virus and how it works. The original entry point in the .EXE header has to be found from within the virus code and the length of the virus subtracted from the length entry in the header. The file length must be adjusted to remove the appended virus code, and most disinfecting programs overwrite the virus code to remove it from the disk.

The programmer must know exactly where the original entry point to the program was stored. If this point is not stored correctly, the program will crash when run. Although GAIII only adjusts two header entries (entry point and length), many other viruses adjust other header entries. All header information must be restored to its original condition before a virus can be removed and the program restored to the uninfected state. If the virus removes header information and does not store it, that information is lost, and disinfecting cannot proceed. This is why many disinfecting programs cannot recover from some viruses.

To disinfect the Galactic Avenger III virus, the cleanup program opens the infected program file and reads the contents into memory. Because GAIII appends the virus code to the end of the program file, the cleanup program calculates the end of the file and uses offsets from the end of the file to find information the virus has stored concerning the original file. The virus code itself is 4,976 bytes long, so the beginning of the infection is the file length less the virus length, rounded to the nearest 16-byte boundary. The beginning of the virus code is a data area 528 bytes long, followed by the code entry point. The original entry point is stored as a double word at offset 516 in the virus data area. This value can be used to restore the header information in the original file. The disinfecting program calculates the original length of the program file and also restores this value to the header. GAIII does not alter any other values in the header, so cleanup is relatively easy.

The cleanup program fills the virus area with zeros to clear out the virus code and writes the memory image back to the disk. At this point, the cleanup program changes the DOS file length to reflect the original program length and returns the extra allocation units to the DOS free pool. That's it. The program is disinfected and operates normally. But...

The "but" occurs when the particular version of GAIII infecting the program is a variation of the GAIII sample that the programmers used in constructing the disinfecting program. I have shown earlier how it is possible to vary the program to hide it from a scanner. If the alteration moves any of the vital areas needed by the disinfecting program, such as the offset of the original entry point, restoration will kill the program. Suppose the signature used by a major antivirus scanner was the following code fragment:

```
MOV          BX,204
MOV          [BX],DX
MOV          [BX+2],AX
    .
    .
    .
JMP          DWORD PTR [BX]
```

This code fragment stores the original entry point during infection into the address pointed to by BX and later uses that entry point to terminate the virus code and begin the legitimate program. But an enterprising malcontent, realizing that the signature is contained in this code segment makes the following change:

```
MOV          BX,206
```

The virus still works, but the entry point is stored 518 bytes into the virus code instead of offset 516. The targeted scanner may miss GAIII entirely unless it is updated with a new signature. Other scanners, using different areas of code as the signature will still identify the virus as GAIII. But is it still GAIII? No.

A disinfecting utility working with the scanner will still pick the double word at offset 516 instead of 518 and write the wrong value to the header. Therefore, it is essential that a scanner be written with some form of checksum or cyclical redundancy checking (CRC) to verify that the virus encountered in the field is the exact virus experienced in the lab. Any unexpected alteration should be cause for termination of the cleanup effort. Care must be taken to ensure that any checksum or CRC does not infringe on areas of the virus subject to change from one infection to another. For instance, the first 512 bytes of the GAIII virus serve as a buffer area for reading and writing infected files and thus reflect values associated with the original program and not the virus itself. As a result, this area is different in every infection.

Boot infectors can be even more dangerous to clean up than file infectors. With a file, if the cleanup does not work properly, the user can replace the program from the original diskette. If a cleanup program does not properly repair a boot infector, the PC may not even boot! Additionally, all files on the computer may be lost in an attempt to cleanup the infection.

As an example, consider the Leif Ericsen virus, an imaginary boot infector. The LE virus is a boot infector that activates on any day after October 10, the day Leif Ericsen discovered America. Upon infection, the LE virus replaces the original MBR with the virus code and moves the original MBR to an unused sector of the disk. The virus makes a hidden directory entry in the root of the infected disk and allocates one cluster to that entry in the FAT to prevent DOS from overwriting the information. Because LE is longer than the 512 bytes allocated for the boot sector, additional virus code is stored in the remaining sectors of the cluster. This code is only used on the activation date.

To disinfect the computer, the cleanup program merely finds the original MBR in the allocated cluster and writes it back to the proper place at side 0, head 0, sector 1. Simple enough. But what happens if the MBR is not in the expected location?

The clean up program then writes bogus information to the MBR, causing a total system crash on a subsequent boot. The PC becomes unbootable from the hard disk. If the machine is booted from a diskette, DOS will not be able to determine the partition information in the MBR and will refuse to recognize the hard disk. In this case, the cure is worse than the disease. With the virus in place, the PC could be booted from a virus-free diskette, and the hard disk was still accessible. After cleanup, the hard disk is virtually dead. Many users may begin from scratch with a full repartition and format of the hard disk, losing every file on the disk.

Sometimes a double infection can prevent the disk from being properly restored. Consider the very real Stoned and Michelangelo viruses, both of which store the original MBR in sector *xx*. When a disk is infected with the Stoned virus, the original MBR is stored in sector *xx*. Subsequently, if the computer is infected with Michelangelo, the MBR containing the Stoned virus is written to sector *xx*, eradicating the original MBR. A disinfecting program recognizes the Michelangelo virus and properly records the contents of sector *xx* into the MBR. The Michelangelo virus is eliminated, but the MBR is now infected with Stoned. To make matters worse, the sector that Stoned uses to store the original MBR is still infected with the Stoned virus. Regardless of how many times the user tries to disinfect the Stoned virus, the same information gets written to the MBR. The original MBR has disappeared. Could things possibly get worse? Of course they could. The program that disinfects from the Michelangelo virus could write sector *xx* with binary zeros after it has transferred that sector to the MBR. A subsequent disinfection of the Stoned virus would cause the zeros in sector *xx* to be written to the MBR, effectively disabling the hard disk entirely.

Cleanup programs work most of the time. It's the rest of the time that disaster occurs. If the virus maintains the partition information as offset 1BE (hex) of the MBR, the use of FDISK /MBR is the easiest solution to a boot virus of the hard disk. Verification of the partition table is as easy as booting the computer from a diskette and trying to access the hard disk. If accessible, the partition information is intact.

Generic Disinfection

There is another way for a program to disinfect a virus. The generic disinfection program relies on storing enough information about an uninfected program file in a database to reconstruct the file in the event of a virus attack. How much is enough? Storing 100 percent of the original file is the only absolute way to restore the original. This can be done with a backup program or by saving the original program distribution diskettes. Generic disinfectors store just enough of the original to disinfect a common virus attack. Viruses that overwrite a file cannot be removed if they overwrite more than the portion of the original stored by the generic disinfector. This makes the generic disinfector less than perfect in the event of a virus attack, but better than nothing.

There is one other consideration when disinfecting a virus: what to do with the virus code itself. If the user deletes an infected file and copies a clean version back to the hard disk, the virus code remains in the sectors unused by the clean program. Although a few viruses search for unused sections of a host, in almost every case, an infected file is longer than the clean version. When the file is deleted, DOS does not erase the sectors used by that file but marks them as available in the FAT. When the clean file is copied back to the disk, it may or may not use the same sectors. In any event, it is highly probable that, because the clean file uses fewer sectors than the infected file and the infected portion was at the end of the file, those sectors that contain the virus code remain on the disk. Is this dangerous?

The answer is simply, no. A virus is never a threat unless it is run. Consider the disks of a virus researcher. There are hundreds of active viruses that could create havoc with the hard disk. However, these files are considered to be data files and not active programs. The researcher can look at and analyze these files with impunity as long as he never runs them. Even an average user may harbor a potential virus in a file or on the boot sector of a diskette. If the file is never executed or the diskette is never used to boot the machine, the virus remains merely a series of flux reversals on a magnetic medium.

Virus code existing on isolated sectors of a disk is not a threat if it cannot be loaded into memory and executed as code. A user who relies on DOS as an operating system is under no threat from isolated sectors containing virus code.

Answering The Question

This chapter started by asking whether antivirus products work. After reading about how they work, you can probably answer for yourself. Yes, they work. If the question were whether antivirus products protect against viruses, the answer would have to be no. They can protect against many (in fact most) viruses, but they cannot offer full protection against all viruses.

As long as the architecture of the PC enables any program to have complete access to the entire memory space and all DOS and BIOS functions, you can never be totally safe from destructive programs. The fault lies within the chips. Microcomputer processors were designed for simplicity, ease of use, and cost effectiveness. Data security was probably not an issue in the design decisions.

The protected mode of Intel processors 80286 and above addresses some of the security problems by isolating memory areas among users and the operating system. However, these chips are dual mode chips capable of operating in real mode where memory cannot be protected. Only by equipping our personal computers with processors that do not allow memory access outside certain bounds can the virus problem be effectively combated. To do this would mean that thousands, if not millions, of pieces of software would become useless, not to mention the installed base of personal computers.

The question becomes how high a price are users willing to pay to eradicate the virus menace?

Perfect Protection

There is, of course, no such thing as perfect protection. But the user can come as close as possible by using a combination approach. The following description assumes a system that is maintained by a single user. If the computer is used by several people or the public at large, then some additional efforts need to be made in the protection sequence.

Scan It

The primary protection should be the scan. A scanner will catch most of the widespread and recognizable viruses. If the computer is a stable environment and no new programs are introduced to the computer, you would only have to scan the computer once. Obviously, if a scanner reported no viruses on the computer, the only viruses that could be present are ones that the scanner does not recognize. Why waste time doing an hourly, daily, or weekly scan if no new programs have been introduced to the computer? Once is sufficient.

If a new program is to be run on the computer, check it with a scanner first. It the scanner finds no viruses, it cannot possibly infect the computer with a virus that the scanner recognizes. It may contain a virus that the scanner does not recognize, but repeated scanning will still not find it, and the user may be lulled into a false sense of security.

Heuristic It

Like the scan, heuristics only needs to be done once per program. If the scanner does not recognize a virus, the heuristic program may flag a program as suspicious or it may not. Whether the program contains a virus or not, the heuristic program will treat the program the same way every time. There is little sense in wasting the time running heuristics on anything other than new programs added to the machine. You should be suspicious of programs that purport to contain possible viruses when run through a heuristics program. Just remember, this does not mean that they do contain viruses. Just be very careful when running such a program after a warning has been given. Be sure you have a reliable integrity checker in operation before running it. You should make a complete backup before running any program flagged as suspicious by a heuristic program.

Integrity Check It

Integrity checking is the next to the last line of defense and should never be ignored. Just because a scanner does not recognize a virus-laden program and heuristics does not find anything suspicious with a program file does not mean that the file is clean. There may be a high probability that there is no virus, but you can never be sure. Running a resident integrity checker will increase the odds that nothing bad is happening that has not been detected to this point. Remember, however, that many new viruses are being developed in an attempt to bypass antivirus measures, and even a resident integrity checker could be fooled.

When introducing a new program to a previously stable system (even one that comes in a shrink-wrapped box), scan it and run heuristics before running the program. Then, after the program has finished, even if the resident integrity checker has not reported a problem, turn the power off. Restart from a reliable DOS diskette and run the integrity checker again. If neither the boot sector nor any file has changed, you can be as close to 100 percent assured as is possible that the program is not infected.

There are no guarantees even if the above procedure is followed to the letter. It is possible for the program to contain a delayed-action virus. For one reason or another there may be some viruses that do not immediately begin to infect other files. Some viruses infect only during certain months of the year as indicated by the system clock. This feature may have been installed to protect the original virus writer or to lull the user into a false sense of security. Naturally, the viruses that are known to have this feature are also known to the scanners. However, because some known viruses have this feature, it is possible that a future virus, unknown to the scanner, may also have a time delay. Therefore, a program that passes the scanner, the heuristics, and the integrity checker may be just waiting in the wings to begin infecting the system.

Multi-User System Protection

If there is more than one person who uses a PC, the above advice needs to be modified. There is no assurance that the other users are as diligent as they should be when introducing new programs to the computer. If there is one person who is placed in charge of the computer, that person should run frequent scans, heuristics, and integrity checks. There is no assurance that user B will not run a program that contains one of the more common viruses known to scanners and infect the system. Therefore, a repeat scan at regular intervals is recommended. Unlike a single-user system, where the user knows to scan a new program and therefore does not need to scan the entire system repeatedly, never assume that all users will scan new programs before running them.

The Final Frontier

The group of antivirus programs known as behavior blockers is the last line of defense against computer viruses. This type of program monitors program and disk activity by remaining resident in memory and intercepting certain interrupt vectors. If, in the determination of the blocker program, an activity seems to be virus related, the user is informed of the activity and given a choice to proceed or not. The type of activity flagged by a behavior blocker is entirely dependent on the antivirus programmers. Behavior blockers can be subject to many false alarms, so many that the average user may be lulled into a sense of complacency and allow a destructive action to take place even after being warned.

A typical warning from a behavior blocker might be an attempt by a program to open another program file, a file with an .EXE or .COM extension. There are legitimate programs that open other program files, but a behavior blocker flags this activity. The user must decide whether the activity is caused by a virus or by a legitimate program. Often the user is not knowledgeable enough to make such a judgment and must call a supervisor or make a guess.

Other behavior blocker activities are easier for the average user to judge. For example, only the program FORMAT should issue a format call to the disk BIOS interrupt. If the user has not requested a format of a disk, then a behavior blocker warning that the disk is about to be formatted will probably prevent a disaster. This assumes that the user knows about formatting and its consequences. The word format means one thing to a computer literate individual and quite another to someone who is just using a computer as an electronic typewriter and has little knowledge of computer terms.

Behavior blockers are best used to try to prevent the damage that computer viruses can cause rather that to prevent the spread of viruses. The instructions contained in a virus that cause it to spread are often the same instructions as those used by legitimate programs. The more false alarms, the more the warnings are ignored. However, when considering the damage that a virus can cause, there probably should be some sort of behavior blocker in effect that will prevent a total trash of the disk. The most damaging virus will erase or alter the vital system areas of the disk, making the disk totally useless and all data stored on the disk inaccessible. A behavior blocker that monitors these vital system areas can become the last line of defense against the unknown virus bent on destruction.

Some known viruses take extraordinary steps to bypass behavior blocker programs. The known virus will be caught by a scanner, but it is entirely within the realm of possibility that an unknown virus can use the same techniques to bypass the system protection.

The Dreaded U Factor

U could mean *use*, *user*, or, phonetically, *you*. No antivirus product—good, bad, or indifferent—can do its work without someone to tell it to work. If a product is a pain to use, it won't get used. If a product has too many false alarms, it won't get used. If it takes too long to run, it won't get used. And so it goes.

A Fortune 50 company paid mega-bucks for a site license of a popular product. Did it find viruses? Of course—at least all those known to the programming staff at the moment of release. But what of the cost of updating thousands of machines when new releases, finding new viruses, were coming out weekly or monthly? The updates sat, unused and uninstalled because of the cost factor.

An antivirus product that enables an unsophisticated user to bypass a warning is almost worse than no antivirus product at all. It's arguable that ignorance is not an excuse, but it's tempting to argue that infection on a broad-scale is the result of choiceful lack of protection rather than a choiceful failure to use or heed the warnings of a product.

Perhaps the best posture is that any antivirus product is better than none as long as the product doesn't instill a false sense of security ("I'm bulletproof! I have KILLVIRUS on my machine!") or do more damage in its disinfection operation than even the most evil viruses might do.

The Dangers of Experts

A favorite definition of expert goes along the lines of someone who knows more than you … or at least says so. A stunning example of an expert widely considered to have gone bad in the virus industry is John McAfee. McAfee's method of giving his products away for free over computer bulletin boards eventually led to an incredible installed (and paid for) base for his products.

As awareness of the virus problem (and the initiative to do something about it) grew in business settings, most savvy managers were aware of a person who knew everything. Chances were that person had downloaded the SCAN product for free and, enjoying a moment of glory by being asked the question, recommended it without hesitation. Unquestionably, this was a fine business strategy for McAfee's fledgling software company, now gone public without McAfee at the helm.

With more and more users turning to the product, the named developer, McAfee, quickly rose to the stature of industry expert. His penchant for hyping the virus threat as well as his creation of a somewhat phantom organization, the Computer Virus Industry Association, quickly turned researchers and developers who considered themselves more professionally responsible against McAfee. Nevertheless, the well-dressed, well-spoken McAfee remained a darling of the media—he always gave them the story they were chasing—Until the day he went too far and the media, to a great extent, was in lock-step with him.

I wrote the following article for *Information Security News*. Rob Rosenberger was the researcher.

Five Million … it's a number, as folks in the Midwest used to say, that's a "helluvamuch" of almost anything. But five million computers harboring a stealthy virus—that could only be contracted if a diskette which was ALREADY infected was mistakenly locked into the A: drive at a PC's bootup—all in peril of complete data destruction on the 517th birthday of Florentine artist Michelangelo Buonarratti? Not. Or, at the very least, not very likely.

Nevertheless, that's what almost the entire world came to believe in five frantic, flaming weeks in the Winter Of Our Virus Discontent.

Boot-sector viruses—Michelangelo, PingPong, Stoned, and their brothers and sisters—don't spread easily. They're second-, third-, fourth- and fifth-generation iterations of the concept used by the celebrated (c)BRAIN virus that first brought the problem of "naughty bits" to public attention, scrutiny, and reaction in the fall of 1987. To "catch" a boot sector virus is difficult, indeed.

A computer must complete the IPL/POST (boot) process with an infected disk in Drive A: to catch one of these buggers. To imagine that, around the world, there were millions of diskettes already infected with Michelangelo lying around and that five million users had powered up five million PCs with not only a diskette locked in the A: drive but a diskette *infected* with Michelangelo in that drive? Add to that the fact that this particular Michelangelo wasn't 517 years old … it was only nine months old when the drums began to beat. And a new chapter in virus history was born.

The last time there was a virus scare like this … mid-October of 1988 … when the DataCrime (Columbus Day) virus and the Jerusalem (Friday the 13th) virus were scheduled to hit concurrently, the media went into hyperspace and sales of antivirus products rocketed. That was nothing compared to Michelangelo.

The following timeline, prepared entirely from media reports, charts the progress of a media event characterized by hype, misinformation, and, say some, outright profiteering and trading on fear.

A careful reading will disclose significant facts: respected news organizations and columnists apparently were unaware that Michelangelo could not spread through computer bulletin board services; the numbers bandied about seemed to come from very few sources; and that nothing, after all, happened.

On January 29, 1992, UPI reporter Jack Lesar filed a newswire saying, "the Michelangelo Virus could erase data from the hard disks of hundreds of thousands of computers around the world on Michelangelo's birthday, March 6."

Winn Schwartau, executive director of the Nashville-based International Partnership Against Computer Terrorism, attributed magical powers to the virus:

It's usually been a rule that a virus can't be propagated by just reading from a data disk. But in this case it appears to no longer be true. You may consciously just be reviewing data, not moving data, but the virus is hidden and executable and it's doing its thing... McAfee said the Michelangelo Virus is the third most common in terms of reports of infection. It accounts for 14 percent of infection reports— a total of about 6,000 last year. And he notes the figure represents the number of sites at which infection has been reported—each of which may have one machine, or 100.

On February 11, 1992, the numbers ante went up. Reuters reporter Wilson daSilva filed a newswire saying that the Michelangelo virus resides on "millions of personal computers around the world." The estimate—five million worldwide—comes from John McAfee. In the story, researcher Wayne Boxall of Australia's Computer Virus Information Group erroneously stated that the virus spreads via computer bulletin boards.

Six days later *Washington Post* reporter John Burgess wrote a Michelangelo story questioning gigantic estimates and the role of people who made those claims: "It remains unclear whether large numbers of computers contain undetected copies of the virus, though estimates of millions of machines have been published in the news media...Past scares about viruses often have proven to be overblown."

"I'm finding virus catastrophes everywhere," said Martin Tibor, a data recovery consultant in San Rafael, CA., whose repeated calls to the media after the Leading Edge incident helped publicize Michelangelo. "These things are replicating like crazy."

On February 19, Symantec/Peter Norton announced it had released a free program to disinfect the Michelangelo virus. The software searches for no other viruses (although it performs a simulated check of the entire drive), unlike Microcom's already released free program that detects 669 different infections. Symantec/Peter Norton also purchased a full-page ad in *Computerworld*'s February 24 issue to warn readers about the virus.

Chris Torchia filed an AP newswire two days later describing how Michelangelo "could send millions of computer users around the world through the ceiling." Tori Case, product manager for Central Point Software, claimed as many as five million computers worldwide may suffer, including 500,000 in the United States.

On February 24, Computer columnist Lawrence Magid offered questionable advice and information both in his print column and on the Prodigy service when he told readers that they could avoid Michelangelo's devastating effects if they activated a computer "on March 5 and leave it running until March 7." Magid claims viruses travel by computer bulletin boards and then oddly advises readers to download antivirus software from a bulletin board.

At the same time, Philip Elmer-DeWitt, writing for *U.S. News and World Report* erroneously reported that Michelangelo could be reliably located on a hard drive through the use of the DOS CHKDSK command.

Four days later Egghead, a national computer store chain, offered to ship a copy of the special Norton AntiVirus Michelangelo Edition for just $4.99. They also offered to send a free brochure about computer viruses, but some customers later complained that it arrived more than a week after the Michelangelo threat had passed.

On March 2, John McAfee, after previously claiming five million computers have Michelangelo, appeared on the "Today" show and said that "there are over a million systems infected now."

That same day AP writer Laura Myers filed a story authoritatively stating Michelangelo "lies dormant in an estimated five million IBM-compatible personal computers worldwide." The story incudes quotes from John McAfee and Martin Tibor.

Computer columnist Lawrence Magid clarified his advice to leave computers on through March 7 to avoid Michelangelo's devastating effects. "This will work in most cases, but if there is a power failure, many personal computers will automatically reboot themselves. Thus, a power failure on March 6 would have the same effect as turning on the computer."

ABC's Ted Koppel devoted a "Nightline" episode to Michelangelo with a lead-in announcement of how it "could be devastating, destroying the memories of millions of computers around the world ... . I just wanted you to understand I'm coming at [this broadcast] with a wealth of ignorance."

John McAfee, Patricia Hoffman, and Martin Tibor contributed to the lead-in story, with Tibor ominously stating viruses are "the equivalent of doing germ warfare in your own neighborhood."

The next day a Reuters reporter filed another erroneous newswire claiming Michelangelo spreads via computer bulletin boards.

"Good Morning America" science editor Michael Gillan claimed "as viruses go, there aren't that many reported incidents [of Michelangelo]... but there is an enormous fear factor." Unfortunately, he advised viewers to leave computers running from March 5 to March 7, following in the footsteps of computer columnist Lawrence Magid.

Another Reuters report about the Michelangelo virus mistakenly claimed "it spreads via computer bulletin boards."

CompuServe's electronic newspaper, *Online Today*, erroneously reported that the Michelangelo virus spreads via online services such as CompuServe. Management will later pull the embarrassing "GO OLT-93" story after receiving complaints from alert readers.

AP writer Laura Myers filed a feature story on Michelangelo. Many TV news anchors read the first paragraph verbatim: "Do you know where that floppy disk has been? Taking a page from safe sex manuals, experts are warning computer users to practice safe computing because of viruses like one called Michelangelo, which could trigger millions of computer crashes and erase data on hard disks this week." TV anchors then followed with the reporter's previous statement: "The virus lies dormant in an estimated 5 million IBM-compatible personal computers worldwide and is poised to strike on Friday, the artist's birthdate."

The numbers ante went up again. Reuters reporter Steve James filed a newswire from Bonn, Germany, with Michelangelo estimates in the tens of millions just for the United States. "Hamburg University computer virus expert Klaus Brunnstein estimates that 15% of all Personal Computers (PCs) in Germany—around half a million—are infected and will lose their data banks on Friday. He also said that 30% of PCs in Britain and 25% in the United States [about 15 million] are believed to have been infected by the Michelangelo virus, as a result of pirated computer games and infected original floppy discs." Note that Brunnstein denies these quotes.

The AP ominously reported, "the Michelangelo computer virus had invaded Capitol Hill, sending congressional staffers scurrying for a cure before Friday's trigger date."

John McAfee appeared in the AP daily quotes column: "This is one of the most widespread viruses. It's out there in a large way and could cause lots of damage if it isn't stopped." The quote comes from a newswire filed by AP reporter Laura Myers.

A Reuters newswire by David Morgan claimed John McAfee receives "about 120 reports [worldwide] of Michelangelo infection a day," prompting some experts to ask how this could justify McAfee's previous estimates of five million. Morgan's story also claims "computer viruses, which first appeared nine years ago, are now growing in number at a rate of about six a day" and that "some experts say the recent proliferation of viruses has much to do with the fall of communism in eastern Europe, specifically Bulgaria."

A Reuters newswire said: "Poland's biggest daily [newspaper] carried a front page story headlined `Michelangelo, The Mass Murderer, Will Attack On Friday.'" Later reports detailed panicked efforts by Polish citizens to obtain antivirus software.

New York Times computer columnist Peter Lewis wrote about both Michelangelo and Jerusalem, stating that the estimates of Michelangelo infections "range wildly from as few as 100 to as many as 2 million." After explaining how the virus spreads, who might be at risk, and proper steps for combatting Michelangelo, he wondered in print "if Michelangelo might more appropriately be called the 'Alamo' virus," because March 6 is also the anniversary of the fall of the Alamo and, like Santa Ana, Michelangelo takes no survivors.

On March 4, numerous reporters logged on to CompuServe, GEnie, America Online, and Prodigy to ask the same question: "Want to be interviewed for a story on the Michelangelo virus?" One *USA Today* reporter, expecting an avalanche of calls, asked people not to tie up his phone unless they actually got hurt by the virus on March 6.

The AP shifted its focus on Michelangelo after receiving phone calls from concerned/outraged virus experts. Stories now began to center on the fear sweeping the world rather than the virus. Bart Ziegler filed the first AP report with contradictory opinions of the situation: "You're more likely to spill a cup of coffee on your keyboard than to get this virus," said Peter Tippett, chairman of Certus International Inc., a maker of antivirus software. "There's definitely hysteria," said Marianne Guntow, a computer analyst at the University of Chicago.

Multiple UPI newswires erroneously claimed Michelangelo spreads via computer bulletin boards.

On March 5, scattered reports from around the globe state that Michelangelo triggered a day early due to a fluke in some computers. Their internal clocks ignore leap days and changed to March 1, 1992 a day too soon.

AP reporter Robert Dvorchak filed the first major newswire with a lead-off paragraph questioning impending sabotage estimates. "Computer users took precautions to disinfect their machines from a virus set to strike on Michelangelo's birthday Friday, although some experts did not expect widespread damage from the electronic prank."

UPI reporter Joe Fasbinder filed a newswire claiming the pending devastation from Michelangelo "is certainly expected to be in the millions of dollars. In addition to the data lost to the virus, millions of dollars in employee time will be needed to re-install damaged software."

On PBS' "McNeil-Lehrer Report," a panel of experts including Dennis Steinauer of NIST, John McAfee, and Charles Rutstein, the National Computer Security Association's staff researcher and a sophomore at Hobart College, are queried about Michelangelo. After Steinauer's careful explanation of how computer viruses are spread, McAfee and Rutstein traded predictions about Michelangelo. Rutstein posited "ten to twenty thousand worldwide," McAfee offered "anywhere from 50,000 to 5 million" and suggested we're "talking sixty million dollars at the very low end" for cleaning up the after-effects of Michelangelo.

March 6, V-day arrives!? Although fear over Michelangelo continued, the major newswires echoed similar stories about a fizzled event. Reuters: "As March 6 dawned in Asia, New Zealand reported scattered infections by the virus—but there was more media hype than electronic havoc." Associated Press: "Personal computer users reported scattered outbreaks today of the

Michelangelo virus but no widespread damage from the much-hyped software invader." UPI: "The long-awaited Michelangelo virus struck around the world Friday, though it did not appear to be the data disaster that some had predicted."

That same day a Reuters newswire claimed Michelangelo "was unwittingly spread round the world by a single Taiwanese software copying house, Dutch police said on Friday. "Taiwan is the source of the mass distribution of the virus," police computer fraud expert Loek Weerd told Reuters. "The Taiwanese authorities have not so far given us the name of the software copy house," Weerd said.

In a freak coincidence, 1,200 automated teller machines in New York shut down due to a power outage. In another freak coincidence, three-fourths of New Jersey's computerized lottery ticket machines shut down because of a computer glitch. Panicked customers incorrectly blamed Michelangelo for the problems. In another freak coincidence, cable subscribers in suburban Philadelphia were "locked" to the channel they last watched on Thursday night. Again, Michelangelo was blamed.

Various UPI newswires finally explained Michelangelo doesn't spread via computer bulletin boards.

Reuters now reported John McAfee "estimated at least 10,000 computers had been hit worldwide" by Michelangelo, in stark contrast to previous Reuters stories where he had estimated five million. Other newswire reports mention McAfee's name while outlining a worldwide "media hype" campaign.

AP reporter Bart Ziegler filed a scathing newswire:

The day of techno-doom turned out to be a dud… For days, news media relayed forecasts of impending doom from Michelangelo. The story had all the right elements: a mysterious invader with a sexy name that could cause havoc by a definite deadline in machines relied upon by millions. The reports often failed to mention that many projections of potential damage were provided by companies that make anti-viral software and stood to benefit from the scare.

One source was John McAfee of McAfee Associates, the largest seller of virus-killing programs. McAfee was widely quoted as saying Michelangelo had infected up to 5 million computers worldwide. Asked Friday whether he had overstated the case, he said the low rate of actual Michelangelo damage was due partly to precautions so many PC users took.

Symantec claimed over 250,000 users around the world obtained a copy of their free Michelangelo disinfector program. Of the online services, Prodigy and GEnie charged nothing for customers to download special antivirus packages; CompuServe pocketed its regular hourly connect fees for the service. Prodigy officials stated that over 100,000 copies had been downloaded.

Michelangelo got another mention in the AP daily quotes column, this time downplaying the scare. "It has been overhyped, without question," said Charles Rutstein, staff researcher for the National Computer Security Association, as computer users braced for a computer virus to strike on Michelangelo's birthday Friday.

AT&T reported Michelangelo erased data on two computers. A spokesman claims the company operates about 250,000 IBM PCs around the world.

The day after, another person rationalized the hype in the AP daily quotes column: "I'd say we would have had serious problems if we hadn't been so worried by all the hype," Joe Pujals, California's computer information manager, on the minimal effect the Michelangelo virus had on computers.

All major newswires ceased reporting about computer viruses by 6:00 a.m. Eastern time.

From March 8-12, no newswire service files a story about computer viruses. On March 13, the scheduled activation date for the Friday the 13th (Jerusalem) virus, no newswire service filed a story about computer viruses—an interesting change considering the media's hype about Friday the 13th in October 1989 and as a footnote to many Michelangelo-related stories. Also, no newswire service filed a story on March 15, the scheduled activation date for the Maltese Amoeba virus.

On March 20, AP writer Larry Blasko filed the first major newswire report since March 7 with another scathing attack on the antivirus industry:

Snake-oil salesmen aren't dead. They've just reprogrammed their pitch. If you believed what you saw in the media in early March, the computerized world was going to end on March 6 when the computer virus Michelangelo would destroy data on disk drives from Kalamazoo to Katmandu. All was doomed on the 517th anniversary

of the artist's birth. But wait. Maybe you were one of the lucky people who owned or could buy virus protection software. Which, by
great coincidence, just happened to be on sale...

So what damage was done? Lots. First, computer viruses are real, just like rat-
tlesnakes and copperheads. But irresponsibly beating the drum and shouting
that they're under every bush—when they aren't—will lead the thoughtless to
conclude that they don't exist. Second, the huge wave of hype created the
notion that low-cost software, whether from bulletin boards or shareware dis-
tributors, was fraught with peril. That's a disservice to a source of many of the
best utility programs, from DOS utilities to the ubiquitous PKZip and LHArc
archiving software. Third, some of the hype was so misinformed that it created
myths. Avoid commercial computer bulletin boards, said one myth. Avoid
office networks, said another. Never buy generic diskettes, said a third.

Hogwash all.

If nothing else, the Michelangelo scare was an example of the global
media community in action. The media fed upon not only sensational statements and press releases from others but upon itself. If Michelangelo—if any
virus—could spread as fast as the coverage of it did, computer users should
indeed worry.

Looking backward, several purveyors of super-inflated infection estimates—both in the press and in the antivirus industry—attempted to put
"spin control" on the story. It was only, they said, through the good offices of
the media that the computing public was made aware of the threat, checked
their PCs, found Michelangelo, and eliminated it. Thus, the very small number of infections.

Some additional numbers may be in order for reality testing. On Prodigy,
the nation's largest on-line service, over 100,000 copies of a Michelangelo
finder were downloaded. Less than one hundred hits were reported on the
service, according to volunteer virus-watcher Henri Delger. A European firm
requested formatted disks (which would show the presence of
Michelangelo) from its client base who had previously experienced viruses.
Of 1500 returned disks, only seven showed boot-sector viruses, only one of
those was Michelangelo.

Applying a sharp pencil to this situation, assume an infection rate of
1:1,000 and further assume that there are 80,000,000 PC/MS-DOS personal
computers in the global community given this, there would have been

80,000 infections (and that means individual PCs infected with Michelangelo) worldwide.

With the 5,000,000 (1:16) number presented, with only 20,000 final hits (1:4000), this means that 4,980,000 DIDN'T have the Michelangelo virus and, according to some, it's because the virus was found and removed with a scanner. To get such a result, 4,980,000,000 PCs would have to have been scanned and cleaned—that's four billion. Add to that the fact that a significant part of the installed base is still comprised of PCs running on the 8088 chip (which are immune to destruction from Michelangelo because their clocks are not on the system board where Michelangelo looked for them), and it makes even less sense.

Were the media victims? Villains? Heroes? Presented with information that appeared to be from "official" organizations with names like the National Computer Security Association, the Computer Virus Industry Association, and the International Partnership Against Computer Terrorism, should they have looked further for the facts? Would the story have been news if only 80,000—or even 20,000—out of 80,000,000 computers were believed to be infected? These questions may remain unanswered if the press doesn't buy the next round of hoopla. As they say in the Midwest, "Fool me once, shame on you; fool me twice, shame on me."

Blame McAfee?

Good question. He seems to blame himself,—which may be a beau geste after he was demoted to chief technical officer of the company he helped found. In an interview with *InfoWorld*'s Rachel Parker he said, "In many cases, I've brought it on myself perhaps by over enthusiasm, stupidity, lack of sufficient background information." The interview went on:

Infoworld: But, frankly, what you were doing was ambulance chasing, by citing the highest numbers?

McAfee: Possibly.

InfoWorld: So if another virus comes around, will you be less visible?

McAfee: I'll do exactly what I did before in terms of simply answering questions when they're asked. It's just that I'll stick to what I know.

As it stands, McAfee's personal financial gain, estimated into the millions of dollars by even more conservative observers, is tarnished. Will he be less visible the next time a virus comes around? It's likely that he and his opinions will dismissed out of hand—and that the boy who cried wolf can spend the rest of his earthly days counting the money he earned by issuing the warning.

But, maybe not. There are persistent rumors of less than open-handed dealing when McAfee Associates, with the assistance of venture capitalists, went public. The Securities and Exchange Commission, when queried, said, though a press officer, "We cannot confirm or deny those rumors."

Blame the Media?

Perhaps. Certain writers who are widely considered to be experts, notably Magid, should have known better. The quick turn-around when AP's Ziegler picked up the beat is important to note. To Koppel's credit, he laid out the caveat of his own massive ignorance on the subject. The Times' Lewis predictably viewed the situation with a practiced and somewhat jaundiced eye and was closest of all to the truth.

Arguably, more people watch television than read the papers. Thus, television had a vast impact on fueling the fires of the Michelangelo scare.

One particularly telling vignette on a TV news show was an older, very tidy-looking gentleman standing in a line to pick up a free anti-Michelangelo program. When asked why he was there, he responded that, since his retirement, he'd spent most of his time working on a family genealogy. If his hard drive failed or his data was destroyed, years of loving work would be gone. Had this gentlemen never heard the term backup?

Because reporters are out for the story they often focus on what people are worried about. Some stories concern subjects that are difficult to understand and quantify, and reporters must base their stories on an expert's advice. Reports based on the statements of police and fire officials, for example, can generally be taken as fact. This is not so in the world of viruses.

Evan Ramstead, who replaced Ziegler at the Associated Press, was straightforward when asked if he would go with an emerging virus story: "I am not sure I would have the acumen to sort the hype from the reality at this point."

The sad fact is that the media has been twice-bitten—with the October 1989/Friday the 13th/Columbus Day hype and again, more deeply, by Michelangelo—and is exponentially shy.

Those Magnificent Magazines

Fortunes and hopes have been hung on reviews by prestigious computer magazines. A Best in Show or Editors' Choice is money in the bank. A bad review, even if the reviewer was asleep at the switch and admits it, can't be taken back with a small correction in a subsequent edition.

Before the results of the most recent (1993) evaluations by *PC Magazine*, a Ziff-Davis publication, wags on Internet's VIRUS-L forum were predicting that the winners would be chosen based on annual advertising budgets that flow into the Ziff empire. Undeniably, the largest antivirus advertisers (based on space taken) in the Ziff chain are Central Point Software and Norton/Symantec. And the winners? Norton Anti-Virus and Central Point Anti-Virus.

While the results were not unexpected, they were painful to many developers whose products had reliably outscored NAV and CPAV in every other testing arena. No doubt their capability to purchase advertising space in Ziff publications was impaired by the testing results, just as the budgets of Central Point and Norton/Symantec were swelled by the influx of sales based on the Editors' Choice designation.

Blame the Testers?

PC Labs performs hundreds of evaluations a year. It is arguably impossible to expect even these talented people to begin to scratch the surface of the highly arcane world of antivirus software when they have other work to do. There are probably less than fifty people in the world who have the knowledge, the talent, and the ability to design a complete testing suite for antivirus products. To the best of current knowledge, none of them works for *PC Magazine*.

Should you trust magazine evaluations? Probably not.

The following article by Sarah Tanner was published in the November 1993 *Virus News International:*

I'm not claiming that all antivirus product reviews conform to the guidelines below but I can tell you I've seen every one of these tricks used in magazine reviews. In some cases, a master reviewer has shown such adroitness that he or she has been able to employ several of the tricks in the same review. In many (if not most) cases, the reviewer was unaware that he was using these tricks but in some cases, it looks as if they have been used deliberately.

The main weapons at your disposal are the choice of what features to review and what to ignore and the weights given to the features you do cover. By a careful use of this, even GrottyScan can be the Editor's Choice.

By the way, GrottyScan and WonderScan are entirely fictitious products and is not meant to stand in for any of the products on the market today. And Grotty Inc. and Wonder Inc. are fictitious companies.

1. Put a lot of weight on User Interface. Then, you can legitimately claim that you liked GrottyScan's user interface better than the others. User Interface is a matter of personal preference. Some people like a command line, others a full screen. Some people like lots of knobs and buttons, others like a clean interface (i.e., no options). If GrottyScan is optionless, give the most points for "a clean, uncluttered, user interface." If GrottyScan is chock-full of bells and whistles, do a tick chart and give the most points for quantity of features.

2. If GrottyScan doesn't have a TSR, then don't test TSRs. You can either just ignore the whole issue or else claim that no-one should use a TSR, perhaps on the grounds of TSR conflict, or on grounds of security, or on any other grounds you choose. In extreme cases, you might say that any vendor offering a TSR is a scoundrel.

3. If GrottyScan doesn't offer file repair, then don't give any points for repair. You could claim that repair is insecure and everyone should delete-and-replace. Or you could explain that some products don't do it very well, so nobody should

use it (even though other products may do it extremely well).

4. If GrottyScan does repair but not very well, then give lots of points for the fact that it does repair but don't actually test it.

5. You're going to have to do a run against a load of viruses. If GrottyScan is really bad at detection, then use just 11 viruses—that way, it doesn't look any worse than the others.

6. If GrottyScan is slow, you can mask that nicely with several deft touches:

   ☛ Scan a floppy disk. That means that the speed is governed by diskette reading speed, not by the product speed.

   ☛ Scan a hard disk without much on it, on a fast machine. That way, all the products take just a few seconds and there isn't much in it. If GrottyScan is ten times slower, that doesn't really look bad if its run time is 10 seconds.

   ☛ Do your timing test on a disk full of viruses. That way, WonderScan will be slowed down by the screen display and other things it has to do when it finds a virus, whereas GrottyScan won't be slowed down, as it won't have found many viruses.

7. If GrottyScan uses its own naming scheme, award half the points for detection and the other half for correctly naming the virus (correct, of course, means using GrottyScan names). Yes, I really have seen this done.

8. If GrottyScan is poor at polymorphic viruses, then use just one specimen of each, thus giving it a 100% score. The NCSA standard testing protocol uses this trick.

9. If GrottyScan can't deal with Stealth viruses in memory, then don't test with a stealth virus in memory (again, the NCSA protocol does this).

10. If GrottyScan has options to run fast and options to detect most viruses, then choose the Fast option in the timing test and Secure in the detection test. Naturally, you won't report this.

11. If GrottyScan has a heuristic analyzer, then make sure you don't run it on a clean machine but only on an infected machine. That way, you don't have to report any false alarms, you can wax lyrical about the way it can detect new viruses, however.

12. If GrottyScan has a behavior blocker, emphasize the fact that it can stop viruses. Don't install the thing and try to use it in daily use, or you'll have to report that all the false alarms it gives makes it unusable. I've seen a journalist rate such an unusable product as the best antivirus product on the market.

13. If the documentation tells you to install WonderScan in a certain way, then install it differently, then give lots of details about how it didn't work when it was wrongly installed.

14. If GrottyScan has a five-page manual, drone on about conciseness and how this is much preferable to the wrist-breaking tomes that come with other products. If GrottyScan has a large manual, emphasis the importance of full documentation.

15. If when you phone Grotty Inc. for technical support, you get put on hold for fifteen minutes and then get given dangerous advice, don't review tech support. On the other hand, if Grotty Inc. gives prompt and accurate support, do a table on how good their technical support is.

16. Take several viruses and patch them; write nulls over part of the virus code. Then, see which scanners still detect the viruses. Patch different places until GrottyScan detects the viruses and the other products don't—even better, get Grotty Inc. to do it for you. After all, they know what part of the virus to patch.

17. You'll need a test suite. Ideally, you should get it from Grotty Inc. You might find that Grotty Inc. doesn't have a virus library, in which case, you should find a collection of files that contains viruses and also lots of corrupted and innocent files. That way, if half the files you use are not viruses, the GrottyScan score of 30 per cent doesn't look too bad compared with the 40 per cent that the best product will get.

18. Give a copy of the exact test files you will be using, to Grotty Inc., three months before the test (this happened in an American review).

19. If GrottyScan finds false alarms in some of your files, count this as a plus, rather than a minus.

20. If GrottyScan doesn't do a self-test to see if it is infected before running, don't test to see if other products do check their own integrity.

21. Use the "faint praise" technique. If you need to say something good about WonderScan, say things like: "suitable for home computer users" or "the packaging was attractive."

22. Use the magnification technique. If you find some minor, unimportant problem with WonderScan, say that "unfortunately, WonderScan is flawed by…" People will read that as "very bad" but you can justify the statement by using the dictionary definition of "flaw," meaning very minor defect.

23. If you find some major problem in GrottyScan that you are forced to report, call the vendor and you'll be able to say, "by the time you read this, this problem will have been fixed." Indeed, since that is true, why bother to tell the reader about the problem!

24. If Wonder Inc. complain and challenge you to produce the "virus" that you claim they cannot find, take refuge behind a non-disclosure agreement that says that you cannot send out the specimen.

25. Don't use viruses at all. Use simulated viruses. Assume that the simulation is perfect and that therefore all products should detect them.

26. Make a mistake in the summary table, accidentally giving WonderScan two stars when you meant four. When they complain, correct this in the next issue, in a little box that no-one will read. You can safely make the opposite mistake with GrottyScan; it is unlikely that they will complain at being given four stars.

Mistakes caused by these techniques are exploited by the marketing departments of all companies in the antivirus market. At the end of the day, it is you the user who is being exploited.

Testing 1-2-3

Just how can the efficacy of a product be shown to a prospective purchaser who has figured out that the magazine evaluations are not The Word of God? Easy. A head-to-head evaluation of your product against the other(s) under consideration. And just what will that hoped-for client understand?

"Numbers. That's all they understand, numbers." Who are "they?" Prospective purchasers of antivirus software. The speaker was the Marketing Director for one of the largest A-V developers.

Thus it became that an entire related industry grew up doing nothing more than "testing" and "certifying" antivirus products.

The early "testing" was, too often, designed by people who were without the first clue as to what an antivirus product ought to be able to do. Most people, however, CAN count so the emphasis was on number of viruses found by a given product. The testing itself was rudimentary at best and, most likely, could have been performed by a bright third-grader. A simple three-step process was employed:

1. Turn on PC loaded with virus library. The "library" consists of executable files known (or, sometimes, presumed) to contain virus code.

2. Install and run scanning product.

3. Count identification "hits."

Depending upon the speed of the scanner, the entire operation could take from three to ten minutes per product. These "results" were widely touted by the testing organizations as "The Word" and consumers believed them.

There were errors. The libraries often contained duplicates, non-viruses, and worse.

Publish or Perish

Like it or not, the Numbers Game was the only game in town. There were two reasons. First was the relative lack of sophistication on the part of the consumer. Without the knowledge (or the virus collection) to run independent tests, reliance on reputed outside experts like the National Computer Security Association or the V-Sum certifications seemed to be the only way to get accurate and reliable information.

The second reason was the perceived reliance by the consumer on the testing results. It became a vicious circle with product developers not only chasing their competitors but their own tails as well.

High Stakes Games

Not only were the testing organizations getting paid, huge contracts were being awarded on the results of those tests. One developer began offering a "bounty" on previously unseen viruses to add to his collection... those new viruses were given, or so it is widely believed, to only ONE certifying organization. Thus, the developer always routinely out-scored every other submission against that particular collection since nobody else had ever seen those viruses and couldn't write a scanner to catch them.

In one memorable test, a small US developer named for a furry black-and-white animal submitted EXACTLY the same scanning program for testing as a major European vendor. The ratings and certifications were not the same. Personal bias or faulty testing?

The National Computer Security Association had, for a while, a thriving business in the testing of antivirus products. The NCSA accumulated a virus library and commenced testing by the 1-2-3 method.

By agreement among the vendor members, the library would be "closed" on a date certain, the library would be distributed to the members, the latest "updates" would be prepared and submitted for testing against the "solid" library. All "members" should have scored 100%. They didn't. The smaller developers were at a distinct advantage in those tests because of their relatively rapid "turn around" time assuming two things: that their products were scanners and they had access to the library. Larger companies suffered because their response time was slow.

Still, any antivirus product developer who chose not to join the NCSA was at a distinct disadvantage. But most chose to join rather than fight in order to at least hope for a level playing field.

In some testing situations, there was the presumption that the developers would continually provide the testers with the latest and greatest version of their product. In this way, if Vendor A wanted a head-to-head challenge against Vendor B, all Vendor A had to do was send money. The testing organization would happily provide the person paying the freight with the latest "library" to check product A before submitting it for testing. Often, the developers of product B never knew the "test" took place.

It was a system full of inequities for everyone concerned.

Is Good Testing Possible?

There's an old saw that states that with enough time and money, anything is possible. Therefore, it is theoretically possible to design a millennium testing suite that would accurately test any antivirus product. Scanners could continue to be tested in a version of the 1-2-3 method but with a few improvements: viruses in memory would have to be reliably found and flagged and almost infinite iterations of a polymorphic virus would have to be identified. The time requirement for even these simple improvements would add exponentially to the time required to test a single product.

Since the wave of the future is clearly integrity checking, it would be useful to be able to test integrity checkers. Here's where it gets really interesting. The integrity checking program would need to be loaded and each and every virus, one at a time, would have to be introduced to the system. If the checker finds it, great. Clean the system and insert virus #2. And so on. With over 3,000 known viruses this becomes time-consuming and labor-intensive. Arguably, the process could be automated.

Testing behavior blockers presents many of the same challenges as integrity checkers but with an added bonus on the labor-intensive side: it's not just the infection with the resulting change to a file that's to be looked at—it's the BEHAVIOR of the destructive program that has to be noticed and stopped. Thus, the tester—man or machine—must invoke an action and observe the results.

The cost of preparing and maintaining such a testing center, let alone staffing it, is monumental.

Experience is the Best Teacher

Probably the best place to actually learn about the various antivirus products is the VIRUS-L conference on Internet and its non-moderated sidekick, comp.virus. There you will find many of the world's leading antivirus experts speaking openly about the pluses and minuses of the various products from their own experiences and hands-on testing. For the most part, these people KNOW THEIR STUFF and pull no punches.

If any newly-released products have problems, you'll learn about it on Internet first.

A Final Warning:

As with anything else, consider the source.

Disk Contents: The DR. PANDA UTILITIES

This disk accompanying this book contains the DR. PANDA UTILITIES. These utility programs can tell you if a virus invades your system.

PANDA Systems has been, according to a *PC Magazine* reviewer, working on the solution since before most people knew there was a problem." Our earliest security programs, in 1984, long before there was a PANDA, were the legendary CHK4BOMB and BOMBSQAD. These early attempts at stopping and identifying destructive programs are still widely circulated today.

With the first release of the DR. PANDA UTILITIES in 1987 (containing the PHYSICAL, MONITOR, and LABTEST programs), this small Wilmington, Delaware, utility developer entered the international area of computer security programming.

As time has passed, computer users have also changed. In the early days, people were more concerned with finding, stopping, and cleaning up after computer virus incursions. That mentality persists, even today, among less sophisticated users and managers.

Many believe that the 1990s will be the decade of secure management of personal computer resources. And the first concern of information services professionals will be proactive management.

The DR. PANDA UTILITIES are known around the world as among the most sophisticated, most elegant, most effective, and easiest to use antivirus products in the marketplace. The modular approach of using individual programs and varying use levels within those programs provides the most efficient possible installation. Furthermore, the completely transparent format requires no training and no support obligations for end users and makes the product the most cost effective antivirus solution available.

It is the belief at PANDA Systems that off-the-shelf software, particularly in the security area, is most likely to stay on the shelf due to difficulty of installation and support, the unmanageable size of "do-all" programs, and the memory requirements of functions not needed by 90 percent of users. PANDA is firmly convinced that PC managers, whether home users or IS managers responsible for thousands of machines, know their needs better than developers ever could. Providing an adjustable product at the lowest possible cost per workstation has been PANDA's goal.

The PANDA Programs

The enclosed diskette contains the following utilities from the DR. PANDA family of PC security programs. Note that these programs require an IBM or fully compatible PC running DOS 3.0 or above.

PHYSICAL	Checks for changes to boot sectors, system files, and program files.
PHYSRES	A TSR program utilizing the database created by PHYSICAL. Checks programs for changes at run-time and creates an audit trail.
PHYSED	A simple point-and-shoot editor to be used with the PHYSICAL data file.
PINSTALL	The installation program for PHYSICAL.EXE and PHYSRES creates the associated data file.

MONITOR	A disk BIOS (INT 13) trap that prevents data destruction. Can also trap Read, Write, and Verify calls in a laboratory setting.
TSRMON	Denies TSR status to unauthorized programs.
LABTEST	A utility to peek inside new or suspicious files before they are run.
DRHOOK	Maps the use of RAM by active programs.

Here is a listing of the DR. PANDA program files:

```
DRHOOK     EXE     25018   04-15-93      9:15a

LABTEST    EXE     34637   04-15-93     11:21a

MONITOR    EXE     8467    04-15-93      5:25a

PHYSED     EXE     41589   04-15-93      9:20a

PHYSICAL   PSK     52975   04-15-93      9:26a

PHYSRES    EXE     10584   04-15-93      9:20a

PINSTALL   EXE     33346   04-15-93     11:10a

TSRMON     COM     4058    04-15-93      6:12a
```

To run PHYSRES, MONITOR, or TSRMON as a TSR program, you need 2,880, 4,608, or 2,304K of memory, respectively.

Along with the program files, a full installation will include three associated data files created as part of the installation process:

PHYSICAL.DAT	A listing of programs to be checked by either PHYSICAL or PHYSRES. Note that this file name may be changed during installation.
TSRMON.DAT	A listing of programs allowed to go TSR. Note that this file name may be changed during installation.
PHYSICAL.HST	A complete audit trail created by PHYSRES.

PHYSICAL/PHYSRES

PHYSICAL and PHYSRES use a proprietary algorithm to test the integrity of program files. If a program file changes characteristics between the time

PHYSICAL is installed and PHYSICAL/PHYSRES is run, a warning is issued. PHYSICAL also checks the partition table and boot sectors of all logical drives on a hard disk and replaces them if they have been changed.

PHYSICAL and PHYSRES report changes to the system and selected files. First, be sure that there are no viruses active when PHYSICAL is installed. Run an antivirus scanner before installing PHYSICAL.

After PHYSICAL is installed on a clean machine, it will report on any changes to files that could indicate a virus attack, whether the virus is a known strain or a new development.

Unlike antivirus scanners, you do not need to update the PHYSICAL data file unless you upgrade existing software or add new programs.

PINSTALL must be used to create the program file, PHYSICAL.EXE. During the installation process, essential information is gathered from the PC itself and stored in PHYSICAL.EXE.

Installing PHYSICAL

Follow these steps to install PHYSICAL:

1. With the DR. PANDA diskette in drive A type:

    ```
    A:
    PINSTALL
    ```

2. A window (Figure 13.1) appears asking if you want to install boot virus protection. The boot sector is the first sector on the hard disk and contains a small program that runs when the computer is first started. Many known viruses replace this program with a virus program. PHYSICAL can write a new self-protecting program to this vital system area to protect against this type of virus. Do not choose this option if you have a special boot program already in place.

3. A prompt appears requesting a name for the program and data files, as shown in Figure 13.2. The default is PHYSICAL.EXE. It is recommended that a unique file name be chosen in the final installation. Unique file

names discourage directed virus attacks against PANDA products. The data file will have the same file name with the extension .DAT.

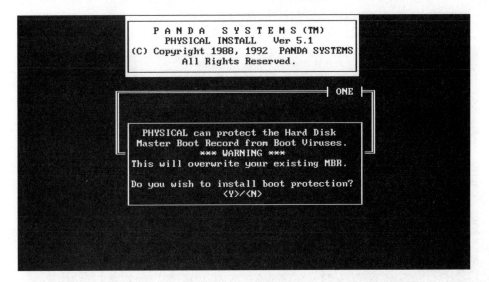

Figure 13.1   Boot protection.

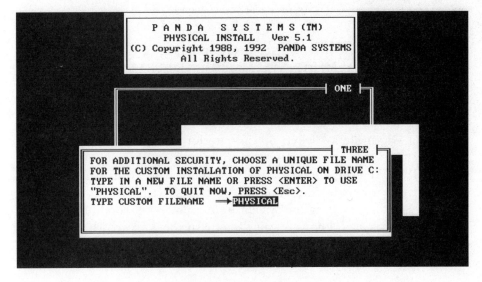

Figure 13.2   Choose a file name.

4. PINSTALL now asks for a directory, as shown in Figure 13.3. The default is /PANDA. You can choose any directory on the disk or create a new one. If the directory does not exist, PINSTALL will make a new directory called PANDA.

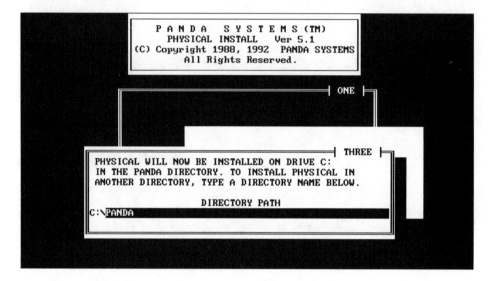

Figure 13.3 Choose a directory.

5. PINSTALL now writes the comparison model of COMMAND.COM, IBMDOS.COM/MSDOS.SYS, IBMBIO.COM/BIO.SYS, and the boot sectors to the PHYSICAL.EXE file.

6. At this point, you are given the option of backing up the PHYSICAL program on a diskette (see Figure 13.4). It is strongly recommended that you make a backup on diskette for several reasons. If a virus becomes active in the system, it could very easily attach itself to the PHYSICAL program before the program can tell you that a virus is active. For truly safe computing, you should always check for viruses after booting the system from a power-off condition using a write-protected, known clean diskette in the A drive. This prevents any virus from entering memory and skewing the results of the PHYSICAL check.

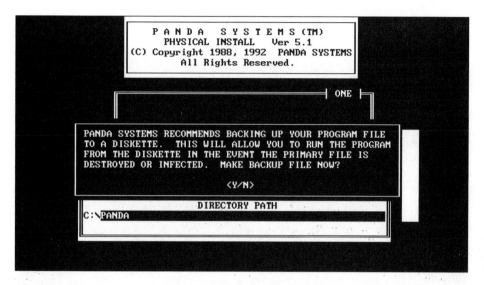

```
        P A N D A    S Y S T E M S (TM)
          PHYSICAL INSTALL    Ver 5.1
      (C) Copyright 1988, 1992   PANDA SYSTEMS
              All Rights Reserved.


                                         ╡ ONE ╞


   PANDA SYSTEMS RECOMMENDS BACKING UP YOUR PROGRAM FILE
   TO A DISKETTE.  THIS WILL ALLOW YOU TO RUN THE PROGRAM
   FROM THE DISKETTE IN THE EVENT THE PRIMARY FILE IS
   DESTROYED OR INFECTED.  MAKE BACKUP FILE NOW?

                       <Y/N>

                 DIRECTORY PATH
   C:\PANDA
```

Figure 13.4 Backup option.

7. Additional files for comparison against the installation model are entered at this time. There are three options in addition to the default (see Figure 13.5):

- No additional files to be checked (default).

- Automatic check of .EXE and .COM files on all logical drives of hard disk.

- Check selected files on any drive. In high security settings, this may include all files on a drive.

- Check and compare selected files on any drive. This is a lengthy and tedious process, but recommended in high security settings. For each file to be compared, the original diskettes are required. It is wise to write-protect them first. As PINSTALL works its way through the selected files, you will be prompted to insert the program disks. If files do not compare properly, a careful examination is indicated.

If this is not the first time you have installed PHYSICAL, you will see a window that offers three choices (see Figure 13.6). You can add to an existing

PHYSICAL data file, begin a new data file, or quit and leave the existing data file in place.

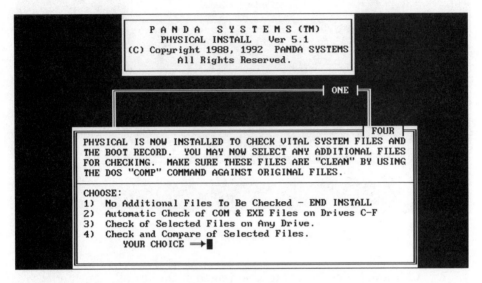

Figure 13.5 Check additional files.

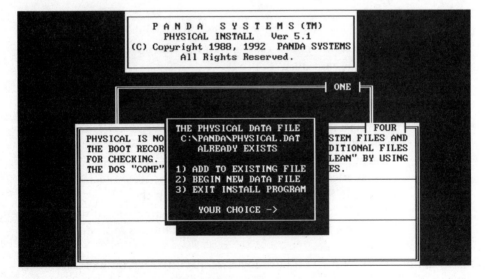

Figure 13.6 Data file exists.

Running PHYSICAL/PHYSRES

All antivirus programs, whether scanners or integrity checkers, are more accurate if the computer is started from a power-off condition with a known uninfected DOS diskette in drive A. This prevents any stealth virus from taking over the operating system and returning false data to the virus checker. You are strongly urged to make a bootable diskette that contains the DOS system files and PHYSICAL.EXE. After you make the diskette, you should write-protect it. For best protection, run PHYSICAL from the diskette after a power-off restart.

Because experience shows that most users will not reboot the computer to run antivirus software, PHYSICAL has built-in safeguards against most stealth techniques. However, it is impossible to guard against every possible method a virus may use to hide from antivirus software.

PHYSICAL/PHYSRES may be run in several different ways:

1. Automatic system check at boot up.
2. Full system check at any time.
3. Automatic check of individual programs at run time.

It is recommended that PHYSICAL be included in each PC's AUTOEXEC.BAT file to ensure that a complete system check is run each time the system is started.

In many settings, PCs run 24 hours a day. We recommend that PHYSICAL be run by typing **PHYSICAL** and pressing **Enter** at the command line at designated intervals.

Make sure that you have included the proper path to the subdirectory where PHYSICAL and PHYSRES are located in your PATH statement. (When the PATH statement or any other portions of AUTOEXEC.BAT are changed, AUTOEXEC must be run to activate the changes.)

If you include PHYSICAL in the AUTOEXEC.BAT file, it is recommended that you use the command line switch "/N" after the name *PHYSICAL* so the program will run automatically with no user intervention unless there is a corrupted file in the system.

PHYSRES should be included in AUTOEXEC.BAT to check each program automatically as it is accessed. PHYSRES is a TSR program. Make sure that it is loaded in AUTOEXEC.BAT before TSRMON so that it is automatically granted TSR status without including it in the approved file. (See the section on TSRMON later in this chapter.)

PHYSICAL may be run at any time by typing the command **PHYSICAL** at the DOS prompt. If you changed the name at installation, the new file name should be typed instead of PHYSICAL.

The installation program automatically records the drive, path, and file name specified for the PHYSICAL.DAT file. If changes are made after installation, PHYSICAL will ask for the new information. If changes are necessary for added security, a re-installation of PHYSICAL is recommended.

PHYSRES shares the same data file created for PHYSICAL by PINSTALL. The audit trail created by PHYSRES is called PHYSICAL.HST and is stored in the /PANDA subdirectory. PHYSICAL.HST simply adds each new program called to a list. You should determine a method for clearing this file at regular intervals.

The PHYSICAL Information Screens

The first screen (see Figure 13.7) displays information about the partition sectors, boot sectors, DOS Files, memory allocation, and companion files.

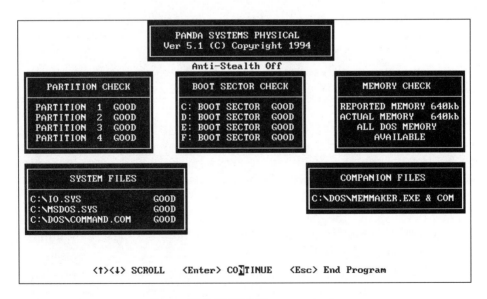

Figure 13.7 PHYSICAL system check.

If the partition sectors, boot sectors, and DOS files match the signatures stored at installation, the status is reported as GOOD. If the signatures do not match, the original sector is written back to the proper place and the status is reported as REPL. If the boot sector needs to be replaced, it could be a sign of a boot sector virus. Sometimes you can change the boot sector by changing DOS versions or running the FDISK program with the /MBR switch. In this case, PHYSICAL should be re-installed after you make the change.

The total amount of memory and the amount of memory known to DOS is displayed. If some memory is hidden from DOS, the cause should be investigated. There are several legitimate programs that use the upper 1K of DOS memory, but any difference greater than 1K may mean a virus has shortened DOS memory for its own use.

Companion files are reported on the first screen. A companion file is a .COM file with the same base name as an .EXE file. DOS will always run a .COM file before an .EXE file, and several viruses make use of this fact by creating a .COM file with the same name as a trusted .EXE file. These companion files are sometimes hidden from a normal directory search and can easily be overlooked. Not all companion files are viruses, but anytime new companion files start appearing, you should be on the alert for a companion virus.

The second PHYSICAL screen displays information about the program files on the system. If the file signature is the same as when the database was created, the status will be reported as GOOD, as shown in Figure 13.8.

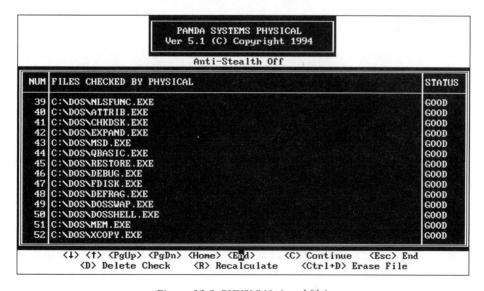

Figure 13.8 PHYSICAL (good file).

If the file has been deleted since the data base was created or updated, the status will be reported as MISSING (see Figure 13.9).

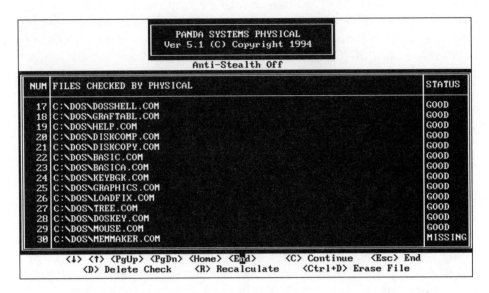

```
                    ┌─────────────────────────────────┐
                    │   PANDA SYSTEMS PHYSICAL         │
                    │   Ver 5.1 (C) Copyright 1994     │
                    └─────────────────────────────────┘
                         Anti-Stealth Off

 NUM FILES CHECKED BY PHYSICAL                          STATUS
  17 C:\DOS\DOSSHELL.COM                                GOOD
  18 C:\DOS\GRAFTABL.COM                                GOOD
  19 C:\DOS\HELP.COM                                    GOOD
  20 C:\DOS\DISKCOMP.COM                                GOOD
  21 C:\DOS\DISKCOPY.COM                                GOOD
  22 C:\DOS\BASIC.COM                                   GOOD
  23 C:\DOS\BASICA.COM                                  GOOD
  24 C:\DOS\KEYBGK.COM                                  GOOD
  25 C:\DOS\GRAPHICS.COM                                GOOD
  26 C:\DOS\LOADFIX.COM                                 GOOD
  27 C:\DOS\TREE.COM                                    GOOD
  28 C:\DOS\DOSKEY.COM                                  GOOD
  29 C:\DOS\MOUSE.COM                                   GOOD
  30 C:\DOS\MEMMAKER.COM                                MISSING

   <↓> <↑> <PgUp> <PgDn> <Home> <End>     <C> Continue    <Esc> End
        <D> Delete Check    <R> Recalculate   <Ctrl+D> Erase File
```

Figure 13.9 PHYSICAL (missing file).

A file whose signature has changed will be reported as BAD (see Figure 13.10). This does not necessarily mean the file contains a virus. It could be a new copy of the program that was installed after PHYSICAL recorded the signature.

At the end of the list of file names stored in the PHYSICAL data file, you see a list of programs that are not checked by PHYSICAL. These are programs that may have been added to the disk after PHYSICAL was installed. These files are reported as NO CHK.

The file status screen will continue to scroll until a file is reached whose status is "BAD." To stop the scrolling at any time, press the **S** key on the keyboard. Pressing the **ESC** key will terminate the program and return to DOS.

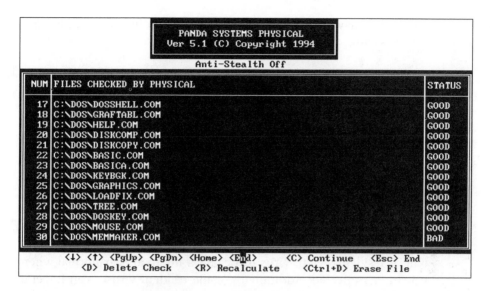

Figure 13.10 PHYSICAL (bad file).

If the scroll is stopped, either by pressing the S key or by a BAD status, the up and down arrow keys will move the display file name by file name (one line at a time). The **PgUp** and **PgDn** keys will advance or retreat one full screen, while the **Home** and **End** keys will move to the first or last page. Pressing the C key will continue the scroll until another BAD status is reached or until the S key is pressed. After the end of the file is reached, the C key will have no effect. In systems with a mouse, screen icons represent each of the possible key presses. A left button click on the icon has the same effect as pressing the key. To remove a known deleted file from checking by PHYSICAL, simply press the D key.

If you are using a mouse pointer, you can move the mouse cursor to the appropriate area of the menu bar and press the left mouse button.

PHYSICAL Options

A command line switch can be set using either the DOS / character or the UNIX - character. Upper- or lowercase can be used for the switch. Following are the switches that can be used by PHYSICAL:

1. **Sort switch (/S):** The /S switch will sort the file name display. Because PHYSICAL must sort drive, path, file name, and extension,

the sorting may take some time. A window will indicate that PHYSI-CAL is sorting the data file.

PHYSICAL /S

2. **No-stop switch (/N):** The /N switch can be used if you want the program to run with no key presses and exit if there are no changed files. In this mode the companion file check is not made. This switch is useful if PHYSICAL is part of the AUTOEXEC.BAT file because it will run and exit if nothing has changed in the system.

    PHYSICAL /N

3. **Anti-stealth switch (/A):** PHYSICAL can bypass any DOS and BIOS calls to the disk system in case a so-called stealth virus is in the system. A resident stealth virus can cause a file to appear normal when it is in fact infected. Additionally, some resident viruses can infect a file when a program like PHYSICAL uses DOS functions to read the file. Even though PHYSICAL uses interrupt trapping to prevent a write to the disk while it is checking the files, there are a few viruses that can bypass such protective measures. Unless PHYSICAL is run after starting the PC from a known clean diskette, you should always use the anti-stealth switch.

    Note that disk compression or other nonstandard DOS disk storage methods make the disk inaccessible to PHYSICAL's anti-stealth functions. Because DOS version 6+ has included disk compression software, PHYSICAL no longer has the anti-stealth mode turned on as a default. If you do not use disk compression software and want to run PHYSICAL in the anti-stealth mode, you must use the /A switch on the command line or include it in a batch file. With the /A switch, if PHYSICAL cannot find a file using non-DOS functions, PHYSICAL reverts to standard DOS calls.

    PHYSICAL /A

4. **Change data file name (/F):** PHYSICAL uses the database created by the PINSTALL program regardless of what file name you chose when you installed PHYSICAL. To use a PHYSICAL database different than the one created by the PINSTALL program, include the file name

following the switch. Note that there is a space after PHYSICAL, but no space between the switch and file name.

PHYSICAL /Fother.one

PHYSICAL Error Conditions

Missing Files

If a file is missing from the system, PHYSICAL will report the status as MISS-ING on the screen. If you are sure that you have intentionally deleted the file, eliminate the missing file from the PHYSICAL database by pressing the **D** key when the file name is highlighted.

Bad Files—Good

Physical will report a BAD status if the file has changed since the signature was calculated. If another file is copied to the same file name, the signature for that file name will change. This is most likely a result of upgrading to a new version of a program. The signature can be recalculated by pressing **R** when the file name is highlighted. (Note that with PHYSRES in memory, the signature may be automatically updated.)

Bad Files—Bad

If you have not changed versions of a program or otherwise changed a file, a BAD status probably indicates that a virus has changed the file. PHYSICAL provides two choices for virus infected files:

1. Do nothing and hope for the best.
2. Delete and reload the infected file. The infected file can be deleted by pressing **CTRL-D**, the Control key and the D key together (at the same time). A window will ask for confirmation of the deletion. After an infected program has been deleted, it may be recopied to the hard disk from a clean version.

Not Checked Files

If PHYSICAL reports NO CHK, it means that the file name is not in the PHYSICAL database. PHYSICAL cannot check a file if it does not have a proper signature for that file. You can use the database editor PHYSED to add the file to the list, but you should scan the file for viruses first.

Bad Partition or Boot Sector

When PHYSICAL is installed, copies of the partition and boot sectors are stored as part of the PHYSICAL.EXE file. These copies can be used to repair an infected partition or boot sector. If PHYSICAL reports a BAD partition or boot sector, the original copy of that sector will be written back to the disk in the appropriate place.

WARNING Some boot infecting viruses hide by directing attempts to access the boot sector to another sector containing a copy of the actual boot sector. Therefore, even though PHYSICAL reports that the sector was replaced, it may not actually be written to the correct sector. If the system is started from a power-off condition with an original write-protected DOS diskette, PHYSICAL will report the condition of the actual partition and boot sectors, and replacements will be properly written.

N O T E If you have repartitioned or reformatted the hard disk since PHYSICAL was installed, an attempt to repair the partition or boot sector could make the hard disk unusable. Be sure to rein-stall PHYSICAL after repartitioning or reformatting a hard disk.

PHYSRES

PHYSRES is the on-the-fly version of PHYSICAL. This is a TSR (terminate and stay resident) program that checks the signature of any program in the PHYSICAL database every time it is accessed. PANDA suggests adding the name *PHYSRES* to the AUTOEXEC.BAT file.

PHYSRES will run in the background with no user intervention unless something happens to change a file in the PHYSICAL database.

If a file is changed, an alarm will sound, and a message is displayed identifying the changed file and the program currently running.

If a file is changed, PHYSRES assumes the worst and will prevent a changed file from executing, being copied, or being renamed. In addition, the program that changed the file is also marked as bad and cannot be run, copied, or renamed. Both files should be deleted and replaced with unaltered copies.

PHYSRES automatically updates the database if a new program file is added to the system or an existing program file is upgraded from the DOS command line using the COPY function. The operation of PHYSRES with install programs may vary.

If a program file is run that is not in the database, a message box appears asking for instructions. There are three choices:

Esc   Do not run the program.

R   Run the program.

A   Add the program to the database.

If you choose to either run the program or add the program's signature to the database, you could be running a virus-infected file. Be especially cautious of any additional PHYSRES warnings such as an attempt to change another program file. This is a sure indication that the program is infected with a virus.

PHYSRES Options

Several options may be entered on the command line following the name *PHYSRES*. If PHYSRES is already in memory, the new switches will take effect immediately without a new copy of the program being placed in memory:

1. **Deactivate switch (/D):** This switch deactivates PHYSRES and, if possible, removes the program from memory.

2. **Professional switch (/P):** PHYSRES assumes normal end user operation of the computer. That means use for word processing, databases, or spreadsheets, perhaps a game or two, and connection to an

on-line service for electronic mail. Normal use constitutes a fairly stable program file content of the computer. Power users who write their own programs and make frequent changes to the file structure may wish to make use of the /P switch. Some operations forbidden by PHYSRES in normal use, may be bypassed by entering a key press.

3. **History switch (/H[filename])**: PHYSRES creates a history file of all programs run. This file is in plain ASCII text and includes the program name and time and date run. The default file name is PHYSICAL.HST.

4. **Filename switch (/Ffilename.exe)**: The name of the PHYSICAL database file is hard-coded into the program during the install process. To override the default name, use this switch.

PHYSED

This is a simple point-and-shoot editor to make changes to the PHYSICAL data file. To access the editing program, type **PHYSED** and press **Enter**.

Editing the PHYSICAL Data File

If PHYSICAL was installed properly, the name of the data file is coded into the PHYSED program. If the data file does not exist, you will be prompted to supply the complete path and name of the file.

PHYSICAL normally checks any file with an executable extension. In DOS these extensions include .COM, .EXE, .SYS, and .OV? (overlay files). If you check any other files, enter the names in the space provided. To accept the default extensions, just press **Enter** (see Figure 13.11).

PHYSED now checks all files in the database against the actual files on the disk. The disk is then checked for files of the proper extension that are not in the database.

While the check is taking place, a "PLEASE WAIT" message will appear, and the disk access light will go on.

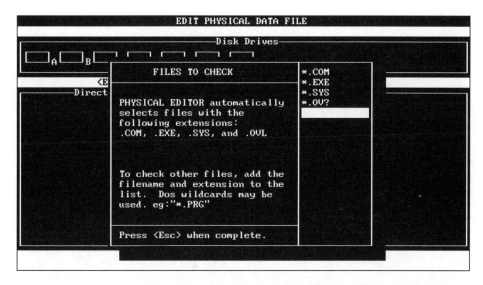

Figure 13.11 PHYSED files to check.

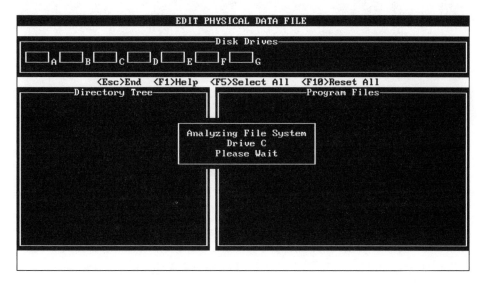

Figure 13.12 PHYSED checking files.

After the check is complete, three windows appear on the screen. These windows are compatible with many popular file system programs. The drives appear across the top of the screen, the directories of the current drive appear to the left, and the files in the current directory appear to the right.

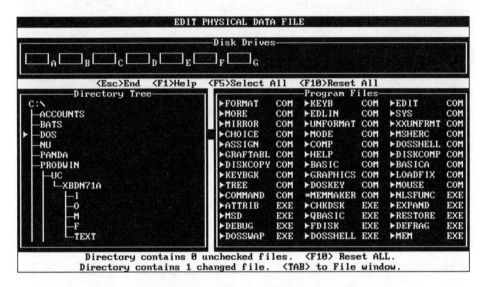

Figure 13.13 PHYSED editing screen.

The **Tab** key will move the highlight cursor from window to window.

If any file on a drive is reported BAD or NOT CHECKED, the drive, directory, and file name will blink. To add the PHYSICAL check to all files on a drive, from the drive window press **F5**. Pressing **F5** from the directory window will add all files in that directory to the database. Checked files have an arrow pointing to their name in the file window.

If a file has changed, an asterisk (*) will appear next to the file name. If you know the file has changed for a legitimate reason, move the highlight cursor to the file name and press **R** to recalculate the signature. If you suspect a virus, do not recalculate the signature because this defeats the purpose of PHYSICAL.

After all files are included in the database and the signatures match, the blinking will stop. Pressing **ESC** will end the PHYSED program. You have to confirm any changes to the PHYSICAL database before exiting.

MONITOR

MONITOR is a small TSR program that constantly tracks calls to INT 13, the disk access interrupt. When a program calls an INT 13 activity, MONITOR will respond. The default level of MONITOR stops only on potentially destructive activities: a FORMAT call, a write to the boot sector, or a write to the partition table. MONITOR also analyzes data before a write to the file allocation table (FAT) and, if improper chaining is present, will terminate the operation. Monitor can be "juiced up" in a lab setting to intercept on READ, WRITE, and VERIFY calls. The /P option for professionals is also available to continue in all trapped situations.

Installing MONITOR

Copy MONITOR into the (pathed) PANDA subdirectory. It can be accessed either through a call in AUTOEXEC.BAT or from the command line.

Normally you would run MONITOR in the default mode, which operates in the background. However, there are several command line switches that make MONITOR a debugging tool. The additional MONITOR switches are:

/R	Intercept all READ calls.
/W	Intercept all WRITE calls.
/V	Intercept all VERIFY calls.
/P	Professional level allowing proceed.

MONITOR prevents the FORMAT call. Should you need to format a disk, you can disable MONITOR by typing **MONITOR X** on the command line. Remember to install MONITOR again after formatting a disk.

TSRMON

Many viruses operate by remaining in memory after the host program finishes. When a program is run, DOS gives it access to all the remaining memory. Most programs return this memory to DOS when they end. However DOS contains routines that allow a program to retain a chunk of memory after it exits. Most TSR programs (including TSRMON) legitimately use this feature to perform useful activities throughout the computing session.

Viruses that use this function can attach themselves to a legitimate host program that does not normally exit and stay in memory.

The TSRMON program is a behavior blocker, antivirus program that limits another program's access to memory after it has ended. When TSRMON is installed, no additional programs will be allowed TSR status through DOS unless pre-approved. This will prevent most resident viruses from activating even if they have slipped through previous screening.

WARNING

Some resident viruses do not use DOS functions to remain in memory. TSRMON will not be able to report these activities.

To install TSRMON, copy TSRMON.COM into the PANDA subdirectory.

Creating the Optional Data File

Using either the **DOS COPY CON TSRMON.DAT** command or an editor, create a file called TSRMON.DAT in the PANDA subdirectory. Include up to ten TSR programs with the full program name, each on an individual line.

Running TSRMON

Either from AUTOEXEC.BAT or the command line, invoke TSRMON with the following command:

TSRMON /fTRSMON.DAT

N O T E

The /f command identifies the associated data file, which may have any name you choose to assign.

If running from AUTOEXEC.BAT, make sure to include the path to the data file as in:

TSRMON /fC:\PANDA\TSRMON.DAT

If running from the \PANDA subdirectory, /fTSRMON.DAT is sufficient.

If you include TSRMON in the AUTOEXEC.BAT file after all legitimate TSR programs have been loaded, you do not have to include the data file. Just remember that after TSRMON is run, all further TSR attempts will be flagged.

LABTEST

LABTEST is a program designed for use by security professionals or other sophisticated users. It is a "peeking" utility that enables you to learn certain information about an unknown file without actually running the program and exposing your system to risk. First, LABTEST reads the code strings and reports on BIOS calls and possible writes to absolute sectors. This information automatically appears on the screen.

Second, all ASCII text strings within the program are displayed. To see the text strings, press **F10**. Occasionally, garbage ASCII characters display with LABTEST. These can be removed with a standard text editor.

Please note that the warning for a read or write to an absolute sector depends on coding that is part of the program. Rarely will the same code strings that indicate a write to an absolute sector be contained in data portions of a program. A skilled technician should examine the program through DOS DEBUG or similar means.

The main purpose of examining text strings is to find hidden hints that virus writers often leave. In this case, illustrated in Figure 13.14, however, it's simply a friendly message from Peter Norton, creator of the well-known Norton Utilities. The file we examined is the main Norton Utility file, NU.COM. The message says, "Best Wishes from Peter Norton."

DRHOOK

This is an extremely sophisticated program for use by computer professionals. It displays the DOS memory usage by TSR programs at the time it is called (see Figure 13.15). Pressing **F3** displays the device driver chain for examination.

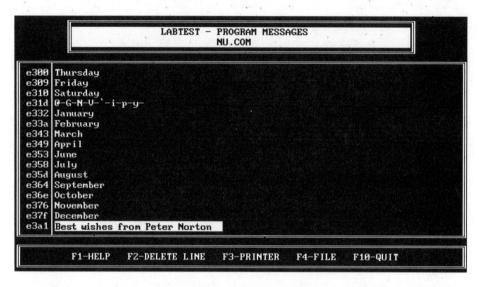

Figure 13.14 LABTEST screen.

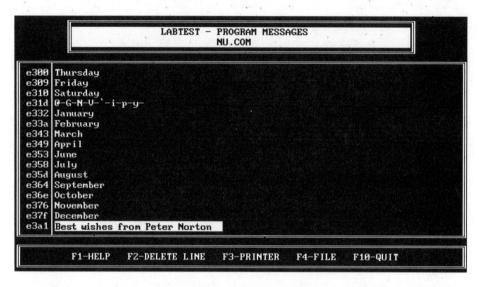

Figure 13.15 DRHOOK screen.

WARNING

PANDA Systems develops utilities to a strict IBM PC-DOS standard. Every effort is made to ensure that their products will work properly with 100% compatibles as well. Experienced PC users are aware that even the smallest changes from the standard can seriously effect the operation of a PC at a number of different levels. You should also be aware that the IBM logo on the outside of the machine does not always guarantee 100% IBM standard components.

Management Considerations

The PANDA Systems philosophy is that computer security (and the associated field of computer viruses) is a management problem that can be solved through technology.

It is becoming increasingly clear that some technological interaction is essential to maintain PC and larger systems security. PANDA products have been designed to be used as cost-effective management tools.

Following are brief outlines of what each major PANDA product does in a real-life setting, the advantages and disadvantages of the program, and a discussion of how they might be defeated.

PHYSICAL/PHYSRES

By definition, virus code must make some changes to an executable file. PHYSICAL is an integrity-checking antivirus program that makes certain that almost any newly-infected file will be identified. As with any integrity check, previously infected programs cannot be identified. However, the purpose of integrity checking is to stop a virus before it spreads to other programs necessitating expensive cleanup procedures. With the rapid proliferation of viruses, integrity checking is an alternative to constant expensive updating of scanning antivirus programs that look for specific viruses. New programs added to the computer should be checked by an antivirus scanner as part of good security management.

PHYSICAL can be run at boot-up (if included in AUTOEXEC.BAT) or from the command line. This can be a disadvantage in a 24-hour setting, where computers are infrequently turned off or where users will not reliably run the program. The addition of PHYSRES to the utility suite eliminates most of this problem. PHYSICAL and PHYSRES are almost impossible to circumvent due to the random, proprietary algorithm. In addition, the renaming of the command files and, particularly, renaming the associated data file, make targeted destruction nearly impossible.

After PHYSICAL and PHYSRES are installed, they require no user interaction. Changes to the underlying data file containing the comparison data are easily accomplished through a simple point-and-shoot editor, PHYSED.

The run-time of PHYSICAL will depend upon the number of files to be compared and the speed of the PC. The run-time of PHYSRES is negligible because only one program file is being checked at a time. When an error condition is encountered, a warning message is displayed on the screen with full information as to the location of the file that has not compared properly.

MONITOR

The elementary nature of DOS allows only a few truly bad things to happen when data are either destroyed or made extremely difficult to recover. These are reformatting of a disk and corruption of the boot sector, file allocation table, or partition data. There are several excellent utilities available that help users recover even from these formerly fatal conditions. Using those utilities, however, is time consuming and requires a technician with a high level of expertise. Each of the destructive acts must happen by a program accessing the DOS interrupt INT 13, the disk access interrupt. MONITOR is a behavior-blocking antivirus program that analyzes each request to use the interrupt and returns an error condition when a potentially destructive request is intercepted. Only on the professional level (/P) is the user allowed to proceed.

There have been lab viruses suggested within the security community where destruction could occur without passing through INT 13. Few have been seen in actual practice. An INT 13 trap program should be considered as an essential final line of defense, not a panacea.

MONITOR also functions as a protective device against an even more common problem, user error. With MONITOR in place, an inadvertent hard drive format cannot occur. Because MONITOR stops all requests to format, an installation where the formatting of floppies is required will need a special .BAT file for the format procedure that disables MONITOR.

When MONITOR encounters an attempted destructive write, full information is displayed to the screen and a warning tone sounds.

TSRMON

The most prevalent of PC/MS-DOS–based viruses, the Jerusalem family, must attain TSR status to either replicate or, on the encoded dates, destroy data. Other viruses also use this technique. In addition, the proper management of TSR programs presents a management challenge.

TSRMON accepts all TSR programs loaded with AUTOEXEC.BAT before it is loaded as well as up to ten additional TSRs identified in the associated data file. If an unapproved TSR makes a load attempt, the user is offered a proceed/fail option with full screen information about the program requesting TSR status.

A small downside risk associated with this technology might occur when an approved program becomes infected with a virus and is allowed TSR status. For example, if a new, infected version of SideKick with the same name as the older, clean version, SK.COM, were run from the A drives, TSR status would be granted and infection could proceed.

There are a few resident viruses that do not use the normal DOS functions to remain resident. TSRMON is not designed to check for nonstandard memory management.

Additional PANDA Security Products

PANDA Systems maintains a full library of additional security programs in addition to the DR. PANDA UTILITIES. These products can be ordered directly from PANDA Systems and are discussed in the following sections.

BEARTRAP

Existing policies and procedures in most large, end user installations include three main points: new or untested software must not be installed without management approval; unapproved software (e. g., games) must not be run; and software licensed for use by the employer must not be copied for home use. This nonintrusive program enforces these policies and procedures. The BEARTRAP warning messages are only seen when an unauthorized activity is attempted. BEARTRAP may also be installed with no warning messages present.

Setting up BEARTRAP is done through an encrypted, password-locked system manager function (BEARMAKE) that creates a data file for comparison. Additional programs or upgrades to current programs may be added to the comparison file with a few keystrokes in the BEAREDIT function.

Numerous additional precautions have been programmed as part of BEARTRAP to eliminate the possibility of bypassing the program. These methods are proprietary and will only be released to prospective clients under proper nondisclosure agreements.

In most end-user settings, BEARTRAP prevents any destructive code from ever entering a user's system. For many installations, it is the only program that may be necessary.

BEARLOCK

BEARLOCK makes the hard disk accessible only if the PC is booted from the hard disk using a special password. If the PC is started from drive A, the hard disk is not recognized by DOS. If the correct password is not entered, the PC will not boot. Unlike other passwording programs, BEARLOCK is not a part of CONFIG.SYS or AUTOEXEC.BAT and cannot be circumvented.

NODEL

NODEL (no delete) prevents users from erasing files by using DEL or ERASE commands from DOS. This program is useful for PCs that are accessible to the public at large and prevents users from deleting programs and data. Additional DOS commands can also be defeated, such as FORMAT, by including the name on the command line when NODEL is loaded.

Putting It All Together

End Users

In most settings, the bulk of PCs are in the hands of end users who use standard applications packages and whose system configurations ought to remain static with the exception of occasionally adding a new application or upgrading an existing one. BEARTRAP presents a comprehensive solution for end users because no new programs are allowed on the PC without management approval. As a practical matter, MONITOR installed on end user machines is an extra level of security for data even in relatively static settings.

Mid-Level Use

For our purposes, mid-level use means those workstations where new programs are often added or evaluated, where the workstation does not remain in a static configuration, or where more freedom is desirable. BEARTRAP is probably not applicable in this setting unless the user assumes the system manager function and uses BEARTRAP to make sure that the PC is protected from unauthorized users running outside programs or copying programs on or off the PC.

The three major DR. PANDA programs, PHYSICAL/PHYSRES, MONITOR, and TSRMON should be used in the mid-level. With the different installation possibilities, it is a simple matter to custom design an individual workstation's security program in a way that will not only protect the PC but be totally transparent to the user.

Power Users

These highly sophisticated users ought not be hemmed in by restrictive products but, rather, given tools that are easy to use and provide a high level of protection. The BEARTRAP function may be used as described above. With the editing functions available, programmers can choose not to have PHYSICAL check work-in-progress that is constantly changing while continuing to check standard files. The professional level and available switches of MONITOR provides a strong debugging tool and protection from some programming errors and the misdeeds of destructive code. TSRMON allows a proceed/fail option that is not burdensome to the talented user.

Troubleshooting

Some of the PANDA utilities rely on system information being in specific locations and were written and tested on pure IBM systems. Some non-IBM systems may not be able to use one or more of the utilities. None of the problems indicated below will in any way compromise the integrity of the system.

MONITOR reads information in the hard disk partition table for head, cylinder, and sector information. If the partition table does not keep this information at the standard IBM/Microsoft location, errors in reporting may occur. The most common problem is reporting a bad FAT write when data is being written. If MONITOR is unable to decipher which are the FAT sectors, an incorrect error may be reported. MONITOR should not be used on these systems.

MONITOR displays messages on the screen using the BIOS screen functions in text mode. Graphics modes are not supported and no windowed message will be displayed in those modes. The distinctive MONITOR siren will sound.

DRHOOK traces the DOS memory allocation chain on start-up. Occasionally, a program will exit and leave the memory chain in a state that causes DRHOOK to enter an endless loop. The system should be rebooted if this happens.

Some TSR programs may conflict with the PANDA TSR programs. All PANDA TSR programs chain to any interrupt handlers already in memory. If a conflict occurs, try loading PANDA TSRs after the TSR causing the conflict.

Some memory management systems are incompatible with PANDA TSR programs. If a conflict occurs, you have to choose between using the memory management system and using the PANDA TSR program.

Out of memory errors may occur on some of the PANDA programs. All available memory is used for global data and should be sufficient for reasonable systems. Systems with little available memory or an unusually large number of directories and files may cause some of the utilities to encounter this error. If LABTEST does not have enough memory to store all the ASCII text within a given file, the display is truncated when memory is exhausted.

Frequently Asked Questions on VIRUS-L/comp.virus

This appendix discusses the VIRUS-L/comp.virus discussion forums. These forums focus on computer virus issues. The following is from the VIRUS-L/comp.virus documentation:

This document is intended to answer the most Frequently Asked Questions (FAQs) about computer viruses. As you can see, there are many of them! If you are desperately seeking help after recently discovering what appears to be a virus on your computer, consider skimming through sections A and B to learn the essential jargon, then concentrate on section C.

If you may have found a new virus, or are not quite sure if some file or boot sector is infected, it is important to understand the protocol for raising such questions, e.g. to avoid asking questions that can be answered in this document, and to avoid sending "live" viruses except to someone who is responsible (and even then in a safe form!).

Above all, remember the time to really worry about viruses is BEFORE your computer gets one!

The FAQ is a dynamic document, which changes as people's questions change. Contributions are gratefully accepted—please e-mail them to me at krvw@cert.org. The most recent copy of this FAQ will always be available on the VIRUS-L/comp.virus archives, including the anonymous FTP on cert.org (192.88.209.5) in the file: pub/virus-l/FAQ.virus-l

Ken van Wyk, moderator VIRUS-L/comp.virus

Primary contributors (in alphabetical order):

Mark Aitchison <phys169@csc.canterbury.ac.nz>

Vaughan Bell <vaughan@computing-department.poly-south-west.ac.uk>

Matt Bishop <matt.bishop@dartmouth.edu>

Vesselin Bontchev <bontchev@fbihh.informatik.uni-hamburg.de>

Olivier M.J. Crepin-Leblond <umeeb37@vaxa.cc.ic.ac.uk>

David Chess <chess@watson.ibm.com>

John-David Childs <con_jdc@lewis.umt.edu>

Nick FitzGerald <cctr132@csc.canterbury.ac.nz>

Claude Bersano-Hayes <hayes@urvax.urich.edu>

John Kida <jhk@washington.ssds.COM>

Donald G. Peters <Peters@Dockmaster.NCSC.Mil>

A. Padgett Peterson <padgett%tccslr.dnet@mmc.com>

Y. Radai <radai@hujivms.huji.ac.il>

Rob Slade <rslade@sfu.ca>

Gene Spafford <spaf@cs.purdue.edu>

Otto Stolz <rzotto@nyx.uni-konstanz.de>

Questions answered in this document

Section A: Sources of Information and Antiviral Software (Where can I find HELP..!)

A1) What is VIRUS-L/comp.virus?

A2) What is the difference between VIRUS-L and comp.virus?

A3) How do I get onto VIRUS-L/comp.virus?

A4) What are the guidelines for VIRUS-L?

A5) How can I get back-issues of VIRUS-L?

A6) What is VALERT-L?

A7) What are the known viruses, their names, major symptoms and possible cures?

A8) Where can I get free or shareware antivirus programs?

A9) Where can I get more information on viruses, etc.?

Section B: Definitions (What is ...?)

B1) What are computer viruses (and why should I worry about them)?

B2) What is a Trojan Horse?

B3) What are the main types of PC viruses?

B4) What is a stealth virus?

B5) What is a polymorphic virus?

B6) What are fast and slow infectors?

B7) What is a sparse infector?

B8) What is a companion virus?

B9) What is an armored virus?

B10) Miscellaneous Jargon and Abbreviations.

Section C: Virus Detection (Is my computer infected? What do I do?)

C1) What are the symptoms and indications of a virus infection?

C2) What steps should be taken in diagnosing and identifying viruses?

C3) What is the best way to remove a virus?

C4) What does the <insert name here> virus do?

C5) What are "false positives" and "false negatives"?

C6) Could an antiviral program itself be infected?

C7) Where can I get a virus scanner for my Unix system?

C8) Why does an antiviral scanner report an infection only sometimes?

C9) Is my disk infected with the Stoned virus?

C10) I think I have detected a new virus; what do I do?

C11) CHKDSK reports 639K (or less) total memory on my system; am I infected?

C12) I have an infinite loop of sub-directories on my hard drive; am I infected?

Section D: Protection Plans (*What should I do to prepare against viruses?*)

D1) What is the best protection policy for my computer?

D2) Is it possible to protect a computer system with only software?

D3) Is it possible to write-protect the hard disk with only software?

D4) What can be done with hardware protection?

D5) Will setting DOS file attributes to READ ONLY protect them from viruses?

D6) Will password/access control systems protect my files from viruses?

D7) Will the protection systems in DR DOS work against viruses?

D8) Will a write-protect tab on a floppy disk stop viruses?

D9) Do local area networks (LANs) help to stop viruses or do they facilitate their spread?

D10) What is the proper way to make backups?

Section E: Facts and Fibs about computer viruses (*Can a virus...?*)

E1) Can boot sector viruses infect non-bootable floppy disks?

E2) Can a virus hide in a PC's CMOS memory?

E3) Can a virus hide in Extended or in Expanded RAM?

E4) Can a virus hide in Upper Memory or in High Memory?

E5) Can a virus infect data files? E6) Can viruses spread from one type of computer to another?

E7) Can DOS viruses run on non-DOS machines (e.g. Mac, Amiga)?

E8) Can mainframe computers be susceptible to computer viruses?

E9) Some people say that disinfecting files is a bad idea. Is that true?

E10) Can I avoid viruses by avoiding shareware/free software/games?

E11) Can I contract a virus on my PC by performing a "DIR" of an infected floppy disk?

E12) Is there any risk in copying data files from an infected floppy disk to a clean PC's hard disk?

E13) Can a DOS virus survive and spread on an OS/2 system using the HPFS file system?

E14) Under OS/2 2.0, could a virus-infected DOS session infect another DOS session?

E15) Can normal DOS viruses work under MS Windows?

Section F: Miscellaneous Questions (I was just wondering...)

F1) How many viruses are there?

F2) How do viruses spread so quickly?

F3) What is the plural of "virus"? "Viruses" or "viri" or "virii" or...

F4) When reporting a virus infection (and looking for assistance), what information should be included?

F5) How often should we upgrade our antivirus tools to minimize software and labor costs and maximize our protection?

Section G: Specific Virus and Antiviral Software Questions...

G1) I was infected by the Jerusalem virus and disinfected the infected files with my favorite antivirus program. However, WordPerfect and some other programs still refuse to work. Why?

G2) I was told that the Stoned virus displays the text "Your PC is now Stoned" at boot time. I have been infected by this virus several times, but have never seen the message. Why?

G3)   I was infected by both Stoned and Michelangelo. Why has my computer became unbootable? And why, each time I run my favorite scanner, does it find one of the viruses and say that it is removed, but when I run it again, it says that the virus is still there?

Section A. Sources of Information and Antiviral Software

A1) What is VIRUS-L/comp.virus?

It is a discussion forum with a focus on computer virus issues. More specifically, VIRUS-L is an electronic mailing list and comp.virus is a USENET newsgroup. Both groups are moderated; all submissions are sent to the moderator for possible inclusion in the group. For more information, including a copy of the posting guidelines, see the file virus-l.README, available by anonymous FTP on cert.org in the pub/virus-l directory. (FTP is the Internet File Transfer Protocol, and is described in more detail in the monthly VIR US-L/comp.virus archive postings—see below.)

Note that there have been, from time to time, other USENET cross-postings of VIRUS-L, including the bit.listserv.virus-l. These groups are generally set up by individual site maintainers and are not as globally accessible as VIRUS-L and comp.virus.

A2) What is the difference between VIRUS-L and comp.virus?

As mentioned above, VIRUS-L is a mailing list and comp.virus is a newsgroup. In addition, VIRUS-L is distributed in digest format (with multiple E-mail postings in one large digest) and comp.virus is distributed as individual news postings. However, the content of the two groups is identical.

A3) How do I get onto VIRUS-L/comp.virus?

Send E-mail to LISTSERV@LEHIGH.EDU stating: "SUB VIRUS-L your-name". To "subscribe" to comp.virus, simply use your favorite USENET news reader to read the group (assuming that your site receives USENET news).

A4) What are the guidelines for VIRUS-L?

The list of posting guidelines is available by anonymous FTP on cert.org. See the file pub/virus-l/virus-l.README for the most recent copy. In general, however, the moderator requires that discussions are polite and non-commercial. (Objective postings of product availability, product reviews, etc., are fine, but commercial advertisements are not.) Also, requests for viruses (binary or disassembly) are not allowed. Technical discussions are strongly encouraged, however, within reason.

A5) How can I get back-issues of VIRUS-L?

VIRUS-L/comp.virus includes a series of archive sites that carry all the back issues of VIRUS-L, as well as public antivirus software (for various computers) and documents. The back-issues date back to the group's inception, 21 April 1988. The list of archive sites is updated monthly and distributed to the group; it includes a complete listing of the sites, what they carry, access instructions, as well as information on how to access FTP sites by E-mail. The anonymous FTP archive at cert.org carries all of the VIRUS-L back issues. See the file pub/virus-l/README for more information on the cert.org archive site.

A6) What is VALERT-L?

VALERT-L is a sister group to VIRUS-L, but is intended for virus alerts and warnings only—NO DISCUSSIONS. There is no direct USE NET counterpart to VALERT-L; it is a mailing list only. All VALERT-L postings are re-distributed to VIRUS-L/comp.virus later. This group is also moderated, but on a much higher priority than VIRUS-L. The group is monitored during business hours (East Coast, U.S.A., GMT-5/GMT-4); high priority off-hour postings can be made by submitting to the group and then telephoning the CERT/CC hotline at 412-268-7090—instruct the person answering the hotline to call or page Ken van Wyk.

Subscriptions to VALERT-L are handled identically to VIRUS-L—contact the LISTSERV.

A7) *What are the known viruses, their names, major symptoms and possible cures?*

First of all, the reader must be aware that there is no universally accepted naming convention for viruses, nor is there any standard means of testing. As a consequence nearly ALL viral information is highly subjective and subject to interpretation and dispute.

There are several major sources of information on specific viruses. Probably the biggest one is Patricia Hoffman's hypertext *VSUM*. It describes only DOS viruses, but almost all of them which are known at any given time. Unfortunately, it is regarded by many in the field as being inaccurate, so we do not advise people to rely solely on it. It can be downloaded from most major archive sites except SIMTEL20.

The second one is the *Computer Virus Catalog*, published by the Virus Test Center in Hamburg. It contains a highly technical description of computer viruses for several platforms: DOS, Mac, Amiga, Atari ST, Unix. Unfortunately, the DOS section is quite incomplete. The *CVC* is available for anonymous FTP from ftp.informatik.uni-hamburg.de (IP=134.100.4.42), directory pub/virus/texts/catalog. (A copy of the *CVC* is also available by anonymous FTP on cert.org in the pub/virus-l/docs/vtc directory.)

A third source of information is the monthly *Virus Bulletin*, published in the UK. Among other things, it gives detailed technical information on viruses (see also A9 below). Unfortunately, it is very expensive (the subscription price is $395 per year). U.S. subscriptions can be obtained by calling 203-431-8720 or writing to 590 Danbury Road, Ridgefield, CT 06877; for European subscriptions, the number is +44-235-555139 and the address is: The Quadrant, Abingdon, OX14 3YS, England.

A fourth good source of information on DOS viruses is the *Computer Viruses* report of the National/International Computer Security Association. This is updated regularly, and is fairly complete. Copies cost approximately $75, and can be ordered by calling 202-244-7875. ICSA/NCSA also publishes the monthly *Virus News and Reviews* and other publications.

Another source of information is the documentation of Dr. Solomon's Anti-virus ToolKit. It is more complete than the *CVC* list, just as accurate (if not more), but lists only DOS viruses. However, it is not available electronically; you must buy his antivirus package and the virus information is part of the documentation.

Yet another source of information is *Virus News International*, published by S & S International. And, while not entirely virus-related, *Computers & Security* provides information on many aspects of computer security, including viruses.

The best source of information available on Apple Macintosh viruses is the on-line documentation provided with the freeware Disinfectant program by John Norstad. This is available at most Mac archive sites.

A8) Where can I get free or shareware antivirus programs?

The VIRUS-L/comp.virus archive sites carry publicly distributable antivirus software products. See a recent listing of the archive sites (or ask the moderator for a recent listing) for more information on these sites.

Many freeware/shareware antivirus programs for DOS are available via anonymous FTP on WSMR-SIMTEL20.ARMY.MIL (192.88.110.20), in the directory PD1:<MSDOS.TROJAN-PRO>. Note that the SIMTEL20 archives are also "mirrored" at many other anonymous FTP sites, including oak.oakland.edu (141.210.10.117, pub/msdos/trojan-pro), wuarchive.wustl.edu (128.252.135.4, /mirrors/msdos/trojan-pro), and nic.fu net.fi (128.214.6.100, /pub/msdos/utilities/trojan-pro). They can also be obtained via E-mail in unencoded form from various TRICKLE sites, especially in Europe.

Likewise, Macintosh antivirus programs can be found on SIMTEL20 in the PD3:<MACINTOSH.VIRUS> directory.

A list of many antiviral programs, including commercial products and one person's rating of them, can be obtained by anonymous ftp from cert.org (192.88.209.5) in pub/virus-l/docs/reviews as file slade.quickref.rvw.

A9) Where can I get more information on viruses, etc.?

There are four excellent books on computer viruses available that should cover most of the introductory and technical questions you might have:

- *Computers Under Attack: Intruders, Worms and Viruses, edited by* Peter J. Denning, ACM Press/Addison-Wesley, 1990. This is a book of collected readings that discuss computer viruses, computer worms, break-ins, legal and social aspects, and many other items related to computer security and malicious software. A very solid, readable collection that doesn't require a highly-technical background. Price: $20.50.

- *Rogue Programs: Viruses, Worms and Trojan Horses*, edited by Lance J. Hoffman, Van Nostrand Reinhold, 1990. This is a book of collected readings describing in detail how viruses work, where they come from, what they do, etc. It also has material on worms, trojan horse programs, and other malicious software programs. This book focuses more on mechanism and relatively less on social aspects than does the Denning book; however, there is an excellent piece by Anne Branscomb that covers the legal aspects. Price: $32.95.

- *A Pathology of Computer Viruses*, by David Ferbrache, Springer-Verlag, 1992. This is a recent, in-depth book on the history, operation, and effects of computer viruses. It is one of the most complete books on the subject, with an extensive history section, a section on Macintosh viruses, network worms, and Unix viruses (if they were to exist).

- *A Short Course on Computer Viruses*, by Dr. Fred B. Cohen, ASP Press, 1990. This book is by a well-known pioneer in virus research, who has also written dozens of technical papers on the subject. The book can be obtained by writing to ASP Press, P.O. Box 81270, Pittsburgh, PA 15217. Price: $24.00.

A somewhat dated, but still useful, high-level description of viruses, suitable for a complete novice without extensive computer background is in *Computer Viruses: Dealing with Electronic Vandalism and Programmed Threats*, by Eugene H. Spafford, Kathleen A. Heaphy, and David J. Ferbrache, ADAPSO (Arlington VA), 1989. ADAPSO is a computer industry service organization and not a publisher, so the book cannot be found in bookstores; copies can be obtained directly from ADAPSO 703-522-5055). There is a discount for ADAPSO members, educators, and law enforcement personnel. Many people have indicated that they find this a very understandable reference; portions of it have been reprinted from many other places, including Denning and Hoffman's books (above).

It is also worth consulting various publications such as *Computers & Security* (which, while not restricted to viruses, contains many of Cohen's papers) and the *Virus Bulletin* (published in the UK; its technical articles are considered good, although there has been much criticism in VIRUS-L of some of its product evaluations).

Section B. Definitions and General Information

B1) *What are computer viruses (and why should I worry about them)?*

According to Fred Cohen's well-known definition, a COMPUTER VIRUS is a computer program that can infect other computer programs by modifying them in such a way as to include a (possibly evolved) copy of itself. Note that a program does not have to perform outright damage (such as deleting or corrupting files) in order to be called a "virus." However, Cohen uses the terms within his definition (e.g. "program" and "modify") a bit differently from the way most antivirus researchers use them, and classifies as viruses some things which most of us would not consider viruses.

Many people use the term loosely to cover any sort of program that tries to hide its (malicious) function and tries to spread onto as many computers as possible. (See the definition of "Trojan.") Be aware that what constitutes a "program" for a virus to infect may include a lot more than is at first obvious—don't assume too much about what a virus can or can't do!

These software "pranks" are very serious; they are spreading faster than they are being stopped, and even the least harmful of viruses could be fatal. For example, a virus that stops your computer and displays a message, in the context of a hospital life-support computer, could be fatal. Even those who created the viruses could not stop them if they wanted to; it requires a concerted effort from computer users to be "virus-aware," rather than the ignorance and ambivalence that have allowed them to grow to such a problem.

B2) *What is a Trojan Horse?*

A TROJAN HORSE is a program that does something undocumented which the programmer intended, but that the user would not approve of if he knew about it. According to some people, a virus is a particular case of a Trojan Horse, namely one which is able to spread to other programs (i.e., it turns them into Trojans too). According to others, a virus that does not do any deliberate damage (other than merely replicating) is not a Trojan. Finally, despite the definitions, many people use the term "Trojan" to refer only to a *non-replicating* malicious program, so that the set of Trojans and the set of viruses are disjoint.

B3) What are the main types of PC viruses?

Generally, there are two main classes of viruses. The first class consists of the FILE INFECTORS which attach themselves to ordinary program files. These usually infect arbitrary .COM and/or .EXE programs, though some can infect any program for which execution is requested, such as .SYS, .OVL, .PRG, & .MNU files.

File infectors can be either DIRECT ACTION or RESIDENT. A direct-action virus selects one or more other programs to infect each time the program which contains it is executed. A resident virus hides itself somewhere in memory the first time an infected program is executed, and thereafter infects other programs when *they* are executed (as in the case of the Jerusalem) or when certain other conditions are fulfilled. The Vienna is an example of a direct-action virus. Most other viruses are resident.

The second category is SYSTEM or BOOT-RECORD INFECTORS: those viruses which infect executable code found in certain system areas on a disk which are not ordinary files. On DOS systems, there are ordinary boot-sector viruses, which infect only the DOS boot sector, and MBR viruses which infect the Master Boot Record on fixed disks and the DOS boot sector on diskettes. Examples include Brain, Stoned, Empire, Azusa, and Michelangelo. Such viruses are always resident viruses.

Finally, a few viruses are able to infect both (the Tequila virus is one example). These are often called "MULTI-PARTITE" viruses, though there has been criticism of this name; another name is "BOOT-AND-FILE" virus.

FILE SYSTEM or CLUSTER viruses (e.g. Dir-II) are those which modify directory table entries so that the virus is loaded and executed before the desired program is. Note that the program itself is not physically altered, only the directory entry is. Some consider these infectors to be a third category of viruses, while others consider them to be a sub-category of the file infectors.

B4) What is a stealth virus?

A STEALTH virus is one which hides the modifications it has made in the file or boot record, usually by monitoring the system functions used by programs to read files or physical blocks from storage media, and forging the results of such system functions so that programs which try to read these areas see the original uninfected form of the file instead of the actual infected form. Thus the viral modifications go undetected by antiviral programs. However, in order to do this, the virus must be resident in memory when the antiviral program is executed.

Example: The very first DOS virus, Brain, a boot-sector infector, monitors physical disk I/O and re-directs any attempt to read a Brain-infected boot sector to the disk area where the original boot sector is stored. The next viruses to use this technique were the file infectors Number of the Beast and Frodo (= 4096 = 4K).

Countermeasures: A "clean" system is needed so that no virus is present to distort the results. Thus the system should be built from a trusted, clean master copy before any virus-checking is attempted; this is "The Golden Rule of the Trade." With DOS, (1) boot from original DOS diskettes (i.e. DOS Startup/Program diskettes from a major vendor that have been write-protected since their creation); (2) use only tools from original diskettes until virus-checking has completed.

B5) What is a polymorphic virus?

A POLYMORPHIC virus is one which produces varied (yet fully operational) copies of itself, in the hope that virus scanners (see D1) will not be able to detect all instances of the virus.

One method to evade signature-driven virus scanners is self-encryption with a variable key; however these viruses (e.g. Cascade) are not termed "polymorphic," as their decryption code is always the same and thus can be used as a virus signature even by the simplest, signature-driven virus scanners (unless another virus or program uses the identical decryption routine).

One method to make a polymorphic virus is to choose among a variety of different encryption schemes requiring different decryption routines: only one of these routines would be plainly visible in any instance of the virus (e.g. the Whale virus). A signature-driven virus scanner would have to exploit several signatures (one for each possible encryption method) to reliably identify a virus of this kind.

A more sophisticated polymorphic virus (e.g. V2P6) will vary the sequence of instructions in its copies by interspersing it with "noise" instructions (e.g. a No Operation instruction, or an instruction to load a currently unused register with an arbitrary value), by interchanging mutually independent instructions, or even by using various instruction sequences with identical net effects (e.g. Subtract A from A, and Move 0 to A). A simple-minded, signature-based virus scanner would not be able to reliably identify this sort of virus; rather, a sophisticated "scanning engine" has to be constructed after thorough research into the particular virus.

The most sophisticated form of polymorphism discovered so far is the MtE "Mutation Engine" written by the Bulgarian virus writer who calls himself the "Dark Avenger." It comes in the form of an object module. Any virus can be made polymorphic by adding certain calls to the assembler source code and linking to the mutation-engine and random-number-generator modules.

The advent of polymorphic viruses has rendered virus-scanning an ever more difficult and expensive endeavor; adding more and more search strings to simple scanners will not adequately deal with these viruses.

B6) What are fast and slow infectors?

A typical file infector (such as the Jerusalem) copies itself to memory when a program infected by it is executed, and then infects other programs when they are executed.

A FAST infector is a virus which, when it is active in memory, infects not only programs which are executed, but even those which are merely opened. The result is that if such a virus is in memory, running a scanner or integrity checker can result in all (or at least many) programs becoming infected all at once. Examples are the Dark Avenger and the Frodo viruses.

The term "SLOW infector" is sometimes used for a virus which, if it is active in memory, infects only files as they are modified (or created). The purpose is to fool people who use integrity checkers into thinking that the modification reported by the integrity checker is due solely to legitimate reasons. An example is the Darth Vader virus.

B7) What is a sparse infector?

The term "SPARSE infector" is sometimes given to a virus which infects only occasionally, e.g. every tenth executed file, or only files whose lengths fall within a narrow range, etc. By infecting less often, such viruses try to minimize the probability of being discovered by the user.

B8) What is a companion virus?

A COMPANION virus is one which, instead of modifying an existing file, creates a new program which (unknown to the user) gets executed by the command-line interpreter instead of the intended program. (On exit, the new program executes the original program so that things will appear normal.) The only way this has been done so far is by creating an infected .COM file with the same name as an existing .EXE file. Note that those integrity checkers which look only for *modifications* in *existing* files will fail to detect such viruses.

(Note that not all researchers consider this type of malicious code to be a virus, since it does not modify existing files.)

B9) What is an armored virus?

An ARMORED virus is one which uses special tricks to make the tracing, disassembling, and understanding of their code more difficult. A good example is the Whale virus.

B10) Miscellaneous Jargon and Abbreviations

BSI   **Boot Sector Infector:** A virus which takes control when the computer attempts to boot (as opposed to a file infector).

CMOS   **Complementary Metal Oxide Semiconductor:** A memory area that is used in AT and higher class PCs for storage of system information. CMOS is battery backed RAM (see below), originally used to maintain date and time information while the PC was turned off. CMOS memory is not in the normal CPU address space and cannot be executed. While a virus may place data in the CMOS or may corrupt it, a virus cannot hide there.

DOS   **Disk Operating System.** We use the term "DOS" to mean any of the MS-DOS, PC-DOS, or DR DOS systems for PCs and compatibles, even though there are operating systems called "DOS" on other (unrelated) machines.

MBR   **Master Boot Record:** The first Absolute sector (track 0, head 0, sector 1) on a PC hard disk, that usually contains the partition

RAM   table (but on some PCs may simply contain a boot sector). This is not the same as the first DOS sector (Logical sector 0).

RAM   **Random Access Memory:** The place programs are loaded into in order to execute; the significance for viruses is that, to be active, they must grab some of this for themselves. However, some virus scanners may declare that a virus is active simply when it is found in RAM, even though it might be simply left over in a buffer area of RAM rather than truly being active.

TOM   **Top Of Memory:** The end of conventional memory, an architectural design limit at the 640K mark on most PCs. Some early PCs may not be fully populated, but the amount of memory is always a multiple of 64K. A boot-record virus on a PC typically resides just below this mark and changes the value which will be reported for the TOM to the location of the beginning of the virus so that it won't get overwritten. Checking this value for changes can help detect a virus, but there are also legitimate reasons why it may change (see C11). A very few PCs with unusual memory managers/settings may report in excess of 640K.

TSR   **Terminate but Stay Resident:** These are PC programs that stay in memory while you continue to use the computer for other purposes; they include pop-up utilities, network software, and the great majority of viruses. These can often be seen using utilities such as MEM, MAPMEM, PMAP, F-MMAP and INFOPLUS.

Section C. Virus Detection

C1) *What are the symptoms and indications of a virus infection?*

Viruses try to spread as much as possible before they deliver their "payload," but there can be symptoms of virus infection before this, and it is important to use this opportunity to spot and eradicate the virus before any destruction.

There are various kinds of symptoms which some virus authors have written into their programs, such as messages, music, and graphical displays. However, the main indications are changes in file sizes and contents, changing of interrupt vectors, or the reassignment of other system resources. The unaccounted use of RAM or a reduction in the amount known to be in the machine are important indicators. The examination of the code is valuable to the trained eye, but even the novice can often spot the gross differences between a valid boot sector and an infected one. However, these symptoms, along with longer disk activity and strange behavior from the hardware, can also be caused by genuine software, by harmless "prank" programs, or by hardware faults.

The only foolproof way to determine that a virus is present is for an expert to analyze the assembly code contained in all programs and system areas, but this is usually impractical. Virus scanners go some way towards that by looking in that code for known viruses; some will even try to use heuristic means to spot viral code, but this is not always reliable. It is wise to arm yourself with the latest antiviral software, but also to pay close attention to your system; look particularly for any change in the memory map or configuration as soon as you start the computer. For users of DOS 5.0, the MEM program with the /C switch is very handy for this. If you have DR DOS, use MEM with the /A switch; if you have an earlier version, use CHKDSK or the commonly-available PMAP or MAPMEM utilities. You don't have to know what all the numbers mean, only that they change. Mac users have "info" options that give some indication of memory use, but may need ResEdit for more detail.

C2) What steps should be taken in diagnosing and identifying viruses?

Most of the time, a virus scanner program will take care of that for you. (Remember, though, that scanning programs must be kept up to date. Also remember that different scanner authors may call the same virus by different names. If you want to identify a virus in order to ask for help, it is best to run at least two scanners on it and, when asking, say which scanners, and what versions, gave the names.) To help identify problems early, run it on new programs and diskettes; when an integrity checker reports a mismatch, when a generic monitoring program sounds an alarm; or when you receive an updated version of a scanner (or a different scanner than the one you have been using). However, because of the time required, it is not generally advisable to insert into your AUTOEXEC.BAT file a command to run a scanner on an entire hard disk on every boot.

If you run into an alarm that the scanner doesn't identify, or doesn't properly clean up for you, first verify that the version that you are using is the most recent, and then get in touch with one of the reputable antivirus researchers, who may ask you to send a copy of the infected file to him. See also question C10.

C3) *What is the best way to remove a virus?*

In order that downtime be short and losses low, do the minimum that you must to restore the system to a normal state, starting with booting the system from a clean diskette. It is very unlikely that you need to low-level reformat the hard disk!

If backups of the infected files are available and appropriate care was taken when making the backups (see D10), this is the safest solution, even though it requires a lot of work if many files are involved.

More commonly, a disinfecting program is used. If the virus is a boot sector infector, you can continue using the computer with relative safety if you boot it from a clean system diskette, but it is wise to go through all your diskettes removing infection, since sooner or later you may be careless and leave a diskette in the machine when it reboots. Boot sector infections on PCs can be cured by a two-step approach of replacing the MBR (on the hard disk), either by using a backup or by the FDISK/MBR command (from DOS 5 and up), then using the SYS command to replace the DOS boot sector.

C4) *What does the <insert name here> virus do?*

If an antivirus program has detected a virus on your computer, don't rush to post a question to this list asking what it does. First, it might be a false positive alert (especially if the virus is found only in one file), and second, some viruses are extremely common, so the question "What does the Stoned virus do?" or "What does the Jerusalem virus do?" is asked here repeatedly. While this list is monitored by several antivirus experts, they get tired of perpetually answering the same questions over and over again. In any case, if you really need to know what a particular virus does (as opposed to knowing enough to get rid of it), you will need a longer treatise than could be given to you here.

For example, the Stoned virus replaces the disk's boot record with its own, relocating the original to a sector on the disk that may (or may not) occur in an unused portion of the root directory of a DOS diskette; when active, it sits in an area a few kilobytes below the top of memory. All this description could apply to a number of common viruses; but the important points of where the original boot sector goes—and what effect that has on networking software, non-DOS partitions, and so on are all major questions in themselves.

Therefore, it is better if you first try to answer your question yourself. There are several sources of information about the known computer viruses, so please consult one of them before requesting information publicly. Chances are that your virus is rather well known and that it is already described in detail in at least one of these sources. (See the answer to question A7, for instance.)

C5) What are "false positives" and "false negatives"?

A FALSE POSITIVE (or Type-I) error is one in which the antiviral software claims that a given file is infected by a virus when in reality the file is clean. A FALSE NEGATIVE (or Type-II) error is one in which the software fails to indicate that an infected file is infected. Clearly false negatives are more serious than false positives, although both are undesirable.

It has been proven by Dr. Fred Cohen that every virus detector must have either false positives or false negatives or both. This is expressed by saying that detection of viruses is UNDECIDABLE. However his theorem does not preclude a program which has no false negatives and *very few* false positives (e.g. if the only false positives are those due to the file containing viral code which is never actually executed, so that technically we do not have a virus).

In the case of virus scanners, false positives are rare, but they can arise if the scan string chosen for a given virus is also present in some benign programs because the string was not well chosen. False negatives are more common with virus scanners because scanners will miss a completely new or a heavily modified virus.

One other serious problem could occur: A positive that is misdiagnosed (e.g., a scanner that detects the Empire virus in a boot record but reports it as the Stoned). In the case of a boot sector infector, use of a Stoned specific "cure" to recover from the Empire could result in an unreadable disk or loss of extended partitions. Similarly, sometimes "generic" recovery can result in unusable files, unless a check is made (e.g. by comparing checksums) that the recovered file is identical to the original file. Some more recent products store information about the original programs to allow verification of recovery processes.

C6) Could an antiviral program itself be infected?

Yes, so it is important to obtain this software from good sources, and to trust results only after running scanners from a "clean" system. But there are situations where a scanner appears to be infected when it isn't.

Most antiviral programs try very hard to identify only viral infections, but sometimes they give false alarms. If two different antiviral programs are both of the "scanner" type, they will contain "signature strings" to identify viral infections. If the strings are not "encrypted", then they will be identified as a virus by another scanner type program. Also, if the scanner does not remove the strings from memory after they are run, then another scanner may detect the virus string "in memory."

Some "change detection" type antiviral programs add a bit of code or data to a program when "protecting" it. This might be detected by another "change detector" as a change to a program, and therefore suspicious.

It is good practice to use more than one antiviral program. Do be aware, however, that antiviral programs, by their nature, may confuse each other.

C7) Where can I get a virus scanner for my Unix system?

Basically, you shouldn't bother scanning for Unix viruses at this point in time. Although it is possible to write Unix-based viruses, we have yet to see any instance of a non-experimental virus in that environment. Someone with sufficient knowledge and access to write an effective virus would be more likely to conduct other activities than virus-writing. Furthermore, the typical form of software sharing in an Unix environment would not support virus spread.

This answer is not meant to imply that viruses are impossible, or that there aren't security problems in a typical Unix environment—there are. However, true viruses are highly unlikely and would corrupt file and/or memory integrity. For more information on Unix security, see the book *Practical Unix Security* by Garfinkel and Spafford, O'Reilly & Associates, 1991 (it can be ordered via E-mail from nuts@ora.com).

However, there are special cases for which scanning Unix systems for non-Unix viruses does make sense. For example, a Unix system which is acting as a file server (e.g., PC-NFS) for PC systems is quite capable of containing PC file infecting viruses that are a danger to PC clients. Note that, in this example, the UNIX system would be scanned for PC viruses, not UNIX viruses.

Another example is in the case of a 386/486 PC system running Unix, since this system is still vulnerable to infection by MBR infectors such as Stoned and Michelangelo, which are operating system independent. (Note that an infection on such a Unix PC system would probably result in disabling the Unix disk partition(s) from booting.)

In addition, a file integrity checker (to detect unauthorized changes in executable files) on Unix systems is a very good idea. (One free program which can do this test, as well as other tests, is the COPS package, available by anonymous FTP on cert.org.) Unauthorized file changes on Unix systems are very common, although they usually are not due to virus activity.

C8) Why does my antiviral scanner report an infection only sometimes?

There are circumstances where part of a virus exists in RAM without being active: If your scanner reports a virus in memory only occasionally, it could be due to the operating system buffering disk reads, keeping disk contents that include a virus in memory (harmlessly), in which case it should also find it on disk. Or after running another scanner, there may be scan strings left (again harmlessly) in memory. This is sometimes called a "ghost positive" alert.

C9) Is my disk infected with the Stoned virus?

Of course the answer to this, and many similar questions, is to obtain a good virus detector. There are many to choose from, including ones that will scan diskettes automatically as you use them. Remember to check all diskettes, even non-system ("data") diskettes.

It is possible, if you have an urgent need to check a system when you don't have any antiviral tools, to boot from a clean system diskette, and use the CHKDSK method (mentioned in C1) to see if it is in memory, then look at the boot sector with a disk editor. Usually the first few bytes will indicate the characteristic far jump of the Stoned virus; however, you could be looking at a perfectly good disk that has been "inoculated" against the virus, or at a diskette that seems safe but contains a totally different type of virus.

C10) I think I have detected a new virus; what do I do?

Whenever there is doubt over a virus, you should obtain the latest versions of several (not just one) major virus scanners. Some scanning programs now use "heuristic" methods (F-PROT, CHECKOUT and SCANBOOT are examples), and "activity monitoring" programs can report a disk or file as being possibly infected when it is in fact perfectly safe (odd, perhaps, but not infected). If no string-matching scan finds a virus, but a heuristic program does (or there are other reasons to suspect the file, e.g., change in size of files) then it is possible that you have found a new virus, although the chances are probably greater that it is an odd-but-okay disk or file. Start by looking in recent VIRUS-L postings about "known" false positives, then contact the author of the antivirus software that reports it as virus-like; the documentation for the software may have a section explaining what to do if you think you have found a new virus. Consider using the BootID or Checkout programs to calculate the "hashcode" of a diskette in the case of boot sector infectors, rather than send a complete diskette or "live" virus until requested.

C11) CHKDSK reports 639K (or less) total memory on my system; am I infected?

If CHKDSK displays 639K for the total memory instead of 640K (655,360 bytes)—so that you are missing only 1K—then it is probably due to reasons other than a virus since there are very few viruses which take only 1K from total memory. Legitimate reasons for a deficiency of 1K include:

1) A PS/2 computer. IBM PS/2 computers reserve 1K of conventional RAM for an Extended BIOS Data Area, i.e. for additional data storage required by its BIOS.

2) A computer with American Megatrends Inc. (AMI) BIOS, which is set up (with the built-in CMOS setup program) in such a way that the BIOS uses the upper 1K of memory for its internal variables. (It can be instructed to use lower memory instead.)

3) A SCSI controller.

4) The DiskSecure program.

5) Mouse buffers for older Compaqs.

If, on the other hand, you are missing 2K or more from the 640K, 512K, or whatever the conventional memory normally is for your PC, the chances are greater that you have a boot-record virus (e.g. Stoned, Michelangelo), although even in this case there may be legitimate reasons for the missing memory:

1) Many access control programs for preventing booting from a floppy.

2) H/P Vectra computers.

3) Some special BIOSes which use memory (e.g.) for a built-in calendar and/or calculator.

However, these are only rough guides. In order to be more certain whether the missing memory is due to a virus, you should: (1) run several virus detectors; (2) look for a change in total memory every now and then; (3) compare the total memory size with that obtained when cold booting from a "clean" system diskette. The latter should show the normal amount of total memory for your configuration.

Note: in all cases, CHKDSK should be run without software such as MS-Windows or DesqView loaded, since GUIs seem to be able to open DOS boxes only on whole K boundaries (some seem to be even coarser); thus CHKDSK run from a DOS box may report unrepresentative values.

Note also that some machines have only 512K or 256K instead of 640K of conventional memory.

C12) I have an infinite loop of sub-directories on my hard drive; am I infected?

Probably not. This happens now and then, when something sets the "cluster number" field of some subdirectory the same cluster as an upper-level (usually the root) directory. The /F parameter of CHKDSK, and any of various popular utility programs, should be able to fix this, usually by removing the offending directory. *Don't* erase any of the "replicated" files in the odd directory, since that will erase the "copy" in the root as well (it's really not a copy at all; just a second pointer to the same file).

Section D. Protection plans

D1) What is the best protection policy for my computer?

There is no "best" antivirus policy. In particular, there is no program that can magically protect you against all viruses. But you can design an antivirus protection strategy based on multiple layers of defense. There are three main kinds of antiviral software, plus several other means of protection (such as hardware write-protect methods).

1) GENERIC MONITORING programs. These try to prevent viral activity before it happens, such as attempts to write to another executable, reformat the disk, etc. Examples: SECURE and FluShot+ (PC), and GateKeeper (Macintosh).

2) SCANNERS. Most look for known virus strings (byte sequences which occur in known viruses, but hopefully not in legitimate software) or patterns, but a few use heuristic techniques to recognize viral code. A scanner may be designed to examine specified disks or files on demand, or it may be resident, examining each program which is about to be executed. Most scanners also include virus removers. Examples: FindViru in Dr. Solomon's Anti-Virus Toolkit, FRISK's F-Prot, McAfee's VIRUSCAN (all PC), Disinfectant (Macintosh). Resident scanners: McAfee's V-Shield, and VIRSTOP. Heuristic scanners: the Analyze module in FRISK's F-PROT package, and SCANBOOT.

3) INTEGRITY CHECKERS or MODIFICATION DETECTORS. These compute a small "checksum" or "hash value" (usually CRC or cryptographic) for files when they are presumably uninfected, and later compare newly calculated values with the original ones to see if the files have been modified. This catches unknown viruses as well as known ones and thus provides *generic* detection. On the other hand, modifications can also be due to reasons other than viruses. Usually, it is up to the user to decide which modifications are intentional and which might be due to viruses, although a few products give the user help in making this decision. As in the case of scanners, integrity checkers may be called to checksum entire disks or specified files on demand, or they may be

resident, checking each program which is about to be executed (the latter is sometimes called an INTEGRITY SHELL). A third implementation is as a SELF-TEST, i.e. the checksumming code is attached to each executable file so that it checks itself just before execution. Examples: Fred Cohen's ASP Integrity Toolkit (commercial), and Integrity Master and VDS (shareware), all for the PC.

3a)   A few modification detectors come with GENERIC DISINFECTION. I.e., sufficient information is saved for each file that it can be restored to its original state in the case of the great majority of viral infections, even if the virus is unknown. Examples: V-Analyst 3 (BRM Technologies, Israel), marketed in the US as Untouchable (by Fifth Generation), and the VGUARD module of V-care.

Of course, only a few examples of each type have been given. All of them can find their place in the protection against computer viruses, but you should appreciate the limitations of each method, along with system-supplied security measures that may or may not be helpful in defeating viruses. Ideally, you would arrange a combination of methods that cover the loopholes between them.

A typical PC installation might include a protection system on the hard disk's MBR to protect against viruses at load time (ideally this would be hardware or in BIOS, but software methods such as DiskSecure and PanSoft's Immunise are pretty good). This would be followed by resident virus detectors loaded as part of the machine's startup (CONFIG.SYS or AUTOEXEC.BAT), such as FluShot+ and/or VirStop together with ScanBoot. A scanner such as F-Prot or McAfee's SCAN could be put into AUTOEXEC.BAT to look for viruses as you start up, but this may be a problem if you have a large disk to check (or don't reboot often enough). Most importantly, new files should be scanned as they arrive on the system. If your system has DR DOS installed, you should use the PASSWORD command to write-protect all system executables and utilities. If you have Stacker or SuperStore, you can get some improved security from these compressed drives, but also a risk that those viruses stupid enough to directly write to the disk could do much more damage than normal; using a software write-protect system (such as provided with Disk Manager or Norton Utilities) may help, but the best solution (if possible) is to put all executables on a disk of their own, protected by a hardware read-only system that sounds an alarm if a write is attempted.

If you do use a resident BSI detector or a scan-while-you-copy detector, it is important to trace back any infected diskette to its source; the reason why viruses survive so well is that usually you cannot do this, because the infection is found long after the infecting diskette has been forgotten with most people's lax scanning policies.

Organizations should devise and implement a careful policy, that may include a system of vetting new software brought into the building and free virus detectors for home machines of employees/students/etc who take work home with them.

Other antiviral techniques include:

(a)   Creation of a special MBR to make the hard disk inaccessible when booting from a diskette (the latter is useful since booting from a diskette will normally bypass the protection in the CONFIG.SYS and AUTOEXEC.BAT files of the hard disk). Example: GUARD.

(b)   Use of Artificial Intelligence to learn about new viruses and extract scan patterns for them. Examples: V-Care (CSA Interprint, Israel; distributed in the U.S. by Sela Consultants Corp.), Victor Charlie (Bangkok Security Associates, Thailand; distributed in the U.S. by Computer Security Associates).

(c)   Encryption of files (with decryption before execution).

D2) *Is it possible to protect a computer system with only software?*

Not perfectly; however, software defenses can significantly reduce your risk of being affected by viruses WHEN APPLIED APPROPRIATELY. All virus defense systems are tools—each with their own capabilities and limitations. Learn how your system works and be sure to work within its limitations.

From a software standpoint, a very high level of protection/detection can be achieved with only software, using a layered approach.

1)   ROM BIOS—password (access control) and selection of boot disk. (Some may consider this hardware.)

2)   Boot sectors—integrity management and change detection.

3) OS programs—integrity management of existing programs, scanning of unknown programs. Requirement of authentication values for any new or transmitted software.

4) Locks that prevent writing to a fixed or floppy disk. As each layer is added, invasion without detection becomes more difficult. However complete protection against any possible attack cannot be provided without dedicating the computer to pre-existing or unique tasks. The international standardization of the world on the IBM PC architecture is both its greatest asset and its greatest vulnerability.

D3) Is it possible to write-protect the hard disk with only software?

The answer is no. There are several programs which claim to do that, but *all* of them can be bypassed using only the currently known techniques that are used by some viruses. Therefore you should never rely on such programs *alone*, although they can be useful in combination with other antiviral measures.

D4) What can be done with hardware protection?

Hardware protection can accomplish various things, including: write protection for hard disk drives, memory protection, monitoring and trapping unauthorized system calls, etc. Again, no tool is foolproof.

The popular idea of write-protection (see D3) may stop viruses spreading to the disk that is protected, but doesn't, in itself, prevent a virus from running.

Also, some of the existing hardware protections can be easily bypassed, fooled, or disconnected, if the virus writer knows them well and designs a virus which is aware of the particular defense.

D5) Will setting DOS file attributes to READ ONLY protect them from viruses?

No. While the Read Only attribute will protect your files from a few viruses, most simply override it, and infect normally. So, while setting executable files to Read Only is not a bad idea, it is certainly not a thorough protection against viruses!

D6) Will password/access control systems protect my files from viruses?

All password and other access control systems are designed to protect the user's data from other users and/or their programs. Remember, however, that when you execute an infected program the virus in it will gain your current rights/privileges. Therefore, if the access control system provides *you* the right to modify some files, it will provide it to the virus too. Note that this does not depend on the operating system used—DOS, Unix, or whatever. Therefore, an access control system will protect your files from viruses no better than it protects them from you.

Under DOS, there is no memory protection, so a virus could disable the access control system in memory, or even patch the operating system itself. On the more advanced operating systems (Unix) this is not possible, so at least the protection cannot be disabled by a virus. However it will still spread, due to the reasons noted above. In general, the access control systems (if implemented correctly) are able only to slow down the virus spread, not to eliminate viruses entirely.

Of course, it's better to have access control than not to have it at all. Just be sure not to develop a false sense of security and to rely *entirely* on the access control system to protect you.

D7) Will the protection systems in DR DOS work against viruses?

Partially. Neither the password file/directory protection available from DR DOS version 5 onwards, nor the secure disk partitions introduced in DR DOS 6 are intended to combat viruses, but they do to some extent. If you have DR DOS, it is very wise to password-protect your files (to stop accidental damage too), but don't depend on it as the only means of defense.

The use of the password command (e.g. PASSWORD/W:MINE *.EXE *.COM) will stop more viruses than the plain DOS attribute facility, but that isn't saying much! The combination of the password system plus a disk compression system may be more secure (because to bypass the password system they must access the disk directly, but under SuperStore or Stacker the physical disk is meaningless to the virus). There may be some viruses which, rather than invisibly infecting files on compressed disks in fact very visibly corrupt the disk.

The "secure disk partitions" system introduced with DR DOS 6 may be of some help against a few viruses that look for DOS partitions on a disk. The main use is in stopping people fiddling with (and infecting) your hard disk while you are away.

Furthermore, DR DOS is not very compatible with MS/PC-DOS, especially down to the low-level tricks that some viruses are using. For instance, some internal memory structures are "read-only" in the sense that they are constantly updated (for DOS compatibility) but not really used by DR DOS, so that even if a sophisticated virus modifies them, this does not have any effect.

In general, using a less compatible system diminishes the number of viruses that can infect it. For instance, the introduction of hard disks made the Brain virus almost disappear; the introduction of 80286 and DOS 4.x+ made the Yale and Ping Pong viruses extinct, and so on.

D8) Will a write-protect tab on a floppy disk stop viruses?

In general, yes. The write-protection on IBM PC (and compatible) and Macintosh floppy disk drives is implemented in hardware, not software, so viruses cannot infect a diskette when the write-protection mechanism is functioning properly.

But remember:

(a)   A computer may have a faulty write-protect system (this happens!)—you can test it by trying to copy a file to the diskette when it is presumably write-protected. (b) Someone may have removed the tab for a while, allowing a virus on. (c) The files may have been infected before the disk was protected.

Even some diskettes "straight from the factory" have been known to be infected in the production processes. So it is worthwhile scanning even write-protected disks for viruses.

D9) Do local area networks (LANs) help to stop viruses or do they facilitate their spread?

Both. A set of computers connected in a well-managed LAN, with carefully established security settings, with minimal privileges for each user, and without a transitive path of information flow between the users (i.e., the objects writable by any of the users are not readable by any of the others) is more virus-resistant than the same set of computers if they are not interconnected. The reason is that when all computers have (read-only) access to a common pool of executable programs, there is usually less need for diskette swapping and software exchange between them, and therefore less ways through which a virus could spread.

However, if the LAN is not well managed, with lax security, it could help a virus to spread like wildfire. It might even be impossible to remove the infection without shutting down the entire LAN.

A network that supports login scripting is inherently more resistant to viruses than one that does not, if this is used to validate the client before allowing access to the network.

D10) *What is the proper way to make backups?*

Data and text files, and programs in source form, should be backed up each time they are modified. However, the only backups you should keep of COM, EXE and other *executable* files are the *original* versions, since if you back up an executable file on your hard disk over and over, it may have become infected meanwhile, so that you may no longer have an uninfected backup of that file. Therefore:

1. If you've downloaded shareware, copy it (preferably as a ZIP or other original archive file) onto your backup medium and do not re-back it up later.

2. If you have purchased commercial software, it's best to create a ZIP (or other) archive from the original diskettes (assuming they're not copy protected) and transfer the archive onto that medium. Again, do not re-back up.

3. If you write your own programs, back up only the latest version of the *source* programs. Depend on recompilation to reproduce the executables.

4. If an executable has been replaced by a new version, then of course you will want to keep a backup of the new version. However, if it has been modified as a result of your having changed configuration information, it seems safer *not* to back up the modified file; you can always re-configure the backup copy later if you have to.

5. Theoretically, source programs could be infected, but until such a virus is discovered, it seems preferable to treat such files as non-executables and back them up whenever you modify them. The same advice is probably appropriate for batch files as well, despite the fact that a few batch file infectors have been discovered.

Section E. Facts and Fibs about Computer Viruses

E1) *Can boot sector viruses infect non-bootable floppy disks?*

Any diskette that has been properly formatted contains an executable program in the boot sector. If the diskette is not "bootable," all that boot sector does is print a message like "Non-system disk or disk error; replace and strike any key when ready," but it's still executable and still vulnerable to infection. If you accidentally turn your machine on with a "non-bootable" diskette in the drive, and see that message, it means that any boot virus that may have been on that diskette *has* run, and has had the chance to infect your hard drive, or whatever. So when thinking about viruses, the word "bootable" (or "non-bootable") is really misleading. All formatted diskettes are capable of carrying a virus.

E2) *Can a virus hide in a PC's CMOS memory?*

No. The CMOS RAM in which system information is stored and backed up by batteries is ported, not addressable. That is, in order to get anything out, you use I/O instructions. So anything stored there is not directly sitting in memory. Nothing in a normal machine loads the data from there and executes it, so a virus that "hid" in the CMOS RAM would still have to infect an executable object of some kind in order to load and execute whatever it had written to CMOS. A malicious virus can of course *alter* values in the CMOS as part of its payload, but it can't spread through, or hide itself in, the CMOS.

A virus could also use the CMOS RAM to hide a small part of its body (e.g., the payload, counters, etc.). However, any executable code stored there must be first extracted to ordinary memory in order to be executed.

E3) *Can a virus hide in Extended or in Expanded RAM?*

Theoretically yes, although no such viruses are known yet. However, even if they are created, they will have to have a small part resident in conventional RAM; they cannot reside *entirely* in Extended or in Expanded RAM.

E4) *Can a virus hide in Upper Memory or in High Memory?*

Yes, it is possible to construct a virus which will locate itself in Upper Memory (640K to 1024K) or in High Memory (1024K to 1088K), and a few currently known viruses (e.g. EDV) do hide in Upper Memory.

It might be thought that there is no point in scanning in these areas for any viruses other than those which are specifically known to inhabit them. However, there are cases when even ordinary viruses can be found in Upper Memory. Suppose that a conventional memory-resident virus infects a TSR program and this program is loaded high by the user (for instance, from AUTOEXEC.BAT). Then the virus code will also reside in Upper Memory. Therefore, an effective scanner must be able to scan this part of memory for viruses too.

E5) *Can a virus infect data files?*

Some viruses (e.g., Frodo, Cinderella) modify non-executable files. However, in order to spread, the virus must be executed. Therefore the "infected" non-executable files cannot be sources of further infection.

However, note that it is not always possible to make a sharp distinction between executable and non-executable files. One man's code is another man's data and vice versa. Some files that are not directly executable contain code or data which can under some conditions be executed or interpreted.

Some examples from the IBM PC world are .OBJ files, libraries, device drivers, source files for any compiler or interpreter, macro files for some packages like MS Word and Lotus 1-2-3, and many others. Currently there are viruses that infect boot sectors, master boot records, COM files, EXE files, BAT files, and device drivers, although any of the objects mentioned above can theoretically be used as an infection carrier. PostScript files can also be used to carry a virus, although no currently known virus does that.

E6) *Can viruses spread from one type of computer to another?*

The simple answer is that no currently known viruses can do this. Although the disk formats may be the same (e.g. Atari ST and DOS), the different machines interpret the code differently. For example, the Stoned virus cannot infect an Atari ST as the ST cannot execute the virus code in the bootsector. The Stoned virus contains instructions for the 80x86 family of CPU's that the 680x0-family CPU (Atari ST) can't understand or execute.

The more general answer is that such viruses are possible, but unlikely. Such a virus would be quite a bit larger than current viruses and might well be easier to find. Additionally, the low incidence of cross-machine sharing of software means that any such virus would be unlikely to spread—it would be a poor environment for virus growth.

E7) Can DOS viruses run on non-DOS machines (e.g. Mac, Amiga)?

In general, no. However, on machines running DOS emulators (either hardware or software based), DOS viruses—just like any DOS program may function. These viruses would be subject to the file access controls of the host operating system. An example is when running a DOS emulator such as VP/ix under a 386 UNIX environment, DOS programs are not permitted access to files which the host UNIX system does not allow them to. Thus, it is important to administer these systems carefully.

E8) Can mainframe computers be susceptible to computer viruses?

Yes. Numerous experiments have shown that computer viruses spread very quickly and effectively on mainframe systems. However, to our knowledge, no non-research computer virus has been seen on mainframe systems. (The Internet worm of November 1988 was not a computer virus by most definitions, although it had some virus-like characteristics.)

Computer viruses are actually a special case of something else called "malicious logic," and other forms of malicious logic—notably Trojan horses—are far quicker, more effective, and harder to detect than computer viruses. Nevertheless, on personal computers many more viruses are written than Trojans. There are two reasons for this: (1) Since a virus propagates, the number of users to which damage can be caused is much greater than in the case of a Trojan; (2) It's almost impossible to trace the source of a virus since viruses are not attached to any particular program.

For further information on malicious programs on multi-user systems, see Matt Bishop's paper, "An Overview of Malicious Logic in a Research

Environment", available by anonymous FTP on Dartmouth.edu (129.170.16.4) as "pub/security/mallogic.ps".

E9) *Some people say that disinfecting files is a bad idea. Is that true?*

Disinfecting a file is completely "safe" only if the disinfecting process restores the non-infected state of the object completely. That is, not only the virus must be removed from the file, but the original length of the file must be restored exactly, as well as its time and date of last modification, all fields in the header, etc. Sometimes it is necessary to be sure that the file is placed on the same clusters of the disk that it occupied prior to infection. If this is not done, then a program which uses some kind of self-checking or copy protection may stop functioning properly, if at all.

None of the currently available disinfecting programs do all this. For instance, because of the bugs that exist in many viruses, some of the information of the original file is destroyed and cannot be recovered. Other times, it is even impossible to detect that this information has been destroyed and to warn the user. Furthermore, some viruses corrupt information very slightly and in a random way (Nomenklatura, Phoenix), so that it is not even possible to tell which files have been corrupted.

Therefore, it is usually better to replace the infected objects with clean backups, provided you are certain that your backups are uninfected (see D10). You should try to disinfect files only if they contain some valuable data that cannot be restored from backups or compiled from their original source.

E10) *Can I avoid viruses by avoiding shareware/free software/games?*

No. There are many documented instances in which even commercial "shrink wrap" software was inadvertently distributed containing viruses. Avoiding shareware, freeware, games, etc. only isolates you from a vast collection of software (some of it very good, some of it very bad, most of it somewhere in between...).

The important thing is not to avoid a certain type of software, but to be cautious of ANY AND ALL newly acquired software. Simply scanning all new software media for known viruses would be rather effective at preventing virus infections, especially when combined with some other prevention/detection strategy such as integrity management of programs.

E11) Can I contract a virus on my PC by performing a "DIR" of an infected floppy disk?

If you assume that the PC you are using is virus free before you perform the DIR command, then the answer is no. However, when you perform a DIR, the contents of the boot sector of the diskette are loaded into a buffer for use when determining disk layout etc., and certain antivirus products will scan these buffers. If a boot sector virus has infected your diskette, the virus code will be contained in the buffer, which may cause some antivirus packages to give the message "xyz virus found in memory, shut down computer immediately." In fact, the virus is not a threat at this point since control of the CPU is never passed to the virus code residing in the buffer. But, even though the virus is really not a threat at this point, this message should not be ignored. If you get a message like this, and then reboot from a clean DOS diskette and scan your hard-drive and find no virus, then you know that the false positive was caused by the fact that the infected boot-sector was loaded into a buffer, and the diskette should be appropriately disinfected before use. The use of DIR will not infect a clean system, even if the diskette it is being performed on does contain a virus.

E12) Is there any risk in copying data files from an infected floppy disk to a clean PC's hard disk?

Assuming that you did not boot or run any executable programs from the infected disk, the answer is generally no. There are two caveats: 1) you should be somewhat concerned about checking the integrity of these data files as they may have been destroyed or altered by the virus, and 2) if any of the "data" files are interpretable as executable by some other program (such as a Lotus macro) then these files should be treated as potentially malicious until the symptoms of the infection are known. The copying process itself is safe (given the above scenario). However, you should be concerned with what type of files are being copied to avoid introducing other problems.

E13) Can a DOS virus survive and spread on an OS/2 system using the HPFS file system?

Yes, both file-infecting and boot sector viruses can infect HPFS partitions. File-infecting viruses function normally and can activate and do their dirty deeds, and boot sector viruses can prevent OS/2 from booting if the primary bootable partition is infected. Viruses that try to directly address disk sectors cannot function because OS/2 prevents this activity.

E14) Under OS/2 2.0, could a virus-infected DOS session infect another DOS session?

Each DOS program is run in a separate Virtual DOS Machine (their memory spaces are kept separated by OS/2). However, any DOS program has almost complete access to the files and disks, so infection can occur if the virus infects files; any other DOS session that executes a program infected by a virus that makes itself memory resident would itself become infected.

However, bear in mind that all DOS sessions share the same copy of the command interpreter. Hence if it becomes infected, the virus will be active in *all* DOS sessions.

E15) Can normal DOS viruses work under MS Windows?

Most of them cannot. A system that runs exclusively MS Windows is, in general, more virus-resistant than a plain DOS system. The reason is that most resident viruses are not compatible with the memory management in Windows. Furthermore, most of the existing viruses will damage the Windows applications if they try to infect them as normal EXE files. The damaged applications will stop working and this will alert the user that something is wrong.

However, virus-resistant is by no means virus-proof. For instance, most of the well-behaved resident viruses that infect only COM files (Cascade is an excellent example), will work perfectly in a DOS window. All non-resident COM infectors will be able to run and infect too. And currently there exists at least one Windows-specific virus which is able to properly infect Windows applications (it is compatible with the NewEXE file format).

Any low level trapping of Interrupt 13, as by resident boot sector and MBR viruses, can also affect Windows operation, particularly if protected disk access (32BitDiskAccess=ON in SYSTEM.INI) is used.

Section F. Miscellaneous Questions

F1) *How many viruses are there?*

It is not possible to give an exact number because new viruses are being created literally every day. Furthermore, different antivirus researchers use different criteria to decide whether two viruses are different or one and the same. Some count viruses as different if they differ by at least one bit in their non-variable code. Others group the viruses in families and do not count the closely related variants in one family as different viruses.

Taking a rough average, as of October 1992 there were about 1,800 IBM PC viruses, about 150 Amiga viruses, about 30 Macintosh viruses, about a dozen Acorn Archimedes viruses, several Atari ST viruses, and a few Apple II viruses.

However, very few of the existing viruses are widespread. For instance, only about three dozen of the known IBM PC viruses are causing most of the reported infections.

F2) *How do viruses spread so quickly?*

This is a very complex issue. Most viruses don't spread very quickly. Those that do spread widely are able to do so for a variety of reasons. A large target population (i.e., millions of compatible computers) helps... A large virus population helps... Vendors whose quality assurance mechanisms rely on, for example, outdated scanners help... Users who gratuitously insert new software into their systems without making any attempt to test for viruses help... All of these things are factors.

F3) *What is the plural of "virus"? "Viruses" or "viri" or "virii" or...*

The correct English plural of "virus" is "viruses." The Latin word is a mass noun (like "air"), and there is no correct Latin plural. Please use "viruses," and if people use other forms, please don't use VIRUS-L/comp.virus to correct them.

F4) When reporting a virus infection (and looking for assistance), what information should be included?

People frequently post messages to VIRUS-L/comp.virus requesting assistance on a suspected virus problem. Quite often, the information supplied is not sufficient for the various experts on the list to be able to help out. Also note that any such assistance from members of the list is provided on a volunteer basis; be grateful for any help received. Try to provide the following information in your requests for assistance:

- The name of the virus (if known);
- The name of the program that detected it;
- The version of the program that detected it;
- Any other antivirus software that you are running and whether it has been able to detect the virus or not, and if yes, by what name did it call it;
- Your software and hardware configuration (computer type, kinds of disk[ette] drives, amount of memory and configuration [extended/expanded/conventional], TSR programs and device drivers used, OS version, etc.).

It is helpful if you can use more than one scanning program to identify a virus, and to say which scanner gave which identification. However, some scanning programs leave "signatures" in memory which will confuse others, so it is best to do a "cold reboot" between runs of successive scanners, particularly if you are getting confusing results.

F5) How often should we upgrade our antivirus tools to minimize software and labor costs and maximize our protection?

This is a difficult question to answer. Antiviral software is a kind of insurance, and these type of calculations are difficult.

There are two things to watch out for here: the general "style" of the software, and the signatures which scanners use to identify viruses. Scanners should be updated more frequently than other software, and it is probably a good idea to update your set of signatures at least once every two months.

Some antiviral software looks for changes to programs or specific types of viral "activity," and these programs generally claim to be good for "all current and future viral programs." However, even these programs cannot guarantee to protect against all future viruses, and should probably be upgraded once per year.

Of course, not every antivirus product is effective against all viruses, even if upgraded regularly. Thus, do *not* depend on the fact that you have upgraded your product recently as a guarantee that your system is free of viruses!

Section G. Specific Virus and Antiviral software Questions...

G1) I was infected by the Jerusalem virus and disinfected the infected files with my favorite antivirus program. However, WordPerfect and some other programs still refuse to work. Why?

The Jerusalem virus and WordPerfect 4.2 program combination is an example of a virus and program that cannot be completely disinfected by an antivirus tool. In some cases such as this one, the virus will destroy code by overwriting it instead of appending itself to the file. The only solution is to re-install the programs from clean (non-infected) backups or distribution media. (See question D10.)

G2) I was told that the Stoned virus displays the text "Your PC is now Stoned" at boot time. I have been infected by this virus several times, but have never seen the message. Why?

The "original" Stoned message was ".Your PC is now Stoned!," where the "." represents the "bell" character (ASCII 7 or "PC speaker beep"). The message is displayed with a probability of 1 in 8 only when a PC is booted from an infected diskette. When booting from an infected hard disk, Stoned never displays this message.

Recently, versions of Stoned with no message whatsoever or only the leading bell character have become very common. These versions of Stoned are likely to go unnoticed by all but the most observant, even when regularly booting from infected diskettes.

Contrary to some reports, the Stoned virus does *NOT* display the message "LEGALISE MARIJUANA," although such a string is quite clearly visible in the boot sectors of diskettes infected with the "original" version of Stoned in "standard" PC's.

G3) I was infected by both Stoned and Michelangelo. Why has my computer became unbootable? And why, each time I run my favorite scanner, does it find one of the viruses and say that it is removed, but when I run it again, it says that the virus is still there?

These two viruses store the original Master Boot Record at one and the same place on the hard disk. They do not recognize each other, and therefore a computer can become infected with both of them at the same time.

The first of these viruses that infects the computer will overwrite the Master Boot Record with its body and store the original MBR at a certain place on the disk. So far, this is normal for a boot-record virus. But if now the other virus infects the computer too, it will replace the MBR (which now contains the virus that has come first) with its own body, and store what it believes is the original MBR (but in fact is the body of the first virus) AT THE SAME PLACE on the hard disk, thus OVERWRITING the original MBR. When this happens, the contents of the original MBR are lost. Therefore the disk becomes non-bootable.

When a virus removal program inspects such a hard disk, it will see the SECOND virus in the MBR and will try to remove it by overwriting it with the contents of the sector where this virus normally stores the original MBR. However, now this sector contains the body of the FIRST virus. Therefore, the virus removal program will install the first virus in trying to remove the second. In all probability it will not wipe out the sector where the (infected) MBR has been stored.

When the program is run again, it will find the FIRST virus in the MBR. By trying to remove it, the program will get the contents of the sector where this virus normally stores the original MBR, and will move it over the current (infected) MBR. Unfortunately, this sector still contains the body of the FIRST virus. Therefore, the body of this virus will be re-installed over the MBR ad infinitum.

There is no easy solution to this problem, since the contents of the original MBR is lost. The only solution for the antivirus program is to detect that there is a problem, and to overwrite the contents of the MBR with a valid MBR program, which the antivirus program will have to carry with itself. If your favorite antivirus program is not that smart, consider replacing it with a better one, or just boot from a write-protected uninfected DOS 5.0 diskette, and execute the program FDISK with the option /MBR. This will re-create the executable code in the MBR without modifying the partition table data.

In general, infection by multiple viruses of the same file or area is possible and vital areas of the original may be lost. This can make it difficult or impossible for virus disinfection tools to be effective, and replacement of the lost file/area will be necessary.

The Antiviral Software of MS-DOS 6

This appendix is a reprint of a broad-based technical review of the Microsoft Anti-Virus program conducted by Yisrael Radai, a virus specialist at the Hebrew University in Jerusalem, Israel. It is reprinted here with his permission.

At the end of March 1993, Microsoft released its long-awaited Version 6 of MS-DOS, and for the first time DOS came equipped with Anti-Viral (AV) software. The very fact that such software is supplied with DOS makes it likely that it will become one of the most widely used AV packages in the world and the de facto standard, regardless of its quality. And precisely for this reason, it will be specifically targeted by virus writers. If there are any weaknesses whatsoever in the software, they will be ruthlessly exploited by these people. Partly for this reason, and partly because many reviewers of AV products seem to be quite unaware of weaknesses due to security holes, much greater emphasis will be placed on such loopholes in this evaluation than is customary in most AV product evaluations.

Microsoft's Anti-Virus (MSAV) software for MS-DOS (this review does not cover AV for Windows) consists of two programs, MSAV and VSafe. Anyone familiar with Central Point's AV programs, CPAV and VSafe, will immediately see the resemblance, and this resemblance is by no means coincidental. (In fact, this is not the second, but the third incarnation of what is essentially the same software, the original being Turbo Anti-Virus of Carmel Software Engineering, Israel.) Actually, Microsoft's AV software lacks several important features of Central Point's, such as the BootSafe program, and MSAV is not quite CPAV, but basically we are dealing with the same software, and except where otherwise noted, almost everything written below about Microsoft's software applies equally well to Central Point's (at least to Version 1.4 and lower).

Together the two programs perform the most common AV functions: (1) scanning for known viruses, (2) removal of known viruses, (3) integrity checking, and (4) generic monitoring of program execution for suspicious activity.

VSafe is a resident program, while MSAV is not; thus function (4) can be performed only by VSafe. On the other hand, only MSAV performs function (2). The other two functions are performed by both programs. The main difference is that MSAV performs them on many files at a time, but only when specifically requested, whereas after VSafe is loaded, it performs them automatically on each program which is about to be executed.

MSAV

As stated above, MSAV is a non-resident program which scans for known viruses and disinfects infected files if desired. Optionally, it also creates and verifies checksums (both options being on by default). MSAV can be activated either interactively (via a menu) or in batch mode (via command-line parameters). If it is activated without parameters, the interactive interface is used, although this can be suppressed, if desired, by means of the parameter /P. Moreover, in interactive mode MSAV can scan only entire drives (this is in contrast to CPAV, with its graphic directory tree). However, one can limit the scan to a desired directory or file by specifying it as a parameter of MSAV:

```
MSAV [drive:][path]filename [options]
```

Although this is not mentioned explicitly in the documentation, wildcard notation within the filename is *not* recognized. (This fact is connected with a serious bug which will be described below.)

N O T E

When used interactively, MSAV displays a simple and pleasant-looking menu containing five choices: Detect, Detect & Clean, Select New Drive, Options, and Exit. There are nine options which can be enabled or disabled, of which the most important are: Create New Checksums, Verify Integrity, Anti-Stealth, and Check All Files. If the user changes any of them (or if he even *enters* the Options menu!), he will be asked, when he tries to exit MSAV, whether he wishes to save the new configuration. If so, a 248-byte file named MSAV.INI will be created or modified accordingly. (In addition to the nine interactive options, this file also includes Fast Detection, Auto Save, and Detection Only. The last mentioned prevents the user from selecting the Detect & Clean option from the Options menu.) Some of the options (e.g. Create New Checksums and Verify Integrity) refer to VSafe as well as to MSAV.

How good is MSAV's scanner? Using a test suite consisting of 2,426 viruses, the VSUM "certification" of Dec. 16, 1993 showed that MSAV, with the 8/93 string update, detected only 48.5% (last place in a field of 11, in which the leader detected 96.7%). (CPAV 2.0, by the way, came in 10th place.)

Unfortunately, scanner comparisons such as this must be taken with a grain of salt, since if one developer has access to the test suite used in a given comparison, his product will have an unfair advantage over the competition. Also, some comparisons do not use the latest version of the scan patterns of the scanners, creating another source of unfairness. Therefore, as a general rule, one should never rely on a single comparison alone. Nevertheless, despite considerable variation in the percentages, almost all other comparisons rank MSAV last and CPAV close to last (e.g. the January, 1994 issue of the *Virus Bulletin* ranks MSAV last and CPAV third-to-last out of 18, with MSAV detecting only 59 of the 80 "in-the-wild" file viruses in *Virus Bulletin's* collection). Moreover, a test conducted by the Virus Test Center in Hamburg showed that detection was sometimes inconsistent, i.e., MSAV detected some, but not all, infections by V2P6 and Anthrax.

Not only are these results very disappointing, but it should also be noted that unlike several other scanners, MSAV does not detect viruses in executable files which were subsequently compressed (e.g. by LZEXE or PKLite).

It has also been reported that MSAV damages some files which it tries to disinfect, e.g. in the case of Niemela-infected files.

Finally, false alarms have been reported with MSAV. For example, MSAV with Version 1.1 of the DOS Anti-Virus Update erroneously reports that the Sydex product CopyQM contains the "Virus Cruncher" virus. The error evidently arose because both CopyQM and the Cruncher virus use the compression software DIET. However, no other leading virus detector which recognizes this virus produces this false alarm. (Sydex reports that Central Point Software ignored its complaints until the matter was turned over to Sydex's attorney.)

Speed: Before starting its file scan, MSAV scans memory (except if asked to scan only a single file). I found that this took 27 seconds on a 386SX computer. (Another scanner which I use requires only seven seconds for this, yet it seems to be no less reliable.) In my opinion this is unacceptably slow. After the memory scan finished, I found that it took an additional 18.8 minutes to scan 40 Mb of files (with Create New Checksums and Verify Integrity both disabled). This also seems a bit slow. I'm quite sure that the great majority of users who choose to insert the line MSAV /P in their AUTOEXEC.BAT file (as suggested on p. 69 of the Upgrade manual) will soon remove it.

In general, it's quite important which setting of each option has been selected by the developers of any product as the default, since that is the setting which most (unsophisticated) users will continue to use. The Create New Checksums and Verify Integrity options are on by default, a reasonable decision. However, the reasoning behind the defaults Anti-Stealth = Off and Check All Files = On is quite beyond my comprehension.

According to the documentation, the Anti-Stealth option causes MSAV to use low-level techniques to detect changes to files when integrity verification is performed. Since presence of an unknown stealth virus in memory at such a time could distort the results, it seems essential to enable this option when booting is performed from the hard disk, as it usually is. Yet by default, this option is off. According to the on-line help, this choice of default is to avoid "a small performance penalty." But when I tested it (with the Verify Integrity option enabled), I found that turning Anti-Stealth on actually *reduced* the file scanning time by 20 to 33%! Perhaps there exists some configuration for which there is some performance penalty, but if so, I have been unable to find it. Therefore, assuming that enabling this option actually produces the effect that it claims, it is difficult for me to understand why it should ever be disabled, let alone be disabled by default.

Turning now to the Check All Files option, turning it off means that only files with specific extensions (EXE, COM, and six others; the list is not customizable by the user) will be checked. On a directory or drive with many non-executable files, this will save a great deal of time. It is therefore a mystery to me why the default for this option is On. It is true that there are a few viruses, such as Frodo, which infect certain types of non-executable files. However, it wouldn't be hard to program the scanner to check such types of files in the special case of *those few viruses*, thus adding very little time to the scan.

To summarize, the default for the Anti-Stealth option is Off, in order (supposedly) to save a little time, while actually making the scan much less secure. On the other hand, the default for the Check All Files option is On, thus increasing the time by a large factor, even though this adds practically no security.

Unfortunately, if one wants to alter any of the options, this cannot be done from the command line. What, then, is the user to do if he wants to temporarily alter one of the options when anything less than an entire drive is to be scanned (i.e. a directory or file, which, as mentioned above, can be requested *only* as a command-line parameter)? One way is to activate MSAV interactively, change options, save them, exit MSAV, then call MSAV with a path or file specification, and finally re-enter MSAV interactively and reset the options. Fortunately, there is a much less tedious way of doing this: The above mentioned file MSAV.INI is a normal ASCII file. The user can therefore edit it before and after executing MSAV. Although this is simpler, providing these options on the command line would be still more convenient.

When used in interactive mode, MSAV provides function keys for partially context-sensitive help in hypertext form (F1), and a list of viruses which MSAV recognizes (F9).

The current version of MSAV requires about 418K of memory in order to run at all, and about 27K more if you wish to use the Help option or see the list of recognized viruses. The MSAV.EXE file is about 168K in size (after compression by LZEXE).

No scanner is worth very much if its list of scan patterns is not frequently updated to detect newly written viruses and new variants of old viruses. Thus Microsoft had to arrange for some means of obtaining updates for MSAV and VSafe. According to the manual, a user can obtain "signatures" of new viruses for MSAV by downloading them from a certain BBS, which turns out, unsurprisingly, to be Central Point's. However, this allows only *detection* of new viruses, not their removal. In order to be able to remove them, it is necessary to update the software. The manual contains two coupons for obtaining Virus Protection Updates (one to be shipped at once, the other in 3-4 months) at a cost of $9.95 each for U.S. residents, much more for others. Just how much *subsequent* updates will cost, or how often new versions will be made available, is not stated. My guess is that the great majority of Microsoft's users will find it too inconvenient and/or too expensive to obtain updates regularly.

As with any other known-virus scanner, even if updates are obtained regularly, there will necessarily be an interval of several months between the time that a new virus (or a sufficiently modified variant of an old one) appears and the time that users can obtain the update necessary to detect and remove it. That is one reason why *generic* detection is so important in an AV package. The most common generic techniques are integrity checking, resident monitoring, and heuristic scanning. Microsoft supplies software for the first two measures, and it is to these that we now turn.

VSafe

VSafe is a resident program which checks for several types of suspicious activities:

1. Warns of attempts to low-level format the hard disk.
2. Warns of attempts to stay resident (by standard DOS methods).
3. Warns of attempts to write to the hard disk.
4. Checks executable files for known viruses when an attempt to open or execute such a file is made (via DOS) and prevents the action if a virus is found.
5. Checks diskettes for known boot-sector viruses whenever a diskette is accessed, and warns the user.

6. Warns of attempts to write to the hard-disk boot sector or MBR.

7. Warns of attempts to write to a diskette's boot sector.

8. Warns of attempts to modify executable files.

By default, (1), (4), (5), and (6) are on; the other options are off.

Regardless of the settings of the above eight options, the program also scans each program which is about to be executed for known viruses (although this is performed in a faster and less sophisticated manner than in MSAV; in particular, it does not use any anti-stealth techniques), scans the boot sector of the diskette in drive A: when Ctrl-Alt-Del is pressed, checks the hard-disk boot sector and the Master Boot Record when VSafe is loaded, and (optionally) performs integrity checking.

When VSafe finds reason to sound an alarm, it usually gives the user a choice between Continue, Stop, or Boot.

Ordinarily, VSafe will be invoked from the AUTOEXEC.BAT file. It is customizable, i.e. the command may contain parameters to indicate changes from the above eight defaults and/or to indicate additional choices such as disabling checksum creation. For example, if one wanted to add options (2) and (8) to the defaults, to turn option (4) off, and to disable checksum creation, he would write

```
VSAFE /2+ /8+ /4- /D
```

After VSafe goes resident, its menu can be called up at any time by pressing Alt-V. (The hot key can be changed to any other Ctrl or Alt combination.) Any of the above 8 options can be toggled on or off at that time, making this one of the most convenient and flexible monitoring programs available. However, I find it most unfortunate that this toggling is not available for checksum creation and integrity checking also. If the user wishes to unload the program at any time, he either presses Alt-U when the menu is up or types VSAFE /U at the command line.

It should be noted that if MSAV is activated while VSafe is resident, MSAV turns off the eight VSafe options until it finishes scanning, and then restores them. (Actually, it does not *always* restore them; see the section Bugs below.)

In order to test the generic features of VSafe without *interference* from its known-virus scanner, it would ordinarily be necessary to restrict oneself to new viruses for which scan strings have not yet been included. I took a different approach. Many of the test viruses which I used were known, but I simulated unknown viruses by first zeroing out all the scan strings inside of VSAFE.COM. Option 2 turned out to be quite successful; it was able to detect all attempts to go resident by the viruses at my disposal (even though the mechanism used to detect this seems to interrupt interception rather than actual memory residence). Option 8, on the other hand, performed rather poorly; there were several situations in which it failed to note that an executable had been modified. In particular, when I deliberately allowed the Frodo virus (which MSAV calls the "100 Years" virus) to go resident, VSafe did not detect subsequent infections of files. Due to time constraints, I was unable to test the options as much as I would have liked to do, but it is safe to assume that all options of VSafe (in fact, those of all other generic monitoring programs as well) can be bypassed by sufficiently clever viruses.

As in the case of MSAV, I question the choice of default options. Why are Options 2, 7 and 8 off by default? True, false alarms will be sounded by Option 2 if the user activates a legitimate resident program after VSafe has been loaded, by Option 7 if he tries to format a diskette, and by Option 8 under some other conditions (e.g. whenever I tried to download an executable file to my PC by means of FTP, VSafe told me that "File xxxxxxx.xxx is about to be changed," even though there was no such file by that name before the download). However, in my experience such false alarms were rare. Moreover, if a program which is about to be executed is infected by a virus which is unknown to VSafe, there is no possibility of preventing it from going resident, of infecting another file, or of infecting a diskette's boot sector without Option 2, 8 (or 3), and 7. In my opinion, the best way to handle such a conflict is to reduce the frequency of the false alarms by making further checks wherever possible, and to set the defaults for such options to On. However, the program developers chose Off as the default settings of these options, apparently considering the risk of viral infection to be less than the annoyance of false alarms.

If expanded memory is available, VSafe will load itself there (7K of conventional memory plus 64K of EMS memory); otherwise in extended memory (23K of conventional plus 23K of XMS); otherwise entirely in conventional memory (44K). There are parameters to prevent loading in EMS or XMS memory if the user so desires.

Usually the additional time required for VSafe to perform its checks is not noticed by the user. I did notice a delay, however, whenever I pressed

Ctrl-Alt-Del, in which case VSafe requires a few seconds to check the boot sector of the diskette in drive A:, but this is probably unavoidable.

Integrity Checking

Integrity checking means detection of modifications in files and boot records. In principle, implementation of such a technique should catch subsequent infections due to almost any type of virus, known or unknown. In MSAV and VSafe, integrity checking is optional, but enabled by default. It can be controlled by the Create New Checksums and the Verify Integrity options of MSAV and the /D option of VSafe. For any given file, the information recorded and checked by either of these programs consists of the date, time, attributes and size of the file, and a 16-bit checksum for it. This information is stored in a database named CHKLIST.MS, 27 bytes per file (12 bytes for the name, 2 for the file checksum, and 13 for the other information, including a special checksum on the rest of the entry), in the directory in which the file resides. (In the following description, I will often speak only of MSAV even though something similar usually applies to VSafe also.)

If the Verify Integrity option is on and the above information already exists in the database, the program computes a checksum of each file in its present form and compares the new information against the recorded information. If a mismatch is found by MSAV, an alarm is sounded and the user is given a choice between Update, Delete, Continue, and Stop, provided MSAV is used interactively.

If the Verify Integrity option is on, the program performs known-virus scanning only if the checksums do not match, or if no checksum is stored for the file in question (except that if the date of the CHKLIST.MS file is older than the date of the MSAV.EXE file, the checksums in CHKLIST.MS are ignored, and re-created if Create New Checksums is on). As a result, not only does integrity checking protect against unknown viruses, but checking usually requires much *less* time when Verify Integrity is on than when it is turned off. It would seem, then, that there is never any reason to disable integrity checking.

MSAV's implementation is such, however, that this conclusion is not entirely justified. One reason is the relatively large amount of disk space which the databases take up due to the unfortunate design decision to have a separate one for each directory. For example, if a user has 150 directories on his disk, the databases will take up a minimum of 300K. Another reason is that in practice, MSAV/VSafe's checksumming is not completely secure (see below), so that the software might erroneously decide that there is no mismatch and therefore skip the known-virus scan.

Because of the first reason, MSAV has a command Delete Checksums, available when the menu is up, by means of a function key (F7). This deletes all the checksum databases on the current drive in order to save disk space, at the expense of losing the integrity checking.

Another MSAV option is called "Create Checksums on Floppy." The description is as follows: "When this option is selected along with Create New Checksums, a CHKLIST.MS file is created for each directory on a floppy disk as it is scanned. This option is useful for creating checksums ... of files on floppy disks before write-protecting the disk." While it is clear that the databases are to be created on a diskette, it is not entirely clear whether the files which are to be checksummed are those on the hard disk or those on that diskette. Some reviewers of CPAV have assumed, apparently without bothering to test it, that the former is the intended interpretation (this could greatly enhance security). However, in actuality, it is the latter which is the true intent.

Note that when a modification is detected by MSAV or VSafe, the user is left to decide for himself whether or not the modification is due to a virus. There are other integrity checkers which apply heuristics in order to help the user to decide this.

Peculiarities in the Documentation

Concerning the Delete Checksums command of MSAV, the on-line help contains an extremely curious passage: "For maximum confidence, delete the checklist files periodically"!! (The "periodically" part makes sense only if the user keeps the Create New Checksums option on, something which the on-line help advises him *not* to do.) In that case, the databases will be built anew, except that meanwhile some of the files might become infected, so that the next time the checksums will be based on *infected* files instead of uninfected ones. How can *deleting the databases* possibly contribute to *confidence*?!?

MSAV's on-line glossary defines a checksum as "a value derived from the executable file's size, attributes, date, and time." This is *not* the way the term is normally used. Ordinarily, a checksum is derived from the *content* of the file. In actuality, MSAV's checksums are functions of the content also (albeit of only a small part of it; see below).

The upgrade manual (p. 64) defines computer viruses as "programs designed to replicate and spread." On p. 65, viruses are divided into three types: boot sector viruses, file infectors, and..."Trojan horse viruses". The last type is defined as a type of virus that "is disguised as a legitimate program... Trojan horse viruses are much more likely to destroy files or damage disks than other viruses."

Aside from the unusual description of Trojan horses as a subset of the viruses, there are several very confusing (if not dangerous) consequences of such a definition and classification: (1) It follows from this definition of a Trojan horse and that of a virus that all Trojan horses replicate (this is incorrect by any accepted definition of a Trojan horse; on the contrary, many people reserve this term precisely for malicious programs which do *not* replicate); (2) the reader is left with the erroneous impression that Trojan horses do not reside in either files or boot sectors (where *do* they reside?), and (3) that file and boot-sector viruses, as opposed to Trojan horses, do little or no damage. (As other people use these terms, both of these types of viruses can do *a great deal* of damage.)

Bugs

MSAV displays the message "Invalid option" in certain cases where it is not at all appropriate, one example occurring if the user specifies the name of a non-existent file on the command line.

A much more serious bug is the following: We mentioned above that if MSAV is activated while VSafe is resident, MSAV turns off the eight VSafe options and later restores them...or rather, is *supposed* to restore them. We also mentioned that while MSAV allows limiting the scan to a specified file, it does not support wildcard notation. But since this shortcoming is not mentioned specifically in the documentation, it is natural for the user to assume that MSAV does support such notation. Yet if he activates MSAV with an asterisk within the file specification on the command line, and the non-asterisked part matches at least one existing file, MSAV will display the message "Access denied" and return to the DOS prompt without performing any action. But meanwhile, MSAV has turned off the eight VSafe options. The bug consists in the fact that in this case, MSAV *fails to turn the VSafe options back on again,* so that although VSafe is still resident, *the user is left without the protection of these options*!

The problem of "ghost positives" has been a long-standing problem with CPAV/VSafe, in that the scan patterns in these programs are left in memory in unencrypted form, and these trigger other antiviral programs which scan memory, i.e. if such programs are activated after MSAV or VSafe, such patterns cause the other programs to think that a virus has been found in memory. A few years ago the developers of CPAV/VSafe made some effort to reduce this problem.

However, they still have much to correct, since patterns which contain wildcards remain unencrypted, and this problem has been carried over from CPAV to MSAV. No other widely used scanner fails to take some measure to prevent such false alarms. The lack of consideration toward other antivirus products creates so many problems that at least one such product displays the following message if it finds VSafe to be active in memory: "Warning! The MSAV/CPAV program is currently resident. As this program leaves virus fragments in memory, it may cause false alarms when scanning memory."

Finally, it seems there are bugs in detection of MtE-encrypted viruses. The Virus Bulletin reports that MSAV consistently locks up after detecting 255 samples of such viruses. Also, Vesselin Bontchev of the VTC has found a file, created during generation of MtE replicants, that when scanned causes MSAV to hang.

Security holes

A *security hole* is a way of circumventing the protection which a program is supposed to provide against attacks. I am aware of the following security holes in the generic features of VSafe and MSAV:

1. It's trivial for a virus to disable VSafe. All it has to do is load certain values into the AX and DX registers and call a certain interrupt (in fact, any one of three interrupts will do), and voilà, VSafe either has all its options disabled or it is completely unloaded from memory (depending on the value loaded into AX), without the user being aware that his protection has disappeared. This trick is used by the Tremor, PC_Weevil, Sterculius.280, and AlphaStrike viruses. By their very nature, resident programs are more vulnerable than non-resident

ones, but to make the protection unloadable by a mere 8 bytes of code is making the job absurdly simple for the virus writers. It's probably only a matter of time until this and several other tricks mentioned below get incorporated into the various virus construction kits available in the virus underground.

2. While VSafe's generic monitoring detects most viral modifications to already existing executable files, it does not detect creation of a new executable file (important for detecting companion viruses), modifications made to a file with a *non*-executable extension, or renaming of files. Thus a virus could alter the extension of an executable file, infect it, then rename it back. Or it could create an infected file under a different name, delete the original file, and rename the infected file to the original name. The Suriv viruses use this technique.

3. Since the earliest that Microsoft's VSafe can be loaded is at the beginning of execution of AUTOEXEC.BAT (in Central Point's software, VSafe can be loaded as a device driver), it cannot be effective when the code in the Master Boot Record, the DOS boot sector, COMMAND.COM, the other system files, or device drivers is executed, hence it cannot prevent viruses in these regions from loading themselves into memory. (Almost all of this is true of other generic monitoring programs as well.) This would not be so bad if MSAV could checksum the DOS boot sector and the Master Boot Record, but it does not. In Central Point's software, there is a program called BootSafe which compares these two regions against previously created copies. However, for some peculiar reason, this program is not included in MS-DOS 6. As a result, "there is no protection in Microsoft's software against unknown boot-record infectors."

4. Although VSafe seems capable of detecting most attempts of viruses to stay resident, there are ways in which a virus could gain as much control as a resident program without hooking interrupts in any sense of the term. Monitoring programs such as VSafe do not prevent these.

5. Since the MSAV.INI file is unencrypted and not normally checked for integrity, a virus could easily modify it so as to disable options such as Verify Integrity and Anti-Stealth.

6. Companion viruses (e.g. Aids-II, Twin-351, Mithrandir) do not modify existing files, but create new ones which get executed before the

target program. The integrity checking of MSAV and VSafe does not detect infection by this type of virus. (As mentioned above, the generic monitoring feature does not detect it either.)

7. A simple way for a virus to defeat the integrity checking is to alter the checksum database, deleting the entry (name and information) for a file just before infecting it. An even simpler way is to delete the entire checksum database. The user will notice nothing unusual, since if a database is deleted (and the Create New Checksums option is on), MSAV will simply start creating the database anew as if one never existed, this time using the *infected* files as a basis for future comparison instead of the original ones. Viruses which exploit this weakness are the Peach, Groove, Encroacher, and Twitch viruses. (Most of these viruses are directed specifically against CPAV's databases, while the Groove virus targets checksum databases of certain other programs as well, but in the case of some of these programs, the user will notice that something unusual has happened.) It is only necessary to add the name of MSAV's checksum databases to make these viruses effective against MSAV as well.

8. A good checksum algorithm for AV use will be based on different (unknown) keys (or passwords) for different users. MSAV/VSafe's algorithm does not do this. Thus even if it were impossible to delete the checksum database or any of its entries, it would still be possible for a virus writer to incorporate the checksumming code from MSAV.EXE or VSAFE.COM into his virus, so that after infecting a file, it could compute the checksum of the infected file and modify the checksum and file length in the database according to the new values.

9. In order to increase speed, MSAV and VSafe do not checksum the entire file, but only its first 63 bytes. Thus a virus which alters only other parts of the file and preserves the file size, date/time, and attributes will not be detected by the integrity checking of MSAV or VSafe. Almost all viruses preserve the date, time and attributes. Considering that there are viruses (e.g. ZeroHunt) which preserve the file size (this is possible also by other tricks not used in any current virus), and viruses (e.g. LeapFrog) which avoid modifying the beginning of files, there is no doubt that such a virus can (and therefore probably will) be written. Another way of exploiting this loophole would be to overwrite the scan strings within MSAV.EXE and/or

VSAFE.COM, thus rendering the scanner completely ineffective. The integrity checking mechanism of MSAV/VSafe would not notice such a modification. (Note also that the programs themselves do not perform an initial self-check which would detect this.)

10. Even if it were made impossible to modify the checksum database, the fact that the checksumming algorithm does not employ a user-dependent key is still a weakness if the algorithm is a relatively trivial one, for in that case it might be easy to forge checksums: i.e. after the virus modifies a file F into a file F it may be able to adjust some data area within F' so that the result has the same checksum as the original file F. (And even if the virus writer cannot find a simple method of doing this, the fact that the checksums of MSAV/VSafe are only 16 bits long may make it feasible to use trial and error to find a suitable adjustment to F'.)

I do not wish to give the impression that Microsoft's (and Central Point's) is the only AV software having such security holes. Nevertheless, the fact is that these holes could have been blocked had the software developers given sufficient thought to the matter. (That this is possible is shown by the fact that there is at least one product whose integrity checker is almost completely free of the relevant security holes mentioned above.)

Note in particular that keeping a separate database for each directory not only uses up a lot of disk space, but also makes it very difficult to block some of these holes. For example, were there only a single database for the entire drive, it would be very simple to store the checksums for the hard disk on a diskette, which could then be write-protected. (Similarly, MSAV could give the user the choice of where to locate the database on the drive, making it more difficult for the virus to find the database, especially if the name of the database were also selectable by the user.)

Note also that I am not revealing any deep secrets by mentioning these security holes. Most are well known to many virus writers, as is evidenced by the examples of existing viruses cited above which exploit them. In fact, sometimes one gets the impression that the only people who *don't* know of these holes are the AV product developers and reviewers of AV software! In the case of the former group, perhaps many of them are indeed aware of some of these holes, but apparently either they think that such holes are too theoretical, obscure or product specific for anyone to exploit them, or else management priorities are such that the developers must devote their energies to the graphic interface and other features which make a good impression on the public and the reviewers rather than to genuine security. In other words, here as in so many other fields, the driving force is often sales at the expense of quality.

Conclusions and Conjectures

The MSAV and VSafe programs have a pleasant user interface and are easy to install and use. However, they have many weaknesses compared to other AV software:

Known-virus Scanning. This part of the software scores lower than most other scanners in speed, and at the bottom of nearly every comparison of products in terms of percentage of viruses detected. Moreover, it cannot detect viruses within compressed executables. Occasional false alarms during detection and destruction of files during disinfection have been reported. Updates of scan patterns and disinfection procedures are available, but probably very few users of MS-DOS 6 will bother obtaining them because of the inconvenience and/or expense.

Generic monitoring. VSafe has 8 optional types of generic monitoring, and supplies them in a manner which is more flexible than most other programs of this type. However, there is considerable room for improvement in some of the monitoring capabilities. Some viral tricks (e.g. companion viruses, or viruses which rename executables, then infect and rename them back) are completely undetectable by VSafe. Moreover, a virus can completely disable the monitoring by loading certain values into certain registers and calling a certain interrupt, and there are already some viruses which do this. (See Security Holes 1 and 2 above.)

Integrity checking. There is no integrity checking on boot sectors or the Master Boot Record, hence an unknown boot-record infector will not be caught. On files, a virus can delete the checksum database (as several existing viruses do), in which case MSAV will build it anew using the *infected* files as a basis for future comparison. It can also bypass the integrity checking by modifying only parts of the file beyond the first 63 bytes and preserving the file length. It does not detect companion viruses. The checksum algorithm is not key-dependent, hence for any given file, all users will have the same checksum; this could be exploited to forge checksums. (For further details, see Security Holes 6-10 above.) The decision to maintain a separate database for each directory is a poor one, since it not only wastes disk space, but also hinders the blocking of some of the security holes.

Default Options. Some are poorly chosen, particularly the MSAV options Anti-Stealth = Off and Check All Files = On.

Conflicts with other Antiviral Software. Scan patterns containing wildcards are not encrypted, causing "ghost positives" when other scanners scan memory after MSAV or VSafe has been activated. No other widely used scanner (except CPAV) fails to take some measure to prevent such false alarms.

One of the things which differentiates a good AV program from a mediocre one is whether the developers concern themselves with guessing what types of tricks a virus writer might adopt in order to bypass the various types of protection offered by the product, and modifying their software accordingly.

Some developers have done this to a greater or less extent. However, it is evident that the developers of MSAV/VSafe have made very little effort in this direction.

Because of its many security holes and the fact that Microsoft's software will probably become the de facto standard, virus writers will probably turn more and more to writing viruses which target specific weaknesses of the generic part of the software.

Will the software be modified to correct these problems? Probably yes, in the case of the default values and minor bugs. However, blocking some of the security holes would require such a radical redesign of the whole system that this is highly unlikely. Moreover, if past experience is any guide, even the problems with less drastic solutions will take years to be corrected, if at all. For years people complained that the developers did not bother to encrypt the scan patterns in CPAV and VSafe, so that if one tried to use any other scanner after CPAV was run or when VSafe was active, the scanner would find such strings in memory, thus producing false alarms (see Section "Bugs" above). The problem was apparently *partially* fixed a few years ago, but it took far too long for even this partial correction to be made.

Despite suggestions to Microsoft that it include validation and/or protection as part of the operating system, it seems to have chosen the easy path. In my opinion, it was a poor choice on Microsoft's part to adopt Central Point's AV software, and probably a mistake on their part to include add-on AV software at all. True, many people who had never before installed AV software will now do so, and this seems to be a benefit. However, they will be under the false impression that they are well protected. Microsoft may shrug its collective shoulders; after all, since when has MS-DOS been noted for high quality? But just as the software will be a tempting target for virus writers, so Microsoft may become a tempting target for lawsuits. If McAfee Associates could be sued by Imageline for a false alarm, what is to be expected when the responsible party is Microsoft?

Acknowledgments

Every effort has been made to make this evaluation as accurate as possible. I wish to express my thanks to Yuval Sherman, head of the Israeli team developing this software, for supplying answers to my many questions, and to Vesselin Bontchev of the Virus Test Center in Hamburg for his comments on an earlier version of this paper. Needless to say, all opinions expressed herein (and errors, if any) are mine alone.

Computer Viruses— What, Where, and When

This appendix presents the complete Virus Catalog release 1.2. This cata log is maintained by Vasselin Bontchev of the Virus Test Center of the University of Hamburg, Hamburg, Germany. It is printed here with his permission. This catalog describes most of the computer viruses extant, what they do and what can be done to prevent or eradicate them.

While the original list was done according to the date of discovery of the virus, it is presented here alphabetically to make it easier for the reader to locate a particular virus. If Panda Pro finds a virus and you really want to know which one it is, run a Scanner to learn the name of your assailant.

Most computer viruses are local in nature. They seldom spread like wildfire as often feared. Even with the popularity of international networks such as Internet, we still don't see them infecting wide areas. The existence of computer viruses in the wild and the freqency of their detection are covered in two successive reports prepared by Joe Wells, a Virus Specialist at Symantec. They are reprinted here with his permission.

"8-Tunes" Virus

```
Entry...............: "8-Tunes" Virus
Alias(es)...........: "1971" Virus
Virus Strain........: ---
Virus detected when.: ---
           where.: ---
Classification......: Link-virus (extending), RAM-resident
Length of Virus.....: .COM files: program length increases by
                       1971-1986 bytes: (length -3) mod 16 = 0.
                      .EXE files: program length increases by
                       1971-1986 bytes: (length -3) mod 16 = 0.
-------------------- Preconditions ----------------------------------
Operating System(s).: MS-DOS
Version/Release.....: 2.xx upward
Computer model(s)...: IBM-PC, XT, AT and compatibles
-------------------- Attributes -------------------------------------
Easy Identification.: Typical texts in Virus body (readable
                      with HexDump-facilities):"COMMAND.COM" in the
                      data area of the virus; increased filelength
                      if the file is infected.
Type of infection...: System: infected if function E00Fh of INT 21h
                      returns the value 4C31h in the AX-register.
                      .Com files: program length increases by 1971-1986
                      bytes; if infected, the bytes 007h,01fh,05fh,
                      05eh,05ah,059h,05bh,058h,02eh,0ffh,02eh,00bh,
                      000h are found 62 bytes before end of file;
                      a .COM file will only be infected once.
                      .COM files will not be infected if
                      filelength<8177  and filelength>63296; virus
                      will be linked to the end of the program.
                      .EXE files: program length increases by 1971-1987
                      bytes. If it is infected the bytes 007h,01fh,
                      05fh,05eh,05ah,059h,05bh,058h,02eh,0ffh,02eh,
                      00bh,000h are found 62 bytes before end of
                      file; an .EXE file will only be infected once;
                      .EXE files will not be infected if
                      filelength<8177; virus will be linked to the
                      end of the program.
Infection Trigger...: Programs are infected during load procedure
                      (Load/Execute-function of Ms-Dos).
Interrupts hooked...: INT21h, INT08h (only if triggered),
                      INT24h (only while infecting a file)
Damage..............: Transient Damage:
                      After 30 minutes, the virus will play one of
                      eigth melodies (random selection). After a short
                      time, the virus will play a melody again.
Damage Trigger......: Damage occurs 90 days after the file infection.
Particularities.....: 1. COMMAND.COM will not be infected.
                      2. Normally, the virus will stay resident at the
                         end of the available memory; only if the
                         memory is fragmented by special software,
                         the virus may become resident (via Dos-
                         function 31h).
                      3. One function (0E00Fh) used by Novell- Netware
                         4.0 can't be accessed anymore.
                      4. The damage occurs immediately when processing
                         a file with creation date before 1984.
                      5. During a file infection, the virus looks for
```

```
                        "BOMBSQAD.COM", an antivirus-tool control-
                        ling accesses to disks; if found, the
                        virus will deactivate it (tested with
                        BOMBSQAD V. 1.2).
                     6. During a file infection, the virus looks for
                        "FSP.COM" (Flushot+), an antivirus tool
                        controlling accesses to disks, files etc.
                        If found, the virus will stop file
                        infection (tested with FLUSHOT V. 1.4).
-------------------- Acknowledgement -------------------------------
Location...........: Virus Test Center, University of Hamburg, Germany
Classification by..: Thomas Lippke, Michael Reinschmiedt
Documentation by...: Michael Reinschmiedt, Thomas Lippke
Date...............: 11-JUN-1990
```

10_Past_3.748 Virus

```
Entry..............: 10_Past_3.748 Virus
Alias(es)..........: Tea Time Virus
Virus Strain.......: 10_Past_3 Virus Strain
Virus detected when.:
              where.: South Africa (common in Jan.1993)
Classification.....: Resident COM infector (appending),armouring
Length of Virus....: 1.Length (Byte) on media:  748 Bytes
                     2.Length (Byte) in memory: 748 Bytes
-------------------- Preconditions ---------------------------------
Operating System(s).: MS-DOS
Version/Release....:
Computer model(s)..: IBM PCs and compatibles
-------------------- Attributes ------------------------------------
Easy Identification.:
Type of infection..: Self-Identification in memory:
                     mem[1ACh..1AFh] = 46h 42h 06h 22h
                     Self-Identification on media: file's end: 06h 22h
Infection Trigger..: Execution of an infected COM program
                     with 4<=LengthCOM<=64496.
Storage media affected:
Interrupts hooked..: INT 21h function 4Bh
Damage.............: Permanent Damage:    ---
                     Transient Damage#1: Reboot during INT 21h.
                     Transient Damage#2: Tamper with interrupt
                                 vectors so as to hang PC.
                     Transient Damage#3: Install new keyboard handler
                                 which affects Shft&Ctrl states.
Damage Trigger.....: Permanent Damage:    ---
                     Transient Damage#1: Reboot on any 22th day in
                                 1991 and any year after.
                     Transient Damage#2: In 1991 and any year after:
                                 If day=29 then trash INT 13h;
                                 If day= 1 then trash INT  9h;
                                 If day=10 then trash INT  Dh;
                                 If day=16 then trash INT 10h.
                     Transient Damage#3: Between 15h10min and 15h13min,
                                 AND if INT 21h occurs
                                 THEN install keyboard handler
                                 which sets Shft & Ctrl states
                                 randomly on about 1 in 11 key-
                                 strokes.
```

```
Particularities.....: Reported in South Africa; purportedly written by
                      a person with the pseudonym Marvin Giskard.
Similarities........: Other variant: 10_Past_3.789
-------------------- Agents --------------------------------------------
Countermeasures.....:
Countermeasures successful:
Standard means......:
-------------------- Acknowledgement -----------------------------------
Location............: CSIR Computer Virus Research Lab, Pretoria, RSA
Classification by...: Paul Ducklin
Documentation by....: Paul Ducklin (CARObase)
                      Klaus Brunnstein (converted to CVC format)
Date................: 1993-February-15
Information Source..: Reverse-Engineering of virus
```

10_Past_3.789 Virus

```
Entry...............: 10_Past_3.789 Virus
Alias(es)...........: ---
Virus Strain........: 10_Past_3 Virus Strain
Virus detected when.:
              where.: South Africa (common in Jan.1993)
Classification......: Resident COM infector (appending),armouring
Length of Virus.....: 1.Length (Byte) on media:  789 Bytes
                      2.Length (Byte) in memory: 789 Bytes
-------------------- Preconditions -------------------------------------
Operating System(s).: MS-DOS
Version/Release.....:
Computer model(s)...: IBM PCs and compatibles
-------------------- Attributes ----------------------------------------
Easy Identification.:
Type of infection...: Self-Identification in memory:
                      mem[1ACh..1AFh] = 46h 42h 06h 22h
                      Self-Identification on media: file's end: 06h 22h
Infection Trigger...: Execution of an infected COM program
                      with 4<=LengthCOM<=64496.
Storage media affected:
Interrupts hooked...: INT 21h function 4Bh
Damage..............: Permanent Damage:    ---
                      Transient Damage#1: Display message and reboot
                                          during INT 21h. Message:
                           Ah Ah Ah Ah Ah "Therese" Ah Ah Ah Ah Ah
                      Transient Damage#2: Tamper with interrupt
                                          vectors so as to hang PC.
                      Transient Damage#3: Install new keyboard handler
                                          which affects Shft&Ctrl states.
Damage Trigger......: Permanent Damage:    ---
                      Transient Damage#1: Display and reboot on aany 22th
                                          day in 1991 and any year after.
                      Transient Damage#2: In 1991 and any year after:
                                          If day=29 then trash INT 13h;
                                          If day= 1 then trash INT  9h;
                                          If day=10 then trash INT 0Dh;
                                          If day=16 then trash INT 10h.
                      Transient Damage#3: Between 15h10min and 15h13min,
                                          AND if INT 21h occurs
                                          THEN install keyboard handler
                                          which sets Shft & Ctrl states
```

```
                              randomly on about 1 in 11 key-
                              strokes.
Particularities.....: Reported in South Africa; purportedly written by
                      a person with the pseudonym Marvin Giskard.
Similarities........: Other variant: 10_Past_3.789
-------------------- Agents -------------------------------------------
Countermeasures.....:
Countermeasures successful:
Standard means......:
-------------------- Acknowledgement ----------------------------------
Location............: CSIR Computer Virus Research Lab, Pretoria, RSA
Classification by...: Paul Ducklin
Documentation by....: Paul Ducklin (CARObase)
                      Klaus Brunnstein (converted to CVC format)
Date................: 1993-February-15
Information Source..: Reverse-Engineering of virus
```

"12-TRICKS" Trojan

```
Entry...............: "12-Tricks" Trojan
Alias(es)...........: ---
Trojan Strain.......: ---
Trojan detected when: ---
              where.: Karlsruhe (West-Germany)
Classification......: Trojan Horse
Carrier of Trojan...: Contained in "CORETEST.COM", a file that will
                      test the speed of a hard disk.
-------------------- Preconditions ------------------------------------
Operating System(s).: MS-DOS, PC-Dos
Version/Release.....: ---
Computer model(s)...: IBM PC, XT, AT and compatibles
-------------------- Attributes ---------------------------------------
Easy Identification.: "MEMORY$", a text within the program, readable
                      with HexDump-utilities.
Infection Trigger...: The trojan searches at different adresses in the
                      ROM-Area of the computer for strings that may
                      be the entry of INT 13h (hard disk).
                       Adresses:            String:
                      C800H:0256H    080H,0FAH,080H,073H,005H,0CDH
                      F000H:2A71H    080H,0FAH,080H,073H,005H,0CDH
                      F000H:A935H    080H,0FAH,079H,077H,005H;0CDH
                      F000H:3772H    0FBH,09CH,022H,0D2H,078H,00CH
                      F000H:D1E7H    0FBH,080H,0FCH,000H,075H,00CH
                      if any such string is found, the damage
                      routine will be installed.
Storage media affected: Partition table of a hard disk.
Interrupts Hooked...: INT 08, INT 09, INT 0D, INT 0E, INT 10, INT 13,
                      INT 16, INT 17, INT 1A.
                      Either one or none of the interrupts will be
                      hooked (random selection).
Damage..............: Permanent damage:
                          Every time the computer boots, one entry in
                          the FAT will be changed.
                          The hard disk will be formatted (Track 0,
                          Head 1, Sector 1, 1 Sector) followed
                          by the message:
                          "SOFTLoK+ V3.0 SOFTGUARD SYSTEMS,INC
                      2840 St.Thomas Expwy,suite 201
```

```
                         Santa Clara,CA 95051 (408)970-9420"
                           (probability 1/4096).
                         Moreover, either one or none of the following
                         permanent or transient damages will occur:
                           permanent: if INT 13 is hooked, *every access*
                           to a floppy drive will be changed to *write-
                           access*.
                           transient damages:
                           INT 08: will slow down the computer by a
                                   random loop;
                           INT 08: will point to a IRET; every routine
                                   that was inserted within the INT 08-
                                   chain will no longer be accessible;
                           INT 09: every keystroke will change the BIOS-
                                   variable [046dh];
                           INT 0D: the interrupt will point to a IRET;
                                   (probability: 1/4);
                           INT 0E: the interrupt will point to a IRET.
                                   (probability: 1/4);
                           INT 10: will slow down the screen by a random
                                   loop;
                           INT 10: every time while scrolling up, the
                                   screen will be blanked;
                           INT 16: the BIOS-variable keyboard flag
                                   [0417h] is modified;
                           INT 17: Every character sent to the printer
                                   is manipulated (randomly);
                           INT 17: every character sent to the printer
                                   is XORed with 020H;
                           INT 1A: sometimes, this routine will return a
                                   random system clock value.
Damage Trigger......: Every boot sequence
Particularities.....: During installation, a mark (0FFH) is set within
                         the partition table at offset 01BDH, so the
                         will be installed only once.
                         The text
                         "SOFTLoK+ V3.0 SOFTGUARD SYSTEMS,INC
                         2840 St.Thomas Expwy,suite 201
                         Santa Clara,CA 95051 (408)970-9420"
                           is readable in the partition table.
-------------------- Acknowledgement --------------------------------
Location............: Virus Test Center, University of Hamburg, Germany
Classification by...: Thomas Lippke, Michael Reinschmiedt
Documentation by....: Thomas Lippke, Michael Reinschmiedt
Date................: 11-June-1990
```

"512" Virus

```
Entry...............: "512" Virus
Alias(es)...........: ---
Virus Strain........: ---
Virus detected when.: January 1990
            where.: Bulgaria
Classification......: COM overwriting/extending/resident.
Length of Virus.....: 512 bytes
-------------------- Preconditions ----------------------------------
Operating System(s).: PC/MS-DOS
Version/Release.....:
```

```
Computer model(s)...: IBM PC/XT/AT/PS and compatibles
-------------------- Attributes ----------------------------------------
Easy Identification.: "666" at offset 509.
Type of infection...: Executable file infection: Overwriting/extending;
                      resident; first 512 bytes placed at free space on
                      last cluster of file, and replaced with the virus
                      code.
                      System infection: RAM-Resident, uses disk buffer
                      space for code in order not to take-up memory.
Infection Trigger...: Any close file (INT 21, Service 3e) or Execute
                      (INT 21, Service 4b) on a .COM file.
Storage media affected: Any Drive
Interrupts hooked...: Int 21 DOS-services
                      Int 13 and Int 24 while infecting.
Damage..............: ---
Damage Trigger......: ---
Particularities.....: If virus is in memory, files are read as unin-
                      fected. Directory never shows size increase, even
                      if the virus is not in memory.
                      Under DOS 3.3, software write protections are
                      bypassed.
Similarities........: ---
-------------------- Agents --------------------------------------------
Countermeasures.....: Monitoring the INT 21 vector.
Countermeasures successful: ---
Standard means......: A Do-it-yourself way: Infect system by running an
                      infected file, ARC/ZIP/LHARC/ZOO all infected COM
                      and EXE files, boot from uninfected floppy, and
                      UNARC/UNZIP/LHARC E etc. all files. Pay special
                      attention to disinfection of COMMAND.COM.
-------------------- Acknowledgement -----------------------------------
Location............: Weizmann Institute Of Science, Rehovot, Israel
Classification by...: Ori Berger
Documentation by....: Yuval Tal (NYYUVAL@WEIZMANN.BITNET), Ori Berger
Date................: 6-March-1990
Information Source..: ---
```

"982" Virus

```
Entry...............: 982 Virus
Alias(es)...........: (Klaeren Virus; see: Particularities/Remark)
Virus Strain........: ---
Virus detected when.: March 1991
            where.: University of Tuebingen (South-West Germany)
Classification......: Resident File Infector
Length of Virus.....: 972-982 Bytes (file)
-------------------- Preconditions -------------------------------------
Operating System(s).: MS-DOS
Version/Release.....: 2.xx upward
Computer model(s)...: IBM-PC, XT, AT and compatibles
-------------------- Attributes ----------------------------------------
Easy Identification.: ---
Scanner Signature...: at end of infected file: 9C FF 1E EB 04 53 51 E8
                      00 00 5B 81 EB AF 03 B9 A5 03 80 37 ?? 43 E2 FA
                      59 5B 3B C1 C3 32 C0 CF 4D 5A
Type of infection...: Program Infector: virus appends itself at end of
                      .COM and .EXE files, enlarging the filesize
                      between 972 and 982 bytes.
```

```
Infection Trigger...:
Interrupts hooked...:
Damage.............: On trigger condition (in May, each year),
                     transient damage is produced.
                     Transient Damage: On trigger condition (May),
                     virus writes several screen pages with
                     text "Klaeren, Ha^s, Ha^s!"
                     (^s = scharfes s, ascii 225; Ha^s=hate),
                     and subsequently erases CMOS RAM thus
                     making disks etc. inaccessible.
                     Permanent Damage: beyond consequences of
                     lost access to devices (e.g. lost data),
                     no permanent damage has been observed.
                     Side Effects: ???
Damage Trigger......: Damage occurs when month=5 (May), each year
Particularities.....: Virus was found in a publicly accessible PC at
                     University of Tuebingen (South-West Germany).
                     The "ha^s" (=hate) message adresses Professor
                     Klaeren (University of Tuebingen).
                     Remark: some antiviruses identify this virus
                     as "Klaeren"; though this name is observed
                     when the virus action is triggered, names
                     of innocent victims should not be used. In-
                     stead, the length-oriented name "982" is
                     preferred as main name.
Similarities........: ---
-------------------- Agents -----------------------------------------
Countermeasures.....:
Countermeasures successful:
Standard means......: Delete infected EXE&COM files, copy uninfected
                     versions from original write-protected disk.
-------------------- Acknowledgement --------------------------------
Location............: Virus Test Center, University of Hamburg, Germany
Classification by...: Klaus Brunnstein
Documentation by....: Klaus Brunnstein
Date................: 15-July-1991
Information source..: (original virus analysis)
```

1260 Virus

```
Entry................. 1260 Virus
Alias(e)............. Variable, Chameleon, Camouflage, Stealth, V2P1
Strain............... distantly related to Vienna strain
Detected: when.......
          where.......
Classification....... Program Virus with direct action, COM infector
Length of virus...... 1260 Bytes
-------------------- Preconditions --------------------------------
Operating System(s)... MS-DOS
Version/Release....... 2.xx and upwards
Computer models....... IBM PC's and compatibles
--------------------Attributes --------------------------------
Easy identification... The seconds field of the timestamp of any
                     infected program will be 62 seconds.
Type of infection..... Program virus with direct action. It only in-
                     fects files with COM extension. It replaces
                     first 3 bytes with a jump to the virus.
Infection trigger..... Execution of an infected file
```

```
Media affected........ The virus will infect any COM file in the
                       current directory.
Interrupts hooked..... INT 1 and INT 3 while virus is executing
Damage................ transient: ---
                       permanent: ---
Particularities....... The actual virus code is encrypted once over
                       the whole code, and various single bytes
                       are also encrypted throughout the virus.
                       These bytes are decrypted prior to exec-
                       ution, using its INT 3 (break point)
                       routine to decrypt, and its INT 1 (trace)
                       routine to encrypt. The encryption routine
                       used to decrypt the entire virus is obscur-
                       red by the addition of irrelevant instruc-
                       tions and by scrambling the order of the
                       instructions from infection to infection.
                       As a consequence of this stealth technique,
                       it is not possible to extract any scan
                       string from this virus at all.
Similarities.......... The virus is similar to Vienna virus, but
                       highly modified, to contain the encryption
                       methods described above.
--------------------- Acknowledgement ----------------------------
Location.............. Virus Test Center, University of Hamburg, Germany
Classification by..... Morton Swimmer
Dokumentation by ..... Morton Swimmer
Date.................. 12-February-1991
```

1701-Virus

```
Entry................: 1701-Virus
Alias(es)...........: Cascade B-Virus
Virus Strain........: Cascade =Autumn =Herbst(laub)-Virus
Virus detected when.:
             where.:
Classification......: Program Virus (extending .COM), RAM resident
Length of Virus.....: .COM-file length increases by 1701 byte
------------------- Preconditions ---------------------------------
Operating System(s).: MS-DOS
Version/Release.....: 2.xx upward
Computer model(s)...: IBM-PC, XT, AT and compatibles
------------------- Attributes ------------------------------------
Easy Identification.: ---
Type of infection...: System: is infected if the call of interrupt 21h
                      with function 4Bh and subfunction FFh is possible
                      and without error and 55AAh is returned in DI-
                      register.
                      .COM file: Program virus: increases COM files by
                        1701 Byte; a .COM file is infected if the
                        first instruction is a three byte jump with
                        DISP16 = (filelength minus viruslength).
                      .EXE file: no infection.
Infection Trigger...: Infects all files that are loaded via the function
                      4Bh and subfunction 00h of the interrupt 21h
                      (MS-DOS uses this function to start any program)
Interrupts hooked...: Int21h, Int28h (only if Clockdevice Year = 1980),
                      Int1Ch (only if damage is triggered)
Damage..............: Transient Damage: Modifies the screen by making the
```

```
                             characters on the screen "fall down" on the screen
                             in connection with clicking noises.
Damage Trigger......: IF function GetDate returns with
                             1. ( year=1988 AND month>=10 ) OR
                             2. ( year=1980 AND
                               2.1 clock is changed by user to year=1988,
                                   month>=10 OR
                               2.2 clock is changed by user to year>1988 )
                             AND a random number generator activates damage.
Similarities........: The 1701-Virus is a patch of the Autumn Virus
                             (=1704-Virus), with the following changes:
                             1) The Filelength will increase by 1701 Bytes.
                             2) The analysis of the BIOS-Copyright string is
                             not active.
                             3) COM-Files up to a length of 63803 will be
                             infected.
Particularities.....: 1. If the system is _not_ infected, the invocation
                             of an infected programm produces errors (system
                             crash is possible).
                             2. COM-files up to a length of 63803 bytes will be
                             infected, but files with a length of more than
                             63576 bytes are not loadable after infection.
                             3. The virus-program is encoded, dependent of
                             the .COM-filelength.
                             4. The distinction between .EXE and .COM files is
                             made by testing the "magic number (MZ)" in the
                             .EXE-Header.
-------------------- Agents --------------------------------------
Countermeasures.....: Category 3: ANTI1701.EXE (VTC Hamburg)
Countermeasures successful: ANTI1701.EXE is an antivirus that only looks
                             for the 1701-Virus and, if requested, will restore
                             the file.
Standard means......: ---
-------------------- Acknowledgement -----------------------------------
Location............: Virus Test Center, University of Hamburg, Germany
Classification by...: Michael Reinschmiedt
Documentation by....: Michael Reinschmiedt
                             Morton Swimmer
Date................: July...... 30, 1989
```

"4096" Virus

```
Entry...............: "4096" virus
Alias(es)...........: "100 years" Virus = IDF Virus = Stealth Virus.
Virus Strain........: ---
Virus detected when.: October 1989.
              where.: Haifa, Israel.
Classification......: Program Virus (extending), RAM-resident.
Length of Virus.....: .COM files: length increased by 4096 bytes.
                             .EXE files: length increased by 4096 bytes.
-------------------- Preconditions --------------------------------
Operating System(s).: MS-DOS
Version/Release.....: 2.xx upward
Computer model(s)...: IBM-PC, XT, AT and compatibles
-------------------- Attributes -------------------------------------
Easy Identification.: ---
Type of infection...: System: Allocates a memory block at high end of
                             memory. Finds original address (inside
```

```
                                DOS) of Int 21h handler. Finds original
                                address (inside BIOS) of Int 13h handler,
                                therefore bypasses all active monitors.
                                Inserts a JMP FAR to virus code inside
                                original DOS handler.
                               .COM files: program length increased by 4096
                               .EXE files: program length increased by 4096
     Infection Trigger...: Programs are infected at load time (using the
                                function Load/Execute of MS-DOS), and whenever
                                a file Access is done to a file with the exten-
                                sion of .COM or .EXE, (Open file AH=3D,
                                Create file AH=3C, File attrib AH=43,
                                File time/date AH=57, etc.)
     Interrupts hooked...: INT21h, through a JMP FAR to virus code inside
                                   DOS handler;
                               INT01h, during virus installation & execution
                                   of DOS's load/execute function (AH=4B);
                               INT13h, INT24h during infection.
     Damage..............: The computer usually hangs up.
     Damage Trigger......: A Get Dos Version call when the date is after the
                               22th of September and before 1/1 of next year.
     Particularities.....: Infected files have their year set to (year+100)
                                of the un-infected file.
                               If the system is infected, the virus redirects
                                all file accesses so that the virus itself can
                                not be read from the file. Also, find first/next
                                function returns are tampered so that files
                                with (year>100) are reduced by 4096 bytes in size.
     -------------------- Agents -------------------------------------------
     Countermeasures.....: Cannot be detected while in memory, so no
                                monitor/file change detector can help.
     Countermeasures successful:
                               1) A Do-it-yourself way: Infect system by running
                                an infected file, ARC/ZIP/LHARC/ZOO all in-
                                fected .COM and .EXE files, boot from unin-
                                fected floppy, and UNARC/UNZIP/LHARC E etc.
                                all files. Pay special attention to disin-
                                fection of COMMAND.COM.
                               2) The JIV AntiVirus Package (by the author of
                                this contribution)
                               3) F. Skulason's F-PROT package.
     Standard means......: ---
     -------------------- Acknowledgement ----------------------------------
     Location............: Weizmann Institute, Israel.
     Classification by...: Ori Berger
     Documentation by....: Ori Berger
     Date................: 26-February-1990
```

"5120" Virus

```
     Entry................ "5120" virus
     Alias(es)............ ---
     Strain............... ---
     Detected: when....... January 1990
               where...... Wuerzburg, West Germany
     Classification....... Program virus
     Length of Virus...... 5120-5135 for EXE and COM files (virus resides
                               on a paragraph boundary)
```

```
----------------------- Preconditions--------------------------------
Operating System(s).... MS-DOS
Version/Release........ 2.00 and upwards
Computer models........ IBM PCs and compatibles
----------------------- Attributes----------------------------------
Easy identification.... The following texts are contained in the virus:
                        "BASRUN", "BRUN", "IBMBIO.COM", "IBMDOS.COM",
                        "COMMAND.COM", "Access denied"
Type of infection...... Program virus. The virus infects in direct
                        action (ie. it only infects on run time), by
                        searching through the directories recursively
                        starting on paths "C:\", "F:\" as well as the
                        current drive an EXE and a COM file to infect.
                        It will infect all files it can find.
                        EXE files will be infected if the length as
                        reported by DOS is less that the file length
                        as reported by the EXE header plus one page.
                        COM files will be infected if the file length
                        is less than 60400 bytes.
                        The virus turns Ctrl-C checking and verify
                        off while in operation.
Infection trigger...... The virus will infect any time it is executed
                        after the 6th of July 1989. However, if an
                        infected file will infect before this date, if
                        it has already been executed once. It doesn't
                        load itself memory resident.
Media affected......... Any logical drive
Interrupts hooked...... ---
Damage................. Any infected file will terminate with the
                        message "Access denied" (this comes from the
                        virus, not from DOS). The file is NOT deleted
                        in any way.
Damage trigger......... Any date after the 1st of June 1992
Particularities........ It seems to be written in a HLL, but I haven't
                        found out which.
Similarities........... ---
------------------------- Agents------------------------------------
Countermeasures........ ---
 - ditto - successful.. Most checksumming programs will find this virus.
                        The program NTI5120 (Virus Test Center) will
                        find and destroy any 5120 virus found.
Standard Means......... Do a string search for any of the strings
                        mentioned above.
----------------------- Acknowledgements-----------------------------
Location............... Virus Test Center, University of Hamburg, Germany
Classification by...... Morton Swimmer
Documentation by....... Morton Swimmer
Date................... 5-June-1990
Information source..... ---
```

Adolf Virus

```
Entry...............: Adolf Virus
Alias(es)...........: ---
Virus Strain........: ---
Virus detected when.: ---
             where.: ---
Classification......: Resident, appending COM-file infector.
```

```
Length of Virus.....: 475 bytes on disk/memory
-------------------- Preconditions ----------------------------------
Operating System(s).: MS-DOS
Version/Release.....: 2.xx and above
Computer model(s)...: IBM PC, XT, AT and compatibles
-------------------- Attributes ------------------------------------
Easy Identification.: The code contains the text: " Adolf Hitler ", and
                      the fourth byte will be an ASCII '5' = 35h.
Self Identification.: The virus will not infect a file, if fourth byte
                      is 35h. It stores itself in memory, starting at
                      position 0000:0200 if there isn't a BBh (the
                      first code-byte).
Type of infection...: Starting an infected file will make the virus
                      resident before executing the file correctly.
                      At execion time of an uninfected file, the virus
                      appends itself to the file's code.
Infection Trigger...: INT 21h load/execute function if the virus is
                      active in memory.
Storage media affected: All files at each locations.
Interrupts hooked...: INT 21h functions 4Bh(load/execute) and 41h(delete),
                      INT 24h.
Damage..............: Nothing except infection.
Damage Trigger......: ---
Particularities.....: If the virus is active in memory and INT 21h
                      function 41h is called, a deletion will only
                      succeed if bits 0 and 1 of BIOS-parameter 046C
                      (Timer) are not set both.
Similarities........: ---
-------------------- Agents ----------------------------------------
Countermeasures.....: Skulasons F-PROT 2.06a, McAfee SCAN V99.
Standard means......: Reboot and delete infected files.
-------------------- Acknowledgement -------------------------------
Location............: Virus Test Center, University of Hamburg, Germany.
Classification by...: Stefan Haack
Documentation by....: Stefan Haack
Date................: 01-FEB-1993
Information Source..: Virus-code analysis
```

"Advent" Virus

```
Entry................. "Advent" Virus
Alias(es)............. ---
Strain................ Syslock/Macho Virus Strain
Detected: when........ Autumn 1988
         where........ Federal Country of Rheinhessen, FR Germany
Classification........ Program Virus (Link virus)
Length of Virus....... 2761 - 2776 (dec) bytes appended on
                              paragraph boundary
---------------------- Preconditions-------------------------------
Operating System(s).... MS/PC-DOS
Version/Release........ 3.00 and upwards
Computer models....... All IBM PC compatibles.
---------------------- Attributes----------------------------------
Easy identification.... Beginning on every "Advent" (the time period
                             beginning at the 4th sunday before
                             Christmas until Christmas eve), the
                             virus displays after every "advent
                             sunday" one more lit candle in a wreath
```

of four, together with the string
"Merry Christmas" and plays the melody
of the German Christmas song "Oh Tannen-
baum". By Christmas all four candles are
lit. This happens until the end of December, when an infected file is run.

Type of infection...... The virus infects both COM and EXE files.
EXE files: it checks the checksum in the EXE
header for 7CB6h, in which case no infection will occure.
COM files: are checked by looking for the
string 39,28,46,03,03,01 (hex) at offset
10h. The virus is not RAM resident,
therefore it will only infect when the
host is run. It infects by searching
through the directories on the current
drive and randomly choosing files and
directories to infect or search. It will
not infect any other drive. It will infect
COMMAND.COM.

Infection trigger...... Virus will infect any time it is run.

Media affected......... All disks that are addressable using
standard DOS functions, as long as it is
the current drive.

Interrupts hooked...... ---

Damage................. Transient damage: displayed picture, melody
(see Easy Identification)

Damage trigger......... Every time the host is run.

Particularities........ The virus checks for the environment variable
"VIRUS=OFF", in which case it will not
infect. The virus encrypts itself using
a variable key.
The virus will only do its transient damage
after 1-Nov-1988.

Similarities........... Macho/Syslock: much of the code is identical,
including the startup code. This means
that Advent will be identified as Syslock
by many scanning programs.
Advent seems to be the precursor to Macho
and Syslock (though detected later).

---------------------------- Agents -----------------------------------

Countermeasures........ Use the environment variable described
above as a first aid measure only. If your
COMMAND.COM in infected, that wont stop
the virus much. Resetting the date will
only stop the damage, not the infection.
Here's one of the few strings that can safely
be searched for:
50,51,56,BE,59,00,B9,26,08,90,D1,E9,8A,E1,
8A,C1,33,06,14,00,31,04,46,46,E2,F2,5E,59;
it should be noted, however, that this
string will also identify Syslock and
Macho.
There is no scanning method that will tell
the 3 apart. "NTIADVEN" uses a checksum.

- ditto - successful.. For proper treatment, my Anti-Virus "NTIADNEN"
is highly recommended (in all humility).
Treatment by hand is very tedious and only
recommendable for experts.

```
Standard Means........  Booting from a write-protected disk and resto-
                        ring all COM and EXE files from the ori-
                        ginal disks.
---------------------- Acknowledgements-----------------------------
Location..............  Virus Test Center, University of Hamburg, FRG
Classification by......  Morton Swimmer
Documentation by.......  Morton Swimmer
Date..................  December 10, 1989
Information source.....  "The Peter Norton Programmer's Guide to the
                        IBM PC" (1985), and members of our group.
                        Also thanks to V-COMM for producing
                        "Sourcer" and making my life easier.
```

"AIDS" Trojan

```
Entry...............:  "AIDS" Trojan
Alias(es)...........:  PC Cyborg Trojan
Trojan Strain.......:  ---
Trojan detected when:  December 1989
            where.:  USA, Europe
Classification......:  Trojan Horse
Carrier of Trojan...:  A hidden file named REM<255> of 146188 bytes;
                       (<255> represents the character ASCII(255));
                       distributed with AIDS.EXE as INSTALL.EXE file
                       on AIDS Information Disk of PC Cyborg, Panama
--------------------- Preconditions -----------------------------
Operating System(s).:  MS-DOS, PC-DOS
Version/Release.....:  ---
Computer model(s)...:  IBM PC, XT, AT and compatibles
-------------------- Attributes -----------------------------
Easy Identification.:  The string "rem<255> PLEASE USE THE auto.bat FILE
                       INSTEAD OF autoexec.bat FOR CONVENIENCE <255>"
                       can be found in AUTOEXEC.BAT
Installation Trigger:  Installing the "AIDS Information Diskette" on
                       hard disk drive C.
Storage media affected:Free space on Partition C:, all directories
Interrupts Hooked...:  ---
Damage..............:  Permanent damage: All directory entry names are
                               encryped by a simple encryption algorithm:
      A -> } , B -> U , C -> _ , D -> @ , E -> 8 , F -> ! , G -> ' ,
      H -> Q , I -> # , J -> D , K -> A , L -> P , M -> C , N -> 1 ,
      O -> R , P -> X , Q -> Z , R -> H , S -> & , T -> 6 , U -> G ,
      V -> 0 , W -> K , X -> V , Y -> N , Z -> I , # -> C , ! -> S ,
      ' -> $ , ^ -> ~ , _ -> 0 , $ -> 3 , 0 -> R , 1 -> F , 2 -> Y ,
      3 -> { , 4 -> J , 5 -> E , 6 -> T , 7 -> ) , 8 -> M , 9 -> - ,
      @ -> L , ~ -> ^ , & -> 7 , } -> 5 , { -> 4 , ) -> % , ( -> B ,
      - -> 2 , % -> W
                       Moreover, 90 extensions known to the program
                       are changed to the following extensions each
                       consisting of one blank plus 2 letters:
COM -> AK , BAK -> AD , EXE -> AU , PRG -> BR , BAT -> AG , DBF -> AN
DOC -> AR , WK1 -> CC , DRW -> DI , NDX -> BK , DRV -> CI , BAS -> AF
OVR -> BN , FNT -> AW , ZBA -> CH , SYS -> BZ , FLB -> DJ , FRM -> AX
DAT -> AL , LRL -> CJ , OVL -> BM , HLP -> BA , PIC -> DK , XLT -> CF
MNU -> BI , TXT -> CB , CAL -> CK , FON -> CL , SPL -> CM , PAT -> DL
MAC -> CN , STY -> BY , VFN -> DM , TST -> CO , GEM -> DN , FIL -> AV
DEM -> AP , REN -> DO , IMG -> DP , RSC -> DQ , MSG -> BJ , MEM -> DR
REC -> BX , GLY -> AZ , CMP -> BI , LGO -> CP , DCT -> AO , GRB -> CQ
CNF -> AJ , INI -> BB , GRA -> CR , DB  -> AM , DTA -> CS , APP -> AC
```

```
CAT -> AH , DIR -> AQ , DVC -> AS , DYN -> AT , INP -> BC , LBR -> BD
LOC -> BF , MMF -> BH , OUT -> BL , PGG -> BO , PIF -> BP , PRD -> BQ
PRN -> BS , SCR -> BU , SET -> BV , SK  -> BW , ST  -> BX , TAL -> CA
WK2 -> CD , WKS -> CE , XQT -> CG , $$$ -> CT , VC  -> CU , TMP -> CV
PAS -> CW , QBJ -> CX , MAP -> CY , LST -> CZ , LIB -> DA , ASM -> DB
BLD -> DC , COB -> DD , DIF -> DH , FMT -> DG , MDF -> BG , FOR -> DF
```

The free space on partition C is filled with
a file containing a number of strings consisting of blanks followed by CR/LF. Every
time the computer boots, a COMMAND.COM is
simulated. Almost all commands are requested
by an error message. DIR shows the directory
before encryption.

Damage..............: Transient damages: from time to time, the following message is displayed:

"It is time to pay for your software lease from PC Cyborg Corporation.
Complete the INVOICE and attach payment for the lease option of your
choice.If you don't use the printed INVOICE, then be sure to refer to
the important reference numbers below in all correspondence.
In return you will recieve:
  - a renewal software package with easy to follow,
    complete instructions;
  - an automatic, self installing diskette
    that anyone can apply in minutes."

Damage Trigger......: Booting the system 90 times (9 in some cases)
Particularities.....: AIDS.EXE will only run after installation on
                      drive C.
                      Some hidden directories are created containing
                      hidden subdirectories and some files which
                      are used by the trojan; filenames contain
                      blanks and can't be accessed via COMMAND.COM.
                      AIDS.EXE and INSTALL.EXE have been written in
                      Microsoft Quick Basic 3.0; according to VTCs
                      retroanalysis, the program quality and the
                      encryption method show moderate quality; more-
                      over, the dialog as well as the function to
                      evaluate the personal risk of an AIDS infect-
                      ion, are rather primitive.
-------------------- Acknowledgement ----------------------------
Location............: Virus Test Center, University of Hamburg, Germany
Classification by...: Ronald Greinke, Uwe Ellermann
Documentation by....: Ronald Greinke
Date................: 10-February-1991
```

# Akuku Virus

```
Entry...............: Akuku virus
Standard CARO name..: Akuku.completely
Alias(es)...........: Russian-A
Virus Strain........: Akuku virus strain
Virus detected when.: ---
            where.: ---
Classification......: Program (COM,EXE) virus, non memory resident
Length of Virus.....: 1. Length in RAM: 1108 bytes
                      2. Length in program: 1111-1114 bytes
-------------------- Preconditions -----------------------------
Operating System(s).: MS-DOS, PC-DOS
Version/Release.....: version 2.xx and higher
```
```

```
Computer model(s)...: IBM-PC, XT, AT and compatibles
-------------------- Attributes ----------------------------------------
Easy Identification.: Virus contains string "Sorry, I'm completely dead."
                      Seconds field in file's time set to 62.
Type of infection...: Installs itself memory-resident when infected
                      program is run. Infects both .EXE and .COM
                      files, including COMMAND.COM, by appending
                      itself to end of file. EXE files are increased
                      by 1114 (45Ah) bytes, COM files by 1111 (457h)
                      bytes, but this amount may increase by up to
                      15 (0Fh) bytes as padding for paragraph align-
                      ment.
Infection Trigger...: Upon running infected file, disk must have 3000
                      (BB8h) bytes of free space. EXE files must be
                      larger than 1000 (3E8h) bytes; COM files must
                      be larger than 1000 (3E8h), but smaller than
                      64000 (FA00h) bytes.
Self Identification.: On disk, virus checks if seconds field of file
                      is set to 62.
Damage..............: Transient damage: virus will display message
                      "Sorry, I'm completely dead.". Virus installs
                      payload in memory, which plays a song.
                      Permanent damage: ---
Damage Trigger......: Trigger for damage is the current time at in-
                      fection time. If the minutes field is one of:
                      32, 33, 34 or 35, the virus displays "Sorry,
                      I'm completely dead, installs the song and
                      plays it every 14 seconds.
Particularities.....: 1. The file date and time will not be altered
                      in the disk directory, except for the seconds,
                      which will be set to 62.
                      2. The drive to be infected is selected according
                      to this rule: if the current time's seconds
                      is =0, select drive A:; if it is >0, but <=22
                      the current drive is selected, and if it is
                      >22, C: is selected.
                      3. Virus will search the whole current directory
                      for files to infect, as well as the first
                      level of all of it's subdirectories. It will
                      infect the first 3 files found. Default
                      drive is reset to the correct drive.
                      4. Virus installs the whole virus body in memory,
                      although only the song is active.
Similarities........: Very similar to Akuku.3 and Cop-Mpl viruses.
                      All Akuku viruses try to infect three files
                      in directory of current disk, but differ on
                      what happens if they cannot be found.
                      The identification by 62 seconds field is similar
                      to Vienna viruses.
-------------------- Agents --------------------------------------------
Countermeasures.....: F-Prot, Anti-Virus Toolkit, ViruScan
Countermeasures successful: F-Prot, Anti-Virus Toolkit
Standard means......: ---
-------------------- Acknowledgement -----------------------------------
Location............: Virus Test Center, University of Hamburg, Germany
Classification by...: Christopher G. Street (guest from Brown Univ)
Documentation by....: Christopher G. Street (guest from Brown univ)
Date................: June 14, 1992
Information Source..: Original virus code
```

Alabama Virus

```
Entry...............: Alabama Virus
Alias(es)...........: ---
Virus Strain........: ---
Virus detected when.: October 1989
             where.: Israel
Classification......: Resident, appending EXE infector.
Length of Virus.....: 1) Length on media: 1408 bytes
-------------------- Preconditions ----------------------------------
Operating System(s).: MS-DOS
Version/Release.....: 2.xx and above
Computer model(s)...: IBM PC, XT, AT and compatibles
-------------------- Attributes -------------------------------------
Easy Identification.: ---
Self Identification.: File create/edit time contains 63 seconds.
                      First 4 bytes of memory are 0h.
Type of infection...: Appends itself to the executed file.
Infection Trigger...: Any INT 21h load/execute function-call.
Storage media affected: All files on each locations.
Interrupts hooked...: INT 21h function 4Bh (load and execute); INT 24h.
Damage..............: Permanent damage: ---
                      Transient damage: One hour after the start of an
                      infected program, the following message will
                      be displayed: "SOFTWARE COPIES ARE PROHIBITED
                      BY INTERNATIONAL LAW",
                      "Box 1055 Tuscambia ALABAMA USA"
                      The message is encrypted by the NOT function.
Damage Trigger......: Permanent damage: ---
                      Transient damage: 1 hour after starting an
                                        infected program.
Particularities.....: ---
Similarities........: ---
-------------------- Agents -----------------------------------------
Countermeasures.....: Skulasons F-PROT 2.06a, McAfee SCAN V99.
Standard means......: Reboot and delete infected files.
-------------------- Acknowledgement --------------------------------
Location............: Virus Test Center, University of Hamburg, Germany.
Classification by...: Michael Haack
Documentation by....: Michael Haack
Date................: 01-FEB-1993
Information Source..: Virus-code analysis
```

"Ambulance Car" Virus

```
Entry...............  "Ambulance Car" Virus
Alias(e)............. REDX-Virus
Strain............... ---
Detected: when........ Germany
          where....... June 1990
Classification........ Program virus, direct action COM infector
Length of virus....... 796 bytes added to COM files
-------------------- Preconditions ---------------------------------
-
Operating System(s)... MS-DOS
Version/Release....... 2.0 and up
Computer models....... Any IBM-compatibles
----------------------Attributes -----------------------------------
```

```
                      to Vienna viruses.
-------------------- Agents ------------------------------------
Countermeasures.....: F-Prot, Anti-Virus Toolkit, ViruScan
Countermeasures successful: F-Prot, Anti-Virus Toolkit
Standard means......: ---
-------------------- Acknowledgement ---------------------------
Location............: Virus Test Center, University of Hamburg, Germany
Classification by...: Christopher G. Street (guest from Brown Univ)
Documentation by....: Christopher G. Street (guest from Brown univ)
Date................: June 14, 1992
Information Source..: Original virus code
```

Alabama Virus

```
Entry...............: Alabama Virus
Alias(es)...........: ---
Virus Strain........: ---
Virus detected when.: October 1989
          where.: Israel
Classification......: Resident, appending EXE infector.
Length of Virus.....: 1) Length on media: 1408 bytes
-------------------- Preconditions -----------------------------
Operating System(s).: MS-DOS
Version/Release.....: 2.xx and above
Computer model(s)...: IBM PC, XT, AT and compatibles
-------------------- Attributes --------------------------------
Easy Identification.: ---
Self Identification.: File create/edit time contains 63 seconds.
                 First 4 bytes of memory are 0h.
Type of infection...: Appends itself to the executed file.
Infection Trigger...: Any INT 21h load/execute function-call.
Storage media affected: All files on each locations.
Interrupts hooked...: INT 21h function 4Bh (load and execute); INT 24h.
Damage..............: Permanent damage: ---
                 Transient damage: One hour after the start of an
                 infected program, the following message will
                 be displayed: "SOFTWARE COPIES ARE PROHIBITED
                 BY INTERNATIONAL LAW",
                 "Box 1055 Tuscambia ALABAMA USA"
                 The message is encrypted by the NOT function.
Damage Trigger......: Permanent damage: ---
                 Transient damage: 1 hour after starting an
                          infected program.
Particularities.....: ---
Similarities........: ---
-------------------- Agents ------------------------------------
Countermeasures.....: Skulasons F-PROT 2.06a, McAfee SCAN V99.
Standard means......: Reboot and delete infected files.
-------------------- Acknowledgement ---------------------------
Location............: Virus Test Center, University of Hamburg, Germany.
Classification by...: Michael Haack
Documentation by....: Michael Haack
Date................: 01-FEB-1993
Information Source..: Virus-code analysis
```

```
                        Released Dec91 Montreal
                          (C) NukE Development Software Inc"
                     Thereafter, the program terminates.
                     2) Upon each INT 21 call, the virus also checks
                     system tick count for being above equivalent
                     of about 16 hours; if this amount of on-time
                     is reached, a green smiley face on black back-
                     ground moves diagonally around the screen
                     bouncing at edges and characters.
Damage Trigger......: 1) For the message: day of the week = Sunday;
                     2) For the smiley:  16 hours of power on time.
Similarities........: ---
Particularities.....: This virus carefully looks for the correct INT 13
                     entry to avoid being trapped by a guardian.
-------------------- Agents ------------------------------------------
Countermeasures.....:
- ditto - successful:
            Removal: Not always possible: a 'NE' type EXE will not
                     work anymore.
Standard means......:
-------------------- Acknowledgement ---------------------------------
Location............: Micro-BIT Virus Center, Univ. Karlsruhe, Germany
Classification by...: Christoph Fischer
Documentation by....: Christoph Fischer
Date................: January 25, 1992
```

Amoeba Virus

```
Entry...............: Maltese Amoeba Virus
Standard CARO name..: Amoeba
Alias(es)...........: Family-N, Irish, Grain of Sand Virus
Virus Strain........: ---
Virus detected when.: UK
            where.: November 1st, 1991 (upon first triggered damage)
Classification......: Program (COM,EXE) infector, variable encryption,
                     memory resident
Length of Virus.....: 1) Length on media:  2 kByte
                     2) Length in memory: 2 kByte
-------------------- Preconditions -----------------------------------
Operating System(s).: MS-DOS
Version/Release.....: 2.xx upward
Computer model(s)...: IBM - PCs, XT, AT, upward and compatibles
-------------------- Attributes --------------------------------------
Easy Identification.: 1) Enlarged file size: using DIR, compare actual
                     file size with original file size.
                     2) Reduction of available memory by 2k Bytes,
                     using CHKDSK.
                     3) Unencrypted text (AMOEBA) in partition sector.
Type of infection...: Upon executing an infected file, the virus makes
                     itself memory resident in highest available
                     2 kByte. Thereafter, upon reading or executing
                     a non-infected file this will be infected.
                     Self-identification: Virus inspects memory (using
                     a Set Date call with invalid date) whether
                     it is in memory; moreover, it checks whether
                     some antivirus programs (Ross Greenberg's
                     FluShot+ or Virex-PC) or PSQR virus are in
                     memory. If any of these are found, virus does
```

```
                              not infect any program. There are unconfirmed
                              reports that this virus checks and deactivates
                              Murphy virus.
Infection Trigger...: Any DOS read or load/execute operation.
Media affected......: Any hard disk and floppy disk.
Interrupts hooked...: INT 24
Crypto method.......: Decryption uses variations of several patterns
                              of instructions, differing for COM and EXE files.
Polymorphic method..: ---
Damage..............: Permanent damage: upon trigger condition, it will
                              overwrite low tracks of a hard disk and any
                              diskette, accompanied by a flashing display,
                              and subsequently hang-up the system. In the
                              overwritten partition sector, the following
                              encrypted text (from Pickering Manuscripts:
                              Blake's Auguries of Innocence, first 4 lines)
                              can be found:
                                  "To see a world in grain of sand
                                   And a heaven in wild flower,
                                   Hold infinity in the palm of your hand
                                   And eternity in a hour."
                                   The Virus 16/3/91
                              When an infected system is booted, this text
                                  is displayed and the system hangs.
                              Moreover, partition sector contains also un-
                                  encrypted texts: "AMOEBA", and the message
                                  that University of Malta "destroyed 5X2
                                  years of human life".
                              Transient damage: ---
Damage Trigger......: November 1st and March 15th, any year.
Similarities........: En/Decryption method similar to V2PX.
Particularities.....: 1) Virus replaces critical error handler INT 24;
                              if virus tries to infect a write-protected
                              diskette, the prompt "Abort, Retry, Fail" is
                              suppressed.
                              2) There is speculation that the uncrypted text
                              may be related to an unhappy fate of 2
                              students of University of Malta, having left
                              after 5 years.
-------------------- Agents -------------------------------------------
Countermeasures.....: McAfee Scan, Skulason F-PROT, Solomon FINDVIRU
                              and some others
Standard means......: Boot from clean system and delete infected files.
-------------------- Acknowledgement ----------------------------------
Location............: Virus Test Center, University of Hamburg, Germany
Classification by...: Klaus Brunnstein
Documentation by....: Virus Bulletin (Dec.91), Stiller's Virus Report
                              (see: Virus-L Vol.5 Issue 30: Feb.14, 1992)
Date................: 15-February-1992
```

"Amstrad" Virus

```
Entry................ "Amstrad" Virus
Alias(es)............ Pixel, V-847 Virus
Strain............... Amstrad Virus Strain
Detected: when....... Fall 1989
          where....... Reported to have been published in PIXEL
                       magazine
```

```
Classification......... Program virus, direct action, prefix
Length of Virus........ COM files increase by 847 bytes, but the
                        actual length of the virus is 591 bytes
                        (the rest is garbage).
----------------------- Preconditions----------------------------------
Operating System(s).... MS-DOS
Version/Release........ 2.xx and upward
Computer models........ IBM-PC's and compatibles
----------------------- Attributes-------------------------------------
Easy identification.... The virus contains the string "Program sick
                        error:Call doctor or buy PIXEL for cure
                        description". The virus identifies
                        infection by checking for the string "IV"
                        at offset 3 in the COM file.
Type of infection...... A program virus that infects all COM files
                        in the current directory by prepending
                        itself to its victim. The virus will not
                        spread very quickly.
Infection trigger...... As it is a direct action virus, it will
                        only infect on run-time, but will do this
                        at any time.
Media affected......... Any logical drive that is the "current" drive
Interrupts hooked...... ---
Damage................. Denial of access
Damage trigger......... The virus carries an evolution counter that
                        is increased every time the virus is
                        executed. When the counter is above or
                        equal to 5, the virus reads the system
                        timer. If the value is odd, the virus will
                        terminate with the message described
                        above. (This is effectively a 50% chance
                        of termination.)
Particularities........ This is a rare example of a prefix program
                        virus.
Similarities........... V-345, V-299, Cancer Viruses
----------------------- Agents----------------------------------------
Countermeasures........ Checksumming programs will detect the changes
                        to the files.
 - ditto - successful.. V847clr by Vesselin Bontchev will successfully
                        search and clear the Amstrad, V-345 and
                        V-299 viruses, and find the Cancer virus.
Standard Means......... Believe it or not, write protecting programs
                        with ATTR will prevent the virus from
                        spreading to them.
----------------------- Acknowledgements-------------------------------
Location............... Bulgarian Academy of Science and
                        Virus Test Center, University of Hamburg, Germany
Classification by...... Vesselin Bontchev
Documentation by....... Morton Swimmer
Date................... 11-June-1990
Information source..... ---
```

Anthrax Virus

```
Entry...............: ANTHRAX Virus
Standard CARO Name..: Anthrax Virus
Alias(es)...........: ---
Virus Strain........: ---
```

```
Virus detected when.: July 1990
              where.: Netherlands
Classification......: Program virus: COM, EXE and partition record
                      (MBR) infector, memory-resident
Length of Virus.....: 1040-1096 Bytes
------------------- Preconditions ---------------------------------
Operating System(s).: MS-DOS
Version/Release.....:
Computer model(s)...: IBM-PC, XT, AT and upwards, and compatibles
------------------- Attributes ------------------------------------
Easy Identification.: The following strings can be found in virus body:
                      "(c) Damage Inc", "1990", "ANTHRAX"
Type of infection...: Virus infects COM, EXE and partition record
                      (MBR). After execution of virus' code, it
                      immediately infects MBR but does NOT stay
                      resident. A second copy of the virus is
                      stored in the last 3 sectors of the hard disk,
                      thus overwriting any data stored there.
                      After having been started from the MBR, virus
                      becomes memory-resident until it has infected
                      one file. It infects a file in the lowest
                      branch of the current directory.
                      Anthrax does NOT infect the Bootrecord of a
                      floppy or hard disk.
Infection Trigger...: Execution of infected program.
Storage media affected: Floppies and hard disks.
Interrupts hooked...: INT13h, INT 1Ah, INT 20h, INT 21h, INT 24h
Damage..............: Transient damage: ---
                      Permanent damage: virus overwrites last 3 sec-
                      tors of hard disk (with it's 2nd copy).
Damage Trigger......: ---
Particularities.....: Virus V2100 installs ANTHRAX in the MBR, if
                      it finds the second copy of ANTHRAX in
                      last 3 sectors of the hard disk.
Similarities........: ---
------------------- Agents ----------------------------------------
Countermeasures.....: F-PROT, SCAN, FindViru
Standard means......: It is very important to clean the last 3 sectors
                       of the harddsik.
------------------- Acknowledgement -------------------------------
Location............: Virus Test Center, University of Hamburg, Germany
Classification by...: Matthias Jaenichen
Documentation by....: Andrzej Kadlof, Virus Information Bank (Poland)
Date................: 14-July-1992
Information Source..: Reverse engineering of virus code
```

AntiCAD Virus

```
Entry...............: AntiCAD Virus
Alias(es)...........: AntiCAD-4096 = Invader Virus
Virus Strain........: Jerusalem Virus Strain, ANTICAD Substrain
Variants............: AntiCAD-A; -B; -C; Chinese; Danube (Donau);
                      Mozart Viruses
Virus detected when.: August 1990
              where.: Australia
Classification......: Program (COM, EXE) & System (Boot, Master Boot)
                      infector; memory resident
Length of Virus.....: 1) Length on media: 4,096 bytes on COM & BOOT;
                                   4,096-4,111 bytes on EXE
```

```
                         2) Length in memory: 5,120 bytes
-------------------- Preconditions ----------------------------------
Operating System(s).: MS-DOS and compatible OS
Version/Release.....: MS-DOS 3.0 and upwards
Computer model(s)...: IBM and compatible PCs
-------------------- Attributes -------------------------------------
Easy Identification.: Virus contains text:
                         "NO SYSTEMDISK...PLEASE INSERT..."
Type of infection...: Depending on type of victim:
                      COM: Prepending but COMMAND.COM not infected;
                      EXE: Appending but ACAD.EXE not infected;
                      BOOT: any diskette without write protection;
                      Master-BOOT: all HD-Drives.
Infection Trigger...: Any Load/Execute operation
Media affected......: All kinds (disks, any diskette)
Interrupts hooked...: 08h (Timer), 09h (Keybord), 13h (Disk),
                      21h (DOS-Calls), 24h (error handler).
Damage..............: Transient: the virus plays some music (variants
                      may play noise), and system is slowed down.
                      This routine activates
                      Permanent: If CTRL-ALT-DEL is pressed while
                      music is playing or ACAD is loaded, *all in-
                      formation on all disks will be overwritten*.
                      CMOS-entries will be deleted.
Damage Trigger......: Transient damage: in original ANTICAD virus,
                      transient damage (playing music, system slow-
                      down) is activated 30 minutes after virus'
                      activation. In ANTICAD variants, activation
                      of transient damage (music/noise) may be de-
                      layed between 7 and 30 days.
                      Permanent damage: one of the following activi-
                      ties will activate permanent damage (over-
                      writing disk media, deleting CMOS entries):
                         P1) pressing CTRL-ALT-DEL when
                             music/noise is played;
                         P2) execution of ACAD;
                         P3) after about 4000 keystrokes.
                      These effects may not be activated every
                      time as activation also depends on several
                      internal triggers.
Particularities.....: ---
Similarities........: Viruses in same (Jerusalem) strain, and esp.
                      those in same (AntiCAD) substrain.
-------------------- Agents -----------------------------------------
Countermeasures.....: According to their documentation, many antivirus
                      products claim recognise and eradicate virus.
-ditto- successful..: Tested: Dr.Solomon's Toolkit, Fridrik Skulason's
                      F-PROT.
Standard means......: 1) Reboot from clean bootdisk.
                      2) Delete all infected files.
                      3) Use SYS-Command to reinstall BOOT sector.
                      4) Use FDISK /MBR to reinstall Master-BOOT
                      sector (MS-DOS 5.0 only).
-------------------- Acknowledgement --------------------------------
Location............: Virus-Test-Center, University of Hamburg, Germany
Classification by...: Matthias Jaenichen
Documentation by....: Matthias Jaenichen
Date................: 31-January-1992
Information Source..: Disassembly, "PC Viruses" by A.Solomon,
                      "VSUM" (P.Hofmann)
```

Anti-Pascal 605 Virus

```
Entry................ Anti-Pascal 605 Virus
Alias(es)............ AP-605, V605, C-605 Virus
Virus Strain......... Anti-Pascal strain
Virus detected when.. June 1990
          where.. Sofia
Classification....... Program Virus extending .COM, direct action
Length of Virus...... 605 Bytes
-------------------- Preconditions ------------------------------------
Operating System(s).. MS-DOS, PC-DOS
Version/Release...... 2.1x upward
Computer models...... IBM PC/XT/AT and compatibles
-------------------- Attributes --------------------------------------
Easy identification.. Infected files begin with "PQVWS". They also
                      contain the string "combakpas???exe" at
                      offset 0x17.0
Self identification.. Files are considered infected if the word at
                      offset 7 contains 0x10C.
VIRSCAN string....... BF00018B360C0103F7B95D021E07EA00, scan COM
                      files only.
Type of infection.... Extends .COM files. The virus overwrites the
                      first 605 bytes of the file. The original 605
                      bytes are moved after the end of the file.
Infection Trigger.... Execution of an infected file.
Storage Media affected Infects .COM files on the current drive and on
                      disk D:.
Interrupts hooked.... INT 24h during infection.
Damage............... transient: ---
                      permanent: may overwrite .BAK and .PAS files.
Damage trigger....... If less than two files in the current directory
                      can be infected, a .BAK or .PAS file is
                      selected and overwritten with the virus
                      body.  The virus tries then to rename the
                      file with a .COM or (if rename is unsuccess-
                      ful) .EXE extension, but due to a bug this
                      never succeeds.
Infective range...... Only files with length 605 to 64930 bytes are
                      infected.
Particularities...... 1. Files larger than 64674 bytes are no longer
                      loadable after infection.
                      2. If the Archive attribute of the file is
                      reset, the virus sets it after infection.
                      3. If the ReadOnly attribute of the file is
                      set, the virus is not able to infect it.
                      4. File date is modified.
Similarities......... ---
-------------------- Agents -----------------------------------------
Countermeasures...... Category 1: Monitoring files
                      Category 2: Alteration detection
                      Category 3: Eradication
-ditto- successful... Category 1: FluShot+, Anti4us
                      Category 2: Sentry
                      Category 3: V605Clr.Com
Standard means....... Setting the attributes of the .COM files to
                      ReadOnly effectivly prevents this virus
                      from infecting/spreading.
-------------------- Acknowledgement --------------------------------
Location............. Bulgarian Academy of Sciences, Sofia
Classification by.... Vesselin Bontchev
```

```
Documentation by .... Vesselin Bontchev
Date................. June 7, 1990
Information Source... ---
```

Armagedon Virus

```
Entry...............: Armagedon Virus
Standard CARO Name..: Armagedon Virus
Alias(es)...........: Greek Virus
Virus Strain........: ---
Virus detected when.: Mai 1990
           where.: Greece
Classification......: Programm/Link (COM) virus
Length of Virus.....: 1079 Bytes
-------------------- Preconditions ---------------------------------
Operating System(s).: MSDOS
Version/Release.....:
Computer model(s)...: IBM-PC, XT, AT and upwards, and compatibles
-------------------- Attributes ------------------------------------
Easy Identification.: Text in virus body: "Armagedon the GREEK"
Type of infection...: Infects COM files only (Int 21h function 4Bh)
                      by prepending the virus before COM file.
Infection Trigger...: Load and execute File by Subfuction 4Bh of Int21h
Storage media affected: diskettes, hard disk
Interrupts hooked...: Int 21h DOS-Services:
                      - function 4Bh changed for infection;
                      - function E0h, returns DADAh;
                      - function E1h, returns the Int21h-Segment;
                      Int08h Timer-Interrupt: Damage-routine added.
Damage..............: Virus sends a string to all 4 COM-ports. This
                      string advises any connected hayes-modem to
                      drop the line and to dial "081<pause>141".
                      In Greece, this would be the time-annouce-
                      ment in Iraklion. Any other device connected
                      to a COM-port would output the String
                      "+++aThOmOs7=35dp081,,,,141"
Damage Trigger......: If time is between 05:00 and 06:00 hours (am)
Similarities........: ---
-------------------- Agents ----------------------------------------
Counterm. successful: McAfee Scan, Skulason F-PROT, Solomon FindViru
Standard means......: Deleting the first 1079 Bytes will disinfect the
                        Programm.
-------------------- Acknowledgement -------------------------------
Location............: Virus Test Center, University of Hamburg, germany
Classification by...: Matthias Jaenichen, VTC Hamburg
Documentation by....: Yuval Tal, Weizmann-Institute, Rehovot, Israel
Date................: June 26, 1990
Information Source..: Yuval Tal
```

Autumn Virus

```
Entry...............: Autumn (Leaves) Virus
Alias(es)...........: Blackjack =1704- =Herbst(laub)= Cascade A-Virus
Virus Strain........: Cascade- = Autumn- =Herbst-Virus
```

```
Virus detected when.: September 1988
             where.: University of Konstanz, FRG
Classification......: Program Virus (extending .COM), RAM resident
Length of Virus.....: .COM filelength increases by 1704 byte
-------------------- Preconditions ------------------------------------
Operating System(s).: MS-DOS
Version/Release.....: 2.xx upward
Computer model(s)...: IBM-PC, XT, AT and compatibles
-------------------- Attributes ---------------------------------------
Easy Identification.: ---
Type of infection...: System: is infected if the call of interrupt 21h
                      with function 4Bh and subfunction FFh is possible
                      and without error and 55AAh is returned in DI-
                      register.
                      .COM file: Program virus, increases COM files by
                         1704 Byte. A .COM file is infected if the
                         first instruction is a three byte jump with
                         DISP16 = (filelength minus viruslength).
                      .EXE file: no infection.
Infection Trigger...: Infects all files that are loaded via the function
                      4Bh and subfunction 00h of the interrupt 21h
                      (MS-DOS uses this function to start any program)
Interrupts hooked...: Int21h, Int28h (only if Clockdevice Year = 1980),
                      Int1Ch (only if damage is triggered)
Damage..............: Transient Damage: Modifies screen by making the
                      characters on the screen "fall down" on the screen
                      in connection with clicking noises.
Damage Trigger......: IF function GetDate returns with
                      1. ( year=1988 AND month>= 10 ) OR
                      2. ( year=1980 AND
                         2.1. clock is changed by user to year=1988
                              month>=10 OR
                         2.2. clock is changed by user to year>1988 )
                      AND a random number generator activates damage.
Particularities.....: 1. If the system is _not_ infected, the invocation
                      of an infected program produces errors (system
                      crash is possible).
                      2. COM-files up to a length of 63800 bytes will
                      be infected, but files with a length of more
                      than 63576 bytes are not loadable after
                      infection.
                      3. The virus-program is encoded, dependent of
                      the .COM-filelength.
                      4. The distinction between .EXE and .COM files is
                      made by testing the "magic number (MZ)" in the
                      .EXE-Header.
-------------------- Agents -------------------------------------------
Countermeasures.....: Category 3: ANTIHBST.EXE (VTC Hamburg)
Countermeasures successful: ANTIHBST.EXE is an antivirus that only looks
                      for the HERBST-virus and, if requested, will
                      restore the file.
Standard means......: ---
-------------------- Acknowledgement ----------------------------------
Location............: Virus Test Center, University of Hamburg, Germany
Classification by...: Michael Reinschmiedt
Documentation by....: Michael Reinschmiedt
                      Morton Swimmer
Date................: July 15, 1989
```

AZUSA Virus

```
Entry...............: AZUSA Virus
Alias(es)...........: ---
Virus Strain........: ---
Virus detected when.: January 1991 (?)
            where.: Ohio, USA
Classification......: Resident Boot sector and Partition Table Infector
Length of Virus.....: 1024 Bytes in memory, 1 sector (400 h) on media
-------------------- Preconditions ----------------------------------
Operating System(s).: MS-DOS
Version/Release.....: 2.xx upward
Computer model(s)...: IBM-PC, XT, AT and compatibles
-------------------- Attributes -------------------------------------
Easy Identification.: 1) Reduction of available memory by 1,024 bytes:
                      CHKDSK returns 654,336 bytes total memory in-
                      stead of 655,360 bytes on 640k machines.
                      2) "E9 8B 00" are first three bytes of infected
                      boot record or partition table.
Scanner Signature...: "E9 8B 00" at 00h on boot sector/partition table
Type of infection...: Virus is extremely virulent and will infect hard
                      disk even if partition table cannot be found
                      (cannot boot thereafter).
                      Hard disk: virus replaces absolute sector 1
                      (partition code & table) with itself, main-
                      taining table data in internal location.
                      Floppy: Virus attempts to infect all floppies
                      previously uninfected; original boot record
                      is stored at track 28h head 1 sector 8
                      regardless of floppy size.
Infection Trigger...: Booting an infected system
Interrupts hooked...: ---
Damage..............: Permanent Damage: Data lost; COM1&LPT1 "hidden"
                      1)Data lost: as virus overwrites 1 sector on
                        floppies, previously stored data are lost;
                        on disk, partition table is overwritten but
                        old table data are stored inside virus.
                      2)COM1 & LPT1 "hidden": after approx.20h re-
                        boots, virus zeroes pointers to COM1 & LPT1
                        thus making those devices unaccessible.
                      3)Virus may cause boot failure on machines
                        with security programs in place.
                      Transient Damage: Reduction of available memory
                      by 1,024 Bytes.
Damage Trigger......: After approx. 20h reboots, COM1 & LPT1 become in-
                      accessible as pointers are zeroed.
Particularities.....: 1) Virus does not use stealth techniques (neither
                      evasive measures nor encryption).
                      2) Odd coding techniques and lack of understand-
                      ing of floppy disk characteristics indicate
                      self-taught writer/experimenter.
Similarities........: ---
-------------------- Agents -----------------------------------------
Countermeasures.....: Reload floppy boot sector; use partition table
                      data maintained inside virus to reconstruct
                      original partition table.
Countermeasures successful: Detection: SCAN v75, DISKSECURE
Standard means......: ---
-------------------- Acknowledgement --------------------------------
Location............: Virus Test Center, University of Hamburg, Germany
```

```
Classification by...: Klaus Brunnstein
Documentation by....: A.Padgett Peterson, Computer Network Security,
                                            Orlando/Florida
Date...............: 18-April-1991
Information source..: A.Padgett Peterson
```

BFD Virus

```
Entry...............: BFD Virus
Standard CARO Name..: BootEXE.452 Virus
Alias(es)...........: BootEXE-452 = Sector Eleven Virus
Virus Strain........: BootEXE Virus Strain
Virus detected when.: July 7, 1992
              where.: U.S.
Classification......: Multipartite (=Program & System) Virus: Resident
                      EXE file (converts EXE format to COM format),
                      diskette boot and system boot infector
Length of Virus.....: System infection: 1 sector on infected disks
                      File infection:   0x01C3h bytes (but files do
                                            NOT grow in length)
-------------------- Preconditions -----------------------------------
Operating System(s).: PC-DOS
Version/Release.....: Any?
Computer model(s)...: Any?
-------------------- Attributes --------------------------------------
Easy Identification.: Infected EXE files begin with EB 39 rather than
                      with "MZ".
Self Identification.: 1) If virus is active in memory, INT13 with F0
                         in AH returns 19 in AH.
                      2) Infected files do not begin with "MZ".
                      3) Infected disks/diskettes contain virus in
                         boot records (compares).
Type of infection...: Any file that begins with "MZ", contains fewer
                      than 0x80 512-bytes pages, has not too many
                      relocation items in the table, has FFFF in
                      the Max Req Para field, and a header size
                      of 0x20 paragraphs.  Any diskette read from,
                      and the first partition on the first hard
                      disk, if it starts on a head other than zero.
Infection Trigger...: Any INT13 that reads the first sector of the file.
Storage media affected: Any diskette can be infected, but only 360K 5.25"
                      diskettes will boot properly. Any hard disk.
Interrupts hooked...: INT13 only.
Damage..............: No apparent intentional damage
Damage Trigger......: ---
Particularities.....: An unusual infection method; the virus installs
                      itself in unused EXE header space when the
                      start of the EXE file is read via INT13.
Similarities........: ---
-------------------- Agents ------------------------------------------
Countermeasures.....: Not stealthed, so scanners with a signature, and
                      modification detectors, should have no trouble.
                      INT21-based monitors won't notice it.
Countermeasures successful: ?
Standard means......: Infected files can be made to work again by
                      changing the first two bytes back to "MZ"
                      (zeroing out the virus code in the unused
                      header space is also a good idea).
```

```
-------------------- Acknowledgement --------------------------------
Location...........: IBM High Integrity Computing Laboratory, USA
Classification by...: David Chess
Documentation by....: David Chess
Date................: 9-July-1992
Information Source..: Analysis of original virus
```

Bouncing-Ball

```
Entry................. Bouncing-Ball Virus
Alias(es).............. Italian; = Ping Pong = Turin-Virus
Strain................. ---
Detected: when........ March 1988
         where........ University of Turin, Italy
Classification........ Bootsector/resident; loads to high-memory.
Length of Virus....... Length on disk: 2 Sectors of 512 Bytes
                       length plus original bootsector  = 3 Sectors.
                       Length in RAM: 1024 Byte.
-------------------- Preconditions----------------------------------
Operating System(s).... MS-DOS
Version/Release........ ---
Computer models........ IBM-PC, XT, AT and compatible
-------------------- Attributes-------------------------------------
Easy identification.... 1.The bootsector contains at the offset
                       01FCh the word 1357h. This is how the
                       virus identifies itself.
                        2.Enter TIME 0, then immediately press any
                       key and Enter; if the virus is present, the
                       bouncing dot will be triggered
                       (->Damage Trigger).
Type of infection...... Infects disk media as follows:
                       1. Determines whether infection is possible
                       2. Secures original bootsector
                       3. Copy the virus's first sector to the
                       bootsector
                       4. Copy the virus's second sector to the
                       first free cluster
                       5. Mark the cluster as bad
                       6. Load and jump to the original boot sector.
Infection trigger...... Every disk that is _read_ using the BIOS
                       function 13h will be infected. (As all read
                       and write operations use this interrupt,
                       any disk operation can lead to infection.)
Media affected........ Infects floppy disks as well as hard disks.
                       The media must fulfill the following criteria:
                       1. 512 bytes per sector (standard)
                       2. There must one free cluster
                       3. A cluster must be at least 2 sectors long.
                       For hard disks: The master boot block (which
                       contains disk and partition data) must conform
                       to the standard.
Interrupts hooked...... BIOS Int 13h
Damage................ Permanent: the boot block is overwritten
                       Transient: A small rhombus (IBM character set:
                              07h) moves like a "bouncing ball" (or
                              ping pong ball) over the screen.
Damage trigger........ Triggered randomly after a disk access within
                       1 second after the system clock reaches a
```

```
                           multiple of 30 minutes (e.g, 00:00, 00:30,
                           01:00, etc.).
Particularities........    1. The virus loads itself to high memory and
                           reduces the memory available to the operating
                           system by modifying a BIOS variable.
                           2. The virus cannot always tell if the hard disk
                           is non-standard, and terminates. Should the
                           virus try to infect a non-standard disk, data
                           may be destroyed on the disk.
Similarities...........    ---
------------------------ Agents----------------------------------------
Countermeasures........    Infected system disks can be cleaned by using
                           the DOS program "SYS.COM". (You must boot from
                           a clean disk.) The "bad" cluster will, however,
                           remain.
Countermeasures successful ---
Standard Means.........    The DOS program "CHKDSK.COM" shows clusters,
                           that contain bad sectors.
--------------------- Acknowledgements -----------------------------
Location...............    Virus Test Center, University of Hamburg, Germany
Classification by......    Michael Reinschmiedt
Documentation by.......    Michael Reinschmiedt
Date...................    July 30, 1989
Updated by.............    Y.Radai, Hebrew University, August 31, 1989
Information source.....    ---
```

Butterflies Virus

```
Entry...............:   Butterflies Virus
Alias(es)...........:   Goddam Butterflies Virus
Virus Strain........:   ---
Virus detected when.:   1993
            where.:     Germany
Classification......:   File Virus (direct action COM Infector)
Length of Virus.....:
-------------------- Preconditions -----------------------------------
Operating System(s).:   MS-DOS
Version/Release.....:   Releases >= 3.2
Computer model(s)...:   IBM and compatibles
-------------------- Attributes --------------------------------------
Easy Identification.:   1) COM Files contain following text strings:
                        "Goddamn Butterflies" and "*.COM"
                        2) 4th Byte of an infected COM file: 01h.
Type of infection...:   1) When executing an infected COM-file, virus will
                        search for up to 4 uninfected COM-files to which
                        it appends it's code.
                        2) When searching for victims, findfirst/findnext
                        is used; therefore, normaly only COM-files in
                        current directory are infected. If DOS append
                        or similar programs are used, victims in other
                        directories will be found also.
Infection Trigger...:   1) Executing an infected program.
                        2) No infection, if COM filesize < 121 Bytes or
                        COM filesize > 64768 Bytes.
Storage media affected: Any disk/diskette
Interrupts hooked...:   ---
Damage..............:   No permanent or transient, except modifying
                        COM-Files.
```

```
Damage Trigger......: ---
Particularities.....: 1) Does not infect COMMAND.COM or any other file,
                         with "ND" at same position (6th and 7th
                         character) in name.
                      2) In some parts of a South German forest, there
                         was a recent invasion of butterfly-larvae with
                         much public attention; this virus may reflect
                         this event.
Similarities........: ---
-------------------- Agents -----------------------------------------
Countermeasures.....:
Countermeasures successful: (no successful detection yet: July 1993)
Standard means......: Delete infected files and restore from a clean
                      source.
-------------------- Acknowledgement --------------------------------
Location............: Virus-Test-Center, University of Hamburg, Germany
Classification by...: Torsten Dargers, Morton Swimmer
Documentation by....: Torsten Dargers
Date................: 31-July-1993
Information Source..: Reverse analysis of virus code
```

"CANCER" Virus

```
Entry................. "CANCER" Virus
Alias(es)............. ---
Strain................ Amstrad Virus Strain
Detected: when........ Fall 1989
         where........ Bulgaria
Classification........ Program virus, direct action, prefix
Length of Virus....... COM file will be increased by multiples of
                       740 bytes, but the actual virus is only
                       228 bytes long!
---------------------- Preconditions--------------------------------
Operating System(s).... MS-DOS
Version/Release........ 2.xx and upward
Computer models........ IBM-PC's and compatibles
---------------------- Attributes-----------------------------------
Easy identification.... An infected file will contain the string "IV"
                        at offset 3 in the COM file. Unlike the
                        other variants of Amstrad, this is never
                        used by this virus.
Type of infection...... A program virus that infects all COM files in
                        the current directory by prepending itself
                        to its victim. The virus will not spread
                        very quickly.
Infection trigger...... As it is a direct action virus, it will only
                        infect on run-time, but will do this at
                        any time.
Media affected......... Any logical drive that is the "current" drive.
Interrupts hooked...... ---
Damage................. The virus will repeatedly infect a file, until
                        it is no longer loadable (hence its name).
Damage trigger........ none, its damage is its infection and the
                        resulting file length increase.
Particularities........ ---
Similarities........... Cancer is a variant of Amstrad.
---------------------- Agents---------------------------------------
Countermeasures....... Checksumming programs will detect the changes
                       to the files.
```

```
        - ditto - successful.. V847clr will find Cancer as a possible variant
                               of Amstrad, but can not destroy it.
        Standard Means........ Believe it or not, write protecting programs
                               with ATTR will prevent the virus from
                               spreading to them.
        ---------------------- Acknowledgements-----------------------------
        Location.............. Bulgarian Academy of Science and
                               Virus Test Center, University of Hamburg, Germany
        Classification by...... Vesselin Bontchev
        Documentation by....... Morton Swimmer
        Date.................. 11-June-1990
        Information source..... ---
```

CHEMNITZ Virus

```
        Entry...............: CHEMNITZ Virus
        Alias(es)...........: ---
        Virus Strain........: ---
        Virus detected when.: University of Chemnitz, Germany
                      where.: December 1992
        Classification......: Memory-resident, appending EXE- and COM-Infector
        Length of Virus.....: 1) Length on media:  772..778 Bytes
                              2) Length in memory: 848 Bytes
        -------------------- Preconditions -----------------------------------
        Operating System(s).: MS-DOS, DR-DOS
        Version/Release.....: MS-DOS 2.xx upward
        Computer model(s)...: IBM - PC, XT, AT, upward and compatibles
        -------------------- Attributes --------------------------------------
        Easy Identification.: 1) Enlarged file size: using DIR, compare actual
                                 file size with original file size.
                              2) Reduction of available memory: using CHKDSK or
                                 MEM, memory size will be reduced by 848 bytes.
                              3) The following signature is found 20Ah (522)
                                 bytes before end of every infected file:
                                 'FMCIKLMOF' = 46 4D 43 49 4B 4C 4D 4F 46 (hex)
        Type of infection...: It infects previously uninfected EXE and COM files
                              when loaded with INT 21, function 4B00h by
                              appending itself to program on media, and
                              makes itself memory-resident.
                              It infects COM and EXE files only once, but does
                              not infect COMMAND.COM.
        Infection Trigger...: Invocation of INT 21h, Function 4B00h
        Interrupts hooked...: INT 21h, function AH=4B (Load&Execute)
        Storage media affected: All COM and EXE files (FD,HD)
                              if not write-protected
        Damage..............: Pernament damage: ---
                              Transient damage: ---
        Damage Trigger......: ---
        Particularities.....: ---
        Similarities........: ---
        -------------------- Agents ------------------------------------------
        Countermeasures.....:
        Countermeasures successful:
        Standard means......: Boot from clean system; delete infected files and
                              replace with uninfected originals from backup.
        -------------------- Acknowledgement ---------------------------------
        Location............: Virus Test Center, University of Hamburg, Germany
        Classification by...: Mark Broecker
```

```
Documentation by....: Mark Broecker
Date................: 19-January-1993
Information Source..: Reverse-Engineering of original virus

                     (received from site of first report: U-Chemnitz)
```

Chinese_Fish Virus

```
Entry...............: Chinese_Fish Virus
Alias(es)...........: Fish Boot Virus
Virus Strain........: ---
Virus detected when.: Early 1992
              where.: ---
Classification......: Memory-resident System (MBR,FBR) infector.
Length of Virus.....: 1.Length (Byte) on media:  1527 bytes (3 sectors)
                      2.Length (Byte) in memory: Does not reserve memory
-------------------- Preconditions ------------------------------------
Operating System(s).: DOS
Version/Release.....:
Computer model(s)...: IBM PCs and compatibles
-------------------- Attributes ---------------------------------------
Easy Identification.: ---
Type of infection...: Self-Identification in memory: ---
                      Self-Identification on disk: BR[B3h] = 2015h
                      System infection:
                       MBR infected at bootup from infected floppy.
                       Virus + ORG.MBR saved at sec 8-10, cyl 0, head 0.
                      FBR infected when accessed from infected system.
                       Virus + ORG.MBR saved at the following:
                              1.44 MB = sec 11-13, cyl 79, head 0
                               720 KB = sec 01-03, cyl 79, head 0
                              1.2 MB = sec 01-03, cyl 79, head 0
                               360 KB = sec 01-03, cyl 39, head 0
Infection Trigger...: Reading or writing HD or FD after booting from
                      infected system or floppy.
Storage media affected: HD and FD
Interrupts hooked...: INT 13h
Damage..............: Permanent Damage:
                      On Harddisk: Sec 8-10, cyl 0, head 0 on HD
                         is overwritten with virus code and ORG.MBR.
                         This is usually non-fatal as these sectors
                         are unused on most machines.
                      On floppy:        Sec   Cyl  Head
                              1.44 MB = 11-13, 79, 0
                               720 KB = 01-03, 79, 0
                              1.2 MB = 01-03, 79, 0
                               360 KB = 01-03, 39, 0
                         These sectors may be in use if floppy is
                         nearly full. Recovery of overwritten
                         sectors is almost impossible.
                      Transient Damage:  Since virus does not reserve
                      any memory for itself, it can easily be over-
                      written after or during startup of machine.
                      If virus is overwritten, machine will crash
                      on next INT 13h issued as virus INT 13h
                      handler no longer exists.
                      When trigger conditions hold, the following
```

```
                        message will be displayed black on white in
                        the upper right corner of the screen:
                            "Hello! I am FISH, please don't kill me.
                            Congratulate 80th year of the Republic Of
                            China Building,Fish will help to kill stone
                            Written by Fish in NTIT. TAIWAIN  80.10.18"
Damage Trigger......: Permanent Damage: Reading/writing HD or FD after
                        booting from infected system or floppy.
                      Transient Damage: Text message displayed on every
                          INT 13h issued the 1st, 11th, 21st and 31st
                          of any month during 1992 (uses INT 1Ah).
Particularities.....: 1) Leaves start of FBR alone, and plays by the
                      rules, making it hard to detect with heuristic
                      scanning.
                      2) Does not reserve the memory it uses.
                      3) Extensive checking for both itself and the
                      Stoned.Michelangelo virus. Making it possible
                      for Chinese_Fish to survive if both viruses
                      infects the same media. Stoned.Michelangelo
                      will always be overwritten by Chinese_Fish,
                      so the virus works like an anti-Michelangelo
                      program, spreading from machine to machine,
                      eradicating Stoned.Michelangelo whereever it
                      comes across it.
                      4) Redirects attempts to read or write sectors
                      where rest of virus + ORG.MBR are stored,
                      as well as the usual redirection of MBR
                      requests.
Similarities........: ---
Stealth techniques..: HD: Gives sec 11, cyl 0, head 0 on read or write
                        requests for sectors 8-10, cyl 0, head 0.
                        And sec 10, cyl 0, head 0 on read or write
                        requests for sec 1, cyl 0, head 0 (MBR).
                      FD: Gives original FBR on requests for boot
                        sector containing virus.
-------------------- Agents -------------------------------------------
Countermeasures.....: F-PROT 2.07 can be used to detect/verify infection
Standard means......: FDISK/MBR after booting from certified virus free
                      system diskette will disinfect harddisk.
-------------------- Acknowledgement ----------------------------------
Location............: The University of Trondheim
                      The Norwegian Institute of Technology
                      Faculty of Electrical Engineering
                      and Computer Science
Classification by...: Henrik Stroem, Stroem System Soft
Documentation by....: Henrik Stroem, Stroem System Soft
Date................: 17-April-1993
Information Source..: Reverse-Engineering of virus code
```

Clone Virus

```
Entry...............: Clone Virus
Alias(es)...........: ---
Virus Strain........: ---
Virus detected when.: Spring 1993
            where.: Sydney, Australia
Classification......: File virus (EXE companion), memory resident.
Length of Virus.....: 1.Length (Byte) on media: 833 Bytes (companion)
```

```
                              2.Length (Byte) in RAM:
-------------------- Preconditions ------------------------------------
Operating System(s).: MSDOS
Version/Release.....:
Computer model(s)...: IBM PCs and Compatibles
-------------------- Attributes ---------------------------------------
Easy Identification.: Companion file contains following text at the end:
                      "Your PC is Cloned!!
                       Clone Virus ver 2.0 ..
                       (c) Cataclysm 1992 Sydney, Australia
                       ....To Create and Mutate...."
Type of infection...: File infection: Upon executing an infected EXE
                      file (precisely: it's hidden COM companion of
                      same name), virus "infects" EXE files by crea-
                      ting a COM file with same name, 833 bytes long,
                      with hidden, system and read only attributes.
                      Self-Identification in file: once in memory,
                      virus intercepts all Int 21 calls with AH = 4B
                      (Load & Execute), 4E (Find First) and 4F (Find
                      Next).  Whenever an EXE file is loaded, a com-
                      panion file is first created (if not already
                      present). Whenever a call to 4E or 4F finds
                      a COM file, it checks if file is one of its
                      companion files; if so, it simply repeats the
                      call until an uninfected file is found.
                      Stealth: By hooking on INT 21 calls Load&Execute,
                      FindFirst and FindNext, used by many utilities
                      e.g. DIR and scanners, virus will not be de-
                      tected by such methods.
                      System infection: virus uses an undefined DOS
                      call to INT 21, to see if it's already in
                      memory; when not yet in memory (=given value
                      in INT 21 register), virus hooks INT 21 and
                      makes itself memory resident.
                      Self-Identification in memory: Checks INT 21
                          functions 4B (Load&Execute), 4E (FindFirst)
                          and 4F (Find Next) register for given value.
Infection Trigger...: Running an infected EXE file (i.e. file with
                      companion virus)
Storage media affected:
Interrupts hooked...: INT 21 functions 4B (Load & Execute),
                      4E (Find First) and 4F (Find Next)
Damage..............: Because of the way COMMAND.COM searches for pro-
                      grams, the hidden .COM files will be run in-
                      stead of user's specified program. Companion
                      will execute it's intended function (see Tran-
                      sient Damage) and subsequently load and start
                      the user's intended "original" program.
                      Permanent Damage: no intended permanent damage.
                      Transient Damage: On trigger condition, following
                      text will be displayed: "Your PC is Cloned!!"
Damage Trigger......: Permanent Damage: ---
                      Transient Damage: If Date = April 1st.
Particularities.....: ---
Similarities........: ---
-------------------- Agents -------------------------------------------
Countermeasures.....: AntiVirus programs
Countermeasures successful: VET 7.3 (CYBEC); no other products tested
Standard means......: Boot from a clean diskette; use proper tool to
                      change Read-Only attribute and delete companion
```

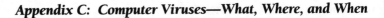

```
                             COM file
-------------------- Acknowledgement ------------------------------------
Location............: CYBEC Pty, Hampton Victoria/Australia
Classification by...: Roger Riordan (riordan.cybec@mhs.oz.au>
Documentation by....: Roger Riordan
                      Klaus Brunnstein (CVC entry)
Date................: 31-July-1993
Information Source..: Analysis of Virus
```

"Dark Avenger" Virus

```
Entry...............: Dark Avenger
Alias(es)...........: ---
Virus Strain........: Dark Avenger
Virus detected when.: November 1989
             where.: USA
Classification......: February 1990
Length of Virus.....: about 1800 Bytes
-------------------- Preconditions ------------------------------------
Operating System(s).: DOS
Version/Release.....:
Computer model(s)...: IBM-compatible
-------------------- Attributes ------------------------------------
Easy Identification.: Two Texts:
                      "Eddie lives...somewhere in time" at beginning
                      and
                      "This Program was written in the City of Sofia
                      (C) 1988-89 Dark Avenger" near end of file
Type of infection...: Link-virus
                      COM-files: appends to the program and installs a
                                 short jump
                      EXE-files: appends to the program at the
                                 beginning of the next paragraph
Infection Trigger...: COM and EXE files are corrupted on any read
                      attempt even when VIEWING!!!
Storage media affected: Any Drive
Interrupts hooked...: Int 21 DOS-services
                      Int 27 Terminate and Stay Resident
Damage..............: Overwrites a random sector with bootblock
Damage Trigger......: each 16th infection; counter located in Bootblock
Particularities.....: -
Similarities........: -
-------------------- Agents ------------------------------------
Countermeasures.....: NONE! All data can be destroyed !!!!
                      There is no way in retrieving lost data.
                      Backups will most probably be destroyed too.
Countermeasures successful: install McAfee's SCANRES.
Standard means......: Good luck! Hopefully the virus did not destroy
                      too many of your programs and data.
-------------------- Acknowledgement ------------------------------------
Location............: Virus Test Center, University of Hamburg, Germany
Classification by...: Matthias Jaenichen
Documentation by....: Matthias Jaenichen
Date................: 31.01.1990
Information Source..: ---
```

Dark Avenger 3 Virus

```
Entry...............: Dark Avenger 3 Virus
Alias(es)...........: V2000 = Eddie 3 Virus
Virus Strain........: Dark Avenger Strain
Classification......: Program Virus, RAM-resident
Length of Virus.....: 2000 Bytes (2076 Bytes in RAM resident mode)
-------------------- Preconditions ---------------------------------
Operating System(s).: MSDOS, PCDOS
Version/Release.....: 3.3
Computer model(s)...: IBM compatibles PCs
-------------------- Attributes ------------------------------------
Easy Identification.: Two Strings : 1) "Copy me - I want to travel"
                                        (at beginning of virus-code)
                                     2) "(c) 1989 by Vesselin Bontchev"
                                        (near end of virus code; but
                                          V.Bontchev is not the author!)
Type of infection...: Link-Virus (postfix infection); virus infects
                      every "COM" and "EXE" file with minimum
                      file-length of 1959 bytes.
Infection Trigger...: Programs are infected at load time (using MsDos
                      function Load/Execute) as well as on every
                      read attempt (viewing, copy etc.)
Storage media affected: Any Drive
Interrupts hooked...:  INT 21h [Dos-Functions] ) hooked by resident
                       INT 27h [TSR]           )      part of virus
                       INT 24h [Critical Error]  > during infection
                       INT 13h [BIOS-Disk Access] > during infection
                                                    and damage
Damage..............: On every 16's execution of an infected file,
                      virus will overwrite a new random data sector
                      on disk; the last overwritten sector will be
                      stored in boot sector.
                      System hang-up, if a program is to be executed,
                      which contains the string "(c) 1989 by
                      Vesselin Bontchev"; V.Bonchev is a Bulgarian
                      author of anti-virus programs.
Damage Trigger......: The virus uses the last byte of "MSDOS-Version"-
                      field in the bootblock as counter; if an
                      infected file is executed, this counter will
                      be invremented.
Particularities.....: On some 386 PCs with different BIOS version,
                      infected programs hang-up the system during
                      virus installation.
                      The virus overwrites the transient part of DOS
                      in RAM to provoke the reload of "command.com",
                      to get a chance for an early infection of
                      this file.
                      The virus intercepts the "Find first" and
                      "Find next" functions, and on "DIR" command
                      execution, virus decreases the file length
                      of marked files by 2000 (virus length).
Similarities........: As in Eddie 2 virus, infected files are marked
                      with "62" in the "seconds"-field of time
                      stamp.
-------------------- Agents ----------------------------------------
Countermeasures.....: The virus will be (for example) detected by :
                      F-FCHK   1.13 (F. Skulason)
                      Findviru 1.8  (Solomon: Virus Tools 4.25)
-------------------- Acknowledgement -------------------------------
```

```
Location............: Virus Test Center, University of Hamburg, Germany
Classification by...: Jörg Steindecker
Documentation by....: Jörg Steindecker
Date................: 14-February-1991
```

"DATACRIME Ia" Virus

```
Entry...............: DATACRIME Ia
Alias(es)...........: DATACRIME 1168-Version = "1168 Virus"
Virus Strain........: DATACRIME
Virus detected when.:
              where.:
Classification......: Link-virus (extending), direct action
Length of Virus.....: .COM file: file length increases by 1168 byte
-------------------- Preconditions ----------------------------------
Operating System(s).: MS-DOS
Version/Release.....: 2.xx upward
Computer model(s)...: IBM-PC, XT, AT and compatibles
-------------------- Attributes -------------------------------------
Easy Identification.: ---
Type of infection...: System: no infection.
                      .COM file: Link-virus, increases COM files by
                        1168 Bytes. A .COM- File is recognized as
                        being infected if the time entry of the
                        last program modification shows the fol-
                        lowing particularities: the last signifi-
                        cant three bytes of the minutes are the
                        same as the seconds. Bit 4,5 of the
                        seconds will be set to zero. For example
                        (H=Hours, M=Minutes, S=Seconds)
                            H H H H H M M M M M S S S S S
                            ? ? ? ? ? ? ? ? 1 0 1 ? ? ? ? ?
                      will be changed to
                            H H H H H M M M M M S S S S S
                            ? ? ? ? ? ? ? ? 1 0 1 0 0 1 0 1
                      .EXE file: no infection.
Infection Trigger...: Every time the virus run it looks for another
                        uninfected .COM- file using the DOS-func-
                        tions Findfirst/Findnext in the current
                        directory or any lower directory. If
                        there is no file that can be infected the
                        virus looks at the drive C: D: A: B: (in
                        this order).
Interrupts hooked...: Int 24 (only when infecting a file)
Damage..............: Permanent Damage: the virus shows the message
                        "DATACRIME VIRUS
                         RELEASED: 1 MARCH 1989"
                        then the first hard disk will be format-
                        ted (track 0, all heads). When formatting
                        is finished the speaker will beep (end-
                        less loop).
Damage Trigger......: if the clock device is October the 13th or
                        later (any year).
Particularities.....: 1. The message "DATACRIME... 1989" is encrypted.
                      2. The virus detects a hard disk if the segment
                           of Int 41 is not zero.
                      3. Cause of a mistake in the code the virus will
                           not use it's format buffer.
```

```
                        4. Cause of a missing segment override Int 24
                            can not be restored every time.
                        5. If the 7th letter of the programname is a 'D',
                            the program will not be infected
                            (e.g. COMMAND.COM).
Similarities........: The differences between Datacrime Ia and Ib
                      are minimal.
------------------ Agents ------------------------------------
Countermeasures.....: ---
- ditto - successful: ---
Standard means......: ---
------------------ Acknowledgement ---------------------------
Location............: Virus Test Center, University of Hamburg, Germany
Classification by...: Michael Reinschmiedt
Documentation by....: Michael Reinschmiedt
Date................: 14-Feb-1990
```

DATACRIME Ib Virus

```
Entry...............: DATACRIME Ib
Alias(es)...........: DATACRIME 1280-Version = "1280" Virus
Virus Strain........: DATACRIME
Virus detected when.: ---
             where.: ---
Classification......: Link-virus (extending), direct action
Length of Virus.....: .COM file: filelength increases by 1280 byte
------------------ Preconditions -----------------------------
Operating System(s).: MS-DOS
Version/Release.....: 2.xx upward
Computer model(s)...: IBM-PC, XT, AT and compatibles
------------------ Attributes --------------------------------
Easy Identification.: ---
Type of infection...: System: no infection.
                      .COM file: Link-virus, increases COM files by
                          1280 Byte. A .COM- File is recognized as
                          being infected if the time entry of the
                          last program modification shows the fol-
                          lowing particularities: the last signi-
                          ficant three bytes of the minutes are the
                          same as the seconds. Bit 4,5 of the
                          seconds will be set to zero. For example:
                          (H=Hours, M=Minutes, S=Seconds)
                              H H H H H M M M M M S S S S S
                              ? ? ? ? ? ? ? ? 1 0 1 ? ? ? ? ?
                          will be changed to
                              H H H H H M M M M M S S S S S
                              ? ? ? ? ? ? ? ? 1 0 1 0 0 1 0 1
                      .EXE file: no infection.
Infection Trigger...: Every time the virus runs it looks for one other
                          uninfected .COM- file using the DOS-func-
                          tions Findfirst/Findnext in the current
                          directory or any lower directory. If there
                          is no file that can be infected the virus
                          looks at the drive C: D: A: B: (in this
                          order).
Interrupts hooked...: Int 24 (only when infecting a file)
Damage..............: Permanent Damage: the virus shows the message
                      "DATACRIME VIRUS
```

```
                                    RELEASED: 1 MARCH 1989"
                                    then the first hard disk will be formatted
                                    (track 0, all heads). If formatting is
                                    finished the speaker will beep (endless
                                    loop).
Damage Trigger......: if the Clock device is October the 13th or
                                    later (any year).
Particularities.....: 1. The message "DATACRIME... 1989" is encrypted.
                                    2. The virus detects a hard disk if the segment
                                       of INT 41 is not zero.
                                    3. Cause of a mistake in the code the virus will
                                       not use it's format buffer.
                                    4. Cause of a missing segment override the INT24
                                       can not be restored every time.
                                    5. If the 7th letter of the programname is a 'D',
                                       the program will not be infected
                                       (e.g. COMMAND.COM).
Similarities........: The differences between Datacrime Ia and Ib
                                    are minimal.
-------------------- Agents -------------------------------------------
Countermeasures.....: ---
- ditto - successful: ---
Standard means......: ---
-------------------- Acknowledgement ---------------------------------
Location............: Virus Test Center, University of Hamburg, Germany
Classification by...: Michael Reinschmiedt
Documentation by....: Michael Reinschmiedt
Date................: 14-Feb-1990
```

"dBase" Virus

```
Entry...............: "dBase" Virus
Alias(es)...........: ---
Virus Strain........: ---
Virus detected when.: October 1989
              where.: ---
Classification......: Link - Virus (extending), RAM - resident
Length of Virus.....: .COM - Files: Program length increases
                                    by 1864 bytes
-------------------- Preconditions -----------------------------------
Operating System(s).: MS-DOS
Version/Release.....: 2.xx upward
Computer model(s)...: IBM - PC, XT, AT and compatibles
-------------------- Attributes --------------------------------------
Easy Identification.: Typical text in Virus body (readable with
                                    HexDump-utilities): "c:\bugs.dat"
Type of infection...: System: RAM-resident, infected if function
                                    FB0AH of INT 21H returns with 0AFBH
                                    in AX register.
                                    .COM file: extended by using EXEC-function.
                                    A file will only be infected once.
                                    .EXE File: no infection.
Infection Trigger...: When function 4B00H of INT 21H (EXEC) is called.
Interrupts hooked...: INT 21H
Damage..............: Permanent Damage:
                                    1. Every time a .DBF file is created in an
                                       infected system with function 3CH, 5BH
                                       or 6CH of INT 21H, the complete filename
```

```
                        of the new .DBF file will be inserted in
                        the hidden file "c:\bugs.dat".
                     2. On every write operation to a file registered
                        in "bugs.dat", all neighboring bytes
                        will be interchanged (e.g.: "01 02 03 04"
                        changed to "02 01 04 03").
                     3. On every read operation from a file regis-
                        tered in "bugs.dat", the bytes will be
                        interchanged again, so that no modifi-
                        cation is visible.
                     4. If the filename of the .DBF file is modified,
                        so that it does not correspond to the
                        filename registered in "bugs.dat", or
                        read/write operations happen in a non-
                        infected system, the bytes will no
                        longer be modified by the virus and they
                        appear defective.
                     Transient Damage:
                     Every time a new .DBF file is created, the
                        virus examines the age of "bugs.dat". If
                        the difference between the month of
                        creation and the current month is greater
                        than 2, the computer will hang in an end-
                        less loop.
Particularities.....: - In case of a program error in the virus,
                        single bytes in the .DBF file could be over-
                        written incorrectly by write operations!
                     - Programs longer than 63415 bytes are no longer
                        loadable.
Special remark......: The original virus contains code which erases
                        (INT 21) the infected DBF file structure
                        after a certain time; Ross Greenberg who detec-
                        ted this virus patched the essential instruc-
                        tion with INT 03 such that the destructive part
                        does no longer work; the rest of the code was
                        not changed. Unfortunately, the changed code
                        escaped one virus expert's computer.
-------------------- Agents -------------------------------------------
-
Countermeasures.....: Category 3: ANTI_DBS.EXE (VTC Hamburg)
- ditto - successful: ANTI_DBS.EXE finds and restores infected
                        programs (only for DBASE).
Standard means......: Notice .COM file length.
                      Typical text in virus body: "c:\bugs.dat",
                        which is also created in the root directory.
-------------------- Acknowledgement ----------------------------------
Location...........: Virus Test Center, University of Hamburg, Germany
Classification by...: Thomas Lippke
Documentation by....: Thomas Lippke
Date................: January 20, 1990
```

Dedicated Virus

```
Entry..............: Dedicated Virus
Alias(es)..........: ---
Virus Strain.......: ---
Polymorphism engine.: Mutating Engine (ME) 0.9
Virus detected when.: UK
```

```
              where.: January 1992
Classification......: Polymorphic encrypted program (COM) infector,
                      non-resident
Length of Virus.....: 3,5 kByte (including Mutating Engine)
-------------------- Preconditions ----------------------------------
Operating System(s).: MS-DOS
Version/Release.....: 2.xx upward
Computer model(s)...: IBM - PCs, XT, AT, upward and compatibles
-------------------- Attributes -------------------------------------
Easy Identification.: COM file growth (no other direct detection means
                      are known as virus encrypts itself, and due
                      to the installed mutation engine, all occu-
                      rences of this virus differ widely)
Type of infection...: COM file infector: all COM files in current
                      directory on current drive (disk,diskette)
                      are infected upon executing an infected file.
Infection Trigger...: Execution of an infected COM file.
Media affected......: Hard disk, any floppy disk
Interrupts hooked...: ---
Crypto method.....: The virus encrypts itself upon infecting a COM
                      file using its own encryption routine; upon
                      execution, the virus decrypts itself using
                      its own small algorithm.
Polymorphic method..: After decryption, the virus' envelope consisting
                      of Mutating Engine 0.9 will widely vary the
                      virus' coding before newly infecting another
                      COM file. Due to this method, common pieces
                      of code of more than three bytes (=signatures)
                      of any two instances of this virus are highly
                      improbable.
                      Remark: Mutating Engine 0.9 very probably was
                      developped by the Bulgarian virus writer
                      "Dark Avenger"; such a program was announced
                      early 1991 as permutating more than 4 billion
                      times, and it appeared in October 1991 or
                      before.
                      The class of permutating viruses is named
                      "polymorphic" to indicate the changing
                      structure which may not be identified with
                      contemporary means. To indicate the relation
                      to such common engine, the term "Polymorhic
                      engine (method)" has been introduced.
                      ME 0.9 was distributed via several Virus
                      Exchange Bulletin Boards, so it is possible
                      that other ME 0.9 related viruses appear.
                      According to (non-validated) information, an-
                      other ME 0.9 based virus (Pogue?) has been
                      detected in North America: COM file infector,
                      memory resident, length about 3,7 kBytes.
Damage..............: Virus overwrites at random times random sectors
                      (one at a time) with garbage (INT 26 used).
Damage Trigger......: Random time
Similarities........: ---
Particularities.....: The virus contains a text greeting a US based
                      female hacker; this text is visible after
                      decryption.
-------------------- Agents -----------------------------------------
Countermeasures.....: Contemporarily, no automatic method for reliable
                      identification of polymorphic viruses known.
- ditto - successful: ---
```

```
Standard means......: ---
-------------------- Acknowledgement --------------------------------
Location............: Virus Test Center, University of Hamburg, Germany
Classification by...: Vesselin Bontchev, Klaus Brunnstein
Documentation by....: Dr. Alan Solomon
Date................: 31-January-1992
```

"den Zuk" Virus

```
Entry................. den Zuk (B)
Alias(es)............. Venezuellan, "The Search"
Strain................ den Zuk
Detected: when........ ---
          where....... ---
Classification........ System (Boot) virus, RAM resident
Length of Virus....... 1 boot sector and 9 sectors on track 40
--------------------- Preconditions -------------------------------
Operating System(s).... MS/PC-DOS
Version/Release........
Computer models........ All IBM PC and AT compatibles.
--------------------- Attributes ----------------------------------
Easy identification.... The label on an infected disk will read:
                        "Y.C.1.E.R.P", where the "." is the F9h
                        character.
Type of infection...... System: the virus resides on the boot sector
                        and at track 40, head 0, sectors 1 - 9.
                        If an infected disk is booted, the virus
                        will load itself into the top of memory.
                        From there it will infect any floppy
                        that is written to.
Infection trigger...... Will infect at any time.
Media affected......... Only floppies. The virus does not identify
                        other types of floppies larger than 360kb.
                        This means that, for instance, the track
                        40 of a 1,2kb disk will be overwritten,
                        and data can be lost, if these sectors
                        were in use.
Interrupts hooked...... Int 13h, Int 9
Damage................. A graphical "DEN ZUK" will stream in from
                        the sides on CGA and EGA screens.
                        (nice effect!)
Damage trigger......... The graphics will appear on every Ctrl-
                        Alt-Delete (reset).
Particularities........ Den Zuk - B will replace an occurance of
                        den Zuk - A (Ohio) as well as the Brain
                        strains of viruses.
                        The virus will mascarade a clean boot
                        sector.
Similarities........... It is a slightly improved version of
                        den Zuk - A.
--------------------- Agents---------------------------------------
Countermeasures........ ---
 - ditto - successful.. ---
Standard Means......... Boot from a clean disk and use SYS to over-
                        write the infected boot sector. It is,
                        however, always better to format the disk.
--------------------- Acknowledgements-----------------------------
Location.............. Virus Test Center, University of Hamburg, Germany
```

```
Classification by...... Morton Swimmer
Documentation by....... Morton Swimmer
Date.................. 15-Feb-1990
Information source..... ---
```

"Devil's Dance" Virus

```
Entry...............: "Devil's Dance"
Alias(es)...........: "Devil","941 Virus"
Virus Strain........:
Virus detected when.: Spring 1990
              where.: Mexico City
Classification......: .COM - file: extending, RAM-resident, link virus
Length of Virus.....: .COM - Files: increased by 941 bytes
-------------------- Preconditions --------------------------------
Operating System(s).: MS-DOS
Version/Release.....: 2.xx upward
Computer model(s)...: IBM - PC, XT, AT and compatibles
-------------------- Attributes -----------------------------------
Easy Identification.: Typical text in Virus body, readable with
                      hexdump-utilities: "Drk", "*.com". If the high-
                      bit of the displayed code is stripped, the mes-
                      sage displayed at system reset time can be read.
                      .COM files: the first three bytes (jmp) and
                      the last three bytes are identical.
                      The file date/time is set to the date/time of
                      the infection (i.e. multiple infected files
                      have the same file date/time).
Type of infection...: System virus: RAM-resident: infected if at the
                      location 3 bytes before INT 21-adress the string
                      "Drk" is found.
                      .COM file: infected by hooking LOAD-function;
                      adds 941 bytes to the end of the file.
                      Only files with extension .COM will be infected.
                      A file will be infected more than once.
                      At first execution of the virus, all .COM files
                      in the current directory will be infected.
                      .EXE File: no infection.
Infection Trigger...: .COM file will be infected, when function 4B00H
                      (LOAD/EXEC) of INT 21H is called.
Interrupts hooked...: INT 21H (functions 4B00H and 49H).
                      INT 09H only for damage.
Damage..............: Permanent Damage:
                      1. Every .COM file executed in an infected
                      system will be infected.
                      2. After pressing 2,500 keys and reset=
                      <CTRL>+<ALT>+<DEL>, the first sector of
                      the hardisk C: will be overwritten.
                      Transient Damage:
                      1. All characters typed will be displayed in a
                      different color on a color card.
                      2. If reset=<CTRL>+<ALT>+<DEL> is pressed, the
                      following message is displayed:
                      "Have you ever danced with"
                      "the devil under the weak light of the moon? "
                      "Pray for your disk! The_Joker..."
                      "Ha Ha Ha Ha Ha Ha Ha Ha Ha Ha".
Damage Trigger......: Keyboard input (characters typed) and
```

```
                          reset=<CTRL>+<ALT>+<DEL>
Particularities.....: - The message "Have you ... Ha Ha"  is encrypted.
                      - All files with .COM extension will be infected
                        (i.e also exe-files with .COM extension).
                      - .COM files with exe-header-id "MZ" will not
                      run after infection.
                      - Virus does not use a self-identification on
                        .COM files; files will be infected many times.
                      - In case of multiple infections of .COM files,
                        system is slowed down on first execution of the
                        virus in a clean system; if, e.g., a file has
                        been infected 10 times, then it will try to
                        infect any accessible .COM file 10 times.
                      - All file attributes are cleared/not restored.
                      - Multiple files have the same date/time.
                      - Programs longer than 64,337 bytes are not exe-
                        cuted correctly after infection.
-------------------- Agents -----------------------------------------
Countermeasures.....: Category 3: NTIDEVIL.EXE (VTC Hamburg)
- ditto - successful: NTIDEVIL.EXE finds and restores infected programs.
Standard means......: Notice .COM file length, file date/time/attribute.
                      Typical text in virus body:  "*.com", "Drk" .
                      Search for hex bytes: E4,E1,EE,E3,E5,E4,A0,F7,E8,
                      F4,E8.Don't use <CTRL>+<ALT>+<DEL> if your screen
                      has been colored; use power-off- or reset-switch
                      to reboot your computer.
-------------------- Acknowledgement --------------------------------
Location...........: Virus Test Center, University of Hamburg, Germany
Classification by...: Stefan Tode
Documentation by....: Stefan Tode
Date...............: 5-June-1990
```

"Do Nothing" Virus

```
Entry..............: The "Do Nothing" Virus
Alias(es)..........: The Stupid Virus, 640K Virus
Virus strain.......: ---
Virus detected when.: 22-October-1989
            where.: BBSs in Israel
Classifications....: COM file infecting virus/extending, resident.
Length of virus....: Infected files grow biggen in 583 bytes.
-------------------- Preconditions ----------------------------------
Operating system(s).: MS-DOS
Version/release.....: 2.0 or higher
Computer model(s)...: IBM PC,XT,AT and compatibles
-------------------- Attributes -------------------------------------
Identification......: .COM files: The first 3 bytes of the infected
                        files are changed.
Type of infection...: System: The virus copies itself to 9800:100h. This
                        means that only computers with 640KB can
                        be infected. Infects other programs by
                        scanning the directory until it finds
                        a .COM file.
                      .COM files: Extends .COM files. Adds 583 bytes to
                        the end of the file.
                      .EXE files: Not infected.
Infection trigger...: The first .COM file of the current directory is
                      infected whether the file is infected or not.
```

```
Interrupts hooked...: 21h, 70h.
Damage..............: None.
Damage trigger......: ---
Particularities.....: 1. Many programs load themself to this area and
                         erase the virus from the memory.
                      2. The virus can work only on 640K systems.
                      3. It changes interrupt 70h to be the same as
                         interrupt 21. In the virus only interrupt
                         70h is used and not interrupt 21h.
-------------------- Agents ---------------------------------------
Countermeasures.....: Virus Buster and more commercial, Israeli anti
                         viral software (JIV, Turbo Anti-Virus).
Countermeasures successful: Virus Buster will locate the virus and upon
                         request, will remove it.
Standard means......: ---
-------------------- Acknowledgement ------------------------------
Classification by...: Yuval Tal (NYYUVAL@WEIZMANN.BITNET)
Documentation by....: Yuval Tal (NYYUVAL@WEIZMANN.BITNET)
Date................: December 19, 1989
```

Dudley Virus

```
Entry...............: Dudley Virus
Alias(es)...........: ---
Virus Strain........: ---
Virus detected when.:
              where.:
Classification......: Polymorphic File (COM,EXE) Infector,Memory resident
Length of Virus.....: 1.Length (Byte) on medium: 1153 Bytes (mod 16)
                      2.Length (Byte) in RAM:    4608 Bytes
-------------------- Preconditions --------------------------------
Operating System(s).: MSDOS
Version/Release.....:
Computer model(s)...: IBM PCs and compatibles
-------------------- Attributes -----------------------------------
Easy Identification.: None (polymorphic)
Type of infection...: Self-Identification methods:
                      File infection: infects COM and EXE files by
                         appending itself. Self recognition in files:
                         virus checks whether EXE_Checksum5045h or
                         COM_start==7100h.
                      System infection: becomes memory resident by
                         TWIXT method. For self-recognition in
                         memory, virus checks for a specific content
                         in AX register upon invocation of INT 21.
Infection Trigger...: Special values in registers upon INT 21 execution
Storage media affected:
Interrupts hooked...: INT 21 functions 4B00h, 3Dh, 56h, 6Ch, 5454h
Damage..............: Permanent Damage: none
                      Transient Damage: none
Damage Trigger......: Permanent Damage: none
                      Transient Damage: none
Particularities.....: 1) Virus contains a text which is not displayed:
                         "<[Oi Dudley!][PuKE]>"
                      2) Virus contains code that attempts to avoid
                         infecting a file with name ????SC??.???,
                         but it has a bug.
Similarities........: ---
```

```
-------------------- Agents ----------------------------------------
Countermeasures.....: Not tested
Countermeasures successful: Not tested
Standard means......:
-------------------- Acknowledgement -------------------------------
Location............: IBM High Integrity Computing Lab, Hawthorne N.Y.
Classification by...: David Chess, HICL
Documentation by....: David Chess (CAROBase entry)
                      Klaus Brunnstein, VTC Hamburg (Virus Catalog)
Date................: March 10, 1993
Information Source..: Reverse analysis of virus code
```

Empire A/B Virus

```
Entry...............: Empire-A Virus
Alias(es)...........: ---
Virus Strain........: Major variant of: Stoned = Marijuana Virus
Known Variant.......: Empire-B Virus
Virus detected when.: April 1991
          where.: Alberta Canada (?)
Classification......: Memory resident Boot + Partition table infector,
                      Stealth virus,undergoing detection mechanisms
Length of Virus.....: Empire-A: 2,048 Bytes in Memory, 2 sector(floppy)
                      Empire-B: 1,024 Bytes in Memory, 1 sector(floppy)
-------------------- Preconditions ---------------------------------
Operating System(s).: MSDOS
Version/Release.....: 2.xx upward (not tested)
Computer model(s)...: IBM-PC, XT, AT and compatibles
-------------------- Attributes ------------------------------------
Easy Identification.: Memory size reduced: CHKDSK will return 653,312
                      "total bytes memory" on a 640k machine.
                      Check first four bytes of MBR or Boot sector
                      for "EA 9F 01 C0",common to Empire-A/B variants.
Scan signature......: When booted from a clean floppy disk, virus can
                      be detected using the string
                      "A3 08 7C A1 13 04 48" (Empire-A)
Type of infection...: Boot sector virus, related to Stoned; virus
                      consists of 2 sectors, the first of which
                      contains its executable code and replaces
                      MBR on a harddisk or BR on floppy.
                      On floppy, the original boot record is stored
                      on track 0 head 1 sector 2, and the message
                      is stored on the next sector, in simply
                      encrypted form.
                      On harddisk, the original MBR is stored on
                      cyl 0 head 0 sector 6, with the message on
                      the next sector.
                      Stealth mechanism: when virus is active in
                      memory,  any request for the MBR will be
                      intercepted by the virus and the real MBR
                      will be returned. Similarly, any attempt
                      to write to the MBR will be changed
                      to a reset by the virus.
Infection Trigger...: ---
Interrupts hooked...: ---
Damage..............: Permanent Damage: Problems on Harddisk/Floppy:
                      High density floppies may experience failures
                         resulting from storage of two original
```

sectors on track 0 head 1 sectors 2-3.
Low density floppies with over 80 directory
entries may also have problems; these can
occur even long after the floppy is disinfected if the directory is not restored.
Harddisk: a disk without "hidden sectors"
will probably experience FAT failures, as
the sectors to which the original boot
sectors have been stored are assumed to
be in the "hidden sector" area.
Transient Damage = Memory reduction, Message:
1) Active Empire-A virus reduces total memory
   by 2,048 bytes (CHKDSK will return 653,312
   "total bytes memory" on a 640k machine)
2) The following message (where each sentence
   is a single line and relies on text-
   wrapping by terminal for legibility) is
   displayed:
    "I'm becoming a little confused as
    to where the "evil empire" is these days.
    If we paid attention, if we cared,
    we would realize just how unethical
    this impending war with Iraq is,
    and how impure the American motives are
    for wanting to force it.
    It is ironic that when Iran held
    American hostages, for a few lives
    the Americans were willing to drag
    negotiation on for months; yet when oil
    is held hostage, they are willing
    to sacrifice hundreds of thousands of
    lives, and refuse to negotiate ...."

```
Damage Trigger......: Message display is triggered by function of
                      realtime clock (details to be analysed)
Particularities.....: Virus tries to avoid reverse analysis: a "cute"
                      at the start will throw a researcher off if
                      a standard STONED opening is expected.
Similarities........: Basically Stoned (I), with major deviations
Known Variant.......: Empire-B, with following major differences:
                      1) Virus occupies 1,024 Bytes in Memory
                      2) Text sector is not used, no message
                      3) Virus uses encryption with different
                         algorithm on each infection, based
                         on time hack
                      4) When resident on fixed disk, the original
                         partition table is stored at sector 3
                         head 0 cyl 0. On floppy, sector 3, head 1,
                         track 0 is used.
                      EMPIRE and EMPIRE-B avoid cross infection by
                      signature checking the first four bytes of
                      MBR or Boot sector for "EA 9F 01 C0".
Remark..............: Other common characteristics indicate that both
                      Empire-A and -B were written by the same
                      person or by two people sharing notes.
-------------------- Agents -------------------------------------------
Countermeasures.....: Detection: CHKDSK, F-DISKINF, DISKSECURE
                                 (SCAN v76C does not pick this up)
Countermeasures successful: Detection: CHKDSK, F-DISKINF, DISKSECURE
Standard means......:
-------------------- Acknowledgement ----------------------------------
```

```
Location............: Virus Test Center, University of Hamburg, Germany
Classification by...: Klaus Brunnstein
Documentation by....: A.Padgett Peterson, Computer Network Security,
                                         Orlando, Florida
Date................: April 18, 1991
Information source..: A.Padgett Peterson
```

Exe_Bug.A Virus

```
Entry...............: Exe_Bug.A Virus
Alias(es)...........: CMOS Virus
Virus Strain........: Exe_Bug Virus Strain
Virus detected when.:
              where.: South Africa (there common in January 1993)
Classification......: Memory-resident System (MBR,FBR) infector,
                      stealth, tunnelling.
Length of Virus.....: 1.Length (Byte) on media:  1 sector
                      2.Length (Byte) in memory: 1 kByte
-------------------- Preconditions ------------------------------------
Operating System(s).: MS-DOS
Version/Release.....:
Computer model(s)...: IBM PCs and compatibles
-------------------- Attributes ---------------------------------------
Easy Identification.: ---
Type of infection...: Self-Identification in memory: ---
                      Self-Identification on disk: MBR[28h] = 7Ch
                      System infection: MBR/FBR infector; saving original
                      boot sector at 0/0/17 (HD), at 40/0/1 (360 kB)
                      and at 80/0/1 (any other floppy).
Infection Trigger...: At bootup from an infected floppy (hard);
                      during INT 13h/AH=02 (floppy)
Storage media affected: HD/FD
Interrupts hooked...: INT 13h/02, INT 13h/03 (stealth mechanism)
Damage..............: Permanent Damage: Sectors on hard drive converted
                                        to disc-trashing trojan; sectors
                                        on floppies converted to virus-
                                        dropping trojan.
                      Transient Damage: ---
Damage Trigger......: Permanent Damage: Condition=Int13h/write AND sect=3
                                        AND buffer[0]='M' AND
                                        ((disc=hard AND 512<=trk<768) OR
                                        (disc=flop AND sect=3))
                      Transient Damage: ---
Particularities.....: CMOS setup is altered to reflect "drive A: not
                      installed", causing some BIOSes to give up
                      bothering to boot from floppy. Virus is thus
                      able to subvert a clean boot by attempting
                      floppy bootup *after* loading itself from the
                      hard drive.
Similarities........: Exe-Bug.Hooker Virus
-------------------- Agents -------------------------------------------
Countermeasures.....:
Countermeasures successful:
Standard means......:
-------------------- Acknowledgement ----------------------------------
Location............:
```

```
Classification by...: Paul Ducklin
Documentation by....: Paul Ducklin (CARObase)
                      Klaus Brunnstein (conversion to CVC format)
Date................: 1993-February-15
Information Source..: Reverse-Engineering of virus code
```

Exe_Bug.Hooker Virus

```
Entry...............: Exe_Bug.Hooker Virus
Alias(es)...........: ---
Virus Strain........: Exe_Bug Virus Strain
Virus detected when.:
              where.: South Africa (there common in January 1993)
Classification......: Memory-resident System (MBR,FBR) infector,
                      stealth, tunnelling.
Length of Virus.....: 1.Length (Byte) on media:  1 sector
                      2.Length (Byte) in memory: 1 kByte
-------------------- Preconditions ----------------------------------
Operating System(s).: MS-DOS
Version/Release.....:
Computer model(s)...: IBM PCs and compatibles
-------------------- Attributes -------------------------------------
Easy Identification.: ---
Type of infection...: Self-Identification in memory: ---
                      Self-Identification on disk: MBR[60h..61h]=BAh 80h
                      System infection: MBR/FBR infector; stores
                      original boot sector at location At 0/0/17 (HD)
                      or at LAST_R (FD)
Infection Trigger...: At bootup from an infected floppy (hard);
                      during INT 13h/AH=02 (floppy)
Storage media affected: HD/FD
Interrupts hooked...: INT 13h/02, INT 13h/03 (stealth mechanism)
Damage..............: Permanent Damage: Sectors on hard drive converted
                                        to disc-trashing trojan.
                      Transient Damage: ---
Damage Trigger......: Permanent Damage: INT13h/write AND buffer[0..1]="MZ"
                                        AND CL=counter
                      Transient Damage: ---
Particularities.....: Can't format floppies. Virus contains encrypted
                      text "HOOKER" (NOT displayed as message).
                      When the Trojan (48 bytes long) is written to
                      disk, string "HOOKER" is appended to it.
Similarities........: Exe-Bug.A Virus
-------------------- Agents -----------------------------------------
Countermeasures.....:
Countermeasures successful:
Standard means......:
-------------------- Acknowledgement --------------------------------
Location............:
Classification by...: Paul Ducklin
Documentation by....: Paul Ducklin (CARObase)
                      Klaus Brunnstein (conversion to CVC format)
Date................: 1993-February-15
Information Source..: Reverse-Engineering fo virus code
```

FEXE Virus

```
Entry...............: FEXE = FEXE 1.0 Virus
Alias(es)...........: ---
Virus Strain........: FICHV Virus Strain
Virus detected when.:
           where.:
Classification......: Program (EXE) infector, memory resident
Length of Virus.....: 1. Length on media:   897 ($381) bytes;
                      2. Length in memory: 2,288 bytes.
-------------------- Preconditions ------------------------------------
Operating System(s).: MS-DOS
Version/Release.....: DOS 2 and upwards
Computer model(s)...: IBM PC/AT & compatibles
-------------------- Attributes ---------------------------------------
Easy Identification.: Infected files are 897 bytes longer than clean
                      EXE files. Free memory space was decreased
                      by 2288 bytes. File time is set to 62 seconds.
                      In memory, the text "** FEXE 1.0 vous a eu **"
                      can be found (28 bytes below Int_21 entrypoint)
Signature...........: AC 32 07 AA 43 3B DA 72 03 BB
                      Remark: this string is a pert of the virus'
                      decryption routine, but is rather unique due
                      to its programming error.
Type of infection...: The virus appends itself to the end of an EXE
                      file and changes the EXE-header.
Infection Trigger...: Whenever an infected file is executed, the virus
                      will go resident and thereby infect the first
                      uninfected EXE-file (found via "Search First",
                      "Search Next"). Upon any "Execute" or "Open
                      file" operation (INT 21, ah=$4B/$3D), virus
                      will infect the first uninfected EXE-file in
                      the same manner.
Storage media affected: EXE files on any disk/diskette
Interrupts hooked...: INT 21 (functions ah=$4B, ah=$3D)
Damage..............: Virus will overwrite the first 6 sectors on both
                      sides of each track, starting from track 0,
                      with the text "** FEXE 1.0 vous a eu **".
Damage Trigger......: Activating an infected file during April (any
                      year).
Particularities.....: Virus uses a simple self-encryption, which was
                      possibly planned as a complex decryption,
                      but due to a programming error operates only
                      in a simple manner (XOR). It always uses
                      standard INT 21 functions (including
                      "Terminate/stay resident": ah=$31).
Similarities........: FICHV viruses (which infect COM files only).
-------------------- Agents -------------------------------------------
Countermeasures.....: No countermeasures known.
Countermeasures successful: Dito. (Tested antivirus do not detect it)
Standard means......: Delete infected EXE files & install clean ones.
-------------------- Acknowledgement ----------------------------------
Location............: Virus Test Center, University of Hamburg, Germany
Classification by...: Toralv Dirro
Documentation by....: Toralv Dirro
Date................: 31-January-1992
Information Source..: In-depth analysis of virus code
```

FICHV 2.0 Virus

```
Entry...............: FICHV 2.0 Virus
Alias(es)...........: ---
Virus Strain........: FICHV Virus Strain
Virus detected when.:
            where.:
Classification......: Program (COM) infector, memopry resident
Length of Virus.....: 1. Length on media:    896 ($380) bytes;
                      2. Length in memory: 1,248 bytes.
------------------- Preconditions ----------------------------------
Operating System(s).: MS-DOS
Version/Release.....: DOS 2 and upwards
Computer model(s)...: IBM PC/AT & compatibles
------------------- Attributes -------------------------------------
Easy Identification.: Infected files are 896 bytes longer than clean
                      COM files. The amount of free RAM is decreased
                      by 1248 bytes. File time is set to 62 seconds.
                      In memory,the text "****FICHV 2.0 vous a eu**"
                      can be found (690 Bytes below Int 21 entry
                      point).
Signature...........: AC 32 07 AA 43 3B DA 72 03 BB
                      Remark: this string is a pert of the virus'
                      decryption routine, but is rather unique due
                      to its programming error.
Type of infection...: The virus appends the first 896 bytes of an in-
                      fected program to the end of the COM file,
                      then overwriting the first 896 bytes.
Infection Trigger...: Whenever an infected file is executed, the virus
                      will go resident and thereby infect the first
                      uninfected EXE-file (found via "Search First",
                      "Search Next"), if the free disk space is
                      >3,000 bytes and the file is longer than
                      1,500 bytes.
                      When the virus is resident, whenever INT 21
                      "Execute" ($4B) is called, the virus will
                      infect the first uninfected COM-file.
Storage media affected: COM files on any disk/diskette
Interrupts hooked...: INT 21 (function ah=$4B).
Damage..............: Virus will overwrite the first 6 sectors on both
                      sides of each track, starting from track 0,
                      with the text "****FICHV 2.0 vous a eu**".
Damage Trigger......: Execution of an infected program during March
                      (any year).
Particularities.....: Virus uses a simple self-encryption, which was
                      possibly planned as a complex decryption,
                      but due to a programming error operates only
                      in a simple manner (XOR). It always uses
                      standard INT 21 functions (including
                      "Terminate/stay resident": ah=$31).
                      Side effect #1: The virus does not check if the
                      file to be infected is smaller than 64,640
                      bytes; therefore, an infected COM file may
                      grow larger than 65,535 bytes and then cannot
                      be executed any longer.
                      Side effect #2: Virus overrides memory at
                      location 6000:0; therefore, conflicts (crash)
                      with other TSR's are possible.
Similarities........: FICHV 2.1, FEXE virus
------------------- Agents -----------------------------------------
```

```
Countermeasures.....: F-Prot 2.02 suspects that virus be a new variant
                      of the FICHV-Virus.
Countermeasures successful: None at classification time.
Standard means......: Delete infected files.
-------------------- Acknowledgement -------------------------------
Location...........: Virus Test Center, University of Hamburg, Germany
Classification by...: Toralv Dirro
Documentation by....: Toralv Dirro
Date................: 31-January-1992
Information Source..: In-depth analysis of virus code
```

FICHV 2.1 Virus

```
Entry...............: FICHV 2.1 Virus
Alias(es)...........: 903 Virus
Virus Strain........: FICHV Virus Strain
Virus detected when.:
           where.:
Classification......: Program (COM) infector, memopry resident
Length of Virus.....: 1. Length on media:    903 ($387) bytes;
                      2. Length in memory: 1,264 bytes.
Length of Virus.....:
-------------------- Preconditions ---------------------------------
Operating System(s).: MS-DOS
Version/Release.....: DOS 2 and upwards
Computer model(s)...: IBM PC/AT & compatibles
-------------------- Attributes ------------------------------------
Easy Identification.: Infected files are 903 bytes longer than clean
                      COM files. The amount of free RAM is decreased
                      by 1264 bytes. File time is set to 62 secons.
                      In memory,the text "****FICHV 2.1 vous a eu**"
                      can be found (693 Bytes below the Int 21
                      entry point).
Signature...........: AC 32 07 AA 43 3B DA 72 03 BB
                      Remark: this string is a pert of the virus'
                      decryption routine, but is rather unique due
                      to its programming error.
Type of infection...: The virus appends the first 903 Bytes of an in-
                      fected program to the end of the file, then
                      overwriting the first 903 bytes.
Infection Trigger...: Whenever an infected file is executed, the virus
                      will go resident and thereby infect the first
                      uninfected EXE-file (found via "Search First",
                      "Search Next"), if the free disk space is
                      >3,000 bytes and the file is longer than
                      1,500 bytes.
                      When the virus is resident, whenever INT 21
                      "Execute" ($4B) or "Open a File" ($3D) is
                      called, the virus will infect the first
                      uninfected COM-file.
Storage media affected: COM files on any disk/diskette.
Interrupts hooked...: INT 21 (functions ah=$4B and ah=$3D).
Damage..............: Virus will overwrite the first 6 sectors on both
                      sides of each track, starting from track 0,
                      with the text "****FICHV 2.1 vous a eu**".
Damage Trigger......: Execution of an infected program during March
                      (nay year).
Particularities.....: Virus uses a simple self-encryption, which was
```

```
                        possibly planned as a complex decryption,
                        but due to a programming error operates only
                        in a simple manner (XOR). It always uses
                        standard INT 21 functions (including
                        "Terminate/stay resident": ah=$31).
                        Side effect #1: The virus does not check for a
                        maximum length of the file to be infected, so
                        the infected files might grow bigger than
                        65,535 bytes and then cannot be executed
                        any longer.
                        Side effect #2: Virus overrides memory at
                        location 6000:0; therefore, conflicts (crash)
                        with other TSR's are possible.
Similarities........: FICHV 2.0, FEXE virus
-------------------- Agents -----------------------------------------
Countermeasures.....: F-Prot v 2.02 recognizes the virus as "FICHV
                        virus"; Scan v85 recognizes it as
                        "903 virus".
Countermeasures successful: Dito.
Standard means......: Delete infected files.
-------------------- Acknowledgement --------------------------------
Location............: Virus Test Center, University of Hamburg, Germany
Classification by...: Toralv Dirro
Documentation by....: Toralv Dirro
Date................: 31-January-1992
Information Source..: In-depth analysis of virus code
```

Fingers Virus

```
Entry...............: Fingers Virus
Alias(es)...........: "08/15" Virus
Virus Strain........: ---
Virus detected when.: ---
            where.: ---
Classification......: Resident Program (COM & EXE) Infector,
                        indirect action.
Length of Virus.....: COM & EXE: 1322 Bytes
                        Memory:         Bytes
-------------------- Preconditions ----------------------------------
Operating System(s).: MS-DOS
Version/Release.....: 3.00 upward
Computer model(s)...: IBM-PC and compatibles
-------------------- Attributes -------------------------------------
Easy Identification.: Virus contains strings (in memory and on file):
                        db "CRITICAL ERROR 08/15: TOO MANY Fi"
                        db 0Fh,"GERS ON KEYBOARD ERROR."
Self-identification.: Infected EXE- and COM-files are recognized by
                            signature "TM" in file's CRC field (offset
                            12h); self-recognition via hooked INT 21h,
                            AX=0FFFEh (returns AX=0815h when virus
                            is resident)
Scanner Signature...: ---
Type of infection...: Infects COM- and EXE-files by appending at end
                            of file.
Infection Trigger...: Upon execution (INT 21h, function AH=4Bh)
Storage media affected: all drives
Interrupts hooked...: INT 21h,INT 24h,INT 09h(from date of activation)
Damage..............: Transient damage: After 1500 keystrokes, the
```

```
                          following message is displayed:
                          "CRITICAL ERROR 08/15: TOO MANY FINGERS
                           ON KEYBOARD ERROR."
                          After the message has been displayed, system
                          is halted by virus.
Damage Trigger......:     Activation date = 11-NOVEMBER-1991
Particularities.....:     ---
Similarities........:     ---
-------------------- Agents -------------------------------------
Countermeasures.....:     McAfee's Scan V80+
Countermeasures successful: McAfee's Scan V80+
Standard means......:     ---
-------------------- Acknowledgement ----------------------------
Location............:     Virus Test Center, University of Hamburg, Germany
Classification by...:     M.Mandelbaum
Documentation by....:     H.Hoppenrath (H+B EDV), M.Mandelbaum VTC
Date................:     15-July-1991
Information Source..:     ---
```

FISH #6 Virus

```
Entry...............:     FISH #6 Virus
Alias(es)...........:     FISH-6 = European Fish Virus
Virus Strain........:     4096 = 4K = FroDo = Stealth strain
Virus detected when.:     October 1990
            where.:       Bonn/Germany ???
Classification......:     Program (extending), RAM-resident, stealth virus
Length of Virus.....:     .COM & .EXE files: length increased by 3584 bytes
                          in RAM: 4096 bytes.
-------------------- Preconditions ------------------------------
Operating System(s).:     MS-DOS
Version/Release.....:     2.xx upward
Computer model(s)...:     IBM-PC, XT, AT and compatibles
-------------------- Attributes ---------------------------------
Easy Identification.:     ---
Type of infection...:     System: Allocates a memory block at the high end
                          of memory. Finds original address of Int 21h
                          handler and original address of Int 13h hand-
                          ler, therefore bypasses all active monitors.
                          Inserts a JMP FAR to virus code inside origi-
                          nal DOS handler.
                          .COM & .EXE files: program length increased by
                          3584. A file will only be infected once.
                          Files with READ-ONLY attribute set can be in-
                          fected; files with SYSTEM attribut set will
                          not be infected (e.g.IBMBIO.COM, IBMDOS.COM).
                          COMMAND.COM is the first file, which will be in-
                          fected in an non infected system.
Infection Trigger...:     Files are infected if function 4B00H (Load/Exe-
                          cute) or function 3EH (Close File) of MS-DOS
                          is called and if last three bytes of file-
                          name sum-up to either 223 (COM) or 226 (EXE),
                          and if free diskspace is >16384 bytes.
Interrupts hooked...:     INT21h, through a JMP FAR to virus code inside
                          DOS handler;
                          INT01h, during virus installation & processing
                          INT13h, INT24h during infection.
Damage..............:     Permanent Damage: a message will be displayed:
```

```
                        "FISH VIRUS #6 - EACH DIFF - BONN 2/90 '~Knzyvo}'"
                        and then the processor stops (HLT instruction).
Damage Trigger......: If (system date>1990) and a second infected .COM
                        file is executed.
Particularities.....: 1. The virus is encrypted in memory and on disk.
                        2. Summing-up the last 3 bytes of the filename
                        for determining .COM and .EXE files for in-
                        fection will also include more than 1200
                        other extensions such as .BMP,.MEM,.OLD,.PIF,
                        .QLB for .COM-files and .LOG,.TBL for .EXE-
                        files and filenames without extension, e.g.
                        READCOM. , TESTFAX. , TEXTOLD. Therefore,
                        virus code will be appended to datafiles (e.g.
                        when using "TYPE TEXTOLD", file TEXTOLD will
                        be infected).
                        4. Only files with id="MZ" or id="ZM" get infected
                        as .EXE.
                        5. If virus is not in memory, infected data files
                        are corrupted.
                        6. Infected files get a new date 100 years ahead:
                        (newyear:=oldyear+100); e.g 1991+100=>2091, but
                        with DIR, the new date is not visible.
                        7. Do not use "CHKDSK /F" in an infected system,
                        as files get damaged (crosslinked-sectors).
                        8. If the system is infected, the virus redirects
                        all file accesses so that the virus itself can
                        not be read from the file (stealth technique).
                        9. Find first/next function returns are tampered
                        so that files with (year>100) are reduced by
                        3584 bytes in size.
                        10.Get/set filedate is also tampered.
                        Remark: the reference to "Bonn" built-into the
                        message (see damage) has lead to the assump-
                        tion that FISH#6 was originated in this Ger-
                        man town; a similar assumption has been made
                        for the related WHALE=MOTHER FISH virus due
                        to a string "Hamburg" appearing in its code.
                        There is *no forther evidence* that both
                        variants of 4096 originated in Germany; the
                        mentioned strings more probably are built-in
                        to masquerade the origin (Russian: MASKIROWKA)
Similarities........: FISH 6 is an optimized 4096 virus as it inherits
                        most of the technology of the 4096 virus.
                        The string '~Knzyvo}' meaning "TADPOLES"
                        is also found in WHALE=MOTHERFISH virus.
-------------------- Agents ----------------------------------------
Countermeasures.....: Cannot be detected on disk while in memory, so no
                        monitor/file change detector can help.
Countermeasures successful:
                        1) A Do-it-yourself way (see 4096 virus):
                        Infect system by running an infected file,
                        ARC/ZIP/LHARC/ZOO all infected .COM and .EXE
                        files, boot from uninfected floppy, and
                        UNARC/UNZIP/LHARC E etc. all files. Pay special
                        attention to disinfection of COMMAND.COM.
                        2) FINDVIRU 1.6    (Solomon)
                        3) F-FCHK   1.12+  (F. Skulason)
                        4) SCAN     6.3V72 (McAfee)
                        5) My NTIFISH6.EXE is an antivirus that only
                        looks for FISH 6 virus, and if requested will
```

```
                            restore the file.
Standard means......: Only sucessful if virus is not in memory!
                     Boot from an uninfected write-protected disk
                     and check century of files (with proper tool).
-------------------- Acknowledgement --------------------------------
Location...........: Virus Test Center, University of Hamburg, Germany
Classification by...: Stefan Tode
Documentation by....: Stefan Tode
Date................: 12-February-1991
Information source..: see: "Virus Bulletin" (also: see 4096)
```

"Flash" Virus

```
Entry................ "Flash" Virus
Alias(e)............. "688" Virus
Strain............... ---
Detected: when....... ---
          where...... ---
Classification....... Program virus, resident virus
Length of virus...... 688 bytes added to infected files
--------------------- Preconditions ---------------------------------
-
Operating System(s)... MS-DOS
Version/Release....... 2.0 and up
Computer models....... Any IBM-compatibles
---------------------Attributes -------------------------------------
-
Easy identification... ---
Type of infection..... The virus makes itself resident and intercepts
                       INT 21 upon subfunction 4Bh (load+execute);
                       the virus TSR tries to infect the loaded
                       file by appending itself to it. If the file
                       to be loaded has an extension starting with
                       "E", the virus assumes it to be an EXE file.
Infection trigger..... Loading of a file triggers infection mechanism.
Interrupts hooked..... INT 21, INT 24 (during infection);
                       INT08 (only upon payload trigger).
Damage................ Starting with June 1990, the virus hooks INT 08,
                       and after a random time it starts to flash
                       the screen image every 7 minutes (5 rapid
                       on/off cycles). This effect is visible on
                       MDA, Hercules, and CGA adapters, but *not*
                       on EGA and VGA cards!
Particularities....... The virus tries to fool debuggers when tracing
                       by self modifying code that executes differ-
                       ently due to the instruction prefetch queue-
                       ing of 80x86 processors.
                       The detection of write protected floppies uses
                       a novel technique: a writeprotected floppy
                       in drive A: will disable the infection
                       mechanism of the resident copy of the virus.
--------------------- Acknowledgement -------------------------------
Location.............. Micro-BIT Virus Center RZ Universitaet Karlsruhe
Classification by..... Christoph Fischer
Dokumentation by ..... Christoph Fischer
Date.................. 3-July-1990
```

FLIP.2343 Virus

```
Entry...............: FLIP.2343 Virus
Alias(es)...........: ---
Virus Strain........: FLIP Virus Strain
Virus detected when.: July 1990
            where.: Germany
Classification......: Multipartite (COM, EXE, Boot, MBR); Encrypted
Length of Virus.....: 1) Length on media:  2343 Bytes
                      2) Length in memory: 3064 Bytes
------------------- Preconditions ------------------------------------
Operating System(s).: MS-DOS
Version/Release.....: Version >=3.0
Computer model(s)...: IBM PCs and Compatibles
------------------- Attributes ---------------------------------------
Easy Identification.: ---
Type of infection...: EXE standard append
                      COM standard append
                      MBR standard;the partition size is decreased
                      by 6 sectors.
                      Boot standard
Infection Trigger...: ---
Storage media affected: HD and Floppy
Interrupts hooked...: INT 01h; INT 10h; INT 13h; INT 1Ch; INT 21h;
                      INT 9Fh
Damage..............: Permanent Damage: ---
                      Transient Damage: the screen ist flipped
                      horizontally. A special character set makes
                      the screen look like if one looks from
                      inside out. This effect only works on EGA or
                      VGA displays.
Damage Trigger......: Permanent Damage: ---
                      Transient Damage: Effects occur on every 2nd
                      of any month between 16:00 and 16:59.
Particularities.....: Due to a bug, an early Flip variant is not able
                      to infect bootsectors of diskettes. The Virus
                      could only be distributed by executing an
                      infected file from floppy or by copying an
                      infected file to diskette.
Similarities........: Virus in Flip strain
Known Variant.......: Flip.2153 Virus
                      1) Length on media:  2153 Bytes
                      2) Length in memory: 2672 Bytes
------------------- Agents -------------------------------------------
Countermeasures.....: Various AntiVirus products detect Flip viruses.
- dito - successful: ---
Standard means......: ---
------------------- Acknowledgement ----------------------------------
Location............: Virus Test Center, University of Hamburg, Germany
Classification by...: Matthias Jaenichen
Documentation by....: (Received from Russian author)
Date................: 20-February-1993
Information Source..: Virus documentation
```

"Form" Virus

```
Entry...............  "Form" Virus
Alias(es)...........  ---
```

```
Strain................. ---
Detected: when......... February 1990
          where....... Zuerich, Switzerland (reported to be very widely
                       spread amongst the Swiss schools in canton Zug)
Classification........ Boot sector virus
Length of Virus....... Exactly 03F9h bytes (approx. 2 sectors)
---------------------- Preconditions------------------------------
Operating System(s).... MS-DOS
Version/Release........ Any
Computer models........ IBM-PS and compatibles
----------------------- Attributes--------------------------------
Easy identification.... The boot sector will contain the following text
                        (amongst others): "The FORM-Virus sends
                        greetings to everyone who's read this text.".
                        (See also: Damage)
Type of infection...... Direct action: at boot time the virus will
                            attempt to infect the hard disk.
                        Indirect: At every read from a floppy, an
                            attempt will be made to infect it.
Infection trigger...... Every read any time.
Media affected........ Any floppy and the first active partition on
                        a harddisk.
Interrupts hooked...... Int 13 (disk) and Int 9 (keyboard) on every
                        24th of the month.
Damage................ The virus makes the keys click and delays key
                        action slightly.
Particularities....... Economically programed. It is a rare example
                        of both direct and indirect action in the same
                        virus.
Similarities.......... ---
------------------------- Agents----------------------------------
Countermeasures........
 - ditto - successful.. Most checksumming programs that check the boot
                        sector.
Standard Means........ The text mentioned above will be found in a
                        cluster marked as bad. Disks can usually be
                        disinfected by booting from a write protected
                        clean boot disk, and using the SYS command on
                        any infected disk.
---------------------- Acknowledgements---------------------------
Location.............. Virus Test Center, University of Hamburg, Germany
Classification by...... Morton Swimmer
Documentation by....... Morton Swimmer
Date.................. 5-June-1990
Information source..... Ralf Brown's interrupt list.
```

"Fumanchu-Virus"

```
Entry..............: "Fumanchu- Virus"
Alias(es)...........:
Virus Strain........: Jerusalem-Virus Strain
Virus detected when.:
          where.:
Classification......: Program-virus (extending), RAM- resident
Length of Virus.....: .COM files: program length increases by
                            2086 bytes
                      .EXE files: program length increases by
                            2080 - 2095 bytes
```

```
-------------------- Preconditions ----------------------------------
Operating System(s).: MS-DOS
Version/Release.....: 2.xx upward
Computer model(s)...: IBM-PC, XT, AT and compatibles
-------------------- Attributes -------------------------------------
Easy Identification.: Typical texts in Virus body (readable with
                      HexDump-facilities):
                      1. "sAXrEMHOr" and "COMMAND.COM" in the
                         data area of the virus and
                      2. "rEMHOr" are the last 6 bytes if the
                         infected program is a .COM file.
Type of infection...: System: infected if function E1h of INT 21h
                      returns the value 0400h in the AX - register.
                      .COM files: program length increases by 2086
                      bytes if it is infected and the last 6 bytes
                      are "rEMHOr" (identification); a .COM file
                      will not be infected more than once.
                      .EXE files: program length increases by 2080
                      - 2095 bytes; if it is infected, the word
                      checksum in the EXE-header is "1988"; an
                      EXE file will not be infected more than once.
Infection Trigger...: Programs are infected when loaded (using the
                      function Load/Execute of Ms-Dos)
Interrupts hooked...: INT08h, INT09, INT16, INT21 (INT24 only while
                      infecting a file).
Damage..............: Transient Damage:
                      1. The message 'The world will hear from me
                      again!  ' is displayed on every warmboot.
                      2. The virus watches the keyboard input and
                      appends slanders about politicians in the
                      keyboard buffer.
Damage Trigger......: Every time the system is infected.
                      Damage 1: always
                      Damage 2: from august 89
Particularities.....: 1. .COM files larger than 63193 bytes are no
                            longer loadable after infection.
                      2. .COM files larger than 63449 bytes are
                            destroyed by overwriting.
                      3. Three functions used by Novell- Netware 4.0
                            cannot be used.
                      4. The virus code contains a routine that will
                            automaticly reboot the system between
                            1 and 16 hours. This code is never
                            activated due to a programming mistake.
                      5. All strings are encrypted.
-------------------- Agents -----------------------------------------
Countermeasures.....: Category 3: ANTIFUMN.EXE (VTC Hamburg)
Countermeasures successful: ANTIFUMN.EXE is an antivirus that only
                      looks for the Fumanchu Virus and, if
                      requested, will restore the file.
Standard means......: Filelength increased if a program is infected.
-------------------- Acknowledgement --------------------------------
Location............: Virus Test Center, University of Hamburg, Germany
Classification by...: Michael Reinschmiedt
Documentation by....: Michael Reinschmiedt
                      Morton Swimmer
Date................: December 15,1989
```

F-Word Virus

```
Entry...............: F-Word Virus
Alias(es)...........: Fuck You Virus
Virus Strain........: ---
Virus detected when.: January 1993
             where.: Italy
Classification......: Program Virus: COM infector, direct action
Length of Virus.....: 383 Bytes
-------------------- Preconditions ------------------------------------
Operating System(s).: MS-DOS, PC-DOS
Version/Release.....:
Computer model(s)...: IBM PC/XT/AT and compatibles
-------------------- Attributes ---------------------------------------
Easy Identification.: Infected files contain strings "FUCK YOU", "*.COM"
Type of infection...: Extends .COM files by replacing first 5 bytes
                      with a portion of the viral code, then extends
                      program by adding rest of code to end of file.
                      Original 5 Bytes will be stored at the end
                      of an infected file.
Infection Trigger...: Execution of an infected file.
Storage media affected: .COM files
Interrupts hooked...: ---
Damage..............:
Damage Trigger......:
Particularities.....: ---
Similarities........:
-------------------- Agents -------------------------------------------
Countermeasures.....: Only Skulason's F-Prot with "Heuristic scan"
                      detects infection (but the alert message
                      is wrong!)
-------------------- Acknowledgement ----------------------------------
Location............: Laboratorio per l'Analisi dei Virus Informatici,
                      Rome
Classification by...: Luca Sambucci
Documentation by....: Luca Sambucci
Date................: February 13, 1993
Information Source..: ---
```

G&H Virus

```
Entry ................ G&H Virus
Alias(es) ............ Demovirus G&H (see: Particularities)
Strain ............... ---
Detected: when ....... February 1991
          where ...... Germany
Classification ....... Program virus: Non-resident COM infector
Length of Virus ...... 1247 bytes
==================== Preconditions ====================================
Operating System(s) ... MS-DOS
Version/Release ....... 2.11 and upwards
Computer models ....... IBM PC and compatibles
==================== Attributes =======================================
Easy identification ... The virus displays a message (in German) every
                        time it infects a file. The message en-
                        compasses a whole screen and includes in-
                        formation on the virus (its length wrongly
                        stated as 1.000 bytes, and virus' behaviour,
```

```
                              the author's address as well as advertise-
                              ment for a brochure on PC security. You must
                              press a key before the message goes away.
Type of infection ..... The virus infects COM files on diskette drive A
                              in direct action and does not go resident.
                              Six bytes are changed in the beginning of
                              the file (the jump to the virus) and the
                              rest is appended to the file.
Infection trigger ..... Execution of an infected program
Media affected ........ Only the physical drive A: (in most cases:
                              first floppy drive).
Interrupts hooked ..... INT 13 for a short time; it is not used for
                              infection or damage.
Damage ................ Transient Damage: message is displayed.
                              Permanent Damage: ---
                              Side Effects: not observed, but possible.
Damage trigger ........ Every time an infected program is run.
Particularities ....... 1) Checks if the drive is a logical drive by
                              seeing whether DOS uses BIOS to access the
                              disk. Virus checks to see if the text has
                              been changed, by building a checksum over
                              the text; if text was changed, the virus
                              terminates.
                              2) This virus was produced by a computer
                              security firm in Germany (near Cologne)
                              and sold for a nominal fee (50 DM) by
                              mail-order; the virus was advertised in a
                              German Data Protection monthly as educa-
                              tional. Only after German Information
                              Security Agency (GISA)'s intervention, the
                              distribution was stopped after apparently
                              a few copies were sent out (with major de-
                              mand unsaturated); in another advertisement
                              the virus was officially withdrawn.
                              3) Even though the names of firm and authors
                              are known and even displayed on screen,
                              VTC anonymizes it by given only the initials
                              as long as virus is not further distributed.
Similarities .......... ---
===================== Agents ========================================
Countermeasures ....... (no contemporary scanner finds this virus)
 - ditto - successful . ---
Standard Means ........ When seeing message, replace infected program
                              with original (non-infected) version.
===================== Acknowledgements ==============================
Location .............. Virus Test Center, University of Hamburg, Germany
Classification by ..... Morton Swimmer
Documentation by ...... Morton Swimmer
Date .................. 15-July-1991
Information source .... (original virus reverse-analysed)
```

"GhostBalls" Virus

```
Entry..............: "GhostBalls"
Alias(es)..........: Ghost
Virus Strain.......: Vienna (DOS-62)
Virus detected when.: Oct. '89
            where.: Iceland
```

```
Classification......: .COM file infecting virus/Extending/Direct/Non-Resident
Length of Virus.....: 2351 bytes added to file
-------------------- Preconditions ------------------------------------
Operating System(s).: MS-DOS
Version/Release.....: 2.0 or higher
Computer model(s)...: IBM PC,XT,AT and compatibles
-------------------- Attributes ---------------------------------------
Easy Identification.: .COM files: "seconds" field of the timestamp
                      changed to 62, as in the original Vienna virus.
                      Infected files end in a block of 512 zero bytes.
Type of infection...: Extends .COM files. Adds 2531 bytes to the end
                      of the file and places a JMP instruction at the
                      beginning.
                      When an infected program is run, it will search for
                      a program to infect, and also try to place a modified
                      copy of the Ping-Pong virus on the boot sector in
                      drive A.
                      The virus will remove the Read-Only attribute from
                      programs in order to infect them. It is replaced
                      afterwards.
Infection Trigger...: One .COM file in the current directory with the
                      "seconds" field not equal to 62 will be infected
                      each time an infected program is run.
Storage media affected: Boot sectors on diskettes.
Interrupts hooked...:
Damage..............: .COM files and boot sectors modified. No permanent
                      damage.
Damage Trigger......:
Particularities.....: The destruction of 1 program in 8 in the original
                      Vienna virus has been disabled. The Ping-Pong
                      copy placed on drive A: has been modified in two ways:
                      It will work on a '286 machine but has been patched
                      so it will not infect other diskettes. Virus contains
                      the text string:
                              "GhostBalls, Product of Iceland"
Similarities........:
-------------------- Agents -------------------------------------------
Countermeasures.....: Any program that identifies the Vienna virus by
                      using signatures should be able to find infected files.
                      VIRSCAN (46) will identify infected files.
                      F-FCHK (by the author of this article) will
                      identify infected files and remove the infection.
Countermeasures successful:
Standard means......:
-------------------- Acknowledgement ----------------------------------
Location............: University of Iceland/Computing Services
Classification by...: Fridrik Skulason  (frisk@rhi.hi.is)
Documentation by....: Fridrik Skulason
Date................: November 2, 1989
Information Source..:
```

GNAT Virus

```
Entry...............: GNAT (1.0) Virus
Alias(es)...........: ---
Virus Strain........:
Virus detected when.: July 1993
             where.: Germany
```

```
Classification......: File virus (EXE infector),memory resident,stealth
Length of Virus.....: 1.Length (Byte) on media: 756-771 Bytes
                      2.Length (Byte) in RAM:    832   Bytes
-------------------- Preconditions ------------------------------------
Operating System(s).: MSDOS
Version/Release.....:
Computer model(s)...: IBM PCs and Compatibles
-------------------- Attributes ---------------------------------------
Easy Identification.: "0103h" in bytes 20-21 of infected files (see Self-
                      Identification in files).
Type of infection...: File infection: After virus became memory resident,
                      EXE and ZM files are infected upon Trigger
                      conditions (see below) by appending virus code.
                      Self-Identification in files: Virus tests if
                      (file[0014h] = 03h)
                      AND (file[0015h] = 01h) {EXE-IP = 0103h}
                      System infection: Upon execution of an infected
                      file, virus makes itself memory resident (using
                      TWIXT method).
                      Self-Identification in memory: Virus tests if
                      memw[0000h:0086h] > 0350h {SEG(INT 21) > 0350h}
Infection Trigger...: If (Exec OR Load w/o Exec) AND
                      (memw[0000h:004Eh] <= 0300h){SEG(INT 13)<=0300h}
                      AND (file[4] >= 1) {Length>=512} AND (file[4] =
                          ((Length SHR 9)+(1; IF Length MOD 512 = 0)))
Storage media affected:
Interrupts hooked...: INT 1C, INT 21/4B00, INT 21/4B02,
                      INT 24 (while in INT 21 ISR).
Damage..............: Permanent Damage: ---
                      Transient Damage: Virus mirrors screen horizontally
                       and vertically.
Damage Trigger......: Permanent Damage: ---
                      Transient Damage: If (Date = October 11)
                       AND (BIOS_timer_low = 0FFFFh)
                       AND at least one new infection at this day.
Particularities.....: 1) Virus is encrypted,with variable key stored in-
                         side decryption routine (form of polymorphism);
                         en/decryption key is low byte of new CS value
                         in EXE-file-header.
                      2) Virus contains encrypted string: "GNAT 1.0".
                      3) Stealth methods: virus sets file r/w for in-
                         fection and restores original file attribu-
                         tes, date and time after infection; hooks
                         interrupts by direct memory access; while
                         running the INT 21h ISR, virus temporarily
                         stores the INT 21 vector saved on infection
                         back to IVT; uses slightly self modifying
                         code; no TSR-call, just jumps to original
                         program at virus' end.
Similarities........: ---
-------------------- Agents -------------------------------------------
Countermeasures.....:
Countermeasures successful:
Standard means......: Delete infected files and replace with clean ones.
-------------------- Acknowledgement ----------------------------------
Location............: Virus Test Center, University of Rostock, Germany
Classification by...: Dirk Haratz (dharatz@informatik.uni-rostock.de)
Documentation by....: Dirk Haratz
                      Klaus Brunnstein (CVC entry)
Date................: 24-July-1993
Information Source..: Reverse analysis of virus code
```

Green Caterpillar Virus

```
Entry..............: Green Caterpillar (A/B/C) Virus
Alias(es)..........: "1575/1591" (15xx) Virus
Virus Strain.......: Caterpillar
Virus detected when.: January 1991
          where.: Ontario, Canada
Classification.....: Resident Program (COM & EXE) Infector
Length of Virus....: Program: 1575 Bytes (modulo 16:1575-1591)
                     Memory:  1760-1840 Bytes
-------------------- Preconditions ---------------------------------
Operating System(s).: MSDOS
Version/Release.....: Version 3.00 and upwards
Computer model(s)...: IBM-Compatibles (only in Real-Mode)
-------------------- Attributes ------------------------------------
Easy Identification.: Text-String found "C:\COMMAND.COM $$$$$"
Type of infection...: Memory: virus installs itself in high memory,
                     but will not protect itself against being
                     overwritten in RAM (A-Variant).
                     COM & EXE files: one COM AND one EXE file are
                     infected upon infection triggered; file-date
                     will be changed to system-Date.
                     COMMAND.COM will be infected immediatly after
                     execution.
Infection Trigger...: Any time a COPY or DIR-Command is executed
Storage media affected: Any media, infection of current path.
Interrupts hooked...: INT 21h; INT 24h; corrupts COPY and DIR commands
Damage.............: Transient damage: a green caterpillar creeps over
                     the screen, starting at the upper left corner.
Damage Trigger......: Two month after 1st infection.
Particularities.....: There are three variants reported:
                     B-Variant installs itself in memory, includ-
                        ing self-protection against overwrite.
                     C-Variant is able to infect a program during
                        its execution.
Similarities........: ---
-------------------- Agents ----------------------------------------
Countermeasures.....: Scan (>V73); VirScan; F-Prot
Countermeasures successful: Scan (>V73); VirScan; F-Prot
Standard means......: Boot from clean system-disk, restore COMMAND.COM,
                     delete all infected files; hide COMMAND.COM
                     in a separate directory, and use the COMSPEC-
                     entry in the CONFIG.SYS file to avoid re-
                     infection of COMMAND.COM.
-------------------- Acknowledgement -------------------------------
Location...........: Virus-Test-Center; University of Hamburg, Germany
Classification by...: Matthias Jaenichen, VTC
                        <jaenichen@rz.informatik.uni-hamburg.dbp.de>
Documentation by....: Matthias Jaenichen, VTC
Date...............: 15-July-1991
Information Source..: Disassembly, Vsum9103 (Patricia Hoffman)
```

Groove Virus

```
Entry..............: Groove Virus
Standard CARO Name..: MtE_0_90.Groove Virus
Alias(es)..........: ---
Virus Strain.......: MtE-based
Virus detected when.: USA
```

```
                    where.: June 1992
Classification......: Polymorphic, memory-resident program (COM and
                      EXE, appending) virus
Length of Virus.....: 1. In RAM: 140 paragraphs;
                      2. on file: variable on disk due to MtE.
-------------------- Preconditions ----------------------------------
Operating System(s).: MS/PC DOS
Version/Release.....: 3.0+ ???
Computer model(s)...: All 80x86-based PCs
-------------------- Attributes -------------------------------------
Easy Identification.: Programs stop running as expected if at all.
Self Identification.: In memory: AX=0FBA0h, INT 21h -> AX = 0ABFh
                      if resident.
                      On files: EXE header checksum = 0FBAh
                                COM 5th byte = 0BAh, 6th byte = 0Fh
Type of infection...: COM & EXE programs (not based on extension)
Infection Trigger...: Execution using INT 21h function 4B.
Storage media affected: All (diskettes,,hard disk)
Interrupts hooked...: INT 21h, INT 24h
Damage..............: Transient damage: the following message will
                      either be displayed after 12:30 midnight
                      based on the tick count returned by INT 1Ah
                      on systems with a RTC, or it is displayed
                      every time when a file is infected:
                      "Dont wory, you are not alone at this hour...
                      This Virus is NOT dedicated to Sara
                      its dedicated to her Groove
                                      (...Thats my name)
                      This virus is only a test virus therefore
                      be ready for my  Next  Test .."
                      This message is not readable in most mutations
                      due to encryption.
                      Permanent damage:
                      Virus will delete the following files upon
                      activation:   C:\NAV_._NO
                                    C:\NOVIRCVR.CTS
                                    C:\NOVIPERF.DAT
                                    C:\CPAV\CHKLIST.CPS
                                    C:\TOOLKIT\FILES.LST
                                    C:\UNTOUCH\UT.UT1
                                    C:\UNTOUCH\UT.UT2
Damage Trigger......: Execution of an infected file
Particularities.....: Virus does not check file extension to determine
                      its type, but rather checks for "MZ" or "ZM"
                      at the start of a file and assumes EXE-type
                      if a match is found; otherwise, it infects
                      as a COM-type file.
                      Infected files will not run properly.
Similarities........: ---
-------------------- Agents -----------------------------------------
Countermeasures.....: CatchMtE 1.0, VDSFSCAN 2.10, VDS 2.10, Gobbler-II
Countermeasures successful: Same as above, but all antivirals that can
                      detect MtE-based viruses 100% of the time
                      should be effective.
Standard means......: Delete infected files and restore clean copies.
-------------------- Acknowledgement --------------------------------
Location............: Baltimore, MD, U.S.A.
Classification by...: Tarkan Yetiser, VDS Advanced Research Group
Documentation by....: Tarkan Yetiser
Date................: 29-June-1992
Information Source..: ---
```

Hafenstrasse Virus

```
Entry..............: Hafenstrasse Virus
Alias(es)..........: ---
Virus Strain.......: ---
Virus detected when.: 22-October-1991
            where.: Hamburg, Germany
Classification......: Program virus, non-resident, EXE-infector
Length of Virus.....: 809 Bytes
------------------- Preconditions --------------------------------
Operating System(s).: MS-DOS
Version/Release.....: 2.xx upward
Computer model(s)...: IBM - PC, XT, AT and compatibles
------------------- Attributes -----------------------------------
Easy Identification.: ---
Type of infection...: The virus infects only EXE files. The virus
                      is not memory-resident.
Infection Trigger...: The virus infects in direct action; when an in-
                      fected program is run, virus tries 5 times
                      to find a file to infect, but will only in-
                      fect one file at a time.
Interrupts hooked...: ---
Damage.............: The message "Hafenstrasse bleibt !" is written
                      to a hidden file. The name of the file is
                      composed of 4 randomly-chosen letters. Even
                      though this seems to be fairly harmless,
                      this will eventually fill the disk, or the
                      capacity of the directory may be exceeded.
                      Remark: the text "Hafenstrasse bleibt!" (=har-
                      bour street remains) is a slogan which some
                      inhabitants (belonging to an "alternative
                      scene") of Hamburg's "harbour street" use
                      to publicly withstand local government plans
                      to replace their old houses by new ones.
Damage Trigger......: A new file is created every time an infected
                      file is run.
Particularities.....: The text is encrypted (only the text).
------------------- Agents ---------------------------------------
Countermeasures.....: ---
- ditto - successful: ---
Standard means......: ---
------------------- Acknowledgement ------------------------------
Location...........: Virus Test Center, University of Hamburg, Germany
Classification by...: Morton Swimmer
Documentation by....: Morton Swimmer
Date...............: 20-November-1991
```

Hafenstrasse-2 Virus

```
Entry..............: Hafenstrasse-2 Virus
Standard CARO name..: Hafenstrasse.1641
Alias(es)..........: Hafenstrasse.e, Red-X-Exe
Virus Strain.......: Both Hafenstrasse & Ambulance (Red-X) strains
Virus detected when.: June 92
            where.: Hamburg
Classification......: Direct action EXE- and COM-infector
Length of Virus.....: 1637-1652 Bytes appended to files
------------------- Preconditions --------------------------------
```

```
Operating System(s).: IBM & Compatibles
Version/Release.....: DOS 2.x and above
Computer model(s)...: IBM PC, XT, AT and higher, and compatibles
-------------------- Attributes -------------------------------------
Easy Identification.: Heavily increased time to access disk, when
                      starting an infected program.
Search string.......: String 3D 00 10 73 1B FE 84 D9 04 06 E8 can be
                      found at about 600 bytes offset from the end.
Type of infection...: EXE-files: standard ways of infecting EXE-files.
                      COM-files: virus behaves as trojan dropper in
                                 releasing Ambulance=Red X virus.
Infection Trigger...: Starting an infected file: virus will search
                      for 1 EXE- and 1 COM-file in path to infect.
Storage media affected: Only files in subdirectories included in the
                      path are infected.
Interrupts hooked...: ---
Damage..............: Permanent damage: system may hang when nearly
                      all files are infected (see Particularities)
                      Transient damage: on COM-files, virus will cause
                      an ambulance car to cross the screen.
Damage Trigger......: On COM files: first time on 6th, then every 8th
                      execution of virus (infection counter).
Particularities.....: 1) First virus to drop a virus from another
                      virus strain (Ambulance car=Red X).
                      2) Virus will check, if the INT-26-vector points
                      to an adress with a segment above $1000; in
                      this case, it will not activate (trying to
                      undergo some online detectors, e.g. Flushot).
                      3) If the files in the PATH are (almost) all
                      infected, the system may hang, because it
                      continues to search for infected files and
                      uses a random function to determine, whether
                      to infect a yet uninfected file.
                      4) No exact match is done do recognize COM- and
                      EXE-files.
                      5) File date and time is not altered.
Similarities........: Hafenstrasse variants, Ambulance car variants
                      (both virus strains use very similar ways to
                      search for a file, to infect; they may come
                      from related authors).
-------------------- Agents -----------------------------------------
Countermeasures successful: F-PROT 2.04a, Antivir from H&B-EDV
Standard means......: Delete and replace infected files.
-------------------- Acknowledgement --------------------------------
Location............: Virus Test Center, University of Hamburg, Germany
Classification by...: Toralv Dirro
Documentation by....: Toralv Dirro
Date................: 07-July-1992
Information Source..: Original virus analysis
```

Hafenstrasse-3 Virus

```
Entry...............: Hafenstrasse-3 Virus
Standard CARO name..: Hafenstrasse.1191
Alias(es)...........: ---
Virus Strain........: Hafenstrasse virus strain
Virus detected when.: July 1992
           where.: Hamburg
```

```
Classification......: Direct action EXE-infector
Length of Virus.....: 1187-1202 Bytes appended to files
-------------------- Preconditions ---------------------------------
Operating System(s).: IBM PC & Compatibles
Version/Release.....: DOS 2.x and above
Computer model(s)...: IBM PC, XT, AT and hiogher, and compatibles
-------------------- Attributes ------------------------------------
Easy Identification.: ---
Scan signature......: String: 3d 00 10 73 14 fe 84 03 01 e8 28 02 e8
                      1f 00 may be found at an offset of about
                      1150 bytes from the end of the file.
Type of infection...: Virus uses standard methods of infecting EXE
                      files searched for in the current path.
Infection Trigger...: Upon starting an infected program, virus
                      searches for an EXE file.
Storage media affected: Only files in subdirectories included in
                      path are affected.
Interrupts hooked...: ---
Damage..............: Permanent damage: ---
                      Transient damage: the first time an infected
                      program is started, virus will display an
                      ambulance car crossing the screen until it
                      reaches the right border, where it will
                      crash against a wall displaying texts
                      "BOOM" and "no more RedX !!!"
Damage Trigger......: The first time an infected program is started.
Particularities.....: 1) This virus does not infect COM files with an
                      Ambulance car dropper, as does the previous-
                      ly found Hafenstrasse-2. Instead, this
                       variant contains a modied ambulance car
                      routine.
                      2) The vector of INT 26 is tested, whether it
                      points to a segment above $1000 or not.
                      As in all (known) Hafentrasse viruses, file
                      and date will not be changed on infection.
Similarities........: Hafenstrasse variants, Ambulance (RedX) variants.
-------------------- Agents ----------------------------------------
Countermeasures.....: ---
Countermeasures successful: F-PROT 2.04a
Standard means......: Delete and replace infected files.
-------------------- Acknowledgement -------------------------------
Location............: Virus Test Center, University of Hamburg, Germany
Classification by...: Toralv Dirro
Documentation by....: Toralv Dirro
Date................: 21-July-92
Information Source..: Original virus analysis.
```

Halloween Virus

```
Entry...............: Halloween Virus
Standard CARO Name..: Halloween Virus
Alias(es)...........: ---
Virus Strain........: ---
Virus detected when.: December 1991
          where.: British Columbia, Canada
Classification......: Program virus (COM&EXE infector, including
                      COMMAND.COM), non-resident
Length of Virus.....: Infected file length: 10,000 bytes (exactly)
-------------------- Preconditions ---------------------------------
```

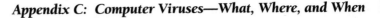

```
Operating System(s).: PC/MS-DOS
Version/Release.....: Any?
Computer model(s)...: Any IBM PC and compatibles?
-------------------- Attributes ---------------------------------------
Easy Identification.: 1) Significant file growth: 10 kByte (exactly).
                      2) Text "Happy HalloweenU" appears near start
                         of infected programs.
Type of infection...: Virus infects COM & EXE programs in the current
                      directory only, but only files with length
                      >= 10,000 (2710h) bytes will be infected.
                      Infection is done through prepending virus to
                      EXE and COM files to be infected file. Date
                      and time of infected file will match the
                      original one's, however the file's position
                      in the directory may change.
Infection Trigger...: Execution of infected program.
Storage media affected: All
Interrupts hooked...: ---
Damage..............: Permanent/transient damage: On October 31
                      (Halloween),  infected files will be
                      truncated to 666 bytes and the message
                              "All Gone Happy Halloween"
                      will appear.
Damage Trigger......: October 31 (Halloween), any year since 1992.
Particularities.....: 1) Search for uninfected files is proceeding
                      from top directory, and each executable file
                      is inspected for previous infection/length.
                      2) During infection, virus holds original code
                      in a temporary file. Moreover, it traps the
                      original file's return code for use when the
                      virus terminates (possibly for tunneling).
Similarities........: ---
-------------------- Agents -------------------------------------------
Countermeasures.....: McAfee Scan, Skulason F-PROT, Solomon FindViru
Countermeasures successful:
Standard means......: On identification, virus may be removed from most
                      programs  (both COM & EXE) by simply stripping
                      off the first 10k bytes.
-------------------- Acknowledgement ----------------------------------
Location............: Orlando/Florida, USA
                      Virus Test Center, University of Hamburg, Germany
Classification by...: Padgett Patterson (USA), Klaus Brunnstein (VTC)
Documentation by....: Klaus Brunnstein (VTC)
Date................: 15-July-1992
Information Source..: Padgett Patterson's report on Halloween virus
```

Headcrash Virus

```
Entry...............: Headcrash Virus
Alias(es)...........: "1067" Virus
Virus Strain........: ---
Virus detected when.: University Giessen (Germany)
           where.: March 1991
Classification......: .COM - file:  RAM-resident program virus
Length of Virus.....: .COM - Files: 1067 bytes
-------------------- Preconditions ------------------------------------
Operating System(s).: MS-DOS
Version/Release.....: 2.xx upward
```

```
Computer model(s)...: IBM - PC, XT, AT and compatibles
------------------- Attributes ------------------------------------
Easy Identification.: .COM files: first three bytes (E9h WXh YZh) and
                       last three bytes are identical. The seconds
                       field of the timestamp is changed to
                       62 sec, similar to Vienna strain.
Type of infection...: RAM-resident: infected if function AX=58CCH of
                       INT 21H is available in system (carry flag
                       not set).
                      .COM file: infected by hooking EXEC-function.
                       If a program is executed, the virus infects
                       the first not-infected .COM file found
                       in the directory of the executed file; it
                       apends 1067 bytes at the end of the file.
                       Only files with extension .COM and with
                       1791 < filesize < 61696 bytes are infected.
                       Files are infected not more than once.
                      .EXE file: no infection.
Infection Trigger...: System will be infected if day is odd and
                       DOS version > 1.00 .
                      .COM file will be infected, when function 4B00H
                       (LOAD/EXEC) of INT 21H is called.
Interrupts hooked...: INT 09H,21H,24H; INT 21H (functions 4B00H,
                       2521H, 3521H, 58CCH and 58DDH);
                       INT 09H only during execution of infected files;
                       INT 24H only during infection of files.
Damage............: Permanent Damage: Every time a file is executed
                       in an infected system, a .COM file will be
                       infected.
                       Transient Damage: Only once per installation of
                       virus before execution of a file, the fol-
                       lowing message is displayed:
                       "Headcrash Industries celebrate 0040hex."
                       (0040H is the infection counter,and may vary)
Damage Trigger......: If a file is executed between 20 and 25 minutes
                       after virus installation AND if realtime
                       clock was not read before virus installation
                       AND if infection counter > 31, then this
                       message is displayed.
Particularities.....: - The message "Headcrash.....hex." is encrypted.
                      - All files with .COM extension will be infected
                        (i.e also exe-files with .COM extension).
                      - .COM files with exe-header-id "MZ" will not
                        run after infection.
                      - Command.com will be infected.
                      - At infection of COMMAND.COM, the free memory
                        is temporaly shrinked to 64k byte; therefore,
                        many programs will no longer execute.
                      - File attributes are restored after infection.
                      - Get/Set interrupt 21H (functions 3521H,2521H)
                        is monitored and modified by virus.
                      - Function AX=58DDH of INT 21H returns:
                        CX = codesegment of virus,
                        ES/BX = segment/offset of old int 21H.
-------------------- Agents ---------------------------------------
Countermeasures.....: Category 3: NTI1067.EXE (VTC Hamburg)
- ditto - successful: NTI1067.EXE finds and restores infected programs.
Standard means......: Notice .COM file length and seconds-timestamp.
                       Search for hex bytes: 01H,B4H,2AH,CDH,21H,F6H,
                       C2H,01H,75H,03H at location 62 of virus.
```

```
--------------------- Acknowledgement ---------------------------------
Location............: Virus Test Center, University of Hamburg, Germany
Classification by...: Stefan Tode
Documentation by....: Stefan Tode
Date................: 15-July-1991
```

Hello Virus

```
Entry...............: Hello Virus
Alias(es)...........: Hello_1a=Hall(oe)chen (German, meaning "Hy!")
Virus Strain........: ---
Virus detected when.: January 1990
            where.: South-West-Germany
Length of Virus.....: 2011 Bytes
-------------------- Preconditions ------------------------------------
Operating System(s).: MS-DOS
Version/Release.....: 3.00+
Computer model(s)...: IBM compatibles
-------------------- Attributes ---------------------------------------
Easy Identification.: Textstring: "Hall(oe)chen, here I'm"
                                "Acrivate Level 1" (wrong syntax!)
Type of infection...: Link-Virus; Infects COM- and EXE-files
Infection Trigger...: Any program file with file-date different
                      from the system-date (only year/month)
Storage media affected: Floppy and harddisk
Interrupts hooked...: INT 21h, function 4Bh
                      INT 08h and INT 16h for Damage
Damage..............: Slows system down, corrupts keyboard-entries
                      (pressing "A" produces "B")
Damage Trigger......: Infection-level greater than 50 or 70
Particularities.....: The damage will not be activated.
Similarities........: ---
-------------------- Agents -------------------------------------------
Countermeasures.....: Scan V57+ (McAfee),
Countermeasures successful: CleanV57+
Standard means......: ---
-------------------- Acknowledgement ----------------------------------
Location............: VTC-Hamburg, BIT-Karlsruhe
Classification......: Matthias Jaenichen, Christoph Fischer
Documentation by....: Matthias Jaenichen
Date................: 31-January-1990
Update..............: 14-February-1991
Information Source..: ---
```

"Hey You" Virus

```
Entry...............: "Hey You" Virus
Alias(es)...........: 923, 928 Virus
Virus Strain........: ---
Virus detected when...: February 1991
            where...: Bulletin Board, Slovenia
Classification........: Program (.COM, .EXE) infector, memory resident
Length of Virus.......: 1) Length on media:  928 (3A0h) - 943 bytes
                        2) Length in memory: 944 bytes
-------------------- Preconditions ------------------------------------
Operating System(s)...: MS/PC-DOS
```

```
Version/Release.......: 2.00 and upwards
Computer model(s).....: All IBM PC compatibles
--------------------- Attributes ------------------------------------
Easy Identification...: Virus contains text (message displayed):
                        "Hey, YOU !!!
                        Something's happening to you !
                        Guess what it is ?!
                        HA HA HA HA ..."
Self identification...: System: infected if INT 21h function BBBBh
                        returns value 6969h in AX-register.
                        .COM files: checks if first byte of file
                        is jump (E9h), calculates jump destination
                        and then compares file contents at destination
                        with first nine bytes of the virus.
                        .EXE files: calculates entry point and compares
                        file contents with first nine bytes of virus.
Type of infection.....: System: Virus first checks MCB if there will
                        be at least 64Kb available after installing
                        itself in memory. It then copies itself at
                        the top of available memory and decreases
                        the value of available memory by 3Bh
                        paragraphs (=944 bytes).
                        Files: virus appends itself at end of .COM
                        (including COMMAND.COM) and .EXE files,
                        enlarging file size between 928 and 943
                        bytes. Files will only be infected once.
Infection Trigger.....: Calling INT 21h (EXEC) function 4B00h
Storage media affected: Files can be infected on all media (HD,FD)
Interrupts hooked.....: INT 21h (functions 4B00h and BBBBh),
                        INT 24h (only during infection of a file)
Damage................: Permanent damage: ---
                        Transient damage: When an infected program is
                        executed, computer beeps (^G), displays
                        the message described above (see: Easy
                        Identification) and exits to DOS.
Damage Trigger........: Transient damage: if during infection function
                        GetDate returns with year>=1991 AND month>=2
                        AND day>=25 AND (Mem[0:46Ch] AND 7=0)
                        (Real Time Clock).
Particularities.......: INT 21h is set directly (not via DOS) and
                        always points to xxxx:00B5h.
                        EXE files with maximum memory requirement equal
                        FFFFh paragraphs will not be infected.
                        Attribute, time and date of an infected file
                        remain unchanged. Read-only and hidden
                        attributes do NOT protect against infection.
Similarities..........: ---
--------------------- Agents ----------------------------------------
Countermeasures.....: F-Prot v2.02 recognizes the virus as "Hey You";
                        McAfee's Scan v80+ recognizes it as "923 virus
                        [923]", McAfee's Scan v89B recognizes it as
                        "Generic Virus [GenF]".
Countermeasures successful: Tested: F-Prot v2.03a detects and removes
                            the virus.
Standard means......: ---
------------------- Acknowledgement ---------------------------------
Location............: ---
Classification by...: Dalibor Cerar
Documentation by....: Dalibor Cerar
Date................: 16-April-1992
Information Source..: (original virus analysis)
```

Horns Virus

```
Entry...............: Horns Virus
Alias(es)...........: ---
Virus Strain........: ---
Virus detected when.:
          where.:
Classification......: File virus (appending AVR infector),stealth,
                      memory resident
Length of Virus.....: 1.Length (Byte) on storage medium: 624 Bytes
                      2.Length (Byte) in RAM:             896 Bytes
-------------------- Preconditions ------------------------------------
Operating System(s).: MSDOS
Version/Release.....:
Computer model(s)...: IBM PCs and compatibles
-------------------- Attributes ---------------------------------------
Easy Identification.: Virus code contains message (not displayed):
                      "[Horns Of Jericho (c) 92 Crom-Cruach/Trident]"
Type of infection...: Appending AVR file infector: virus infects .AVR
                      files opened for read-only when file is being
                      closed. Virus appends itself (624 bytes) to
                      end of an infected file and recalculates .AVR
                      specific checksum to bypass AVR integrity check.
                      Remark: AVR format is COM-like, but starts at
                          offset 0000h rather than 0100h; an AVR file
                          is loaded to XXXX:0000, where XXXX is ar-
                          bitrary segment. Module's entry point is at
                          offset +48h.
                      Self-identification in file:  File[0x48] = 0xE9
SELFREC_IN_MEMORY: INT_21;AX=44A0 -> AH=FF
                      System infection: upon execution of an infected
                      file, virus makes itself memory resident using
                      TWIXT method.
                      Self-identification in memory: special content
                          of register upon INT 21 invocation.
Infection Trigger...: Infection occurs when the following conditions
                      hold: (Open for Read-Only + Close)
                          AND FileName[0..1]=='C:'
                          AND FileExt=='.AVR' AND File[0x48] != 0xE9
                          AND File[0x41..0x43]==0x000100
                          AND (File[0x3c..0x3d] & 0xf)==0
Storage media affected: Virus infects only files on disk drive C:
Interrupts hooked...: INT 21 (functions 3D00, 3E, 44A0)
Damage..............: Permanent Damage: none (except infection)
                      Transient Damage: An infected AVR module will
                      report correct result (whether a file being
                      scanned is infected or not) with a probability
                      1/4. In 3/4 of cases, it will report "not
                      infected" regardless on actual state. IN FACT,
                      due to a bug, an infected .AVR will always
                      report "not infected".
Damage Trigger......: (BIOS_TIMER_TICKS & 03) != 0
Particularities.....: 1) Stealth method: Recalculates the AVR checksum
                      for an infected file, to undergo AVR integrity
                      check.
                      2) Virus is distributed by dropper HORNS.COM.
                      3) AVR file format was used some time ago by some
                      scanners (e.g. TBScan) but is no longer used.
Similarities........: ---
-------------------- Agents -------------------------------------------
```

```
Countermeasures.....:
Countermeasures successful: None (at publication time)
Standard means......: Delete infected file, replace with clean file.
-------------------- Acknowledgement -----------------------------
Location............: Program Systems Institute, Russian Academy of
                      Sciences, Pereslavl-Zalessky, Russia
Classification by...: Dmitry O. Gryaznov
Documentation by....: Dmitry O. Gryaznov
                      Klaus Brunnstein (VTC, Virus Catalog entry)
Date................: 21-July-1993
Information Source..: Reverse analysis of virus code
```

Icelandic#1 Virus

```
Entry...............: Icelandic virus (Version #1)
Alias(es)...........: Disk-eating virus
Virus Strain........: Icelandic Virus
Virus detected when.: Mid-June '89
              where.: Iceland
Classification......: .EXE file infecting virus/Extending/Resident
Length of Virus.....: 1. 656-671 bytes added to file
                      2. 2048 bytes in RAM
-------------------- Preconditions -------------------------------
Operating System(s).: MS-DOS
Version/Release.....: 2.0 or higher
Computer model(s)...: IBM PC,XT,AT and compatibles
-------------------- Attributes ----------------------------------
Easy Identification.: .EXE Files: Infected files end in 18 44 19 5F (hex).
                      System: Byte at 0:37F contains FF (hex)
Type of infection...: Extends .EXE files. Adds 656-671 bytes to the end
                      of the file. Length MOD 16 will always be 0.
                      Stays resident in RAM, hooks INT 21 and infects
                      other programs when they are executed via function
                      4B. It will remove the Read-Only attribute if
                      necessary, but it is not replaced. .COM files are
                      not infected.
Infection Trigger...: Every tenth program run is checked. If it is an
                      uninfected .EXE file it will be infected.
Storage media affected: ---
Interrupts hooked...: INT 21
Damage..............: If the current drive is a hard disk larger than
                      10M bytes, the virus will select one cluster and
                      mark it as bad in the first copy of the FAT.
                      Diskettes and 10M byte disks are not affected.
Damage Trigger......: The damage is done whenever a file is infected.
Particularities.....: The virus modifies the MCBs in order to hide
                      from detection. It will not be activated if INT 13
                      contains something other than 0070:xxxx or
                      F000:xxxx when an infected program is run.
Similarities........: ---
-------------------- Agents --------------------------------------
Countermeasures.....: All programs which check for .EXE file length
                      changes will detect infections.
                      Any virus prevention program that changes INT 13
                      will prevent the activation of the virus.
                      F-SYSCHK (by the author of this article) will
                      detect the system infection.
                      F-FCHK (by the author of this article) will
```

```
                               identify infected files.
Countermeasures successful: F-SYSCHK, F-FCHK (from F.Skulason's
                            ANTIVIRUS package)
Standard means......: Use DEBUG to check the byte at 0:37F.
                            Running any program which stays resident and
                            modifies INT 13 (like PRINT) will prevent the
                            virus from being activated.
-------------------- Acknowledgement --------------------------------
Location............: University of Iceland/Computing Services
Classification by...: Fridrik Skulason  (frisk@rhi.hi.is)
Documentation by....: Fridrik Skulason
Date................: July 8, 1989
Information Source..:
```

Icelandic#2 Virus

```
Entry...............: Icelandic virus (Version #2)
Alias(es)...........:
Virus Strain........: Icelandic Virus
Virus detected when.: July 20 1989
            where.: Iceland
Classification......: .EXE file infecting virus/Extending/Resident
Length of Virus.....: 1. 632-647 bytes added to file
                      2. 2048 bytes in RAM
-------------------- Preconditions ----------------------------------
Operating System(s).: MS-DOS
Version/Release.....: 2.0 or higher
Computer model(s)...: IBM PC,XT,AT and compatibles
-------------------- Attributes -------------------------------------
Easy Identification.: .EXE Files: Infected files end in 18 44 19 5F (hex).
                      System: Byte at 0:37F contains FF (hex).
Type of infection...: Extends .EXE files. Adds 632-647 bytes to the end
                      of the file. Stays resident in RAM, hooks INT 21 and
                      infects other programs when they are executed via
                      function 4B. It will remove the Read-Only attribute if
                      necessary, but it is not restored.
                      .COM files are not infected.
Infection Trigger...: Every tenth program run is checked. If it is an
                      uninfected .EXE file it will be infected.
Storage media affected: ---
Interrupts hooked...: INT 21
Damage..............: none
Damage Trigger......:
Particularities.....: The virus modifies the MCBs in order to hide from
                      detection. The INT 13 checking in the Icelandic-1
                      has been removed. The virus uses the name of the
                      file to determine if it is an .EXE file, but not
                      the true type, as determined by the first 2 bytes.
                      The virus assumes the program reserves all available
                      memory (FFFF paragraphs needed). Programs that donot
                      will cause a system crash when infected and run.
                      This virus is a version of the Icelandic-1 virus,
                      modified so that it does not use INT 21 calls to DOS
                      services. This is done to bypass monitoring programs.
Similarities........:
-------------------- Agents -----------------------------------------
Countermeasures.....: All programs which check for .EXE file length
                      changes will detect infections.
```

```
Countermeasures successful:
                        Detection of infection:
                          F-FCHK (from F.Skulason's F-PROT package)
                          VIRUSCAN
                        Prevention of infection:    F-FCHK
                        Removal:                    F-FCHK
Standard means......: Use DEBUG to check the byte at 0:37F.
-------------------- Acknowledgement -------------------------------
Location............: University of Iceland/Computing Services
Classification by...: Fridrik Skulason  (frisk@rhi.hi.is)
Documentation by....: Fridrik Skulason
Date................: Sept 20, 1989
Information Source..:
```

Invisible Virus

```
Entry...............: Invisible Virus
Alias(es)...........: ---
Virus Strain........: ---
Virus detected when.: Spring 1993
            where.: Italy
Classification......: System (MBR) and File (COM,EXE) Infector,
                      memory resident, slightly tunnelling
Length of Virus.....: 1.Length (Byte) on storage medium:
                        1a. Length in COM files:       2926 Bytes
                        1b. Length in EXE files:       2926+15 Bytes
                        1c. Length of MBR:             7 sectors.
                      2.Length (Byte) in RAM:
                        2a. when loaded from file:     3456 bytes
                        2b. when loaded from MBR:      4096 bytes.
-------------------- Preconditions ---------------------------------
Operating System(s).: MSDOS
Version/Release.....:
Computer model(s)...: IBM PCs and compatibles
-------------------- Attributes ------------------------------------
Easy Identification.: ---
Type of infection...: File infection: virus infects COM and EXE files
                      if the normal way (appending).
                      Self-Identification in file: checksum
                      of entrypoint.
                      System infection: virus makes itself memory
                      resident, using TWIXT method when loaded from
                      a file, or TOP when loaded by MBR.
                      Self-Identification in memory: virus checks
                      for specila value in INT 21 register.
Infection Trigger...: Executing, opening, renaming or mode changing
                      a COM or EXE file; virus avoids certain files
                      by doing a checksum on the name.
Storage media affected: Infects MBR on disks, and COM or EXE files on
                      disk or diskette. Does NOT infect floppy boot
                      records.
Interrupts hooked...: INT 21 (functions 2521,3521,4B00,3D,43,56,1C)
                          (during boot from infected MBR only, later
                      unhooked)
Damage..............: Permanent Damage: Overwrites some files instead
                      of infecting.  The replacement code displays
                      some song lyrics (see below) and plays noise
                      on the speaker.
```

```
                       Transient Damage: Virus plays some noise on the
                       speaker. Trojanized files display message:
                                 "I'm the invisible man,
                                  I'm the invisible man,
                                  Incredible how you can
                                  See right through me.
                                  I'm the invisible man,
                                  I'm the invisible man,
                                  It's criminal how I can
                                  See right through you."
                       This text is encrypted in virus, but not in
                       Trojanized files.
Damage Trigger......: Permanent Damage: Complex and pseudo-random, but
                       becoming more likely with time-since-infection.
                       Transient Damage: Execution of trojanized file.
Particularities.....: 1) Not stealth, and only slightly tunnelling in
                       attempting to hide INT 21 being intercepted.
                       2) Mildly polymorphic both on files and MBR.
                       3) Virus contains the following text which is NOT
                       displayed: "The Invisible Man - Written in
                       SALERNO (ITALY), October 1992.  Dedicated to
                       Ester: I don't know how or when, but I will
                       hold you in my arms again.". Text encrypted.
INTERRUPTS_HOOKED: 21/2521, 21/3521, 21/4B00, 21/3D, 21/43, 21/56,
                       1C (during boot from infected MBR only, later
                       unhooked)
Similarities........: ---
-------------------- Agents ------------------------------------------
Countermeasures.....:
Countermeasures successful:
Standard means......:
-------------------- Acknowledgement ---------------------------------
Location............: IBM High Integrity Computing Lab, Hawthorne N.Y.
Classification by...: David M. Chess, IBM HICL
Documentation by....: David M. Chess, IBM HICL
                       Klaus Brunnstein (VTC, Virus Catalog entry)
Date................: 31-July-1993
Information Source..: Reverse analysis of virus code
```

Involuntary Virus

```
Entry...............: Involuntary Virus
Alias(es)...........: ---
Virus Strain........: ---
Virus detected when.: 1992
              where.: USA
Classification......: File and System virus (EXE, SYS infector),
                       encrypted, sometimes memory resident
Length of Virus.....: 1.Length (Byte) on media: 14xx bytes (see text)
                       2.Length (Byte) in RAM:
-------------------- Preconditions -----------------------------------
Operating System(s).: MSDOS
Version/Release.....:
Computer model(s)...: IBM PCs and Compatibles
-------------------- Attributes --------------------------------------
Easy Identification.: 1) No simple scan string is available for EXE files
                       due to the encryptive nature of the beast (but
                       24 bytes of the decryptor seem to be constant,
```

only filled with variable number of NOPs)

2) In memory (INT 21h handler) and SYS files, you can check for the following string:

```
3d 00 4b 74 03 e9 45 02 50 53
52 1e 06 b8 02 3d cd 21 73 03
```

Type of infection...: File infection: Upon infection (by appending virus' code), program entry is modified to point to the virus decryption code. File size will grow by 14xx bytes; size change can be observed with a DIR command (no stealth attempt made by virus).

When virus first activates, it will try to read C:\CONFIG.SYS file and look for device drivers to infect. It checks EXE victims fo 'MZ' signature, not for extension; therefore, any program loaded via 4B00 not having MZ signature is infected.

File access during infection is via handle-oriented DOS functions. If victim is write-protected, it will NOT be infected since virus does not attempt to clear the file attribute if a request to OPEN for READ/WRITE fails.

Self-Identification in files: Virus avoids multiple infections by checking: if difference between SS and SP fields in EXE header is =5Ch, then it assumes file already to be infected; otherwise, file will be infected now.

System infection: Virus becomes memory resident when activated from a device, but when in an EXE file, it functions as a non-resident SYS infector. When running an infected EXE, it looks around for SYS files to infect, but does not go resident. When booting with an infected SYS file in CONFIG.SYS, it goes resident and infects EXE files that are executed.

Self-Identification in memory: ?

Infection Trigger...: Execution of infected EXE files or booting from an infected SYS (see System infection).

Storage media affected: Disks

Interrupts hooked...: INT 21h via direct access to IVT; checks for AX = 4B00, LOAD/EXEC request.

Damage..............: Permanent Damage:

1) On trigger conditions (see below), virus displays following message:

"You have helped spread this virus
This has been a message from your friendly neighborhood infection service.
Thank you for your involuntary cooperation."

2) When having displayed the message, virus will overwrite the first 10 sectors of first FAT on C: using INT 26h (absolute disk write).

Transient Damage: ---

Damage Trigger......: Permanent Damage: 14th day of every month

Remark: David Chess reports a variant with trigger date = 19th any month.

Transient Damage: ---

Particularities.....: 1) This virus uses a crude 16-bit XOR type encryption routine to evade identification. Encryption key is obtained from BIOS timer (low word only). The decryption loop contains a bunch of

```
                              NOPs for confusion. The general routine used
                              for encryption is fixed; virus does not qualify
                              for fully polymorphic.
Similarities........: ---
-------------------- Agents --------------------------------------------
Countermeasures.....:
Countermeasures successful:
Standard means......: Delete infected files and replace with clean ones.
-------------------- Acknowledgement ----------------------------------
Location............: VDS Advanced Research Group, Baltimore, MD
Classification by...: Tarkan Yetiser <TYETISER@ssw02.ab.umd.edu>
Documentation by....: Tarkan Yetiser (in Virus-L: August 26, 1992)
                      David Chess IBM HICL (in Virus-L: Sept.2, 1992)
                      Klaus Brunnstein (CVC entry)
Date................: 31-July-1993
Information Source..: Virus-L (see authors)
```

Israeli-Virus

```
Entry...............: Israeli-Virus
Alias(es)...........: Jerusalem (A) ="Friday 13th" Virus
Virus Strain........: Israeli-Virus
Virus detected when.: December 1987
           where.: Hebrew University, Jerusalem, Israel
Classification......: Program Virus (extending), RAM-resident
                          overwriting under certain conditions.
Length of Virus.....: .COM files: length increases by 1813 bytes.
                      .EXE files: length increases by 1808-1823 bytes.
                           (.EXE file length must be a multiple of
                            16 bytes, as in any .EXE file)
-------------------- Preconditions ------------------------------------
Operating System(s).: MS-DOS
Version/Release.....: 2.xx upward
Computer model(s)...: IBM-PC, XT, AT and compatibles
-------------------- Attributes ---------------------------------------
Easy Identification.: Typical texts in Virus body (readable
                      with HexDump-facilities):
                      1. "MSDOS" and "COMMAND.COM" in the Data area
                      of the virus and
                      2. "MSDOS" are the last 5 bytes if the infected
                      program is a .COM file.
Type of infection...: System: infected if function E0h of INT 21h
                              returns value 0300h in the AX-register.
                      .Com files: program length increases by 1813
                              bytes if it is infected and the last 5
                              bytes are "MsDos" (identification). .COM
                              files are infected only once; COMMAND.COM
                              will not be infected.
                      .EXE files: program length increases by 1808
                              - 1823 bytes, and no identification is
                              used; therefore, .EXE files can be
                              infected more than once.
                              The virus uses the file length in the EXE
                              header to decide where to copy itself;
                              if this field contains a value smaller
                              than the actual length of the file,
                              then the virus will *overwrite* the file
                              instead of extending it!
Infection Trigger...: Programs are infected at load time (using the
```

```
                          function Load/Execute of MS-DOS).
Interrupts hooked...: INT21h, INT08h
Damage.............: Permanent Damage: On every "Friday the 13th",
                          every loaded program is deleted.
                     Transient Damage: On every other day, after 30
                          minutes a loop is bound into the
                          operating system, which slows the
                          system; At this moment, a 12-by-12
                          region of the screen is scrolled up by
                          two lines, leaving a black 2-by-12
                          rectangle on the screen.
Damage Trigger......: Every time the system is infected, one of the
                     damages will be used.
Particularities.....: 1. .COM files larger than 63.466 bytes are no
                          longer loadable after infection.
                     2. .COM files larger than 63.723 bytes are
                          destroyed by overwriting.
                     3. .EXE files can be infected many times.
                     4. Three functions used by Novell Netware 4.0
                     can't be used.
-------------------- Agents --------------------------------------
Countermeasures.....: Category 3: ANTIIS#1.EXE (VTC Hamburg)
                     Remark: 1) The well-known UnVirus (developed at
                          Hebrew University) safely detects and
                          disinfects this virus (plus 5 more).
                             2) Several Antiviruses do not work safe,
                          e.g. M-JRUSLM (McAfee) destroys 10%
                          of the .EXE-files during disinfection.
Countermeasures successful: ANTIIS#1.EXE is an antivirus that only
                     looks for the Israeli Virus and, if requested,
                     will restore the file.
Standard means......: ---
-------------------- Acknowledgement ------------------------------
Location............: Virus Test Center, University of Hamburg, Germany
Classification by...: Thomas Lippke, Michael Reinschmiedt
Documentation by....: Michael Reinschmiedt, Thomas Lippke
                     Morton Swimmer
Date................: July 15, 1989
Updates by..........: Y.Radai, Hebrew University, August 31, 1989
```

Joshi Virus

```
Entry...............: Joshi Virus
Alias(es)...........: Joshua Virus
Virus Strain........: ----
Virus detected when.: ?
              where.: India, Germany
Classification......: Master Bootsector and Bootsector Virus,
                     memory resident, stealth
Length of Virus.....: 4 KByte
-------------------- Preconditions --------------------------------
Operating System(s).: MS-DOS
Version/Release.....: any
Computer model(s)...: IBM - PC, XT, AT, upward and compatibles
-------------------- Attributes -----------------------------------
Easy Identification.: CHKDSK will report 6KB memory less than
                     installed.
                     On hard disks, the Master Bootsector contains
```

```
                             EB 1F 90 as first Bytes; at end of sector 3
                             and beginning of sector 4 on track 0, string
                             "Type Happy Birthday Joshi" can be found.
Type of infection...:        Hard disk: Master Bootsector will be infected;
                             the original Master-Bootsector will be saved
                             in sector 9. The virus resides on track 0,
                             sectors 1-8.
                             Floppy-Disk: Bootsector will be infected; the
                             original Bootsector will be saved on additio-
                             nal track 40/80 in sector 9. Virus resides
                             on track 40/80 in sectors 2 to 6. On 720 kB
                             diskettes, virus will overwrite original
                             data on track 40.
Infection Trigger...:        Actions: Read, write, verify track 0/sector 1
Storage Media affected:      Any hard disk, any floppy
Infection targets:..:        Hard disk Master Bootrecord; Floppy Bootrecord
Interrupts hooked...:        INT 8, INT 9, INT 13h, INT 21h
Interrupts used.....:        INT 8, INT 9, INT 10H, INT 13h, INT 19h
Damage..............:        Permanent damage: on 720 kByte floppies,
                             original data on track 40 will be overwrit-
                             ten during infection.
                             Transient damage: virus displays message
                             "Type Happy Birthday Joshi".
Damage Trigger......:        On January 5th, a DOS call (INT 21h) of any
                                of the following functions
                                - 48h (memory allocation)
                                - 49h (free allocated memory block)
                                - 4Ah (resize allocated memory block)
                                - 2Ah (get date)
                                - 2Bh (set date)
                                - 2Ch (get time)
                                - 2Dh (set time)
Particularities.....:        1) Joshi prevents being overwritten by the
                             STONED-virus
                             2) With Hercules graphic cards, problems may
                             occur as JOSHI does not save Hercules screen
                             memory.
-------------------- Agents -----------------------------------------------
Countermeasures.....:        According to their documentation, many antivirus
                             products claim to recognise/eradicate virus.
-ditto- successful..:        Tested: Dr.Solomon's Toolkit 4.15,
                             Fridrik Skulason's F-PROT 2.04a,
                             H&B-EDV Antivir-IV 4.03 and McAfee Scan93.
Standard means......:        1) Reboot from clean bootdisk.
                             2) Use SYS-Command to reinstall BOOT sector on
                             floppies.
                             3) Use FDISK /MBR to reinstall Master-BOOT
                             sector on Harddisk (MS-DOS 5.0 only).
-------------------- Acknowledgement --------------------------------------
Location............:        Virus Test Center, University of Hamburg, Germany
Classification by...:        Torsten Dargers, Ulf Heinemann
Documentation by....:        Torsten Dargers, Ulf Heinemann
Date................:        26-June-1992
```

Junior Virus

```
Entry...............:        Junior Virus
Alias(es)...........:        ---
```

```
Virus Strain........: ---
Virus detected when.: July, 1992
           where.: Sofia, Bulgaria
Classification......: Memory resident, appending, COM file infector
Length of Virus.....: 234 bytes
-------------------- Preconditions ------------------------------------
Operating System(s).: PC/MS-DOS. Uses several undocumented and version-
                      dependent tricks. Does not work under DR-DOS.
Version/Release.....: Works under PC-DOS 3.30. Haven't checked for other
                      versions.
Computer model(s)...: Any MS-DOS computer
-------------------- Attributes ---------------------------------------
Easy Identification.: ---
Self Identification.: The first instruction of infected files is a JMP
                      which points at 56 bytes before end of file.
Type of infection...: Any executable file, the first 2 bytes of which
                      are not 'MZ' or 0C4h. Virus is appended to file.
Infection Trigger...: Execution of a file.
Storage media affected: Any storage media with MS-DOS compatible file
                      system.
Interrupts hooked...: INT 78h, 21h, 24h (only during infection),
                      INT 13h (only during infection, and only if it
                      is not already intercepted).
Damage..............: ---
Damage Trigger......: ---
Particularities.....: The virus traps INT 21h/AX=4B00h in a very unusual
                      way. It puts an INT 78h instruction at
                      TerminateAddress-2 and intrcepts INT 78h itself.
Similarities........: ---
-------------------- Agents -------------------------------------------
Countermeasures.....: Any up-to-date scanner; any integrity checker.
                      Monitoring programs which trap only INT 13h may
                      not be able to detect the virus.
Countermeasures successful: ---
Standard means......: Delete infected files, restore clean copies.
-------------------- Acknowledgement ----------------------------------
Location............: Virus Test Center, University of Hamburg, Germany
Classification by...: Vesselin Bontchev
Documentation by....: Vesselin Bontchev
Date................: 10-August-1992
Information Source..: Reverse analysis of virus code
```

Kampana Virus

```
Entry..............: Kampana Virus
Alias(es)..........: Telefonica = Spanish Telecom Virus
Virus Strain.......: Kampana Virus Strain
Virus detected when.: December 1990
           where.: Spain
Classification......: Program Virus: memory-resident, self-encrypting
                      appending COM infector, stealth
Length of virus.....: 1) Length on media: 3700 bytes
                      2) Length in RAM:   3700 bytes
Variants............:
-------------------- Preconditions ------------------------------------
Operating system(s).: MS-DOS
Version/release.....: 2.0 and higher
Computer model(s)...: All MS-DOS machines
```

```
-------------------- Attributes -----------------------------------------
Easy identification.: The following text can be found in memory:
           "Virus Anti - C.T.N.E. (c)1990 Grupo Holokausto.",0h,
           "Kampanya Anti-Telefonica. Menos tarifas y mas servicio.",0h,
           "Programmed in Barcelona (Spain). 23-8-90. - 666 -",0h
Type of infection...: Self-Identification: The time stamp of an
                     infected file is changedby adding 200 to actual
                     year (19xx ==> 21xx); this will not be
                     visible when virus is resident.
                     When executing an infected file, virus will
                     decrypt and install itself resident in memory.
                     Subsequently, Kampana Boot Virus is installed
                     on hard disk (see Kampana Boot).
                     A previously non-infected .COM file is infected
                     when virus is memory-resident by appending the
                     viral code to it; small COM files (size<128)
                     and large COM files (size>=61000 bytes) are not
                     infected.
Infection trigger...: Execution of a .COM-file (but not IBM*.COM
                     or ??MAND*.COM), this is
Storage media affected: Files on all media. (See boot-virus, too.)
Interrupts hooked...: INT21h only.
Damage..............: Permanent Damage: Kampana Virus overwrites HD
                              boot sector with Kampana Boot.
Damage trigger......: Permanent Damage: accessing a file on disk.
Particularities.....: The virus ignores all attributes of a file.
                     It encryptes itself in a file using two
                     different techniques, including many changes
                     of dummy bytes to reduce the length of scan
                     strings; it looks for interrupts 13h, 21h,
                     40h to access BIOS and DOS directly; if file-
                     length is looked for, virus displays original
                     length of an infected file.
-------------------- Agents ---------------------------------------------
Countermeasures.....: Very difficult because of encryption and stealth!
Countermeasures successful: ---
Standard means......: FindViru, F-Prot and Scan (etc)
-------------------- Acknowledgement ------------------------------------
Location............: Virus Test Center, University of Hamburg, Germany
Classification by...: Daniel Loeffler
Documentation by....: Daniel Loeffler
Date................: January 25, 1993
Information Source..: Reverse-Engineering of virus code
```

Kampana Boot Virus

```
Entry...............: Kampana Boot Virus
Alias(es)...........: Antitelefonica = Antitel Boot Virus
Virus Strain........: Kampana Virus Strain
Virus detected when.: Summer 1991
            where.: Spain
Classification......: Boot Virus, memory resident, stealth
Length of virus.....: 1) Length in memory: 1024 bytes
                     2) Lenght on media:  1024 bytes = 2 sectors
-------------------- Preconditions --------------------------------------
Operating system(s).: MS-DOS
Version/release.....: 2.0 and higher
Computer model(s)...: All MS-DOS machines
```

```
-------------------- Attributes ----------------------------------------
Easy identification.: Start of infected boot-sector contains empty
                      entries (8*" ") as manufacturer-ID  and DOS-ID.
                      This is readable ONLY if booted from a clean
                      disk.
Type of infection...: Self-Identification: Word 9EBCh at offset 4Ah in
                      the infected boot-sector (=location where
                      the encrypted message starts)
                      Hard disk #1 infected by Kampana file virus:
                      boot virus is written to HD position at
                      head 0, track 0, sector 1 and 6; the old
                      boot sector is moved to sector 7.
                      The virus will enter at top of memory during
                      boot process and will intercept INT13h.
Infection trigger...: Every access to a non-write-protected diskette
                      will infect it (via INT 13h).
Storage media affected: FD in drive A: and B:
Interrupts hooked...: INT13h
Damage..............: Permanent damage: virus writes garbage
                      (from 0000:0000h) to all sectors on all floppy
                      disk drives (or harddisks) many times.
                      Transient damage: Virus displays the text:
                      "Campaña Anti-TELEFONICA (Barcelona)",0ah,0dh
Damage trigger......: Every 400th boot.
Particularities.....: Virus intercepts INT13h to control any access
                      to itself, so the original content is displayed.
                      Changed content is displayed ONLY if booted
                      from a clean disk.
-------------------- Agents ------------------------------------------
Countermeasures.....: Very difficult because of encryption / stealth!
Countermeasures successful: ---
Standard means......: FindViru, F-Prot, Scan (etc)
-------------------- Acknowledgement ---------------------------------
Location............: Virus Test Center, University of Hamburg, Germany
Classification by...: Daniel Loeffler
Documentation by....: Daniel Loeffler
Date................: January 25, 1993
Information Source..: Reverse-Engineering of virus code
```

Keypress Virus

```
Entry...............: Keypress Virus
Alias(es)...........: ---
Virus Strain........: ---
Virus detected when.: January 1991 (when VTC received virus copy)
            where.: Frankfurt    (in an international hotel)
Classification......: Program virus (extending), RAM-resident
Length of Virus.....: .COM-file length increased by 1232-1247 bytes;
                      .EXE-file length increased by 1472-1487 bytes.
-------------------- Preconditions ------------------------------------
Operating System(s).: MS-DOS
Version/Release.....: 2.xx upward
Computer model(s)...: IBM - PC, XT, AT and compatibles
-------------------- Attributes ---------------------------------------
Easy Identification.: Typical text in virus body (readable with
                      HexDump-utilities): ".COM",00h,".EXE",00h
Type of infection...: System: RAM-resident, infected if the word
                      0001h is found at position 0000h:0600h.
```

```
                          .COM - Files: if DOS version>=3.00 then ex-
                          tended by using EXEC-function else ex-
                          tended by using open file function and no
                          system file infection. Only files with length
                          from 1217 to 64064 bytes can be infected;
                          files may only be infected once.
                          .EXE - Files: if DOS version>=3.00 then extended
                          by using EXEC-function else extended by using
                          open file function and no system file infec-
                          tion; files may only be infected once.
Infection Trigger...: When function 4B00h (EXEC), or function 3D0x
                          (open file) of INT 21h is called.
Interrupts hooked...: INT 21h and INT 1Ch always; INT 23h and INT 24h
                          during infection.
Damage.............: Transient damage: every 10 minutes, the virus
                          will look at INT 09h (keyboard interrupt) for
                          2 seconds; if a keystroke is recognized
                          during this time, it will be repeated depend-
                          ing on how long the key is pressed; it thus
                          appears as a "bouncing key".
                          Permanent damage: ---
Particularities.....: Date and time of last file modification is set
                          to the current date.
                          .COM files longer than 64032 bytes are no longer
                          loadable.
-------------------- Agents -------------------------------------------
Countermeasures.....: ---
- ditto - successful: ---
Standard means......: Notice file length.
                          Notice date and time of last file modification.
-------------------- Acknowledgement ---------------------------------
Location............: Virus Test Center, University of Hamburg, Germany
Classification by...: Thomas Lippke
Documentation by....: Thomas Lippke
Date................: 10-February-1991
```

Last-Year Virus

```
Entry...............: Last-Year Virus
Alias(es)...........: ---
Virus Strain........: ---
Virus detected when.:
             where.:
Classification......: File virus(appending COM infector),memory resident
Length of Virus.....: 1.Length (Byte) on storage medium: 604 Bytes
                       2.Length (Byte) in RAM:            880 Bytes
-------------------- Preconditions -----------------------------------
Operating System(s).: MSDOS
Version/Release.....:
Computer model(s)...: IBM PCs and compatibles
-------------------- Attributes --------------------------------------
Easy Identification.: ---
Type of infection...: Self-Identification methods:
                       File infection: infects COM files by appending
                          it's code. For self-identification, tests
                          whether 4th and 5th byte is "88 31".
                       System infection: virus makes itself memory
                          resident via TWIXT method. For self-identi-
                          fication, virus checvks whether 2 bytes
```

```
                            before the byte that the INT21 vector points
                            to are "61 6D". Can therefore load more than
                            once if another INT21-hooker intervenes.
Infection Trigger...: Finding an executable file and if DS:DX ends
                            in "COM".
Storage media affected:
Interrupts hooked...: Int 21: functions 4B, 0A, 2A
Damage..............: Permanent Damage: none
                            Transient Damage: INT21 handler subtracts one
                             from the year on INT21/2A (Get Date) calls.
Damage Trigger......: Permanent Damage: none
                            Transient Damage: Always
Particularities.....: 1) No side effects, except transient damage and
                            usual MCB-munging due to TWIXT method.
                            2) Virus code is rather explicit in handling
                            (ignoring) write-protect errors in INT 24
                            handler but coding of INT 21 handler shows
                            some unused flag; potentially more variants
                            are intended.
Similarities........: ---
-------------------- Agents --------------------------------------------
Countermeasures.....: Not tested
Countermeasures successful: Not tested
Standard means......:
-------------------- Acknowledgement -----------------------------------
Location............: IBM High Integrity Computing Lab, Hawthorne, N.Y.
Classification by...: David Chess, IBM HICL
Documentation by....: David Chess, IBM HICL (CAROBase entry)
                            Klaus Brunnstein, VTC (Virus catalog entry)
Date................: June 24, 1993
Information Source..: Reverse analysis of virus code
```

Lehigh Virus

```
Entry...............: Lehigh Virus
Alias(es)...........: ---
Virus strain........: ---
Virus detected when.: November 1987
             where.: Lehigh University (Bethlehem/USA)
Classification......: System virus (COMMAND.COM), RAM-resident
Length of virus.....: 555 bytes
-------------------- Preconditions -------------------------------------
Operating system(s).: MS-DOS
Version/release.....: 2.0 and higher
Computer model(s)...: All MS-DOS machines
-------------------- Attributes ----------------------------------------
Easy identification.: Last two bytes of COMMAND.COM = A9h 65h,
                            COMMAND.COM grows by 555 bytes.
Type of infection...: COMMAND.COM only (stack space at end of file
                            overwritten); RAM resident (no check if
                            RAM infected before).
Infection trigger...: Uninfected COMMAND.COM in the root directory of
                            used or current drive (checked by INT 21h)
Storage media affected: Any COMMAND.COM on hard disk or diskette.
Interrupts hooked...: INT 21h: Ah = 4Bh(load) and Ah = 4E(find file)
                            INT 44H: Set as old INT 21h
Damage..............: If A: or B: selected (if it is not the current
                            drive), then sector 1 to 32 are overwritten
                            with garbage read from BIOS and print-text
```

```
                             (also from BIOS).
Damage trigger......: Infection counter = 4
Particularities.....: Not hardware-dependent: INT 21h, 26h used only
Similarities........: ---
------------------- Agents -----------------------------------------
Countermeasures.....: ---
Countermeasures successful: Several antiviruses (McAfee, Solomon,
                           Skulason et.al.) successfully detect and
                           eradicate this virus.
Standard means......: ---
------------------- Acknowledgement --------------------------------
Location............: Virus Test Center, University of Hamburg, Germany
Classification by...: Daniel Loeffler (disassembly by Joe Hirst)
Documentation by....: Daniel Loeffler
Date................: December 18, 1989
Information Source..: ---
```

"Lehigh" Virus

```
Entry...............: "Lehigh" Virus
Alias(es)...........: ---
Virus strain........: ---
Virus detected when.: November 1987
            where.: Lehigh University (Bethlehem/USA)
Classification......: System virus (COMMAND.COM), RAM-resident
Length of virus.....: 555 bytes
------------------- Preconditions ----------------------------------
Operating system(s).: MS-DOS
Version/release.....: 2.0 and higher
Computer model(s)...: All MS-DOS machines
------------------- Attributes -------------------------------------
Easy identification.: Last two bytes of COMMAND.COM = A9h 65h;
                      text found: ":\command.com".
Type of infection...: COMMAND.COM only (stack space at end of file
                      overwritten); RAM resident (no check if
                      RAM infected before).
Infection trigger...: Uninfected COMMAND.COM in the root directory of
                      used or current drive (checked by INT 21h)
Storage media affected: Any COMMAND.COM on hard disk or diskette.
Interrupts hooked...: INT 21h; INT 44h (Set as old INT 21h).
Damage..............: If A: or B: selected (if it is not the current
                      drive), then sector 1 to 32 are overwritten
                      with garbage read from BIOS and print-text
                      (also from BIOS).
Damage trigger......: Infection counter = 4
Particularities.....: Not hardware-dependent: INT 21h, 26h used only
Similarities........: ---
------------------- Agents -----------------------------------------
Countermeasures.....: ---
Countermeasures successful: Several antiviruses (McAfee, Solomon,
                           Skulason et.al.) successfully detect and
                           eradicate this virus.
Standard means......: ---
------------------- Acknowledgement --------------------------------
Location............: Virus Test Center, University of Hamburg, Germany
Classification by...: Daniel Loeffler (disassembly by Joe Hirst)
Documentation by....: Daniel Loeffler
Date................: June 30, 1990
Information Source..: ---
```

Leningrad.543 Virus

```
Entry...............: Leningrad.543 Virus
Standard CARO name..: Leningrad.543
Alias(es)...........: Sov1, Sov-543, USSR-543, C-543, PANIKER
Virus Strain........: Leningrad virus strain
Virus detected when.: Mid 1990
            where.: Leningrad (St.Petersburg), Russia (ex USSR)
Classification......: Non-resident program (COM) infector
Length of Virus.....: COM files increased by 543 bytes
-------------------- Preconditions ---------------------------------
Operating System(s).: MS-DOS
Version/Release.....: 2.xx upward
Computer model(s)...: IBM-PC, XT, AT and compatibles
-------------------- Attributes ------------------------------------
Wasy Identification.: Infected files contain strings "*.COM", "PATH="
                      and "That could be a crash, crash, crash !".
Type of infection...: Virus searches path and current directory. It
                      infects using standard DOS INT 21h calls.
Infection Trigger...: Any start of an infected file.
Storage media affected: Hard disk, any floppy disk
Interrupts hooked...: ---
Damage..............: Transient damage: Upon starting an infected pro-
                      gram on a Friday 13th, the virus will display
                      "That could be a crash, crash, crash !"
                      Permanent damage: an infected files may grow
                      > 64KB, so it cannot be started afterwards.
Damage Trigger......: Any Friday 13th.
Particularities.....: ---
Similarities........: Leningrad.600 = Sov2 virus
-------------------- Agents ----------------------------------------
Countermeasures successful:McAfee Scan,Skulason F-PROT,Solomon FINDVIRU
Standard means......: Delete infected COM files, copy uninfected
                      versions from original write protected disk.
-------------------- Acknowledgement -------------------------------
Location............: Virus Test Center, University of Hamburg, Germany
Classification by...: Torsten Dargers
Documentation by....: Dr. Eldar Musaev, Leningrad, Russia
Date................: 07-July-1992
Information Source..: ----
```

"Lisbon Virus"

```
Entry...............: "Lisbon" Virus
Alias(es)...........: ---
Virus strain........: Vienna Virus strain
Virus detected when.: ---
            where.: ---
Classification......: Program virus (extending), direct action
Length of virus.....: 648 bytes
-------------------- Preconditions ---------------------------------
Operating system(s).: MS-DOS
Version/release.....: 2.0 and higher
Computer model(s)...: All MS-DOS machines
-------------------- Attributes ------------------------------------
Easy identification.: Last five bytes of file = "@AIDS" (Ascii)
Type of infection...: Self-Identification: The time stamp of an
                        infected file is changed: the seconds are
```

```
                         set to 62 (= 2 * 1Fh).
                         When infected file is executed, .COM-files
                         in the current directory as well as in the
                         directories in the DOS-PATH are extended
                         by appending the viral code; no infection if
                         the file size<10 or file size>64000 bytes.
Infection trigger...: A selected .COM-file is infected by "random" IF
                         (system seconds AND 58h) <> 0 ELSE damaged!
Storage media affected: Current media and media accessed via DOS-PATH.
Interrupts hooked...: --
Damage..............: A selected .COM-file is damaged permanently:
                         Overwriting the first five bytes by "@AIDS"
Damage trigger......: IF (system seconds AND 58h) = 0, ELSE infection!
Particularities.....: The virus ignores READ-ONLY and HIDDEN attributes.
Similarities........: Dissimilarities to Vienna:
                         Different trigger byte (7);
                         the five damage bytes are changed.
-------------------- Agents -------------------------------------------
Countermeasures.....: Category 3: ANTI!LIS.EXE (d:) (/f)
Countermeasures successful: My Antivirus ANTI!LIS.EXE looks for
                         infected files on a given drive (d:) and
                         optionally removes the virus (if /f given).
Standard means......: ---
-------------------- Acknowledgement ----------------------------------
Location............: Virus Test Center, University of Hamburg, Germany
Classification by...: Daniel Loeffler
Documentation by....: Daniel Loeffler
Date................: June 5, 1990
Information Source..: ---
```

Little_Red Virus

```
Entry...............: Little_Red Virus
Alias(es)...........: ---
Virus Strain........: ---
Virus detected when.: Summer 1993
            where.: Sydney University, Australia
                         (presumably Chinese origin)
Classification......: File virus (COM,EXE infector), memory resident,
                         limited stealth, partly encrypted
Length of Virus.....: 1.Length (Byte) on media: 1465 Bytes
                         2.Length (Byte) in RAM:
-------------------- Preconditions ------------------------------------
Operating System(s).: MSDOS
Version/Release.....:
Computer model(s)...: IBM PCs and Compatibles
-------------------- Attributes ---------------------------------------
Easy Identification.:
Type of infection...: File infection: Virus infects all files loaded by
                         DOS function 4B ("Load & Execute"), and one COM
                         or .EXE file on each DIR command. Virus in-
                         creases length of infected files by 1465 bytes.
                         This increase in length is hidden from DIR, but
                         programs which use DOS functions 4E & 4F will
                         reveal the change in length.  Top of memory is
                         set down from A000 to 9F30.
                         Encryption: two small sections of virus are en-
                         crypted, using a fixed key (easy to detect).
```

```
                         Self-Identification in file:
                         System infection: upon starting an infected file,
                         virus makes itself memory resident.
                         Self-Identification in memory: virus uses DOS
                         function 30 (get version) for self-recognition,
                         and returns a particular value if resident.
Infection Trigger...: Starting an infected program.
Storage media affected: Disk
Interrupts hooked...:
Damage.............: Permanent Damage: No intended permanent damage.
                         Side effects: during test, author experienced
                         damage of COMMAND.COM, thus preventing booting.
                         Transient Damage: no visible messages, but virus
                         contains 2 tunes, with separate trogger:
                         1) A song named after the town where Mao
                            Tse Tung was born, and
                         2) a Chinese patriotic song called
                            Dong Fong Hong (or Mao's song);
                         3) Virus slows systems (disk activities).
Damage Trigger......: Permanent Damage: ---
                         Transient Damage: Both tunes are played on a
                         given day, from 1994 onward, starting one
                         hour after virus' activation and then
                         played continously. Date trigger conditions:
                         1) Tune #1 played on each December 26,
                            from 1994 onward; this is Mao's birthday
                            where it is traditionally sung in China;
                         2) Tune #2 is played on September 9th, from
                            1994; on this day, Mao died.
Particularities.....: Virus author has gone to some trouble to try to
                         make virus inconspicuous until Sept 1994, but
                         the decision to check files accessed by DOS
                         functions 11 & 12 (the old style Find first
                         and find next, used by DIR) causes obvious
                         additional disk activity.  In a test on an XT,
                         it took over 5 secs to do a DIR of a disk with
                         21 files, all infected, whereas this took only
                         2.1 secs when virus was not active.
Similarities........: ---
-------------------- Agents -----------------------------------------
Countermeasures.....:
Countermeasures successful:
Standard means......: Delete infected files and replace with clean ones.
-------------------- Acknowledgement --------------------------------
Location............: CYBEC Pty, Hampton Victoria/Australia
Classification by...: Roger Riordan (riordan.cybec@mhs.oz.au>
Documentation by....: Roger Riordan
                         Klaus Brunnstein (CVC entry)
Date................: 31-July-1993
Information Source..: Analysis of Virus
```

Loren Virus

```
Entry...............: Loren Virus
Alias(es)...........: ---
Virus Strain........: ---
Virus detected when.: Summer 1993
            where.: Australia (high school)
```

```
Classification......: File virus (COM,EXE infector), memory resident
Length of Virus.....: 1.Length (Byte) on media: 1387 Bytes
                      2.Length (Byte) in RAM:
-------------------- Preconditions ------------------------------------
Operating System(s).: MS DOS
Version/Release.....:
Computer model(s)...: IBM PCs and Compatibles
-------------------- Attributes ---------------------------------------
Easy Identification.:
Type of infection...: File infection: virus infects .COM & .EXE files,
                      increasing length by 1387 bytes, by appending
                      itself to the end of the file; first 5 bytes of
                      COM files are saved, and replaced with a jump
                      to the virus, followed by a signature. It in-
                      fects all files opened for execution, and all
                      COM & EXE files referenced by INT 21 (functions
                      11&12, Find First & Find Next). As these are
                      used by DIR command, if virus is in memory,
                      DIR will infect all .COM or .EXE files opened.
                      Stealth: handler for INT 21 (fct 11&12) contains
                      code to fake file size, so that DIR does NOT
                      not reveal the increase in file length.
                      Due to interception of INT 24, critical errors
                      are not reported. An infected file's date,
                      time & attributes are preserved, and R/O files
                      are infected.
                      Self-Identification in files: virus checks bytes
                      3 & 4 in COM files, which are set to 52 43
                      ('RC'); in infected EXE file, CRC field in
                      header is set to sum of initial CS and IP
                      fields plus 1b3.
                      System infection: when an infected file is run,
                      virus decodes a block containing the recovery
                      information, and then issues INT 1. If virus
                      is already active this is intercepted, and
                      interrupt handler restores the file and runs
                      it.  Otherwise the virus reduces the size of
                      last memory block by 60h paras, and copies
                      itself to offset 40h in block thus reserved.
                      Self-Identification in memory: test INT 1 values.
Infection Trigger...: Execution of an infected file, and after infec-
                      tion of memory, any use of INT 21 function 4B00
                      (Find First/Find Last), e.g. issuing a DIR
                      command.
Storage media affected:
Interrupts hooked...: INT 21 functions 11, 12, 4B00, & B5; INT 24.
Damage..............: Permanent Damage: Upon trigger condition, virus
                      attempts to format cylinder zero, head zero,
                      on drive C.  If this fails, virus then tries
                      drives A, then B.  If it succeeds in formatting
                      any drive, it gives a message (see Transient
                      Damage) and then resets the counter.
                      Transient Damage: if virus succeeded in formatting
                      any drive, it issues the message:
                        "Your disk is formated by the LOREN virus.
                         Written by Nguyen Huu Giap.
                         Le Hong Phong School *** 8-3-1992"
                      Then, the damage counter is set to zero.
and then resets the infection counter.
Damage Trigger......: Permanent Damage: virus counts number of files
```

```
                          infected after last boot; upon counter=20,
                          Permanent Damage function is triggered.
                          Transient Damage: this is triggered upon success-
                          ful completion of the Permanent Damage.
Particularities.....: 1) As damage counter is reset when virus is loaded
                          into memory, damage function (payload) will
                          only be triggered if 20 files are infected in
                          a single session. This may easily be achieved
                          using multiple DIRs.
                          2) Message (see Transient Damage) is encrypted.
Similarities........: ---
-------------------- Agents ---------------------------------------
Countermeasures.....:
Countermeasures successful:
Standard means......: Delete infected files and replace with clean ones.
-------------------- Acknowledgement -------------------------------
Location............: CYBEC Pty, Hampton Victoria/Australia
Classification by...: Roger Riordan (riordan.cybec@mhs.oz.au>
Documentation by....: Roger Riordan
                          Klaus Brunnstein (CVC entry)
Date................: 31-July-1993
Information Source..: Analysis of Virus
```

LoveChild Trojan

```
Entry...............: LoveChild Trojan Horse
Alias(es)...........: ---
Virus Strain........: Lovechild Strain
Virus detected when.:
              where.:
Classification......: Trojan Horse
Length of Trojan....: 64 Bytes
-------------------- Preconditions ----------------------------------
Operating System(s).: MS-DOS
Version/Release.....: all DOS-versions
Computer model(s)...: IBM-PC, XT, AT and compatibles
-------------------- Attributes -------------------------------------
Easy Identification.: Text "LoveChild in reward for software sealing."
                          is contained within the file.
                          The trojan has a lenght of 64 bytes.
Scanner Signature...: 4C 6F 76 65 43 68 69 6C 64 20 69 6E 20 72
Type of infection...: This trojan is installed by LoveChild virus.
Infection Trigger...: ---
Storage media affected: The first harddisk.
Interrupts hooked...: ---
Damage..............: Trojan writes garbage onto the first harddisk,
                          starting with track 0 and using the first
                          4 heads. This trojan counts through all
                          tracks, overwriting each, until the harddisk
                          is completely thrashed.
Damage Trigger......: Execution of the trojan.
Particularities.....: See: LoveChild Virus (Computer Virs Catalog)
Similarities........: ---
-------------------- Agents ----------------------------------------
Countermeasures.....: Scan v80 by McAfee finds this trojan.
Countermeasures successful: Clean v80 by McAfee deletes this trojan.
Standard means......: Delete infected files, copy uninfected versions
                          from original write-protected disk.
```

```
-------------------- Acknowledgement -------------------------------
Location............: Virus Test Center, University of Hamburg, Germany
Classification by...: Toralv Dirro, Gerald Schrod
Documentation by....: Toralv Dirro, Gerald Schrod
Date................: 15-July-1991
Information Source..: ---
```

LoveChild Virus

```
Entry...............: LoveChild Virus
Alias(es)...........: ---
Virus Strain........: ---
Virus detected when.:
            where.:
Classification......: Memory-resident Program Infector (COM)
Length of Virus.....: COM-files: 488 Bytes
-------------------- Preconditions ---------------------------------
Operating System(s).: MS-DOS
Version/Release.....: Version 3.30 (all other versions crash)
Computer model(s)...: IBM-PC, XT, AT and compatibles
-------------------- Attributes ------------------------------------
Easy Identification.: The text "(c) Flu Systems (R)" and "LoveChild in
                      reward for software sealing.." can be found at
                      the end of infected COM-files as well as in
                      memory at the adress 0:1e0.
Scanner Signature...: 4C 6F 76 65 43 68 69 6C 64 20 69 6E 20 72
Type of infection...: The virus appends itself to the end of COM-files;
                      first 3 bytes are saved und used for it's
                      identification-byte ($fb) and a jump; these
                      will be restored after execution of virus.
Infection Trigger...: Execution of an infected program.
Storage media affected: Files can be infected on all media.
Interrupts hooked...: INT 21, functions 4b (open/execute)
                                        3d (open with handle)
                                        56 (rename)
                                        3c (create file)
                                        40 (write to file)
                      are used to infect com-files and for the
                      effects (see: particularities).
Damage..............:Permanent damage:
                      1) If an EXE-file is write-accessed (INT 21,
                      ah=40), virus reads a random number and some-
                      times rewrites the file with a trojan horse.
                      If the trojan is executed, it will write gar-
                      bage to harddisk on first four heads, star-
                      ting with track 0 and continuing until reset!
                      (for description of the trojan: see Virus
                      Catalog entry of LoveChild Trojan)
                      2) If a file is created (INT 21,ah=3c), virus
                      sometimes (randomly) decides to call INT 21,
                      ah=39, thus creating a subdirctory instead.
                      3) If a file which is not a COM-file is opened,
                      renamed or executed (ah=3d/56/4b), virus
                      sometimes (randomly) calls INT 21, ah=41,
                      thus deleting the entire file.
                      Transient damage: ---
Damage Trigger......: 1) Any Write-to-a-file operation (e.g. copying)
                      2) Create-a-file operation
```

```
                     3) Open or execute non-COM-files or rename file.
                     A random number is used to decide wether to per-
                     form the respective damage or not.
Particularities.....: Due to an error in the virus, it will crash on
                     all versions other than MS-DOS 3.30; this is
                     probably due to unsufficient testing; change
                     of one byte only allows virus to run on all
                     DOS versions available.
                     On MS-DOS 3.30, the virus rewrites INT 13; there-
                     fore, any protection-software hooking INT 13
                     is deactivated. Virus doesn't hook INT 21
                     directly; it tries to hide, by installing a
                     jump to itself within the INT 21-routine.
                     On other DOS-versions, virus hooks INT 21 vec-
                     tor, but the INT 13 vector is not affected.
                     The virus can always be found at adress 0:1e0 in
                     memory, the entry is 0:2cd.
Similarities........: ---
-------------------- Agents -------------------------------------------
Countermeasures.....: Scan v80 by McAfee finds virus and trojan.
Countermeasures successful: Clean v80 by McAfee removes virus, as well
                           as LOVEKILL.EXE by Toralv Dirro.
Standard means......: Delete infected files, copy uninfected versions
                     from original write-protected disk.
-------------------- Acknowledgement ----------------------------------
Location............: Virus Test Center, University of Hamburg, Germany
Classification by...: Toralv Dirro, Gerald Schrod
Documentation by....: Toralv Dirro, Gerald Schrod
Date................: 15-July-1991
Information Source..: ---
```

Mabuhay Virus

```
Entry...............: Mabuhay Virus
Alias(es)...........: ---
Virus Strain........: ---
Virus detected when.: Mid 1993
             where.: Manila, Philippines
Classification......: File Virus (COM,EXE Infector), Memory resident
Length of Virus.....: 1.Length (Byte) on media: 2660 (+16) Bytes
                     2.Length (Byte) in RAM:   2688 Bytes
-------------------- Preconditions ------------------------------------
Operating System(s).: MSDOS
Version/Release.....: DOS 2.0 or later
Computer model(s)...: IBM PCs and Compatibles
-------------------- Attributes ---------------------------------------
Easy Identification.: ---
Type of infection...: File infection: Infexts COM and EXE files by
                     appending itself to file.
                     Self-Identification in files: Compares entry
                     point code with its own code.
                     System infection: Upon executing an infected file,
                     virus makes itself resident in low memory.
                     Self-Identification in memory: test for given
                     value in INT 21 register.
Infection Trigger...: Once resident, any file executed will be infected.
Storage media affected:
Interrupts hooked...: INT 21
```

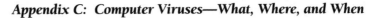
```
Damage..............: Permanent Damage: Virus damages EXE/COM files of
                     opposite type as it checks only file extension.
                     Transient Damage: Plays music and displays color
                     graphic an following text on screen:
                     "June 12 - the Independence Day of the Philippines.
                             ++
                        *    ++
                                 ++
                          \|/       ++
                          -----    *    +++++++++++++++++
                          /|\       ++
                             ++
                        *    ++
                        ++
                                   MABUHAY ANG PILIPINAS!
                                 Dedicated to Manong Eddie."
                     The image in the middle (displayed in graphic,
                        above approximated in ASCII) displays the
                        Philippine flag and is blue on top, red
                        below with a gray (gray background and
                        yellow foreground) field inside horizontal
                        V (">") on left side of the flag.
Damage Trigger......: Permanent Damage: ---
                     Transient Damage: June 12th, any year
Particularities.....: 1) Message is encrypted in virus.
                     2) Virus was captured by integrity check on
                     several machines in metro Manila.  It is "in the
                     wild" in Philippines and not detected by
                     scanners existing in July 1993.
Similarities........: ---
-------------------- Agents ---------------------------------------
Countermeasures.....:
Countermeasures successful: No scanner detects this virus on publication
Standard means......: Delete infected file and replace by clean one.
-------------------- Acknowledgement -------------------------------
Location............: Stiller Research, Tallahassee, FL
Classification by...: Wolfgang Stiller
Documentation by....: Wolfgang Stiller (CAROBase entry)
                     Klaus Brunnstein (Virus Catalog entry)
Date................: 15-July-1993
Information Source..: Reverse analysis of virus code
```

MachoSoft-Virus

```
Entry................. MachoSoft Virus
Alias(es)............. ---
Strain................ ---
Detected: when........ September 1989
          where....... Wilhelmshaven, West Germany
Classification........ Program Virus (Link virus)
Length of Virus....... 3550-3560 (dec) bytes appended on
                       paragraph boundary
---------------------- Preconditions----------------------------
Operating System(s)... MS/PC-DOS
Version/Release....... 3.00 and upwards
Computer models....... All IBM PC compatibles.
---------------------- Attributes-------------------------------
Easy identification.... Any string "Microsoft" is replaced with
```

```
                          "Machosoft" on the hard disk.
Type of infection......   The virus infects both COM and EXE files.
                          In the case of EXE files, it checks the
                          checksum in the EXE header for 7CB6h, in
                          which case no infection will occure. COM
                          files are checked by looking for the
                          string 39,28,46,03,03,01 (hex) at offset
                          10h. The virus is not RAM resident,
                          therefore it will only infect when the
                          host is run. It infects by searching
                          through the directories on the current
                          drive and randomly choosing files and
                          directories to infect or search. It will
                          not infect any other drive. It will infect
                          COMMAND.COM.
Infection trigger......   None, it will infect any time it is run.
Media affected.........   All disks that are addressable using
                          standard DOS functions.
Interrupts hooked......   ---
Damage.................   Will replace any occurance of "MicroSoft"
                          with "Machosoft". It does this by using
                          the DOS (not BIOS) interrupts 25h and 26h,
                          and searching the disk from beginning to
                          end, sector by sector. It tries 20h
                          sectors at a time, and stores the last
                          sector infected in the file
                          "\IBMNETIO.SYS", which is marked "system"
                          and "hidden". After reaching the last sector,
                          it will start from the beginning again.
Damage trigger.........   Every time the host is run.
Particularities........   The virus checks for the environment
                          variable "VIRUS=OFF", in which case it
                          will not infect. The virus in encrypted
                          using a variable key.
                          The virus will only do damage after January 1,
                          1985.
                          The virus has some trouble searching the
                          directories. Most of the effort go into
                          infecting the beginning of the disk. Macho
                          may not even reach the end of the disk on
                          larger systems.
                          As the programmer was otherwise very
                          professional in his programming, we may
                          see a version with a better directory
                          searching algorithm soon.
                          I've been told that DOS interrupts 25h and
                          26h are no longer supported by Microsoft
                          in DOS 4.0. This would obviously have its
                          consequences.
Similarities...........   ---
--------------------------- Agents----------------------------------
Countermeasures........   Use the environment variable described
                          above as a first aid measure only. If your
                          COMMAND.COM in infected, that wont stop
                          the virus much. Resetting the date will
                          only stop the damage, not the infection.
                          Here's one of the few strings that can
                          safely be searched for:
                            50,51,56,BE,59,00,B9,26,08,90,D1,E9,8A,E1,
                            8A,C1,33,06,14,00,31,04,46,46,E2,F2,5E,59
```

```
- ditto - successful...  For proper treatment, my Anti-Virus
                         "NTIMACHO" is highly recommended (in all
                         humility). Treatment by hand is very
                         tedious and only for experts.
Standard Means........   Booting from a write-protected disk and
                         restoring all COM and EXE files from the
                         original disks is the only way.
--------------------- Acknowledgements--------------------------------
Location..............   Virus Test Center, University of Hamburg, Germany
Classification by......   Morton Swimmer
Documentation by.......   Morton Swimmer
Date..................   1-Nov-1989
Information source.....   "The Peter Norton Programmer's Guide to
                         the IBM PC" (1985), and the members of our
                         group.
```

Marijuana Virus

```
Entry...............:  Marijuana Virus
Alias(es)...........:  Stoned Virus, New Zeeland Virus
Classification......:  System Virus (= Bootsector virus)
Length of Virus.....:  440 bytes (occupies one sector on storage medium)
                       2 kbyte in RAM
-------------------- Preconditions -----------------------------------
Operating System(s).:  MS-DOS,
Version/Release.....:  2.xx and upward
Computer model(s)...:  IBM-PC/XT/AT
-------------------- Attributes --------------------------------------
Easy Identification.:  'Your PC is now Stoned!.....LEGALISE MARIJUANA!'
                       in the bootsector at offset 18Ah
Type of infection...:  Self-identification: The virus regards a disk as
                       infected if the bootsector starts with
                       EA 05 00 C0. The virus installs itself 2 kbyte
                       below the end of available memory, removes that
                       space from DOS, and infects the first hard disk
                       when booting from an infected floppy disk. It
                       captures all read and write calls to drive A:,
                       checks for infection and if not present, infects
                       the disk. Infection occurs by transferring the
                       original bootsector on a floppy drive to head 1,
                       track 0, sector 3 or on a hard disk to head 0,
                       track 0, sector 7, and the original bootsector is
                       replaced with the virus bootsector. When the
                       virus installs itself from a floppy drive and the
                       last three bits of the system clock counter are
                       all zero, the PC beeps and the message 'Your PC
                       is now Stoned!' is printed on the screen.
Infection Trigger...:  Infection of drive A: disks at any activity
                       that invokes an int 13h read or write call
                       (e.g. DIR, TYPE)
                       Infection of the hard disk: when booting from an
                       infected floppy disk.
Storage media affected: Infects only disks in drive A: (media type
                        doesn't matter) and the first hard disk
Interrupts hooked...:  Int 13h functions 2, 3 (read, write)
Damage..............:  Indirect damage through infection:
                       1. Floppy disks: The overwritten sector is
                       usually a part of the root directory, so
```

```
                            directory entries may be destroyed.
                            2. Hard disk: Overwrites sector 7. Usually this
                            sector is not used, but in some non-standard
                            cases the hard disk may become inaccessible.
Damage Trigger......: Infection, booting
Particularities.....: Normal formating will not remove the virus from
                            an infected hard disk
-------------------- Agents --------------------------------------------
Countermeasures.....: Category 3: ANTIMARI.COM (VTC Hamburg)
Countermeasures successful: ANTIMARI.COM deactivates the resident
                            Marijuana-Virus in RAM and restores the
                            bootsector to it's correct place
-------------------- Acknowledgement -----------------------------------
Location............: Virus Test Center, University of Hamburg, Germany
Classification by...: Rainer Anscheit
Documentation by....: Rainer Anscheit
Date................: Jan. 14, 1990
```

Merritt Virus

```
Entry...............: Merritt
Alias(es)...........: =Yale  =Alameda (A) -Virus
Virus Strain........: Merritt/Alameda-Strain
Virus detected when.: November 24, 1988
              where: University of New Brunswick, Fredericton, CANADA
                            First detection: Merritt College, California, 1987
Classification......: System Virus (= BootSector-Virus)
Length of Virus.....: 512 Bytes
-------------------- Preconditions -------------------------------------
Operating System(s).: MS-DOS
Version/Release.....:
Computer Models.....: IBM PCs and Compatibles (not ATs=80286).
-------------------- Typical Attributes --------------------------------
Easy Identification.: No characteristic text (in code, Vol-labels etc).
Type of infection...: Boots when infected disk is inserted and system
                            is booted. Installs itself in high memory, removes
                            that memory from DOS. Installs itself as the
                            Warm-start (CTRL+ALT+DEL) interrupt handler
                            (actually the keyboard handler); spreads by
                            CTRL+ALT+DEL interrupt handler. Moves "real" boot
                            sector to track 39, sector 8. Does not infect
                            .COM or .EXE files.
Damage..............: Permanent Damage: moves boot block to track 39,
                            sector 8 (if there was a file, it is corrupted).
                            This sector is not marked as bad, so a file may
                            overwrite the real boot block so that the disk may
                            become "NOT bootable". It will count to 39 and
                            Blast the FAT (`0'). It counts a certain key
                            stroke (there is also code for decrementing the
                            count by another keystroke).
Particularities.....: Hangs-up 80286-systems.
Similarities........: With other members of Merritt/Alameda-strain.
-------------------- Agents --------------------------------------------
Tested vaccines.....: Michael MacDonalds own vaccine, which identifies
                            virus and overwrites the boot block.
Vaccines successful.: Michael MacDonald's own vaccine.
Standard means......: Compare boot sector of infected disk with a
                            "real" system disk. If different: check track 39,
```

```
                             sector 8; if this contains the real boot block,
                             execute a SYS command to reinstall real boot block
                             and system files.
-------------------- Classification ----------------------------------
Location............: School of Computer Science,
                      University of New Brunswick
Classification by...: Michael J. MacDonald
Documentation by....: Michael J. MacDonald, Software Specialist
                      University of New Brunswick, P.O.Box 4400
                      Fredericton, New Brunswick, CANADA  E3B 5A3
                      BITNET: MIKEMAC@UNB.CA
Date of Entry.......: June 5, 1989
Information Source..: ---
```

Michelangelo Virus

```
Entry...............: Michelangelo Virus
Alias(es)...........: Ninja Turtle Virus (in Taiwan)
Virus Strain........: Stoned Virus Strain
Virus detected when.: Summer 1991
           where.:
Classification......: System virus (boot, partition table), resident
Length of Virus.....: Fits well into code space of partition table
                      Memory: 2,048 bytes just below end of DOS
-------------------- Preconditions ----------------------------------
Operating System(s).: MS-DOS
Version/Release.....: 2.xx upward
Computer model(s)...: IBM - PC, XT, AT, upward and compatibles
-------------------- Attributes -------------------------------------
Easy Identification.: ---
Direct Detection....: Original partition table or original boot sector
                      can be found in sector 7 of a hard disk
                      and specific sectors of 5.25"/3.5" diskette.
                      CHKDSK "total memory bytes" shows that available
                      memory is reduced by 2,048 bytes.
Type of infection...: Upon booting from an infected floppy, virus will
                      make itself memory resident and infect par-
                      tition table. Any INT13 is intercepted there-
                      after. Any floppy A: operation will infect
                      disk in drive A: provided the motor was off;
                      this reduces excessive infection testing.
Infection Trigger...: Booting from an infected disk will infect a com-
                      puter. Usage of the floppy A: drive (read,
                      write, or format) can cause an infection of
                      that medium.
Infection targets:..: Partition table of harddisks and bootsectors
                      of floppy disks.
Interrupts hooked...: INT 13
Damage..............: Data destruction by overwriting the medium, from
                      which system was booted from: on harddisks,
                      virus will overwrite sector 1-17 on head 0-3
                      of all tracks; on floppies, virus will over-
                      write sector 1-9 or 1-14 (depending on FAT
                      type) on both heads and all tracks.
Damage Trigger......: Data destruction occurs when system's date
                      equals March 6 of any year. This is birthdate
                      of Michelangelo Buonarotti, Italian artist,
                      architect and engineer (born March 6, 1475
```

```
                            in Caprese, died February 18, 1564 in Rome)
                            Remark: there is *no evidence* in the virus
                            that it's programmer related March 6 to
                            Michelangelo B.; the name probably is the
                            interpretation of the first person to
                            (possibly partially) analyse this virus.
   Similarities........: Virus seems to be an enhanced Stoned virus
   Particularities.....: 1) Virus uses BIOS directly.
                            2) As virus overwrites hard disk sector 7, it
                            may also affect other operating systems which
                            use an infected disk.
   -------------------- Agents ----------------------------------------
   Countermeasures.....:
   - ditto - successful: Fridrik Skulason's F-PROT and Dr. Solomon's
                            FINDVIRU detect and eradicate this virus.
   Standard means......: Boot from a clean disk and move original sector
                            to its proper location (sector 1, head 0,
                            track 0). On systems where an early FDISK (no
                            hidden sectors) was used to low-level format
                            hard disk, FAT copy 1 might be damaged; an
                            additional copying of FAT 2 onto FAT 1 might
                            then be necessary.
   -------------------- Acknowledgement -------------------------------
   Location............: Micro-BIT Virus Center, Univ.Karlsruhe, Germany
   Classification by...: Christoph Fischer
   Documentation by....: Christoph Fischer
   Date................: 17-September-1991
   Update..............: Padgett Patterson, Orlando/Florida (31-Jan-1992)
```

Minimal Virus Strain

```
   Strain............... Minimal Virus Strain
   Classification....... All Minimal Viruses:
                          Overwriting COM infectors, direct action;
                          not memory-resident.
   Size of Viruses...... On media: various (see entries)
                          ======================================
   Virus Entry#1........ Minimal.Psycho = Minimal.Hastings Virus
   Detected: when....... ---
             where...... ---
   Size of virus........ Length: 200 bytes (overwriting)
                          ------------------------------
   Virus Entry#2........ Minimal.Hanger Virus
   Detected: when....... ---
             where...... ---
   Size of virus........ Length: 143 bytes (overwriting)
                          ------------------------------
   Virus Entry#3........ Minimal.Banana Virus
   Detected: when....... ---
             where...... ---
   Size of virus........ Length: 139 bytes (overwriting)
                          ------------------------------
   Virus Entry#5........ Minimal.50 Virus
   Detected: when....... ---
             where...... ---
   Size of virus........ Length: 50 bytes (overwriting)
                          ------------------------------
   Virus Entry#6........ Minimal.46 = DeathCow Virus
```

```
Detected: when........  ---
          where.......  ---
Size of virus........  Length: 46 bytes (overwriting)
Variant..............  Minimal.42
Size of virus........  Length: 42 bytes (overwriting)
                       ------------------------------
Virus Entry#7........  Minimal.45.A = Shortest Virus
Detected: when........  ---
          where.......  ---
Clones...............  Minimal.45.B virus, Minimal.45.C virus
Size of virus........  Length: 45 bytes (overwriting)
Variant..............  Minimal.35 Virus
Size of virus........  Length: 35 bytes (overwriting)
                       ------------------------------
Virus Entry#8........  Minimal.44 Virus
Detected: when........  ---
          where.......  ---
Length of virus......  Length: 44 bytes (overwriting)
                       ------------------------------
Virus Entry#9........  Minimal.39 Virus
Detected: when........  ---
          where.......  ---
Length of virus......  Length: 39 bytes (overwriting)
Variant..............  Minimal.38 Virus
Length of virus......  Length: 38 bytes (overwriting)
                       ------------------------------
Virus Entry#10.......  Minimal.31.A Virus
Detected: when........  ---
          where.......  ---
Clone................  Minimal.31.B = Miniscule Virus
Size of virus/clone...  Length: 31 bytes (overwriting)
                       ------------------------------
Virus Entry#11.......  Minimal.30.A Virus
Detected: when........  ---
          where.......  ---
Clones...............  Minimal.30.B, Minimal.30.C Virus
Size of virus/clones..  Length: 30 bytes (overwriting)
                       ------------------------------
Virus Entry#12.......  Minimal.25 Virus
Detected: when........  ---
          where.......  ---
Length of virus......  Length: 25 bytes (overwriting)
Variant..............  Minimal.26 Virus
Length of virus......  Length: 26 bytes (overwriting)
--------------------- Preconditions --------------------------------
Operating System(s)...  MS/PC-DOS 3.x upwards
Computer models.......  All IBM PC/AT compatibles
--------------------- Common Attributes of Strain Viruses ----------
Easy identification...  Infected files will not run as they are over-
                        written by the resp. virus; only virus code
                        will be executed, and system will then crash.
Type of infection.....  Self-identification: none (just overwriting)
                        COM files: not increased, unless infected file
                        is shorter than virus. Files can only be
                        infected when an infected host is started;
                        first bytes of infected file (length depending
                        on virus/variant) will be overwritten by virus.
                        EXE files: no infection.
Infection trigger.....  Any time an infected file is run, the viruses
                        infects one or all .COM files in the current
                        directory.
```

```
Affected media........ Files on HardDisk or any FloppyDisk.
Interrupts hooked..... ---
Damage................ Permanent damage: infected file is overwritten.
Damage trigger........ Execution of an infected file.
Particularities....... The file date/time will be set to the date
                       of the infection.
Similarities.......... In stepwise reduction of size, MINIMAL viruses
                       aim at achieving the shortest code suitable
                       for infection. Though probably different
                       authors worked on the viruses, this common
                       goal is explicitly mentioned in some texts.
                       While early version contain several texts,
                       later versions contain essentially code suf-
                       ficient to infect files by overwriting them;
                       but texts may be deposited in infected files
                       at remote locations.
                       Every virus in Minimal strain infects one or
                       all *.COM or *.C* or *.* files in the
                       current directory, by overwriting the first
                       bytes of the files with itself. If the file
                       to be infectes is smaller than the resp.
                       virus, the file size will grow to the virus'
                       size.
--------------------- Special Attributes of Minimal.Hastings ----------
Virus name............ Minimal.Psycho or Minimal.Hastings
Size.................. 200 bytes
Type of infection..... Infects the 1st .COM file in current directory
                       by overwriting it.
Easy identification... Texts found in virus at offset 40dez
                          '*.COM by' (encrypted name deleted)
                          'AKA Nick Haflinger...'
                          'Zopy me I want' to travel'
                          'I can now program in assembler'
                          'This program was written in the town'
                          'of Hastings hehehehe!'
--------------------- Special Attributes of Minimal.Hanger ------------
Virus name............ Minimal.Hanger Virus
Size.................. 143 bytes
Type of infection..... Infects all *.C* files (*.COM, but also *.C)
                       in current directory by overwriting them.
Easy detection........ Infected files contain (unencrypted) message
                       (see Transient damage) at offset 59dez.
Damage................ Permanent damage: Overwriting infected files.
                       Transient damage: After infection, virus displays
                       the message:  'System Hanger! Enjoy! '
                       'Note: Your system is now hanged.'
                       'Press Reset to continue.'
                       Then systems may hang (HLT instruction)
--------------------- Special Attributes of Minimal.Banana ------------
Virus name............ Minimal.Banana Virus
Size.................. 139 bytes
Type of infection..... Infects all *.COM files in current directory
                       by overwriting them.
Easy identification... The following text is found in infected files
                       at offset 80dez:
                       'BANANA, coded by Morbid Angel'
                       '-92 in Stockholm/Sweden*.COM'
Particularities....... Upon infection, file-attribute, time and date
                       are saved and correctly restored.
--------------------- Special Attributes of Minimal.50 ---------------
```

```
Virus name........... Minimal.50 Virus
Size................. 50 bytes
Type of infection..... Infects all *.COM files in current directory
                       by overwriting them.
-------------------- Special Attributes of Minimal.46 ----------------
Virus name........... Minimal.46 = DeathCow Virus
Size................. 46 bytes
Type of infection..... Infects all *.COM files by overwriting the,.
Variants.............. Optimized version is Minimal.42,
Size................. 42 bytes
Easy identification... The following text is visible in infected files
                       'DeathCow, Strain B' '(C) 1991'
                       'Nowhere Man and [NuKE] WaErZ'
                       'Written by Nowhere Man, derived from'
                       'DeathCow (author unknown)'
-------------------- Special Attributes of Minimal.45 ----------------
Virus name........... Minimal.45.A = Shortest Virus
Size................. 45 bytes
Type of infection..... Infects all *.COM files by overwriting them.
Clones............... Minimal.45.B and Minimal.45.C (same size)
Variants.............. Minimal.35 Virus
Size................. 35 bytes
-------------------- Special Attributes of Minimal.44 ----------------
Virus name........... Minimal.44 Virus
Size................. 44 bytes
Type of infection..... Infects all *.COM files in current directory
                       by overwriting them
-------------------- Special Attributes of Minimal.39 ----------------
Virus name........... Minimal.39 Virus
Size................. 39 bytes
Type of infection..... Infects all *.COM files in current directory
                       by overwriting them.
Variants.............. Minimal.38 Virus
Size................. 38 bytes
Remark............... A slightly optimized version of Minimal.39 Virus
-------------------- Special Attributes of Minimal.35 ----------------
Virus name........... Minimal.35 Virus
Size................. 35 bytes
Type of infection..... Infects one file with pattern *.C* by overwriting
Easy identification... Infected files contain following unencrypted text
                       'Copyright (C) by Line Noise 1992'
Remark............... A significantly optimized version of Minimal.45
-------------------- Special Attributes of Minimal.31.A --------------
Virus name........... Minimal.31.A Virus
Size................. 31 bytes
Type of infection..... Infects one file with pattern *.C* by overwriting
-------------------- Special Attributes of Minimal.31.B --------------
Virus name........... Minimal.31.B = Miniscule Virus
Size................. 31 bytes
Type of infection..... Infects one file with pattern *.* by overwriting
Easy identification... The following text is found in infected files
                       'Miniscule: the world's smallest'
                       'generic virus (only 31 bytes'
                       'long!) (C) 1992 Nowhere Man and'
                       '[NuKE] WaReZ' 'Written on January'
                       '22, 1991'
-------------------- Special Attributes of Minimal.30.A/B/C ----------
Virus name........... Minimal.30.A Virus
Size................. 30 bytes
Type of infection..... Infects one file with pattern *.* by overwriting
```

```
Variant#1............. Minimal.30.B
Particularities....... Minimal.30.B overwrites 256 bytes of a file
Remark................ Uses two different opcodes for same purpose
Variant#2............. Minimal.30.C Virus
Remark................ Some opcodes swapped, but 98% same code
Particularities....... Minimal.30.C overwrites 30 bytes of a file
--------------------- Special Attributes of Minimal.25 ---------------
Virus name............ Minimal.25 Virus
Size.................. 25 bytes (or longer);
                       infected file size will vary, due to some
                       optimization in virus code, in the range
                       of overwritten bytes  25 <= size <= 33049.
Type of infection..... Infects one .COM file by overwriting
Particularities....... Virus only works under specific conditions.
Variants.............. Minimal.26 Virus
Size.................. 26 bytes
Type of infection..... Infects one *.* file
Particularities....... As Minimal.25, this virus also works only
                       under specific conditions
--------------------- Agents -----------------------------------------
Countermeasures.......
Standard Means........ Notice file length and file date/time.
                       Use ReadOnly attribute.
                       Infected files can only be disinfected by
                       replacing them with the original files.
--------------------- Acknowledgements -------------------------------
Location.............. Virus Test Center, University of Hamburg, Germany
Classification by..... Stefan Tode
Documentation by...... Stefan Tode
Date.................. 31-January-1993
Information source.... ---
```

Mirror Virus

```
Entry................. Mirror Virus
Alias(es)............. Flip Clone Virus
Strain................ ---
Detected: when........ 18-December-1990 (when VTC received virus code)
          where....... Hamburg, Germany
Classification........ Program Virus, indirect action, postfix
Length of Virus....... File: either 925 or 933 bytes
                       RAM:  928 bytes
--------------------- Preconditions ----------------------------------
Operating System(s)... MS/PC-DOS
Computer models....... All IBM PC compatibles.
--------------------- Attributes -------------------------------------
Easy identification... ---
Type of infection..... Program virus that only infects files with the
                       extension EXE. The virus loads itself into
                       RAM and hooks various INT 21h functions.
                       When one of these are called, the virus will
                       search the current directory for EXE files
                       to infect. The virus will be located behind
                       the host program. A generation counter is
                       incremented whenever an infected file is run
                       again.
Infection trigger..... Any time an infected file is run.
Media affected........ Any logical disks.
```

```
Interrupts hooked..... INT 21h Functions 0fh,16h,3ch,3dh,4b00h,4b03h
Damage............... Permanent damage: ---
                      Transient Damage: when triggered, the screen
                       will flip horizontally character for
                       character, but not as sophisticatedly as
                       Flip virus.
Damage trigger........ If a program is run with a generation counter
                       of 10, a routine will be installed with
                       INT 1ch pointing to it. After approximately
                       10 minutes, the damage will trigger.
Particularities....... There are a number of possible design bugs in
                       the virus, that may cause unpredictable
                       behaviour.
Similarities......... Although having a similar damage to Flip, this
                       is a completely different virus.
-------------------- Agents ----------------------------------------
Countermeasures....... ---
 - ditto - successful. McAfee's Scan version 72
Standard Means........ ---
-------------------- Acknowledgements ------------------------------
Location............. Virus Test Center, University of Hamburg, Germany
Classification by..... Morton Swimmer
Documentation by...... Morton Swimmer
Date.................. 12-February-1991
Information source.... ---
```

"MIX1" Virus

```
Entry................: MIX1 Virus
Alias(es)...........: Mixer1
Virus strain........: Icelandic Virus
Virus detected when.: August 22, 1989
            where.: BBSs in Israel
Classification......: Program virus (.EXE files) - Extending,
                      RAM-resident.
Length of virus.....: 1. Infected .EXE files enlarged by 1618-1634
                      bytes (depends on the original file size).
                      2. 2048 bytes in RAM.
-------------------- Preconditions ---------------------------------
Operating system(s).: PC/MS DOS version
Version/Release.....: 2.0 or later.
Computer model(s)...: IBM-PC, XT, AT and compatibles
-------------------- Attributes ------------------------------------
Easy Identification.: 1. "MIX1" are the last 4 bytes of the infected
                         file.
                      2. In DEBUG to check byte 0:33C. If this equals
                         77h, then the virus is in memory.
Type of infection...: System: Infected if byte 0:33C equals 77h.
                      .EXE files: Only files which do not have a
                            signature at their end are infected.
                            File length is increased by 1618 -
                            1634 bytes.
Infection trigger...: When executing/load .EXE files through interrupt
                      21h service 4bh.
Interrupt hooked....: 21h, 14h, 17h, optionally 8,9 (after 6th level
                      of infection).
Damage..............: Garbled output on parallel and serial connec-
                      tions, after 6th level of infection boot
```

```
                         will crash the system (a bug), num-lock
                         is constantly on, a ball will start boun-
                         cing.
Damage trigger......: After executing and infected file is executed
Particularities.....: 1. Booting may crash the computer (possibly
                         a bug).
                      2. Memory allocation is done through direct
                         MCB control.
                      3. Does not allocate stack, and therefore makes
                         some files unusable.
                      4. Infects only files which are bigger than 8K.
-------------------- Agents -------------------------------------------
Countermeasures.....: Virus Buster and more commercial, Israeli anti
                         viral software (JIV, Turbo Anti-Virus).
Countermeasures successful: Virus Buster will locate the virus and
                         upon request, will remove it.
Standard means......: Check byte 0:33C (cf: Easy identifications).
-------------------- Acknowledgement ----------------------------------
Classification by...: Yuval Tal (NYYUVAL@WEIZMANN.BITNET), Ori Berger
Documentation by....: Yuval Tal (NYYUVAL@WEIZMANN.BITNET), Ori Berger
Date................: December 19, 1989
```

Mummy 1.2 Virus

```
Entry...............: Mummy 1.2 Virus
Standard CARO Name..: Jerusalem.Mummy.1_2 Virus
Alias(es)...........: ---
Virus Strain........: Jerusalem Virus strain, Mummy substrain
Virus detected when.: Spring 1992
             where.: Germany
Classification......: Program (EXE) virus (appending), memory resident
Length of Virus.....: Appends 1399-1414 bytes
-------------------- Preconditions ------------------------------------
Operating System(s).: MS-DOS
Version/Release.....: All versions above 2
Computer model(s)...: PC and all compatibles
-------------------- Attributes ---------------------------------------
Easy Identification.: File growth; no plain text in files visible.
                      Virus self-identification: EXE header checksum
                      (file offset 12h) contains 0C0Bh.
Type of infection...: All files starting with "MZ" (normal EXE header)
                      that are executed or opened will be infected
                      provided there is enough space left on volume.
Infection Trigger...: Load & Execute or Open of a file containing "MZ"
                      as first two bytes.
Storage media affected: All (diskettes, hard disks)
Interrupts hooked...: INT 24 (hooked); INT 21 and 26 (used)
Damage..............: Transient damaga: there is an encrypted text in
                      the virus, that is decrypted when the virus
                      goes memory resident. This text is never
                      displayed!
                      Memory dump (typical text!):
                      0D 0A 20 04 20 4D 75 6D  ... . Mum
                      6D 79 20 56 65 72 73 69  my Versi
                      6F 6E 20 31 3E 32 20 04  on 1.2 .
                      20 0D 0A 0A 4B 61 6F 68  ...Kaoh
                      73 69 75 6E 67 20 53 65  siung Se
                      6E 69 6F 72 20 53 63 68  nior Sch
                      6F 6F 6C 0D 0A 0A 54 7A  ool...Tz
```

```
65 6E 67 20 4A 61 75 20    eng Jau
4D 69 6E 67 20 70 72 65    Ming pre
73 65 6E 74 73 0D 0A 0A    sents...
53 65 72 69 65 73 20 4E    Series N
75 6D 62 65 72 20 3D 20    umber =
5B 78 78 78 78 78 5D 0D    [xxxxx].
0A 24                      .$
```

Permanent damage: virus contains a counter (16bit) being decremented upon every loading or opening of an infected file; this counter is reset to zero every time an OEM call to DOS is made (INT 21 AH=FFh and AL<>FFh) (this function is used by several programs).
Upon each attemted infection, this counter is checked whether having reached zero; if so, the current logical drive is overwritten with the virus code and memory garbage. 99 sectors are being overwritten starting with the bootsector (logical sector 0). This acitivity destroys the bootsector, FAT 1 and FAT 2, and the root directory as well as some data.

Damage Trigger......:	If trigger counter becomes zero.
Particularities.....:	Trigger counter is forced to zero if DOS INT 21h is invoked, e.g. by specific programs or another virus. New infection sinherit trigger counter in infecting file.
Similarities........:	Jerusalem/Mummy virus strain

-------------------- Agents -----------------------------

Countermeasures.....:	McAfee Scan, Skulason F-PROT, Solomon FindViru Removal not recommended, might not work on special EXE files!
Standard means......:	Replace infected file with uninfected original.

-------------------- Acknowledgement ----------------------------

Location...........:	Micro-BIT Virus Center, Univ Karlsruhe, Germany
Classification by...:	Christoph Fischer (Klaus Brunnstein, VTC)
Documentation by....:	Christoph Fischer
Date...............:	April-1992
Information Source..:	---

"Murphy-1" Virus

Entry...............:	"Murphy-1" Virus
Alias(es)...........:	---
Strain..............:	Murphy Virus Strain
Detected: when......:	December, 1989
where......:	Sofia, Bulgaria
Classification......:	Program virus, indirect action
Length of Virus.....:	1277 bytes added to EXE and COM files.

---------------------- Preconditions -----------------------------

Operating System(s)....:	MS-DOS
Version/Release........:	3.xx and upward
Computer models........:	IBM-PC's and compatibles

------------------------ Attributes------------------------------

Easy identification....:	The virus contains the string: "Hello, I'm Murphy. Nice to meet you friend. I'm written since Nov/Dec. Copywrite (c)1989 by Lubo & Ian, Sofia, USM Laboratory." See also damage.
Type of infection......:	Murphy is a program virus that appends itself

to any COM or EXE file larger than
1277 bytes. COM files must be smaller than
64226 bytes, however if a COM file larger
than 64003 is infected, it will not run.
A file is judged as infected if the length
between program entry and end of file is
the same as the virus length.
The virus also locates the original INT 13
handler and unhooks any other routines
that have been hooked onto this interrupt
and restores the interrupt to the original
handler.
Murphy installs itself into memory by
modifying the MCB chain. It determines
whether it is already in memory by
executing INT 21 function 4B59h. If the
carry flag is not set on return, then the
memory is assumed to be not infected.

Infection trigger......	Infects file on execution and opening.
Media affected.........	Any logical drive.
Interrupts hooked......	INT 21 functions 4B, 3D00, 6C00 (b1=0) are used to infect files, and INT 24 and 13 are captured to mask out errors.
Damage.................	The speaker is turned on and off which produces a clicking noise.
Damage trigger.........	This happens between 10:00 and 11:00 (AM).
Particularities.......	INT 21 function 6C00 is the DOS 4.xx extended open/create function. This makes Murphy-1 one of the first viruses to make use of DOS 4.xx
	The virus knocks out the transient part of COMMAND.COM forcing it to be reloaded and thereby infected.
Similarities..........	Much of the code was taken from Eddie-1 /Dark Avenger.
	This is the precursor to Murphy-2.

-------------------------- Agents ----------------------------------

Countermeasures.......	Checksumming programs will detect the virus, but have the side-effect of infecting every file on the disk if the virus is in memory. F-DLOCK in Fridrik Skulason's F-PROT package prevents files from being infected.
- ditto - successful..	---
Standard Means.........	---

---------------------- Acknowledgements -----------------------------

Location..............	Bulgarian Academy of Science and Virus Test Center, University of Hamburg, Germany
Classification by......	Vesselin Bontchev
Documentation by.......	Morton Swimmer
Date..................	12-June-1990
Information source.....	---

"Murphy-2" Virus

Entry.................	"Murphy-2" Virus
Alias(es).............	---
Strain................	Murphy Virus Strain
Detected: when........	April, 1990

```
           where........ Sofia, Bulgaria
Classification......... Program virus, indirect action
Length of Virus........ 1521 bytes added to EXE and COM files.
---------------------- Preconditions ----------------------------
Operating System(s).... MS-DOS
Version/Release........ 3.xx and upward
Computer models........ IBM-PC's and compatibles
----------------------- Attributes ------------------------------
Easy identification.... The virus contains the string: "It's me -
                        Murphy. Copywrite (c)1989 by Lubo & Ian,
                        Sofia, USM Laboratory." See also damage.
Type of infection...... Murphy is a program virus that appends itself
                        to any COM or EXE file larger than 1521
                        bytes. COM files must be smaller than
                        63982 bytes.
                        A file is judged as infected if the length
                        between program entry and end of file is
                        the same as the virus length.
                        The virus also locates the original INT 13
                        handler and unhooks any other routines
                        that have been hooked onto this interrupt
                        and restores the interrupt to the original
                        handler.
                        Murphy installs itself into memory by
                        modifying the MCB chain. It determines
                        whether it is already in memory by
                        executing INT 21 function 4B59h. If the
                        carry flag is not set on return, then the
                        memory is assumed to be not infected.
Infection trigger...... Infects file on execution and opening.
Media affected......... Any logical drive.
Interrupts hooked...... INT 21 functions 4B, 3D00, 6C00 (bl=0) are
                        used to infect files, and INT 24 and 13
                        are captured to mask out errors.
Damage................. A ball (character 07) bounces over the screen.
Damage trigger......... This happens if the virus is active between
                        10:00 and 11:00 (AM).
Particularities........ INT 21 function 6C00 is the DOS 4.xx
                        extended open/create function. This makes
                        Murphy (1/2) one of the first viruses to
                        make use of DOS 4.xx
                        The virus knocks out the transient part of
                        COMMAND.COM forcing it to be reloaded and
                        thereby infected.
Similarities........... This virus was derived from Murphy-1. The
                        code has been cleaned up a bit, but the
                        main difference is in the damage.
                        Much of the code was taken from Eddie-1
                        /Dark Avenger.
                        The bouncing ball effect looks very much
                        like the Italian-virus, but the code shows
                        no similarities.
-------------------------- Agents -------------------------------
Countermeasures........ Checksumming programs will detect the virus,
                        but have the side-effect of infecting
                        every file on the disk if the virus is in
                        memory.F-DLOCK in Fridrik Skulason's F-PROT
                        package prevents files from being infected.
                        (It was loaded before the virus was.)
   - ditto - successful.. ---
```

```
Standard Means........  ---
--------------------- Acknowledgements ----------------------------
Location..............  Virus Test Center, University of Hamburg, Germany
Classification by......  Morton Swimmer. The source listing came
                        from Lubomir Mateev, one of the "authors"
                        of this virus. It was nicely commented in
                        Bulgarian.
Documentation by......  Morton Swimmer
Date..................  12-June-1990
Information source.....  ---
```

NGUYEN Virus

```
Entry...............: NGUYEN Virus
Alias(es)...........: ---
Virus Strain........: ---
Virus detected when.:
          where.:
Classification......: File Virus (EXE, COM infector), memory resident
Length of Virus.....: 1.Length on storage media: 1740 Bytes (appended)
                      2.Length in memory:        3082 Bytes
-------------------- Preconditions ----------------------------------
Operating System(s).: MSDOS
Version/Release.....: Release 2.x and above
Computer model(s)...: IBM compatibles
-------------------- Attributes -------------------------------------
Easy Identification.: 1) Texts "Hacker: NGUYEN HIEU VINH" and "South of
                         Viet Nam" can be found near end of an in-
                         fected file ($200 bytes offset approx).
                      2) Infected files have date/time: 8.8.88, 8.08.
                      3) If virus is resident, chkdsk or mem will report
                         3082 bytes less total memory than expected.
Scan String.........: String "cd 21 81 f9 04 41 75 09 81 fa 08 11"
                      can be found near the end of an infected file.
Type of infection...: EXE-files: standard ways of infecting EXE-files.
                      COM-files: standard appending method.
Infection Trigger...: Virus will become resident when an infected program
                      is executed. After becoming resident, every file
                      executed via INT 21, AH=4B (Load and Execute)
                      will be infected.
Storage media affected: Any files executed will be infected.
Interrupts hooked...: INT 21, INT 24 (only during infection),
                      INT 1C (see particularities).
Damage..............: Permanent Damage: If file is created or opened to
                      Read Only, depending on random choice, virus
                      overwrites file from beginning with text
                      "Hacker: NGUYEN HIEU VINH <adress>" where
                      <adress> may be related to virus' author.
                      Permanent/Transient Damage: Denial of service,
                      message "ATV, VDW and LF to kill me!!!" dis-
                      played and potentially INT 21 code trashed
                      (see Particularities 2).
                      Transient Damage: Overwriting 1st line of screen
                      with text: "DBSoft-Doàn Thàn Tú là 1 ke trôm
                      cap software. He's a professional thief...".
Damage Trigger......: Permanent Damage: Creating or opening a file with
                      Read-Only attribute will trigger the damage
                      function when virus is resident.
```

```
                             Permanent/Transient Damage: given number of
                             infections AND detection of files starting
                             with "AV", "VD" and "LF".
                             Transient Damage: Given number of infections.
Particularities.....:  1) The file date/time stamp is used as infection
                             flag, with Date/Time=8.8.88, 8.08 indicating
                             infection by this virus.
                             2) After a given number of total infections,
                             if a file is executed whose name starts with
                             "AT", "VD","LF" it's execution will be denied;
                             this may be intended as attack on some AV soft-
                             ware. Then a message will be written that you
                             should not use "ATV, VDW and LF to kill me!!!".
                             Virus also seems to trash INT 1B vector on
                             this occasion (ctrl-break-check).
                             3) After a given numbers of total infection,
                             virus will additionally hook INT 1C and after
                             some time will display the text "DBSoft-Doàn
                             Thàn Tú là 1 ke trôm cap software. He's a pro-
                             fessional thief..." on screen's first line
                             (writing directly to the screen, not caring
                             about the actual videomode).
                             4) Infected files will be shown with their normal
                             length in a directory if virus is resident.
                             5) Virus does not check length of COM files before
                             infection, which may result in COM files with
                             length > 64 kBytes which cannot be executed
                             after infection.
Similarities........: ---
-------------------- Agents -----------------------------------------
Countermeasures.....: None
Countermeasures successful: At publication time, no AV product detects
                             or clean this virus successfully.
Standard means......: Delete and replace infected files.
-------------------- Acknowledgement --------------------------------
Location............: Virus Test Center, University of Hamburg, Germany
Classification by...: Toralv Dirro
Documentation by....: Toralv Dirro
Date................: 31-July-1993
Information Source..: Reverse analysis of virus code
==================== End of Nguyen Virus ============================
```

NoInt Virus

```
Entry...............: NoInt Virus
Alias(es)...........: ---
Virus Strain........: Stoned Virus Strain
Virus detected when.:
            where.:
Classification......: System virus (MBR,FBR infector), memory resident
Length of Virus.....: 1.Length on media:      1 Sector
                      2.Length in memory:      1 KByte
                      3.Length of virus code: 363 Bytes.
-------------------- Preconditions ----------------------------------
Operating System(s).: MSDOS
Version/Release.....: 2.xx upward
Computer model(s)...: IBM-PC, XT, AT and compatibles
-------------------- Attributes -------------------------------------
```

```
Easy Identification.: 1) Memory size reduced: CHKDSK will report 2KBytes
                         less memory than installed.
                      2) FBR/MBR contain following hex-string at offset
                         00CB, which may be used as scanstring:
                         "33 DB 33 C9 33 D2 2E FF 2E D6 00 00 7C 00 00"
                         (part of virus' stealth function).
Type of infection...: File infection: ---
                      System infection: Upon booting from an infected
                         diskette, virus will make itself memory re-
                         sident and infect disk's Master Bootrecord.
                         Subsequently, any access to any non-infected
                         diskette will result in it's infection. Upon
                         infection, a disk's MBR is saved at Head 0,
                         Cylinder 0, Sector 7; a diskette's original
                         FBR is saved at Head 1,Cylinder 0,Sector 3.
Infection Trigger...: Booting from an infected diskette; when virus is
                         memory resident: accessing any diskette.
Storage media affected: Hard disk, diskette
Interrupts hooked...: INT 13h
Damage..............: Transient damage: ---
                      Permanent damage: On diskette, virus will store
                         original Bootsector in part of root-directory;
                         entries previously referenced there are lost.
Damage Trigger......: Transient damage: ---
                      Permanent damage: accessing a diskette.
Particularities.....: ---
Similarities........: Variant of Stoned Virus
-------------------- Agents ----------------------------------------
Countermeasures.....: According to their documentation, many antivirus
                         products claim to recognize/eradicate virus.
Countermeasures successful:
Standard means......: 1) Reboot from clean bootdisk.
                      2) Use SYS-Command to reinstall BOOTsector on
                         floppies.
                      3) Use FDISK /MBR to reinstall Master Boot sector
                         on hard disk (MS-DOS 5.00 or higher only).
-------------------- Acknowledgement --------------------------------
Location............: Virus Test Center, University of Hamburg, Germany
Classification by...: Ulf Heinemann
Documentation by....: Ulf Heinemann
Date................: 31-July-1993
Information Source..: Reverse analysis of virus code
```

Nomenklatura Virus

```
Entry...............: Nomenklatura Virus
Alias(es)...........: ---
Virus Strain........: ---
Virus detected when.:
             where.:
Classification......: RAM-resident Program (COM & EXE) Infector
Length of Virus.....: COM & EXE fles: 1024 Bytes
                      Memory: 1072 Bytes
-------------------- Preconditions ----------------------------------
Operating System(s).: MS-DOS
Version/Release.....: 2.xx upward
Computer model(s)...: IBM compatibles
-------------------- Attributes -------------------------------------
```

```
    Easy Identification.: Textstring: 'Nomenklatura' at offset 4 followed
                          by string "00 80 FC 4B 74 0A 80 FC 3D 74 14"
    Self Identification : Checks length of code after execution of initial
                          jump; infects only if this length isnot 1024.
    Type of infection...: System: Allocates a memory block at high end of
                          memory, finds original adress of INT 13h
                          handle, collects and changes INT 21h vector.
                          COM&EXE files: program length increased by 1024.
                          Required size of files for infection:
                            .EXE: more than 1024 bytes
                            .COM: filesize between 1024 and 64000 bytes.
                          Files will only be infected once. COMMAND.COM
                          is normally first file that will be infected.
                          If ReadOnly attribute of file is set, virus
                          is not able to infect it.
                          File date & time will not be changed.
    Infection Trigger...: Programs are infected at load time (using MsDos
                          function 4Bh) as well as when MsDos function
                          3Dh is invoked.
Storage media affected: Any drive
    Interrupts hooked...: INT 13h during virus installation in RAM,
                          INT 21h hooked by resident part of virus.
                          INT 13h, INT 24h during infection.
    Damage.............: Permanent Damage: by exchanging random words.
                          Any file containing exchanged words will sud-
                          denly contain totally different data. Any
                          type of file and both FATs may be affected.
                          Transient damage: ---
    Damage Trigger......: random trigger
    Particularities.....: While virus is in memory, every virus scanning
                          program will infect all files on the system,
                          as virus uses MsDos function 3Dh (open file).
    Similarities........: ---
    -------------------- Agents --------------------------------------
    Countermeasures.....: Detection in RAM: McAfee's Scan 7.2V77
                                            Skulason's f-syschk V 1.16+
    Countermeasures successful: Detection in files & succesful desinfect:
                                            Skulason's f-fchk V 1.15+
    Standard means......: Set ReadOnly attribute
    -------------------- Acknowledgement -----------------------------
    Location............: Virus Test Center, University of Hamburg, Germany
    Classification......: Soenke Spehr
    Documentation by....: Soenke Spehr
    Date................: 15-July-91
    Information Source..: ---
```

"Ogre" Virus

```
    Entry................. Ogre Virus
    Alias(es)............. Disk Killer 1.00
    Strain................ ---
    Detected: when........ ---
              where....... ---
    Classification........ Boot sector virus, RAM resident
    Length of Virus....... 2560 bytes of code, 5 sectors on disk
                           (+1 where original bootsector is saved)
    ---------------------- Preconditions-----------------------------
    Operating System(s).... MS-DOS
```

```
Version/Release........ not relevant
Computer models........ IBM-PC/AT and compatibles
---------------------- Attributes---------------------------------
Easy identification.... Word at offset 003Eh in the boot sector
                            will contain the value 3CCBh.
Type of infection...... System virus: Ogre will infect any boot
                            sector it comes in contact with. On flop-
                            pies the virus will reserve 5 sectors by
                            marking them as bad. On hard disks the
                            "Special Reserved Sectors" are used, if
                            sufficiently abundent.
Infection trigger...... Any read to a drive will provoke an infection.
Media affected......... Floppies and hard disks
Interrupts hooked...... Int 13 function 2, Int 9, Int 8.
Damage................. It will destroy (encode) the entire disk.
Damage trigger......... The virus has a counter hooked to the timer
                            interrupt. The counter is updated on
                            any infected disk that is found. After
                            about 48 hours of work time, damage is
                            done if within that hour a read to disk
                            is done, else the virus must wait an-
                            other 255 hours.
Particularities........ An disk detroyed (encoded) by Ogre can be
                            restored by an appropriate decoding
                            routine.
Similarities........... ---
---------------------- Agents------------------------------------
Countermeasures........ FindViru in Dr. Solomon's Toolkit will
                            find Ogre.
 - ditto - successful.. AntiOgre will identify and restore an
                            infected disk. RestOgre will restore a
                            destroyed disk.
Standard Means......... Boot from a clean disk and use the SYS command
---------------------- Acknowledgements---------------------------
Location............... Virus Test Center, University of Hamburg, Germany
Classification by...... Morton Swimmer
Documentation by....... Morton Swimmer
Date................... 2-Feb-1990
Information source..... ---
```

OROPAX-Virus

```
Entry...............: OROPAX Virus
Alias(es)...........: Music Virus
Virus Strain........: ---
Virus detected when.: February 1989
Classification......: Program Virus (extending), Direct Action,
                      RAM-resident
Length of Virus.....: COM-files: length increased by 2756-2806 Byte,
                            always divisable by 51.
-------------------- Preconditions --------------------------------
Operating System(s).: MS-DOS
Version/Release.....: 2.xx upward
Computer model(s)...: IBM-PC, XT, AT and compatibles
-------------------- Attributes -----------------------------------
Easy Identification.: Typical texts in Virus body (readable with HexDump
                            facilities): "????????COM" and "COMMAND.COM"
Type of infection...: System: RAM-resident, infected if function 33E0h
```

```
                          of interrupt 21h returns 33E0h in AX-register.
                          .COM File: extending by using FindFirst/FindNext-
                          function in the home directory until a COM File
                          is encountered with a different Attribute than
                          N or A. Files are only infected once.
                          The following .COM-files will not be infected:
                          - COMMAND.COM,
                          - COM files with length divisible by 51,
                          - COM file with an attribute other than N or A,
                          - COM files longer than 61980 Bytes.
                          .EXE File: no infection.
Infection Trigger...: When any of the following INT 21h functions: 39h,
                          3Ah, 3Ch, 3D01h, 41h, 43h, 46h, 13h, 16h, or 17h
                          are called; these functions are also used by other
                          resident DOS commands, e.g. MD, RD, DEL, REN,
                          and COPY.
Interrupts hooked...: INT08h, INT20h, INT21h, INT27h
Damage..............: Transient Damage: After 5 minutes, the virus will
                          start to play three melodies repeatly with a
                          7 minute interval in between. This can only be
                          stopped with a reset. OROPAX and earcaps can be
                          used to avoid "music overload".
Damage Trigger......: Using a random number generator, the virus decides
                          whether to become active.
-------------------- Agents -------------------------------------------
Countermeasures.....: Category 3: ANTIORO.EXE (VTC Hamburg)
Countermeasures successful: ANTIORO.EXE finds and restores infected
                          programs (only for OROPAX).
Standard means......: notice .COM file length
-------------------- Acknowledgement ----------------------------------
Location............: Virus Test Center, University of Hamburg, Germany
Classification by...: Thomas Lippke
Documentation/Translation: Morton Swimmer
Date................: July 15, 1989
```

Parity_Boot Virus

```
Entry...............: Parity_Boot (A) Virus
Alias(es)...........: P-Check Virus (see: CVC entry July 1992)
Virus Strain........: Parity_Boot Virus Strain
Virus detected when.: April 1992
            where.:
Classification......: System (bootsector/partition table (MBR)) virus,
                          stealth
Length of Virus.....: Length on medium: 512 Bytes (=1 sector)
-------------------- Preconditions ------------------------------------
Operating System(s).: MS-DOS
Version/Release.....:
Computer model(s)...: IBM PC and compatibles
-------------------- Attributes ---------------------------------------
Easy Identification.: Memory decreased by 1 kBytes after infection;
                          no plain text in bootsector or MBR, like
                          "Non system disk..." or "Bad partition....".
Type of infection...: Boot sectors and partition table of media.
Infection Trigger...: Booting from an infected disk will infect the
                          hard disk; from this time, all read accesses
                          to the boot sector of any physical drive will
                          infect the medium in this drive.
```

```
Storage media affected: All media: Floppy disk, hard disk.
Interrupts hooked...: INT 09, INT 13.
Damage..............: Transient/Permanent damage:
                      Some built-in mechanism simulates a parity error
                      message on the screen after 1 hour of opera-
                      tion plus an additional hour for each infec-
                      tion: the more infections, the longer till
                      the parity check display.
                      The parity error simulation switches to 40 x 25
                      mode, displays 'PARITY CHECK' and then halts
                      the processor.
                      Virus constantly garbles the INT01&INT03 entries,
                      so that debug will not work; this is not tied
                      to a trigger.
Damage Trigger......: The internal timer tick (not the CMOS clock) is
                      used for timing. Trigger= 1+n hours after
                      boot up (n=number of infections since booting).
Particularities.....: 1) Message text "PARITY CHECK" is constantly
                      encrypted with key 55h.
                      2) In summer 1993, virus (variant B) is "in the
                      wild" in Germany.
Similarities........: Parity_Boot Virus Strain: variants B,C
-------------------- Agents ---------------------------------------
Countermeasures.....: Up-to-date antiviral products, e.g. McAfee Scan,
                      Skulason F-PROT, Dr.Solomon FindViru.
                      Remark: invoking Scan or F-PROT after another
                      scanner having detected and deleted this virus
                      may result in a "false positive" diagnosis as
                      both scanners scan also DOS buffers (where
                      virus would NOT reside) which may not be
                      cleared by the AV product used before.
                      Removal: SYS on floppies; FDISK /MBR (DOS 5.0)
Standard means......:
-------------------- Acknowledgement -----------------------------
Location............: Micro-BIT Virus Center, Univ Karlsruhe, Germany
Classification by...: Christoph Fischer (Klaus Brunnstein, VTC)
Documentation by....: Christoph Fischer
                      Klaus Brunnstein (VTC, update)
Date................: April-1992 (original entry: P-Check)
                      31-July-1993 (update)
Information Source..: reverse analysis of virus code
```

P-Check Virus

```
Entry...............: P-Check Virus
Alias(es)...........: ---
Virus Strain........: ---
Virus detected when.: April 1992
             where.:
Classification......: System (bootsector/partition table (MBR)) virus,
                      stealth
Length of Virus.....: Length on medium: 512 Bytes (=1 sector)
-------------------- Preconditions --------------------------------
Operating System(s).: MS-DOS
Version/Release.....:
Computer model(s)...: IBM PC and compatibles
-------------------- Attributes -----------------------------------
Easy Identification.: Memory decreased by 1 kBytes after infection;
```

```
                              no plain text in bootsector or MBR, like
                              "Non system disk..." or "Bad partition....".
Type of infection...: Boot sectors and partition table of media.
Infection Trigger...: Booting from an infected disk will infect the
                              hard disk; from this time, all read accesses
                              to the boot sector of any physical drive will
                              infect the medium in this drive.
Storage media affected: All media: Floppy disk, hard disk.
Interrupts hooked...: INT 09, INT 13.
Damage..............: Transient/Permanent damage:
                              Some built-in mechanism simulates a parity error
                              message on the screen after 1 hour of opera-
                              tion plus an additional hour for each infec-
                              tion: the more infections, the longer till
                              the parity check display.
                              The parity error simulation switches to 40 x 25
                              mode, displays 'PARITY CHECK' and then halts
                              the processor.
                              Virus constantly garbles the INT01&INT03 entries,
                              so that debug will not work; this is not tied
                              to a trigger.
Damage Trigger......: The internal timer tick (not the CMOS clock) is
                              used for timing. Trigger= 1+n hours after
                              boot up (n=number of infections since booting)
Particularities.....: ---
Similarities........: ---
-------------------- Agents --------------------------------------------
Countermeasures.....: Up-to-date antiviral products.
                              Removal: SYS on floppies; FDISK /MBR (DOS 5.0)
Standard means......:
-------------------- Acknowledgement -----------------------------------
Location............: Micro-BIT Virus Center, Univ Karlsruhe, Germany
Classification by...: Christoph Fischer (Klaus Brunnstein, VTC)
Documentation by....: Christoph Fischer
Date................: April-1992
Information Source..: ---
```

Peach Virus

```
Entry...............: Peach Virus
Standard CARO Name..: Peach Virus
Alias(es)...........: ---
Virus Strain........: ---
Virus detected when.:
            where.:
Classification......: Program (COM&EXE) Virus (appending), resident
Length of Virus.....: On media: 887 Bytes.
-------------------- Preconditions -------------------------------------
Operating System(s).: MS-DOS
Version/Release.....: 2.00 and above
Computer model(s)...:
-------------------- Attributes ----------------------------------------
Easy Identification.: The following text can be found in infected files:
                              "Roy XuatroNo 2 Peach GardenMeyer Rd. Spore 1543"
Self Identification.: In memory: at position 0040:00fc, the string
                              "Roy" can be found.
                              In file: in the EXE header, the IP field will con-
                              tain 01fch at position 14h; in COM file, virus
```

```
                        compares the COM startup code it inserts.
Type of infection...: Virus infects COM and EXE files. It identifies
                      EXE files by looking for "Z" at position 1.
                      Virus goes memory-resident.
Infection Trigger...:Load and Execute (Int 21h function 4B00)
Storage media affected:Anything that can be addressed using DOS calls
                      (floppy diskettes, hard disks)
Interrupts hooked...: Int 21h, Int 23h and Int 24h (Control-C and
                      Critical Error Handler) during infection.
Damage..............: Transient Damage: ---
                      Permanent Damage: if file "chklist.cps" (crea-
                      ted by Central Point AntiVirus) is found,
                      this file is deleted.
Damage Trigger......: If file "chklist.cps" is found.
Particularities.....: ---
Similarities........: ---
-------------------- Agents ------------------------------------------
Countermeasures.....: Skulason F-PROT 2.02, Solomon FindViru 3.5
Standard means......: ---
-------------------- Acknowledgement ---------------------------------
Location............: Virus Test Center, University of Hamburg, Germany
                      S&S International (Deutschland)
Classification by...: Morton Swimmer
Documentation by....: Morton Swimmer
Date................: 7-July-1992
Information Source..: Original virus
```

"Perfume" Virus

```
Entry................ "Perfume" Virus
Alias(e)............. = "4711" = "765" Virus
Strain............... ---
Detected: when....... ---
          where...... ---
Classification....... Program virus, resident COM infector
Length of virus...... 765 bytes added to COM files
--------------------- Preconditions --------------------------------
Operating System(s)... MS-DOS
Version/Release....... 2.0 and up
Computer models....... Any IBM-compatibles
----------------------Attributes ----------------------------------
Easy identification... Contains in one version the following strings:
                       "G-VIRUS V2.0",0Ah,0Dh,
                       "Bitte gebe den G-Virus Code ein : $" <CRLF>
                       0Ah,0Dh,"Tut mir Leid !",0Ah,0Dh,"$"; (trans-
                       lated 2nd and 3rd strings: "please input
                       G-virus code"; "sorry"); in another version
                       there is a block of 88(dec) bytes that
                       contain 00h.
Type of infection..... The virus makes itself resident and intercepts
                       INT 21 upon subfunction 4Bh (load+execute);
                       virus TSR tries to infect the loaded file
                       by appending itself to it. Infectable files
                       have extension COM and are less than FC00h
                       (64512d) bytes long.
Infection trigger..... Loading of a file triggers infection mechanism.
Interrupts hooked..... INT 21
Damage............... A password is demanded after an infected file
```

has been invoked more than 80 times. Initial
message is the first string given above. If
the given password is not "4711" (name of a
well known German perfume), the virus will
display the second message and terminate the
program. In the hacked version of the virus,
all messages have been zeroed out including
the termination characters ("$") which causes
the virus to output its code as text till the
first $-character. Also the input buffer size
for the password iterrogation has been zeroed
which causes unpredictable results upon entry
of too many characters.
```
Particularities.......  Under a rare circumstance, the virus can
                        produce a variant of itself which won't be
                        able to identify itself and thus will infect
                        a file more than once; this is one of several
                        bugs in the virus.
--------------------- Acknowledgement -----------------------------
Location.............. Micro-BIT Virus Center RZ Universitaet Karlsruhe
Classification by..... Christoph Fischer
Dokumentation by ..... Christoph Fischer
Date.................. 14-April-1990
```

Peter Virus

```
Entry...............: Peter Virus
Alias(es)...........: ---
Virus Strain........: ---
Virus detected when.: May 1993
           where.: Japan
Classification......: System virus (MBR,FBR infector)
Length of Virus.....: 1.Length (Byte) on media: 5 sectors
                      2.Length (Byte) in RAM:   4 kBytes
-------------------- Preconditions ------------------------------------
Operating System(s).: MSDOS
Version/Release.....:
Computer model(s)...: IBM PCs and Compatibles: models > 80286, CMOS
-------------------- Attributes ---------------------------------------
Easy Identification.:
Type of infection...: File infection: ---
                      Self-Identification in files: ---
                      System infection: When booting from an infected
                      disk or diskette, virus installs itself in
                      hi-memory. On media, virus code is 5 sectors
                      long, stored at at 0/0/2 (disk), an at 50/0/2
                      (floppy, only if sectors/track is at least 15)
                      Self-Identification on disks:
                      MBR [0x1FD] == 0xBB, FBR [0x1FD] == 0x11
                      Self-Identification in memory: ---
Infection Trigger...: MBR: (Boot) & (MBR[0x1FD]!=0xBB)
                      FBR: (INT13) & (AX==02 | AX==03) &
                       (FBR[0x1FD]!=11) & (FBR[0x18]>=0x0F)
                      That is, when booting from an infected floppy,
                      virus infects hard disk unless its mark is
                      already there, and when using a floppy in A:
                      it gets infected unless the mark is there,
                      or it has less than 15 sectors/track.
```

```
Storage media affected: Hard disk, floppy disks
Interrupts hooked...: INT 13/02, 13/03
Damage..............: Permanent Damage: If user answers any of the
                      questions (see Transient Damage) incorrectly,
                      virus returns without restoring the garbled
                      part of hard disk.  If user answers correctly,
                      virus restores garbled part of hard disk and
                      boots normally.  (Not actually tested)
                      Transient Damage: Upon trigger conditions (see
                      Transient Damage Trigger), virus displays a
                      message (see below), garbles part of hard disk
                      by XORing with hex 78, and asks four questions
                      about pop music.
                      Message, questions and replies (excrypted):
                         "Good morning,EVERYbody,I am PETER II
                          Do not turn off the power, or you will
                          lost all of the data in Hardisk!!!
                          WAIT for 1 MINUTES,please...
                          Ok.If you give the right answer to the
                          following questions,I will save your HD:
                          A. Who has sung the song called
                             "I`ll be there" ?
                             1.Mariah Carey  2.The Escape Club
                             3.The Jackson five  4.All  (1-4):
                          B. What is Phil Collins ?
                             1.A singer  2.A drummer  3.A producer
                             4.Above all  (1-4):
                          C. Who has the MOST TOP 10 singles
                             in 1980`s ?
                             1.Michael Jackson  2.Phil Collins
                             (featuring Genesis)
                             3.Madonna  4.Whitney Houston  (1-4):
                          CONGRATULATIONS !!! YOU successfully pass
                             the quiz!
                          AND NOW RECOVERING YOUR HARDISK ......
                          Sorry!Go to Hell.Clousy man!"
Damage Trigger......: Permanent Damage: If user answers a question
                      in the quiz wrong.
                      Transient Damage: If CMOS clock bytes 7 and 8
                      contain 27 and 2.
Particularities.....: 1) Correct answers are: 4,4,2 (at least in the
                      virus author's opinion)
                      2) Coding style (and English) is very odd and
                      self-taught-looking; e.g. Virus author seems
                      not to know about direct addressing modes.
                      3) Limitations: Virus executes only if CPU >= 286
                      (uvirus ses PUSHA and POPA), CMOS (for date
                      for payload)
Similarities........: ---
-------------------- Agents ---------------------------------------------
Countermeasures.....:
Countermeasures successful:
Standard means......:
-------------------- Acknowledgement ------------------------------------
Location............: IBM High Integrity Computing Lab, Hawthorne, NY
Classification by...: David Chess, HICL
Documentation by....: David Chess (CAROBase entry)
                      Klaus Brunnstein, VTC Hamburg (Virus Catalog)
Date................: 24-May-1993, 1993
Information Source..: Reverse analysis of virus code
```

Plovdiv 1.3 Virus

```
Entry................: Plovdiv 1.3 Virus
Alias(es)............: Damage 1.3 Virus
Virus Strain.........: Damage Virus Strain
Virus detected when..: September 1991
             where..: Plovdiv, Bulgaria
Classification.......: Program virus, Extending, Resident
Length of Virus......: 1,000 in files, 1,328 bytes in memory
-------------------- Preconditions ----------------------------------
Operating System(s)..: MS-DOS
Version/Release......: 2.xx and upward, special support for 3.30
Computer model(s)....: IBM-PC, XT, AT and compatibles
-------------------- Attributes -------------------------------------
Easy identification..: The virus contains the string
                       "(c)Damage inc. Ver 1.3 1991 Plovdiv S.A.".
Type of infection....: Self-Identification: The virus identifies
                       infection by seconds field in file time.
                       Executable Files: Size increased by 1,000 bytes.
                       System infection: RAM-resident. Allocates a
                       memory block at high end of memory by
                       1,344 bytes. If MS-DOS version is 3.30, virus
                       finds original address of INT 21h and INT 13h
                       handlers, thus bypassing active monitors.
Infection Trigger....: Programs are infected at load time (using the
                       function Load/Execute of MS-DOS), and when-
                       ever a *.COM or *.EXE file is Opened.
Media affected.......: Any logical drive that is the "current" drive.
Interrupts hooked....: INT 21h functions 4Bh, 3Dh are used to infect
                       files. Functions 11h and 12h are used to hide
                       virus infection in files.
                       INT 24h and INT 13h are temporary captured to
                       mask out errors.
                       INT 32h contains original INT 21h handler.
Damage...............: The virus formats all available tracks on the
                       current drive.
Damage trigger.......: The virus carries an evolution counter that
                       is decreased every time the virus is executed.
                       Upon counter = 0, the virus reads the system
                       timer. If the value of hundreds is greater
                       than 50, the virus will format all available
                       tracks on the current drive (effectively a
                       50% chance of destruction). "Current" drive
                       is any logical drive on which file is opened,
                       executed or searched thru FindFirst/FindNext.
Particularities......: The virus knocks out the transient part of
                       COMMAND.COM forcing it to be reloaded and
                       thereby infected.
Similarities.........: Damage 1.1 Virus
-------------------- Agents -----------------------------------------
Countermeasures......: VirusClinic 2.00.007+ (Ivan Trifonoff)
Countermeasures successful: VirusClinic 2.00.007+ (Ivan Trifonoff)
Standard means.......: text search of string "Damage"
-------------------- Acknowledgement --------------------------------
Location.............: Laboratory of Computer Virology,
                       Bulgarian Academy of Sciences, Sofia
Classification by....: Ivan Trifonoff
Documentation by.....: Ivan Trifonoff
Date.................: 2-October-1991
Information Source...: ---
```

PS-MPC Virus Generator

```
Entry...............: PS-MPC Virus Generator
Alias(es)...........: Phalcon-Skism Mass Produced Code Generator
Virus Strain........: PS-MPC generated Viruses
Virus detected when.: Summer 1992
            where.: North America (USA)
Classification......: Virus-Generator: creates Assembly Code for
                      Non-resident File Infectors, optionally
                      Self-encrypting.
Length of Virus.....: Depends on creation options and infection routine
-------------------- Preconditions -----------------------------------
Operating System(s).: MS-DOS 4.0 and above
Version/Release.....: Versions 0.90 ß, 0.91 ß
Computer model(s)...: IBM & compatibles
-------------------- Attributes --------------------------------------
Easy Identification.: Variable self-identification
Type of infection...: COM and EXE appending
Infection Trigger...: Every INT 21 call in resident viruses
Storage media affected: EXE and COM files are infected (v.0.90 ß);
                        COMMAND.COM may be infected (v.0.91 ß)
Interrupts hooked...: INT 21 all functions, (INT 24)
Damage..............: To be written by oneself and linked to
                      asm-code of generated code.
Damage Trigger......: Various time-checks may be selected.
Particularities.....: - Viruses decrease memory in high memory-area
                        if resident.
                      - Normally files in the current directory will
                        be infected. It is possible to make the virus
                        traversal (infects current directory and below)
                      - Major Skeleton configuration options v.0.91 ß:
                      * Infection C(OM)/E(XE)
                      * CommandCom (Yes/No): infect COMMAND.COM
                      * Resident (Yes/No)
                      * Traversal (same dir/subdirectories)
                      * Residence Methods (Interrupt,Direct DOS
                         manipulation,BIOS manipulation)
                      * Encrypted (Yes/No)
                      * IDWord (2 character:self-identification)
                      * MinSize/MaxSize: minimum/maximum size
                         of COM files to be infected
                      * Infections#: max.number of infections
                      * ErrorHandler: critical error handler for
                         Abort,Retry,Fail messages
                      * VirusName, AuthorName: strings
                      * Activation Conditions: IfMonth,IfDay,
                         IfYear,IfDayofWeek,IfMonthDay,IfHour,
                         IfMinute,IfSecond,Percentage(counter)
Similarities........: More than 20 viruses have appeared which have
                      clearly been produced with this virus generator:
                      1) 203 Virus
                      2) 644 Virus
                      3) Abraxas Virus
                      4) ARCV Virus Strain
                           ARCV-1 ,-2, -3, -4, -5, -6, -7, -8, -9
                      Remark: ARCV group has also produced viruses
                              with TPE engine (see TPE strain)
                              and developed the ARCV strain.
                      5) Joshua Virus
                      6) Kersplat Virus
```

```
                          7) McWhale Virus
                          8) Mimic Virus
                          9) Small_ARCV Virus
                         10) Small_EXE Virus
                         11) Swan_Song Virus
-------------------- Agents ------------------------------------------
Countermeasures.....:
Countermeasures successful: FindViru, F-Prot (etc)
Standard means......:
-------------------- Acknowledgement ---------------------------------
Location............: Virus Test Center, University of Hamburg, Germany
Classification by...: Holger Prescher
Documentation by....: Holger Prescher
Date................: 02-January-1993
Information Source..: Reverse-Analysis of Generator, Skeleton files.
```

PS-MPC2 Virus Generator

```
Entry...............: PS-MPC2 Virus Generator
Alias(es)...........: PS-MPC G2 =
                      Phalcon-Skism G2 0.70 beta Virus Generator
Virus Strain........: Phalcon-Skism G2 generated Viruses (generates com-
                      pact easily modifiable commented source code)
Virus detected when.:
             where.:
Classification......: Virus-Generator: Creates Assembly Code for
                      Resident and Non-resident File Infectors,
                      optionally Self-encrypting.
Length of Virus.....: Depends on creation options and action routine
-------------------- Preconditions -----------------------------------
Operating System(s).: MS-DOS
Version/Release.....: Versions 4.0 and upward
Computer model(s)...: IBM & compatibles
-------------------- Attributes --------------------------------------
Easy Identification.: Variable self-identification
Type of infection...: COM and EXE infector, appending
Infection trigger...: 1) Execution of an infected program.
                      2) Every INT 21 call in resident viruses.
Storage media affected: EXE and or COM files infected;
                      COMMAND.COM may be infected (parameter)
Interrupts hooked...: INT 21 all functions, (INT 24)
Damage..............: To be written by specific virus author and to
                      be linked to PS-MPC G2 generated code.
Damage Trigger......: Depending on specific virus.
Particularities.....: - PS-MPC G2 Viruses decrease memory in high
                        memory-area if resident.
                      - The PS-MPC G2 generator offers the following
                        major Skeleton configuration options:
                        * Infection C(OM)/E(XE) (may be both)
                        * CommandCom (Yes/No): infect COMMAND.COM
                        * Resident (Yes/No)
                        * Encrypted (Yes/No), Encryption: xor, add
                        * IDWord (2 character:self-identification)
                        * MinSize/MaxSize: minimum/maximum size
                            of COM files to be infected
                        * Infections#: max.number of infections
                        * ErrorHandler: critical error handler for
                            Abort,Retry,Fail messages
```

```
                          * VirusName, AuthorName: strings
                          * AntiDebugger (Yes/No): If this option is
                             set to Yes, the CPU-generated Breakpoint
                             Interrupt INT3 points to INT21 and is
                             also used from the virus itself instead
                             of INT21.
Similarities........: 1) PS-MPC (original version)
                      2) Following PS MPC G2 generated viruses are
                      known:
-------------------- Agents --------------------------------------
Countermeasures.....:
Countermeasures successful: FindViru, F-Prot (etc) detect PS MPC G2
                            generated viruses.
Standard means......:
-------------------- Acknowledgement -----------------------------
Location............: Virus Test Center, University of Hamburg, Germany
Classification by...: Holger Prescher & Frank Bohnsack
Documentation by....: Holger Prescher & Frank Bohnsack
Date................: 31-July-1993
Information Source..: Reverse-Analysis of Generator, Skeleton files.
```

Qrry Virus

```
Entry...............: Qrry Virus
Alias(es)...........: ---
Virus Strain........: ---
Virus detected when.: March 1993
               where.: USA
Classification......: System virus (MBR, FBR infector), memory resident
Length of Virus.....: 1.Length (Byte) on media:  1 Sector
                      2.Length (Byte) in RAM:    1 kByte
-------------------- Preconditions -------------------------------
Operating System(s).: MSDOS
Version/Release.....:
Computer model(s)...: IBM PCs and Compatibles
-------------------- Attributes ----------------------------------
Easy Identification.: Test if bootrec[0]==EBh & bootrec[0170h]==ABCDh
Type of infection...: File infection: ---
                      Self-Identification in files: ---
                      System infection: Virus code stored at 27h/01h/09h.
                      Upon booting from an infected disk, virus makes
                      itself memory resident (in hi-memory).
                      Self-Identification in memory: ---
                      Self-Identification on disk:
                       bootrec[0]==EBh & bootrec[0170h]==ABCDh
Infection Trigger...: If given values in INT 13 registers are found.
Storage media affected: Hard disk, floppy disks
Interrupts hooked...: INT 13/0201
Damage..............: Permanent Damage: overwrites the first 9 sectors
                      of the first 3 tracks on any disk or diskette
                      head that's read from.
                      Transient Damage: ---
Damage Trigger......: Permanent Damage: All days in December:
                      Real_Time_Clock_Month == 12
                      Transient Damage: ---
Particularities.....: Name "QRRY" is taken from some ASCII characters
                      that happens to appear in virus code; no other
                      obvious characteristic for naming.
```

```
Similarities........: ---
-------------------- Agents ---------------------------------------
Countermeasures.....:
Countermeasures successful:
Standard means......:
-------------------- Acknowledgement -------------------------------
Location............: IBM High Integrity Computing Lab, Hawthorne, NY
Classification by...: David Chess, HICL
Documentation by....: David Chess (CAROBase entry)
                      Klaus Brunnstein, VTC Hamburg (Virus Catalog)
Date................: March 8, 1993
Information Source..: Reverse analysis of virus code
```

Requires Virus

```
Entry...............: Requires Virus
Alias(es)...........: Requires.981 = Demise = Later Virus
Virus Strain........: ---
Virus detected when.: Russia
              where.: ---
Classification......: Resident, appending-EXE and prepending-COM file
                         infector
Length of Virus.....: In files: 981 bytes (EXE files are first padded
                            to a multiple of 16 bytes).
                      In memory: 1952 bytes after the last MCB.
-------------------- Preconditions ---------------------------------
Operating System(s).: MS/PC DOS
Version/Release.....: 3.0+
Computer model(s)...: Any MS-DOS compatible computer
-------------------- Attributes ------------------------------------
Easy Identification.: All infected files contain the message
                      "This program requires MS-DOS 3.00 or later$".
Self Identification.: In memory: INT 21h/AH=0B3h returns 9051h in AX.
                      In COM files: if the first two bytes of the file
                                 are 50h 8Ch, it is considered as
                                 infected. However, the first  two
                                 bytes of the virus are actually
                                 50h 0B4h, which causes COM files
                                 to be re-infected multiple times.
                      In EXE files: if the two bytes at offset 10h in
                                 EXE header are 5Ch 09h (in the SP
                                 field), then file is considered
                                 as infected.
Type of infection...: Files with extension 'COM' and 'EXE'. The true
                      file type is determined by checking the first
                      two bytes for 'MZ', however. No check is made
                      for 'ZM'. Files ??????D.COM is not infected.
Infection Trigger...: OpenFileHandle and LoadAndExec (INT 21h/AH=3Dh
                      and INT 21h/AX=4B00h).
Storage media affected: Any MS-DOS file system which contains infectable
                      objects.
Interrupts hooked...: INT 21h and INT 24h (only during infection).
Damage..............: Transitive damage: infected programs executed
                         under a version of DOS below 3.0 display
                         message "This program requires MS-DOS 3.00
                         or later" and refuse to run.
                      Permanent damage: ---
Damage Trigger......: Transitive damage: Execution of an infected file
```

```
                       under a version of DOS below 3.0.
                       Permanent damage: ---
Particularities.....: 1) When an infected file is executed,virus removes
                       itself from there, in an attempt to hide the
                       source of infection and to prevent from being
                       detected by self-checking programs.
                       2) COM files can be infected multiple times.
                       3) Due to some bugs, multiply infected files can
                       not always be restored to their original state
                       but will still contain parts of the virus.
                       Those parts, however, will be inactive and will
                       never receive control. However, they may cause
                       "ghost positive" alerts by some scanners (since
                       a significant part of the virus potentially
                       containing scan strings used by scanners,
                       remain in such incompletely "cleaned" files).
Similarities........: ---
-------------------- Agents -----------------------------------------
Countermeasures.....: Virus uses no full stealth, tunneling, or poly-
                       morphism, so most integrity checkers, monitors,
                       and up-to-date scanners should have no problems
                       detecting it.
Countermeasures successful: F-Prot 2.04a was tested and was able to
                       successfully remove virus when removable.
Standard means......: If you can remove it without any anti-virus progs
-------------------- Acknowledgement --------------------------------
Location............: Virus Test Center, University of Hamburg, Germany
Classification by...: Vesselin Bontchev
Documentation by....: Vesselin Bontchev
Date................: 27-Jul-1992
Information Source..: Reverse analysis of virus code
```

RMBD Virus

```
Entry...............: RMBD Virus
Alias(es)...........: ---
Virus Strain........:
Virus detected when.: July 1993
             where.: USA
Classification......: System virus (MBR,FBR infector), memory resident
Length of Virus.....: 1.Length (Byte) on media: 1 (or 0) sector
                       2.Length (Byte) in RAM:   1 kByte
-------------------- Preconditions ----------------------------------
Operating System(s).: MSDOS
Version/Release.....:
Computer model(s)...: IBM PCs and Compatibles
-------------------- Attributes -------------------------------------
Easy Identification.: Text in virus:  "RMBDRMCC B WRM"
Type of infection...: File infection: ---
                       Self-Identification in files: ---
                       System infection: Upon booting from infected media,
                       virus makes itself memory resident (hi-memory).
                       By manipulating INT 13, virus hides it's pre-
                       sence in memory (stealth mechanism).
                       Self-Identification in memory: none
                       Self-identification on disks:  none
Infection Trigger...: MBR of drive 80 is infected on every boot from an
                       infected diskette or hard disk. Diskette boot
```

```
                          records are infected on any INT13 read or write.
Storage media affected: Hard disk, floppy disks
Interrupts hooked...: INT  13/02, 13/03
Damage..............: Permanent Damage:
                          1) Overwrites 0x0E sectors, starting at
                             sector 4, of some tracks on cylinder 0.
                          2) Side effects: Infected diskettes will not
                             have a valid BPB, and will often not be
                             readable at all.  When a machine is booted
                             from an infected diskette, the virus will
                             infect the hard disk, and then boot from
                             the bootable partition on the hard disk!
                             (Rather than booting from diskette.)
                          Transient Damage: ---
Damage Trigger......: Permanent Damage:
                          1) If INT13 AND (AH=02 or AH=03) AND
                             (0040:0071 & 0x80 set)
                             [The BIOS "break" bit, high bit of 0040:0071,
                             is set during an INT13 read or write]
                          2) ---
                          Transient Damage: ---
Particularities.....: 1) Hard disk required, even to boot from an
                          infected floppy.
                          2) Very unusual infection methods, in that it
                          saves neither original MBR of hard disks nor
                          original DBR of diskettes.  Instead, it contains
                          essentially all of the code from the normal MBR,
                          and uses that to boot the system.  Even when
                          booting from an infected floppy, virus reads
                          MBR of hard disk, copies partition table, and
                          (after infecting of hard disk) uses MBR code to
                          boot from hard disk.
                          3) Meaning of text "RMBDRMCC B WRM" unclear.
Similarities........: ---
-------------------- Agents --------------------------------------------
Countermeasures.....:
Countermeasures successful:
Standard means......:
-------------------- Acknowledgement -----------------------------------
Location............: IBM High Integrity Computing Lab, Hawthorne, NY
Classification by...: David Chess, HICL
Documentation by....: David Chess (CAROBase entry)
                      Klaus Brunnstein, VTC Hamburg (Virus Catalog)
Date................: 6-July-1993
Information Source..: Reverse analysis of virus code
```

RPVS Virus

```
Entry..............: RPVS Virus
Alias(es)..........: TUQ = 453 Virus
Strain.............: ---
Detected: when.....: 1-August-1990
          where....: Suedwestdeutscher Bibliotheksverbund
                        (located at University of Konstanz, Germany)
Classification.....: Link virus, direct action COM infector
Length of virus....: 453 bytes added to COM files
-------------------- Preconditions -------------------------------------
Operating System(s): MS-DOS
```

```
Version/Release....: 2.0+
Computer models....: All MS-DOS-Machines
------------------- Attributes -----------------------------------
Easy identification: File size increased by 453 bytes. The following
                     offsets are taken relative to the address
                     the JMP instruction (cf. infra) points to:
                     offset | string / bytes found
                     -------+----------------------------------
                       007  | "VIRUS"
                       00D  | "*.COM"
                       013  | "????????COM"
                       030  | file-id of the infected program
                       043  | original contents of 1st 3 bytes
                       052  | "TUQ(?)RPVS"
Self-identification: Last two bytes = 9090(hex). When an infected file
                     is executed, one uninfected .COM-file in cur-
                     rent directory is infected by appending the
                     viral code.
Type of infection..: Direct action. Begin of program is overwritten
                     with JMP instruction pointing to appended
                     viral code.
Infection trigger..: Executing an infected file will trigger the
                     infection attempt in the local directory.
                     Virus has been tested with one bait (at most)
                     available, so it is not clear whether multiple
                     programs will be infected. No files outside
                     the local directory have been infected during
                     tests.
Storage media affected: Current media (current directory).
Interrupts hooked..: ---
Damage.............: ---
Particularities....: ---
------------------- Agents ---------------------------------------
Countermeasures....: Category 3: ANTI!453.EXE (d:) (/f)
Countermeasures successful: ANTI!453.EXE (Daniel Loeffler,VTC-Hamburg)
                     looks for infected files on a given drive (d:)
                     and optionally removes the virus (if /f given).
Standard means.....: ---
------------------- Acknowledgement ------------------------------
Location...........: Rechenzentrum der University Konstanz
Classification by..: Otto Stolz <RZOTTO at DKNKURZ1.BITNET>
                     Daniel Loeffler (VTC-Hamburg)
Documentation by ..: Otto Stolz <RZOTTO at DKNKURZ1.BITNET>
                     Daniel Loeffler (VTC-Hamburg)
Date...............: 10-February-1991
```

RPVS/TUQ Virus

```
Entry..............: RPVS Virus
Alias(es)..........: TUQ = "453" Virus
Strain.............: ---
Detected: when.....: August 1, 1990
          where....: Suedwestdeutscher Bibliotheksverbund
                     (located at University of Konstanz)
Classification.....: Program virus: direct action COM-infector
Length of virus....: .COM files: 453 bytes appended
```

```
---------------------- Preconditions ----------------------------
Operating System(s): MS-DOS
Version/Release....: Version 2.0 upwards
Computer models....: All MS-DOS-Machines
----------------------Attributes ------------------------------------
Easy identification: File size increases by 453 bytes.
                     Diverse texts are visible (with proper tool) in
                         the virus; the offsets given are relative to
                         the address the JMP instruction (cf. infra)
                         points to:
                     offset | string / bytes found
                     -------+------------------------------------
                     007    | "VIRUS"
                     00D    | "*.COM"
                     013    | "????????COM"
                     030    | file-id of the infected program
                     043    | original contents of 1st 3 bytes
                     052    | "TUQ(?)RPVS"
Self-identification: Last two bytes = 9090(hex).
                     When an infected file is executed, one
                     uninfected .COM-file in current directory
                     is infected by appending the viral code.
Type of infection..: Direct action; begin of program is overwritten
                     with JMP to appended viral code.
Infection trigger..: Executing an infected file will trigger the
                     infection attempt in the local directory.
                     No files outside the local directory have
                     been infected during tests.
Storage media affected: Current media (Current directory).
Interrupts hooked..: ---
Damage.............: Transient damage: ---
                     Permanent damage: ---
Damage trigger.....: ---
Particularities....: ---
-------------------- Agents ----------------------------------------
Countermeasures....: Category 3: ANTI!453.EXE (d:) (/f)
Countermeasures successful: ANTI!453.EXE (Daniel Loeffler,VTC-Hamburg)
                            looks for infected files on a given drive
                            (d:) and optionally removes the virus
                            (if /f given).
Standard means.....: ---
-------------------- Acknowledgement ---------------------------
Location...........: Rechenzentrum der University Konstanz
Classification by..: Otto Stolz <RZOTTO at DKNKURZ1.BITNET>
                     Daniel Loeffler (VTC-Hamburg)
Dokumentation by ..: Otto Stolz <RZOTTO at DKNKURZ1.BITNET>
                     Daniel Loeffler (VTC-Hamburg)
Date...............: 15-July 1991
```

Runtime Virus

```
Entry..............: Runtime Virus
Alias(es)..........: Runtime-err412 Virus
Virus Strain.......: ---
Virus detected when.: July 1993
             where.: USA
```

```
Classification......: File virus (COM, COMMAND.COM infector)
Length of Virus.....: 1.Length (Byte) on media: 365 Bytes
                      2.Length (Byte) in RAM:   0 (not memory resident)
-------------------- Preconditions -----------------------------------
Operating System(s).: MSDOS
Version/Release.....: MSDOS >= 3.0
Computer model(s)...: IBM PCs and Compatibles
-------------------- Attributes --------------------------------------
Easy Identification.: Text in virus code: "Runtime error 412"
Type of infection...: File infection: virus infects COM files, including
                      COMMAND.COM. To hide itself against detection
                      (stealth), it restores original time and date
                      stamps to files after infection.
                      Self-Identification in files: code intends to check
                       for initial NEAR CALL (0eh), doesnot work.
                      System infection: not memory resident.
                      Self-Identification in memory: ---
Infection Trigger...: Upon execution of an infected file
Storage media affected: Disk and diskette
Interrupts hooked...: None
Damage..............: Permanent Damage: no intended permanent damage.
                      Side effect: Uncontrolled file growth due to
                      multiple infections.
                      Transient Damage:
                      1) Hangs system occasionally on trigger conditions.
                      2) Displays message "Runtime error 412" followed by
                      possible garbage.
Damage Trigger......: Permanent Damage: ---
                      Transient Damage:
                      1) On Fridays before 11:00 AM if clock
                           @ 40:06Ch >0b0h.
                      2) Execution of infected file.
Particularities.....: Virus cannot infect read-only files.
Similarities........: ---
-------------------- Agents ------------------------------------------
Countermeasures.....:
Countermeasures successful: At publication date, virus was not detected
                       by tested scanners (VIRx,McAfee's Scan,F-Prot,
                       IBM anti-virus, and TBscan602).
Standard means......: Delete infected files and replace with clean ones.
-------------------- Acknowledgement ---------------------------------
Location............: Stiller Research, Tallahassee, FL
Classification by...: Wolfgang Stiller
Documentation by....: Wolfgang Stiller (CAROBase entry)
                      Klaus Brunnstein (Virus Catalog entry)
Date................: 6-July-1993
Information Source..: Reverse analysis of virus code
```

Sadam Virus

```
Entry...............: Sadam Virus
Alias(es)...........: =Saddam Virus
Virus strain........: Stupid Virus Strain (?)
Virus detected when.: 1-October-1989
            where.: BBS in Israel
Classifications.....: COM file infecting virus/extending, resident.
Length of virus.....: 917-924 bytes, depending on size of name
                      of infected file.
```

```
Length of Virus.....: 919 bytes appendend (CBh+2CCh)
-------------------- Preconditions ----------------------------------
Operating system(s).: MS-DOS
Version/release.....: 2.0 or higher
Computer model(s)...: IBM PC,XT,AT and compatibles
-------------------- Attributes -------------------------------------
Identification......: Memory: INT 6Bh points to original INT 21h.
                      (see Particularities [4])
                      .COM files: The encryped message; to decrypt
                      the string, add 6 to each char, the terminat-
                      ing char is 24h before adding 6. The name of
                      the infected file is stored with the virus.
                      (name is stored at infection time; later
                      renaming will not be recognized!)
Type of infection...: System: The virus copies itself to high memory
                      at the adress    [0:413]*40h-867h.
                      The virus does not diminish the memory size
                      by what is written in [0:413], nor will DOS
                      regard that area as used; therefore, big
                      programs may hang-up the system.
                      .COM files: Extends .COM files; appends 919
                      bytes to the end of the file.
                      .EXE files: Not infected.
Infection trigger...: Several file services of INT 21h
Interrupts hooked...: INT 21h, INT 6Bh.
Damage..............: Displays the message:
                      "HEY SADAM"{LF}{CR}
                      "LEAVE QUEIT BEFORE I COME" (wrong syntax)
Damage trigger......: Counts the number of infections; on every 8th
                      infection, the string will be displayed.
Particularities.....: 1. Many programs load themself to this area and
                      therefore erase the virus from memory.
                      2. The virus uses INT 6BH replacement for the
                      original INT 21H.
                      3. The virus infects just files in the current
                      directory.
                      4. If the disk is write-protected, the message
                      from DOS about write protection will be dis-
                      played when the virus tries to spread.
                      5. The virus will not be able to change files
                      that have the Read-Only attribute set.
-------------------- Agents -----------------------------------------
Countermeasures.....: F-Prot 1.13 RESIDENT PART ONLY: identifies the
                      virus as The Stupid Virus and does not let
                      the program get into memory.
-------------------- Acknowledgement --------------------------------
Classification by...: Baruch Even (NYEVENBA@WEIZMANN.BITNET)
                      Matthias Jaenichen, VTC-Hamburg
Documentation by....: Matthias Jaenichen, VTC-Hamburg
Date................: 5-October-1990
Update..............: 14-February-1991
Information Source..: ---
```

Saratoga Virus

```
Entry...............: "Saratoga virus"
Alias(es)...........:
Virus Strain........: Icelandic Virus
```

```
Virus detected when.: July '89
            where.: Saratoga (California)
Classification......: .EXE file infecting virus/Extending/Resident
Length of Virus.....: 1. 642-657 bytes added to file
                      2. 2048 bytes in RAM
-------------------- Preconditions ------------------------------------
Operating System(s).: MS-DOS
Version/Release.....: 2.0 or higher
Computer model(s)...: IBM PC,XT,AT and compatibles
-------------------- Attributes ---------------------------------------
Easy Identification.: .EXE Files: Infected files end in "PooT".
                      System: Byte at 0:37F contains FF (hex)
Type of infection...: Extends .EXE files. Adds 642-657 bytes to the end
                      of the file. Stays resident in RAM, hooks INT 21 and
                      infects other programs when they are executed via
                      function 4B. It will remove the Read-Only attribute if
                      necessary, but it is not restored.
                      .COM files are not infected.
Infection Trigger...: One out of every two programs run is checked. If it is
                      an uninfected .EXE file it will be infected.
Storage media affected: ---
Interrupts hooked...: INT 21
Damage..............: If the current drive is a hard disk larger than
                      10M bytes, the virus will select one cluster and
                      mark it as bad in the first copy of the FAT.
                      Diskettes and 10M byte disks are not affected.
Damage Trigger......: The damage is done whenever a file is infected.
Particularities.....: The virus modifies the MCBs in order to hide
                      from detection. The INT 13 checking in the original
                      version has been removed.
                      The virus uses the name of the file to determine
                      if it is an .EXE file, but not the true type, as
                      determined by the first two bytes.
                      The virus assumes the program reserves all available
                      memory (FFFF paragraphs needed). Programs that donot
                      will cause a system crash when infected and run.
Similarities........: This virus is just a minor variant of Icelandic-1.
-------------------- Agents -------------------------------------------
Countermeasures.....: All programs which check for .EXE file length
                      changes will detect infections.
Countermeasures successful:
                      Detection of infection:
                       F-FCHK (from F.Skulason's F-PROT package)
                       VIRUSCAN
                      Removal:  F-FCHK
Standard means......:
-------------------- Acknowledgement ----------------------------------
Location............: University of Iceland/Computing Services
Classification by...: Fridrik Skulason  (frisk@rhi.hi.is)
Documentation by....: Fridrik Skulason
Date................: Sept 20, 1989
Information Source..: ---
```

Scrambler Trojan

```
Entry...............: Scrambler Trojan
Alias(es)...........: KEYBGR Trojan
Virus strain........: ---
```

```
Virus detected when.: June 1990
            where.: West Germany
Host.................: Keybgr.com
Virus detected when.: November 1987
            where.: Lehigh University (Bethlehem/USA)
-------------------- Preconditions ----------------------------------
Operating system(s).: MS-DOS
Version/release.....: It is not bound to any particular DOS version,
                      but keybgr is not used on standard DOS later
                      than 3.3 Computer models PC's with standard
                      keyboards.
Computer model(s)...: All MS-DOS machines
-------------------- Attributes -------------------------------------
Easy identification.: The Trojan contains many copies of the string
                      "nothing".
Interrupts hooked...: INT 9 is captured for the host program, and
                      INT 1C is used for the damage.
Damage..............: A smiley face moves in a random fashion about
                      the screen displacing characters as it moves.
                      The face is either ascii 2 or 1 with a 50%
                      probability.
Damage trigger......: About 60 minutes after the trojan keybgr is
                      started.
Particularities.....: ---
Similarities........: ---
-------------------- Agents -----------------------------------------
Countermeasures.....: ---
Detectors...........: ---
Standard Means......: ---
-------------------- Acknowledgement --------------------------------
Location............: Virus Test Center, University Hamburg, FRG
Classification by...: Morton Swimmer
Documentation by....: Morton Swimmer
Date................: June 30, 1990
Information Source..: ---
```

Semtex Virus

```
Entry...............: Semtex Virus
Alias(es)...........: Screen Trasher Virus
Virus Strain........:
Virus detected when.: September 1991
            where.: Germany
Classification......: Program (appending) virus, resident
Length of Virus.....: 1,000 Bytes
-------------------- Preconditions ----------------------------------
Operating System(s).: MS-DOS
Version/Release.....: 1.xx upward
Computer model(s)...: IBM - PC, XT, AT, upward and compatibles
-------------------- Attributes -------------------------------------
Direct Detection....: Every hour, the screen is overwritten by trash.
Easy Identification.: Infected files will contain the string:
                      "  S E M T E X  by Dusan Toman, CZECHOSLOVAKIA"
                      " (7)213-040 or (804)212-23  "
Type of infection...: All *.COM that are executed or opened will be
                      infected if their length <= 61,000 Bytes.
                      COMMAND.COM will also be infected; there is
                      explicit code in the virus that exploits
```

```
                           the comspec.
Infection Trigger...: Any Load/Execute or Open of a *.COM file.
Infection targets:..: All *.COM files with length <= 61,000 Bytes.
Interrupts hooked...: INT 08 (hooked); INT 10, INT 21 (used);
                           INT 61 (occupied)
Damage..............: At an hourly intervall, virus will trash screen
                           contents by overwriting with garbage.
Damage Trigger......: A Counter that counts the timer tics.
Similarities........: ---
Particularities.....: 1) This virus does not intercept INT 24, so a
                           write error will occur upon each infection
                           attempt.
                           2) Windows 3.0 will not like what virus does
                           to the memory allocation.
                           3) INT 61 usage will render the following pro-
                           ducts inoperative:
                               Atari Portfolio (system management)
                               HP 95LX System (system management)
                               JPI topspeed modula (procedure exit trap)
                               FTP PC/TCP (function calls)
                               Adaptec and Omti controller
                               Banyan Vines (network)
                               Sangoma CCIP (CCPOP3270)
-------------------- Agents ---------------------------------------
Countermeasures.....:
- ditto - successful:
Standard means......:
-------------------- Acknowledgement ------------------------------
Location............: Micro-BIT Virus Center, Univ Karlsruhe, Germany
Classification by...: Christoph Fischer
Documentation by....: Christoph Fischer
Date................: 31-January-1992
```

Seventh Son Virus

```
Entry...............: Seventh Son Virus
Standard CARO name..: Seventh_Son.284 Virus
Alias(es)...........: Seventh Son-284 Virus
Virus Strain........: Seventh Son virus strain
Virus detected when.: October 1991
               where.: Eastern Europe
Classification......: File (COM) virus
Length of Virus.....: 284 Bytes
-------------------- Preconditions --------------------------------
Operating System(s).: DOS
Version/Release.....:
Computer model(s)...: IBM compatibles
-------------------- Attributes -----------------------------------
Easy Identification.: The displayed text "Seventh son of a seventh son"
                           can be found in infected programs.
Type of infection...: Infects only COM files
Infection Trigger...: Execution of an infected program.
Storage media affected: Infects any diskette and hard disks
Interrupts hooked...: ---
Damage..............: Permanent damage: ---
                           Transient damage: displays the text
                                      "Seventh son of a seventh son"
Damage Trigger......: Permanent damage: ---
```

```
                          Transient damage: executing an infected program
Particularities.....:     ---
Similarities........:     Seventh Son variants (.332, .350)
-------------------- Agents -----------------------------------------
Countermeasures.....:     McAfee Scan,Skulason F-PROT,Solomon FINDVIRU
Standard means......:     Delete infected files and replace with un-
                          infected originals or backups.
-------------------- Acknowledgement --------------------------------
Location............:     Virus Test Center, University of Hamburg, Germany
Classification by...:     Michaela Schroeder, Peter Liem, Doerte Hachfeld,
                          Holger Prescher
Documentation by....:     Holger Prescher, Doerte Hachfeld, Peter Liem,
                          Michaela Schroeder
Date................:     20-July-1992
Information Source..:     Reverse-Engineering of virus code
```

SHOE-B v9.0

```
Entry..................   SHOE-B v9.0
Alias(es)..............   ---
Strain.................   Brain/Pakistani
Detected: when.........   November 1988
          where........   Houston University
Classification.........   System (Boot sector) virus
Length of Virus........   approx. 3k (not all is actually used)
---------------------- Preconditions--------------------------------
Operating System(s)....   MS-DOS
Version/Release........   Should work with all versions
Computer models........   IBM-PC's and compatibles
---------------------- Attributes-----------------------------------
Easy identification....   The volume label of the infected disk will
                          read: "(c) Brain"
Type of infection......   The virus installs itself in high memory after
                          booting with an infected disk. It captures all
                          read and  write calls to the disk, checks for
                          infection and, if not yet present, infects the
                          disk. Infection occurs by flagging five blocks
                          as bad, copying itself and the original boot
                          sector into those five blocks, and replacing the
                          boot sector with its own. The virus identifies
                          itself by checking the boot sector for the
                          word 1234h at position 0004h in the boot sector.
Infection trigger......   Counter: will attempt to infect initially
                          after 31 read/write calls, subsequently after
                          every fourth call.
Media affected.........   Only floppy disks; Hard disks not infected.
Interrupts hooked......   Int 13h functions 2,3 (read,write).
Damage.................   Destroys five blocks (as well as the boot
                          sector) upon infection, otherwise nothing.
Damage trigger.........   ---
Particularities........   The virus looks whether attempts are made to
                          read the boot sector; in this case, the virus
                          transfers the original boot sector. The virus
                          can therefore not be identified with utilities
                          such as PC-TOOLS or NORTON  UTILITIES.
                          An infected boot sector contains the following
                          typical text: "Welcome to the Dungeon
                          (c) 1986 Basit & Amjads (pvt) Ltd
```

```
                          VIRUS_SHOE RECORD v9.0 Dedicated to the dynamic
                          memories of millions of virus who are no longer
                          with us today - Thanks GOODNESS!! BEWARE OF THE
                          er..VIRUS: \this program is catching   program
                          follows after these messeges..... $#%$!!   ";
                          this text is never displayed.
Similarities........... Similar to all viruses of Pakistani/Brain strain.
---------------------- Agents -------------------------------------------
Countermeasures........ ----
Countermeasures successful ---
Standard Means......... The DOS command "SYS n:" (where n is the drive
                          of the infected disk) will disinfect the disk
                          IF AND ONLY IF you have booted from a clean disk.
                          You will have to use utilities such as PC-TOOLS
                          to recover the "bad" sectors.
---------------------- Acknowledgements----------------------------------
Location............... Virus Test Center, University of Hamburg, Germany
Classification by...... Morton Swimmer
Documentation by....... Morton Swimmer
Date................... June 29, 1989
Information source..... PC VIRUS LISTING (Jim Goodwin)
```

Silly Willy Trojan

```
Entry...............: Silly Willy Trojan
Standard CARO Name..: Silly_Willy Trojan
Alias(es)...........: ---
Virus Strain........: Silly Willy (Trojan/Virus) Strain
Virus detected when.: March 92
            where.: Munich, Germany
Classification......: Trojan
Length of Virus.....: 803 Bytes
-------------------- Preconditions ----------------------------------
Operating System(s).: IBM PC & Compatibles
Version/Release.....: DOS 2.x and above
Computer model(s)...: IBM PC, XT, AT and upwards, and compatibles
-------------------- Attributes -------------------------------------
Easy Identification.: ---
Scan signature......: The string: 0e 1f b0 49 be 11 00 b9 24 03 2b ce
                          28 04 can be found at begin of an trojanized
                          file.
Type of infection...: ---
Infection Trigger...: ---
Storage media affected: Any floppy diskette, hard disk
Interrupts hooked...: ---
Damage..............: Transient/Permanent damage: The trojan displays
                          a face, telling that he is Silly Willy and
                          right now formatting the hard disk. But
                          instead, it writes a hidden file, so the
                          user observes some hard disk activities. The
                          hidden file has a length between 154,622 and
                          459,952 bytes and contains the text
                            "The User of This Computer Is Stupid!".
                          After some time, another message will appear:
                            "ERROR: o SYSTEM found!
                             No Files on drive C:
                             Insert SYSTEM diskette in drive A:
                                and push a key!"
```

```
                              After pushing a key, the first 9 sectors on
                              the first five tracks will be overwritten
                              with the text
                                 "The User of This Computer Is Stupid!"
                              Then, the system hangs.
Damage Trigger......: Starting a trojanized EXE-file
Particularities.....: Silly Willy Trojan is dropped by Silly Willy
                      Virus which overwrites EXE files with trojan.
Similarities........: ---
-------------------- Agents -------------------------------------------
Countermeasures.....: Solomon FindViru 4.23, Antivir from H&B-EDV
Standard means......: Delete/replace trojanized files with clean ones.
-------------------- Acknowledgement ----------------------------------
Location............: Virus Test Center, University of Hamburg, Germany
                      Siemens Nixdorf AG (SNI), Munich
Classification by...: Toralv Dirro (VTC), Ralph Dombach (SNI)
Documentation by....: Toralv Dirro
Date................: 16-July-92
Information Source..: Original virus analysis
```

Silly Willy Virus

```
Entry...............: Silly Willy Virus
Standard CARO Name..: Silly_Willy Virus
Alias(es)...........: ---
Virus Strain........: Silly Willy (Trojan/Virus) Strain
Virus detected when.: March 91
              where.: Munich, Germany
Classification......: Direct action COM-infector, Trojan dropper (EXE)
Length of Virus.....: Length in COM-files: 2261-2314 bytes
-------------------- Preconditions ------------------------------------
Operating System(s).: IBM PC & Compatibles
Version/Release.....: DOS 2.x and above
Computer model(s)...: IBM PC, XT, AT and upward, and compatibles
-------------------- Attributes ---------------------------------------
Easy Identification.: Increased file size; unusual long loading time.
Scan signature......: The string : BE 15 00 8B 1A B9 D0 08 81 E9 can be
                      found at about 2300 bytes offset from the end
                      of an infected file.
Type of infection...: COM-files will be searched via FindFirst,FindNext,
                      starting with root directory, and in sub-
                      directories, if no uninfected files are found
                      in the root.
                      EXE-files will be overwritten with Silly Willy
                      Trojan (see separate Virus Catalog entry).
Infection Trigger...: Starting an infected file; virus will search
                      for one COM-file to infect and for one EXE-
                      file to trojanize.
Storage media affected: Only files on drive C: will be affected.
Interrupts hooked...: ---
Damage..............: Transient damage: ---
                      Permanent damage: EXE-files are overwritten
                         with Silly Willy Trojan (see separate Virus
                         Catalog entry).
Damage Trigger......: Start of an infected program
Particularities.....: 1) The virus uses polymorphic methods to hide
                         from detection in COM-files. At offset 0,
                         16 Bytes are inserted in COM-files; these
```

```
                         can hold 16 different values of code. The
                         virus merges two 8 byte strings, and each
                         string has four different values; moreover,
                         a random number of bytes is inserted, too.
                         Due to a very simple decryption algorithm
                         (XOR) and some uncrypted code, the poly-
                         morphic routine is rather ineffective.
                         2) Date and time of infected programs will not
                         be changed.
                         3) Only COM-files with a length between 1087
                         and 58,932 bytes will be infected.
                         4) No exact match to recognize EXE and COM
                         files is performed.
Similarities........: ---
-------------------- Agents ------------------------------------
Countermeasures.....: Checksums, etc.
Countermeasures successful: Solomon FindViru 4.23, H&B-EDV AntiVir
Standard means......: Delete and replace infected files.
-------------------- Acknowledgement ---------------------------
Location............: Siemens Nixdorf AG (SNI), Munich, Germany
                      Virus Test Center, University Hamburg, Germany
Classification by...: Ralph Dombach (SNI), Toralv Dirro (VTC)
Documentation by....: Toralv Dirro
Date................: 16--July-1992
Information Source..: Orignal virus analysis
```

South African Friday 13

```
Entry...............: South African Friday the 13th virus
Alias(es)...........: Miami, Munich
Virus Strain........:
Virus detected when.: 1987
             where.: South Africa
Classification......: .COM file infecting virus/Extending/Direct
Length of Virus.....: 419 bytes
-------------------- Preconditions -----------------------------
Operating System(s).: MS-DOS
Version/Release.....: 2.0 or higher
Computer model(s)...: IBM PC,XT,AT and compatibles
-------------------- Attributes --------------------------------
Easy Identification.: Text "INFECTED" found near start of virus.
Type of infection...: Virus adds itself to end of file and places a
                      three-byte jump at the beginning.
Infection Trigger...: When an infected file is run, it will infect every
                      .COM file in the current directory, with the excep-
                      tion of COMMAND.COM.
Storage media affected:
Interrupts hooked...: ---
Damage..............: Every infected file run on a Friday the 13th will
                      be deleted.
Damage Trigger......: Current date, as reported by DOS.
Particularities.....: ----
Similarities........: The effect is similar to that of other, unrelated
                      viruses. VIRUS-B is a modified variant of this
                      virus.
-------------------- Agents ------------------------------------
Countermeasures.....: All programs which check for .COM file length
                      changes will detect infections.
```

```
                        Simply making all .COM files read-only is effective
                        against this virus.
Countermeasures successful:
                        Detection of infection:
                          F-FCHK (from F.Skulason's F-PROT package)
                          VIRUSCAN
                        Removal:  F-FCHK
Standard means......:   Write-protect every .COM file with "attrib +r *.COM".
-------------------- Acknowledgement --------------------------------
Location............:   University of Iceland/Computing Services
Classification by...:   Fridrik Skulason  (frisk@rhi.hi.is)
Documentation by....:   Fridrik Skulason
Date................:   Sept 20, 1989
Information Source..:   ---
```

Su Virus

```
Entry...............:   Su Virus
Alias(es)...........:   Susan Virus
Virus Strain........:   ---
Virus detected when.:   April 1993
            where.:     USA
Classification......:   Overwriting File (EXE) Virus, memory resident
Length of Virus.....:   1.Length (Byte) on media: 864 Bytes
                        2.Length (Byte) in RAM:   571 Bytes
-------------------- Preconditions ----------------------------------
Operating System(s).:   MSDOS
Version/Release.....:   MSDOS>=3.30  (Bug: Checks for DOS 3.03)
Computer model(s)...:   IBM PCs and Compatibles
-------------------- Attributes -------------------------------------
Easy Identification.:   Virus contains the following texts, unencrypted:
                        "Bad command or file name", "Susan", "*.*",
                        "*.EXE", "DIR"
Type of infection...:   File infection: Virus infects EXE files by over-
                        writing it's code over the first 864 bytes.
                        Self-Identification in files: FileTime.Seconds=1Fh
                        System infection: Upon executing an infected EXE
                        file, virus makes itself memory resident (in
                        low memory)
                        Self-Identification in files: if given value in
                        INT 2Fh register found.
Infection Trigger...:   If (a single "DIR" issued) AND
                        (FindFirst finds an uninfected .EXE file)
Storage media affected:
Interrupts hooked...:   INT 2F/10F, 2F/AE00, 2F/AE01
Damage..............:   Permanent Damage:
                        1) Infected files are overwritten and destroyed.
                        2) Deletion of all files in current directory.
                        Transient Damage: Instead of executing the infected
                        program, virus displays the message:
                        "Bad command or file name" and then terminates.
Damage Trigger......:   Permanent Damage:
                        1) Upon infection (see Infection Trigger)
                        2) 16 Infections since activation
                        Transient Damage: Staring an infected program.
Particularities.....:   1) Virus does not hand control over to infected
                        program; instead, it terminates with afore-
                        mentioned message.
```

```
                            2) Virus uses INT 21;AX=5D00h to delete files.
                            3) Hooked interrupts (AH=0AEh) are reportedly
                            called by COMMAND.COM just before executing
                            commands from keyboard.
                            4) Naming: "Susan" found in text; "Su" used as
                            register content.
Similarities........:      ---
-------------------- Agents --------------------------------------
Countermeasures.....:
Countermeasures successful:
Standard means......:      Delete infected files and replace with clean ones.
-------------------- Acknowledgement -----------------------------
Location............:
Classification by...:      Snorre Fagerland
Documentation by....:      Snorre Fagerland (CAROBase entry)
                           Klaus Brunnstein (VTC, Virus Catalog entry)
Date................:      25-June-1993
Information Source..:      Reverse analysis of virus code
```

Sunday A&B Viruses

```
Entry...............:      Sunday A & B Viruses
Alias(es)...........:      ---
Virus Strain........:      Israeli-Virus
Classification......:      Program Virus (extending), RAM-resident
Length of Virus.....:      .COM files: length increases by 1636 bytes.
                           .EXE files: length increases by 1638-1647 bytes.
                           .OVL files: length increases by 1638-1647 bytes.
-------------------- Preconditions -------------------------------
Operating System(s).:      MS-DOS,PC-DOS
Version/Release.....:      2.xx upward
Computer model(s)...:      IBM-PC, XT, AT and compatibles
-------------------- Attributes ----------------------------------
Easy Identification.:      Typical texts in Virus body (readable
                           with HexDump-facilities):
                           "Today is SunDay" (Part of Message)
Type of infection...:      System: infected if function FFh of INT 21h
                           returns value 0400h in the AX-register.
                           Files : The virus infects .COM, .EXE and overlay
                           files. Generaly, files only infected once.
Infection Trigger...:      Programs are infected at load time (using the
                           function Load/Execute of MS-DOS).
Interrupts hooked...:      INT21h, INT08h
Damage..............:      Sunday Version A:
                           30 minutes after the FIRST infected programm
                           was run, the virus displays this message:
                           "Today is SunDay! Why do you work so hard?
                            All  work and no play make you a dull boy!
                            Come on! Let's go out and have some fun!"
                           Sunday Version B:
                           If the first infected file was run, every
                           loaded program is deleted.
Damage Trigger......:      Every Sunday, if year of date not equal 1989
Particularities.....:      The version of the SUNDAY that we have named
                           "B" includes version "A", except that the
                           typical message is not displayed on Sunday.
```

```
-------------------- Agents ------------------------------------------
Countermeasures.....: The virus will be detected by :
                      VIRSUCH  2.15 (D. Hoppenrath)
                      SCAN     3.1  (McAfee)
-------------------- Acknowledgement ---------------------------------
Location............: Virus Test Center, University of Hamburg, Germany
Classification by...: Jörg Steindecker
Documentation by....: Jörg Steindecker
Date................: June 15, 1990
Updates by..........: ---
```

"SURIV 2.01" Virus

```
Entry...............: "SURIV 2.01"
Alias(es)...........: "APRIL 1ST"
Virus Strain........: Jerusalem-Virus
Virus detected when.: ---
              where.: ---
Classification......: Link - Virus (extending), RAM - resident
Length of Virus.....: .EXE - Files: Program length increases
                          by 1488 bytes
-------------------- Preconditions -----------------------------------
Operating System(s).: MS-DOS
Version/Release.....: 2.xx upward
Computer model(s)...: IBM - PC, XT, AT and compatibles
-------------------- Attributes --------------------------------------
Easy Identification.: Typical text in Virus body (readable with
                      HexDump-utilities): "sURIV 2.01"
Type of infection...: System: RAM-resident.
                      .EXE file: extended by using EXEC-function;
                       files will not be infected more than once.
                      .COM File: no infection.
Infection Trigger...: When function 4B00H of INT 21H (EXEC) is called.
Interrupts hooked...: INT 1C, INT 21H, INT 24H
Damage..............: Permanent Damage: --
                      Transient Damage:
                      The virus examines the current date. On every
                      1st April, the virus will display the message
                      "APRIL 1ST HA HA HA YOU HAVE A VIRUS", and
                      the computer will hang in an endless loop.
                      In 1980 and on every Wednesday after 1. April
                      1988, the computer will hang at latest 55
                      minutes after system infection in an endless
                      loop.
Particularities.....: One function (0DEH) used by Novell - Netware 4.0
                      can't be used.
-------------------- Agents ------------------------------------------
Countermeasures.....: ---
- ditto - successful: ---
Standard means......: Notice .EXE file length.
                      Typical text in virus body: "sURIV 2.01"
-------------------- Acknowledgement ---------------------------------
Location............: Virus Test Center, University of Hamburg, Germany
Classification by...: Thomas Lippke
Documentation by....: Thomas Lippke
Date................: 5-June-1990
```

"Suriv 3.00" Virus

```
Entry...............: Suriv 3.00
Alias(es)...........: Jerusalem (B) = Israeli #3 Virus
Virus Strain........: Israeli-Virus
Classification......: Program Virus (extending), RAM-resident
Length of Virus.....: .COM files: length increases by 1813 bytes.
                      .EXE files: length increases by 1808-1823 bytes.
                             (.EXE file length must be a multiple of
                              16 bytes, as in any .EXE file)
-------------------- Preconditions -----------------------------------
Operating System(s).: MS-DOS,PC-DOS
Version/Release.....: 2.xx upward
Computer model(s)...: IBM-PC, XT, AT and compatibles
-------------------- Attributes --------------------------------------
Easy Identification.: Typical texts in Virus body (readable with HexDump
                      facilities): "sURIV 3.00".
Type of infection...: System: infected if function E0h of INT 21h
                              returns value 0300h in the AX-register.
                      .Com files: program length increases by 1813; files
                              are infected only once; COMMAND.COM will
                              not be infected.
                      .EXE files: program length increases by 1808
                              - 1823 bytes, and no identification is
                              used; therefore, .EXE files can be
                              infected more than once.
Infection Trigger...: Programs are infected at load time (using the
                      function Load/Execute of MS-DOS).
Interrupts hooked...: INT21h, INT08h
Damage..............: 1. 30 seconds after the 1st infected program
                      was run, the virus scrolls up 2 Lines in a
                      small window of the screen ( left corner 5,5;
                      right corner  16,16).
                      2. The virus slows down the system by about 10 %.
Damage Trigger......: Every time when the system is infected.
Particularities.....: 1. The version of the Suriv 3.00 which we have
                      analyzed compares the system-date with
                      "Friday 13th", but is not able to recognize
                      "Friday 13th", because of a "bug"; if it cor-
                      rectly recognized this date, it would delete
                      any program started on "Friday 13th".
                      2. .EXE files can be infected many times.
                      3. Novell Netware 4.0 functions, esp. "Print
                      Spooling" (INT21h/E0h), "Set Error Mode"
                      (INT21h/DDh) and "Set Broadcast Mode"
                      (INT21/DEh) cannott be used.
-------------------- Agents ------------------------------------------
Countermeasures.....: The virus will be detected by :
                      VIRSUCH  2.15 (D. Hoppenrath) as Israeli #3
                      F-FCHK   1.08 (F. Skulason)   as Israeli/Jerusalem
                      SCAN     3.1  (McAfee)        as Jerusalem Ver. B
                      FINDVIRU 6.04 (Solomon)       as Suriv 3
                      Several Antiviruses do not work safely.
-------------------- Acknowledgement ---------------------------------
Location............: Virus Test Center, University of Hamburg, Germany
Classification by...: Jörg Steindecker
Documentation by....: Jörg Steindecker, Joe Hirst (BCVRC)
Date................: 5-June-1990
Updates by..........: ---
```

Sverdlov Virus

```
Entry................: Sverdlov Virus
Alias(es)............: Hymn = Hymn of USSR Virus
Virus Strain.........: 1990
Virus detected when..: USSR
              where..: September 1991
Classification.......: Program virus, postfix, memory resident
Length of Virus......: On media: 1,974 bytes
-------------------- Preconditions ------------------------------
Operating System(s)..: MS-DOS and compatible
Version/Release......: 3.0 and upwards
Computer model(s)....: IBM and compatible PC/XT/AT upwards
-------------------- Attributes --------------------------------
Easy Identification..: Infected files grows by 1,971 bytes.
Type of infection....: Program infector: The virus will make itself
                       memory-resident and infect infect every
                       program which uses INT21 (functions 3c,
                       3d, 3e, 43, 4b)
Infection Trigger....: At any time but not if system date's Day=Month
Media affected.......: Any (hard disk, floppy disk)
Interrupts hooked....: INT 21h, INT 1Ch, INT 24h
Damage...............: Permanent: ---
                       Transient: The virus shows a nice spectacle
                       on the screen, in displaying a V-shaped
                       window in different colors; inside the
                       window you, the text is displayed:
                       " USSR (c) 1991 ". Moreover, the national
                       anthem of USSR is played.
Damage Trigger.......: When becoming memory resident, virus sets a
                       random number. When random number=1,
                       damage is triggered.
Particularities......: ---
Similarities.........: ---
-------------------- Agents ------------------------------------
Countermeasures......: ---
  - dito - successful: Tested: Fridrik Skulason's F-PROT
Standard means.......: ---
-------------------- Acknowledgement ---------------------------
Location.............: Virus Test Center, University of Hamburg, Germany
                       and Technical University of Dresden, Germany
Classification by...: Frank Schwarz
Documentation by....: Frank Schwarz
Date.................: 31-January-1992
Information Source..: ---
```

"Swap" Virus

```
Entry................: Swap Virus
Alias(es)............: = Israeli Boot Virus
Virus Strain.........: ---
Virus detected when.: June, 1989
              where.: Israel
Classification......: Boot Sector infection, resident in RAM
Length of Virus.....: 1.   740 Byte on storage medium
                      2. 2.048 Byte in RAM
-------------------- Preconditions ------------------------------
Operating System(s).: MS-DOS
```

```
Version/Release.....: versions 2.0 or later
Computer model(s)...: ---
-------------------- Attributes ------------------------------------
Easy Identification.: A) Boot sector:
                      A1) Bytes from $16A in boot sector are:
                          31 C0 CD 13 B8 02 02 B9 06 27 BA 00
                          01 CD 13 9A 00 01 00 20 E9 XX XX
                      A2) First 3 bytes in boot sector are:
                          JMP 0196 (this is, the boot sector was
                                         loaded to CS:0)
                      B) FAT: track 39 sector 6-7 are marked as bad.
                      C) The message:
                         "The Swapping-Virus. (C) June, by the CIA"
                      located in bytes 02B5-02E4 on track 39,sector 7.
Type of infection...: Resident in RAM. A diskette is infected when it is
                      inserted into the drive and ANY command that reads
                      from or writes to the diskette is executed.
Infection Trigger...: Virus starts to work after 10 minutes.
Storage media affected: Infects diskettes; hard disks are NOT infected.
Interrupts hooked...: Int $8 Timer-Tick: responsible for letter-dropping
                      Int $13 Disk Drive: Infects!
Damage..............: Permanent Damage: track 39 sector 6-7 will be
                      marked as bad.
Damage Trigger......: Whenever a diskette is infected.
Particularities.....: A diskette will be infected only if track 39
                      sectors 6-7 are empty.
Similarities........: ---
-------------------- Agents ----------------------------------------
Countermeasures.....: Category 1: .1 Monitoring Files:          ---
                                  .2 Monitoring System Vectors: ---
                                  .3 Monitoring System Areas:   ---
                      Category 2: Alteration Detection:         ---
                      Category 3: Eradication:                  ---
                      Category 4: Vaccine:                      ---
                      Category 5: Hardware Methods:             ---
                      Category 6: Cryptographic Methods:        ---
Countermeasures successful: ---
Standard means......: ---
-------------------- Acknowledgement --------------------------------
Location............: Weizmann Institute, Rehovot, Israel
Classification by...: Yuval Tal
Documentation by....: Yuval Tal
Date................: August 1989
Information Source..:
```

"Sylvia 2.1" Virus

```
Entry...............: Sylvia V2.1
Alias(es)...........: Holland Girl Virus
Virus Strain........: Sylvia
Classification......: File Virus (Not RAM-resident), infects COM-files
Length of Virus.....: 1332 bytes
-------------------- Preconditions ---------------------------------
Operating System(s).: PCDOS/MSDOS
Version/Release.....: 2.xx upward
Computer model(s)...: IBM-PC, XT, AT and compatibles
-------------------- Attributes ------------------------------------
Easy Identification.: Typical texts in Virus body (readable with
                      Hexdump-facilities) :
```

```
                         1. "39 38 39 38 4F 45 4F 52 61 59
                            1E 56 5D 5A 52 61 62" (encoded text)
                         2. 'Text-Virus V2.1'
                         3. 'Sylvia Verkade'
Type of infection...: The virus infects only COM-files with less
                     than 30 KB; it does not infect COMMAND.COM,
                     IBMBIO.COM, IBMDOS.COM.
                     1301 bytes of the virus-code are written
                     in front of and 31 bytes are written behind
                     the original code; files are only infected once,
                     because the virus checks the existence of its
                     signature (808h) at the beginning of the file.
Infection Trigger...: When an infected file is started, the virus
                     tries to infect 5 COM-files on default drive.
Interrupts hooked...: INT24h
Damage..............: The virus displays the following message :
                     "FUCK YOU LAMER !!!! (CRLF)  system halted..."
                     and stops system by jumping into an endless loop.
                     The message is encoded in the program. In this
                     version (V2.1), the message typical for original
                     Sylvia virus ("This program is infected by a
                     HARMLESS ... ") is NOT displayed.
Damage Trigger......: After being activated, the virus checks itself
                     by creating a check-sum of the first 144 words.
                     When the check-sum is incorrect (# 46A3h) the
                     damaging part of the virus is activated.
-------------------- Agents -------------------------------------------
Countermeasures.....: The virus will be detected by :
                        VIRSUCH 2.15 (D. Hoppenrath)
                        F-FCHK 1.08  (F. Skulason)
                        SCAN 2.3 & 3.1 (McAfee)
Countermeasures successful: F-FCHK 1.08 successful disinfects programs
-------------------- Acknowledgement ----------------------------------
Location............: Virus Test Center, University of Hamburg, Germany
Classification by...: Jörg Steindecker
Documentation by....: Jörg Steindecker
Date................: 5-June-1990
```

"Syslock" Virus

```
Entry................. Syslock
Alias(es)............. ---
Strain................ Advent/Macho/Syslock family
Detected: when........ July 1989 (?)
          where....... USA
Classification........ Program Virus (postfix)
Length of Virus....... 3550-3560 (dec) bytes appended on
                             paragraph boundary
---------------------- Preconditions----------------------------------
Operating System(s).... MS/PC-DOS
Version/Release........ 3.00 and upwards
Computer models........ All IBM PC compatibles.
---------------------- Attributes-------------------------------------
Easy identification.... Any string "MICROSOFT" is replaced with
                            "MACROSOFT".
Type of infection...... The virus infects both COM and EXE files.
                        EXE files: the virus checks the checksum in
                           the EXE header for 7CB6h, in which case
                           no infection will occure.
```

COM files: are checked by looking for the
string 39,28,46,03,03,01 (hex) at offset
10h. The virus is not RAM resident,
therefore it will only infect when the
host is run. It infects by searching
through the directories on the current
drive and randomly choosing files and
directories to infect or search. It will
not infect any other drive than the
current one. It will infect COMMAND.COM.

Infection trigger...... Virus will infect any time it is run.
Media affected......... All disks that are addressable using standard
DOS functions.
Interrupts hooked...... ---
Damage................. Will replace any occurance of "MICROSOFT"
with "MACROSOFT". It does this by using
the DOS (not BIOS) interrupts 25h and 26h,
and searching the disk from beginning to
end, sector by sector. It tries 20h
sectors at a time, and stores the last
sector infected in the file
"\DOS\KEYB.PCM", which is marked "system"
and "hidden". After reaching the last
sector, it will start from the beginning
again.
Damage trigger......... Every time the host is run, after 1-Jan-1985.
Particularities........ The virus checks for the environment variable
"SYSLOCK=@" (therefore its name), in
which case it will not infect. The virus
is encrypted using a variable key.
The functions of DOS interrupts 25h and
26h have been changed in DOS 4.0.
Similarities........... See Macho virus documentation
----------------------- Agents---
Countermeasures........ Use the environment variable described
above as a first aid measure only. Here's
one of the few strings that can safely be
searched for:
50,51,56,BE,59,00,B9,26,08,90,D1,E9,8A,E1,
8A,C1,33,06,14,00,31,04,46,46,E2,F2,5E,59
This string will however identify Advent
and Macho as well.
- ditto - successful.. For proper treatment, my antivirus "NTISYSL"
is highly recommended (in all humility).
Treatment by hand is very tedious and
only for experts.
Standard Means......... Booting from a write-protected disk and
restoring all COM and EXE files from the
original disks is the only way.
---------------------- Acknowledgements----------------------------
Location............... Virus Test Center, University of Hamburg, Germany
Classification by...... Morton Swimmer
Documentation by....... Morton Swimmer
Date................... 1-Dec-1989
Information source..... ---

Techno Virus

```
Entry...............: Techno Virus
Alias(es)...........: ---
Virus Strain........: ---
Virus detected when.: December 1992
            where.: Pforzheim, Germany
Classification......: Direct action, Program (COM) Infector, appending.
Length of Virus.....: 1.Length (Byte) on media:  1123-1138 Bytes
                      2.Length (Byte) in memory: ---
------------------- Preconditions -----------------------------------
Operating System(s).: MS-DOS
Version/Release.....: Version >= 2.00
Computer model(s)...: IBM PCs and Compatibles
------------------- Attributes --------------------------------------
Easy Identification.: Infected Files contain two plain text strings
                      near the end: "TECHNO",
                                    "Don't touch the keyboard".
Type of infection...: Self-Identification on disk:
                      (FILE[0]=E9) and (FILE[A]=78) and (FILE[C]=79)
                      Appending file virus. The virus first tries to
                      infect COMMAND.COM by checking for the COMSPEC
                      entry in the environment and then does a
                      find_first/next_loop on *.COM, which is
                      limited by a timer to about 1.15 sec
                      (probably to hide the activity).
Infection Trigger...: Executing an infected file if Length of destination
                      file is 10<=FileLength<61439.
Storage media affected: COM files on HD/FD
Interrupts hooked...: INT 1C and INT 24 are hooked;
                      INT 10, INT 16 and INT 21 are used.
Damage..............: Permanent Damage: ---
                      Transient Damage: Displaying message, Techno music:
                      Virus writes "TECHNO" all over the screen, while
                      playing techno music. If a key is touched this
                      is intercepted and the string "Don't touch the
                      keyboard" is written instead. Finally it
                      displays a box in the middle spelling in big
                      letters the word "TECHNO".
Damage Trigger......: Permanent damage: ---
                      Transient damage: Executing an infected file will
                      trigger a random number renerator with a 0.25%
                      probability of triggering the transient effects
                      (messages/music).
Particularities.....: Limits the infection process to 1.15 sec to reduce
                      the chance of being detected.
Similarities........: ---
------------------- Agents ------------------------------------------
Countermeasures.....:
Countermeasures successful:
Standard means......: 1) For detection, search for "TECHNO" and
                      "Don't touch the keyboard" in COM files.
                      2) For removal: delete or overwrite infected files.
------------------- Acknowledgement ---------------------------------
Location............: Micro-BIT Virus Center, Univ Karlsruhe, Germany
Classification by...: Christoph Fischer
Documentation by....: Christoph Fischer
Date................: 28-December-1992
Information Source..: Reverse-engineering of Virus
```

"Tequila" Virus

```
Entry................... "Tequila" Virus
Alias(es).............. ---
Strain................. ---
Detected: when........ April 1991
          where....... Steinhausen, Switzerland
Classification........ Memory-resident Program AND System Infector,
                       Stealth, complex Self-Encryption Virus
Length of Virus....... EXE-Files: 2,468 Bytes
                       System:    6 sectors (including original MBR)
                       Memory:    3 kBytes
=================== Preconditions ===============================
Operating System(s)... MS/PC-DOS
Version/Release....... 2.00 and upwards
Computer models....... All IBM PC compatibles.
===================== Attributes ===============================
Easy identification... A text is contained in 2nd sector AFTER last
                       sector of first active partition. This
                       text is also displayed if INT 21h is
                       called with AX = FE03h. The text is:
                      "Welcome to T.TEQUILA's latest production
                       Contact T.TEQUILA/P.o.Box 543/6312 St'hausen/
                                              Switzerland. <CR> <CR>
                       Loving thoughts to L.I.N.D.A <CR> <CR>
                       BEER and TEQUILA forever !"
                       There will be a gap of 6 sectors between
                       the active partition and the next one.
Type of infection..... The virus infects EXE files as well as the
                       Master Boot Record and becomes resident.
                       Memory: when an infected EXE-file is execute
                       virus makes itself memory resident (at TOM).
                       EXE-FILES:virus appends 2468 bytes when infec-
                       ting a file. The code segment and offsets
                       in EXE header are changed to point to the
                       virus. In some cases, the stack segment is
                       modified so that the virus will not be over-
                       written in memory. The growth of infected
                       files is invisible when virus is resident
                       in memory, due to its stealth technique.
                       The virus modifies the file's time stamp to
                       read 62 seconds and changes the checksum in
                       the EXE header to be one of a finite set of
                       values.
                       No EXE-files are infected with "SC" or "V"
                       in name (thus excluding most antiviruses).
                       EXE-File encryption: virus is encrypted in
                       file; it selects 1 of 3 possible encryption
                       algorithms and 1 of 2 methods to implement
                       it. Moreover, a random number of random
                       junk code is inserted between instructions.
                       Therefore, no scan signature is valid. The
                       encryption routine uses itself as the key
                       (which makes debugging rather tricky.)
                       Master Boot Record: the virus reduces the ac-
                       tive partition's size by 6 sectors and in-
                       serts into this space the original MBR and
                       the entire virus. Original MBR is patched
                       with virus code. The virus is not encrypted
                       in the MBR. Virus stealth method intercepts
```

```
                           Read/Write to MBR and makes original MBR
                           available.
                           No Boot Sector Infection.
Infection trigger......    The virus will infect the MBR ONLY when started
                           from file. After the next system start, the
                           virus will infect files from memory.
Media affected........     Files can be infected on all media. MBR is ONLY
                           infected on hard disk, not on floppies.
Interrupts hooked......    Interrupts 21h function 4Bh (LOAD/EXEC) is used
                           to infect files;
                           Interrupt 21 functions 11h, 12h, 4Eh, 4Fh, and
                           Interrupt 13h are used to mask its operation;
                           Interrupt 21h function FE02h is the virus'
                           memory installation check;
                           Interrupt 21h funtion FE03h displays message.
Damage................     Transient Damage: at certain time/date,virus
                           will display a fractal at program termina-
                           tion of any file, even if not infected.
                           Permanent Damage: virus searches for files
                           that have been given a validation string
                           by McAfee's Scan and destroy such files.
Damage trigger........     The fractal is displayed at program termina-
                           tion after a certain time; but there seems
                           to be bug in the code somewhere so that it
                           is not executed "normally".
                           The strings are patched any time.
Particularities........    1) Like 1260, V2P2 and V2P6 viruses, virus
                           tries to avoid being scanned for.Generally,
                           virus authors seem to know contemporary
                           virus developments; techniques of older
                           viruses (SHOE-B) and recent stealth methods
                           are used, but encryption methods have no
                           ancestors.
                           2) Virus spread rapidly in Europe when an in-
                           fected game was downloaded to a shareware
                           BBS. Two authors (18 and 21 years) were ex-
                           amined soon after detection by Swiss police.
Similarities...........    ---
===================== Agents ==========================================
Countermeasures........    ---
 - ditto - successful..    Solomon's Toolkit vers. 5 and Morton Swimmer's
                           NTIteq will find and disinfect TEQUILA.
                           Michael Weiner's inoculator ATEQUILA prevents
                           Tequila infection.
Standard Means.........    ---
===================== Acknowledgements ===========================
Location...............    Virus Test Center, University of Hamburg, Germany
Classification by......    Morton Swimmer
Documentation by.......    Morton Swimmer
Date...................    15-July-1991
Information source.....    Michael Weiner's trace of the virus
                           Further information: Morton Swimmers evaluation
```

Terminator II

```
Entry................:  Terminator II Virus
Alias(es)............:  ---
Virus Strain.........:  ---
```

```
Virus detected when.:
              where.:
Classification......: File virus (COM,EXE infector); memory resident;
                      stealth.
Length of Virus.....: 1.Length (Byte) on media: 2294 Bytes
                      2.Length (Byte) in RAM:   2448 Bytes.
-------------------- Preconditions ------------------------------------
Operating System(s).: MSDOS
Version/Release.....:
Computer model(s)...: IBM PCs and Compatibles.
-------------------- Attributes ---------------------------------------
Easy Identification.: 1) Last two bytes of infected are equal to 1000h,
                      seconds value of FileTime set to 56 (see: Self-
                      Identification in files).
                      2) File allocation errors shown by CHKDSK. Amount
                      of free memory is decreased by 2448 bytes.
Type of infection...: File infection: virus appends itself to end of an
                      EXE or COM file and changes the CS:IP in EXE
                      header or places JMP to virus code in COM files.
                      Only files larger than 1388 bytes will be in-
                      fected. File with names containing "SCAN" in
                      any place of name will not be infected.
                      Self-Identification in files: Last two bytes of
                       virus are equal to 1000h, seconds value of
                       FileTime set to 56.
                      System infection: When starting an infected file,
                      virus makes itself memory resident at top of
                      system memory but below 640K boundary (usually
                      at 9f67:0000). Virus allocates memory by de-
                      creasing size of the last "Z" Memory Control
                      Block by 2448 bytes.
                      Self-Identification in memory: function 4BFEh of
                      DOS services reconstruct and execute program
                      if virus is in memory, otherwise virus conti-
                      nues execution and installs itself in memory.
Infection Trigger...: Executing an infected file, or Opening, Loading
                      and Executing any file when memory is infected.
Storage media affected:
Interrupts hooked...: INT 21h(Dos-Services): functions: 0Fh (Open_FCB),
                      11h (Find1st_FCB),12h (FindNxt_FCB),3dh (Open),
                      3eh (Close),3fh (Read),42h (Seek),4eh (Find1st),
                      4fh (FindNxt),4B00h (Load/Execute),4B01h (Load),
                      6ch (Extended_Open).
Damage..............: Permanent Damage:
                      1) Virus slows down speed of computer, mixing
                         output to printer: case of every 16th
                         character will be reversed and 0 will be
                         changed to 9.
                      2) Displays string "TERMINATOR", overwrites
                         CMOS, overwrites 1 side of all hard drives.
                      Transient Damage: ---
Damage Trigger......: Permanent Damage:
                      1) Damage 1) will be triggered two month after
                         infection, if second bit of date is non-zero.
                      2) Damage 2) will be triggered if date is
                         bigger than date of infection plus two month
                         plus ten days.
                      Transient Damage: ---
Particularities.....: Due to his setalth technique, virus is almost in-
                      visible when active in memory. It has prevention from
```

```
                      "curing" by packing infected files, mostly
                      stealth viruses can be disinfected by such a
                      trick, because usually stealth virus returns
                      clean file to system, and file becomes clean
                      during packing.
Similarities........: NOT related to Terminator as described in VSUM!
-------------------- Agents ----------------------------------------
Countermeasures.....:
Countermeasures successful: Detection: Gobbler-II v3.0
                          Disinfection: Gobbler-II v3.0+
Standard means......: Delete infected files and replace with clean ones.
-------------------- Acknowledgement -------------------------------
Location............:
Classification by...: Received from unnamed contributor outside VTC
Documentation by....:
                      Klaus Brunnstein (VTC, CVC entry)
Date................: 31-July-1993
Information Source..:
```

"Thursday 12" Virus

```
Entry...............: Thursday-12 Virus
Alias(es)...........: ---
Virus Strain........: ---
Virus detected when.: June 27, 1991
            where.: Tornado Bulletin Board (TECS), Hamburg
Classification......: Memory-resident Program Infector
                      Simple self-encryption
Length of Virus.....: EXE-files: 2270 Bytes; COM-Files: 2168 Bytes
                      Memory:    2161 Bytes
-------------------- Preconditions ---------------------------------
Operating System(s).: MS-DOS
Version/Release.....: 2.xx upward
Computer model(s)...: IBM-PC, XT, AT and compatibles
-------------------- Attributes ------------------------------------
Easy Identification.: INT 21 Vector is hooked to adress xxxx:026d;
                      EXE-files start at adress xxxx:100 with jump
                      to 106 and call to 10c (at 106);
                      COM-files start with jump, at the target of
                      this jump, identical code will be found.
                      The virus' text (see: transient damage) can be
                      found near the end of memory, 52dh bytes
                      behind the INT 21 target adress.
Scanner Signature...: String 83 f9 00 74 09 51 56 30 24 46 is con-
                      tained near end of EXE and COM files.
Type of infection...: The virus appends itself at the end of EXE and
                      COM files. It will not infect programs con-
                      taining any of the following strings in their
                      name: SCAN, CLEAN, VIR, ARJ, FLU or COMMAND.
Infection Trigger...: Execution of an infected program.
Storage media affected: Files can be infected on all medias.
Interrupts hooked...: INT 21, functions 0f,3d (both open a file),
                          4b (load/execute)
                          6c (extended open and create (DOS 4.0))
                      are used to infect a file.
Damage..............: Permanent damage: ---
                      Transient damage: The virus draws a litte box,
                      containing the following text:
```

```
                       "VirCheck V1.2 (C) 1991
                       Be aware of those worms out there, violating
                       your machine on Friday 13th - it's tomorrow!
                       Special thanks to Ross M. Greenberg
                       Patricia M. Hoffmann and John McAfee
                       Press any key to continue..."
                       The box disappears after pressing any key and
                       system continues working, completely unaffected.
                       No side effects have been observed, although
                       heavy damage was reported, when running this
                       virus with a hard-disk realtime-packer.
Damage Trigger......: The text appears only on Thursday 12th, after
                       execution of 4 programs that were already
                       infected, if the virus is in memory.
Particularities.....: The virus was found on a public domain PAC-MAN
                       game (CD-MAN), which could be downloaded from
                       the Tornado BBS, Hamburg. The infected program
                       was downloaded 19 times before detection of
                       contamination; at this time (1st generation),
                       it was also reported in Kiel (100 km north
                       of Hamburg). After report, infected program
                       was deleted from BBS.
                       (It is known, who actually put the program
                       onto BBS, and we try to get more information
                       where the virus actualy comes from)
Similarities........: ---
-------------------- Agents --------------------------------------
Countermeasures.....: (no contemporary scanner finds the virus)
Countermeasures successful: ANTITH12 of Toralv Dirro finds and
                             eradicates this virus.
Standard means......: Delete infected EXE&COM files, copy uninfected
                       versions from original write-protected disk.
-------------------- Acknowledgement -----------------------------
Location............: Virus Test Center, University of Hamburg, Germany
Classification by...: Toralv Dirro, Stefan Tode
Documentation by....: Toralv Dirro
Date................: 15-July-1991
Information Source..: (original virus analysis)
```

"Tiny" Virus

```
Entry................ "Tiny" Virus
Alias(e)............. V163 Virus
Strain............... ---
Detected: when....... ---
          where...... ---
Classification....... Program virus, direct action COM infector
Length of virus...... 163 bytes added to COM files
-------------------- Preconditions -------------------------------
Operating System(s)... MS-DOS
Version/Release...... 2.0 and up
Computer models...... Any IBM-compatibles
-------------------- Attributes ----------------------------------
Easy identification... File size increases by 163 bytes
Type of infection.... Direct action; appending 163 bytes to COM files
Infection trigger.... Executing an infected file will trigger the
                       infection attempt in the local directory.
Interrupts hooked.... ---
```

```
Damage............... ---
Particularities....... No payload. Will only infect COM files starting
                       with E9h (JMP instruction).
-------------------- Acknowledgement -----------------------------
Location.............. Micro-BIT Virus Center RZ Universitaet Karlsruhe
Classification by..... Christoph Fischer
Dokumentation by ..... Christoph Fischer
Date.................. 16-June-1990
```

Tonya Virus

```
Entry...............: Tonya Virus
Alias(es)...........: ---
Virus Strain........: ---
Virus detected when.: Summer 1993
            where.: Melbourne, Australia
Classification......: File virus (COM infector), memory resident,
                      variably encrypted
Length of Virus.....: 1.Length (Byte) on media:  971 Bytes
                      2.Length (Byte) in RAM:   2016 Bytes
-------------------- Preconditions -------------------------------------
Operating System(s).: MSDOS
Version/Release.....:
Computer model(s)...: IBM PCs and Compatibles
-------------------- Attributes ----------------------------------------
Easy Identification.: Virus is variably encrypted, no signature possible
                      (after decryption, text may be identified)
Type of infection...: File infection: COM files are infected upon
                          opening (INT 21/3D) or loading for execution
                          (INT 21/4B), if not too short (<50) or too long
                          (>64,303). Upon detecting an yet uninfected COM
                          file with proper size, virus appends it's code
                          at the end and restores date, time and attributes
                          previously saved. Length of COM files increase
                          by 971 bytes.
                      Self-Identification in files:
                      Stealth: Virus is variably encrypted. Virus inter-
                      cepts DOS functions OpenFile and Load&Execute,
                      and it saves date&time attributes, to avoid
                      detection.
                      System infection: When an infected COM file is
                      executed, virus after decryption first tries to
                      make itself memory resident, using a non-
                      standard DOS function; if not yet resident,
                      virus loads itself to top-of-memory, reducing
                      available memory by 2016 bytes.
                      Self-Identification in memory: checking register
                      value of an undocumented DOS function.
Infection Trigger...: Executing an infected file, or (when virus is
                      memory resident) invoking DOS functions
                      Open File or Load&Execute, as long as
                      50<filesize<64,303 bytes.
Storage media affected:
Interrupts hooked...: INT 21/3D (OpenFile), INT 21/4B (Load&Execute)
Damage..............: Permanent Damage: No intended permanent damage
                      Transient Damage: Following text is displayed
                      at screen's bottom, with nominal height of
                      screen reduced to 21 lines (with an unusual
```

```
                              screen function), so that this message re-
                              mains at screen's bottom also upon scrolling:
                                  "I love Tonya Harding,
                                   The best womens Figure Skater in history.
                                   Now Tonya, Do that triple axle
                                   and kick Kristi Yamaguchi's arse
                                   - Australian Parasite -"
Damage Trigger......: Permanent Damage: ---
                              Transient Damage: Upon each invocation of INT 21,
                              a counter is incremented; if this reaches
                              30,000, the display is triggered.
Particularities.....: The message contains many names which may cause
                              different names choosen from some AV authors
                              (most probably "Australian Parasite").
Similarities........: ---
-------------------- Agents ---------------------------------------------
Countermeasures.....:
Countermeasures successful:
Standard means......: Delete infected files and replace with clean ones.
-------------------- Acknowledgement ------------------------------------
Location............: CYBEC Pty, Hampton Victoria/Australia
Classification by...: Roger Riordan (riordan.cybec@mhs.oz.au>
Documentation by....: Roger Riordan
                              Klaus Brunnstein (CVC entry)
Date................: 31-July-1993
Information Source..: Analysis of Virus
```

"Traceback" Virus

```
Entry...............: "Traceback" Virus
Alias(es)...........: "3066" Virus
Virus Strain........: Traceback
Virus detected when.: June 1989
            where.: ---
Classification......: Program extending, RAM-resident
Length of Virus.....: .COM and .EXE files increased by 3066 bytes.
-------------------- Preconditions --------------------------------------
Operating System(s).: MS-DOS
Version/Release.....: 2.xx upward
Computer model(s)...: IBM-PC, XT, AT and compatibles
-------------------- Attributes -----------------------------------------
Easy Identification.: Typical text in Virus body (readable
                              with hex-dump-utilities):
                              1. "VG1" in the data area of the virus
                              2. "VG1" is found at offset of near-jmp-
                              displacement if program is a .COM file.
                              3. The complete name of the file, which infected
                              the currently loaded file, is in the code.
                              4. Search .COM or .EXE files for the hex-string:
                              58,2B,C6,03,C7,06,50,F3,A4,CB,90,E8,E2,03,
                              8B (the last 16 bytes of an infected program).
Type of infection...: System: infected if signature string "VG1"
                                    is found in specific location in memory.
                              .COM files: program length increased by 3,066
                                    bytes if it is infected. Infects files up
                                    to 62,218 bytes. The first byte of an infec-
                                    ted file is a near-jump (E9h,XXh,YYh) to the
                                    virus code; program is infected if the string
```

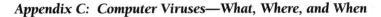

```
                            "VG1" is at offset (viruscode_entry)-03h.
                            .Com files are infected only once.
                            .EXE files: program length increased by 3066 bytes
                              string "VG1" is used for identification.
                            .EXE files are infected only once.
     Infection Trigger...: Programs are infected the first time the virus is
                            run, and at load time (using the function
                            Load/Execute (4Bh) of MS-DOS).
     Interrupts hooked...: INT 21h, INT 1Ch, INT 09h, INT 20h, INT 27h,
                            (INT 24h only during infection of a file).
     Damage.............: Transient Damage: One hour after system infection,
                            the characters will fall down the screen. Af-
                            ter 1 minute, screen is automaticly restored.
                            During damage, INT 09h will be hooked.
                            Characters typed during damage will move
                            "fallen-down" characters back to their
                            start position. Damage repeats every hour.
                            Permanent Damage: ---
     Damage Trigger......: Every time an infected file is run, system date
                            is checked; apart from diverse conditions before
                            Dec.28 1988, the relevant routine checks:
                            If (system date >= 28th of December 1988)
                            then "cascade damage" (same as Autumn Virus).
     Particularities.....: - The virus infects all files, which will be
                              loaded via INT 21h (function 04Bh, including
                              .EXE, .COM and other files as .APP(GEM),.OVL).
                            - Some files will not run after infection.
     Similarities........: There are some variants of this virus.
     -------------------- Agents ------------------------------------------
     Countermeasures.....: Category 3: NTI3066.EXE (VTC Hamburg)
     Countermeasures successful: NTI3066.EXE is an antivirus that only
                            looks for the Traceback-3066 Virus and,
                            if requested, will restore the file.
     Standard means......: Notice file-length and search after the strings.
     -------------------- Acknowledgement ---------------------------------
     Location...........: Virus Test Center, University of Hamburg, Germany
     Classification by...: Stefan Tode
     Documentation by....: Stefan Tode
     Date................: 5-June-1990
     Information source... PC VIRUS LISTING (Joe Hirst)
```

Trivial Virus Strain

```
     Strain............... Trivial Virus Strain
     Classification....... All Trivial Viruses:
                           Overwriting COM infectors, direct action;
                           not memory-resident.
     Size of Viruses...... On media: various (see specific entries)
                           =========================================
     Virus Entry#1........ Trivial.Psycho = Trivial.Hastings Virus
     Detected: when....... ---
              where....... ---
     Size of virus........ Length: 200 bytes (overwriting)
                           -------------------------------
     Virus Entry#2........ Trivial.Hanger Virus
     Detected: when....... ---
              where....... ---
     Size of virus........ Length: 143 bytes (overwriting)
```

```
                              ---------------------------------
Virus Entry#3......... Trivial.Banana Virus
Detected: when........ ---
          where....... ---
Size of virus........ Length: 139 bytes (overwriting)
                              ---------------------------------
Virus Entry#5......... Trivial.50 Virus
Detected: when........ ---
          where....... ---
Size of virus........ Length: 50 bytes (overwriting)
                              ---------------------------------
Virus Entry#6......... Trivial.46 = DeathCow Virus
Detected: when........ ---
          where....... ---
Size of virus........ Length: 46 bytes (overwriting)
Variant............... Trivial.42
Size of virus........ Length: 42 bytes (overwriting)
                              ---------------------------------
Virus Entry#7......... Trivial.45.A = Shortest Virus
Detected: when........ ---
          where....... ---
Clones................ Trivial.45.B virus, Trivial.45.C virus
Size of virus........ Length: 45 bytes (overwriting)
Variant............... Trivial.35 Virus
Size of virus........ Length: 35 bytes (overwriting)
                              ---------------------------------
Virus Entry#8......... Trivial.44 Virus
Detected: when........ ---
          where....... ---
Length of virus....... Length: 44 bytes (overwriting)
                              ---------------------------------
Virus Entry#9......... Trivial.39 Virus
Detected: when........ ---
          where....... ---
Length of virus...... Length: 39 bytes (overwriting)
Variant............... Trivial.38 Virus
Length of virus...... Length: 38 bytes (overwriting)
                              ---------------------------------
Virus Entry#10........ Trivial.31.A Virus
Detected: when........ ---
          where....... ---
Clone................. Trivial.31.B = Miniscule Virus
Size of virus/clone... Length: 31 bytes (overwriting)
                              ---------------------------------
Virus Entry#11........ Trivial.30.A Virus
Detected: when........ ---
          where....... ---
Clones................ Trivial.30.B, Trivial.30.C Virus
Size of virus/clones.. Length: 30 bytes (overwriting)
                              ---------------------------------
Virus Entry#12........ Trivial.25 Virus
Detected: when........ ---
          where....... ---
Length of virus....... Length: 25 bytes (overwriting)
Variant............... Trivial.26 Virus
Length of virus....... Length: 26 bytes (overwriting)
--------------------- Preconditions ---------------------------------
Operating System(s)... MS/PC-DOS 3.x upwards
Computer models....... All IBM PC/AT compatibles
--------------------- Common Attributes of Strain Viruses -----------
```

```
Easy identification...  Infected files will not run as they are over-
                        written by the resp. virus; only virus code
                        will be executed, and system will then crash.
Type of infection.....  Self-identification: none (just overwriting)
     -                  COM files: not increased, unless infected file
                        is shorter than virus. Files can only be
                        infected when an infected host is started;
                        first bytes of infected file (length depending
                        on virus/variant) will be overwritten by virus.
                        EXE files: no infection, unless virus infects
                        with the *.* pattern.
Infection trigger.....  Any time an infected file is run, the viruses
                        infects one or all .COM files in the current
                        directory (see entries for details).
Affected media........  Files on HardDisk or any FloppyDisk.
Interrupts hooked.....  ---
Damage...............   Permanent damage: infected file is overwritten.
Damage trigger........  Execution of an infected file.
Particularities.......  The file date/time will be set to the date
                        of the infection.
Similarities.........   In stepwise reduction of size, Trivial viruses
                        aim at achieving the shortest code suitable
                        for infection. Though probably different
                        authors worked on the viruses, this common
                        goal is explicitly mentioned in some texts.
                        While early version contain several texts,
                        later versions contain essentially code suf-
                        ficient to infect files by overwriting them;
                        but texts may be deposited in infected files
                        at remote locations.
                        Every virus in Trivial strain infects one or
                        all *.COM or *.C* or *.* files in the
                        current directory, by overwriting the first
                        bytes of the files with itself. If the file
                        to be infected is smaller than the resp.
                        virus, the file size will grow to the virus'
                        size. The wildcard pattern *.* includes the
                        files .COM .EXE .OVL .SYS .DOC .TXT etc.
--------------------  Special Attributes of Trivial.Hastings ----------
Virus name...........   Trivial.Psycho or Trivial.Hastings
Size.................    200 bytes
Type of infection.....  Infects the 1st .COM file in current directory
                        by overwriting it.
Easy identification...  Texts found in virus at offset 40dez
                           '*.COM by' (encrypted name deleted)
                           'AKA Nick Haflinger...'
                           'Zopy me I want' to travel'
                           'I can now program in assembler'
                           'This program was written in the town'
                           'of Hastings hehehehe!'
--------------------  Special Attributes of Trivial.Hanger ------------
Virus name...........   Trivial.Hanger Virus
Size.................    143 bytes
Type of infection.....  Infects all *.C* files (*.COM, but also *.C)
                        in current directory by overwriting them.
Easy detection........  Infected files contain (unencrypted) message
                        (see Transient damage) at offset 59dez.
Damage...............   Permanent damage: Overwriting infected files.
                        Transient damage: After infection, virus displays
                        the message:  'System Hanger! Enjoy! '
```

```
                        'Note: Your system is now hanged.'
                        'Press Reset to continue.'
                        Then systems may hang (HLT instruction)
--------------------- Special Attributes of Trivial.Banana ------------
Virus name............ Trivial.Banana Virus
Size.................. 139 bytes
Type of infection..... Infects all *.COM files in current directory
                        by overwriting them.
Easy identification... The following text is found in infected files
                        at offset 80dez:
                        'BANANA, coded by Morbid Angel'
                        '-92 in Stockholm/Sweden*.COM'
Particularities....... Upon infection, file-attribute, time and date
                        are saved and correctly restored.
--------------------- Special Attributes of Trivial.50 ---------------
Virus name............ Trivial.50 Virus
Size.................. 50 bytes
Type of infection..... Infects all *.COM files in current directory
                        by overwriting them.
--------------------- Special Attributes of Trivial.46 ---------------
Virus name............ Trivial.46 = DeathCow Virus
Size.................. 46 bytes
Type of infection..... Infects all *.COM files by overwriting the,.
Variants.............. Optimized version is Trivial.42,
Size.................. 42 bytes
--------------------- Special Attributes of Trivial.45 ---------------
Virus name............ Trivial.45.A = Shortest Virus
Size.................. 45 bytes
Type of infection..... Infects all *.COM files by overwriting them.
Clones................ Trivial.45.B and Trivial.45.C (same size)
Variants.............. Trivial.35 Virus
Size.................. 35 bytes
--------------------- Special Attributes of Trivial.44 ---------------
Virus name............ Trivial.44 Virus
Size.................. 44 bytes
Type of infection..... Infects all *.COM files in current directory
                        by overwriting them
--------------------- Special Attributes of Trivial.39 ---------------
Virus name............ Trivial.39 Virus
Size.................. 39 bytes
Type of infection..... Infects all *.COM files in current directory
                        by overwriting them.
Variants.............. Trivial.38 Virus
Size.................. 38 bytes
Remark................ A slightly optimized version of Trivial.39 Virus
--------------------- Special Attributes of Trivial.35 ---------------
Virus name............ Trivial.35 Virus
Size.................. 35 bytes
Type of infection..... Infects one file with pattern *.C* by overwriting
Remark................ A significantly optimized version of Trivial.45
--------------------- Special Attributes of Trivial.31.A --------------
Virus name............ Trivial.31.A Virus
Size.................. 31 bytes
Type of infection..... Infects one file with pattern *.C* by overwriting
--------------------- Special Attributes of Trivial.31.B --------------
Virus name............ Trivial.31.B = Miniscule Virus
Size.................. 31 bytes
Type of infection..... Infects one file with pattern *.* by overwriting
Easy identification... The following text is found in infected files
--------------------- Special Attributes of Trivial.30.A/B/C ----------
```

```
Virus name............ Trivial.30.A Virus
Size.................. 30 bytes
Type of infection..... Infects one file with pattern *.* by overwriting
Variant#1............. Trivial.30.B
Particularities....... Trivial.30.B overwrites 256 bytes of a file
Remark............... Uses two different opcodes for same purpose
Variant#2............. Trivial.30.C Virus
Remark............... Some opcodes swapped, but 98% same code
Particularities....... Trivial.30.C overwrites 30 bytes of a file
-------------------- Special Attributes of Trivial.25 ---------------
Virus name............ Trivial.25 Virus
Size.................. 25 bytes (or longer);
                       infected file size will vary, due to some
                       optimization in virus code, in the range
                       of overwritten bytes  25 <= size <= 33049.
Type of infection..... Infects one .COM file by overwriting
Particularities....... Virus only works under specific conditions.
Variants.............. Trivial.26 Virus
Size.................. 26 bytes
Type of infection..... Infects one *.* file
Particularities....... As Trivial.25, this virus also works only
                       under specific conditions
-------------------- Agents -------------------------------------------
Countermeasures.......
Standard Means........ 1) Notice file length and file date/time.
                       2) Use ReadOnly attribute.
                       3) Infected files can only be disinfected by
                       replacing them with the original files.
-------------------- Acknowledgements --------------------------------
Location.............. Virus Test Center, University of Hamburg, Germany
Classification by..... Stefan Tode
Documentation by...... Stefan Tode
Date................. 31-July-1993 (Update of Feb-93 entry)
Information source.... ---
```

V163 Virus

```
Entry................: V163 Virus
Alias(es)...........: ---
Virus Strain........: ---
Virus detected when.: January 1993
            where.: Zeuthen, Germany
Classification......: Memory-resident Program (COM) Infector, Appending
Length of Virus.....: 1.Length (Byte) on media:   163 Bytes
                      2.Length (Byte) in memory:  163 Bytes
-------------------- Preconditions ------------------------------------
Operating System(s).: MS-DOS
Version/Release.....: All versions
Computer model(s)...: IBM PCs and Compatibles
-------------------- Attributes ---------------------------------------
Easy Identification.: All files without an EXE-Header (MZ) will grow by
                      163 bytes and will have a 'M' as first byte
                      followed by a intra segment jump (E9h).
Type of infection...: Self-Identification in memory: [0000:0086]=60
                      Self-Identification on disk:   FILE[0]=4D ='M'
                      File infection: Appending file virus. The virus
                      infects all files that do not contain an 'M'
                      as first byte.
```

```
Infection Trigger...: Executing a file.
Storage media affected: HD/FD
Interrupts hooked...: INT 21/4B
Damage..............: Permanent Damage: ---
                     Transient Damage: ---
Damage Trigger......: Permanent Damage: ---
                     Transient Damage: ---
Particularities.....: 1) Does not bypass the R/O-flag of files.
                     2) Uses the DOS data area at 60:00 to 60:A2 to go
                     resident; this will not always work!
                     3) Newer EXE-headers like NE or LE will not be
                     handled, thus these files will be damaged!
                     4) Virus doesnot properly self-recognize itself in
                     memory; anything resident process hooking INT21
                     will cause the virus to become resident again!
Similarities........: ---
-------------------- Agents -------------------------------------------
Countermeasures.....:
Countermeasures successful:
Standard means......: 1) Detection: COM files grow by 163 bytes.
                     2) Removal:   Delete or overwrite infected files.
-------------------- Acknowledgement ----------------------------------
Location............: Micro-BIT Virus Center, Univ Karlsruhe, Germany
Classification by...: Christoph Fischer
Documentation by....: Christoph Fischer
Date................: 18-Febuary-1993
Information Source..: Reverse-Engineering of virus code
```

"V-277" Virus

```
Entry................. "V-277" Virus
Alias(es)............. "Viki" Virus
Strain................ Amstrad Virus Strain
Detected: when........ Spring 1990
         where........ Bulgaria
Classification........ Program virus, direct action, prefix
Length of Virus....... 277 bytes
----------------------- Preconditions ----------------------------
Operating System(s)... MS-DOS
Version/Release....... 2.xx and upward
Computer models....... IBM-PC's and compatibles
----------------------- Attributes -------------------------------
Easy identification.... The virus identifies infection by checking for
                        the string "UM" at offset 3 in the COM file
Type of infection...... A program virus that infects all COM files
                        in the current directory by prepending
                        itself to its victim.
Infection trigger...... As it is a direct action virus, it will only
                        infect on run-time, but will do this at
                        any time.
Media affected......... Any logical drive that is the "current" drive.
Interrupts hooked...... ---
Damage................. Denial of access. It also similates a RAM
                        parity error. This doesn't mean however
                        that it has destroyed the hardware.
Damage trigger......... The virus carries an evolution counter that
                        is increased every time the virus is
                        executed. When the counter is above or
```

```
                        equal to 5, the virus reads the system
                        timer. If the value is odd, the virus will
                        terminate with parity error. (This is
                        effectively a 50% chance of termination.)
Particularities........ This is a variant of the V-299 virus. It
                        is now vying for recognition as the
                        smallest known virus.
Similarities........... Amstrad, V-345, V-299, Cancer Viruses.
                        I don't know why anyone would bother to
                        modify such a stupid virus as the Amstrad.
------------------------ Agents ----------------------------------
Countermeasures........ Checksumming programs will detect the changes
                        to the files.
 - ditto - successful.. ---
Standard Means......... Believe it or not, write protecting programs
                        with ATTR will prevent the virus from
                        spreading to them.
--------------------- Acknowledgements ---------------------------
Location............... Bulgarian Academy of Science and
                        Virus Test Center, University of Hamburg, Germany
Classification by...... Morton Swimmer, VTC
Documentation by....... Vesselin Bontchev
Date................... 11-June-1990
Information source..... ---
```

"V-299" Virus

```
Entry.................. "V-299" Virus
Alias(es).............. ---
Strain................. Amstrad Virus Strain
Detected: when......... Winter 1989
          where........ Bulgaria
Classification......... Program virus, direct action, prefix
Length of Virus........ 299 bytes
----------------------- Preconditions ----------------------------
Operating System(s).... MS-DOS
Version/Release........ 2.xx and upward
Computer models........ IBM-PC's and compatibles
------------------------ Attributes ------------------------------
Easy identification.... The virus contains the string "Program sick
                        error:Call doctor or buy PIXEL for cure
                        description". The virus identifies
                        infection by checking for the string "IV"
                        at offset 3 in the COM file.
Type of infection...... A program virus that infects all COM files
                        in the current directory by prepending
                        itself to its victim. The virus will not
                        spread very quickly.
Infection trigger...... As it is a direct action virus, it will only
                        infect on run-time, but will do this
                        at any time.
Media affected......... Any logical drive that is the "current" drive
Interrupts hooked...... ---
Damage................. Denial of access
Damage trigger......... The virus carries an evolution counter that
                        is increased every time the virus is
                        executed. When the counter is above or
                        equal to 5, the virus reads the system
```

```
                          timer. If the value is odd, the virus will
                          terminate with the message described
                          above. (This is effectively a 50% chance
                          of termination.)
Particularities........   This is an optimized variant of the V-345
                          virus. At the time of its creation it was
                          the smallest known virus.
Similarities...........   Amstrad, V-345, Cancer Viruses
--------------------------- Agents ----------------------------------
Countermeasures........   Checksumming programs will detect the changes
                          to the files.
 - ditto - successful..   V847clr by Vesselin Bontchev will successfully
                          search and clear the Amstrad, V-345 and
                          V-299 viruses, and find the Cancer virus.
Standard Means.........   Believe it or not, write protecting programs
                          with ATTR will prevent the virus from
                          spreading to them.
---------------------- Acknowledgements -----------------------------
Location...............   Bulgarian Academy of Science and
                          Virus Test Center, University of Hamburg, Germany
Classification by......   Morton Swimmer
Documentation by.......   Vesselin Bontchev
Date...................   11-June-1990
Information source.....   ---
```

"V-345" Virus

```
Entry..................   "V-345" Virus
Alias(es)..............   ---
Strain.................   Amstrad Virus Strain
Detected: when.........   Winter 1989
          where........   Bulgaria
Classification.........   Program virus, direct action, prefix
Length of Virus........   345 bytes
----------------------- Preconditions -------------------------------
Operating System(s)....   MS-DOS
Version/Release........   2.xx and upward
Computer models........   IBM-PC's and compatibles
----------------------- Attributes ----------------------------------
Easy identification....   The virus contains the string "Program sick
                          error:Call doctor or buy PIXEL for cure
                          description". The virus identifies
                          infection by checking for the string "IV"
                          at offset 3 in the COM file.
Type of infection......   A program virus that infects all COM files
                          in the current directory by prepending
                          itself to its victim. The virus will not
                          spread very quickly.
Infection trigger......   As it is a direct action virus, it will
                          only infect on run-time, but will do this
                          at any time.
Media affected.........   Any logical drive that is the "current" drive
Interrupts hooked......   ---
Damage.................   Denial of access
Damage trigger.........   The virus carries an evolution counter that is
                          increased every time the virus is executed.
                          When the counter is above or equal to 5,
                          the virus reads the system timer. If the
```

```
                            value is odd, the virus will terminate
                            with the message described above. (This is
                            effectively a 50% chance of termination.)
Particularities........ This is an optimized variant of Amstrad virus
Similarities........... Amstrad, V-299, Cancer Viruses
-------------------------- Agents ----------------------------------
Countermeasures........ Checksumming programs will detect the changes
                            to the files.
 - ditto - successful.. V847clr by Vesselin Bontchev will successfully
                            search and clear the Amstrad, V-345 and
                            V-299 viruses, and find the Cancer virus.
Standard Means......... Believe it or not, write protecting programs
                            with ATTR will prevent the virus from
                            spreading to them.
---------------------- Acknowledgements -----------------------------
Location............... Bulgarian Academy of Science and
                            Virus Test Center, University of Hamburg, Germany
Classification by...... Morton Swimmer
Documentation by....... Vesselin Bontchev
Date................... 11-June-1990
Information source..... ---
```

Vacsina (1,2) Virus

```
Entry...............: "Vacsina Virus" (#1/#2)
Alias(es)...........:
Virus Strain........:
Virus detected when.: August 1989
             where.: University of Cologne, Germany
Classification......: Link-virus (extending), RAM- resident
Length of Virus.....: .COM files: program length increases by
                               1206-1221 bytes
                      .EXE files: program length increases by
                               132 bytes
-------------------- Preconditions ----------------------------------
Operating System(s).: MS-DOS
Version/Release.....: 2.xx upward
Computer model(s)...: IBM-PC, XT, AT and compatibles
-------------------- Attributes -------------------------------------
Easy Identification.: 1. Typical texts in Virus body (readable
                         with HexDump-facilities): "VACSINA" in
                         data area of the virus.
                      2. The length of an infected file is increased.
                      2. The date/time of the last program modification
                         is different between an infected program and
                         its original version.
Type of infection...: System: infected if the segment:offset of INT31h
                         points to 0539h:7fxxh.
                      .Com files: with a program length of 1207-62866
                         bytes will be infected if the first instruc-
                         tion is a JMP_DISP_16 (Opcode E9) and the
                         program length increases by 1206-1221 bytes.
                         The last 4 bytes are 0F4h,07Ah,005h,000h
                         (identification); therefore, a .COM file
                         will not be infected more than once.
                      .EXE files: with a program length up to 64946
                         bytes will not be infected, but converted
                         in a COM-format and the program length
```

```
                        increases by 132 bytes. The virus adds code
                        to the EXE-file that is able to relocate
                        the file while loading it. If a converted
                        EXE-file is started again in an infected
                        system, it will be infected like a COM-file.
Infection Trigger...:   Programs are infected when they are run (using
                        the function Load/Execute of Ms-Dos).
Interrupts hooked...:   INT21h, INT24h (only while infecting a file).
                        INT31 (identification that system is infected)
Damage.............:    Transient damage: every time a file is infected,
                        the loudspeaker will beep.
Damage Trigger......:   ---
Particularities.....:   The date/time of the last program modification
                        will not be restored.
-------------------- Agents -------------------------------------------
Countermeasures.....:   Category 3: ANTIVACS.EXE (VTC Hamburg)
- ditto - successful:   ANTIVACS.EXE is an antivirus that specifically
                        looks for the VACSINA virus and, if re-
                        quested, will restore the file.
Standard means......:   ---
-------------------- Acknowledgement ----------------------------------
Location...........:    Virus Test Center, University of Hamburg, Germany
Classification by...:   Michael Reinschmiedt
Documentation by....:   Michael Reinschmiedt
Date................:   January 3, 1990
```

VACSINA Rev. 2

```
Entry.................   VACSINA virus
Alias(es).............   ---
Strain................   ---
Detected: when........   Early August 1989
          where.......   University of Cologne, West-Germany
Classification........   Filevirus/resident   with update facility
Length of virus.......   length added to a COM-type file 1206-1221 bytes
                         length added to a EXE-type file 132 bytes and
                         then like a COM-type file
--------------------- Preconditions------------------------------------
Operating System(s)....  MS-DOS
Version/Release........  ---
Computer models.......   IBM-PC, XT, AT, PS/2 and compatibles
--------------------- Attributes---------------------------------------
Easy identification....  The string 'VACSINA' in the viruscode
                         the last 4 bytes of an infected file show
                         F4 7A 05 00
                         memorysegment 0000:00C5 contains 7F 39 05
                         when VACSINA is resident.
                         The bytes 05 00 at the end of the file and
                         the 05 in memory 0000:00C7 are version-
                         numbers of VACSINA (see below).
Type of infection......  VACSINA installs a TSR that trapps INT 21H
                         function 4BH (load & execute). Every file
                         that is loaded via this function will be
                         infected (provided some constraints are met
                         see below)
                         VACSINA checks the version number (current is
                         0005) and will remove earlier versions of itself
                         and substitute with the newer virus code!
```

```
Infection trigger...... Executing an uninfected file after an infected
                        file was used.
Media affected......... Any via INT 21H funtion 4BH loadable file,
                        that either starts with E9H (jump) or 'MZ'
                        (EXE header). This includes COM, EXE, OVL, and
                        APP (GEM) files.
                        Files with the leading E9 must be bigger
                        than 1206 and smaller than 62867
                        Files with a EXE-Header must not be bigger
                        than 64947 for the 132 loader attachment.
                        after that they have to meet the constraints
                        of a E9H headed file.
Interrupts hooked...... INT 21H (function 4BH), INT 24H
                        The INT 31 table entry is used as the VACSINA
                        present flag.
Damage................. After a successfull infection of a COM-type file
                        a beep (DOS-BELL) is issued.
                        NO OTHER PAYLOAD !
                        This looks like test code for the infection-
                        mechanism.
Damage trigger......... The beep is triggered when a COM-Type file is
                        successfully infected.
Particularities........ Probably a testversion that prematurely escaped
                        since there is no payload, the beep when
                        infecting another file, and some incomplete
                        codesections.
                        The virus opens a file 'VACSINA' and closes it
                        after a while, never writing or reading from it.
                        The returncodes of the open and close operations
                        are ignored.
                        The words for vaccine are written with two Cs in
                        all languages that use latin letters except for
                        norvegian (they write vaksine).
                        The virus has an update facility and will replac
                        old versions with new versions of itself!
Similarities........... ---
----------------------- Agents----------------------------------------
Countermeasures........ ANTI-VD of the MVC (University of Karlsruhe)
                        detects and removes the virus from any file.
                        EXE-headers are reconstructed!
Countermeasures successful ---
Standard Means......... The DEL command after booting from a clean
                        systemdisk.
---------------------- Acknowledgements -----------------------------
Location............... Micro-BIT Virus Center University of Karlsruhe,
                                                                 Germany
Classification by...... C. Fischer, T. Boerstler, R. Stober
Documentation by....... C. Fischer, T. Boerstler, R. Stober
Date................... Nov. 13, 1989
Information source..... The update feature was first discovered by
                        David M. Chess, Yorktown Heights
```

VCL Authoring Package

```
Entry..............: Virus Construction Language (VCL)
Standard CARO name..: VCL
Alias(es)..........: ---
Virus Strain.......: ---
```

```
Virus detected when.: ---
             where.: ---
Classification......: Virus Authoring Package: generates file (COM,EXE)
                      infectors or trojans, depending on selection
                      of options. They are generated in source code.
Length of Virus.....: ---
-------------------- Preconditions -------------------------------
Operating System(s).: MS-DOS
Version/Release.....: Version 2.x and above
Computer model(s)...: IBM PC, XT, AT and higher, and compatibles
-------------------- Attributes ----------------------------------
Easy Identification.: (depends on generated virus)
Search string.......: (depends on generated virus)
Type of infection...: EXE-files: Overwriting or Companion
                      COM-files: Overwriting or Appending
Infection Trigger...: (depends on generated virus)
Storage media affected: (depends on generated virus)
Interrupts hooked...: ---
Damage..............: The following types of transient or permanent
                      damage can be implemented in all classes of
                      viruses and trojans generated:
                       1) Beep a desired amount of times.
                       2) Change size of RAM available under 1 meg.
                       3) Clear the screen.
                       4) Cold Reboot of the system.
                       5) Corrupt files, using a random encryption.
                       6) Disable a parallel prot.
                       7) Disable the Print Screen Key.
                       8) Disable a serial port.
                       9) Display a string on the screen.
                      10) Drop a program into a file.
                      11) Delete files.
                      12) Lock up the computer.
                      13) Send a value to a port.
                      14) Send random values to all ports.
                      15) Play a tune / Sound effects.
                      16) Send a string to the printer.
                      17) Switch to ROM BASIC (if available).
                      18) Send a string to a serial port.
                      19) Swap two parallel ports.
                      20) Swap two serial ports.
                      21) Trash one or more drives (starting with the
                          highest drive).
                      22) Uncrunch and display a run-length encoded
                          ANSI string.
                      23) Warm reboot.
                      It is possible to implement any other routine
                      as a transient or permanent damage.
Damage Trigger......: Condition can be choosen from the following menu:
                       1) Country code (DOS).
                       2) Kind of CPU installed in the computer.
                       3) Day / Month / Year / Weekday.
                       4) DOS-version.
                       5) Ammount of EMS.
                       6) Number of floppy drives.
                       7) Number of game ports.
                       8) Hour / Minute / Second.
                       9) Number of prallel ports.
                      10) Amount of RAM.
                      11) Random.
```

```
                     12) BIOS rollover flag (indicates wether the
                         computer has been on for 24 hours continu-
                         ously or not)
                     13) Number of serial ports.
                     14) All files infected.
                     15) Is 4DOS installed?
                     The condition can be choosen freely and the
                     trigger may be set for all damages individually,
                     responding to whether conditions are true,false,
                     or relations (equal,bigger,lesser) hold. Various
                     conditions can be combined.
Particularities.....: 1) VCL Toolkit also offers the opportunity to build
                     Trojans and Logic bombs with all possibilities
                     as described above.
                     2) VCL Toolkit offers the feature to use encryption
                     for Viruses and Trojans but not for Logic bombs.
                     Encryption method is a simple XOR with variable
                     key and 2 slightly different routines (use of
                     di/si).
                     3) It is also possible to install a trace-stopper,
                     but it should stop no longer than 5 min.
                     4) The infection rate of created viruses can also
                     be modified.
                     5) Generated viruses can search their victims either
                     in actual directory, all directory tree, path
                     or only the first file, depending on the user.
General comments....: It's not that easy, creating viruses with this
                     tool as it may seem: most viruses generated with
                     VCL have difficulties during assembly,  and if
                     they are successfully assembled they dont work
                     in most cases.
Similarities........: 1) Some parts of the code are stolen from various
                     other sources.
                     2) Among others, the following viruses generated
                     with VCL have appeared:
                         CodeZero, Diarrhea, Diarrhea II,
                         Diogenes, Donatello, Earth_Day, Enun,
                         Kinison, Mimic, Pearl_Harbour, VMessiah,
                         Venom, Yankee.A, Yankee.B
                     The following trojan developped with VCL has
                     appeared:
                         Richards
-------------------- Agents --------------------------------------------
Countermeasures successful: (depends on virus and AV product)
Standard means......: Delete and replace infected files.
-------------------- Acknowledgement -----------------------------------
Location...........: Virus Test Center, University of Hamburg, Germany
Classification by...: Toralv Dirro
Documentation by....: Toralv Dirro
Date................: 25-February-1993
Information Source..: Original virus analysis
```

VCS V1.0 Virus

```
Entry................ VCS V1.0 Virus
Alias(es)............ Virus-Construction-Set V1.0 = VDV Virus
                    (VDV = "Verband Deutscher Virenliebhaber";
                       = "community of German virus lovers")
```

```
Strain................ ---
Detected: when........ March 1991
          where....... Bulletin Board, Hamburg, Germany
Classification........ Program Virus, direct action; overwriting
                       AUTOEXEC and CONFIG.SYS; encrypted.
Length of Virus....... File: 1077 bytes
-------------------- Preconditions ------------------------------
Operating System(s)... MS/PC-DOS
Computer models....... All IBM PC compatibles.
-------------------- Attributes ---------------------------------
Easy identification... Files containing C350h at offset 03h regarded
                       as infected (self identification)
                       Search string at offset 00h:
                       E8 14 00 8A A4 2F 05 8D BC 20 01 B9 0F 04 89 FE
Type of infection..... .COM files: increased by 1077 bytes; virus
                       is not RAM resident, files can only be in-
                       fected when an infected host is started;
                       files are randomly infected in the current
                       directory or in root directory and below.
                       Files are not infected if word at offset
                       03h of file contains C350H.
                       .COM files are infected only once.
                       .EXE files: no infection.
Infection trigger..... Any time an infected file is run, the virus
                       infects up to 10 files, but only if the
                       Int 26h (=absolute-disk-write-vector) is
                       not hooked by a program.
Interrupts hooked..... ---
Damage................ Permanent damage: when triggered, the files
                       'C:\AUTOEXEC.BAT' and 'C:\CONFIG.SYS' will
                       be overwritten with 512 bytes of text.
                       Transient Damage: when AUTOEXEC and CONFIG.SYS
                       have been overwritten, a text which was
                       deliberately choosen by the installator
                       (see: Particularities:Generating the virus)
                       may be displayed.
Damage trigger........ If generation counter > damage counter, the
                       permanent/transient damage is performed.
Particularities....... Virus is encrypted; on each infection, en-
                       cryption key and generation counter are
                       changed; virus therefore mutates.
                       Files with ReadOnly attribute set will not
                       be infected.
                       .COM files longer than 64,190 bytes are no
                       longer loadable.
Particularities/Generating this virus: VCS virus was created by
                       program VCS.EXE ('Virus Construction Set
                       V1.0'), which was written by a "Verband
                       Deutscher Virenliebhaber" (=community of
                       German virus lovers) and was available via
                       a BBS in Hamburg. Using VCS.BIN and a
                       textfile, VCS.EXE generates the program
                       VIRUS.COM (1077 bytes). In constructing
                       this virus, the user can adjust the damage
                       counter (1st active generation: 1..199)
                       and specify his own textfile of 512 bytes.
                       In VCS' menu (22 lines), detailed informa-
                       tion is given how to generate 1st virus,
                       ending with:
                           "3) Start VIRUS.COM ...
```

The infected program is now 1077 Bytes
longer than before and can be given to
known persons, friends and enemies.."
The textfile (in German, 29 lines) distributed with VCS is essentially:

"Virus Construction Set"

"All have waited for it, here it is!
Who didnot want to shove a little virus
under his best enemy, but had none at his
hand? ....."

"This virus copies itself when invoked on
.COM files in actual drive, after speci-
fied number of generations a specified
text will be displayed, AUTOEXEC.BAT and
CONFIG.SYS will be deleted. Virus detects
FLUSHOT in memory and keeps quiet."

"This program is a community exercise of
VDV Hamburg. We can be reached in BBS
Hamburg (local tel#) under 'VDV'...."

"In case of interest, version 2 of VCS
will soon be available, with more possibilities to tune the virus."

"Now to the legal aspect: herewith, a
user is explicitly warned that this
program generates viruses which may
damage data. By using this program, the
user accepts full responsibility for the
viruses which he generates. We are not
responsible under any circumstances.
Nevertheless we renounce, due to evident
reasons, to mention our adress here..."

"... donate 20 DM to Red Cross. Generally,
this program may be copied and used as
desired."

"We wish much fun with our viruses...."

```
Similarities........... ---
--------------------- Agents -------------------------------------
Countermeasures....... Searchstring at offset 00h of virus:
                       E8 14 00 8A A4 2F 05 8D BC 20 01 B9 0F 04 89 FE
 - ditto - unsuccessful. McAfee's Scan version 75 and below
 - ditto -   successful. Tode's NTI-VCS.EXE is an antivirus that
                       only looks for VCS virus, and if requested
                       will restore the file.
Standard Means........ Notice file length. Use ReadOnly attribute.
--------------------- Acknowledgements ----------------------------
Location.............. Virus Test Center, University of Hamburg, Germany
Classification by..... Stefan Tode
Documentation by...... Stefan Tode and Matthias Jaenichen
Date.................. 15-July-1991
Information source.... ---
```

VCS V1.0 Manta Virus

```
Entry................. VCS V1.0 Manta Virus
Standard CARO Name.... VCS.Manta Virus
Alias(es)............. ---
Strain................ VCS Virus Strain
Detected: when........ Summer 1992
```

```
            where....... Bulletin Board, Hamburg, Germany
Classification........ Clone of VCS V1.0 Virus
                       Program Virus, direct action; overwriting
                       AUTOEXEC and CONFIG.SYS; encrypted.
Length of Virus....... Increase of file length: 1077 bytes
-------------------- Preconditions ------------------------------
Operating System(s)... MS/PC-DOS
Computer models....... All IBM PC compatibles with CPU > 8088
-------------------- Attributes ---------------------------------
Easy identification... Same as VCS V1.0 virus:
                       Files containing C350h at offset 03h regarded
                       as infected (self identification)
                       Search string at offset 00h:
                       E8 14 00 8A A4 2F 05 8D BC 20 01 B9 0F 04 89 FE
Type of infection..... Same as VCS V1.0 virus
Infection trigger..... Same as VCS V1.0 virus
Interrupts hooked..... ---
Damage................ Same as VCS V1.0 virus:
                       Permanent damage: when triggered, the files
                       'C:\AUTOEXEC.BAT' and 'C:\CONFIG.SYS' will
                       be overwritten with 512 bytes of text.
                       Transient Damage: when AUTOEXEC and CONFIG.SYS
                       have been overwritten, a text which was
                       deliberately choosen by the installator
                       (see: Particularities:Generating the virus)
                       may be displayed.
Damage trigger........ Same as VCS V1.0 virus
Particularities....... Same as VCS V1.0 virus
Particularities/Generating this virus: VCS V1.0 Manta was generated
                       with the VCS V1.0 (see catalog entry VCS V1.0).
                       In addition to the characteristics of VCS V1.0,
                       the following text will be displayed until
                       a key is pressed:
                       "RAM Parity Error at 0F67:1B2C"
                       "(C)ontinue  (S)hut off NMI  (R)eboot ".
                       The files C:\AUTOEXEC.BAT and C:\CONFIG.SYS will
                       be overwritten with this text, as well as with
                       the following text referring to popular jokes
                       about some people which drive a special Opel
                       car type called "Manta". The text is:
                       "Ein Mantafahrer haelt an einer Ampel. Neben ihm
                        haelt ein Porsche. Beide kurbeln die Scheiben
                        runter, und der Porschefahrer fragt: 'Was hat
                        vier Beine und ist unheimlich bloed?'
                        Mantafahrer: 'Keine Ahnung'
                        Porschefahrer: 'Du und deine Freundin'
                        An der naechsten Ampel haelt ein Golf neben dem
                        Manta. Mantafahrer: 'Was hat vier Beine und ist
                        unheimlich doof ?' Golffahrer: 'Keine Ahnung'
                        Mantafahrer: 'Meine Freundin und ich'."
                       Translation:
                       "A Manta driver stops at a traffic lights.
                        A Porsche stops beside him. Both of them open
                        the window and the Porsche driver asks:
                        'What has four legs and is very very mad?'
                        Says Manta driver: 'I do not know'
                        Says Porsche driver: 'You and your girlfriend'
                        At next traffic lights, a Golf stops beside the
                        Manta. Says Manta driver: 'What has four legs
                        and is very very mad ?'
```

```
                          Says Golf driver: 'I do not know'
                          Says Manta driver:'My girlfriend and me.' "
                          Moreover, VCS V1.0 Manta uses opcode 68h (push
                          constant on stack) which is not defined on
                          8088 processors; so, virus will not work on
                          such systems.
Similarities........... ---
--------------------- Agents -----------------------------------------
Countermeasures....... Searchstring at offset 00h of virus:
                          E8 14 00 8A A4 2F 05 8D BC 20 01 B9 0F 04 89 FE
  - ditto -   successful. Actual versions of McAfee Scan, Skulason
                          F-PROT, Solomon FindViru.
                          Tode's NTI-VCS.EXE is an antivirus that
                            only looks for VCS virus, and if requested
                            will restore the file.
Standard Means........ Notice file length. Use ReadOnly attribute.
--------------------- Acknowledgements -----------------------------
Location.............. Virus Test Center, University of Hamburg, Germany
Classification by..... Stefan Tode
Documentation by...... Stefan Tode and Matthias Jaenichen
Date.................. 15-July-1991
Information source.... ---
```

VCS V1.1a Virus

```
Entry................. VCS V1.1a Virus
Alias(es)............. Virus-Construction-Set V1.1a
Strain................ VCS Virus Strain
Detected: when........ JAN 1992
           where....... Bulletin Board, Hamburg, Germany
Classification........ Clone of VCS V1.0 Virus
                          Program Virus, direct action; overwriting,
                          AUTOEXEC.BAT and CONFIG.SYS; encrypted.
Length of Virus....... Increased File Length: 1077 bytes
--------------------- Preconditions --------------------------------
Operating System(s)... MS/PC-DOS
Computer models....... All IBM PC compatibles with CPU > 8088.
--------------------- Attributes -----------------------------------
Easy identification... Files containing C390h at offset 03h regarded
                          as infected (self identification).
Scan signature........ Searchstring at offset 00h (same as VCS V1.0):
                          E8 14 00 8A A4 2F 05 8D BC 20 01 B9 0F 04 89 FE
                          same as VCS V1.0
Type of infection..... same as VCS V1.0
Infection trigger..... same as VCS V1.0
Interrupts hooked..... ---
Damage................ same as VCS V1.0
Particularities....... same as VCS V1.0
Particularities/Generating as VCS 1.0, generated by Virus Construction
                          Set Version 1.0
DisSimilarities....... Virus is similar to VCS V1.0 virus and uses the
                          same code, except the self identification
                          routine. Only the version number is changed, so
                          the following string can be found in VCS V1.1a:
                          "Virus Construction Set V1.1a"
--------------------- Agents ---------------------------------------
Countermeasures....... Searchstring at offset 00h of virus:
                          E8 14 00 8A A4 2F 05 8D BC 20 01 B9 0F 04 89 FE
```

```
            - ditto - successful. Skulason's F-PROT V2.04  detects as VCS variant.
                                  McAfee's Scan version 93 as Manta
                                  Tode's NTI-VCS.EXE is an antivirus that
                                  only looks for VCS viruses, and if requested
                                  will restore the file.
Standard Means........ Notice file length. Use ReadOnly attribute.
--------------------- Acknowledgements ----------------------------
Location.............. Virus Test Center, University of Hamburg, Germany
Classification by..... Stefan Tode
Documentation by...... Stefan Tode
Date.................. 21-July-1992
Information source.... ---
```

VCS V1.3 Virus

```
Entry................. VCS V1.3 Virus
Standard CARO Name.... VCS.RUF
Alias(es)............. Virus-Construction-Set V1.3 Virus=VCS1.3.RUF
Strain................ VCS Virus Strain
Detected: when........ March 1992
          where....... Bulletin Board, Hamburg, Germany
Classification........ Clone of VCS V1.0 Virus;
                       Program Virus, direct action; overwriting
                       AUTOEXEC and CONFIG.SYS; encrypted.
Length of Virus....... Increase of file length: 1077 bytes
--------------------- Preconditions ----------------------------
Operating System(s)... MS/PC-DOS
Computer models....... on IBM PC compatibles with CPU > 8086.
--------------------- Attributes ----------------------------
Easy identification... Files containing C350h at offset 03h regarded
                       as infected (self identification)
                       Search string at offset 00h:
                       E8 14 00 8A 9C 2F 05 8D BC 20 01 B9 0F 04 89 FE
Type of infection..... same as VCS V1.0
Infection trigger..... same as VCS V1.0
Interrupts hooked..... ---
Damage................ same as VCS V1.0
Particularities....... same as VCS V1.0
Particularities/Generating
                       VCS1.3 = VCS.RUF is a virus which was generated
                       by the Virus Construction Set V1.3.
                       The textbuffer in the damage routine contains
                       the strings "Deutsche Bundespost" (=German
                       Post Office) and "Telekom". A blockgraphics
                       displaed consists of a telephone icon and
                       the German Telecom's slogan:
                       "RUF DOCH MAL AN" (=You should call").
Similarities.......... 1) Virus is similar to VCS 1.0 virus and uses
                          the same code, except for the encrypt-
                          ion routine.
                       2) VCS 1.3 is a patched version of VCS 1.0.
                          It was created by someone who calls
                          himself "Hanswurst".
                       3) The textstrings of VCS.EXE are also
                          patched. The following strings can be
                          found in the VCS.EXE:
                          "(C) 1991 by VDV, 1992 by Hanswurst"
                          "Virus Construction Set V1.3, gepatcht"
```

```
                                  " von Hanswurst 1992"
-------------------- Agents -----------------------------------------
Countermeasures....... Searchstring at offset 00h of virus:
                       E8 14 00 8A 9C 2F 05 8D BC 20 01 B9 0F 04 89 FE
 - ditto - successful. Tode's NTI-VCS.EXE is an antivirus that only
                       looks for VCS viruses, and if requested will
                       restore the file.
 - ditto - unsuccessful. Presently, no AV product identifies VCS V1.3.
Standard Means........ Notice file length. Use ReadOnly attribute.
-------------------- Acknowledgements --------------------------------
Location.............. Virus Test Center, University of Hamburg, Germany
Classification by..... Stefan Tode
Documentation by...... Stefan Tode
Date.................. 21-July-1992
Information source.... ---
```

VDV-853 Virus

```
Entry................. VDV-853 Virus
                       (VDV = "Verband Deutscher Virenliebhaber";
                          = "community of German virus lovers")
Alias(es)............. ---
Strain................ VCS Virus Strain
Detected: when........ December 1991
          where....... Hamburg, Germany
Classification........ Program (COM) infector, encrypted, appending,
                       direct action; not memory resident
Length of Virus....... on media: 853 bytes
-------------------- Preconditions -----------------------------------
Operating System(s)... MS/PC-DOS 2.x upwards
Computer models....... All IBM PC/AT compatibles with CPU > 8088.
-------------------- Attributes --------------------------------------
Easy identification... ---
Signature............. Search string at offset 00h:
                       E8 14 00 8A A4 4F 04 8D BC 20 01 B9 2F 03 89 FE
Type of infection..... Self-identification: files containing C350h at
                       offset 03h regarded as infected.
                       EXE files: no infection.
                       COM files: are infected only once. Files are
                       randomly infected in the current directory
                       or in root directory and below if word at
                       offset 03h of file doesnot contain C350h.
                       File size is increased by 853 bytes. Virus
                       is not RAM resident; files can only be in-
                       fected when an infected host is started.
Infection trigger..... Any time an infected file is run, the virus
                       infects up to 10 files, but only if the
                       INT 26h (=absolute-disk-write-vector) is
                       not hooked.
Affected media........ Files on hard disk or any diskette.
Interrupts hooked..... ---
Damage................ Permanent damage: when triggered, all files in
                       the root directory will be overwritten with
                       273 bytes of text including a Christmas tree
                       and message (see Particularities).
                       Transient Damage: when the file has been over-
                       written, message (see: Particularities) will
                       be displayed until a key is pressed.
```

```
Damage trigger........ Permanent or transient damage is activated when
                       month of system date = December and day of
                       system date = 24, 25 or 26 (Christmas).
Particularities....... 1) Virus is encrypted; upon each infection, en-
                       cryption key is changed.
                       2) Virus uses opcode 68h (push constant on
                       stack) which isnot defined on 8088 processors;
                       so, virus will not work on such machines.
                       3) Files with ReadOnly attribute will not be
                       infected.
                       4) VDV-853 virus was written by some "Verband
                       Deutscher Virenliebhaber" (=community of
                       German virus lovers). This virus is realated
                       to VCS virus (see Catalog edition July 91)
                       but may have been created before the release
                       of the VCS 1.0.
                       The following message can be found in over-
                       written (damaged) files and will be display-
                       ed under damage trigger conditions:
                       "Froehliche Weihnachten wuenscht
                               der Verband Deutscher Virenliebhaber
                        Ach ja, und dann wuenschen wir auch noch
                        viel Spasz beim Suchen nach den Daten von
                        der Festplatte!
                        gez. VDV, Dezember 1990."
                       Translation:
                       "Happy Christmas wishes the community of
                        German virus lovers
                        Oh yes, and then we wish you a lot of fun,
                        by searching for your data on your
                        harddisk!"
                        Yours  VDV, December 1990.";
                       On the left side of the message, a stylized
                       Christmas tree is displayed in textgraphic.
Similarities.......... 1) Virus is similar to VCS 1.0 virus and uses
                       the same code, except that damage routine
                       and some address functions are changed.
                       2) In distinction to VCS 1.0 virus, VDV-853
                       has no generation counter and a different
                       damage routine. Probably, is was not
                       created with Virus Construction Set 1.0
-------------------- Agents -------------------------------------------
Countermeasures.......
 - ditto -   successful. Solomon's Findviru V4.01 detects as VDV-853.
                       Skulason's F-PROT V2.02  detects as VDV-853.
                       Tode's NTI-VDV.EXE is an antivirus that only
                           looks for VDV-853 virus, and if requested
                           will restore the original file.
 - ditto - unsuccessful. McAfee's Scan version 86b and below
Standard Means........ Notice file length. Use ReadOnly attribute.
                       Or use FLU-Shot or another program, which
                       monitors INT 26h.
-------------------- Acknowledgements ----------------------------------
Location.............. Virus Test Center, University of Hamburg, Germany
Classification by..... Stefan Tode
Documentation by...... Stefan Tode
Date.................. 31-January-1992
Information source.... ---
```

Vienna Virus

```
Entry...............: Vienna Virus
Alias(es)...........: "648 Virus", Austrian Virus
Classification......: Programm Virus (Extending), Direct Action
Length of Virus.....: 648 Bytes
-------------------- Preconditions ------------------------------------
Operating System(s).: PC-DOS, MS-DOS
Version/ Release....: 2.xx and upward
Computer model(s)...: IBM-PC XT AT
-------------------- Attributes ---------------------------------------
Type of infection...: Self-Identification: The second-entry of the
                      time stamp of an infected file is set to 62 dec.
                      Infects .COM-files (with length between 10 and
                      64.000 bytes) in the current directory of the
                      current drive and in all directories that are
                      accessible via the PATH-definition.
                      Virus code is appended at the end of the file.
Infection Trigger...: Execution of an infected file.
Storage media affected: Hard and Floppy disks.
Damage..............: The first five bytes of the selected file will
                      be overwritten a long jump to the BIOS
                      initialisation routine.
Damage Trigger......: IF (7 AND second-bits of system-time) equals 0.
Particularities.....: For infection, the virus selects an appropriate
                      file and, depending on the value of the damage
                      trigger, either infects that file or overwrites
                      the first five bytes. The attribute, time- and
                      date-stamp of an infected file remains unchanged
                      with exception of the seconds-bits. The READ-ONLY
                      and HIDDEN attributes do not protect against
                      infection.
-------------------- Agents: ------------------------------------------
Countermeasures.....: ----
Countermeasures successful: ---
Standard Means......: ----
-------------------- Acknowledgements: --------------------------------
Location............: Virus Test Center. University of Hamburg, Germany
Classification by...: Rainer Anscheit (July 4, 1989)
Documentation by....: Rainer Anscheit (July 4,1989)
Updated by..........: Klaus Brunnstein
Date................: October 31, 1989
```

"Vienna 348" Virus

```
Entry...............: "Vienna 348" Virus
Alias(es)...........: ---
Virus strain........: Vienna Virus strain
Virus detected when.: ---
             where.: ---
Classification......: Program virus (extending), direct action
Length of virus.....: 348 bytes
-------------------- Preconditions ------------------------------------
Operating system(s).: MS-DOS
Version/release.....: 2.0 and higher
Computer model(s)...: All MS-DOS machines
-------------------- Attributes ---------------------------------------
Easy identification.: Bytes found in virus = EAh,06h,00h,00h,C8h;
```

```
                         text found: "*.COM",00h,"PATH=".
Type of infection...: Self-Identification: The time stamp
                         of an infected file is changed:
                         the seconds are set to 62 (= 2 * 1Fh).
                         When infected file is executed, .COM-files
                         in the current directory as well as in the
                         directories in the DOS-PATH are extended
                         by appending the viral code; no infection
                         if the filesize<10 or filesize>64000 bytes.
Infection trigger...: A selected .COM-file is infected by "random" IF
                         (system seconds AND 7) <> 0 ELSE damaged!
Storage media affected: Current media and media accessed via DOS-PATH.
Interrupts hooked...: INT 24h diverted to own error-handler only
                         during virus-runtime to suppress
                         error-messages send out by DOS.
Damage..............: A selected .COM-file is damaged permanently:
                         Overwriting the first five bytes
                         with a far jump to the HD-low-level-format-
                         routine (XT only).
Damage trigger......: IF (system seconds AND 7) = 0, ELSE infection!
Particularities.....: The virus ignores READ-ONLY and HIDDEN attributes;
                         The PATH-search is corrected!
Similarities........: Dissimilarities to Vienna (648 bytes):
                         Code optimized and length decreased;
                         the five damage-bytes are changed.
-------------------- Agents ------------------------------------
Countermeasures.....: ---
Countermeasures successful: ---
Standard means......: Do not execute .COM files with time stamp seconds
                         equal 62; restore them from a backup-disk.
-------------------- Acknowledgement ---------------------------
Location............: Virus Test Center, University of Hamburg, Germany
Classification by...: Uwe Ellermann, Daniel Loeffler
Documentation by....: Daniel Loeffler, Uwe Ellermann
Date................: June 28, 1990
Information Source..: ---
```

"Vienna 353" Virus

```
Entry...............: "Vienna 353" Virus
Alias(es)...........: ---
Virus strain........: Vienna Virus strain
Virus detected when.: ---
            where.: ---
Classification......: Program virus (extending), direct action
Length of virus.....: 353 bytes
-------------------- Preconditions -----------------------------
Operating system(s).: MS-DOS
Version/release.....: 2.0 and higher
Computer model(s)...: All MS-DOS machines
-------------------- Attributes --------------------------------
Easy identification.: Bytes found in virus = EAh,06h,00h,00h,C8h;
                         text found: "*.COM",00h,"PATH=".
Type of infection...: Self-Identification: The time stamp
                         of an infected file is changed:
                         the seconds are set to 62 (= 2 * 1Fh).
                         When infected file is executed, .COM-files
                         in the current directory as well as in the
```

```
                         directories in the DOS-PATH are extended
                         by appending the viral code; no infection
                         if the filesize<10 or filesize>64000 bytes.
Infection trigger...: A selected .COM-file is infected by "random" IF
                         (system seconds AND 7) <> 0 ELSE damaged!
Storage media affected: Current media and media accessed via DOS-PATH.
Interrupts hooked...: INT 24h diverted to own error-handler only
                         during virus-runtime to suppress
                         error-messages send out by DOS.
Damage.............: A selected .COM-file is damaged permanently:
                         Overwriting the first five bytes
                         with a far jump to the HD-low-level-format-
                         routine (XT only).
Damage trigger......: IF (system seconds AND 7) = 0, ELSE infection!
Particularities.....: The virus ignores READ-ONLY and HIDDEN attributes;
                         The PATH-search is corrected!
Similarities........: Dissimilarities to Vienna (648 bytes):
                         Code optimized and length decreased;
                         the five damage-bytes are changed.
-------------------- Agents -------------------------------------------
Countermeasures.....: ---
Countermeasures successful: ---
Standard means......: Do not execute .COM files with time stamp seconds
                         equal 62; restore them from a backup-disk.
-------------------- Acknowledgement ----------------------------------
Location............: Virus Test Center, University of Hamburg, Germany
Classification by...: Uwe Ellermann, Daniel Loeffler
Documentation by....: Daniel Loeffler, Uwe Ellermann
Date................: June 28, 1990
Information Source..: ---
```

"Vienna 367" Virus

```
Entry...............: "Vienna 367" Virus
Alias(es)...........: ---
Virus strain........: Vienna Virus strain
Virus detected when.: ---
              where.: ---
Classification......: Program virus (extending), direct action
Length of virus.....: 367 bytes
-------------------- Preconditions ------------------------------------
Operating system(s).: MS-DOS
Version/release.....: 2.0 and higher
Computer model(s)...: All MS-DOS machines
-------------------- Attributes ---------------------------------------
Easy identification.: Bytes found in virus = EAh,06h,00h,00h,C8h;
                         text found: "*.COM",00h,"PATH=".
Type of infection...: Self-Identification: The time stamp
                         of an infected file is changed:
                         the seconds are set to 62 (= 2 * 1Fh).
                         When infected file is executed, .COM-files
                         in the current directory as well as in the
                         directories in the DOS-PATH are extended
                         by appending the viral code; no infection
                         if the filesize<10 or filesize>64000 bytes.
Infection trigger...: A selected .COM-file is infected by "random" IF
                         (system seconds AND 7) <> 0 ELSE damaged!
Storage media affected: Current media and media accessed via DOS-PATH.
```

```
Interrupts hooked...: INT 24h diverted to own error-handler only
                          during virus-runtime to suppress
                          error-messages send out by DOS.
Damage..............: A selected .COM-file is damaged permanently:
                          Overwriting the first five bytes
                          with a far jump to the HD-low-level-format-
                          routine (XT only).
Damage trigger......: IF (system seconds AND 7) = 0, ELSE infection!
Particularities.....: The virus ignores READ-ONLY and HIDDEN attributes;
                          The PATH-search is corrected!
Similarities........: Dissimilarities to Vienna (648 bytes):
                          Code optimized and length decreased;
                          the five damage-bytes are changed.
-------------------- Agents -------------------------------------------
Countermeasures.....: ---
Countermeasures successful: ---
Standard means......: Do not execute .COM files with time stamp seconds
                          equal 62; restore them from a backup-disk.
-------------------- Acknowledgement ----------------------------------
Location............: Virus Test Center, University of Hamburg, Germany
Classification by...: Uwe Ellermann, Daniel Loeffler
Documentation by....: Daniel Loeffler, Uwe Ellermann
Date................: June 28, 1990
Information Source..: ---
```

"Vienna 435" Virus

```
Entry...............: "Vienna 435" Virus
Alias(es)...........: ---
Virus strain........: Vienna Virus strain
Virus detected when.: ---
            where.: ---
Classification......: Program virus (extending), direct action
Length of virus.....: 435/367/353/348 bytes
-------------------- Preconditions ------------------------------------
Operating system(s).: MS-DOS
Version/release.....: 2.0 and higher
Computer model(s)...: All MS-DOS machines
-------------------- Attributes ---------------------------------------
Easy identification.: Bytes found in virus = EAh,05h,00h,00h,C8h;
                          text found: "*.COM",00h,"PATH=".
Type of infection...: Self-Identification: The time stamp
                          of an infected file is changed:
                          the seconds are set to 62 (= 2 * 1Fh).
                          When infected file is executed, .COM-files
                          in the current directory as well as in the
                          directories in the DOS-PATH are extended
                          by appending the viral code; no infection
                          if the filesize<10 or filesize>64000 bytes.
Infection trigger...: A selected .COM-file is infected by "random" IF
                          (system seconds AND 7) <> 0 ELSE damaged!
Storage media affected: Current media and media accessed via DOS-PATH.
Interrupts hooked...: INT 24h diverted to own error-handler only
                          during virus-runtime to suppress
                          error-messages send out by DOS.
Damage..............: A selected .COM-file is damaged permanently:
                          Overwriting the first five bytes
                          with a far jump to the HD-low-level-format-
                          routine (XT only).
```

```
Damage trigger......: IF (system seconds AND 7) = 0, ELSE infection!
Particularities.....: The virus ignores READ-ONLY and HIDDEN attributes;
                      The PATH-search is corrected!
Similarities........: Dissimilarities to Vienna (648 bytes):
                      Code optimized and length decreased;
                      the five damage-bytes are changed.
-------------------- Agents -------------------------------------------
Countermeasures.....: ---
Countermeasures successful: ---
Standard means......: Do not execute .COM files with time stamp seconds
                      equal 62; restore them from a backup-disk.
-------------------- Acknowledgement ----------------------------------
Location............: Virus Test Center, University of Hamburg, Germany
Classification by...: Uwe Ellermann, Daniel Loeffler
Documentation by....: Daniel Loeffler, Uwe Ellermann
Date................: June 28, 1990
Information Source..: ---
```

"Vienna 623" Virus

```
Entry...............: "Vienna 623" Virus
Alias(es)...........: ---
Virus strain........: Vienna Virus strain
Virus detected when.: ---
              where.: ---
Classification......: Program virus (extending), direct action
Length of virus.....: 623 bytes
-------------------- Preconditions ------------------------------------
Operating system(s).: MS-DOS
Version/release.....: 2.0 and higher
Computer model(s)...: All MS-DOS machines
-------------------- Attributes ---------------------------------------
Easy identification.: Bytes found in virus = EAh,00h,00h,00h,C8h;
                      text found: "*.COM" and "PATH=".
Type of infection...: Self-Identification: The time stamp
                      of an infected file is changed:
                      the seconds are set to 62 (= 2 * 1Fh).
                      When infected file is executed, .COM-files
                      in the current directory as well as in the
                      directories in the DOS-PATH are extended
                      by appending the viral code; no infection
                      if the filesize<10 or filesize>64000 bytes.
Infection trigger...: A selected .COM-file is infected by "random" IF
                      (system seconds AND 7) <> 0 ELSE damaged!
Storage media affected: Current media and media accessed via DOS-PATH.
Interrupts hooked...: INT 24h diverted to own error-handler only
                      during virus-runtime to suppress
                      error-messages send out by DOS.
Damage..............: A selected .COM-file is damaged permanently:
                      Overwriting the first five bytes
                      with a far jump to the HD-low-level-format-
                      routine (XT only).
Damage trigger......: IF (system seconds AND 7) = 0, ELSE infection!
Particularities.....: The virus ignores READ-ONLY and HIDDEN attributes;
                      The PATH-search is not correct:
                      First xxxPATH=C:\xxx in environment is found.
Similarities........: Dissimilarities to Vienna (648 bytes):
```

```
                          Code optimized and length decreased;
                          the five damage-bytes are changed.
-------------------- Agents -------------------------------------------
Countermeasures.....: ---
Countermeasures successful: ---
Standard means......: Do not execute .COM files with time stamp seconds
                          equal 62; restore them from a backup-disk.
-------------------- Acknowledgement ----------------------------------
Location............: Virus Test Center, University of Hamburg, Germany
Classification by...: Uwe Ellermann, Daniel Loeffler
Documentation by....: Daniel Loeffler, Uwe Ellermann
Date................: June 28, 1990
Information Source..: ---
```

"Vienna 627" Virus

```
Entry...............: "Vienna 627" Virus
Alias(es)...........: ---
Virus strain........: Vienna Virus strain
Virus detected when.: ---
             where.: ---
Classification......: Program virus (extending), direct action
Length of virus.....: 627 bytes
-------------------- Preconditions ------------------------------------
Operating system(s).: MS-DOS
Version/release.....: 2.0 and higher
Computer model(s)...: All MS-DOS machines
-------------------- Attributes ---------------------------------------
Easy identification.: Last five bytes of file = EAh,0Bh,02h,13h,58h;
                          text found: "*.COM" and "PATH=".
Type of infection...: Self-Identification: The time stamp
                          of an infected file is changed:
                          the seconds are set to 62 (= 2 * 1Fh).
                          When infected file is executed, .COM-files
                          in the current directory as well as in the
                          directories in the DOS-PATH are extended
                          by appending the viral code; no infection
                          if the filesize<10 or filesize>64000 bytes.
Infection trigger...: A selected .COM-file is infected by "random" IF
                          (system seconds AND 7) <> 0 ELSE damaged!
Storage media affected: Current media and media accessed via DOS-PATH.
Interrupts hooked...: --
Damage..............: A selected .COM-file is damaged permanently:
                          Overwriting the first five bytes with an
                          jump somewhere into the RAM.
Damage trigger......: IF (system seconds AND 7) = 0, ELSE infection!
Particularities.....: The virus ignores READ-ONLY and HIDDEN attributes;
                          The PATH-search is not correct:
                          First xxxPATH=C:\xxx in environment is found.
Similarities........: Dissimilarities to Vienna (648 bytes):
                          Code optimized and length decreased;
                          the five damage-bytes are changed.
-------------------- Agents -------------------------------------------
Countermeasures.....: ---
Countermeasures successful: ---
Standard means......: Do not execute .COM files with time stamp seconds
                          equal 62; restore them from a backup-disk.
-------------------- Acknowledgement ----------------------------------
```

```
Location............: Virus Test Center, University of Hamburg, Germany
Classification by...: Uwe Ellermann, Daniel Loeffler
Documentation by....: Daniel Loeffler, Uwe Ellermann
Date................: June 28, 1990
Information Source..: ---
```

Violetta Virus

```
Entry...............: Violetta Virus
Alias(es)...........: ---
Virus Strain........: ---
Virus detected when.: January 1992
              where.:
Classification......: Program virus, resident
Length of Virus.....: 3,840 Bytes
------------------- Preconditions -----------------------------------
Operating System(s).: MS-DOS
Version/Release.....: 2.xx upward
Computer model(s)...: IBM - PC, XT, AT, upward and compatibles
------------------- Attributes --------------------------------------
Easy Identification.: Infected files will contain the string
                      "VIOLETTA" twice (offset 2H and 202H in file)
Type of infection...: All *.COM files except COMMAND.COM when executed
                      will be infected. The virus saves the first
                      3,840 bytes of the host to the end of the file
                      and overwrites the first 3,840 bytes with the
                      virus code. Files smaller than 3,840 bytes
                      are first enlarged to 3,840 bytes.
Infection Trigger...: Load and Execute of a *.COM file.
Infection targets:..: All *.COM files except COMMAND.COM
Interrupts hooked...: INT 21
Interrupts used.....: INT F1, INT FF both used, but not chained; this
                      might cause trouble with Zenith Z100 warm
                      boot procedure.
Damage..............: No active payload
Damage Trigger......: ---
Similarities........: ---
Particularities.....: Unusual coding, much dead code, several code
                      sections overwritten with NOPs.
------------------- Agents ------------------------------------------
Countermeasures.....:
- ditto - successful:
             Removal: Not always possible: correct size of files
                      smaller than 3,840 cannot be restored.
Standard means......:
------------------- Acknowledgement ---------------------------------
Location............: Micro-BIT Virus Center, Univ Karlsruhe, Germany
Classification by...: Christoph Fischer
Documentation by....: Christoph Fischer
Date................: January 25, 1992
```

VOID_POEM Virus

```
Entry...............: VOID_POEM Virus
Alias(es)...........: Poem Virus
Virus Strain........: ---
```

```
Virus detected when.:
             where.: South Africa
Classification......: Memory-resident Program (COM) infector, appending.
Length of Virus.....: 1.Length (Byte) on media:  1825 + 31 Bytes
                      2.Length (Byte) in memory: 1825 Bytes
-------------------- Preconditions ------------------------------------
Operating System(s).: MS-DOS
Version/Release.....: Version >=3.10
Computer model(s)...: IBM PCs and compatibles
-------------------- Attributes ---------------------------------------
Easy Identification.: ---
Type of infection...: Self-Identification in memory:
                      memw[0:1F0h] XOR memw[0:1F2h] = ACDCh
                      Self-Identification on disk:
                      file[last_byte-1] XOR D9h=file[last_byte]
Infection Trigger...: Execution of a COM program with
                      580<=LengthCOM<=62464.
Storage media affected: FD/HD
Interrupts hooked...: INT 21h/4Bh, INT 21h/6Dh.
Damage..............: Permanent Damage: Poem (the same one) written
                                        over LSN 1..1220 on drive C:
                      Transient Damage: Long Poem (very adolescent!)
                                        displayed on screen; long text
                                        (not included here) encrypted.
Side-effect.........: PC may hang due to direct residency.
Damage Trigger......: Permanent Damage: IF Day=21 AND Month=12
                      Transient Damage: IF Day=21 AND Month<>12
                                        AND counter=2112
Particularities.....: The poem printed by the virus states that it was
                      written by "Marvin Giskard", the pseudonym of
                      the person claiming to have written
                      10_Past_3.748. The poem is dedicated to "T";
                      10_Past_3.789, a rework of .748, includes code
                      to print the name "Therese".
Similarities........: ---
-------------------- Agents -------------------------------------------
Countermeasures.....:
Countermeasures successful:
Standard means......:
-------------------- Acknowledgement ----------------------------------
Location............:
Classification by...: Paul Ducklin
Documentation by....: Paul Ducklin (CAERObase)
                      Klaus Brunnstein (conversion to CVC format)
Date................: 1993-February-15
Information Source..: Reverse-engineering of virus
```

V-Sign Virus

```
Entry...............: V-Sign Virus
Standard CARO name..: V-Sign (.3F,.1F) Virus
Alias(es)...........: Cansu = Sigalit Virus
Virus Strain........: V-Sign Virus Strain
Known Variants......: V-Sign.3F, V-Sign.1F
Virus detected when.: Turkey
             where.: February 1992
```

```
Classification......: Boot sector and partition table infector,
                      oligomorphic, memory resident
Length of Virus.....: 1) Length on media:  38 bytes + 2 sectors
                      2) Length in memory: 2 kByte
-------------------- Preconditions --------------------------------
Operating System(s).: MS-DOS
Version/Release.....: ---
Computer model(s)...: IBM - PCs, XT, AT, upward and compatibles
-------------------- Attributes -----------------------------------
Easy Identification.: Search string (hex pattern) with wildcards (?):
                      1272 FA?? ???? ???? ???? ????
                      ???? ??CD 1372 EAE9 A601 7698
Type of infection...: Upon booting from an infected diskette, the
                      virus makes itself memory resident in highest
                      available 2 kByte below 640 kByte; system
                      space is decreased by 2,048 bytes. After
                      that, virus hooks INT 13h and modifies the boot
                      sector image in memory by restoring the 38
                      bytes previously overwritten; control is then
                      transferred to the original boot sector. On a
                      previously not-infected hard disk, memory
                      resident virus will infect HD partition table
                      on first HD access; moreover, boot sectors on
                      any not write-protected diskette accessed
                      during memory residence of virus will be
                      infected. The second part of the virus body
                      is located at different places, depending on
                      the size of the infected medium:
                      Track: Head: Sectors: Medium:
                        0     0     4-5     Hard disk
                        0     1     2-3     5.25" DD diskette
                        0     1     13-14   5.25" HD diskette
                        0     1     4-5     3.5"  DD diskette
                        0     1     14-15   3.5"  HD diskette
                      Upon every infection, virus increments a counter;
                      when Counter AND Mask=0, transient damage is
                      triggered (see below).
                      Self-identification: After intercepting all
                      read/write operations, virus checks for an
                      existing infection using 9876h marker.
Infection Trigger...: Booting from an infected medium (floppy boot
                      sector, HD partition table)
Media affected......: Any hard disk and floppy diskette.
                      Remark: due to a bug, all diskettes infected in
                      drive B: will try to load the second part of
                      the virus body from that drive and thus will
                      be non-infective (except if you happen to have
                      two infected diskettes of one and the same
                      size and capacity in both drives during the
                      bootstrap). When booting from such floppies,
                      virus attempts to read 2 sectors from B: and,
                      if unsuccessful, system hangs.
Interrupts hooked...: INT 13h
Crypto method.......: ---
Polymorphic method..: V-Sign is oligomorphic (mild form of polymorphism),
                      so it can be detected with a search string con-
                      taining wildcards (see Search string). Oligo-
                      morphism is generated in the 38 byte code.
```

```
Damage..............: Permanent HD damage: upon HD infection, V-Sign
                      saves 38 bytes of partition table in its
                      code and overwrites Side 0, Cyl.0, Sector 1;
                      moreover, it saves the rest of its code on
                      Side 0, Cyl.0, Sectors 4+5. Partition table
                      is NOT saved.
                      Permanent FD damage: upon floppy infection, virus
                      saves 38 bytes of floppy boot sector in its
                      code and overwrites original bootsector;
                      moreover, it saves the rest of its code in
                      last 2 sectors of root directory (see remark).
                      Original boot sector is NOT saved.
                      Transient damage: dependent on trigger con-
                      dition, the virus displays a block graphic
                      showing a Victory sign; then, system hangs.
Damage Trigger......: Permanent (HD,FD) damage trigger: overwriting
                      action during infection process.
                      Transient damage: triggered when
                      Infection Counter AND Mask = 0; Mask differs
                      between variants:
                            Variant 3F: every 64th infection
                            Variant 1F: every 32nd infection.
Similarities........: Infection method similar to Stoned viruses
Known variants......: 2 minor variants (clones) are known which differ
                      in 1 mask containing either 1F or 3F.
Particularities.....: ---
-------------------- Agents -------------------------------------------
Countermeasures.....: McAfee Scan V95+, Skulason F-PROT 2.05+,
                      Solomon FINDVIRU 6.02, IBM's VirScan 2.2.3A
                      and VirX 2.5+ detect V-Sign (other scanners
                      may also detect V-Sign but were not tested).
Standard means......: 1) Boot from clean system; reconstruct 38 original
                      boot sector bytes from virus analysis.
                      2) Use SYS to destroy virus; reformat diskette
                      after COPYing essential files.
                      3) Use FDISK/MBR (DOS 5) to reconstruct MBR.
-------------------- Acknowledgement ----------------------------------
Location............: Virus Test Center, University of Hamburg, Germany
Classification by...: Klaus Brunnstein
Documentation by....: 1) Fridrik Skulason: Virus Bulletin July 1992
                      2) David Chess, IBM High-Integrity Computing Lab
                      3) Patty Hoffman VSUM (October 1992/with errors)
Date................: 22-December-1992
```

Warlock Virus

```
Entry...............: Warlock Virus
Alias(es)...........: ---
Virus Strain........: ---
Virus detected when.: April 1993
            where.: Kazakhstan
Classification......: File Virus (COM,EXE,OVL;DBF infector), memory
                      resident, partly (messages) encrypted
Length of Virus.....: 1.Length (Byte) on media:
                         1a.          EXE files: 1817 (+16)   Bytes
                         1b.          COM files: 1817 (+16)+4 Bytes
```

```
                            2.Length (Byte) in RAM:    3648 Bytes
-------------------- Preconditions ------------------------------------
Operating System(s).: MS-DOS/PC-DOS
Version/Release.....: MS-DOS/PC-DOS >= 2.0
Computer model(s)...: IBM PCs and Compatibles
-------------------- Attributes ---------------------------------------
Easy Identification.: --- (File[EOF-4] == 0B0Dh (0Dh, 0Bh))
Type of infection...: File infection: infects COM and EXE files
                      by appending it's code (adapting to 16 bytes
                      adress boundary); for COM files, virus adds
                      extra 4 bytes after appending itself. Damages
                      OVL and DBF files (though not infecting them).
                      Self-Identification in file: checks bytes before
                      EOF: File[EOF-4] == 0B0Dh (0Dh, 0Bh)
                      System infection: upon starting an infected file,
                      virus makes itself memory resident in memory
                      (using TWIXT method).
                      Self-Identification in memory: tests INT 21
                      register for given value. Additional check is
                      made by a resident virus: it compares a piece
                      of it's code to that of the caller (with bug).
Infection Trigger...: Infection occurs if the following condition holds:
                      Exec OR (Open OR Rename OR ChMod) AND
                      FileExt IN [.EXE, .COM, .OVL, .DBF]) AND
                      (FileName != "COMMAND.COM") AND
                      (LengthCOM > 1024) AND (LengthCOM < 62687) AND
                      (LengthEXE <= EXE_Image_Size (i.e.EXE file is
                      not segmented)) AND
                      (EXE_IP != 0eh (all LZEXE-packed files, in par-
                      ticular AIDSTEST scanner)) AND
                      (EXE_stack < EXE_Image_Size OR
                          EXE_stack > EXE_Image_Size+72h
                      (a bug - should be 720h)
Storage media affected:
Interrupts hooked...: INT 21/4B, 21/3D, 21/43, 21/56, 21/D000, 24, 2A
Damage..............: Permanent Damage:
                      1) First 32 bytes of DBF files are overwritten
                         with 0C3H value.
                      2) Side Effects: Overlays are damaged, some EXE
                         files won't operate properly - virus body
                         might be overwritten by program's stack.
                      Transient Damage: ---
Damage Trigger......: Permanent Damage:
                      1) File[0]==03 (usually .DBF files signature)
                         and executing or opening or renaming or
                         Get/Set File Attribute of infected file.
                      2) Executing such OVL or EXE files.
                      Transient Damage: ---
Particularities.....: 1) Virus contains following emcrypted strings
                      (not displayed): "Revenge of WARLOCK!",
                      "STACK    STACK    STACK    STAC",
                      "COMMAND.COM", "EXE", "OVL", "DBF".
                      2) For some MS-DOS versions (prev. to 4.0), virus
                      patches direct DOS entry. Otherwise, it simply
                      intercepts INT 21 vector.
Similarities........: Tunnelling is borrowed from Yankee_Doodle.TP.
-------------------- Agents -------------------------------------------
Countermeasures.....:
```

```
Countermeasures successful:
Standard means......: Delete infected files, replace wth clean ones.
-------------------- Acknowledgement --------------------------------
Location...........: Program Systems Institute, Russian Academy of
                     Sciences, Pereslavl-Zalessky, Russia
Classification by...: Dmitry O. Gryaznov
Documentation by....: Dmitry O. Gryaznov
                     Klaus Brunnstein (VTC, Virus Catalog entry)
Date................: 17-July-1993
Information Source..: Reverse analysis of virus code
```

"XA1" Virus

```
Entry................ "XA1" Virus
Alias(e)............. V1539 Virus
Strain............... ---
Detected: when....... March 1990
          where...... West-Germany (Altena)
Classification....... Program virus, direct action COM infector
Length of virus...... 163 bytes added to COM files
---------------------- Preconditions -------------------------------
Operating System(s)... MS-DOS
Version/Release....... 2.0 and up
Computer models....... Any IBM-compatibles
----------------------Attributes ----------------------------------
Easy identification... The virus contains the following German string:
                       "Und er lebt doch noch : Der Tannenbaum !",0Dh,
                       0Ah,00h, "Frohe Weihnachten ...",0Dh,0Ah,07h,
                       00h (translated in English: "And he lives:
                       the Christmas tree", "Happy Christmas").
Type of infection..... Direct action; prepending 1539 bytes to
                       COM files.
Infection trigger..... Executing an infected file will trigger the
                       multiple infection attempts searching the
                       PATH variable in the environment.
Interrupts hooked..... INT 24
Damage............... When an infected program is run between December
                       24th and 31st (any year), the virus will
                       display a full screen image of a christmas
                       tree and german seasons greetings.
                       When an infected program is run on April 1st
                       (any year), it drops a code into the boot-
                       sectors of floppy A: and B: as well as into
                       the partition table of the harddisk. The old
                       partition sectors are saved but most likely
                       destroyed since running another infected
                       file will save the modified partition table
                       to the same location. On any boot attempt
                       from an infected harddisk or floppy, the text
                       "April April" will be displayed and the PC
                       will hang.
Particularities....... The virus is self-encrypting and tries to fool
                       debuggers. The decrypting routine is slightly
                       modified upon each infection.
---------------------- Acknowledgement ----------------------------
Location............. Micro-BIT Virus Center RZ Universitaet Karlsruhe
```

```
Classification by..... Christoph Fischer
Dokumentation by ..... Christoph Fischer
Date.................. 16-March-1990
```

XREH Virus

```
Entry...............: XPEH-4016 Virus in (kyrillic letters)
                      CHREN-4016 Virus (in Latin letters)
Alias(es)...........: ---
Virus Strain........: XREH Virus Strain
Virus detected when.: ?
             where.: Russia
Classification......: Program (COM & EXE) Virus, memory-resident
Length of Virus.....: 1. Length on media:  4016 bytes (appended)
                      2. Length in memory: 3872 bytes.
-------------------- Preconditions ----------------------------------
Operating System(s).: MS-DOS
Version/Release.....: DOS 2.x and above
Computer model(s)...: IBM & Compatibles
-------------------- Attributes -------------------------------------
Easy Identification.: Total memory size decreased by 4032 bytes, disk
                      access slows down, when virus is active.
Scan signature......: The following bytes can be found at the INT-21-
                      entrypoint: 80 FC 4E 74 12 80 FC 4F 74 0D 2E 3A
Type of infection...: a) COM-files : The virus appends itself to the
                         end of the file, changing the first
                         32 Bytes of the victim (restored later).
                      b) EXE-Files : Virus uses standard ways of
                         infecting EXE-files.
Infection Trigger...: Execution of COM & EXE files, when month>March
                      and year>1991.
                      Usage of INT 21, AH=4E/4F (FindFirst/FindNext),
                      when the date is above March and 1991. (For
                      details ).
Storage media affected: Files on all accessible media are affected.
Interrupts hooked...: INT 21, functions: AH=4E (FindFirst),
                         AH=4F (FindNext), AH=4B (Load&Execute)
                      INT 1C (Timer),
                      INT 01 (Trace) and INT 03 are hooked temporarily
                      (For details see Particularities)
Damage..............: Files with the Extension ".    ", ".LEX", ".TXT",
                      ".BAK" can be garbled, during September-December
                      of any year above 1991.
Damage Trigger......: System-date (see Damage).
Particularities.....: The virus hooks INT 21, AH=4E/4F for infecting
                      files and encrypting files (damage!), as well
                      as subtracting his length from COM/EXE with
                      filetime 30 seconds. Filetime will be set
                      to 30 sec, when it has been infected or garb-
                      led.
                      This routine will garble files, in months
                      >=September of any year above 1991 and in-
                      fecting COM and EXE files in months >=March
                      of any year above 1991, using a 1:4 random-
                      routine to determine whether to be active.
                      The virus uses the EXE-signature (MZ/ZM) to
```

recognize EXE-files.
COM files will only be infected, when their size
is >=288 and <=61,815 bytes. As the maximum
size of COM-files seems to have been forgotten
to be changed, while writing a new version of
the virus (there are shorter versions!), COM-
files can get bigger than 65k and won't run.
If the date is >=September and >1991, ".   ",
".LEX", ".TXT", ".BAK" files can be garbled,
decrypting up to 64k of them with the kyrillic
letters XPEH (hex: 95 80 85 8D) (xor).
The INT 1C (Timer) is used to check, wether the
entrance of INT 1 and INT 3 (Trace/Breakpoint)
is an IRET-instruction; if not, the entrypoint
is overwritten with a CALL FAR into the virus.
Here the virus determines, from where the INT
has been called, and if it was a INT 1 or INT 3.
After that, it is decided whether only the
Trace-flag is disabled, or if it should hang
the system.
The virus copies itself to the top of RAM, de-
creasing the total amount of memory by 4032
bytes.
When the virus installs itself into memory, it
uses a kind of TRACER, to find the original
INT 21 entry (decission is made via the segment: if it is below 200, virus assumes that
original INT 21 entry has been reached).
While running, the virus constantly de/encrypts
parts of it to disable reassembling of itself,
making analysis very difficult.

```
Similarities........: XREH variants
-------------------- Agents ----------------------------------------
Countermeasures.....: F-PROT 2.02D in Quick-scan recognises the virus as
                      a new variant of Cascade.
Countermeasures successful: The Antiviral Package v. 4.6 from Kaspersky
                      (Moscow) recognizes and removes the virus.
Standard means......: Delete and replace infected files.
-------------------- Acknowledgement -------------------------------
Location............: Virus Test Center, University of Hamburg, Germany
Classification by...: Toralv Dirro
Documentation by....: Toralv Dirro
Date................: 05-May-1992
Information Source..: Original virus analysis
```

"Zero Bug" Virus

```
Entry...............: "Zero Bug"
Alias(es)...........: "ZBug","Palette"
Virus Strain........:
Virus detected when.: October 1989
            where.:
Classification......: Link-Virus (extending), RAM - resident
Length of Virus.....: .COM-Files increased by 1536 bytes
                      in RAM : 1792 bytes + environment
-------------------- Preconditions ---------------------------------
```

```
Operating System(s).: MS-DOS
Version/Release.....: 2.xx upward
Computer model(s)...: IBM - PC, XT, AT and compatibles
-------------------- Attributes ------------------------------------
Easy Identification.: Typical text in Virus body (readable with
                      HexDump-utilities): "ZE","COMSPEC=C:",
                      "C:\COMMAND.COM".
                      .COM files: "seconds" field of the timestamp
                      changed to 62 sec (similar to GhostBalls
                      original Vienna viruses).
Type of infection...: System: RAM-resident, infected if string "ZE"
                      is found at offset 0103h (INT 60h).
                      .COM file: extended by using CREATE-function.
                      Adds 1536 bytes to the beginning of the
                      file; a file will not be infected more
                      than once.
                      .EXE File: no infection.
Infection Trigger...: When function 3C00h (CREATE) and 4000h (WRITE)
                      of INT 21h is called (e.g. if you use
                      "COPY *.COM <destination>", then every
                      destination-file will be infected).
Interrupts hooked...: INT 60h,  INT 21h, INT 1Ch
Damage..............: Permanent Damage:
                      1.  Every time a .COM file is created in an
                      infected system with function 3Ch of INT 21h,
                      the file will be infected.
                      Transient Damage:
                      1.  If INT 1Ch is hooked, every 14 sec INT 21h
                      will be set to the viruscode (programs which
                      hooked INT 21h will be unhooked and hang).
                      2.  All characters "0" (zero) will be exchanged
                      with other characters. Exchange characters
                      are 01h, 2Ah, 5Fh, 3Ch, 5Eh, 3Eh and 30h,
                      in which case the attribute is set to back-
                      ground color (i.e. the character is invi-
                      sible). This routine uses about 10% of CPU-
                      time (system is slowed down accordingly).
                      3.  Modifies the filelength in the Disk
                      Transfer Area (DTA): files doesnot appear
                      as infected. The length of the files with
                      seconds field of timestamp set to 62 sec
                      will be modified in DTA accordingly:
                      filelength := filelength - viruslength.
Damage Trigger......: Only if "C:\COMMAND.COM" is infected, INT 1Ch is
                      hooked  and damage is done.
                      After 240 reboots of system, the first damage
                      occurs. The next damage occurs after every
                      fifth reboot.
Particularities.....: In case of MS-DOS error in 2.xx, system can hang
                      by infection of "C:\COMMAND.COM".
                      Programs longer than 63728 bytes are not
                      executed correctly after infection.
-------------------- Agents ----------------------------------------
Countermeasures.....: Category 3: ANTI_ZBG.EXE (VTC Hamburg)
- ditto - successful: ANTI_ZBG.EXE finds and restores infected
                      programs.
         unsuccessful: Programs which check only the filelength of
                      infected files in an infected system may fail.
```

```
Standard means......: Notice .COM file length.
-------------------- Acknowledgement --------------------------------
Location...........: Virus Test Center, University of Hamburg, Germany
Classification by...: Stefan Tode
Documentation by....: Stefan Tode
Date................: January 20, 1990
```

ZeroHunt Virus

```
Entry................ ZeroHunt Virus
Clones............... ZeroHunt-415, ZeroHunt-411 (minor variations)
Alias(es)............ Minnow, Minnow-1 Virus
Strain............... Zero-Hunt Virus Strain
Detected: when........
          where.......
Classification....... Program (COM) infector, but not increasing;
                      stealth, indirect action, memory resident
Length of Virus...... 1) Length on media:  no increase in file length
                      2) Virus code in memory/inside file:
                          Length (ZeroHunt-411) = 411 bytes;
                          Length (ZeroHunt-415) = 415 bytes;
-------------------- Preconditions ----------------------------------
Operating System(s)... MS/PC-DOS 2.x and upwards
Computer models....... All IBM PC compatibles.
-------------------- Attributes -------------------------------------
Easy identification... ---
Type of infection..... EXE files: not infected;
                      COM files: are infected only once.
                      Self-identification: files containing F5E9h
                      at begin of file, and containing E8h at
                      memory address 0:021Ch are regarded as
                      infected.
                      Virus searches for 411/415 bytes, depending
                      on the clone, for 00h's; if found (typic-
                      ally a buffer), virus copies itself into
                      this part of file: therefore, size of in-
                      fected files do not increase!
                      Virus makes itself RAM resident and copies
                      itself into the interrupt table (in low
                      memory at location 0:021Ch, INT 87h).
                      Files are infected when executed.
Infection trigger..... Any file, which is executed via function 4B00h
                      of INT 21h, will be infected, only if 1st
                      byte of file is E9h and if 411/415 bytes
                      containing 00h's are found.
Interrupts hooked..... INT 21h (always pointing to 0:02D5h);
                      INT 24h (during infection);
                      INT 8Bh (points to EE83:019Bh for ZH-411 virus,
                          and to    EE83:019Fh for ZH-415 virus).
Damage............... No intentional damage.
                      Side effect: system or programs may hang, if
                      they are using the interrupt table as a
                      buffer or if they are using Interrupts
                      > INT 87h (possibly BASIC or LAN Adapters).
                      Moreover, files may get corrupted if one variant
                      tries to infect a file while the other vari-
                      ant is yet active in memory. If ZeroHunt-415
```

```
                               is active in memory, 4 bytes of a file in-
                               fected with ZeroHunt-411 will be corrupted
                               (4 bytes overwritten with 00h).
Damage trigger........         ---
Particularities.......         Stealth method: Virus cannot be found in an
                               infected file, because it monitors all DOS
                               read access functions and may temper them
                               (detail: INT 21h fct. 14h not monitored),
                               thus removing itself from an infected file.
                               Virus may also hook Interrupts > 87h (due to
                               the location of virus).
Similarities.........          ZeroHunt-411 is an optimized version of
                               ZeroHunt-415; due to this optimization,
                               some code/data differs.
--------------------- Agents --------------------------------------------
Countermeasures.......
- ditto - successful..         McAfee's Scan version 85+ (both variants)
                               Solomon's FindViru V4.01+ ( "        "   )
                               Skulasons F-PROT V.2.02 recognizes:
                               ZeroHunt.415 correctly, disinfects wrongly;
                               ZeroHunt.411 as new variant.
Standard Means........         Easy disinfection (only if virus is active in
                               memory): copy all *.COM files to different
                               extension (maybe *.MOC), then reboot system
                               from an clean disk and then rename all *.MOC
                               files back to *.COM.
--------------------- Acknowledgements ----------------------------------
Location..............         Virus Test Center, University of Hamburg, Germany
Classification by.....         Stefan Tode
Documentation by......         Stefan Tode
Date..................         31-January-1992
Information source....         Full reverse engineering of both viruses
```

PC Viruses in the Wild — February 1, 1994

This is a cooperative listing of viruses reported as being in the wild by 16 virus information professionals. The basis for these reports are virus incidents where a sample was received, and positively identified by the participant. Rumors and unverified reports have been excluded.

The list should not be considered a list of currently common viruses however. No provision is made for commonness. A currency basis for the list has been set. Reports date from September of 1992 to the present.

This data indicates only which viruses have been found in the wild.

Table C.1 below gives the names of participants, along with their organization, antivirus product (if any), and geographic location.

Table C.1

Key	Participant	Organization	Product	Location	Scope
As	Alan Solomon	S&S Int'l	Toolkit	UK	
Dc	Dave Chess	IBM	IBM AntiVirus	USA	Int'l
Ek	Eugene Kaspersky	KAMI	AVP	Russia	
Fb	F. Bonsembiante	Virus Report	None	Argentina	Reg'l
Fs	Fridrik Skulason	Frisk Int'l	F-Prot	Iceland	
Gj	Glenn Jordan	Datawatch	VirexPC	USA	
Jw	Joe Wells	Symantec	NAV	USA	Int'l
Pd	Paul Ducklin	CSIR Virus Lab	None	So Africa	
Pp	Padgett Peterson	Hobbyist	DiskSecure	USA	
Rf	Richard Ford	Virus Bulletin	None	UK	
Rh	Richard Head	Jade Corp	None	Japan	Reg'l
Rr	Roger Riordan	CYBEC	VET	Australia	
Sg	Shimon Gruper	EliaShim	ViruSafe	Israel	
Vb	Vesselin Bontchev	U of Hamburg	None	Germany	
Ws	Wolfgang Stiller	Stiller Res.	Integ Master	USA	
Yr	Yuval Rakavi	BRM	Untouchable	Israel	

Table C.2 is based on two or more participants reporting a virus. Therefore, these viruses are probably more geographically scattered.

Table C.2

CARO Name of Virus	AsDcEkFbFsGjJwPdPpRfRhRrSgVbWsYr	Alias(es)
AntiEXE	| . . . x . x . . . . . . x . . |	
Athens	| . . . x . x . . . . |	Trajector
Barrotes.A	| x . . . . . x x . . . . |	Barrotos
Brasil	| . . . . . x . x . . . . |	
Butterfly	| . . . . . x . . . . . . x . x |	
Cascade.1701.A	| x x . x x . . . . x x . x x . . |	1701
Cascade.1704.A	| x x x . x . x . . . . . x . . x |	1704
Changsha	| . . . . x . . . . x x . . . . |	Century
Chinese Fish	| x x . . x x x x . . . x . . . x |	Fish Boot
CPM	| . . . . . . x . x . . . . . . |	Chile, Meirda

Table C.2   *continued*

CARO Name of Virus	AsDcEkFbFsGjJwPdPpRfRhRrSgVbWsYr	Alias(es)
Dark_Avenger.1800.A	x x . x x x x . . x x x . . x x	Eddie
Dark_Av.2100.SI.A	x . . . . . x	V2100
Datalock.920	x x . . . . x . . . . . x . . x	V920
Dir-II.A	x x x x x . x x . x x x x x x x	Creeping Death
Disk_Killer.A	x . x . . x . x x . . x	Ogre
Even_Beeper	x x	
EXE_Bug.A	x . . . . x x . x . . . x . x .	CMOS 1
EXE_Bug.C	. . . . . x . . . . x . x .	
Fichv.2_1	x . . x . . . . . . x . . x	905
Filler	. . . . x x	
Flip.2153.A	x x . x x . x . . x x . x . . .	Omicron
Flip.2343	x . . x	Omicron
Form	x x . x x x x . x x x . x x x x	Form 18
Freddy_2	. . . x	
Frodo.Frodo.A	x x . x x . x . . . x x x . . x	4096, 100 Year
Ginger	. . . . . x . . . . . x . . .	Gingerbread
Green Caterpillar	x x . . x x . x x x x . x x	Find,1591,1575
Helloween.1376	x . . . . . x . . x x x . . x x	1376
Jerusalem.1244	x x	1244
Jerusalem.1808.Std.	x x . x x x x x x x x . x . x x	1808, Israeli
Jer.Anticad.4096.B	x . . . x . . . . . . x . . .	Invader
Jerusalem.Fu_Manchu	x . . . . . x . . . . x . . .	2080, 2086
Jerusalem.Mummy.2_1	x . . . x . . x . . x . x . . .	PC Mummy
Jerusalem.Sunday.A	. . . . . . x . . x x	Sunday
Jer.Zerotime.Austr.	x x . . . . x x . x x	Slow
Joshi.A	x x . . x x x . x x x x x . x .	
Kampana.3700:Boot	x x . x x x x . . x x . . . x .	Telecom, Drug
Keypress.1232.A	x x . . . . x . x x x x . x x	Turku, Twins
Liberty	. x . . x . x . . x x . . x x	Mystic, Magic
Maltese Amoeba	x x . . x . x . x x . . x . x x	Irish
Music_Bug	. . . . x x . x . . . . . x .	
Necros	x . . . . . x	Gnose, Irish3
NJH-LBC	x x	Korea Boot
No_Frills.Dudley	x . . . . x	Oi Dudley

Table C.2 continued

CARO Name of Virus	AsDcEkFbFsGjJwPdPpRfRhRrSgVbWsYr	Alias(es)
No_Frills.No_Frills	. . . . . x . . . . x	
Nomenklatura	x x	Nomen
November_17th.855.A	x x . . x . x	V855
NPox.963.A	. . . . x . x x	Evil Genius
Ontario.1024	. x . . . . x x	SBC, 1024
Parity_Boot.B	x . . . . x x . x x . . x . . .	
Ping_Pong.B	x x . x . . . . x . . x . x . .	Italian
Predator.2448	. . . x . x	2448
Print_Screen	x x . . . x x	PrnScn
Quit.A	x x	555, Dutch
Quox	. x . . x . x	Stealth 2
Ripper	x x . . x . x	Jack Ripper
Screaming_Fist.696	x x . . . x x . . . . . . x . .	Screamer, 696
Stealth.B	. x . . . x . x	STB
Stoned.16	x x . . . x x	Brunswick
Stoned.Azusa	x x . . x . x x x . x x x . x .	Hong Kong
Sto'd.Empire.Monkey	. . . . x x x . x . . x . x x .	Monkey
Stoned.Flame	. . . . x . . . . . x . x . . .	Stoned(3C)
Stoned.June_4th	x . . . x x . . x x . x x . . .	Bloody!,Beijing
Stoned.Lzr	. . . x . x x	Stoned.Whit
Stoned.Manitoba	. . . . x . x	Stonehenge
Stoned.Michelangelo	x x x x x x x x x x x x x x x .	March 6
Stoned.NoINT	x x . . x x x x . x . x . . x .	Stoned 3
Stoned.NOP	. . . . . . x . . . . x .	NOP
Stoned.Standard.B	x . x x x x x x x x x x x x x .	New Zealand
Sto'd.Swed._Dis.	x . . . x	
Stoned.W-Boot	. . . . x . . . . x	W-Boot
Stardot.789	. x . . . . x	805
SVC.3103	x . x . . x . . . x . x	SVC 5.0
Swiss_Phoenix	. . . . x x	
Tequila	x x . x . x x . x x . x x x x x	
Tremor	. . . x . . . . x . . x x . . .	
V-Sign	x x . . x x x . . x x x x . x .	Cansu, Sigalit
Vacsina.TP-05	x x . . x x x . . x x . . . x .	RCE-1206

Table C.2 continued

CARO Name of Virus	AsDcEkFbFsGjJwPdPpRfRhRrSgVbWsYr	Alias(es)
Vacsina.TP-16	| x x . . x . . . . |	RCE-1339
Vienna.648.Reboot	| x x x . . . . |	DOS-62
WXYC	| . x . . . x . . . . |	
Yankee Doodle.TP-39	| x . . . x . . . . |	RCE-2772
Yankee D.TP-44.A	| x . x . x . x . . x x . . x . x |	RCE-2885
Yankee D.XPEH.4928	| . . . x . . . . x . |	Micropox
Yeke.1076	| . x . . . x . . . . |	

Table C.3 is based on a single participant noting more than one infection site and may signify limited regional virus outbreaks.

Table C.3

CARO Name of Virus	AsDcEkFbFsGjJwPdPpRfRhRrSgVbWsYr	Alias(es)
10_Past_3.748	| . . . . . . x . . . . |	
Boot-437	| . . . . x |	
BootEXE	| . . . . x . . . . |	BFD-451
Brain	| . . . . . . x . . . . |	Pakistani
Cascade.1701.G	| . . . . x . . . |	1701
Coffeeshop:MtE_090	| . . . . . x . . . . |	
Darth_Vader.3.A	| . . . . x . . |	
Datalock.828	| . . . . x . |	
Den_Zuko.A	| x . . . . |	Den Zuk
DosHunter	| . x . . . . |	
Emmie.3097	| . . . . x . |	
EXE_Engine	| . . . . x . . . |	
Grower	| . . . . . x . . . . |	V270x, 268+
Hafenstrasse	| . . . . x . . . |	Hafen
Hi	| . . . . x |	Hi.460
Involuntary.A	| . . . . . . x . . . . |	Invol
Japanese_Xmas	| . . . . x . . . . . |	Xmas in Japan
Jerusalem.1808.CT	| . x . . . . |	Capt Trips

Table C.3 *continued*

CARO Name of Virus	AsDcEkFbFsGjJwPdPpRfRhRrSgVbWsYr	Alias(es)
Jerusalem.1808.Null	. x	
Jerusalem.Carfield	x	
Jerusalem.Moctezuma	. x	
Jerusalem.Mummy.1_2	. . . . . . x	
Jerusalem.Sunday.II	. x	Sunday 2
Joshi.B	. x	
KampanaGalicia:Boot Drug	. . . . . x	Telecom,
Keypress.1744	. . . . x .	
Little Brother.307	. . . . x	
Lyceum.1788	. . x	
MacGyver	. . . . . x	Shoo
MISiS NIKA	. . . . x .	Zharinov,
Murphy.Smack.1841	. . . . . x	Smack
Necropolis	. . . . x .	1963
November_17th.800	. . . . . x	Jan1, 800
Number_of_the_Beast	. . . x	512, 666
Parity_Boot.A	. . . . x . .	
Sat_Bug	. . . . . x	Satan Bug
Scream._Fist.NuWay	. . . . . x	Sticky
Sleepwalker	. . . . x . . .	
Stinkfoot	. . . . x	
Stoned.Bunny.A	. . . . . x . . . . x . .	
Stoned.Dinamo	. . . . x .	
Sto'd.EmpireIn_Love	. . . . x	
SVC.2936	. . . . . x	
Sto'd.Empire.Int_10	. . . . x	
Swiss_Boot	. . . x	Swiss Army
Syslock.Syslock.A	x	
Vmem	. . . . x .	
Voronezh.1600	. . x	RCE-1600
Yale	. x	Alameda

Frequency of PC Viruses Confirmed in the Wild (Based on the January 1, 1994 WildList)

This list adds currency and frequency factors to the WildList. For the currency factor a base date of September 1, 1992 has been chosen. How often a virus has been reported (the frequency factor) is indicated by a number from 1 to 4 that represents a feel for how often each virus has been found in the wild. So far six of the WildList participants have provided their frequency information. Here are the frequency factors:

4=Very frequent. 3=Fairly frequent. 2=Barely frequent. 1=Rarely found.

Table C.4 below gives the names of participants, along with their organization, antivirus product (if any), and geographic location.

Table C.4

Key	Participant	Organization	Product	Location
AS	Alan Solomon	S&S Int'l	Toolkit	UK
DC	Dave Chess	IBM	IBM AntiVirus	USA
FS	Fridrik Skulason	Frisk Int'l	F-Prot	Iceland
JW	Joe Wells	Symantec	NAV	USA
RF	Richard Ford	Virus Bulletin	None	UK
VB	Vesselin Bontchev	U of Hamburg	None	Germany

Table C.5

CARO Name of Virus	AS	DC	FS	JW	RF	VB	Aliases
1 Form	4	4	4	4	4	4	
2 Stoned.Standard.B	4	4	1	3	4	3	New Zealand, Marijuana
3 Stoned.Michelangelo	2	3	4	3	2	3	March 6
4 Kampana.3700:Boot	2	2	4	3	3	.	Telecom,Drug, Telefonica
V-Sign	2	3	3	3	3	.	Cansu, Sigalit
5 Tequila	2	3	2	2	3	1	

Table C.5 continued

CARO Name of Virus	AS	DC	FS	JW	RF	VB	Aliases
6 Yankee_Doodle.TP-44.A	2	3	2	1	2	2	RCE-2885, TP-44, Doodle
7 Joshi.A	2	4	1	2	3	.	
8 Jerusalem.1808.Standard	3	4	1	2	1	.	1808, Israeli, Friday13
Stoned.NoINT	1	3	1	3	3	.	Stoned 3, Bloomington
9 Cascade.1701.A	2	3	1	.	3	1	1701, Falling Letters
Flip.2153.A	2	3	2	1	2	.	Omicron
Green_Caterpillar	2	3	1	2	2	.	Find,1591,1575
Parity_Boot.B	1	2	.	2	1	4	
10 Stoned.Empire.Monkey.B	.	2	3	3	.	2	
11 Dir-II.A	1	2	1	1	2	1	Creeping Death, FAT
12 Vacsina.TP-05	2	2	1	1	2	.	RCE-1206, TP-05
13 Stoned.Azusa	1	3	3	1	.	.	Hong Kong
14 Tremor	.	.	3	.	1	4	
15 Cascade.1704.A	1	1	4	1	.	.	1704
Dark_Avenger.1800.A	2	2	1	1	1	.	Eddie
16 Maltese_Amoeba	2	1	1	1	1	.	Irish, Grain of Sand
17 Liberty	.	3	1	1	1	.	Mystic, Magic
November_17th.855.A	2	1	1	2	.	.	V855
18 EXE_Bug.A	2	.	.	3	1	.	CMOS1
Helloween.1376	1	.	.	2	3	.	1376
Ping_Pong.B	2	2	.	.	2	.	Italian
Quox	.	2	1	3	.	.	Disk Infect, Stealth 2
19 Ripper	1	1	1	2	.	.	Jack Ripper
20 Chinese_Fish	1	.	1	3	.	.	Fish Boot
Keypress.1232.A	2	2	.	.	1	.	Turku, Twins
Screaming_Fist.696	1	2	.	2	.	.	Screamer 2B, 696
Stoned.16	1	3	.	1	.	.	Brunswick
21 Datalock.920	1	2	.	1	.	.	V920
Stoned.June_4th	2	.	.	1	.	1	Bloody!, Beijing
22 Fichv.2_1	1	.	3	.	.	.	905
Vacsina.TP-16	2	.	2	.	.	.	RCE-1339, TP-16

Table C.5 continued

CARO Name of Virus	AS	DC	FS	JW	RF	VB	Aliases
Yankee_Doodle.TP-39	2	.	2	.	.	.	RCE-2772, TP-39, Doodle
23 Barrotes.A	1	1	.	1	.	.	Barrotos
Disk_Killer.A	1	.	.	1	1	.	Ogre
Frodo.Frodo.A	1	.	1	1	.	.	4k, 4096, 100 Years
Print_Screen	1	1	.	1	.	.	PrnScn
24 AntiEXE	.	.	.	1	.	2	
Flip.2343	1	.	2	.	.	.	Omicron
Jerus.Zerotime.Aust.	2	1	.	.	.	.	Slow
Stardot.789	.	2	.	1	.	.	805
Stealth.B	.	1	.	2	.	.	STB
Stoned.Manitoba	.	.	1	2	.	.	Stonehenge

Notes on Interpreting the Data

The 48 viruses listed above have a mean frequency of .5 or above. This means each virus has been found by at least three participants, if the virus is rarely found; by two participants, if one has found it on more occasions; or by one participant, who has found it fairly often. Other viruses on the WildList, found less frequently, are here omitted.

Since some viruses are of equal frequency, the data here has been fine tuned by modifying the mean frequency. A virus reported by more of the participants is ranked slightly higher than one of the same frequency that is reported by fewer participants. Based on this modification, the viruses below are placed in frequency slots. Form is the most often reported virus and is in slot 1, Kampana.3700:Boot and V-Sign (which have the same frequency even after modification) share slot 4, etc.

On the other hand, the data may be interpreted by modifying each mean frequency in an opposite manner. That is, by ranking a virus slightly lower if it's reported by more participants. The logic here would be that the virus received its mean frequency through fewer, but higher, frequency factors. For example, Stoned.Azusa could be viewed as more frequent than Vacsina.TP-05 since it got two "Fairly frequent" ratings and the most Vacsina got was "Barely frequent" from any participant.

Even so, using this later method of interpretation would simple juggle the order slightly; no viruses would move onto, or drop off the list. I have chosen the first method simply because it leans more towards answering the question: "How widespread is the virus?"

The collation of this material is done by Joe Wells, Virus Specialist at Symantec, Peter Norton Group, who is solely responsible for its contents. The material presented is implicitly copyrighted under various laws, but may be freely quoted or cited. However, its source and cooperative nature should be duly referenced. Other antivirus product developers are invited to participate. If you wish to do so, please contact me.

The FreqList by Joe Wells—jwells@symantec.com—70750,3457—Vol 2.01.

Index

What's on the Disk and How to Install It

For a more complete description of all the programs, please see Chapter 13.

The enclosed diskette contains eight (8) programs from the DR. PANDA family of PC security programs. They are:

PHYSICAL	Checks for changes to boot sectors, system file, and program files.
PHYSRES	A TSR program utilizing the database created by PHYSICAL. Checks programs for changes at runtime and creates an audit trail.
PHYSED	A point-and-shoot editor to be used with the PHYSICAL data file.
PINSTALL	The installation program for PHYSICAL.EXE and PHYSRES creates the associated data file.
MONITOR	A Disk BIOS (INT 13) trap which prevents data destruction. Can also trap Read, Write, and Verify calls in a laboratory setting.
TSRMON	Denies TSR status to unauthorized programs.
LABTEST	A utility to "peek" inside new or suspicious files before they are run.
DRHOOK	Maps the use of RAM by active programs.

NOTE You have to use PINSTALL to install the DR. PANDA family of PC security programs, because it creates several associated files that are necessary for the running of the rest of the program.

To install, first insert this diskette in either drive A: or B:. If you are in Windows, Quit, and then go to the DOS root directory prompt. Change directory to either drive A: or B: by typing either CD\a: or CD\B:, then type PINSTALL. Follow the instructions as prompted. A full installation will create three associated data files created as part of the installation process. They are:

PHYSICAL.DAT	Listing of programs to be checked by either PHYSICAL or PHYSRES. Note: This filename may be changed at installation.
TSRMON.DAT	Programs allowed as "OK" to go TSR. Note: This filename may be changed at installation.
PHYSICAL.HST	A complete audit trail created by PHYSRES.